Corporate Governance and Ethics

Zabihollah Rezaee, Ph.D., CPA, CMA, CIA, CGFM, CFE

Thompson-Hill Chair of Excellence &
Professor of Accountancy
Fogelman College of Business and Economics, University of Memphis

WILEY

JOHN WILEY & SONS, INC.

VICE PRESIDENT AND PUBLISHER   *Donald Fowley*
ASSOCIATE PUBLISHER   *Christopher DeJohn*
PRODUCTION SERVICES MANAGER   *Dorothy Sinclair*
PRODUCTION EDITOR   *Janet Foxman*
EXECUTIVE MARKETING MANAGER   *Amy Scholz*
SENIOR MARKETING MANAGER   *Julia Flohr*
CREATIVE DIRECTOR   *Harry Nolan*
SENIOR DESIGNER   *Kevin Murphy*
EDITORIAL ASSISTANT   *Kathryn Fraser*
ASSISTANT MARKETING MANAGER   *Carly DeCandia*
SENIOR MEDIA EDITOR   *Allison Morris*
PROJECT EDITOR   *Ed Brislin*
PRODUCTION SERVICES   *Dennis Free/Aptara, Inc.*
COVER DESIGN   *David Levy*
COVER IMAGE   © *Anthony Harvie/Getty Images*

This book was set in Times Roman by Aptara, Inc. and printed and bound by RRD Crawfordsville. The cover was printed by RRD Crawfordsville.

The book is printed on acid-free paper. ∞

Library of Congress Cataloging-in-Publication Data:
Rezaee, Zabihollah, 1953-
    Corporate governance and ethics / Zabihollah Rezaee.
       p. cm.
    Includes index.
    ISBN 978-0-471-73800-8 (pbk.)
  1. Corporate governance–United States.   2. Business ethics–United States.   I. Title.
    HD2741.R479 2009
    174′.4–dc22

                                                       2008012274

Printed in the United States of America

10 9 8 7 6 5 4 3 2 1

This book is dedicated to my son, Nick, and my daughter, Rose—two parts of my biggest dream—for their love, understanding, and encouragement to write this book aimed at developing competent and ethical future business and academic leaders.

Acknowledgments

This book has benefited from the assistance of numerous professionals and colleagues. I would like to specifically thank Lynn Turner and Cynthia Richson for their invaluable review of earlier chapters of the book. I would also like to extend my appreciation to Todd DeZoort, Patrick Kelly, and Michelle McGowen for the comments they contributed during the development of this textbook. I thank the publishing team at Wiley & Sons for their help, particularly Chris DeJohn, Katie Fraser, and Julia Flohr; Dennis Free at Aptara; and the copyeditor, Kris Lynch.

I am grateful to Barbara Haertl for her assistance in managing and editing the chapters. The assistance of my graduate students, Joseph Nowell, Siddhi Shastra, Chetan Jain, and my student worker, Jacob Foltz-Gray, is also appreciated. I am thankful for the love, patience, and support of my wife, Soheila, my son, Nick, and my daughter, Rose, which made it easier for me to focus on completing this book.

Preface

Ineffective corporate governance at the two biggest bankrupt companies in U.S. history (Enron and WorldCom) created incentives and opportunities for earnings management, fraudulent financial reporting, and an unethical corporate culture in which these and other companies (Adelphia, Waste Management, Tyco) failed. Failure of these high-profile companies, which resulted in the loss of hundreds of billions of dollars to investors, paved the way for recent corporate governance reforms, including the Sarbanes-Oxley Act of 2002 (SOX), U.S. Securities and Exchange Commission (SEC) rules, listing standards, and best practices. Corporate governance and business ethics are regarded as the most influential theme of the twenty-first century, having transformed from a compliance requirement to a strategic business imperative and ethical corporate culture. Colleges and universities play an important role in training competent and ethical future academic and business leaders. In today's global business environment, with volatile worldwide capital markets and eroded investor confidence in corporate accountability, the demand for effective corporate governance and ethical conduct in ensuring reliable financial information is higher than ever before.

Effective corporate governance assists management in better running its organization; promotes a vigilant oversight function by the board of directors; encourages shareholders to take an active role in monitoring their organizations; promotes gatekeepers (auditors, legal counsel, investment banks, financial advisors, and analysts) to fulfill their professional duties; and improves public trust in the organization's affairs and performance. Organizations of all types (for profit or not-for-profit), sizes, and complexities (simple operation or multinational) can benefit from effective corporate governance. Studying corporate governance and ethics can further our understanding of the roles and responsibilities of all corporate governance participants in improving corporate governance practices, stimulate dialogue among business students who will eventually be business leaders, and promote research in the emerging field of corporate governance and ethics. More than twenty business schools now offer a separate course in corporate governance and ethics, and the demand for and interest in this emerging area of education is expected to increase.

This book is developed based on five overriding themes:

1. Study of corporate governance and ethics is by its nature interdisciplinary and requires knowledge of laws, rules, regulations, finance, economics, politics, organizational behavior, accounting, information systems, psychology, and other disciplines.

2. There is a need for a conceptual framework and knowledge base to collect comprehensively all aspects of corporate governance in a single setting such as in this book.

3. There should be a broad and integrated approach in studying the embedded roles and responsibilities of all corporate governance participants, including investors, the board of directors, management, auditors, legal counsel, financial advisors, policymakers, regulators, and the global business and academic communities.

4. Corporate governance is a global phenomenon, and thus, there should be an international approach because corporate governance reforms in different countries are shaped by their legal, political, and cultural environment. Today's corporate governance has emerged as best practices worldwide.

5. Ethics consist of moral values, personal integrity, professional accountability, business legitimacy, equity, and fairness, all of which are viewed differently by various people as acceptable standards of behavior.

Many factors in the early 2000s contributed to the erosion of investor confidence, including an economic slowdown, threats of terrorism, a three-year equity bear market, and, particularly, the many reported financial scandals. Financial scandals of high-profile companies and ethical debacles in corporations have eroded investor confidence and public trust in corporate America and its corporate governance, financial reporting, and audit functions. Congress responded to the scandals by passing SOX to hold public companies more accountable for the information they release to the public. SOX and its related SEC rules are intended to improve corporate governance, enhance the quality of financial reports, improve audit effectiveness, and increase civil and criminal liabilities for violation of securities laws.

Reported financial scandals at the turn of the twenty-first century and related regulatory responses reinvigorated interest in corporate governance and business ethics. Although business schools did not contribute to the perceived ethical debacles in corporations, the report issued by the Ethics Education Task Force of the Association to Advance Collegiate Schools of Business International (AACSB) reemphasizes the importance of ethics education in better training business majors for the challenging career awaiting them. The report specifically states, "The time has come for business schools—supported by AACSB International—to renew and revitalize their commitment to the centrality of ethical responsibility at both the individual and corporate levels in preparing business leaders for the twenty-first century." This report identifies the four important areas viewed by AACSB as the "cornerstones of a comprehensive and viable ethics education curriculum in business schools." These areas are (1) responsibility of business in society, (2) ethical decision making, (3) ethical leadership, and (4) corporate governance. Corporate governance and business ethics have been fundamental components of business schools' curriculum in recent years. This book is the first to present a comprehensive framework of the theory and practice of corporate governance and business ethics by focusing on the four cornerstones promoted by the AACSB. This book presents a comprehensive primer of corporate governance and business ethics to provide a framework for business schools in training future leaders.

There are several plausible reasons for integrating corporate governance and business ethics education into the business curriculum:

1. Reported financial scandals and regulatory responses underscore the importance of effective corporate governance and ethical behavior and conduct by corporations and, thus, business schools in training future corporate leaders.

2. SOX is intended to improve corporate governance by enforcing more accountability for public companies and requiring the adoption of a code of ethics for their executives.

3. Corporate governance and business ethics are not properly integrated into business education.

4. Teaching and research in corporate governance and business ethics have been strongly recommended and encouraged.

5. There is an inventory of support materials for teaching ethics and corporate governance in the post-Enron era. There are sufficient resources (textbooks such as this book, published articles, Web sites, videos) to offer a stand-alone course in business ethics and corporate governance or to integrate ethics and corporate governance modules into business courses.

6. It is easier in the post-SOX era to obtain administrative support to offer ethics and corporate governance courses.

The ever-improving corporate governance and accountability for business organizations appears to be a national trend. Two areas that have recently received long-awaited attention are business ethics and corporate governance. Business schools play an important role in preparing the next generation of business leaders, who will experience lifelong training in acting with integrity, upholding the highest level of ethical conduct, and carrying the heavy burden of public trust. These next generations of business leaders must understand the importance of ethical conduct and corporate governance to our society and its role in ensuring that high-quality financial and nonfinancial information is disseminated to the capital markets by public companies. Thus, ethical behavior, professional accountability, and personal integrity must be promoted throughout the business curriculum. This book is intended to develop an awareness and understanding of the main themes, perspectives, frameworks, concepts, and issues pertaining to corporate governance and business ethics from historical, global, institutional, commercial, best practices, and regulatory perspectives.

The fifteen chapters of this book are organized into three parts. Part One contains three chapters that present the free market system and business, importance of financial information to investors and the capital markets, and emergence of corporate governance and business ethics practice and education. In Part Two, Chapters 4 to 11 provide a framework for the discussion of roles and responsibilities of participants in the oversight, managerial, compliance, auditing, advisory, and monitoring functions of corporate governance. Part Three includes Chapters 12 to 15, which present emerging trends in corporate governance and business ethics, including governance of private and not-for-profit organizations.

Chapter objectives, summaries, key terms, review questions, discussion questions, and cases are provided for each chapter. A test bank and other supplemental teaching aids are also provided.

This book goes far beyond existing books on corporate governance that address only limited aspects of responsibilities of the board of directors, management, and shareholders. This book is different from the existing books on corporate governance and business ethics in many ways:

1. *Relevance:* This book exposes readers to all functions of corporate governance (oversight, managerial, compliance, internal audit, external audit, legal and advisory, and monitoring).

2. *Comprehensiveness:* Unlike existing books, this book presents an integrated approach to corporate governance and business ethics by focusing on important drivers of corporate governance, including state laws, federal laws, listing standards, and best practices worldwide.

3. *Content materials:* This book incorporates corporate governance reforms and best practices from a global perspective and business ethics from behavioral and applied aspects.

4. *Approach in presentation:* This book provides maximum flexibility in presenting the amount and order of materials on corporate governance and business ethics.

5. *Organization:* Each chapter begins with a brief introduction, learning objectives, and text, followed by a summary, key learning points, and the end-of-chapter materials.

Corporate governance is in transition—its role has evolved from compliance with applicable laws, rules, and regulations to a strategic business imperative of creating shareholder value, while protecting the interests of other stakeholders. Corporate governance has become an integral part of business culture in promoting ethical conduct; strengthening the quality of both financial and nonfinancial information about sustainable organizations' key performance indicators (KPIs); ensuring efficiency, safety, and liquidity of the capital markets; and improving investor confidence in financial reports and capital markets.

As this book was going to production, two important advisory committees were established by the U.S. Treasury Department and the SEC to examine the U.S. financial reporting system and audit process. The final reports of these advisory committees are expected to have significant impacts on corporate governance attributes, particularly addressing complexity and making improvements in financial reporting and in the audit process to strengthen the usefulness of financial information to investors and the capital markets. These and other regulatory reforms and best practices in the post-SOX era have brought corporate governance and ethics to the center stage of business curriculum. Business schools play an important role in preparing the next generation of business and academic leaders with life-long education and training to conduct themselves with integrity, competency, and professional accountability. It is the author's hope that the comprehensive corporate governance and ethics education compiled in this book will contribute to this important role of business schools. *Corporate Governance and Ethics* is designed to provide an adequate knowledge base for students in business, law, and other fields interested in corporate governance and ethics.

Brief Contents

Contents

Part Two	Roles and Responsibilities of Corporate Governance Participants 87

Chapter 4. Board of Directors' Roles and Responsibilities   89

Chapter 5. Board Committee Roles and Responsibilities   117

Part One

Private Enterprise and Public Trust

Chapter 1

The Free Market System and Business

INTRODUCTION

This chapter presents the dynamics of relationships between capital markets and businesses as perceived by investors and transformed through corporate governance. Corporate and accounting scandals at the turn of the twenty-first century eroded public trust and investor confidence in corporate America and its financial reports. Several initiatives and reforms, including the Sarbanes-Oxley Act of 2002 (SOX), listing standards of national stock exchanges, corporate governance best practices, and business ethics guidance were established to restore investor confidence in public financial information. These reforms are a continuous process, creating new measures and practices for public companies and their directors, officers, accountants, auditors, legal counsel, financial analysts, investing banks, and others to effectively fulfill their responsibilities and discharge their accountability. This chapter provides an introduction and background as a plan for corporate governance and business ethics presented throughout the book.

Primary Objectives

The primary objectives of this chapter are to

- Learn the free market system and business.
- Understand the role and responsibility of business in society.
- Understand the primary goal of corporate governance.
- Recognize that effective corporate governance is established through power sharing among all participants, particularly shareholders, boards of directors, and management.
- Exemplify the importance of reliable and transparent financial information.
- Be aware of the effect of corporate governance on investor confidence.
- Present various definitions of corporate governance.
- Provide an overview of corporate governance reforms.
- Introduce business ethics.
- Provide an overview of costs and benefits of corporate governance reforms.
- Address the impacts of corporate governance reforms on accountability.

THE FREE ENTERPRISE SYSTEM AND CAPITAL MARKETS

The free enterprise system is a bedrock principle of the U.S. economy, and its capital markets are the backbone of such systems. Understanding of the free enterprise system and its contribution to continuous economic growth in the United States is important in assessing the global competitiveness of U.S. financial markets. It has made the U.S. financial markets the world's largest, deepest, and safest marketplaces and home to the world's largest financial institutions. The U.S. free enterprise system has transformed from private ownership of businesses to dispersed public ownership of corporate shares by nearly 60 million Americans.

Businesses play an important role in creating safe, efficient, and competitive capital markets to ensure economic growth, low costs of capital, entrepreneurship, innovation, and job creation. Capital provided by investors to public companies is the lifeblood of the markets. Thus, investor protection in providing the most cost-effective capital is essential to the survival and competitiveness of capital markets. More than 100 million Americans have provided capital to the markets, and companies have had access to sufficient funding at the lowest cost of capital possible worldwide. Investors must not only be encouraged and rewarded for investing in the capital markets, but also protected through appropriate regulations, effective corporate governance, and optimal market mechanisms. The preservation of the integrity, reputation, and efficiency of the capital markets is the responsibility of all participants, including investors, corporations, regulators, government entities, and society at large, and serves the best interests of all participants. William Donaldson, former chairman of the U.S. Securities and Exchange Commission (SEC), regarding the importance of the reputation of the capital markets, states that "capital will always go where it is welcome, and stay where it is well treated."[1]

Investor confidence in U.S. capital markets was eroded at the turn of the twenty-first century as a result of high-profile financial scandals, the economic downturn, the September 11, 2001, terrorist attacks, and ineffectiveness of market mechanisms. Congress responded by passing SOX to establish a new regime of investor protection. This new regulatory reform was aimed at identifying and managing conflicts of interest by improving the scope and speed of corporate disclosures. Investors providing capital and companies raising capital usually participate in markets where they feel safe through appropriate regulations and fair and transparent enforcement.

The question that remains on the minds of many corporate governance activists and critics is whether the history of financial scandals normally caused by relaxed regulations and ineffective corporate governance measures is doomed to repeat itself. Examples of these financial scandals are (1) corporate and accounting scandals of the early 1930s, which promoted congressional response with the passage of the Securities Act of 1933 and the Securities Exchange Act of 1934, and the creation of the SEC; (2) the savings and loan debacles of the 1980s and the resultant Federal Deposit Insurance Corporation (FDIC) Improvements Act of 1991; and (3) the wave of financial scandals of high-profile companies in the late 1990s and early 2000s that prompted the passage of SOX, the creation of the Public Company Accounting Oversight Board (PCAOB), and the issuance of more than twenty rules by the SEC in implementing provisions of SOX. Any future financial scandals would cause devastating impacts today, as more than half of all households in the United States are now investing in the securities markets through private investment in company shares, mutual funds, and pension funds. Moreover, as the United States moves to a more global economy and large pension funds fail (e.g., United Airlines), Americans are being forced to take on increasing responsibility to ensure the security of their financial future and retirement funds. These investors demand more accountability, and public companies have responded by making improvements in their corporate governance practices and accountability above and beyond regulatory compliance in the post-SOX era.

The free enterprise system in the United States and its dispersed capital ownership structure necessitate the effective functioning of corporate governance and business ethics guided by cost-effective, efficient, and enforceable regulations; optimal market mechanisms; and best practices. From the early stage of the free enterprise system, promoted in the book *The Wealth of Nations*, written by Adam Smith in 1776, lawmakers, regulators, economists, and business leaders shared the belief that a free and competitive market economy enables corporations to efficiently and effectively use society's resources in creating value, and market mechanisms prevent corporations from abusing their power and defrauding their stakeholders. Recent financial scandals prove that market mechanisms by themselves may not be adequate to monitor, control, and discipline business affairs, and corporate governance reforms were needed to correct the perceived failures of market mechanisms.

A healthy financial sector and efficient capital markets are vital to the economic growth and prosperity of the nation. However, U.S. capital markets in recent years have faced ever-increasing competition from other global financial markets, including those in London and Hong Kong. Ironically, it has been suggested that relaxing some market regulations in the United States can improve the capital market's competitiveness. Although regulations should not drive away good business and should attract investors seeking proper protection, they should not be perceived as constraints in entering into the capital markets. Effectiveness of regulations and market mechanisms in protecting investors and maintaining efficient, transparent, and competitive capital markets can best be measured in terms of investor confidence in the markets. Establishing and enforcing appropriate securities laws are essential in sustaining investor confidence. Securities laws that are not cost effective, efficient, or scalable and are not enforced can contribute to the erosion of investor confidence. Market mechanisms that are not optimal or effective can make public companies susceptible to financial scandals and prone to earnings management and fraud, thus damaging the integrity of the capital markets. Although legal and regulatory laws and practices have played a role in establishing U.S. preeminence in global capital markets, the primary drivers of the shift in capital markets are economic and geographic factors. Fair and mutually beneficial relations between the U.S. and foreign capital markets can strengthen the global capital markets. Enabling U.S. investors to invest in foreign capital markets and reciprocally allowing foreign investors to access the U.S. capital markets can promote global competition and the raising of capital by profitable companies worldwide.

PUBLIC TRUST AND INVESTOR CONFIDENCE

Public trust and investor confidence in the nation's economy and its capital markets are the key drivers of economic growth, prosperity, and financial stability. The U.S. capital markets have for several decades been regarded as the most transparent, efficient, and fair markets worldwide, which have (1) facilitated efficient allocation of a scarce resource of capital, (2) enabled public companies to raise capital for establishing or expanding their businesses, and (3) provided a safe and lucrative financial marketplace for individual investors to invest their money in order to fund their retirement goals or to save enough for their children's education. Thus, the liquidity, robustness, and safety of the capital markets are vital to the nation's economic welfare. Corporate governance reforms have made U.S. capital markets the largest, most liquid, robust, fair, and lucrative worldwide.

Lynn Turner, a former chief accountant at the SEC, in testifying before the Senate Banking Committee, states that

> ... the ability of the U.S. capital markets to attract capital depends on investors having confidence in the integrity and transparency of the markets. Confidence is earned over time through honest and fair markets that provide investors with the material information they need to make informed decisions.[2]

Investors are considered to be confident when stock prices are high, the news about future stock performance is optimistic, and financial information is perceived to be reliable. The financial scandals in the late 1990s and the early 2000s, along with the economic downturn, have had a substantial negative impact on investor confidence. Corporate governance reforms, including SOX, SEC-related rules, listing standards of national stock exchanges, and best practices, have been established to rebuild public trust and investor confidence in corporate America, its corporate governance, its financial reports, and its capital markets. Investors would like to see changes in the corporate governance structure that require not only compliance with these reforms, but also address managerial incentives and pressures, the vigilance and independence of boards of directors, the quality and independence of auditors, the objectivity of financial analysts, and shareholder democracy in director elections.

The post-SOX era is characterized by (1) legislation and regulations (SOX, SEC rules) to strengthen corporate accountability and improve corporate governance; (2) a change in the regulatory framework for the auditing profession through the establishment of the PCAOB; (3) the move toward more transparent and timely financial reports; and (4) a redefining of roles and responsibilities of those who are directly or indirectly involved in the financial reporting process (e.g., directors, officers, auditors, legal counsel, financial advisors, investors). The SEC's success in achieving its mission of protecting investors and maintaining efficient, transparent, and competitive capital markets can only be measured in terms of investor confidence in the markets. Establishing appropriate securities laws and maintaining effective enforcement of the laws is essential in sustaining investor confidence. Securities laws that are not cost effective, efficient, or scalable and are not effectively enforced can erode investor confidence.

The improvement in investor confidence has become a daily concern and priority of public companies. As stated by three former SEC chief accountants, "In our capital markets a single catastrophic reporting failure is a disaster in which losses to investors and the public can be, and often are, overwhelming, wiping out decades of hard work, planning, and saving."[3] Investor confidence in public financial information is a complex issue that "cannot be legislated . . . the investment community is requiring individual companies, one by one, to earn back market trust."[4] Investor confidence in corporate America, its financial information, and capital markets is vital in ensuring the sustainability of the free enterprise system.

THE ROLE AND RESPONSIBILITY OF BUSINESS IN SOCIETY

Public companies are a major engine of economic growth and prosperity of the free enterprise system in advanced capitalist economies such as the one in the United States. More than half of the population in the United States invest in public companies and are affected by corporations' performance. This unprecedented accumulation of economic power within public companies underscores the importance of corporate governance, accountability, and business ethical conduct. Shareholders who invest capital are often remote by distance or knowledge from those managing corporations. The report of The Conference Board Commission on Public Trust and Private Enterprise states that

> . . . the corporate form has proven to be a superior means for attracting capital, organizing labor, stimulating ideas, and providing efficient systems of production and distribution. Therefore, sustaining confidence and trust in the performance of that corporate system is a matter of enormous public concern.[5]

Corporations in the United States are viewed as creators of value for all concerned stakeholders as depicted in Figure 1.1. As separate legal entities, corporations obtain their financial capital, labor capital, and skills (managerial capital) from their stakeholders, conduct value-added activities, and return sustainable and enduring value to their stakeholders. All stakeholders contribute to the successful operation of corporations in creating value. For example, equity and debt holders provide financial capital, employees offer labor capital, management provides managerial skills, boards of directors oversee corporate affairs, and the government sets rules to protect stakeholders. In return, corporations grant (1) limited liability measuring the maximum that stakeholders, including shareholders, can lose of

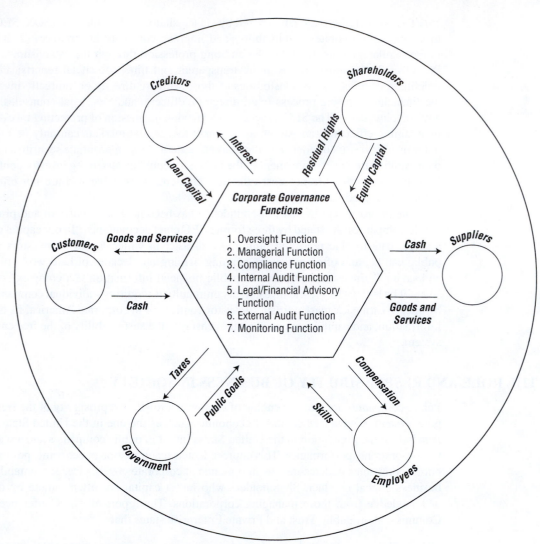

Figure 1.1 Corporations' role in society.

Source: Rezaee, Z. 2007. *Corporate Governance Post-Sarbanes-Oxley Act: Regulations, Requirements, & Integrated Processes*. John Wiley & Sons, Hoboken, NJ.

their contribution and investment in corporations; and (2) increased stakeholder value, in the normal course of their business, with shareholders having a residual claim.

All stakeholders are provided with incentives and opportunities to reward corporations for good performance and discipline them for poor performance. For example, suppliers and customers reward good corporate performance by actively and favorably doing business with the company, and discipline the company by restricting business with the company. Lenders and investors reward good performance by investing in the company at the lower desired rate of return on investment (cost of capital) and discipline poor corporate performance by disinvesting or demanding a higher rate of return on their investment. Thus, the roles and responsibilities of each group of stakeholders are defined by a set of rules, laws, norms, standards, and commonly accepted business practices and contracts.

The rash of financial scandals has raised serious concerns about public companies' corporate governance and the quality of financial disclosures, and has contributed to the erosion of investor confidence in financial disclosures of public companies, raising the relevant question of whether companies achieved their goal of creating sustainable shareholder value, and how public company performance can be improved. The primary mission of public companies is regarded as creating enduring value, and the corporate governance structure is designed to ensure the accomplishment of this mission. The mission of corporate governance can be further classified into two goals of value creation and value protection. The value creation goal of corporate governance focuses on shareholder value creation and enhancement through the development of long-term strategies to ensure sustainable and enduring operational performance. The value protection goal concentrates on the accountability of the way the company is managed and monitored to protect the interests of shareholders and other stakeholders.

Corporate stakeholders are classified into several layers as depicted in Figure 1.2 and are categorized into three general tiers.

The First Tier: Investors

The first tier of stakeholder hierarchy is composed of investors or shareholders who own the company. Shareholders are the primary stakeholders; without them, the company would not exist. Many argue that the primary purpose of the company is to maximize shareholder wealth. Thus, the company's corporate governance structure should reduce the agency costs raised from the separation of ownership and control by aligning the interests of management with those of shareholders. Shareholders provide capital to the company in return

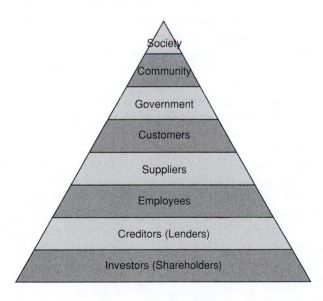

Figure 1.2 Eight layers of shareholders and stakeholders.

for sustainable return on their investment in terms of periodic dividends and stock price appreciations. Payment of dividends reduces the amount of discretionary funds available to management and, thus, can be used as a deterrent to opportunistic managerial behavior and as a vehicle for controlling management actions. Shareholders participate and shape the company's corporate governance structure by exercising their voting rights to elect the members of the board of directors who are directly responsible for protecting their interests and are ultimately accountable to them for the company's business affairs.

Corporations are owned by shareholders who have a variety of risk and return preferences. Owners can be individual investors, institutional investors, banks, pension funds, and industrial companies. Conceptually, institutional investors represent small shareholders as pensioners or beneficiaries. To ensure that institutional investors effectively protect the interests of their beneficiaries or trustees, they should disclose their corporate governance and voting policies as well as potential conflicts of interest and how they manage them. These owners have different identities, strategic interests, financial interests, and time horizons. Financial interest derives from investor motivation to obtain a desired return on investment. Financial interests of return on investment can be achieved by either dividends received from the company profits or the realization of capital gains through stock price appreciation. Institutional and individual investors are typically motivated by the maximization of financial return and exercise their control efforts through a shareholder voting process. Strategic interests are often motivated by nonfinancial objectives and are associated with attempts to exert control over a company through the use of ownership stakes. Strategic interests can be pursued to secure markets, underwrite relational contracts, manage technological dependence, protect managerial autonomy, and regulate competition between firms.

Liquidity is another factor being considered by investors when they invest in a company. Liquidity is determined by the investor's ability to sell their shares in a relatively short time and without a reduction in price or substantial cost. The liquidity preference of investors may result in a diversified portfolio, fragmented shareholders, and stable capital markets that enable exit without negatively affecting share prices. Ownership by individual and institutional investors is often motivated by financial interests and high liquidity, whereas ownership by the state, banks, and industrial corporations is typically centered around highly committed stocks with sustainable strategic interests.

Corporate governance and reforms, including state and federal laws, are aimed at protecting shareholder rights by allowing shareholders to (1) inspect and copy the company's stock ledgers, its list of shareholders, and certain books and records; (2) approve certain business transactions (e.g., mergers and acquisitions); (3) receive proxy materials; and (4) obtain significant disclosures for related party transactions. Shareholder democracy empowering shareholders to nominate, elect, or remove directors has been extensively debated in the literature. Under the current plurality voting system of uncontested director elections, even a single vote for a nominee will elect that director to a board regardless of the number of withholding votes. The majority voting system, which requires a director who received a majority of "against" or "withhold" votes to resign, has received a great deal of attention. Despite its many legal concerns and complications (e.g., plurality voting is allowed under state law), the majority voting system has been advocated by institutional investors and investor activists. A modified version of "majority voting," better known as "majority voting lite" or "Pfizer majority voting," has been suggested. Under the "majority voting lite" system, directors who receive a majority of against or withhold votes are required to submit their resignation to the board. The company's board of directors then decides whether to accept the resignation and, if so, would appoint its own candidate.

The Second Tier: Creditors

Lenders and creditors are considered as the second tier of stakeholders in the company. A typical ownership structure of a public company usually consists of three distinct components: debt securities held by creditors, internal equity securities held by directors and officers, and external equity held by shareholders. Debt and equity securities may have a different impact on the value of the company, as well as differing effects on the company's corporate governance structure.

The proportion of debt equities to the total capital of the company determines the extent of debt holders' concerns that management may be motivated to transfer wealth from them to shareholders and also determines the agency costs assumed by debt holders and their demand for monitoring.[6] Thus, debt holders demand some control over managerial actions by entering into debt covenant contracts designed to protect their interests and determine whether breaches of contractual provisions have occurred.

The extent to which an organization derives its funding from equity or debt may significantly affect the business decisions of the company. For example, the United States and the United Kingdom rely on shareholder funding, whereas Germany derives a significant portion of its capital from creditors. As a result, the United States and UK tend to favor their shareholders, and Germany lends favorability to its creditors. Because creditors tend to be more conservative in weighing business risk (shareholders are usually more likely to encourage business decisions that would result in large capital gains, although creditors do not benefit from such gains), companies largely funded by creditors often choose to minimize risk instead of maximizing wealth.[7]

The Third Tier: Others

The third tier of stakeholders consists of employees, suppliers, customers, government, community, and society. Organizations are now realizing that their stakeholders consist of more than just corporate debt and equity holders. Stakeholders are now identified as those who influence or are influenced, either directly or indirectly, by organizational activities. Many companies today are reaching out to these stakeholders in order to overcome various challenges, such as improving customer perception and reputation, entering viable markets, and resolving conflicts with stakeholder activists. Communication with all stakeholders of the organization is central to improving decision-making processes, strengthening relationships, gathering important information, and building an accord among dissimilar views.[8]

THE ROLE OF FINANCIAL INFORMATION IN THE CAPITAL MARKETS

The sustainability and financial health of public companies, public trust, and investor confidence in financial reports play a crucial role in the integrity and efficiency of the capital markets and the economic growth and prosperity of the nation. Investors, by investing in

401(k), mutual funds, or retirement accounts, or actively playing the stock market, become interested in public companies' governance and are more sensitive to the companies' affairs and the virtues of their directors and officers, including their honesty, integrity, ethics, accountability, and reliability, and the transparent communication of these virtues to investors. The sustainability of public companies is key to keeping investor confidence high and requiring accurate financial reports for investors to make informed investment decisions. Reliability, accuracy, and transparency of financial information play a vital role in the efficiency, integrity, and safety of the capital markets. The ever-increasing demand for high-quality financial information makes the role of individuals involved in the corporate financial reporting supply chain, including the board of directors, the audit committee, management, and auditors, a value-added function under intense scrutiny. Financial disclosures under SEC regulations are necessary to provide investors with reliable, meaningful financial information so they can make informed investment decisions.

Our society, particularly the investing community, relies on the quality of corporate financial reports in making rational decisions. Accurate financial information assists investors with making informed, sound investment decisions, whereas inaccurate financial information is likely to mislead them into making bad investment decisions. William McDonough, the former chairman of the PCAOB, states that "confidence in the accuracy of accounting statements is the bedrock of investors being willing to invest, in lenders to lend and for employees knowing their firms' obligations to them can be trusted."[9] A greater number of people are now investing through retirement funds or actively managing their portfolios and are affected by the financial information disseminated to the market.

Public companies in the United States are required to file their financial reports with the SEC, including audited annual financial statements on Form 10-K, reviewed quarterly financial statements on Form 10-Q, and extraordinary transactions on a current basis on Form 8-K (e.g., departure of directors, officers, auditors), in addition to proxy financial statements submitted to investors. SOX requires financial statements filed with the SEC to be certified by the company's senior executives (chief executive officer [CEO], chief financial officer [CFO]). Section 404 of SOX also requires public companies (as of 2004, large companies known as accelerated filers) to file management and auditor reports on their internal control over financial reporting. These regulated disclosures and filings are further discussed in Chapter 6.

Financial statements are a vital source of information to the capital markets and their participants. The quality of investment and voting decisions by investors depends on the accuracy, completeness, and reliability of financial information disseminated to them by public companies. Thus, high-quality financial information improves investor decisions and, in turn, efficiency, liquidity, and safety of the capital markets, which may result in prosperity and economic growth for the nation. Financial disclosures under SEC regulations are necessary to prevent fraud and financial manipulation. Our society, particularly the investing community, relies on the quality of corporate financial reports in making rational decisions. However, there is an expectation gap between what users of financial reports expect to receive and what they actually receive. Several factors have contributed to this expectation gap, including (1) deficiencies in auditing and reporting standards in the sense that they are not suitable for the existing knowledge-based Internet economic environment, (2) lack of motivation on the part of corporate executives to completely adhere to the standards in providing high-quality and reliable financial information, (3) lack of financial literacy and training of financial statement users to effectively use financial information in making decisions, and (4) complexity of accounting standards.

The ever-growing complexity of business transactions (e.g., derivatives, fair value measurements), recent regulatory reforms, and a litigious environment have contributed to the intricacy of accounting standards. Overly complex accounting standards may not provide the necessary guidance for preparers and auditors to produce high-quality financial information and can create a significant cost burden with little value to investors. Users of financial reports desire high-quality, reliable, useful, and transparent financial information that reflects the economic substance of the business. Regulators (SEC), standard setters (Financial Accounting Standards Board [FASB] and PCAOB), and the business community should work together to address this complexity. Although regulators should review the accuracy and completeness of financial reports as well as proper disclosures of business transactions to ensure investor protection, they should avoid second guessing professional judgments by management. Standard setters should make their reporting guidance cost effective, efficient, and scalable. Corporations should regard the dissemination of high-quality financial reports as their ultimate goal and fiduciary duty to the investing public. Management should attempt to present the economic realities of the business through financial reports and prepare them at a reasonable cost.

The reliability of financial reports and the quality of audit reports are essential to maintaining investor confidence and promoting efficient capital markets. Integrated financial and internal control reporting (IFICR) is financial information contained in published financial statements and reports on internal control over financial reporting (ICFR). Reporting of financial statements and ICFR is vital because it assists shareholders to make appropriate investment and voting decisions, enables them to exercise their ownership rights on an informed basis, and protects them from receiving misleading financial information. Public companies in the United States are required to publish audited annual financial statements prepared in conformity with generally accepted accounting principles (GAAP) along with reviewed quarterly financial reports. In the post-SOX period since 2004, the majority of public companies known as accelerated filers, with $75 million in market capitalization, have also been required to publish management and auditor reports on their ICFR. These two disclosure requirements, collectively referred to as IFICR, are intended to facilitate companies' abilities to attract investors, strengthen their competitive edge, and maintain confidence in capital markets.

Figure 1.3 shows that high-quality financial information is more accurate, complete, transparent, trustworthy, and value relevant compared to low-quality financial reports. High-quality financial reports enable users, including investors, to better assess the risk and return associated with their investment. Figure 1.4 shows that financial statements are typically scrutinized through several processes for the verification of their accuracy, completeness, and reliability. The six layers of financial statement scrutiny are (1) management certification of accuracy and completeness of financial statements in presenting fair and true financial condition and results of operation as required by Sections 302 and 906 of SOX; (2) corporate governance oversight of financial statements, particularly by the company's audit committee; (3) management certification of the effectiveness of ICFR in compliance with Section 404 of SOX; (4) independent audit reports on both fair presentation of financial statements and effectiveness of ICFR; (5) SEC reviews of published financial statements and PCAOB inspections of audit quality; and (6) monitoring of published

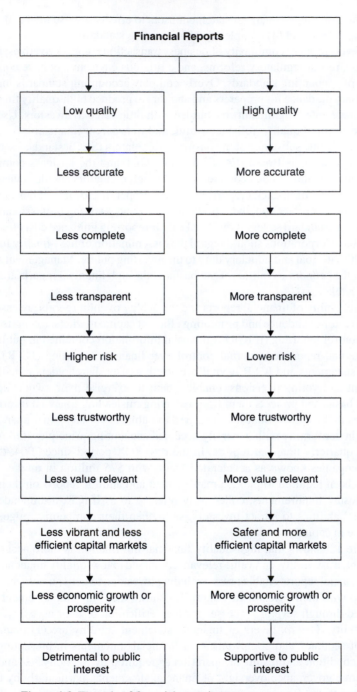

Figure 1.3 The role of financial reporting.

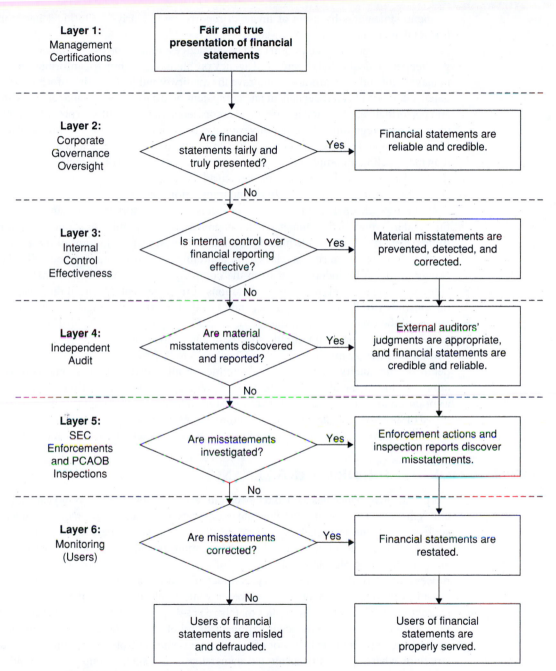

Figure 1.4 Layers of financial statement scrutiny.

financial statements by users of financial reports, particularly institutional investors and financial analysts.

Corporate governance reforms and best practices require the establishment of four key gatekeepers to deal with the perceived agency problems of asymmetric information between management and investors and to improve the quality of public financial information. These gatekeepers are (1) an independent and competent board to oversee management's strategy and performance; (2) an independent and competent external auditor to provide a high level of assurance regarding the reliability, quality, and transparency of the financial reports; (3) objective and competent legal counsel in providing legal advice and in ensuring more than mere technical compliance with applicable regulations; and (4) objective and competent financial advisors and investment bankers to advise company management and the board in conducting legitimate business affairs and transactions that have a valid economic purpose.

These gatekeepers are responsible for protecting investors from obtaining misleading financial information disseminated to the capital market by public companies in their public filings. Reported high-profile financial scandals suggest that the failures of these gatekeepers are significant contributory factors in continuing corporate malfeasance. Gatekeepers should (1) be fully independent from the company, (2) exercise professional skepticism when attesting to or relying on representations of management, (3) fulfill their professional responsibility to the investing public, and (4) withdraw from the engagement when the integrity of their work is compromised due to factors beyond their control. The value-adding activities, roles, and responsibilities of these gatekeepers and other corporate governance participants are examined in detail in Chapters 3 to 9. Effective corporate governance depends on the quality of value-adding activities of all gatekeepers. It should be noted that attorneys and financial advisors are generally viewed as advocates for those they represent as opposed to being representatives of investors. The role of the other two gatekeepers (the board of directors and the independent auditor) is legally and conceptually regarded as being a representative of investors with the keen purpose of protecting investor interests.

INTRODUCTION TO CORPORATE GOVERNANCE

Corporate governance has gained renewed interest and relevance in recent years and is now emerging as a central issue within public companies. Companies have recently undergone a series of corporate accountability reforms resulting from government regulations (SOX), the emergence of powerful institutional investors, listing standards of national stock exchanges, and guiding principles and best practices of investor activism. Corporate governance is a process affected by legal, regulatory, contractual and market-based mechanisms, and best practices to create substantiate shareholder value while protecting the interests of other shareholders. This definition implies that there is a dispersed ownership structure, and thus, the role of corporate governance is to protect shareholders and other stakeholders' interests by limiting opportunistic behavior of management who controls their interests. In a capital structure where there is concentrated ownership and a small group of shareholders can exercise ownership control, corporate governance should ensure the alignment of interests of controlling shareholders with those of minority or individual shareholders.

The primary role of all corporate governance participants, as defined in this book, should center around the fundamental theme of protecting shareholders, restoring investor confidence, and supporting strong and efficient capital markets. Corporate governance is conceived broadly in this book in terms of institutional arrangements and mechanisms affecting and affected by the role of corporate governance participants (the board of directors, senior executives, management, auditors, financial advisors, regulators, investors, and other stakeholders). Corporate governance can be defined as a process through which shareholders induce management to act in their interests, providing a degree of investor confidence that is necessary for the capital markets to function effectively.

Effective corporate governance ensures corporate accountability, enhances the reliability and quality of public financial information, enhances the integrity and efficiency of the capital market, and, thus, improves investor confidence. Poor corporate governance can have detrimental effects on a company's potential, performance, and accountability and can pave the way for financial difficulties and even fraud. Corporate governance in the twenty-first century goes beyond focusing on shareholder value enhancement because companies play a vital role in the global economy and capital markets by relying on private sector institutions to manage personal savings and secure retirement income. Corporate governance defines a set of contracts and relationships between the company, its directors, its officers, and its stakeholders. It is expected to not only define the relationship between the company's management, board, and shareholders, but also to focus on its impact on overall economic performance and market integrity, as well as public trust of its financial information.

Public companies are required to comply with the corporate governance requirements of state and federal statutes as well as the listing standards of national stock exchanges. However, mere compliance will not guarantee effective corporate governance, and companies should integrate the best practices suggested by investor activists and professional organizations into their corporate governance structure. In addition, companies may be penalized by investors if they fail to consider best practices. Effective corporate governance can only be achieved when all participants (1) add value to the company's sustainable long-term performance; (2) effectively carry out their fiduciary duty and professional responsibilities; (3) are held accountable and personally responsible for their performance; and (4) develop a practice of not only complying with applicable regulations, but also committing to doing the right thing and observing ethical principles of professional conduct in avoiding potential conflicts of interest.

Corporate governance is ultimately about leadership and accountability (1) for efficiency and effectiveness of operations to compete in the global markets; (2) for disclosure of accurate, complete, and transparent information regarding corporate performance in areas of economic and social activities; and (3) that is transparent to ensure trustworthiness of corporations and their leaders in contributing to the achievement of the company's sustainable performance and success, the integrity and efficiency of capital markets, economic growth, prosperity of the nation, and the sustainability of the global market.

Corporate Culture and Integrity

The lack of investor confidence in corporate America and its financial reports has continued to adversely affect the vibrancy of the capital market as corporate scandals of high-profile companies such as Enron and WorldCom tarnished corporate trustworthiness. This challenged business leaders to change their culture, behavior, and attitudes to restore confidence and trust in business. Corporate culture is continuously affected by its leadership in setting a "right tone at the top" and is often informal in establishing powerful norms and standards that influence behavior. Laws, regulations, rules, and standards are effective measures in changing the structure, process, and composition of corporate governance, whereas corporate culture is developed over time and derived from shared values. The engaged board of directors can significantly influence the corporate culture by (1) setting an appropriate "tone at the top" and promoting personal integrity and professional accountability, (2) rewarding high-quality and ethical performance, (3) disciplining poor performance and unethical behavior, and (4) maintaining the company's high reputation and stature in the industry and the business community. The extent and nature of the impact of corporate culture depends on the company's values and norms, the commitment of its directors and officers in promoting and enforcing ethical conduct, and the effectiveness of responses to internal and external changes.

The revised federal sentencing guidelines (FSG) emphasize the need for a culture of compliance and ethics.[10] This amendment revised FSG's provisions regarding compliance and ethics programs to strengthen the criteria that organizations must follow to prevent and detect criminal conduct. The revised FSG require organizations to (1) exercise due diligence to prevent and detect criminal conduct; (2) promote an organizational culture that encourages ethical conduct and compliance with applicable regulations; (3) assign oversight compliance responsibilities to specific senior executives (e.g., chief compliance officer [CCO]); (4) define specific roles and reporting relationships of personnel relevant to their compliance and ethics program responsibilities; (5) exercise oversight pertaining to the implementation of the compliance and ethics program by the company's board of directors or the organization's highest-level governing body; (6) require compliance and ethics training for everyone within the company, including directors, officers, employees, and agents, as appropriate; (7) establish proper policies, procedures, and steps to achieve compliance; (8) enforce compliance and ethics standards through disciplinary measures; (9) provide incentives for performance in accordance with compliance and ethics programs; (10) take reasonable steps to respond to and prevent criminal conduct by focusing on the establishment and maintenance of an ethical culture; and (11) assess periodically the effectiveness of the company's compliance and ethics program through monitoring, auditing to detect criminal misconduct, self-reporting, and cooperation with authorities.[11]

The compliance culture requires the establishment and implementation of proper programs, policies, and procedures to effectively comply with applicable regulations, standards, and best practices. However, compliance just for the sake of compliance and the development of a "check box" mentality is not enough. Corporations should create an ethical culture that encourages all corporate governance participants to do the right thing and understand that this is vital to the company's sustainable financial performance. To effectively integrate the culture of ethics and compliance into corporate governance, corporations should set an appropriate tone at the top that promotes (1) the development of roles and responsibilities for all corporate governance functions (oversight, managerial, auditing, compliance, assurance, monitory); (2) directors, officers, and employees to do the right thing; (3) the acceptance of responsibility and accountability of all personnel for their actions and actions of others under their supervision; (4) free discussion of concerns and issues without fear of retaliation; (5) proper consideration of ethical issues throughout the company when difficult and complex decisions are made; (6) understanding of the incentives and rationalization factors affecting individuals' decisions when the pressure that may drive unethical behavior exists; (7) proper oversight and management of all compliance activities and ongoing monitoring of compliance policies to adopt changes in applicable laws and regulations; (8) emphasis by directors and officers on an ethical tone at the top; and (9) reporting of unethical and noncompliance instances through the proper channels to top level management and, if necessary, to the board of directors or its designated committee (e.g., audit committee).

The compliance culture can be promoted through the establishment of a centralized CCO who is primarily responsible for ensuring compliance with all applicable laws, regulations, rules, standards, codes of ethics, policies, and procedures, and oversees all compliance functions. The CCO maintains a close working relationship with the company's directors in setting compliance strategies, properly communicating procedures to business units' compliance officers, and continuously monitoring and enforcing compliance policies and procedures. The promotion and enforcement of compliance culture starts from the board of directors by possibly establishing a compliance committee to establish strategies and ensure that related functions are being overseen and monitored. Compliance policies should be enforced and monitored by managers at each reporting business unit. All employees should adhere to compliance procedures, and legal counsel should update and revise them as necessary to ensure that they are relevant and adhere to legal and regulatory changes.

Corporate Accountability

To improve corporate accountability, corporations must also assess the impact of emerging corporate governance reforms, including the provisions of SOX, SEC-related implementation rules, PCAOB professional standards, listing standards, and best practices, and ensure compliance with these reforms. Ever-increasing global initiatives have extended corporations' accountability not only to their investors, but also to all stakeholders on a variety of issues from economic measures to governance, ethical, social, and environmental performance. Traditionally, public companies have primarily focused on achieving their economic objective of making a profit and enhancing shareholder wealth by engaging in operating, investment, and financing activities to provide and distribute goods and services. This narrow focus on achieving economic performance has been criticized for ignoring other ethical responsibilities of corporations. The multiple bottom lines (MBL) objectives of economic, social, ethical, and environmental (ESEE) performance have been advocated by global business and investment communities.[12] With the MBL objectives, the primary goal is to achieve economic performance while proper consideration is given to other measures, including social, ethical, and environmental (SEE) issues. The perceived benefits of reporting both financial and nonfinancial key performance indicators (KPIs) are improved quality of information, enhanced communications with analysts and investors, and integration of the organization's operating, financial, and social performance.

In today's business environment, global businesses are under close scrutiny and profound pressures from lawmakers, regulators, the investment community, and their diverse stakeholders to accept responsibility for their MBL of governance and ESEE performance. A study released by the United Nations in October 2005 concluded that "the integration of environmental, social, and governance (ESG) issues into investment analysis, so as to more reliably predict financial performance, is clearly permissible and is, arguably, required in all jurisdictions."[13] Institutional investors should incorporate MBL performance in these areas into their investment and voting decisions.

In October 2005, Mercer Investment Consulting (Mercer IC) announced that its research of investment managers will now include systematic evaluations of "their performance with regard to 'active ownership' practices (including proxy voting and shareholder engagement) and the incorporation of environmental, social, and corporate governance (ESG) analysis into mainstream decision making."[14] Mercer also announced that it would start rating managers on their share voting habits, engagement practices, and the extent to which they incorporate ESG issues in portfolio analysis. Although the primary focus and goal of corporate governance in the foreseeable future will continue to be an economic issue of creating long-term shareholder value, the trend toward emphasis on social, ethical, and environmental issues will continue to increase as more shareholders become concerned about these issues, file proposals, and bring these proposals to a vote. Corporate accountability reporting in areas of economic, social, ethical, environmental, and governance activities is presented in Chapter 14.

INTRODUCTION TO BUSINESS ETHICS

Ethics is defined in *Merriam-Webster's Dictionary* as "a set of moral principles: a theory or system of moral values."[15] Ethics in the literature is defined as value systems by which individuals assess their and others' behavior according to a set of previously established standards driven by a variety of religious, cultural, societal, or philosophical sources.[16] Ethics is also described as "a process by which individuals, social groups, and societies evaluate their actions from a perspective of moral principles and value."[17] Although there is not a single commonly accepted definition of business ethics, obvious examples of possible violations range from manipulation of financial information and backdating practices of executive stock options grants to spying on outside directors. Ethical violations include the behavior of the convicted executives of such high-profile companies as Enron, WorldCom, Adelphia, and Tyco. The trend in business shows a decline in business ethics in recent years, which can be reversed through (1) more education of business ethics, (2) establishment of business codes of ethical conduct, and (3) enforcement of ethical conduct.

The wave of financial scandals at the turn of the twenty-first century along with congressional responses and related regulations have brought corporate governance and business ethics into the center stage of corporate accountability and business education. Given the current culture of corporate accountability and ethical business climate as reflected in the extant literature, corporate governance and business ethics education is becoming more important to business students. Reports of professional organizations have recommended that ethics, integrity, and accountability be integrated into business and accounting curriculum.

Ethics in business assumes an important underlying postulate that the majority of the business leaders, managers, and other personnel are honest and ethical in conducting their business, and the minority who engage in unethical conduct will not prevail in the long term. Thus, the corporate culture and compliance rules should provide incentives and opportunities for ethical individuals to maintain their honesty and integrity and provide measures for the minority of unethical individuals to be monitored, punished, and corrected for their unethical conduct. Companies should promote a spirit of integrity that goes beyond compliance to the letter of the law by creating a business culture of doing what is right.

Codes of business ethics and conduct are intended to govern behavior, but they cannot substitute for moral principles, culture, and character. Warren Buffet, a veteran of corporate governance, rightfully states that the five most dangerous words in the business culture are "everybody else is doing it" as a rationale for business decision making.[18] This phrase has often been used to justify the morality and legitimacy of business actions. One obvious misuse of this phrase is the rationale by many companies for providing backdated or manipulated option grants to their directors and officers.

Corporate governance should create an ethical business environment in which all employees are encouraged and empowered to "do the right thing." Secretary of Treasury Henry Paulson believes that "we must rise above a rules-based mindset that asks 'is this legal?' and adopt a more principles-based approach that asks 'is this right?'"[19] Companies need to have ethics and business programs to address (1) their diversity of personnel services; (2) their expectations of the public and their stakeholders; (3) their legal, professional, and regulatory environment; and (4) compliance with applicable regulations, including SOX, FSG, SEC rules, and listing standards of national stock exchanges.

Business schools are being criticized for overemphasizing technical training and underemphasizing ethical considerations, professionalism, accountability, and responsibility of future business leaders, the business students.[20] The goal of business ethics education is to teach students accountability to their profession and society, and there is a general consensus among academicians and practitioners that corporate governance and business ethics should be part of business education. However, the means of and strategy for providing such education is not clear. Most states require certified public accountant (CPA) candidates to pass an ethics exam and report the ethics component in their continuing education requirements. One approach to teaching business ethics is to integrate it across the curriculum by exposing students to corporate governance issues and common ethical dilemmas and methods of resolving them.

Business ethics requires that corporations promote a culture of moral responsibility to society. Thus, in educating future business leaders, business schools attempt to incorporate and integrate business ethics into their curriculum. In light of recent high-profile cases of unethical behavior on the part of management, who once received their education in business schools, business schools are being criticized for not providing sufficient ethical education to their students. This suggests that management education should affect a person's ethics composition and shape his or her awareness and appreciation of ethical behavior and consequences. Proponents of an integrated approach suggest that ethics be an essential part of the business curriculum. Business education should introduce students to ethical issues and provide them with tools and skills to meet the ethical challenges of the business world.

There are some who believe that ethical thinking and accountability should be explored throughout the education process by either integrating them into business courses and programs or teaching them as a stand-alone subject. The National Association of State Boards of Accountancy's (NASBA's) Exposure Draft of proposed changes to the Uniform Accounting Act, Rules 5-1 and 5-2, promotes increased attention to ethics, corporate governance, communication, research, and analytical skills. The American Accounting Association (AAA) Task Force's consideration is that the strategy suggested in the proposal would not achieve NASBA's stated goals, and its implementation would impose significant costs.[21]

There are generally two schools of thought on whether ethics can be taught in the classroom among academicians, professionals, and students.[22] One view suggests that ethics can and should be taught in the classroom, and the other alludes to the fact that a person is either ethical or not and thus ethics cannot be taught. Regardless, business schools and particularly accounting students should be aware of their code of professional conduct, accountability, and professionalism, as well as the responsibilities of all participants in the financial reporting. Thus, this book focuses on both corporate governance and business ethics to provide students with the education to better understand their professionalism, leadership responsibilities, accountability, personal integrity, and ethical conduct.

An important aspect of the emerging trend toward increased corporate accountability and governance is reflected in the role and relevance of business ethics and codes of professional conduct. The diversity of people, existence of various value systems, and sensitivity of moral issues make it difficult to achieve a consensus and central theme for ethics. Thus, the "situation ethics theory" is used in this book to build a consensus as to appropriate ethical practices and professional responsibilities.[23]

CLASSROOM IMPLICATIONS OF THIS BOOK

This book is the first to compile corporate governance reforms, including state and federal statutes, rules, regulations, listing standards, guiding principles, and best practices, as well as business ethics theory and practice, into a single book to assist in corporate governance and business ethics education. The quality and quantity of corporate governance and ethics coverage in business texts has been criticized. Critics argue that business education is not adequate in areas such as ethics, corporate governance, professional judgment, accountability, and responsibility.

There are several plausible reasons for integrating corporate governance and business ethics education into the business curriculum:

1. Reported financial scandals (e.g., Enron, WorldCom, Global Crossing, Adelphia, Qwest) underscore the importance of vigilant corporate governance and ethical conduct by corporations.

2. SOX is intended to improve corporate governance by enforcing more accountability for public companies and requiring adoption of a code of ethics for their executives.

3. Anecdotal evidence and academic studies suggest that corporate governance and business ethics are not properly integrated into business education, and coverage of these issues should be increased.

4. Teaching and research in corporate governance and business ethics have been strongly recommended and encouraged.

5. There is an inventory of support materials for teaching business ethics and corporate governance in the post-Enron era. There are sufficient resources (textbooks such as this book, published articles, Internet Web sites, videos) to offer a stand-alone course or integrate business ethics and corporate governance modules throughout accounting courses.

6. It is easier to obtain administrative support to offer business ethics and corporate governance courses in the post-SOX era.

7. Several business schools have developed innovative strategies for engaging students in the challenge of providing ethical leadership by focusing on both positive and negative examples of everyday conduct in business.

8. There is an increasing trend toward incorporation of business ethics and corporate governance education into the business curriculum worldwide.

9. Accounting programs should integrate provisions of SOX on corporate governance, financial reporting, and audit functions into the curriculum.

10. Corporate governance has evolved from compliance requirements to a business imperative.

11. NASBA, in its Exposure Draft of Uniform Accounting Rules 5-1 and 5-2 regarding NASBA 150-hour education, emphasized the need for six semester credit hours in ethical and professional responsibilities that was subsequently tabled.

12. The Association to Advance Collegiate Schools of Business International (AACSB) has promoted the integration of business ethics and corporate governance into the business curriculum.

SUMMARY

Corporate governance involves relationships and power sharing between a company's management, board, shareholders, and other stakeholders, including the way the board oversees the running of a company by its managers and how board members are, in turn, accountable to shareholders and the company. Corporate governance also provides the structure for determining the objectives of the company, attaining those objectives, and monitoring its performance. It should provide proper incentives for the board and management to pursue objectives that are in the interests of the company and its shareholders. An effective corporate governance system helps provide a level of confidence that is necessary for the proper functioning of a market economy.

Good corporate governance lays the foundation for the integrity and efficiency of financial markets. Conversely, poor corporate governance weakens a company's potential and, at worst, can pave the way for financial difficulties and fraud. Companies that are well governed will usually outperform poorly governed companies and will be able to attract investors to help finance further growth. As a result, companies are encouraged to use their resources more efficiently, and the cost of capital is lower. Simply stated, good corporate governance strengthens market and investor confidence, integrity, and efficiency, thereby promoting economic growth and financial stability.

The Key Points of This Chapter are

- The primary goal of corporate governance is to create a right balance of power sharing among all participants, particularly shareholders, boards of directors, and management, to create and enhance shareholder value while protecting the interests of other stakeholders.

- The investment community is requiring companies to earn back public trust; therefore, the roles of individuals involved in corporate financial reporting have become a value-added function under intense scrutiny.

- Reliable and transparent financial information contributes to the efficient function of the capital markets and economic growth.

- Corporate government reforms require four key corporate gatekeepers: an independent and competent board, an independent and competent auditor, objective and competent legal counsel, and objective and competent financial advisors.

- Corporate governance, for the purpose of this book, is defined as the process affected by a set of legislative, regulatory, and legal market mechanisms; listing standards; best practices; and efforts of all corporate governance participants, which creates a system of checks and balances with the goal of creating and enhancing sustainable value for shareholders while protecting the interests of other stakeholders.

- Market-based mechanisms alone cannot solve corporate governance problems because they are often initiated and enforced after the occurrences of management abuse and after shareholders sell their shares, depressing the price.

- Corporate governance reforms, including SOX, SEC-related implementation rules, listing standards of national stock exchanges, auditing standards of the PCAOB, guiding principles of professional organizations, and best practices, are intended to improve the vigilance and effectiveness of corporate governance; reliability, integrity, transparency, and quality of financial reports; the effectiveness of internal controls and related risk management assessment; the credibility of the audit function; the independence and objectivity of other gatekeepers, such as legal counsel, financial analysts, and shareholders; monitoring; and democracy.

- The net benefit of corporate governance reforms is expected to aid in improving investor confidence and public trust in corporate America, identify and manage potential conflicts of interest that may exist, and address the professional accountability and personal integrity of all corporate governance participants.

- Corporations should set an appropriate "tone at the top" to effectively integrate a culture of ethics and compliance.

- Global initiatives have extended corporations' accountability, not only to their investors, but also to all stakeholders, on a variety of issues from economic measures to governance, ethical, social, and environmental performance. Therefore, corporations are focusing on MBL objectives of ESEE performance.

KEY TERMS

corporate accountability reporting	Generally Accepted Accounting Principles (GAAP)	Sarbanes-Oxley Act of 2002 (SOX)
corporate culture	listing standards	Securities Act of 1933
corporate gatekeeper	multiple bottom lines (MBL)	Securities Exchange Act of 1934
corporate governance	Public Company	Securities and Exchange
ethical accountability	Accounting Oversight	Commission (SEC)
federal sentencing guidelines	Board (PCAOB)	social accountability

REVIEW QUESTIONS

1. What is the primary goal of corporate governance?

2. What is the primary mission of a public company?

3. What is the role of a corporate governance gatekeeper?

4. Corporate governance reforms and best practices require the establishment of four key gatekeepers to deal with the perceived agency problems of asymmetric information between management and investors and to improve the quality of public financial information. Who are these gatekeepers and what role do they play in corporate governance?

5. How does an effective corporate governance structure improve investor confidence?

6. What is the primary intent of corporate governance reforms?

7. What benefits are obtained by the proper implementation of SOX?

8. How can the board of directors influence the corporate culture?

9. What is the intention of organizational codes of business ethics and conduct?

10. What are the three key best practices that make corporate governance effective?

11. Why is there no universal definition of corporate governance?

12. How have SOX provisions, SEC-related rules, and listing standards influenced the corporate governance structure?

13. What business entities are currently affected by SOX?

14. What is the difference between a shareholder and a stakeholder aspect of corporate governance?

15. What are the primary differences between financial reporting and corporate accountability reporting?

16. What is the relationship between corporations and stakeholders, and what is the corporations' role in that relationship?

17. What is the primary difference between the first and second tier of the stakeholder hierarchy?

18. To whom are corporations accountable?

19. Explain the relationship between corporations and the capital markets in the United States.

DISCUSSION QUESTIONS

1. In your own words, briefly explain the concepts of value creation and value protection.

2. Has Sarbanes-Oxley thus far had a positive, negative, or neutral effect on public companies? Defend your answer.

3. Discuss the following quote from Lori A. Richards, the SEC's director of the Office of Compliance Inspections and Examinations:

   It's not enough to have policies. It's not enough to have procedures. It's not enough to have good intentions. All of these can help. But to be successful, compliance must be an embedded part of your firm's culture.

4. What are the benefits of an MBL approach in evaluating the organization KPIs related to both financial and nonfinancial information?

5. Who are first-tier, second-tier, and third-tier stakeholders, and why are they significant to the organization?

6. What is the significance of quality financial statements and other financial reporting information?

7. What are the responsibilities of corporate governance gatekeepers?

8. What should the board of directors do to promote a positive corporate culture?

9. Will compliance with applicable laws, rules, and regulations ensure effective corporate governance? Explain your answer.

10. What are some reasons for integrating corporate governance and business ethics education into the business curriculum?

11. As noted in the text, corporate governance has no universally accepted definition. Define corporate governance and explain your definition.

12. The following is a list of eight entities and conventional systems that shape corporate governance. Provide examples of how or what they have done.
    (a) Federal legislation
    (b) State statutes
    (c) SEC regulation
    (d) The courts
    (e) Listing standards
    (f) Investor activists
    (g) Investors
    (h) Other corporate governance participants

13. The book mentions many examples of the give–take relationship between corporations and society. What are some other examples of the corporation–society relationship? Provide a minimum of three examples.

14. Discuss the significance and importance of investors (shareholders) as the first tier of the stakeholder hierarchy.

NOTES

1. Whitehouse, K. 2006, July 25. Former SEC Head Supports Efforts Stop Quarterly Guidance. *Dow Jones News Service.*

2. Turner, L. E. 2006, September 6. Hearing on: Stock Options Backdating before U.S. Senate Committee on Banking, Housing, and Urban Affairs.

3. Schuetze, E., M. Sutton, and L. Turner. 2003, January 4. A letter sent to the PCAOB by the three former chief accountants of the SEC. A copy can be obtained from lynneturner@aol.com.

4. Woodward, R., J. Dittmar, and C. Munoz. 2003. The Currency of Good Governance. *Platts Energy Business & Technology* 5(4): 30.

5. The Conference Board. 2003. Commission on Public Trust and Private Enterprise. Available at: www.conference-board.org/pdf_free/SR-03-04.pdf.

6. Jensen, M. C., and W. H. Meckling. 1976. Theory of the Firm: Managerial Behavior, Agency Costs and Ownership Structure. *The Journal of Financial Economics* 3: 305–360.

7. Mintz, S. M. 2005. Corporate Governance in an International Context: Legal Systems, Financing Patterns and Cultural Variables. *Corporate Governance* 13(5): 582–597.

8. Business for Social Responsibility. 2003, April. Stakeholder Engagement Issue Brief. Available at: www.bsr.org/CSRResources/IssueBriefDetail.cfm?DocumentID=48813.

9. Solomon, D., and C. Bryan-Low. 2003. 'Tough' Cop for Accounting Beat. *The Wall Street Journal* April 16: Cl.

10. U.S. Sentencing Commission. 2004. 2004 Federal Sentencing Guideline Manual. Available at: www.ussc.gov/2004guid/TABCON04.htm.

11. Ibid.

12. Global Reporting Initiative (GRI). 2002. Sustainability Reporting Guidelines. Available at: www.celb.org/lmageCache/CELB/content/travel_2dleisure/gri_5f2002_2epdf/vl/gri_5f2002.pdf.

13. Freshfields Bruckhaus Deringer. 2005, October. A Legal Framework for the Integration of Environmental, Social and Governance Issues into Institutional Investment: Produced for the Asset Management Working Group of the UNEP Finance Initiative. Available at: www.unepfi.org/fileadmin/documents/freshfields_legal_resp_2005.pdf.

14. Mercer IC. 2005, October 25. Mercer IC Evaluates Investment Managers' Involvement in Active Ownership and Integrated Analysis. Available at: www.mercer.com/referencecontent.jhtml?idContent=1199370.

15. Merriam-Webster's Online Dictionary, n.d. Available at: www.m-w.com/dictionary/ethics.

16. Hurley, M. 1992. Ethical Problems of the Association Executive in Study Guide for Institutes of Organizational Management, Chamber of Commerce of the United States, Washington, DC, p. 2.

17. Cordiero, W. P. 2003. The Only Solution to the Decline in Business Ethics: Ethical Managers. *Teaching Business Ethics* 7: 3.

18. *Financial Times*. 2006, September 27. Full Text of Warren Buffet's September 27 Memo. Available at: us.ft.com/ftgateway/superpage.ft?news_id=ftol00920061710250260&page=2.

19. Paulson, H. M. 2006, November 20. Remarks by Treasury Secretary Henry M. Paulson on the Competitiveness of U.S. Capital Markets Economic Club of New York. New York, NY. Available at: www.treas.gov/press/releases/hpl74.htm.

20. Bernardi. R. A., and D. F. Bean. 2006. Ethics in Accounting Education: The Forgotten Stakeholders. *The CPA Journal* July.

21. American Accounting Association (AAA). 2005, August 26. Letter to NASBA Education Committee (regarding creation of AAA Task Force). August 2006. AAA, Sarasota, FL. Available at: www.nasba.org/nasbaweb/NASBAWeb.nsf/PLT/2D5B2F21CEAE871E862571B900755B45/$file/AmericanAccountingAssociation(AAA).pdf.

22. See note 20 above.

23. McCarthy, I. N. 1997. Professional Ethics Code Conflict Situations: Ethical and Value Orientation of Collegiate Accounting Students. *Journal of Business Ethics* 16: 1467–1474.

Chapter 2

Corporate Governance

INTRODUCTION

Many initiatives and developments during the past several decades have shaped corporate governance. The early developments underscored the need to ensure that management acts in the sustainable well-being of the company and its shareholders. Recent developments of the late 1990s and the early 2000s reinvigorated interest in, and focus on, effective corporate governance to protect shareholders and other stakeholders (e.g., employees, creditors, customers) from managerial misconduct and corporate malfeasance. Corporate governance reforms, including SOX and related SEC implementation rules, listing standards of national stock exchanges (New York Stock Exchange [NYSE], Nasdaq, American Stock Exchange [AMEX]), and best practices and guiding principles of professional organizations (National Association of Securities Dealers [NASD], The Conference Board), came in response to the wave of financial scandals in high-profile public companies. These reforms require professional accountability, personal responsibility, and integrity for all participants. Corporate governance has transformed from compliance requirements to the business strategic imperative of creating shareholder value and protecting the interests of other stakeholders. These developments aim at improving public trust and investor confidence in corporate America, its corporate governance, its capital markets, and financial reporting. This chapter presents the fundamentals of corporate governance.

Primary Objectives

The primary objectives of this chapter are to

- Identify the corporate governance developments in the post-SOX era.
- Understand that corporate governance is designed to ensure the public companies' goals of shareholder value creation and stakeholder value protection.
- Define corporate governance structure and its components of principles, functions, and mechanisms.
- Illustrate how corporate governance has evolved from compliance function to a strategic imperative of creating shareholder value and protecting the interests of other stakeholders.
- Provide an overview of corporate governance aspects and principles, and define the principles on which an effective corporate governance structure should be based.
- List and define the seven essential corporate governance functions.
- Identify significant improvements resulting from corporate governance reforms in the United States.
- Become familiar with best practices of corporate governance.
- Become familiar with corporate governance reporting and its components as well as corporate governance ratings.

DEFINITION OF CORPORATE GOVERNANCE

Corporate governance is a relatively new term often used to describe the way a company is managed, monitored, and held accountable. There is no universally accepted definition of corporate governance primarily because its concept is not well defined, it covers various distinct economic phenomena, and it is often described from the shareholders' view of what a company should and should not do. The business literature and authoritative guides have defined corporate governance in different ways and from different perspectives. Some define it from a regulatory perspective as "the system of laws, rules, and factors that control operations at a company."[1] Others define corporate governance from points of view of corporate governance participants and related constraints as dealing "with the ways in which suppliers of finance to corporations assure themselves of getting a return on their investment."[2] Others view corporate governance as more than merely the relationship between the company and its capital providers by focusing on the broader aspects of stakeholders. Corporate governance is a field in economics that investigates how to motivate management of corporations by the use of incentive mechanisms, such as contracts, organizational design, and legislation.[3]

The legal definition of corporate governance focuses on the enforcement of shareholders' rights by stating that "the field of corporate governance is concerned with the rules and principles that regulate the power relationship among owners [shareholders], directors, and managers."[4] In the United States, corporate governance is shaped by (1) federal legislation, including the Securities Act of 1933 and the Securities Exchange Act of 1934 and SOX; (2) state statutes defining corporation legal boundaries; (3) regulatory rules established by the SEC; (4) the courts' deliberation in interpreting and enforcing federal and state laws; (5) listing standards of national stock exchanges; (6) investor activists (e.g., The Conference Board, public pension funds, investor organizations, the Council of Institutional Investors) in suggesting best practices and policies; (7) investors, especially institutional shareholders in communicating with corporations through active engagement, proxy voting, and sponsoring shareholder proposals; and (8) other corporate governance participants, particularly the company's independent directors in implementing corporate governance measures.

Corporate governance, for the purpose of this book, is defined as

The process affected by a set of legislative, regulatory, legal, market mechanisms, listing standards, best practices, and efforts of all corporate governance participants, including the company's directors, officers, auditors, legal counsel, and financial advisors, which creates a system of checks and balances with the goal of creating and enhancing enduring and sustainable shareholder value, while protecting the interests of other stakeholders.

ASPECTS OF CORPORATE GOVERNANCE

Corporate governance has evolved from its role of reducing agency costs to creating long-term shareholder value, and, recently, to increasing value for all stakeholders. Under the emerging reforms, in the past several decades it has further evolved to the integrated aspect of meeting both compliance requirements and promoting a strategic business imperative. Three aspects of corporate governance examined in this chapter are shareholder aspect, stakeholder aspect, and an integrated aspect. The shareholder aspect focuses on the shareholder value creation and enhancement goal of corporate governance, whereas the stakeholder aspect emphasizes the value protection goal for all stakeholders; the integrated approach combines the two. Corporate governance reforms in the United States typically focus on the shareholder aspect, whereas in Europe the emphasis is on the integrated aspect.

Shareholder Aspect

Shareholders own corporations. The board of directors is elected and executives are hired to make business decisions on behalf of the shareholders. Directors appoint management to manage the business and allocate resources for their optimal use. As corporations grew and their stocks were widely distributed among smaller groups of investors, ownership became dispersed, and individual shareholder control diminished. As investors continue to lose the control of corporations they own, the senior officers, particularly the CEOs, gain more control and ability to influence business affairs, presumably in the best interest of shareholders. Thus, corporate accountability to ensure interests of management align with those of shareholders becomes a centerpiece of corporate governance and its effectiveness in protecting and creating shareholder value.

The shareholder aspect of corporate governance is based on the premise that shareholders provide capital to the corporation that exists for their benefit. It supports the agency theory that fiduciary duties of corporate directors and executives are to shareholders who have a residual claim on the company's residual assets and cash flows. Shareholders (principals) provide capital to the company, which is run by management (agent). The principal–agent problem exists because corporations are separate entities from their owners—management needs physical capital (investment funds), and investors need skilled human capital to run the company. According to the principal–agent theory, also called the shareholder model of corporate governance, the primary objective of the company is to maximize shareholder wealth, and, thus, the role of corporate governance is to ensure the enhancement of shareholder wealth and to align the interests of management with those of the shareholders. The principal–agent problem arises from two factors: the separation of ownership and control, and, most importantly, incomplete contracts or costly enforceable contracts between the agents and the principals, known as agency costs.

The corporate governance structure should consist of mechanisms (internal and external) designed to effectively align the behavior of management (agents) with the desires of the principals (shareholders). The agency problem exists when the interests of management and shareholders are not in accord and when there are difficulties in verifying management activities. Agency costs also arise where there is an "information asymmetry" between management and shareholders and when the company's board of directors fails to fulfill its fiduciary duties of effectively carrying out its assigned oversight role.

In the real world, the agency problem can never be perfectly solved, and agency costs cannot be totally eliminated. If complete contracts were feasible and efficiently enforceable, there would be no agency costs, in the sense that investors would have known exactly what management was doing with their funds, and management would know investors' expectations. However, complete contracts are neither feasible nor enforceable, which results in the occurrence of "residual contract rights" of making decisions based on the rights not specified in the contract or based on unforeseen circumstances. The residual contract rights may cause asymmetric information problems because management possesses information that is not disclosed or available to investors, which may result in management entrenchment. Two types of managerial failures may prevent management from acting in the best interest of shareholders: (1) failure of managerial competence resulting from unintentional mistakes or negligence in discharging fiduciary duties; and (2) failures of managerial integrity caused by willful or opportunistic behaviors (fraudulent activities, fabrications, embezzlement, illegitimate earnings management) that have detrimental effects on the value of the firm's assets.[5]

Under the shareholder aspect, corporate governance is designed to reduce the agency costs and align the interests of management with those of investors through (1) providing incentives and opportunities for management to carry out its function effectively, and to maximize shareholder wealth by providing executive compensation plans, ownerships, or stock options; (2) strengthening shareholder rights to monitor, control, and discipline management through enforceable contracts or legal protection; (3) promoting shareholder democracy; (4) improving the vigilance of the board's oversight function; (5) holding directors accountable and liable for the fulfillment of their fiduciary duties; and (6) improving the effectiveness of both internal corporate governance mechanisms (board of directors, internal controls) and external corporate governance mechanisms (external audit, monitoring, and regulatory functions).

Stakeholder Aspect

The stakeholder model of corporate governance focuses on the broader view of the company as the nexus of contracts among all corporate governance participants with the common goal of creating value. The emerging model concentrates on maximization for all stakeholders, including (1) contractual participants such as shareholders, creditors, suppliers, customers, and employees; and (2) social constituents, including the local community; society and global partners; local, state, and federal governments; and environmental matters. Under this view, public companies must be socially responsible—good citizens granted the use of the nation's physical and human capital, managed in the public interest. Thus, the performance of public companies is measured in terms of key financial indicators (earnings, market share, stock price), social indicators (employment, customer satisfaction, fair trading with suppliers), ethical indicators (proper business culture, business code of conduct), and environmental indicators (antipollution, preservation of natural resources).

Stakeholders are individuals or groups who affect the company's strategic decisions, operations, and performance, and are also affected by its decisions or activities. Traditionally, shareholders have been the primary users of the company's financial reports, which reflect the company's financial condition and the results of operations. Although shareholders are still the primary recipient of the company's reports on economic performance, stakeholders are now becoming more engaged and interested in the company's MBL performance on a variety of economic, governance, ethical, social, and environmental issues.

Integrated Aspect

The shareholder aspect of corporate governance implies that shareholders, by virtue of their ownership investment in the company, are entitled to direct and monitor its business and affairs. Shareholders influence corporate governance by exercising their right to elect directors, who then appoint management to run the company. Directors and officers, as agents of the company, act as trustees on behalf of shareholders, and their primary responsibilities and fiduciary duties are to shareholders. Although directors' and officers' legal fiduciary duties are only extended to shareholders who invested in the company, they may have many nonfiduciary duties to other stakeholders, who may have various interests and claims to the company's welfare. Shareholders' rights, including the right to elect, the right to put propositions before the annual shareholder meetings, and the right to reliable and accurate financial information, are legally enforceable, and offending directors and officers can be brought to justice through the courts. Stakeholders such as employees, creditors, customers, suppliers, social responsibility activists, and communities, who are affected by and can affect the success of the company, do not have the right to direct or monitor the company. Nonetheless, the interests of stakeholders are protected under the contract and tort laws.

Anecdotal evidence and academic research suggest that (1) companies and their directors and officers should pay attention to the interests of various stakeholders; (2) the interests of stakeholders have intrinsic value to the company; (3) stakeholders contribute to and have some claim to the company's success; (4) directors and officers have many nonfiduciary duties to stakeholders under contract and tort laws; and (5) the shareholder–management relationship, in an ethical sense, is not different than that with other stakeholders, although, legally, the relationship may be different.[6] U.S. corporate governance has traditionally been geared toward increasing shareholder value with little focus on protecting the interests of other stakeholders. Thus, until recently, there was no guidance on how the board should treat stakeholders other than shareholders.

The primary goal of corporate governance is not simply to reduce agency costs, but to create a right balance of power sharing among all corporate governance participants, particularly shareholders, directors, and management, driven by the responsibility to create and enhance long-term shareholder value while protecting the interests of other stakeholders. Modern corporate governance emphasizes both financial aspects of increasing shareholder value and an integrated approach that considers the rights and interests of all stakeholders. Corporate governance should be viewed as a dynamic and integrated approach of addressing financial, social, environmental, and economic concerns of all stakeholders. Regardless of what aspect of corporate governance is accepted, the corporate governance structure should be based on the following premises:

1. The primary purpose of corporate governance is to create and enhance sustainable and enduring shareholder value while protecting the interests of other shareholders.

2. The board of directors, as representatives of investors, has direct authority and responsibility to govern business affairs of the company and is ultimately accountable to investors for the company's strategic performance, achievement of goals, and prevention of surprises.

3. The board of directors delegates the authority of managing the company to the top management team (senior executives, CEO, CFO) and holds senior executives accountable for their decisions, actions, and performance without micromanaging business affairs and decisions.

4. The chairperson of the board of directors is directly responsible for coordinating and organizing the board's activities and is ultimately accountable to the entire board, not the CEO.

5. The CEO is directly responsible for managing the company and is ultimately accountable to the board for the assigned managerial functions and decisions.

6. Corporate governance participants' roles (e.g., oversight, managerial, compliance, internal audit, advisory, external audit, monitoring) should be viewed as "value added."

7. Corporate governance should promote and facilitate shareholder democracy through majority voting and shareholders' access to proxy materials for the nomination and election of directors.

8. Proper communications through proxy statements and periodic financial reports assist shareholders in their investment and voting decisions.

9. Well-governed companies outperform poorly governed companies in the long term, and thus, more capital will flow to companies with good governance.

10. Directors' and officers' accountability should be achieved through a proper evaluation system that rewards good and ethical performance while punishing poor performance and misconduct.

11. Executive compensation should be linked to performance, be established and approved by the board of directors, and receive the advisory approval of shareholders.

12. The board of directors should have a proper executive succession plan and appropriate strategies to deal with potential crisis management.

CORPORATE GOVERNANCE STRUCTURE

Corporate governance was traditionally viewed as the mechanism for aligning the interests of management and those of shareholders, which arose from the separation of ownership and control of public companies. The role of corporate governance has been to reduce agency costs and to create long-term shareholder value by focusing on the decision control responsibilities of the board of directors and decision management functions of senior executives. This section presents a much broader view, an integrated approach to corporate governance, by focusing on the value-adding role of corporate governance participants, including the board of directors, management, auditors, financial advisors, legal counsel, standard-setting bodies and regulators, and other stakeholders.

There is no globally accepted corporate governance structure. Different structures of corporate governance reflect the nature of cultural, social, legal, regulatory, business, and economic systems. The Anglo-Saxon structure focuses on managerial functions to maximize shareholders' wealth, whereas the German structure emphasizes the interests of a wide range of stakeholders, including shareholders, creditors, employees, and communities. The corporate governance structure presented in this chapter is based on three interrelated components of corporate governance principles, functions, and mechanisms, as depicted in Figure 2.1.

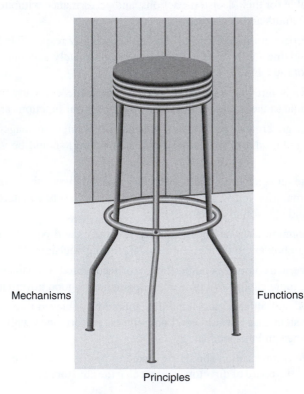

Mechanisms

Functions

Principles

Figure 2.1 Corporate governance structure.

Source: Rezaee, Z. 2007. *Corporate Governance Post-Sarbanes-Oxley Act: Regulations, Requirements, & Integrated Processes.* John Wiley & Sons, Hoboken, NJ.

Corporate Governance Principles

No globally accepted set of corporate governance principles can be applied across a broad range of board structures; business practices; and legal, political, and economic environments. In 2004, the Organisation for Economic Co-operation and Development (OECD) released its revised Principles of Corporate Governance. These principles are (1) fairness, (2) transparency, (3) accountability, and (4) responsibility. The OECD's set of core principles of corporate governance is applicable to a wide range of jurisdictions. These principles were subsequently adopted by the International Corporate Governance Network (ICGN). Figure 2.2, Panels A to C, summarize corporate governance principles, policies, and rules of several organizations, including the NYSE, the OECD, and the ICGN. These corporate governance principles, policies, and rules are discussed in depth throughout the book.

Panel A: NYSE Corporate Governance Rules: Section 303A

1. **Independent Directors**
   Listed companies must have a majority of independent directors.

2. **Independence Tests**
   To tighten the definition of independent director for purposes of these standards, no director qualifies as independent unless the board of directors affirmatively determines that the director has no material relationship with the listed company (directly or as a partner, shareholder, or office of an organization that has a relationship with the company). Companies must identify which directors are independent and disclose the basis for that determination. [The rules then stipulate a number of criteria for determining whether a director is independent.]

3. **Executive Sessions**
   To empower nonmanagement directors to serve as a more effective check on management, the nonmanagement directors of each listed company must meet at regularly scheduled executive sessions without management.

4. **Nominating/Corporate Governance Committee**
   - Listed companies must have a nominating/corporate governance committee composed entirely of independent directors.
   - The nominating committee must have a written charter. [The rules then stipulate what the charter should address.]

5. **Compensation Committee**
   - Listed companies must have a compensation committee composed entirely of independent directors.
   - The compensation committee must have a written charter. [The rules then stipulate what the charter should address.]

6. **Audit Committee**
   Listed companies must have an audit committee that satisfies the requirements of Rule 10A-3 under the Exchange Act.

7. **Audit Committee Additional Requirements**
   - The audit committee must have a minimum of three members.
   - In addition to any requirement in Rule 10A.3(b)(1), all audit committee members must satisfy the requirements for independence set out in Section 303A.02.

- The audit committee must have a written charter. [The rules then stipulate what the charter should address.]
- Each listed company should have an internal audit function.

8. **Shareholder Approval of Equity Compensation Plans**
   The shareholders must be given the opportunity to vote on all equity-compensation plans and material revisions thereto, with limited exemptions defined by the NYSE corporate governance rules.

9. **Corporate Governance Guidelines**
   Listed companies must adopt and disclose corporate governance guidelines that address certain subjects.

10. **Code of Business Conduct and Ethics**
    Listed companies must adopt and disclose a code of business conduct and ethics for directors, officers, and employees, and promptly disclose any waivers of the code for directors or executive officers.

11. **Foreign Private Issuer Disclosure**
    Listed foreign private issuers must disclose any significant ways in which their corporate governance practices differ from those followed by domestic companies under NYSE listing standards.

12. **Certification Requirements**
    - Each listed company CEO must certify to the NYSE each year that he or she is not aware of any violation by the company of NYSE corporate governance listings standards, qualifying the certification to the extent necessary.
    - Each listed company CEO must promptly notify the NYSE in writing after any executive officer of the company becomes aware of any material noncompliance with any applicable provisions of Section 303A.
    - Each listed company must submit an executed Written Affirmation annually to the NYSE.

13. **Public Reprimand Letter**
    The NYSE may issue a public reprimand letter to any listed company that violates an NYSE listing standard.

14. **Web Site Requirement**
    Listed companies must have and maintain a publicly accessible Web site.

Source: Final NYSE Corporate Governance Rules: Section 303A. Available at: www.nyse.com/pdfs/finalcorpgovrules.pdf.

Panel B: OECD Principles of Corporate Governance

1. **Ensuring the basis for an effective corporate governance framework.**
   The corporate governance framework should promote transparent and efficient markets, be consistent with the rule of law, and clearly articulate the division of responsibilities among different supervisory, regulatory, and enforcement authorities.

2. **The rights of shareholders and key ownership functions.**
   The corporate governance framework should protect and facilitate the exercise of shareholder's rights.

3. **The equitable treatment of shareholders.**
   The corporate governance framework should ensure the equitable treatment of all shareholders, including minority and foreign shareholders. All shareholders should have the opportunity to obtain effective redress for violation of their rights.

4. **The role of shareholders in corporate governance.**
   The corporate governance framework should recognize the rights of stakeholders established by law or through mutual agreements and encourage active co-operation between corporations and stakeholders in creating wealth, jobs, and the sustainability of financially sound enterprise.

5. **Disclosure and transparency.**
   The corporate governance framework should ensure that timely and accurate disclosure is made on all material matters regarding the corporation, including the financial situation, performance, ownership, and governance of the company.

6. **The responsibilities of the board.**
   The corporate governance framework should ensure the strategic guidance of the company, the effective monitoring of management by the board, and the board's accountability to the company and the shareholders.

Source: Organisation for Economic Co-operation and Development (OECD). (2004). OECD Principles of Corporate Governance. Available at: www.oecd.org/dataoecd/32/18/31557724.pdf.

Panel C: International Corporate Governance Network (ICGN) Statement on Global Corporate Governance Principles

1. **Corporate Objective**
   Corporate governance practices should optimize returns to the shareholders and develop and implement a strategy for the long-term prosperity of the business.

2. **Disclosure and Transparency**
   The corporation should disclose relevant and material information concerning the corporation on a timely basis. The information should include things like whether the company is meeting market guidelines where they exist, the relationship of the company with other companies, major shareholders in the company, information on special voting rights, shareholders' agreements, significant cross-shareholding relationships, cross-guarantees, and information on differential voting rights and related party transactions.

3. **Audit**
   ICGN supports the development of the highest-quality international accounting and financial reporting standards. Annual audits should be carried out on behalf of the shareholders by external auditors, proposed by the audit committee, and approved by the shareholders. The audit committee should represent the shareholders' interests all the time. The annual audit should provide an opinion on whether the financial statements fairly represent the financial position and performance of the company in all material respects, give a true and fair view of the affairs of the company, and are in accordance with applicable laws and regulations. The board of directors or the officers as required by the applicable laws should affirm the company's financial reports and internal controls at least annually.

4. **Shareholders' Ownership, Responsibilities, Voting Rights, and Remedies**
   Corporations should facilitate exercising shareholders' rights. All shareholders should be treated equally. One common share should have one vote, and access to voting should be facilitated by following the ICGN's Global Share Voting principles.

5. **Corporate Boards**
   Corporate boards should be independent and monitor the effectiveness of the company's governance practices and making changes as needed. They should

set performance benchmarks and oversee major decisions for the corporation. In all cases, the boards should work in shareholders' best interests and represent them.

6. **Corporate Remuneration Policies**
Corporations should follow the best practices for remuneration set out in the most current policy of the ICGN.

7. **Corporate Citizenship, Stakeholder Relations, and the Ethical Conduct of Business**
The board is accountable to shareholders and responsible for managing successful and productive relationships with the corporation's stakeholders. Cooperation between corporations and their stakeholders is essential for creating wealth, employment, and financially sound enterprise over time. Corporations should comply with all applicable laws and regulations, disclose their policies, encourage employee participation, adopt a code of ethics, promote and implement a culture of integrity, and be socially responsible.

8. **Corporate Governance Implementation**
Corporations should comply with a widely recognized national corporate governance code which is generally in line with ICGN principles. Where such a code does not exist, investors and others should insist on developing one. Corporate governance issues between shareholders, the board, and management should be addressed through dialogue and, where appropriate, with government regulatory representatives as well as other concerned bodies, so as to resolve disputes, if possible, through negotiation, mediation, or arbitration.

Source: International Corporate Governance Network (ICGN). Draft Statement on Global Corporate Governance Principles. Available at: www.icgn.org/members/consultations/cgp/exposure_draft.pdf.

Figure 2.2 Global corporate governance principles, rules, and policies.

Several corporate governance principles of honesty, resilience, responsiveness, and transparency are discussed in the following paragraphs.

1. **Honesty.** Honesty means telling the truth at all times, regardless of the consequences. Honesty is important in establishing a trusting relationship among all corporate governance participants. This also means that corporate communications with both internal and external audiences, including public financial reports, should be accurate, fair, transparent, and trustworthy. A reputation for honesty can be earned over time through truthful and transparent corporate communication, and it can be easily destroyed through lies, deceptions, malfeasance, concealments, and fraud. In today's information technology environment, access to verifiable information on corporation trustworthiness and honesty is easily and conveniently available. Thus, public companies should continuously maintain honesty and a good reputation.

2. **Resilience.** A resilient corporate governance structure is sustainable and enduring in the sense that it will easily recuperate from setbacks and abuses. A possible drawback to a flexible corporate governance structure is the potential for abuse because

the open and responsive structure is more susceptible to exploitation. Corporate governance mechanisms, both internal and external, are designed to prevent, detect, and correct such abuse.

3. **Responsiveness.** The company's timely and appropriate responses to the requests or desires of all stakeholders show the company has respect for the concerns and interests of others. Effective corporate governance is also responsive to emerging initiatives and changes in political, regulatory, social, and environmental issues.

4. **Transparency.** Openness and understandability of the company's disclosures to both internal and external audiences can result in trust in its corporate governance. Transparency means that the company is not hiding relevant information, and disclosures are fair, accurate, and reliable. Transparent corporate governance is open and understandable to all concerned parties in terms of its goals, principles, mechanisms, and functions.

A key principle of effective corporate governance is its transparency and well-balanced, fair disclosure of not only financial information, but also operations and structures. One important element of the financial reporting process is the disclosure of significant events and transactions that could possibly affect the judgment and decisions of stakeholders in dealing with the company. One obvious example is identification and disclosure of related parties and related party transactions. In the case of Enron, that would be the nature, relevance, and significance of those "Special Purpose Entities" that were established to exaggerate earnings and hide liabilities. Another example would be the reputation, integrity, and shareholdings of executives' restricted stocks and stock options. Whether the nature of these disclosures should be continuous or periodic depends on the company's culture of openness and its corporate governance structure.

In October 2004, the European Commission (EC) released a proposal intended to improve corporate governance transparency in the following ways: (1) the company's board of directors would be directly responsible for financial statements; (2) proper disclosure of all material off balance sheet arrangements would be required in the notes to the financial statements; (3) proper disclosure of transactions with related parties would be required; and (4) a corporate governance statement as an integral part of annual reports would be required to reflect information about the company's risk management system, internal controls, shareholders' rights and meetings, and the board of directors and its committees.[7]

A joint report by the CFA Institute and the Business Roundtable Institute for Corporate Ethics makes the following recommendations for improving corporate communications and transparency: (1) encourage companies to provide more transparent financial reports and more meaningful and frequent communications about their long-term vision, strategic goals, and performance metrics, including key financial indicators; (2) encourage greater use of plain language communications, as opposed to the current communications dominated by legal and accounting language; (3) endorse the use of corporate sustainable investment statements to shareholders above and beyond the requirements of the current practice reporting and operating model; (4) improve corporate disclosure and communication processes to adequately inform investors and analysts rather than create complexity and confusion regarding the company's sustainable performance; and (5) encourage institutional investors to provide sustainable investment statements to their beneficiaries similar to those companies are required to make to their shareholders.[8]

In summary, corporate governance structure should be developed based on the following principles:

1. *Value-adding philosophy*—Corporate governance should provide foundations for all corporate governance functions to add value to the company's sustainable performance.

2. *Ethical conduct*—Corporate governance should promote ethical conduct for all participants throughout the company. This entails setting an appropriate tone at the top and a firm commitment by corporate governance participants to adhere to ethical behavior and conduct.

3. *Accountability*—Corporate governance should foster accountability and responsible decision making throughout the company. All participants should be held accountable for their decisions, actions, and performance. Accountability is the cornerstone of corporate governance in continuously monitoring best practices. Main drivers of accountability are the acceptance of responsibility, ethical decision making, transparency, and candor, which result in the establishment of trust and a mutually beneficial working relationship between the company and its shareholders. In today's environment, global businesses are under close scrutiny and profound pressures from lawmakers, regulators, the investment community, and their diverse stakeholders to accept accountability and responsibilities for their MBL or governance, economic, ethical, social, and environmental performance.

4. *Shareholder democracy and fairness*—Corporate governance should promote shareholder democracy in director elections by recognizing and respecting the rights of shareholders. Furthermore, the rights and interests of all stakeholders should also be acknowledged and respected. Shareholders have the right to (a) vote for the election of directors; (b) receive annual audited financial statements and quarterly reviewed financial statements; (c) demand access to corporate documents, including minutes of board meetings; (d) submit shareholder resolutions that are placed in the annual proxy statement; (e) vote on important business transactions, such as mergers and acquisitions; and (f) bring shareholder derivative lawsuits. Shareholder democracy is enhanced when shareholders are granted majority voting for the election of directors, advisory voting for the approval of executive compensation, and access to proxy materials for the nomination of director candidates.

5. *Integrity of financial reporting*—Corporate governance should safeguard the integrity of financial reporting by enhancing the quality, reliability, and transparency of financial reports. The achievement of integrity in financial reporting depends on the competent and ethical conduct of all participants in the financial reporting process and the efficacy of regulations and standards governing the process. The erosion of confidence in financial reporting integrity may result in more regulations that are often not cost effective, efficient, or scalable.

6. *Transparency*—The companies' actions, governance, and financial and nonfinancial aspects of its business should be easily available and understandable by all parties concerned.

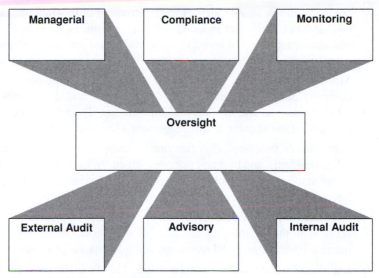

Figure 2.3 Corporate governance functions.

7. *Independence*—The concept of independence in corporate governance determines the extent to which the corporate governance process and its related mechanism minimize or avoid conflicts of interests and self-dealing actions of its key personnel.

Corporate Governance Functions

Corporate governance functions constitute an important element of the corporate governance structure. Figure 2.3 shows the seven essential functions of oversight, managerial, compliance, internal audit, advisory, external audit, and monitoring. A well-balanced implementation of these interrelated functions can produce responsible corporate governance, reliable financial reports, and credible audit services. This integrated approach underscores and reaffirms the primary goal of corporations to create shareholder value while protecting the interests of other stakeholders. Given the primary purpose of any business, particularly public companies, is to create substantial and enduring value, then the goal of corporate governance is to ensure all participants are working effectively to achieve this goal and that their roles in corporate governance are viewed as value-added functions.

The seven interactive functions of corporate governance are important in creating a well-balanced and effective operation. Three of these functions, however, are crucial to the achievement of sustainable corporate performance. These three functions are the oversight function assumed by the board of directors, managerial function delegated to management, and monitory function exercised by shareholders. The effectiveness of these functions largely depends on well-balanced working relationships among shareholders, the board of directors, and management. The primary focus of state and federal statutes has been on defining the power-sharing relationship between these three.

1. **Oversight function.** This function is granted to the board of directors with the fiduciary duty of overseeing the managerial function in the best interests of the

company and its shareholders. The effectiveness of this function depends on directors' independence, due process, authority, resources, composition, qualifications, and accountability. The board of directors should provide strategic advice to management and oversee managerial performance, yet avoid micromanaging.

2. **Managerial function.** This function is given to management in order to run the company and manage its resources, operations, and disclosures of relevant and reliable financial and nonfinancial information. The effectiveness of this function depends on the alignment of management's interests with those of shareholders.

3. **Compliance function**. This function is composed of a set of laws, regulations, rules, standards, and best practices developed by state and federal legislators, regulators, standard-setting bodies, and professional organizations to create a compliance framework for public companies in which to operate and achieve their goals.

4. **Internal audit function**. This function provides both assurance and consulting services to the company in the areas of operational efficiency, risk management, internal controls, financial reporting, and governance processes.

5. **Legal and financial advisory function**. This function provides legal advice and assists the company, its directors, officers, and employees in complying with applicable laws and other legal obligations and fiduciary duties. Financial advisers provide financial advice and planning to the company.

6. **External audit function**. This function is performed by external auditors in expressing an opinion that financial statements truly and fairly represent, in all material respects, the company's financial position and the results of operations in conformity with generally accepted accounting principles (GAAP). External auditors lend credibility to the company's financial reports and thus add value to its corporate governance through their integrated audit of both internal control over financial reporting and financial statements.

7. **Monitoring function**. This function is exercised by shareholders, particularly institutional shareholders, who are empowered to elect and, if warranted, remove directors. Shareholders can influence corporate governance through their proposals and nominations to the board of directors. Shareholders elect directors, and directors appoint officers (CEO, CFO) to manage the company. Other stakeholders such as creditors, employees, financial analysts, and investor activists can also affect corporate policies and practices.

Corporate Governance Mechanisms

The corporate governance structure is shaped by internal and external governance mechanisms, as well as policy interventions through regulations. Both internal and external corporate governance mechanisms of the company have evolved over time to monitor, bond, and control management. Internal mechanisms are designed to manage, direct, and monitor corporate activities in order to create sustainable stakeholder value. Examples of internal governance mechanisms are the board of directors, particularly independent directors; the audit committee; management; internal controls; and internal audit functions. External governance mechanisms are intended to monitor the company's activities, affairs, and performance to ensure that the interests of insiders (management, directors, and officers) are aligned with the interests of outsiders (shareholders and other stakeholders). Examples of external mechanisms are the capital market, the market for corporate control, and the labor market, as well as state and federal statutes, court decisions, shareholder proposals, and best practices of investor activists. Recent financial scandals indicate that a combination of both mechanisms is needed to protect investors and other stakeholders from corporate abuse and misconduct. Thus, policy interventions, including legislation and regulations, are often necessary to ensure effective functioning of corporate governance.

In a dispersed ownership structure, a typical shareholder may have little power to control the company's affairs beyond voting power to elect members of the board of directors. Management may act in its own interest and violate its fiduciary responsibility, which raises the agency conflict between management and owners. The existence of potential agency conflicts may result in substantial costs to shareholders in the sense that management's actions may not always be taken in the best interests of shareholders. Internal corporate governance mechanisms are employed to monitor management actions and align management incentives with shareholder interests. Market-based external mechanisms are also being used as a means of controlling management behavior. For example, the managerial labor market can discipline managers because their past performance is evaluated by the market in their future employment, thus providing a source of competition that encourages managers to behave responsively. The capital markets, through their role in pricing securities, can discipline managers because their option value is often related to the company's market value. Therefore, under the agency theory, both internal and external corporate governance mechanisms are intended to induce managerial actions that maximize profit and shareholder value.

Corporate governance mechanisms can also substitute for each other. For capital markets, monitoring can be substituted with direct monitoring by shareholders. Corporate governance mechanisms do not often operate independently, but rather they operate as imperfect substitutes, partial complements, and in aggregate. Thus, corporate governance mechanisms are viewed as a nexus of contracts that is designed to align the interests of management with those of its shareholders. These mechanisms are collectively shaping the company's corporate governance structure by creating a system of checks and balances. Their effectiveness is related to the cost–benefit trade-offs among these mechanisms, their availability, the extent to which they are being used, whether their marginal benefits exceed their marginal costs, and the company's corporate governance structure.

It has been argued that there is no need for corporate governance reforms beyond state statutes, policy interventions, or regulations because product market competition provides sufficient incentives for public companies to adopt the most effective corporate governance structure. Companies that do not adopt an effective corporate governance structure would presumably be inefficient and in the long-term would be disciplined by the capital markets. Thus, there is no need for policy or governmental interventions because market mechanisms correct any corporate governance inefficiencies. In this context, market competition is viewed to be significantly influential and has shaped corporate governance with no justification for public or governmental intervention. Nonetheless, the rash of financial scandals in the late 1990s and the early 2000s, and the persistence of these scandals in recent years as evidenced by pervasive option backdating practices, prove that market-based mechanisms alone could not solve corporate governance problems. The capital markets hit rock bottom in the early 2000s primarily because market correction mechanisms, lax regulations and oversight, and poorly developed disclosure standards failed to protect investors and thus diminished public trust in the capital markets.

Pension funds are usually indexed and do not have the flexibility of readily divesting in poorly governed companies. Furthermore, market correction mechanisms are often initiated and enforced after the occurrences of substantial management abuse and after shareholders either sell their shares and depress the stock price or lose millions of dollars as a result of accounting and other fraud. The sale of shares has transaction costs and does not directly remove assets from management control because they are simply passing shares to other investors who ultimately suffer the same management malfeasance. Market correction mechanisms may affect corporate governance after significant wealth is destroyed and after considerable transaction costs for other stakeholders, including employees in the form of layoffs and lost wages and pension funds, and society in the form of lost taxes. When scandals surface, as was the case with Enron, Adelphia, Tyco, and WorldCom, the investing public often learns of misleading or omitted disclosures that had been made, thus causing investors and the markets to make poor decisions based on incorrect data, at least in the short term. Over a longer period of time, as reliable information is provided to the markets, investors are able to correct and discipline the unethical and improper conduct of market participants.

SOURCES OF CORPORATE GOVERNANCE

The primary sources of corporate governance in the United States are corporate laws, securities laws, listing standards, and best practices.

Corporate Laws

State corporate law establishes standards of conduct for corporations and defines fiduciary duties, authorities, and responsibilities of shareholders, directors, and officers. Corporate law differs from one state to another, which may result in some variation in responsibilities of directors and officers as well as shareholders' rights. Most states, excluding Delaware, adopt the Model Business Corporation Act (discussed in Chapter 7) as their corporate law.

The Federal Securities Laws

Federal securities laws are passed by Congress and are intended to protect investors by ensuring efficient and transparent capital markets and mitigating the risk of misleading public financial information. The two fundamental laws pertaining to public companies are the Securities Act of 1933 and Securities Exchange Act of 1934. These acts are primarily disclosure-based statutes that require public companies to file a periodic report with the SEC and disclose certain information to their shareholders. SOX expanded the role of federal statutes by providing measures to improve corporate governance, financial reports, and audit activities.

Listing Standards

Listing standards adopted by national stock exchanges establish corporate governance standards for listing companies to promote high standards of shareholder democracy, corporate responsibility, and accountability to shareholders, and to monitor the operation of securities markets. Corporate governance listing standards address a variety of issues such as uniform voting rights, mandatory audit committee formation, and shareholder approvals of broad-based option plans. These standards are applicable to all public companies listing their equity shares with some exceptions (foreign companies, companies with controlling shareholders of more than 50 percent voting power).

Best Practices

Corporate governance best practices recommended by professional organizations (e.g., The Conference Board, the Business Roundtable Institute) and investor activists (e.g., Council of Institutional Investors) are nonbinding guidelines intended to improve corporate governance policies and practices of public companies beyond and above state and federal statutes and listing standards.

CORPORATE GOVERNANCE REFORMS

Corporate governance in the United States is shaped by state and federal statutes, listing standards of national stock exchanges, and best practices recommended by professional organizations and shareholder proposals. These requirements and initiatives are collectively referred to in this book as corporate governance reforms. The erosion in investor confidence in the early 2000s has been caused by many factors, including the collapse of the dot.com market, the economic downturn, reported financial scandals, and numerous earnings restatements of high-profile companies. Several corporate governance reforms in the United States have been established, including SOX, SEC-related implementation rules, listing standards of national stock exchanges, auditing standards of the PCAOB, guiding principles of professional organizations (The Conference Board, Council of Institutional Investors, and National Association of Corporate Directors), and best practices. These reforms were intended to improve the vigilance of corporate governance; the reliability, integrity, transparency, and quality of financial reports; the effectiveness of internal control over financial reporting and related risk management assessment; the credibility of the external audit function; the independence and objectivity of other gatekeepers such as legal counsel and financial analysts; and shareholder monitoring and democracy. Corporate governance has been and will continue to be the main theme of the twenty-first century. Sound corporate governance requires proper legal, regulatory, and institution structure and practices. Reforms promote shareholder democracy and empower shareowners as corporations influence the integrity of the capital markets and the overall financial well-being of society.

Market mechanisms failed to prevent the corporate debacles of Enron, WorldCom, Global Crossing, and others that were devastating to shareholders, employees, pensioners, and society because almost all corporate wealth was destroyed. The relaxation of regulations and too much reliance on market mechanisms to correct poor corporate governance toward the end of the twentieth century contributed to the wave of financial scandals in the early

2000s, which led to the passage of SOX in 2002. The history of regulation in the United States appears to follow the pattern of lax regulation (early twentieth century) followed by corporate and accounting scandals (the stock market crash of 1929), countered with more regulation (the Securities Act of 1933 and the Securities Exchange Act of 1934), then again relaxed or compromised regulation (the end of the twentieth century), yet another wave of financial scandals (the late 1990s and early 2000s), and the resulting additional regulation (SOX, SEC rules, listing standards of the early 2000s). The intent of regulation has been to restore public trust in corporate America, its financial reports, and capital markets pursuant to the occurrences of massive financial scandals. Thus, corporate governance reforms should create an environment that promotes strong marketplace integrity as well as restores investor confidence in the quality, reliability, and transparency of financial disclosures and information.

SARBANES-OXLEY ACT OF 2002

Many factors, including high-profile business failures (e.g., WorldCom, Enron, Global Crossing, Adelphia) caused by the reported financial statement fraud; well-publicized restatements of financial reports (e.g., Xerox, AOL, Tyco); and concerns over auditors' independence, objectivity, and credibility (e.g., Andersen) have resulted in the loss of investor confidence in corporate America. Several initiatives have been taken to address the use of aggressive accounting practices by public companies. SOX was signed into law on July 30, 2002, to reinforce corporate accountability and rebuild investor confidence in public financial reports.[9]

SOX was designed to (1) establish an independent regulatory structure for the accounting profession, (2) set high standards and new guiding principles for corporate governance, (3) improve the quality and transparency of financial reporting, (4) improve the objectivity and credibility of audit functions and empower the audit committee, (5) create more severe civil and criminal remedies for violations of federal securities laws, and (6) increase the independence of securities analysts. The SEC has also issued several rules (CEO and CFO certification of financial reports, disclosure controls and procedures, and ethics for corporate senior executives' auditor independence) to implement provisions of SOX. Table 2.1 summarizes various sections of SOX.

Several provisions of SOX became effective immediately on its passage (i.e., enhanced criminal penalties for securities fraud, the extension of the statute of limitations for securities fraud, a prohibition against personal loans to corporate insiders), and some provisions became effective shortly after the passage of SOX (i.e., executive certification requirements, the acceleration of the filing deadlines). The SEC has issued rules to implement other provisions (e.g., audit committee, auditor independence, financial analyst independence). Provisions of SOX and SEC-related implementation rules are long-term continuous measures taken by legislators and regulators that affect many professionals involved with corporate governance and the financial reporting process, including corporate executives, independent directors, audit committee members, external auditors and auditing standard setters, accountants and accounting standard setters, corporate lawyers, securities analysts, investment banks and financial advisors, and credit rating agencies. SOX also directs nine studies to be conducted by the SEC and the Comptroller General (e.g., audit industry consolidation, investment banks and financial reports, mandatory audit firm rotation, comparative

Table 2.1 Summary of Provisions of SOX

Corporate governance	Financial reporting	Audit functions	Others
1. Enhanced audit committee responsibility for hiring, firing, compensating, and overseeing auditors and preapproval of nonaudit services.	1. CEO/CFO certification of financial reports.	1. Establishment and operation of the Public Company Accounting Oversight Board (PCAOB), an independent nongovernmental agency that regulates and oversees the audit of public companies.	1. Professional responsibilities for attorneys appearing and practicing before the SEC.
2. Disclosure, in the periodic reports, of whether the audit committee has at least one member who is a "financial expert," and if not, why not.	2. Internal control report by management.	2. Registration with the PCAOB of public accounting firms that audit public companies.	2. Disclosures of corporate code of ethics.
3. CEOs' and CFOs' certification of the accuracy and completeness of quarterly and annual reports.	3. Attestation and report by auditors on management's assessment of internal controls.	3. PCAOB authority to issue auditing standards, inspect registered accounting firms' operations, and investigate potential violations of Securities laws.	3. Collection and administration of funds for victim investors.
4. Management assessment and reporting of the effectiveness of disclosure controls and procedures.	4. Disclosures of off balance sheet arrangements.	4. Requirement that auditors be appointed, compensated, and overseen by the audit committee.	4. Analyst conflicts of interest (regulation AC).
5. Ban on personal loans by companies to their directors or executives other than certain regular consumer loans.	5. Disclosures of contractual obligations.	5. Many nonaudit services are prohibited from being performed contemporaneously with an audit.	5. Whistleblower protection.
6. Establishment of procedures by each audit committee for receiving, retaining, and handling complaints received by the company concerning accounting, internal controls, or auditing matters.	6. Disclosures of reconciliation of non-GAAP financial measures pertaining to pro forma financial information.	6. Rotation of the lead (or coordinating) audit partner and the lead review partner every five years.	6. Debts nondischargeable in bankruptcy.
7. Review of each quarterly and annual report (Forms 10-Q and 10-K) by officers.	7. Disclosures of material correcting adjustments by auditors.	7. Auditors report to the audit committee.	7. Temporary freeze authority for SEC.
8. Forfeiture by CEO or CFO of certain bonuses and profits when the company restates its financial statements due to its material noncompliance with any financial reporting requirements.	8. Disclosures of transaction involving management and principal stockholders.	8. Prohibiting where CEO or CFO previously employed by auditor.	8. SEC censures or bars any person who is not qualified, lacks the requisite character or integrity, or with unethical conduct from appearing before the SEC.
9. Improper influence on conduct of audits.	9. Accelerated filing of changes in beneficial ownership by insiders.	9. Auditors attestation to and reporting on management assessment of internal controls.	9. Lengthened statute of limitations for securities fraud.
10. Insider trades during pension fund blackout periods.	10. Real-time disclosures of information concerning material changes in financial condition or operations (Form 8-K disclosures).	10. Limitations on partner compensation.	10. Criminalization of corporate misconducts.
11. Officers' and directors' bars and penalties for violations of securities laws or misconduct.	11. Periodic review of published financial statements by the SEC at least once every three years.	11. Disclosure of fees paid to the auditor.	11. Criminal penalties for defrauding shareholders of public companies.
	12. SEC-enhanced authority to determine what constitutes U.S. GAAP.	12. Requirements for preapproval of audit and permitted nonaudit services by the audit committee.	12. Retaliation against informants.
		13. Retention of audit work papers and documents for five years.	13. Increased criminal penalties under securities laws and mail and wire fraud.
		14. Increased penalties for destruction of corporate audit records.	14. Future studies on consolidation of public accounts by firm, audit firm rotation, accounting standards, credit rating agencies, and investment banks.

Source: Extracted from the Sarbanes-Oxley Act of 2002. Available at: www.whitehouse.gov/infocus/corporateresponsibility.

accounting, rating agencies). The SEC has issued more than twenty rules pertaining to the implementation of provisions of SOX.

SOX provisions encourage and enforce a rules-based approach to corporate governance by addressing all seven corporate governance functions (oversight, managerial, compliance, internal audit, advisory, external audit, and monitory). SOX does not represent a comprehensive and systematic approach to corporate governance, but rather it addresses potential conflicts of interest that may exist among corporate governance functions and those who carry out these functions. Indeed, almost all provisions of SOX provide measures for identifying and managing conflicts of interest relevant to corporate governance, financial reporting, and the audit activities of public companies.

SOX provisions, SEC-related rules, and listing standards influence corporate governance structure in at least three ways.[10] First, auditors, analysts, and legal counsel who were not traditionally considered components of corporate governance are now brought into the realm of internal governance as gatekeepers. Second, the legal status and fiduciary duty of company directors and officers, particularly the audit committee and CEO, have been more clearly defined and, in certain instances, significantly enhanced. Third, certain aspects of state corporate law were preempted and federalized. For example, Section 402 of SOX prohibits loans to directors and officers, whereas state law permits such loans. Under Section 304, officers must reimburse certain compensation received, such as bonuses based on erroneous numbers, if the company has to restate its financial statements as a result of fraud. Section 301 of SOX grants more direct statutory responsibilities to the audit committee than state law (e.g., direct responsibility for hiring, compensating, and firing independent auditors).

As with any regulation, shareholder wealth effects of SOX are a function of both the expected benefits and the expected costs imposed on public companies with its passage. The overall benefit induced by SOX in improving investor confidence must be weighted with the imposed compliance costs for the majority of public companies. Academic research suggests that (1) good (poor) corporate governance is associated with higher (lower) profits, less (more) risk, less (more) stock price volatility, higher (lower) values, and larger (smaller) cash payouts; and (2) firms with stronger corporate governance experienced higher stock returns than those with weaker corporate governance during the 1990s.[11] SOX requires a poor (good) governance firm to make many (few) changes to its pre-SOX governance structure. Thus, compliance with provisions of SOX would be more costly to poor governance firms than good governance firms.

The cost–benefit of compliance with SOX has been extensively debated. Particularly, its burden of creating certain competition disadvantages for the U.S. market is being examined. Like any regulations, compliance with provisions of SOX is not without cost. The direct and most debated cost of SOX is Section 404 compliance, requiring mandatory internal control reporting by companies' management and independent auditors. A 2007 survey of 2000 corporate executives reveals that (1) the compliance costs of SOX for the second consecutive year declined substantially; (2) the cost dropped 23 percent in 2006; (3) total compliance costs decreased to an average $2.9 million per company in 2006, which is down 35 percent from the $4.51 million average costs in 2006; (4) there was no significant change in audit fees; and (5) the majority of surveyed executives (78 percent) reported that the costs to comply with Section 404 still outweigh any benefits.[12] More manageable and cost-effective Section 404 compliance is currently being addressed by the SEC and the PCAOB.

Several reports (e.g., the U.S. Chamber of Commerce, Capital Markets Regulation, Bloomberg/Schumber) have criticized the potential adversarial effects of SOX on U.S. capital markets' global competitiveness and have suggested SOX requirements be relaxed or rolled back. Their rationale is that SOX compliance costs are disproportionately high for smaller companies and have also scared foreign companies away from U.S. stock markets. Several other reports have suggested that SOX provisions are working in rebuilding investor confidence, and thus its implementation rules must be made more cost effective, efficient, and scalable. Their rationale is that recent reforms have made the United States a nation of shareowners, with more than 57 million American households owning stocks (either directly or through mutual funds). Furthermore, regulators (SEC) and standard setters (PCAOB) have proposed relaxing some of the seemingly costly implementation rules of SOX (Section 404).

The U.S. Chamber of Commerce and many public companies and their executives have blamed the extensive compliance costs of SOX (estimated as high as $6 billion in 2006) as a major contributing factor to the decline in U.S. stock market listings, particularly initial public offerings (IPOs).[13] Much of the compliance cost is attributed to ineffective, inefficient, excessive, and ambiguous implementation rules. The SEC and the PCAOB have addressed cost justifiability, efficiency, and scalability of SOX implementation rules. Christopher Cox, the SEC's chairman, opposes weakening SOX by stating, "We don't need to change the law [SOX]. We need to change the way it is implemented."[14] During the past five years, SOX has been both appraised as a sweeping measure in restoring investor confidence in corporate America and financial reporting and criticized as being detrimental to the global competitiveness of the U.S. capital markets. Nonetheless, some of the costly provisions of SOX (e.g., Section 404) have been fine-tuned by regulators, and many of its provisions (e.g., internal control reporting, regulation of the accounting profession) have been adopted in other countries such as Canada, China, France, and Japan. The unprecedented performance of financial markets post-SOX is perhaps an indication of the efficacy of SOX in restoring confidence in financial markets. Another measure of SOX's effectiveness is the significant reduction in the number of reported material weaknesses in internal controls. Despite the high compliance costs of Section 404, the United States continues to be the world's leading capital market because SOX has brought fairness to the financial reporting process, affecting investor confidence and efficiency of capital markets.

Investor protection provided by corporate governance reforms is the backbone of fair, efficient, and robust capital markets in the United States. The post-Enron period is characterized by substantial corporate governance reforms, including SOX, SEC-related implementation rules, and new listing standards. Time will tell whether these vital and well-suited reforms will diminish over time and lose their relevance. Nonetheless, what is obvious is that as more U.S. households invest in the capital markets (now more than 90 million Americans own shares), the next wave of scandals and their devastating effects on investors and the capital markets could cripple the economy. It is the author's hope that public companies rise above the "check-box compliance" mentality and employ corporate governance best practices that go above and beyond regulations.

CORPORATE GOVERNANCE RATING

The rash of financial scandals of high-profile companies caused investors to be more active in monitoring companies in which they invested. They have begun to consider corporate governance effectiveness in their investment decisions. The well-deserved, long-awaited investor focus on corporate governance generated a demand for and interest in the development of ratings metrics or systems that gather, analyze, rank, and compare corporate governance practices of public companies. National and international organizations, including Institutional Shareholder Services (ISS), the Corporate Library, Standard & Poor's, Moody's Investment Service, CoreRatings, Governance Metrics International (GMI), and Glass Lewis & Co., have developed and published variations of corporate governance ratings that are often used by shareholders in assessing their stock returns and bondholders in determining the costs of lending.

GMI established its scoring algorithm with hundreds of metrics relevant to the governance quality and risk assessment of each rated company into six categories of board accountability, financial disclosure, shareholder rights, executive compensation, takeover defenses, and reputation/regulatory problems.[15] GMI updates its governance scores daily and posts them on its Web site or red flags them as special alerts. GMI, by not soliciting consulting contracts, pension-proxy voting arrangements, or other potentially conflicting business relations, has attempted to establish objective, fair, and independent governance scoring of rated companies and, thus, influence corporate governance issues. Companies were ranked worldwide on their working relationships with their investors, community members, employees, and activists. Companies were ranked based on their governance issues, business strategy, performance management, nonfinancial reporting, overall internal controls and decision making, and social and environmental issues. Table 2.2 provides information about corporate governance rating organizations.

CORPORATE GOVERNANCE REPORTING

Public companies do not usually report their corporate governance activities. Corporate governance reporting (CGR) goes beyond the mandatory periodic financial reports or filings with regulatory bodies. It reports on the company's vision, strategies, and missions in creating stakeholder value and its financial, economic, social, and environmental indicators. CGR entails assessing the quality and effectiveness of the organization's corporate governance and reporting findings to interested stakeholders, including the board of directors, executives, auditors, regulatory agencies, and shareholders. CGR should (1) disclose all relevant information about the effectiveness of the company's corporate governance, (2) focus on the company's sustainability performance, (3) provide transparent information about the company's performance and its impacts on all stakeholders, and (4) assess the company's responsiveness to the needs of its stakeholders.

From a theoretical standpoint, well-governed companies are expected to have a competitive advantage over poorly governed companies. The empirical question to be addressed is whether investors value corporate governance policies and practices of public companies and consider governance factors in their investment decision-making process as reflected in stock price changes—more specifically, whether the capital markets place a premium (discount) on stock prices and cost of capital based on perceived corporate governance strengths (weaknesses). Prior research[16] finds companies with higher corporate governance ratings/indexes outperform those with lower ratings as measured by stock returns. Other studies[17,18] find that firms with higher corporate governance ratings have lower cost of equity capital because of the perceived lower agency risk to shareholders, lower

Table 2.2   Corporate Governance Rating Organizations

Organization	Description	Web site
Glass Lewis & Co. (GLC)	1. Provides global proxy research and advice for approximately 8,000 public companies and several stock indexes, including the Russell 3000, S&P 500, S&S Mid Cap 400, Wilshire 5000, S&P Small Cap 600, and others. 2. Focuses on the economic consequences of corporate governance issues (e.g., board independence, executive compensation, majority voting) and their potential effects on shareholder value. 3. Establishes a proprietary method for rating public companies' executive compensation practices by using a pay-for-performance model focusing on several performance measures of one-year total shareholder return, two-year change in book value, two-year stock price performance, one-year ROE, two-year EPS growth, and one-year ROA. The top five officers' compensation in a company is compared to the median paid by the competition in its own industry, sector, and similar-size firms. A letter grade from A to F is then assigned to the company's overall compensation practice that used by the compensation committee. 4. Provides its corporate governance services to institutional investors, mutual funds, and pension funds, without seeking consulting services.	www.glasslewis.com
Institutional Shareholder Services (ISS)	1. Provides several services, including corporate governance quotient (CGQ) ratings, proxy recommendations, research services, and voting analytics, as well as consulting services. 2. The ISS CGQ database provides company ratings based on their corporate governance practices that assist institutional investors in assessing the effectiveness of public companies' governance and quality of corporate boards. 3. The ISS gathers corporate governance data about 5,000 public companies and classifies them into sixty-three ratings criteria based on their corporate governance practices and structures. 4. The ISS calculates the raw score for each company and then compares companies on a relative basis to an index and industry group to determine the separate index and industry CGQ scores.	www.issproxy.com
Council of Institutional Investors (CII)	The CII annually publishes a focus list of underperforming companies. The selected companies to be included in the focus list should have the largest underperformance relative to their industry group's five-year median return, and they must lag both their market index and industry group returns for one-, three-, and five-year periods ending June 30.	www.cii.org

(Continued)

Table 2.2   (*Continued*)

Organization	Description	Web site
The Corporate Library	1. The Corporate Library's Board Analyst provides data on more than 2,000 U.S. and 500 large international companies. 2. The Corporate Library provides comparative corporate governance data for large companies and their directors, a corporate governance best practices score, and a unique board effectiveness rating system. 3. The Corporate Library performs no consulting services, is fully independent of the companies it rates, and does not offer any investment or proxy recommendations. 4. Board effective rating identifies potential areas of the board's ineffective oversight rated from A to F, where firms with F ratings have exhibited major governance-related problems. 5. The best practices compliance score determines how well a company meets generally accepted governance practices suggested by professional organizations (e.g., CII, the Business Roundtable, International Corporate Governance Network, ICGN). 6. The Corporate Library also provides CEO compensation ratings by identifying red flags such as base pay over $1 million, CEO bonus of more than double the annual salary, excessive amounts of options granted to the CEO, high tax payments (gross-ups), a declining number of shares owned by the CEO, and lack of adequate disclosure on CEO compensation.	www.thecorporatelibrary.com
Governance Metrics International (GMI)	1. GMI provides corporate governance ratings and research on more than 3,200 global companies. Its rating criteria are based on securities regulations, stock exchange listing standards, and various corporate governance principles and best practices. 2. GMI establishes global ratings and makes market ratings by using hundreds of data points to determine an overall GMI score and separate scores for each of GMI's six research categories of board accountability, financial disclosure and internal controls, shareholder rights, remuneration, market for control, and corporate behavior. GMI ratings are scored from 1 to 10, where 10 indicates the highest ratings.	www.gmiratings.com
Equilar	Equilar provides detailed compensation data based on more than 75 unique data elements gathered from proxy and annual reports for all top executives of 4,000 companies, including Russell 3000. Executive compensation elements included in the database are cash compensation, long-term awards, and option grants using the Black-Scholes and binomial lattice models, employment agreements, and company financial performance.	www.equilar.com

(Continued)

Table 2.2 (*Continued*)

Organization	Description	Web site
FTSE/ISS Corporate Governance Indexes (CGI)	FTSE in collaboration with ISS has developed a global corporate governance index since April 2004. The CGI covers about 2,200 large and midcap stocks in the 24 developed countries of the FTSE Global Equity Index Series (GEIS). The CGI rating system covers about 60 corporate governance criteria regarding five general areas of (1) board of directors (composition, nominating committee, voting policies, succession planning, and size); (2) audit (audit committee, audit fees, and auditor rotation); (3) shareholder rights and protections (capital structure and antitakeover provisions); (4) compensation (director compensation, cost of equity awards, pension provisions); and (5) ownership (percentage of total equity owned by directors and director/executive ownership guidelines).	www.ftse.com
Standard and Poor's/Glass Lewis & Co. Board Accountability Index (BAI)	The BAI is structured based on correlation between stock performance and the extent to which boards are accountable to their shareholders. The BAI is regarded as an enhanced corporate governance index because it tracks its benchmark index closely through quantitative algorithms and its robustness in controlling for risk. The BAI only covers the S&P 500 companies and makes constant updates on its weightings and closing prices. The BAI evaluates S&P 500 companies (underweights and overweights) based on the following five corporate governance criteria of (1) staggered boards, (2) ability of shareholders to amend corporate bylaws, (3) poison pills, (4) golden parachutes, and (5) supermajority merger requirements. The BAI overweights companies with less than three of these criteria classified as good governance companies and underweights them with three or more entrenching provisions reflecting bad governance companies.	www.glasslewis.com/ solutions/bai.php

Source: Rezaee, Z. 2007. *Corporate Governance Post-Sarbanes-Oxley Act: Regulations, Requirements, & Integrated Processes.* John Wiley & Sons, Hoboken, NJ.

systematic risk, and lower idiosyncratic risk. Corporate governance measures and performance indicators that could be included in CGR are (1) descriptions of an organization's culture, appropriate tone at the top, board of directors, internal controls, and commitment to economic, social, and environmental goals; (2) major risks facing the organization in achieving its economic, social, and environmental goals and measures taken to address such risks; (3) the percentage of the board of directors who are independent and non-executive directors; (4) the existence of an audit committee comprising all independent and financially literate directors; (5) the adequacy of internal controls; (6) corporate governance principles and mechanisms to which the organization adheres; (7) the status of the organization's compliance with applicable laws, rules, regulations, and standards, and disclosure of areas of noncompliance; and (8) the organization's financial and nonfinancial KPIs. The corporate governance report should include

1. The company's objectives and management's visions to achieve these objectives
2. Major share ownership and voting rights
3. A summary of financial position and results of operations
4. The compensation policy for directors and officers
5. Significant issues relevant to employees and other stakeholders
6. The corporate governance structure, including aspects, principles, and functions
7. Material information on MBL sustainability performance
8. The company's initiatives on risk management, including foreseeable risk factors and responses
9. The company's voting system (majority vs. plurality)
10. The duality of CEO positions or separation of the positions of the chairperson of the board and the CEO
11. The percentage of independent directors
12. The number of meetings of the board of directors and its committees
13. The annual evaluation of the board of directors, its committees, and the committee members
14. The company's compliance with corporate governance reforms, including SOX, SEC-related rules, listing standards, and best practices
15. All relevant information about the effectiveness of the company's corporate governance
16. Assessment of the company's responsiveness to the needs of its stakeholders
17. Other information deemed necessary and relevant to the company's shareholders and other stakeholders pertaining to corporate governance

There are substantial differences between financial reporting and CGR: (1) unlike financial reporting, corporate governance reporting is not a legal requirement; (2) financial reporting must be prepared in accordance with GAAP, whereas corporate governance reporting has no single set of standards that are widely agreed on; (3) the financial reports audit is required for financial reporting to lend credibility to financial reports, while there is no mandatory assurance report on the corporate governance reporting; (4) unlike the financial audit report, there are no guidelines specifying the type and level of assurance on corporate governance reports; (5) financial reports and audits are prepared primarily for shareholders, while corporate governance reports and related assurance reports can be provided to a broad range of stakeholders with different and often competing interests; and (6) corporate governance reports and assurance entail both financial (quantitative) and nonfinancial (qualitative) information that requires special skills in assessing credibility and reliability.

GLOBAL CONVERGENCE IN CORPORATE GOVERNANCE

There are no globally accepted corporate governance reforms and best practices. Differences are mainly driven by the country's statutes, corporate structures, and culture. Country statutes could pose challenges for regulators in adopting corporate governance reforms and financial reporting disclosures for home companies as well as multinational corporations. The United States and UK, for example, operate under common law, which tends to give more antidirector privileges to minority shareholders compared to countries under code law (e.g., Germany), in the sense that regulators allow too many or too few rights to minority shareholders. Another example is that regulations in the United States are typically regulator led, being established by the SEC, to protect investors, whereas reforms in the UK are normally shareholder led, indicating that investors are responsible for safeguarding their interests.

Corporate and capital structure can also influence corporate governance and financial disclosure requirements. One of the key differences in corporate structure is ownership of the company. In the United States, ownership of shares is dispersed because more than 100 million Americans own company's shares through direct investment and retirement plans. Comparative stock ownerships in Europe are more concentrated, and thus controlling shareholders are in a better position to influence corporate governance and business operations. Corporate governance in a dispersed share ownership is designed to align the interests of management with those shareholders because management may have incentives to engage in earnings management and focus on short-term considerations at the expense of sustainable shareholder value creation and long-term performance. Conversely, with concentrated ownership, corporate governance creates a right balance between the interests of minority and majority shareholders. The primary purpose of corporate governance in the United States is to enhance shareholder value creation while protecting the interests of other stakeholders, whereas in Germany the focus is more on protecting creditors because banks play an important role in financing companies.

The board system can also influence corporate governance. In one-tier boards in the United States, directors are elected to oversee management in running the company, whereas in the two-tier board system in Germany, the supervisory board advises, appoints, and supervises the management board in managing the operation of the company; however, Japan's companies operate through a complex system of committees, and these committees oversee and run the company. Cultural and political differences can also influence corporate governance because some cultures are more collective and risk averse than others (e.g., Germany compared to the United States). An appropriate question is whether these differences in corporate governance can be reconciled and whether convergence is possible. A move toward corporate governance integration was attempted in 1999 by the OECD.

Differences between U.S. and European Models of Corporate Governance

Several differences exist between U.S. and European models of corporate governance. The most significant differences are[19]

1. *Definition of corporate governance*—Corporate governance in the United States primarily focuses on aligning the interests of management with those of the shareholders. In contrast, European corporate governance emphasizes the protection of all stakeholders' interests, including shareholders, and particularly alignment of the interests of controlling shareholders with those of minority or individual shareholders.

2. *Dispersed versus concentrated ownership*—The capital ownership structure in the United States is more dispersed because about 100 million Americans own shares of public companies through direct or managed ownership. Conversely, capital ownership in Europe is more concentrated with majority ownership and controlling shareholders. Thus, corporate governance mechanisms in Europe are designed to protect the rights of minority individual shareholders and protect divergent controlling shareholders.

3. *Fiduciary duties*—The so-called Anglo-Saxon legal regime in both the United States and the UK establishes an enforceable set of fiduciary duties for directors to act as agents in the best interest of both controlling and minority shareowners. In civil law countries (most of Europe), the fiduciary principle is not well developed and thus the rules-based approach often allows controlling shareholders to extract private benefits at the expense of individual or minority shareholders.

4. *Regulator led versus shareholder led approach*—The U.S. disclosure system is viewed as a regulator led approach in the sense that state statutes enact laws pertaining to corporate governance matters, and federal statutes establish rules aimed at protecting shareholders of all sizes regarding disclosures and other matters relevant to public companies. Conversely, the UK promotes shareholder monitoring to protect their interests, giving the appearance that shareholders have more rights in the UK than in the United States regarding director nomination and election as well as major business transactions.

5. *Plurality versus majority voting*—The board election process in the United States is governed by plurality voting by shareholders coupled with limited ability to even nominate director candidates. Conversely, in the UK and other European countries, directors are elected by a simple majority voting that empowers shareholders to remove at annual or extraordinary meetings incompetent and unethical directors. Shareholders in the United States are lagging behind their counterparts in Europe to have access to proxy materials for the nomination of director candidates to vote against underperforming directors and to have advisory votes in approving executive compensation.

6. *Different types of fraud*—Different capital ownership systems, namely, dispersed versus concentrated, may be susceptible to different types of fraud. The dispersed ownership structure in the United States is more prone to short-term earnings management and quarterly reporting frauds perpetrated to overstate earnings to positively influence stock prices and thus greater value executive stock options. Conversely, in Europe, shareholders are not susceptible to short-term earnings management fraud; instead, they are concerned about the extraction of private benefits from the company and its controlling shareholders to the detriment of minority shareholders.

SUMMARY

The scandals of the late 1990s and early 2000s were devastating, resulting in the erosion of investor confidence and public trust in financial reports disseminated by public companies. The financial scandals of high-profile companies such as Enron, WorldCom, Global Crossing, and Qwest (better known as the Big Four scandals) alone cost investors and pensioners more than $460 billion. The scandals raised a fundamental question: "Where were directors, officers, auditors, legal counsel, financial analysts, investment banks, and even standard-setting bodies and regulators?" That is, what role did lack of responsible, vigilant, and effective corporate governance play in these scandals? The relaxation of regulations and too much reliance on market mechanisms to correct corporate governance ineffectiveness toward the end of the twentieth century contributed to the wave of financial scandals in the early 2000s, ultimately leading to the passage of SOX in 2002. This chapter presented the corporate governance definition, aspects, structure, principles, seven interrelated functions, mechanisms, sources, and reforms, including state and federal statutes, Congressional actions (SOX), and regulations (SEC rules, PCAOB standards, listing standards, best practices), that have shaped modern corporate governance.

The key points of this chapter are

- Corporate governance participants must structure the process to ensure the goals of both shareholder value creation and stakeholder value protection for public companies.

- The corporate governance structure is shaped by internal and external governance mechanisms, as well as policy interventions through regulations.

- Corporate governance mechanisms are viewed as a nexus of contracts that is designed to align the interests of management with those of the shareholders.

- The effectiveness of both internal and external corporate governance mechanisms depends on the cost–benefit trade-offs among these mechanisms and is related to their availability, the extent to which they are being used, whether their marginal benefits exceed their marginal costs, and the company's corporate governance structure.

- There are three aspects of corporate governance: the shareholder aspect, the stakeholder aspect, and the integrated aspect.

- Corporate governance structure should be based on the principles of value-adding philosophy, ethical conduct, accountability, shareholder democracy and fairness, integrity of financial reporting, transparency, and independence.

- A well-balanced operation of the seven corporate governance functions—oversight, managerial, compliance, internal audit, legal and financial advisory, external audit, and monitoring—can contribute toward effective corporate governance.

- Corporate governance effectiveness is defined as the extent to which the company's corporate governance is achieving its objectives in three categories: (1) promoting efficient and effective operational, financial, and social performance; (2) creating shareholder value while protecting the interests of other stakeholders (employees, suppliers, customers, and creditors); and (3) ensuring the integrity, quality, reliability, and transparency of financial reporting.

KEY TERMS

corporate governance effectiveness	internal governance mechanisms	shareholder aspect
corporate governance rating	oversight	stakeholder
external governance mechanisms	oversight board	stakeholder aspect
integrated aspect	remuneration	transparency
	shareholder	

REVIEW QUESTIONS

1. What are the three "legs" of the corporate governance structure discussed in this chapter?

2. What is the underlying focus of the shareholder aspect of corporate governance?

3. What types of managerial failures prevent management from acting in the best interest of the shareholders?

4. Is value creation or value protection the primary goal of corporate governance?

5. What is corporate governance resilience, and how is it maintained?

6. What is corporate governance responsiveness?

7. Explain corporate governance transparency.

8. What are the seven essential corporate governance functions?

9. What are the roles and responsibilities of inside and outside directors?

10. What items are likely to be recorded in a corporate governance report?

11. What is the basic cause of corporate agency problems?

DISCUSSION QUESTIONS

1. What are the versions of corporate governance mechanisms? How are they effective? How can they be ineffective?

2. Identify and define the three aspects of corporate governance.

3. What entities or groups of individuals are responsible for the oversight, managerial, and monitoring functions, and what are their basic responsibilities and duties?

4. Compare and contrast the internal and external audit functions.

5. Corporate governance reforms are intended to reduce many potential conflicts of interest among corporate governance participants, including directors, management, auditors, financial analysts, corporate counsel, and investors. What conflicts of interest are possible among these groups?

6. As an investor, would you find use in corporate governance reports? Explain.

7. Use your research skills to search the Internet for information regarding the most recent GMI ratings. Do the ratings show an improvement in corporate governance procedures? Briefly comment on your findings.

8. Many "best practices" are mentioned in the text. Which three best practices do you agree with, and which three best practices do you disagree with? Explain.

9. In your own words, what is honesty?

10. Hypothetically, what are the agency problems that exist in your work and school environment?

11. Perform an Internet search for the Securities Acts of 1933 and the Securities Exchange Act of 1934. What are some of the key provisions of these acts?

12. Are internal or external corporate governance mechanisms more influential to the effectiveness of corporate governance? Defend your answer.

13. Which approach do you prefer: principles based or rules based of corporate governance? Why?

14. Search the Internet for the global regulators' perspectives on convergence in corporate governance.

15. Discuss the advantages and disadvantages of both a regulatory-led and a shareholder-led approach to corporate governance.

NOTES

1. Gillan, S. L., and L. T. Starks. 1998. A Survey of Shareholder Activism: Motivation and Empirical Evidence. *Contemporary Finance Digest* 2(3): 10–34.

2. Shleifer, A., and R. Vishny. 1997. A Survey of Corporate Governance. *Journal of Finance* 52(2): 737–775.

3. The Encyclopedia about Corporate Governance. n.d. What is Corporate Governance? Available at: www.encycogov.com/WhatIsGorpGov.asp.

4. Goodman, A., and B. Schwartz. 2004. *Corporate Governance: Law and Practice.* Matthew Bender & Co., Albany, NY.

5. Moldoveanu, M., and R. Martin. 2001, February 2. *Agency Theory and the Design of Efficient Governance Mechanisms.* University of Toronto, Rotman School of Management. Available at: www.rotman.utoronto.ca/rogermartin/Agencytheory.pdf.

6. Etzion, A. 1998. A Communication Note on Stakeholder Theory. *Business Ethics Quarterly* 8(4).

7. European Commission (EC). 2004. Commission Recommendation of 14 December 2004. Fostering an Appropriate Regime for the Remuneration of Directors of Listed Companies. Available at: europa.eu.int/eur-lex/lex/LexUriServ/site/en/oj/2004/l_385/l_38520041229en00550059.pdf.

8. Krehmeyer, D., M. Orsagh, and K. N. Schacht. 2006, July 24. *Breaking the Short-Term Cycle.* CFA Institute Centre Publications. Available at: www.cfapubs.org/toc/ccb/2006/1.

9. Sarbanes-Oxley Act of 2002. 2002, July 30. Available at: www.law.uc.edu/CCL/SOact/soact.pdf.

10. Mitchell, L. E. 2003. The Sarbanes-Oxley Act and the Reinvention of Corporate Governance. *Villanova Law Review* 48(4): 1189–1216.

11. Gompers, P. A., J. L. Ishii, and A. Metrick. 2003. Corporate Governance and Equity Prices. *Quarterly Journal of Economics* 118(1): 107–155.

12. Siegel, A. 2007, May 16. Lower SOX Costs Don't Assuage Execs. *Investment News.*

13. Westbrook, J. 2007, March 14. SEC's COX Says He Opposes Weakening Sarbanes-Oxley. *Bloomberg News.*

14. Ibid.

15. Governance Metrics International (GMI). n.d. GMI Ratings Reports. Available at: www.gmiratings.com/(ppt5c345mxxnihj2d5o4pw3q)/Default.aspx.

16. Governance Metrics International (GMI). 2003. GMI Governance and Performance Study. Contact GMI to purchase this study: www.gmiratings.com/(13uzfz25qer35d451kf3ny55)/ContactGMI.aspx.

17. Skaife, H. A., D. W. Collins, and R. LaFond. 2004, December. Corporate Governance and the Cost of Equity Capital (Abstract). Available at: papers.ssrn.com/sol3/papers.cfm?abstract_id=639681.

18. European Center for Corporate Engagement (ECCE). 2006. Corporate Governance and the Cost of Equity Capital: Evidence from GMI's Governance Ratings. ECCE Research Note 06-01.

19. Campos, R. C. 2007, February 8. Speech by SEC Commissioner: Remarks before the CNMV Corporate Governance and Securities Markets Conference. Available at: www.sec.gov/news/speech/2007/spch020807rcc.htm.

Chapter 3

Introduction to Business Ethics

INTRODUCTION

This chapter starts with the general definition of "ethics"; its field of study, including metaethics, normative ethics, and applied ethics; and proceeds with business ethics. Ethics are broadly described in the literature as moral principles about right and wrong, honorable behavior reflecting values, or standards of conduct. Honesty, openness, responsiveness, accountability, due diligence, and fairness are core ethical principles. An online poll conducted in January 2005 by the Dallas chapter of the International Association of Business Communicators (Dallas/IABC) reveals that (1) about 30 percent of respondents indicate that they have been asked to compromise their integrity often, very often, or extremely often; (2) of these, more than 10 percent responded that they have been asked to compromise their integrity extremely often; and (3) the remaining 69 percent said they have never or not often been asked by management to compromise their integrity.[1] Those results suggest that employees and even executives are still under pressure to compromise their integrity despite the requirements of corporate governance reforms (SOX, listing standards) for the establishment of a code of business ethics for senior executives and employees that promotes ethical conduct by setting a "right tone at the top." Organizations should ensure an ethical work environment free of pressures or incentives for senior executives and other employees to compromise their integrity and professional responsibility. This chapter presents an introduction to business ethics, its implications for business, and curriculum developments.

Primary Objectives

The primary objectives of this chapter are to

- Present the definition of ethics in general and business ethics in particular.
- Recognize the need for a code of ethics that is upheld especially by setting the right "tone at the top."
- Become familiar with the SEC rules and regulations relating to ethics.
- Provide an overview of listing standards and suggestions relating to ethics.
- Understand the board's role in setting the company's ethical codes.
- Recognize the benefits of and need for an ethical workplace.
- Identify incentive programs and their roles in promoting an ethical workplace.
- Illustrate that actions speak louder than words in promoting an ethical workplace.
- Discuss the integration of business ethics into the business curriculum.
- Provide an example of proficient implementation of an ethical code by examining the Defense Industry Initiatives on Business Ethics and Conduct.

ETHICAL THEORIES

There are several broadly accepted ethical theories. The consequentialist theory advocates that ethical behavior or the moral rightness of one's actions are determined by the results of the act and its impact on either the individual (egoism) or all involved (utilitarianism).[2] Nonconsequentialists, in contrast, assess the nature of the act as being either ethical or unethical regardless of its results. The individualist dimension of ethical decision making asserts that individuals are only concerned with the impact of their decisions on their own and their immediate family's well-being and interests.[3] Collectivism postulates that individuals tend to belong to groups and thus focus on the group's interests when making ethical decisions.

Metaethics focus on ethical theories, their evolution, and the social, religious, spiritual, and cultural influences shaping those theories. Normative ethics emphasize practical aspects by providing principles of appropriate behavior and guidance for what is right or wrong, good or bad in behavior (e.g., principles of justice, honesty, social benefits, lawfulness). Applied ethics deal with the application of moral principles and reasoning as well as codes of conduct for a particular profession or segment of the society (e.g., business ethics, environmental ethics, medical ethics).

Business ethics, the focus of this chapter, are a subset of applied ethics that deals with ethical issues, conflicts of interest, and the morality of business decisions. Business ethics are defined as the moral principles and ethical standards that guide business behavior. An appropriate code of ethics that sets the appropriate tone at the top of promoting ethical and professional conduct is the backbone of effective corporate governance and establishes the moral structure for the entire organization. Integrity and ethical conduct are key components of an organization's control environment as set forth in both reports of the Committee of Sponsoring Organizations of the Treadway Commission (COSO): "Internal Control—Integrated Framework" and "Enterprise Risk Management—Integrated Framework."[4]

A corporate code of ethics has been defined in several authoritative guides and in the business literature. The SEC's definition of code of ethics focuses on ethical conduct of the company's specified officers involved in financial reporting. Public companies are encouraged to define codes of ethics broadly to address the ethical conduct of all personnel within the company, with broad coverage of both financial and nonfinancial activities. The SEC rule describes the term code of ethics as written standards designed to deter wrongdoing and to promote[5]

1. Full, fair, accurate, timely, and transparent disclosures in reports and documents filed or submitted to the SEC and in other public communications

2. Honest and ethical conduct throughout the company, including the ethical handling of apparent or actual conflicts of interest between personal and professional activities and relationships

3. Accountability for compliance with the established code of ethics

4. Compliance with applicable regulations and professional standards

5. The timely and effective internal reporting of noncompliance and any violations of the established code of ethics to an appropriate person or persons designated in the code

Ethical crises have occurred throughout the history of humankind and will continue to occur particularly when there is a conflict of interest. Many tragedies and scandals can be traced back to the ethical behavior of individuals involved and their activities. For example, reported financial scandals might have been prevented had executives, directors, and auditors behaved more ethically. Codes of business ethics and conduct are intended to govern behavior, but they cannot substitute for moral principles, culture, and character. There has been a discussion of whether ethics and ethical behavior can be taught. There are some who believe that moral principles and ethics are part of family values that cannot be taught. Although we are not taking any position on this issue, we believe that business ethics can be promoted and taught to improve professional reputation, accountability, integrity, judgment, and other qualities of the business decision-making process. Setting the appropriate "tone at the top" promoting ethical organization, culture, and policies can effectively influence individuals' behavior. Teaching business ethics should provide incentives, opportunities, and rationalization for individuals, particularly professionals, to uphold their personal integrity and professional accountability.

ETHICS IN THE WORKPLACE

Ethics in the workplace are receiving a considerable amount of attention as the emerging corporate governance reforms require setting an appropriate tone at the top promoting ethical conduct. A review of the reported financial scandals proves that most ethical dilemmas have financial consequences and dimensions. There is increased interaction between the board of directors, audit committees, internal auditors, external auditors, executives, and employees in general regarding ethical conduct in the workplace. SOX is reported to have a positive impact on business codes of ethics. However, SOX is only one element in the complex corporate culture that determines the ethical conduct of participants in the current corporate business model. The other elements require changes in corporate culture in promoting competency and integrity among all participants.

A survey of ethics and workplace conducted by Deloitte & Touche in 2007 finds a strong link between ethics and work–life balance, as 91 percent of respondents believed that workers are more likely to behave ethically at work when they have a work–life balance.[6] Survey results suggest that providing a balance between work and life through a more flexible work schedule provides incentives and opportunities for job satisfaction and fostering an ethical workplace culture. The survey identifies the following key factors in promoting an ethical workplace: (1) behavior of management (42 percent); (2) behavior of direct supervisor (35 percent); (3) positive reinforcement for ethical behavior; (4) compensation, including salary and bonus (29 percent); and (5) behavior of peers (23 percent). These results clearly indicate that the majority of respondents (77 percent) believe that the behavior of top management and the direct supervisor in setting an appropriate tone at the top foster an ethical workplace environment. Management can create a workplace environment that is conducive to ethical behavior by setting examples and acting as a role model for employees to behave ethically. Furthermore, a slight majority of respondents reported that they have observed supervisors setting positive examples of ethical behavior daily or several times per week.

The survey finds that more than half of the respondents believed that their job causes conflict between their work responsibilities and personal priorities. The major aspects of respondents' jobs that can cause such conflicts are (1) high levels of stress (28 percent), (2) long hours (25 percent), (3) fast-paced environment (14 percent), (4) inflexible schedule (13 percent), (5) conflicts between personal values and company's core values (9 percent), and (6) highly competitive environment (7 percent). The survey finds the following reasons people make unethical decisions in the workplace: (1) lack of personal integrity (80 percent), (2) job dissatisfaction (60 percent), (3) financial rewards (44 percent), (4) pressure to meet goals (41 percent), and (5) ignorance of code of conduct (39 percent).

Establishing an appropriate tone at the top and the existence of an enforceable corporate code of conduct can promote an ethical workplace environment, as the majority of respondents believe that (1) their company's values promote an ethical workplace environment, (2) they agree with their company's values, and (3) their company's values emphasize a healthy work–life balance. The survey shows the following results pertaining to questionable behavior in the workplace environment: (1) stealing petty cash (99 percent), (2) cheating on expense reports (95 percent), (3) taking credit for another person's accomplishment (94 percent), (4) lying on time sheets about hours worked (92 percent), (5) coming into work hungover (76 percent), (6) telling a demeaning joke (75 percent), and (7) taking office supplies for personal use (70 percent). Ironically, the majority of respondents believed that it was acceptable to (1) use company technology for personal use (72 percent), (2) take a sick day when not actually ill (66 percent), (3) date a subordinate (57 percent), and (4) ask a colleague for a personal favor (63 percent).

All organizations, regardless of their mission (e.g. profit oriented, not for profit) and size (large vs. small), should establish an "organizational ethical culture." The phrase "organizational ethical culture" consists of three words: (1) organization, which is defined as a group of individuals or entities bound to achieve a shared goal; (2) ethics, which are honorable behavior conforming to the norm of the group; and (3) culture, which is a pattern of shared beliefs adopted by the group in dealing with its internal and external affairs. Thus, organizational ethical culture is an environment of beliefs, ethical behavior, and practices shared by members in pursuing their goals and fulfilling their responsibilities. Ethical behavior and value creation may produce the same consequences in many corporate settings. Management has a fiduciary responsibility for stakeholder value creation, enhancement, and protection within the boundaries of ethical standards. The effective fulfillment of these responsibilities ensures that directors not only carry out their fiduciary duties of care, loyalty, and due diligence, but that they also abide by corporate governance best practices.

A survey conducted by The Conference Board in February 2004 examines the role of the board of directors in promoting ethical conduct from a large sample of global companies.[7] The survey reveals that the oversight activities and involvement of the board, particularly the audit committee, in establishing, maintaining, and monitoring ethics programs is growing. About 66 percent of all surveyed companies in the United States report that their company's codes of ethics were established by a board resolution. The increasing trend toward more involvement of the board of directors in a company's ethics program was influenced by the devastating consequences of reported financial scandals rooted in ethical conduct by directors, officers, and auditors of high-profile companies and the development of corporate governance reforms in promoting ethical conduct throughout the organization.

The survey also reports that (1) more than half of the surveyed board members indicate that they review their company's ethics programs regularly with a range of 54 percent in Japan and 78 percent in the United States; (2) about 50 percent said they review their company's ethics training programs with a range of 42 percent of companies in Western Europe and 61 percent in the United States; (3) audit committees in the United States were more involved in overseeing their companies' ethics programs than in other countries (e.g., 77 percent in the United States compared to 63 percent in Japan and 40 percent in India); and (4) independent directors made up the ethics oversight committees in 85 percent of U.S. companies, 82 percent of Japanese companies, and 37 percent of Western European companies. Overall, the survey results indicate that all 165 of the surveyed global companies have taken measures to ensure compliance with corporate ethics programs, with U.S. companies leading the effort.

BUSINESS ETHICS

Ethics are a branch of philosophy with no clear-cut definition of what behaviors are ethical and which are unethical when judging one's behavior. There is no general or global consensus for defining ethical behavior for individuals because it may change from time to time and from one place to another. There is no universal measure or standard as to what constitutes ethical behavior. The problem of defining business ethics is more severe because a business is a collection of individuals, often with conflicting interests, who make decisions on behalf of the organization. Business ethics are most simply described as a process of promoting moral principles and standards that guide business behavior. Four different levels of business ethics have been identified based on what type of business and how their actions are evaluated.[8] These levels are

1. The society level, which defines ethical behavior and assesses the effect of business on society

2. The industry level, which suggests that different industries have their own set of ethical standards (e.g., chemical industry vs. pharmaceutical industry)

3. The company level, under which different companies have their own set of ethical standards

4. The individual manager level, at which each manager and other corporate participants are responsible for their own ethical behavior

Companies need to have ethics and business programs to address (1) their diversity of personnel services; (2) their expectations of the public and their stakeholders; (3) their legal, professional, and regulatory environments; (4) compliance with applicable regulations including SOX, FSG, SEC rules, and listing standards of national stock exchanges; and (5) integration of ethics and business conduct programs into their corporate governance. Thus, one feasible way to judge ethical behavior is to focus on determinants of business ethics and behavior such as corporate culture, incentives, opportunities, and choices.

Corporate Culture

A corporate culture of setting an appropriate tone at the top of promoting ethical and honorable behavior can play an important role in establishing ethical behavior throughout the company. Corporate culture is influenced by the delegation of authority, assignment of responsibilities, and the process of accountability. Proper communication of corporate culture such as code of conduct and job descriptions throughout the company is essential in promoting and enforcing ethical behavior.

Ethics in business have an important underlying postulate that the majority of business leaders, managers, and other personnel are honest and ethical in conducting their business, and the minority who engage in unethical conduct will not prevail in the long term. Thus, corporate culture and compliance rules should provide incentives and opportunities for the majority of ethical individuals to maintain their honesty and integrity and provide measures for the minority of unethical individuals to be monitored, punished, and corrected for their unethical conduct. Companies should promote a spirit of integrity that goes beyond compliance with the established code of business ethics or compliance to the letter of the law by creating a business culture of doing what is right.

Incentives

Incentives are perhaps the most essential determinant of business ethics. Individuals within the company (managers, employees) tend to act according to incentives provided to them in terms of rewards and the performance evaluation process. The company's incentive plans can be structured to direct managers' and employees' behavior in the desired manner. The diversity of people, existence of various value systems, and sensitivity of moral issues make it difficult to achieve a consensus and central theme for ethics. Thus, "situation ethics theory" is used in this chapter to build a consensus as to appropriate ethical practices, professional responsibilities, and honorable behavior through the promotion, establishment, and compliance with business and professional codes of conduct.[9] Situation ethics are "a moral pattern allowing circumstances to overrule principle and allegiance. Principle here is interpreted as definable moral, criminal, or civil law. Allegiance refers to group loyalty."[10]

This suggests that individuals should do what is right rather than comply with specific principles when facing ethical challenges.

Opportunity

Corporate culture and incentives can encourage individuals to behave in the desired ethical manner. However, if opportunities exist, wrongdoers will take advantage and behave in an opportunistic manner. Thus, effective corporate governance, internal controls, and enterprise risk management can reduce the opportunity for unethical conduct. Attributes of an ethical integrity-based corporate culture are sense of employee responsibility, freedom to raise concerns without fear of retaliation, managers modeling ethical behavior and expressing the importance of integrity, an understanding by leadership of the pressure points that drive unethical behavior, and processes to find and fix these areas of pressure.[11]

Dark Reading's 2006 "security scruples" survey reveals that entities operate differently in private than they say they do in public. A survey of 648 IT and security professionals was conducted to determine their beliefs and behaviors in both real and hypothetical security situations. The results indicate that (1) a large majority agreed on how to "do the right thing"; (2) more than 27 percent have accessed unauthorized data; (3) only 53 percent said they would report a colleague who was abusing security privileges; and (4) although many entities maintain codes of ethics and related policies to protect their ethical and legal positions, their actual enforcement of these policies varies with the situation.[12] These results suggest that situational ethics where the ends justify the means prevail more in the workplace than the codes of ethics focusing on good versus bad or acceptable behavior versus unacceptable conduct.

Choices

Individuals, in general, are given the freedom to make choices and usually choose those that will maximize their well-being. Managers and employees make decisions, take actions, and exercise their choices on behalf of the company as agents of their company. Nevertheless, their choices are often influenced by corporate culture, incentives, opportunities, and actions because other individuals in the organization do not work in isolation. Although there is not a single commonly accepted definition of business ethics, there are numerous examples of possible violations of ethics in business ranging from backdating practices of executive stock options grants to spying on outside directors. Ethical violations include the behavior of the convicted executives of the high-profile companies Enron, WorldCom, Adelphia, and Tyco. The trend in business shows a decline in business ethics in recent years. The actual decline or the perception of such is not good for business and modern society for the following reasons. This trend of dealing in business ethics should be reversed through (1) more education of business ethics, (2) establishment of business codes of ethical conduct, (3) enforcement of ethical conduct, and (4) increased promotion of ethical behavior in the business culture.

TRIANGLE OF BUSINESS ETHICS

Figure 3.1 shows the triangle of business ethics consisting of (1) ethics sensitivity, (2) ethics incentives, and (3) ethical behavior.

Figure 3.1 Triangle of Business Ethics.
Source: Rezaee, Z. 2007. *Corporate Governance Post-Sarbanes-Oxley Act: Regulations, Requirements, & Integrated Processes*. John Wiley & Sons, Hoboken, NJ.

Ethics Sensitivity

An organization consists of diverse individuals with a variety of value systems and ethical theories. An individual (e.g., accountant) in an organization works in collaboration and coordination with others in fulfilling his or her responsibilities. Gamesmanship, loyalty, peer pressure, and other factors influence one's ethical decisions and actions. Ethics sensitivity is defined as moral principles, workplace factors, gamesmanship, loyalty, peer pressure, and job security that influence one's ethical decisions and are derived from the organization's ethical culture.

Ethics Incentives

Ethics incentives encompass rewards, punishments, and requirements for behaving either ethically or unethically. Examples of ethics incentives are an organization's appropriate tone at the top promoting ethical conduct, various professional codes of conduct (e.g., American Institute of Certified Public Accountants [AICPA] Code of Conduct), and ethics rules (SEC's ethics rule for principal financial officers). Incentives for ethical behavior come from several sources, including (1) individual-based incentives, (2) organization-based incentives, (3) market-based incentives, (4) profession-based incentives, and (5) regulatory-based incentives.

1. **Individual-based incentives.** Individual-based incentives for ethical behavior pertain to one's ethical values and moral principles to do the right thing. The fundamental individual-based incentive is the need and desire of individuals to maximize their own good and minimize their discomfort.[13]

2. **Organization-based incentives.** Organization-based incentives come from setting an appropriate tone at the top and establishing, maintaining, and enforcing ethical behavior throughout the organization. They include measures for motivating and mandating individuals to comply with the company's applicable regulations and ethical standards and act within ethical and legal constraints.[14]

3. **Profession-based incentives.** Profession-based incentives are defined by a professional affiliation of individuals. For example, practicing accountants should observe the AICPA's and PCAOB's code of professional ethics. Professional codes of

conduct serve as a reference and a benchmark for individuals, establish rules of conduct relevant to the profession, and provide a means of facilitating enforcements of rules and standards of conduct.

4. **Market-based incentives.** Market-based incentives are provided by markets in imposing substantial costs on organizations and individuals that engage in unethical behavior. For example, reducing costs by lowering the quality of products and services would cause a market reaction.

5. **Regulatory-based incentives.** Regulatory-based incentives are induced through rules and regulations by imposing sanctions, fines, and penalties on organizations and individuals who engage in unethical and unacceptable behavior. Organizations and individuals assess expected future loss in terms of potential penalties, the probability of being caught, and the possible gains from opportunistic behavior in making decisions.

Business ethical conduct addressed in this chapter is based on the premises that (1) individuals respond to a variety of incentives provided to them in logical, systematic, and creative ways; (2) individual-based incentives relate to personal integrity and are the primary driver of ethical behavior; (3) organization-based incentives should be established through corporate culture; (4) professional-based incentives establish rules of conduct relevant to individuals' professional behavior and responsibility; (5) market-based incentives influence the reputation and impose potentially significant costs on organizations and individuals who engage in unethical behavior; and (6) regulatory-based incentives impose severe penalties on those who engage in unlawful and unethical behavior. These incentives alone or in aggregate promote ethical behavior. These incentives should be identified, addressed, and used to promote and enforce ethical behavior.

Ethical Behavior

The company's directors and executives should demonstrate, through both their actions and their policies, a firm commitment to ethical behavior throughout the company and a culture of trust within the company. Although a "right tone at the top" is very important in promoting an ethical culture, actions often speak louder than words. The following quotes were made by high-profile executives who were subsequently indicted and convicted of corporate malfeasance.[15] These CEOs promoted ethical and social values in words yet violated them in their actions.

> *Boards should be absolutely certain that the company is run properly from a fiduciary standpoint in every degree. I am a great believer in the audit committee having full access to the auditors in every way, shape and form.—Al Dunlap (Sunbeam)*

> *You'll see people who in the early days . . . took their life savings and trusted this company with their money. And I have an awesome responsibility to those people to make sure that they've done right.—Bernard Ebbers (WorldCom)*

> *We are offended by the perception that we would waste the resources of a company that is a major part of our life and livelihood, and that we would be happy with directors who would permit that waste. . . . So as a CEO, I want a strong, competent board.—Dennis Koskoski (Tyco)*

It's more than just dollars. You've got to give back to the community that supported you.—John Rigas (Adelphia)

People have an obligation to dissent in this company.—Jeffrey Skilling (Enron)

SEC Rules on Corporate Code of Ethics

A corporate code of ethics has been defined in several authoritative guides and the business literature. The SEC's definition of code of ethics focuses on the conduct of the company's specified officers involved in financial reporting. Public companies are encouraged to define code of ethics broadly to address the conduct of all personnel within the company with the broad coverage of both financial and nonfinancial activities. The SEC rule describes the term "code of ethics" as written standards designed to deter wrongdoing and to promote[16]

1. Full, fair, accurate, timely, and transparent disclosure in reports and documents filed or submitted to the SEC and in other public communications made by public companies

2. Avoidance of conflicts of interest, including disclosure of any material transaction or relationship that reasonably could be expected to give rise to such a conflict to an appropriate person or persons identified in the company's adopted code

3. Honest and ethical conduct throughout the company, including the ethical handling of apparent or actual conflicts of interest between personal and professional activities and relationships

4. Accountability for compliance with the established code of ethics

5. Compliance with applicable laws, rules, regulations, and professional standards

6. The prompt internal reporting of noncompliance and any violations of the established code of ethics to an appropriate person or persons designated in the code

The SEC extended code of ethics requirements to both the company's principal financial officers (SOX's Section 406) and principal executive officers (SOX's Section 407). The SEC rules in implementing Section 406 of SOX require public companies to disclose whether they have adopted a code of ethics for their principal officers, including principal executive officers, principal financial officers, principal accounting officers, controller, or other personnel performing similar functions in the annual report filed with the SEC. If the company has not adopted such a code of ethics, it must disclose the reason for not doing so.

Public companies must make their code of ethics publicly available through

1. Filing their code of ethics as an exhibit to their SEC annual reports

2. Posting their code of ethics on their Web site, and annual reports filed with the SEC must specify the URL and its purpose

3. Disclosing in their annual reports that a copy of their code of ethics is available without charge on request

The SEC rules on corporate codes of ethics neither specify the content and format of such a code nor prescribe the procedure for monitoring, enforcing, or sanctioning any violations. The SEC recommends (1) adoption of codes of ethics that are more comprehensive and broader than ones that mainly meet the new disclosure requirements; (2) establishment of a code of ethics that describes the company's policies and procedures for internal reporting of code violations; (3) designation of individuals with adequate authority and status (e.g., the chair of the audit committee and ethics officer) within the company to receive, investigate, and take action on the reported code violations; (4) providing of guidelines for avoiding material transactions or relationships associated with potential conflicts of interest; (5) disclosure of consequences of noncompliance or violation of the company's established code of ethics; and (6) establishment of policies and procedures to ensure that individuals receiving code violations are recused when they are involved in any matters related to an alleged violation.

SEC rules require public companies to report significant amendments to their code of ethics, or any waiver affecting specified officers to the SEC pursuant to the filing of their first annual report on their code of ethics. These should be disclosed within five business days and can be provided in a Form 8-K filed with the SEC or disclosed on the company's investor relations Web site. The Web site disclosure must be maintained online for at least 12 months or otherwise be retained for at least five years. Public companies that do not have a code of ethics must establish a code that meets the requirements of the SEC final rule. Public companies with an existing code of ethics must ensure that their existing code satisfies SEC requirements or otherwise revise their code to meet the requirements; if not, they must be prepared to disclose why they have not adopted a qualifying code of ethics.

Listing Standards

The listing standards of the NYSE further expanded on the SEC rules by requiring listed companies to (1) adopt and disclose a code of business conduct and ethics for directors, officers, and employees; and (2) promptly disclose any waivers of the adopted code for directors and executive officers.[17] The NYSE listing standards recommend that each company determine its own business conduct and ethics policies, but provide an extensive list of matters that should be addressed by the company's code, including conflicts of interest, corporate opportunities, confidentiality, protection of proper use of the company's assets, fair dealing, reporting of any illegal or unethical conduct, and compliance with applicable regulations. NASD ethics rules for Nasdaq-listed companies are similar to those of the NYSE and further require the company's adopted code to provide for an enforcement mechanism and any waivers of the code for directors or executive officers to be approved by the board and disclosed not later than the next periodic report.

The emerging corporate governance reforms (SOX, SEC rules, listing standards) require public companies to adopt a code of conduct for key financial officers. Public companies have adopted codes of conduct, offered employee training programs in ethics, and often appointed chief ethics officers to oversee the establishment and maintenance of codes of ethics and ethics programs. The established codes of conduct and ethics programs address the following:

1. Avoidance and resolution of conflicts of interest between the company and employee
2. Compliance with all applicable regulations
3. Emphasis on customer relations to enhance the company's reputation

4. Avoidance of improper use of the company's confidential information

5. Encouragement of whistleblowers to reveal dishonesty, wrongdoings, and improper behavior

The process of making ethical decisions starts with the commitment to do the right thing by (1) recognizing the relevant issue, event, or decision; (2) evaluating all alternative courses of action and their impacts on one's well-being as well as the well-being of others possibly affected by the decisions; (3) deciding on the best course of action available; (4) consulting appropriate ethical guidance; (5) continuously assessing the consequences of the decision and adopting appropriate changes; and (6) implementing the decision.

ETHICS TEACHING IN BUSINESS SCHOOLS

Institutions of higher education, particularly business colleges and accounting programs, are responding to changes in corporate governance, business environment, and the accounting profession. The observed changes are (1) more academic courses are being offered in areas of corporate governance, business ethics, forensic accounting, enterprise risk management, internal auditing, and information technology; (2) the acceptance and appeal of an accounting career is growing as the public is becoming more educated about the important role that accountants and financial advisers can play in our society; (3) enrollment in accounting programs increased 19 percent from 2000 to 2004; and (4) new accounting graduates hiring increased by 17 percent between 2003 and 2004.[18] Indeed, SOX has conspicuously been referred to as the "Accountants Full Employment Act." Business schools and accounting programs can also influence corporate governance by training competent and ethical future business leaders. Thus, the emerging corporate governance reforms have had a positive impact on academic programs. Conversely, the reported financial scandals have had negative impacts on business students' ethical conduct because a survey finds that the majority of students (77 percent) use recent corporate and political scandals to justify their cheating behavior.[19]

The wave of financial scandals at the turn of the twenty-first century along with congressional responses and related regulations have brought corporate governance and business ethics to the center stage of business education. Given the current culture of corporate accountability as reflected in the extant literature, corporate governance and business ethics education are becoming more important to business students. Reports of professional organizations, including the AICPA, the Association to Advance Collegiate Schools of Business (AACSB), and NASBA and academic studies (e.g., Albrecht and Sack, AAA) have recommended that ethics, integrity, and accountability be integrated into the business and accounting curriculum.

The goal of corporate governance and business ethics education is to teach students their responsibilities and accountability to their profession and society. Almost all states require CPA candidates to pass an ethics exam before licensing and report the ethics component in their continuing education requirements. Almost all states require a minimum amount of ethics education for their practicing CPAs. One approach to teaching business ethics is to integrate it across the curriculum by exposing students to corporate governance issues and common ethical dilemmas and methods of resolving these issues and dilemmas.

Business ethics require that corporations promote a culture of moral responsibility to society. Thus, business schools, in educating future business leaders, attempt to incorporate and integrate business ethics into their curriculum. Business schools are being criticized for not providing ethical awareness and education to students in light of recent high-profile cases of unethical behavior on the part of management who once received their education in business schools. This suggests that management education should influence a person's ethics composition and shape his or her awareness and appreciation of ethical behavior and consequences. Proponents of an integrated approach to ethics in business education recommend that ethics be an essential part of the business curriculum. Business education should introduce students to ethical issues and provide them with tools and skills to meet the ethical challenges of the business world.

The Ethical Resource Center (ERC) has strongly supported teaching ethics education in business schools by stating

> It is crucial that [business] students are exposed at the core level not simply to finance, accounting, management, and marketing, but also to ethical reasoning and methods for resolving the difficult problems in these disciplines . . . the AACSB and schools of business [must] ensure the proficient education of students of business in the area of business ethics so as to develop both their knowledge and competency in this area. . . . It requires positive attention in standard business courses, as well as special attention in separate courses in business ethics.[20]

The AACSB in its task force report promotes coverage of ethics in the business curriculum but stopped short of requiring AACSB-accredited schools to offer specific ethics courses or integrate ethical education throughout the curriculum.[21] It is left up to business schools to determine whether to provide ethics education to business students in a single course or integrated across the curriculum. The questions of "should business education teach ethics" and "how should it be taught" are yet to be answered and remain debatable in the business and education communities. Another relevant question is whether ethics education should be a core competency or be treated separately in each of the traditional functional areas (e.g., accounting, finance, management, marketing). AACSB's treatment of ethics through infusion in the business curriculum has been criticized for being too ambiguous and encouraging meaningless superficial measures to satisfy accreditation.

Offering a stand-alone course in business ethics requires defining the goal of such a course and its topical content. The purpose of an ethics course should be to teach ethical concepts and analytical skills that enhance students' ethical awareness and understanding of ethical reasoning. The moral issues facing their personal and professional lives encourage them to assess the moral implications of their decisions and develop their personal integrity and professional responsibility, and ultimately enable them to be an ethical leader. The objective is to educate and train moral individuals who will make ethical decisions and provide students with insights and skills that will prepare them to apply high ethical standards in their business career.

Four years after the passage of SOX, businesses have taken appropriate measures to improve their professional accountability. Yet, many business schools are still struggling with how to teach ethics, leadership, corporate governance, and accountability more effectively. Craig Smith, associate dean at London Business Schools, states that while all full-time and executive MBA students are required to study ethics, "It's often just an elective offering at best, arguably preaching to the converted."[22] The emerging corporate governance reforms require a high standard of professional conduct for corporate directors, officers, and accountants, yet at many business schools faculty "resent being forced to squeeze ethics lessons into an already jam-packed syllabus, while students grumble that ethics classes tend to be preachy and philosophical."[23]

The quality and quantity of ethics coverage in accounting texts have been criticized.[24] Critics argue that accounting education is not adequate in areas such as ethics, corporate governance, professional judgment, accountability, and responsibility. Professional ethical orientation (knowledge of their profession's code of conduct) is expected to be improved through ethics education and to influence individuals' ethical behavior and conduct. The improvement of accounting ethics education can be achieved through (1) undergraduate exposure to both ethical theory and applied ethics, (2) inputs from practitioners and academicians, (3) systematic exposure of undergraduates to professional ethics scenarios and problems, and (4) the development of students' ability to identify ethical issues and apply values and a reasoning process to professional ethical problems.[25]

Many business schools are facing difficulties in either offering a stand-alone ethics course or integrating the ethics model into the business curriculum. For example, in Columbia's MBA program "when a professor said it was time for the ethics module, it felt very forced and students didn't participate very much and a lot of students were also upset about being graded on a curve. If you received a low grade, you felt you would be viewed as a bad person."[26] Although the integration model sounds justifiable and feasible, "many faculty members have no training in ethics and the law and don't know how to incorporate them well."[27] Thus, many national leading MBA programs (Columbia, Harvard) have taken a broader approach to teaching business ethics by blending it with social responsibilities, leadership, corporate accountability, and corporate governance. This approach of placing ethics within a larger framework (1) is preferred and has worked well "because instead of a lot of philosophical musings, it focuses on how to apply ethics lessons in the real world"[28]; and (2) is being promoted by both academic organizations (AACSB) and professional organizations (NASBA). This is the approach taken in this book and the framework used throughout the book.

NASBA, in its Exposure Draft of Uniform Accountancy Rules 5–1 and 5–2 regarding NASBA 150-hour Education, emphasizes the need for six semester credit hours in ethical and professional responsibilities education.[29] NASBA defines education in ethical and professional responsibilities as "a program of learning that provides potential professional accountants with a framework of professional values, ethics, and attributes for exercising professional judgment and for acting in an ethical manner that is in the best interest of the public and the profession." This requires that professional and ethical accountants comply with all applicable regulations and codes of ethical conduct. NASBA recommends that the process of ethics education starts with the discussion of broad philosophical ethical concepts and then proceeds to the application of these concepts to the accounting and business environment. NASBA states that an acceptable ethics education program should contain (1) three semester credit hours in ethical and professional responsibilities of CPAs, and (2) three semester hours in ethical foundations and applications in business. NASBA also suggests that neither of the two requirements be integrated with the legal and regulatory environment of business or business law courses. These ethical content requirements can be integrated with each other or other content requirements (e.g., corporate governance, accounting, auditing). Nonetheless, these proposed ethics requirements subsequently were not approved by NASBA's board.

Ethics in Institutions of Higher Education

Financial scandals of the twenty-first century have reinvigorated interest in business ethics and academic programs because investors are now more educated about the impacts of unethical behavior on their investment, and business schools realize the importance of training future ethical business leaders. Several incidents of ethical violations and cheating have been reported at highly rated business schools. Recently, thirty-four business students in the Duke MBA program were accused of violating the school's honor code by cheating on an exam. Those students are expected to receive stiff penalties: nine will be expelled, fifteen will be suspended for one year and receive an "F" in the class, nine will receive an "F" in the course, and one will receive a failing mark on an assignment.[30] These and other cases call for business schools to (1) adopt *zero tolerance* ethics and honor codes, (2) establish appropriate policies and procedures to implement honor codes, (3) properly communicate the honor code and related policies and procedures to students, (4) require business students to certify their understanding of honor codes and related policies and procedures, and (5) establish a due diligence process for the strict enforcement of honor codes and related policies. The honor code should describe (1) the purpose of the honor code in creating a culture of integrity, fairness, honesty, respect for others, and trustworthiness; (2) policies in determining the scope of the honor code measures taken to assure the achievement of its objectives and details of its violations, including lying, cheating, and stealing; (3) enforcement procedures and actions determining due judicial process and penalties; and (4) the appeal process.

Another incident of unethical behavior occurred at Texas A&M University's Mays Business School, where twenty-four undergraduate students were given disciplinary action for allegedly cheating on a quiz in a business ethics class. Students enrolled in the course took the quiz for fellow students who were absent, and as a result of their cheating, received grades "D" or "F" for the course. Student cheating on an ethics exam at Columbia University, one of the premier journalism schools, also received significant media coverage and discussion in 2004. Academic integrity and ethical conduct by students and faculty are important to the sustainable well-being and reputation of institutions of higher education. This academic integrity can be achieved when (1) there is an effective and fairly enforceable academic honor code, (2) faculty are willing to take proper action against suspected cheaters, (3) adequate research is conducted to identify factors that affect academic integrity, including fundamental ethical values, and (4) ethics are integrated into the business curriculum, and pedagogies are developed to teach and encourage adherence to ethical values and conducts.

PROFESSIONAL ETHICS

Characteristics of a profession are (1) existence of a common body of knowledge consisting of an intellectual skill obtained through education, training, certification, and continuing professional education; (2) adoption and adherence to a common code of conduct guiding professional behavior and action and holding members accountable for their actions; and (3) acceptance of a duty to society, the profession, and its members. Thus, the acceptance of ethical duties or responsibilities is the cornerstone of a profession. The accounting profession is characterized by (1) serving the public interest; (2) performing responsibly with integrity, competency, objectivity, and transparency; (3) exercising due diligence in maintaining independence and improving the quality of services provided; and (4) protecting investors from receiving misleading audited financial reports.

In addressing an auditor's bias in judgment, one should realize that (1) accountants do not work in isolation, but rather as team players, where their work ethics and behaviors are influenced by the ethics and conduct of coworkers, superiors, and even subordinates within the company; and (2) like other human, they can be pressured and motivated when the opportunity is given and thus be tempted to engage in unethical behavior (e.g., manipulation of financial reports).

In June 2005, the International Ethics Standards Board for Accountants (IESBA), part of the International Federation of Accountants (IFAC), issued its revised Code of Ethics for use by professional accountants worldwide.[31] The key principles of the IESBA's code of ethics are (1) integrity, (2) objectivity, (3) professional competence and due care, (4) confidentiality, and (5) professional behavior. Standard 2130, Assurance Engagement of the ETA's International Standards for the Professional Practice of Internal Auditing, requires internal auditors to "evaluate the design, implementation, and effectiveness of the organization's ethics-related objectives, programs and activities."[32] The audit committee should ask internal auditors to evaluate the company and the extent of compliance of its major functions (key units) with its established code of business conduct. The purpose of this evaluation is to reinforce the company's commitment to ethical values and integrity. Many states have started to require mandatory ethics education and training as a part of their continuing professional education (CPE) requirements to maintain a CPA license in good standing. For example, Table 3.1 shows that New York requires four hours of ethics CPE for a triennial license period, while the state of Virginia requires two hours of ethics CPE reporting each year.

REPORTING BUSINESS ETHICS AND CONDUCT

Ethical accountability refers to the behavior of individuals and the organization's commitment to conduct their activities in an honorable manner. Social accountability refers to the effects of the organization's activities and behavior of its stakeholders, including society, the environment, competitors, suppliers, customers, employees, directors, officers, and other profit-oriented and not-for-profit organizations. As corporate scandals come to light, even three years after the passage of SOX (e.g., Refco), the issue of business ethics becomes more prominent. Section 406 of SOX requires public companies to disclose in their annual financial statements the establishment (or lack of) a corporate code of conduct. Nevertheless, public companies may choose to report their business ethics and conduct as a separate report to their shareholders or as part of their regular filings with the SEC.

The Conference Board suggests that the establishment of ethical conduct, corporate culture, and related policies and procedures is crucial for all companies. Boards should set a right tone at the top promoting ethical conduct, and management should establish policies and procedures that define, communicate, and demand ethical conduct and enforce companies' codes of conduct. The 2006 survey conducted by the Ethics and Compliance Officer Association (ECOA) and salary.com indicates that (1) organizations recognize the

Table 3.1 Ethics Requirements of CPE

Jurisdiction	Hours of ethics CPE every triennial (Three Years)
1. Alabama	None
2. Alaska	Four every two years
3. Arizona	Four every two years
4. Arkansas	Four every three years
5. California	Eight every six years
6. Colorado	Two every two years
7. Connecticut	Four every three years
8. Delaware	Four every two years
9. District of Columbia	Four every two years
10. Florida	Four every two years
11. Georgia	None
12. Guam	Six every three years
13. Hawaii	Four every two years
14. Idaho	None
15. Illinois	Four every three years
16. Indiana	Two every three years
17. Iowa	Four every three years
18. Kansas	Two every two years
19. Kentucky	None
20. Louisiana	Two every three years
21. Maine	Four every three years
22. Maryland	Four every two years
23. Massachusetts	Four every two years
24. Michigan	Two every year
25. Minnesota	Eight every three years
26. Mississippi	Three every three years
27. Missouri	Two every year
28. Montana	Two every three years
29. Nebraska	Four every two years
30. Nevada	Four every two years
31. New Hampshire	Four every three years
32. New Jersey	Four every three years
33. New Mexico	None
34. New York	Four every three years
35. North Carolina	Two every year in group setting or four every year if self-paced
36. North Dakota	None
37. Ohio	Three every three years
38. Oklahoma	Two every year
39. Oregon	Four every four years
40. Pennsylvania	None

(Continued)

Table 3.1   *(Continued)*

Jurisdiction	Hours of ethics CPE every triennial (Three Years)
41. Puerto Rico	None
42. Rhode Island	Six every three years
43. South Carolina	None
44. South Dakota	None
45. Tennessee	None
46. Texas	Four every two years
47. Utah	None
48. Vermont	Four every two years
49. Virgin Islands	N/A*
50. Virginia	Two every year
51. Washington	Four every three years
52. West Virginia	None
53. Wisconsin	N/A*
54. Wyoming	Two every three years

*No requirements for continuing education.
Source: VanZante, N. R., and R. B. Fritzsch. 2006. Comparing State Board of
Accountancy CPE Requirement with an Emphasis on Professional Ethics Requirements.
The CPA Journal October: New York State Society of CPAs. Available at:
www.nysscpa.org/cpajournal/2006/1006/essentials/p58.htm.

importance of their ethics and compliance office; (2) the compensation of ethics and compliance officers, on average, increased by 12 percent in 2006; (3) top global ethics and compliance executives earned a median annual salary of $206,800, median total cash compensation of $285,000, and median long-term incentives of $342,100; (4) top domestic ethics and compliance executives earned a median annual salary of $180,000, with a median total cash compensation of $202,300 and median long-term incentives of $81,600; and (5) ethics and compliance officers add value to their organization as reflected in their increased compensation.[33]

The defense industry has been under observation for improving its ethics conduct. Certain defense contractors have adopted six principles of business ethics and conduct set forth in the Defense Industry Initiatives (DII) on Business Ethics and Conduct, better known as Initiatives. DII was established in 1986 to adopt and implement a set of business ethics and conduct principles.[34] These six principles require that defense contractors (1) comply with a written code of business conduct; (2) provide sufficient training to all personnel within their organization regarding personal responsibility under the code; (3) encourage internal reporting of violations of the code with the promise of no retaliation for such reporting; (4) self-govern their activities by implementing controls to monitor compliance with all applicable laws and regulations (e.g., federal procurement laws); (5) share their best practices in implementing the DII principles through participation in an annual Best Practices Forum; and (6) be accountable to the public, particularly through the completion of an annual Public Accountability Questionnaire.

Those defense contractors participating in the Initiatives (signatory companies) are required to complete the questionnaire by answering a series of questions regarding their policies, procedures, and programs designed to comply with the Initiatives during their reporting period. These signatories, as part of their public accountability process, are required to conduct internal audits, assess their compliance, and provide officer certifications regarding the completeness, accuracy, and timeliness of their responses to the questionnaire. Alternatively, signatories may engage an independent public accountant to examine or review their responses to the questionnaire and express a conclusion regarding their appropriateness in a public report. The performance of such engagements by an independent public accountant (practitioner) raised several questions about whether this is considered as an attest engagement under Section 101 of the AICPA's Attest Engagements, what criteria should be used by the practitioner for such an attest engagement, what procedures should be applied to the questionnaire responses, and what report format should be used for such an engagement.

The AICPA, in offering guidance to practitioners for performing such services to signatories, provides interpretations of Section 101 Attest Engagements by answering the previous questions.[35] The AICPA states that (1) Section 101 is applicable when a practitioner is engaged by a signatory (defense contractor) to review or examine its certification of an annual public accountability questionnaire; (2) the criteria for assessing the defense contractor's responses are contained in the questionnaire and its related instructions and should be used by the practitioner in the review or examination; (3) the objective of procedures performed is to gather sufficient and competent evidential matter that the defense contractor has designed and implemented policies and programs to adequately respond to all questions in the questionnaire, not to provide assurance on the effectiveness of the designed policies and procedures in compliance with the signatory's code of business ethics and conduct; and (4) Figures 3.2 and 3.3 illustrate the standards of reporting that provide guidance regarding report content and wording appropriate for various circumstances.

FINANCIAL REPORTING INTEGRITY

Financial reporting integrity is vital in rebuilding investor confidence in corporate America, its financial reports, and the capital markets. Integrity is also important to individuals and society in providing a basis for (1) establishing trust, (2) relying on information, (3) developing markets, (4) achieving desired outcomes, and (5) inspiring public policy.[36] The five key aspects of integrity are moral values, motives, communication, qualities, and achievements.

The integrity of the financial reporting process can create investor confidence in financial information required for the efficient functioning of the capital markets. The integrity of the process is a function of trustworthiness of all individuals involved including the board of directors, particularly the audit committee, management, both internal and external auditors, legal counsel, investment banks, and financial analysts. Specifically, the integrity and competence of those engaged directly in the financial reporting process, such as management, the audit committee, and external auditors, greatly influence the quality and reliability of financial reports. Table 3.2 presents a framework for reporting with integrity consisting of (1) five key aspects of moral values, motives, commitments, qualities, and achievements; (2) five organizational drivers of leadership, strategy, policies, information, and culture; and

Defense Industry Questionnaire on Business Ethics and Conduct

Illustration 1: Unqualified Opinion Unrestricted with Criteria Attached to the Presentation

Defense Contractor Assertion

Statement of Responses to the Defense Industry Questionnaire on *Business Ethics and Conduct for the period from* _____ *to* _____.

The affirmative responses in the accompanying *Questionnaire on Business Ethics and Conduct with Responses by the XYZ Company for the period from* _____ *to* _____ are based on policies and programs in operation for that period and are appropriately presented in conformity with the criteria set forth in the *Defense Industry Initiatives on Business Ethics and Conduct*, including the questionnaire.

Attachments:

Defense Industry Initiatives on Business Ethics and Conduct

Instructions and Questionnaire on Business Ethics and Conduct with Responses by the XYZ Company for the period from _____ to _____.

Examination Report

Independent Accountant's Report

To the Board of Directors of the XYZ Company:

We have examined the XYZ Company's *Statement of Responses to the Defense Industry Questionnaire on Business Ethics and Conduct for the period from* _____ *to* _____, and the questionnaire and responses attached thereto. XYZ Company's management is responsible for its responses to the questionnaire. Our responsibility is to express an opinion based on our examination.

Our examination was conducted in accordance with attestation standards established by the American Institute of Certified Public Accountants and, accordingly, included examining, on a test basis, evidence as to whether XYZ Company had policies and programs in operation during that period that support the affirmative responses to the questionnaire and performing such other procedures as we considered necessary in the circumstances. We believe that our examination provides a reasonable basis for our opinion. Our examination procedures were not designed, however, to evaluate whether the aforementioned policies and programs operated effectively to ensure compliance with the Company's *Code of Business Ethics and Conduct* on the part of individual employees or to evaluate the extent to which the Company or its employees have complied with federal procurement laws, and we do not express an opinion or any other form of assurance thereon.

In our opinion, the affirmative responses in the questionnaire accompanying the *Statement of Responses to the Defense Industry Questionnaire on Business Ethics and Conduct for the period from* _____ *to* _____ referred to above are appropriately presented in conformity with the criteria set forth in the *Defense Industry Initiatives on Business Ethics and Conduct*, including the questionnaire.

Source: Adapted from AICPA's Professional Standards AT §9101.21.

Figure 3.2 Illustrative defense contractor assertions and examination reports.

Defense Industry Questionnaire on Business Ethics and Conduct

Defense Contractor Assertion

Statement of Responses to the Defense Industry Questionnaire on *Business Ethics and Conduct for the period from* _____to_____.

The affirmative responses in the accompanying *Questionnaire on Business Ethics and Conduct with Responses by the XYZ Company for the period from* _____to_____ are based on policies and programs in operation during that period and are appropriately presented in conformity with the criteria set forth in the *Defense Industry Initiatives on Business Ethics and Conduct,* including the questionnaire.

Attachments: None

Review Report

Independent Accountant's Report

To the Board of Directors of the XYZ Company:

We have reviewed the XYZ Company's *Statement of Responses to the Defense Industry Questionnaire on Business Ethics and Conduct for the period from* _____to_____. XYZ Company's management is responsible for the Statement of Responses to the Defense Industry Questionnaire on Business Ethics.

Our review was conducted in accordance with attestation standards established by the American Institute of Certified Public Accountants. A review is substantially less in scope than an examination, the objective of which is the expression of an opinion on the affirmative responses in the questionnaire. Accordingly, we do not express such an opinion. Additionally, our review was not designed to evaluate whether the aforementioned policies and programs operated effectively to ensure compliance with the Company's *Code of Business Ethics and Conduct* on the part of individual employees or to evaluate the extent to which the Company or its employees have complied with federal procurement laws and we do not express an opinion or any other form of assurance thereon.

Based on our review, nothing came to our attention that caused us to believe that the affirmative responses in the questionnaire referred to above are not appropriately presented in conformity with the criteria set forth in the *Defense Industry Initiatives on Business Ethics and Conduct,* including the questionnaire.

This report is intended solely for the information and use of the XYZ Company and [*identify other specified parties---for example*, the Defense Industry Initiative] and is not intended to be and should not be used by anyone other than these specified parties.

Source: Adapted from AICPA's Professional Standards AT §9101.25.

Figure 3.3 Illustrative defense contractor assertion and review report restricted because criteria are available only to specified parties.

Table 3.2 Framework for Reporting with Integrity

Key aspects	Organizational drivers	Reporting process attributes
1. Moral values	1. Leadership	1. Honesty and truthfulness
2. Motives	2. Strategy	2. Fairness
3. Commitments	3. Policies	3. Compliance
4. Qualities	4. Information	4. Public interests
5. Achievements	5. Culture	5. Remediations
		6. Consistency

Source: Extracted from publication of The Institute of Chartered Accountants in England and Wales (ICAEW). 2007, April. Information for Better Markets: Reporting with Integrity. Available at www.icaew.com/ bettermarkets.

(3) six reporting processes of honesty, fairness, compliance, public interest, transparency, remediations, and consistency.

The five key aspects of integrity in reporting are

1. *Moral values*—All financial reporting participants should embrace honesty, trustworthiness, and fairness, and observe moral values in fulfilling their reporting responsibilities with a keen focus on substance over form reporting attributes.

2. *Motives*—Reporting should be motivated by a desire to provide relevant, useful, reliable, and transparent information to enable users of reports to make informed decisions rather than a preference for self-interested goals of focusing on maximizing personal wealth through bonuses, stock options backdating, or saving face.

3. *Commitments*—All participants in the financial reporting process should be committed to and accountable for creating shareholder value while protecting the interests of other stakeholders.

4. *Qualities*—All participants in the financial reporting process should be competent, possess the knowledge and experience needed to discharge their reporting responsibilities, be courageous enough to resist pressure and report both good and bad news, and be capable of exercising independent judgment.

5. *Achievements*—All participants in the financial reporting process should strive to achieve the stated financial reporting goals.

Organizational Drivers of Integrity in Reporting

The five organizational drivers of integrity in reporting are

1. *Leadership*—An appropriate tone at the top set by senior executives in promoting ethical behavior and commitment to high-quality financial reporting is vital in ensuring the integrity of financial reports.

2. *Strategy*—A proper strategy should be established for achieving the stated financial reporting goals of providing high-quality financial information with a keen focus on assisting users to make informed decisions. This strategy should identify users' information needs and financial reporting goals as well as recruit competent and

ethical senior executives and other professionals (e.g., accountants, auditors) to achieve these goals.

3. *Policies*—Proper policies should be established to support the stated strategy, and these policies should be reviewed periodically and on an ongoing basis for their adequacy, appropriateness, and effectiveness. Reporting policies and procedures are normally concerned with accounting policies, internal control procedures, and risk assessment policies and procedures. Effective implementation of these policies substantially reduces the risk of misleading financial information.

4. *Information*—An organization's policies and procedures should ensure the production of relevant, useful, reliable, and high-quality financial information to assist users in making informed decisions.

5. *Culture*—A culture of ethical behavior and financial reporting integrity should be promoted throughout the organization by linking rewards systems to high-quality reporting and sustainable performance rather than short-term performance or pressure to make the numbers.

The integrity reporting process promotes the attributes of honesty, fairness, and compliance with applicable regulations; ensures public interests are subject to proper remediation; and should be applied consistently as depicted in Table 3.2.

SUMMARY

A well-established and effectively enforced code of conduct provides ethical standards and guidelines on resolution of conflicts of interest; compliance with applicable regulations, confidentiality and proprietary of information; and fair dealing with investors, customers, suppliers, employees, and other interested parties. The emerging corporate governance reforms require public companies to establish a code of conduct for their executives and other key personnel and publicly disclose their business code of conduct.

The key points of this chapter are

- Ethics are broadly described in the literature as moral principles about right and wrong, honorable behavior reflecting values, or standards of conduct. Honesty, openness, responsiveness, accountability, due diligence, and fairness are the core ethical principles.

- Business ethics are a specialized study of moral right and wrong. It concentrates on moral standards as they apply to business policies, institutions, and behavior. It includes not only the analysis of moral norms and moral values, but also attempts to apply the conclusion of this analysis to that assortment of institutions, technologies, transactions, activities, and pursuits that we call business.

- An appropriate code of ethics that sets the right tone at the top of promoting ethical and professional conduct and establishing the moral structure for the entire organization is the backbone of effective corporate governance.

- SEC rules require public companies to report significant amendments or any waiver affecting specified officers pursuant to the filing of their first annual report on their code of ethics.

- Corporate culture and compliance rules should provide incentives and opportunities for the majority of ethical individuals to maintain their honesty and integrity, and provide measures for the minority of unethical individuals to be monitored, punished, and corrected for their unethical conduct.

- Attributes of an ethical corporate culture or an integrity-based culture are sense of employee responsibility, freedom to raise concerns without fear of retaliation, managers modeling ethical behavior and expressing the importance of integrity, an understanding by leadership of the pressure points that drive unethical behavior, and processes to find and fix these areas of pressure.

- The company's directors and executives should demonstrate, through their actions as well as their policies, a firm commitment to ethical behavior throughout the company and a culture of trust within the company. Although a "right tone at the top" is very important in promoting an ethical culture, actions often speak louder than words.

- There is a need for the development of business ethics reporting similar to the one in the defense industry and assurance provided on business ethics reports as suggested by the AICPA.

KEY TERMS

business ethics
code of ethics
Committee of Sponsoring
   Organizations of the
   Treadway Commission
   (COSO)

The Conference Board
Defense Industry Initiatives
   on Business Ethics and
   Conduct

ethical behavior
ethics incentives
ethics sensitivity

REVIEW QUESTIONS

1. What are the three ethical classifications and their purposes discussed by the author?

2. What factors can lead to a company engaging in corporate misconduct of misrepresenting their financial position?

3. Explain the terms of the phrase "organizational ethical culture."

4. From start to finish, what are the steps required to make an ethical decision?

5. What are situational ethics?

6. What are the attributes of an ethical culture?

7. What is meant by the term "ethics sensitivity"?

8. What are the sources of incentives for ethically based behavior?

9. What are the differences between organization-based incentives and profession-based incentives?

10. What is meant by the term "ethical behavior"?

11. What are the six principles of business ethics and conduct?

DISCUSSION QUESTIONS

1. What are ethics? Explain.

2. Do you believe moral principles and ethics are part of family values that cannot be taught? Substantiate your answer.

3. Companies that do not have a code of ethics must either establish such a code or disclose why they have not implemented a code. What factors would lead a company to not develop a code of ethics?

4. Do you believe that a company should provide incentives and opportunities for the majority of ethical individuals to maintain their honesty and integrity, and at the same time, provide measures for the unethical individuals to be monitored, punished, and corrected for their unethical conduct? Explain why.

5. In what ways can doing what is right contrast with established principles and procedures?

6. Are people motivated more by incentives to do what is right or by the self-pride of doing what is right? Explain.

7. Has the ethical downfall of major corporations ultimately helped build a more ethical business world? Defend your answer.

NOTES

1. Miller, R. 2005, January. Dallas/IABC Quick Poll: Communicators Face Integrity Issues. News release. Available at: dallasiabc.com/content/view/400/151/.

2. Shaw, W. H. 1999. *Business Ethics.* Wadsworth, Belmont, CA.

3. Hofstede, G. 1980. *Culture's Consequences: International Differences in Work-Related Values.* Sage, Beverly Hills, CA.

4. Committee of Sponsoring Organizations (COSO). 1998. Internal Control—Integrated Framework: Executive Summary. Available at: www.coso.org/publications/executive_summary_integrated_framework.htm. Committee of Sponsoring Organizations (COSO). 2004, September. Enterprise Risk Management—Integrated Framework: Executive Summary. Available at: www.coso.org/Publications/ERM/COSO_ERM_ExecutiveSummary.pdf.

5. U.S. Securities and Exchange Commissionsee (SEC). 2003, January. Disclosure Required by Sections 406 and 407 of the Sarbanes-Oxley Act of 2002. Available at: www.sec.gov/rules/final/33-8177.htm.

6. Deloitte & Touche. 2007, April 16. Deloitte & Touche USA LLP Survey Finds Strong Relationship Between Work-Life Balance and Ethical Behavior. Available at: www.deloitte.com/dtt/press_release/0,1014,sid%253D%2526cid%253D153527,00.html.

7. Berenbeim, R. E., and Kaplan, J. M. 2004, February. *Ethics Programs . . . The Role of the Board: A Global Study.* Report R-1344-04-RR. The Conference Board, New York. Available at: www.conference-board.org/publications/describe.cfm?id=762.

8. Steiner, G., and J. Steiner. 2006. *Business, Government and Society* (Seventh Edition), pp. 206–208. McGraw-Hill, New York.

9. McCarthy, I. N. 1997. Professional Ethics Code Conflict Situations: Ethical and Value Orientation of Collegiate Accounting Students. *Journal of Business Ethics* 16: 1467–1474.

10. Milton, D. G. 1971. Entrepreneurial Style and the Situation Ethic. *Business* 11(2): 18.

11. Gebler, D. 2005, May/June. Why Is It So Hard to Create an Ethical Culture? Available at: accounting.smartpros.com/x48460.xml.

12. Wilson, T. 2006, October 4. Security's Rotten Apples. Available at: www.darkreading.com/document.asp?doc_id=105282.

13. Cohen, J. 2001. Appreciating, Understanding and Applying Universal Moral Principles. *Journal of Consumer Marketing* 18(7): 578-594.

14. Jenkins, R. 2001. April. Corporate Codes of Conduct: Self-Regulation in a Global Economy. Technology, Business and Society Programme Paper Number 2. United Nations Research Institute for Social Development, Geneva, Switzerland. Available at: www.unrisd.org/unrisd/website/document.nsf/0/e3b3e78bab9a886f80256b5e00344278/$ FILE/jenkins.pdf.

15. Grace, H. S., Jr. 2005, May. Effective Governance in an Ethicless Organization. Available at: www.nysscpa.org/cpajournal/2005/505/perspectives/p6.htm.

16. See note 5 above.

17. New York Stock Exchange (NYSE) 2003. Final NYSE Corporate Governance Rules. Available at: www.nyse.com/pdfs/finalcorpgovrules.pdf.

18. SmartPros. 2006, January 31. Accounting Grads Better Prepared, Survey Says. Available at: accounting.smartpros.com/x51625.xml.

19. Oh, H. 2006, February 6. Class Notes: Biz Majors Get an F for Honesty. *Business Week.* Available at: www.businessweek.com/magazine/content/06_06/c3970008.htm.

20. Ethics Resource Center. 2003, May. Proposed Standards and Business School Responsibilities. Available at: www.ethics.org/resources/articles-organizational-ethics.asp?aid=958.

21. Association to Advance Collegiate Schools of Business (AACSB) International. 2007. Report of the AACSB International: Impact of Research: Task Force. Available at: www.aacsb.edu/Resource_Centers/Research/Impact_of_Research_Report-DRAFT.pdf.

22. Alsop, R. 2005. At M.B.A. Programs, Teaching Ethics Poses Its Own Dilemma. *The Wall Street Journal* April 12: B4.

23. Ibid.

24. Lawrence, J. E. 1997. The Ethical Construction of Auditors: An Examination of the Effects of Gender and Career Level. *Managerial Finance* 23(12): 52.

25. See note 9 above.

26. See note 22 above.

27. Ibid.

28. Ibid.

29. National Association of State Boards of Accountancy (NASBA). 2005, February. Rules 5-1 and 5-2 Exposure Draft. Article 5: Certified Public Accountants. Available at: www.nasba.org/nasbaweb/NASBAWeb.nsf/PS/264D55C613B9747D862571B900755C7F/$file/UAA%20Education%20Rules%20Exposure%20Draft.pdf.

30. Damast, A. 2007. Duke MBAs Fail Ethics Test. *Business Week* April 30.

31. International Federation of Accountants' (IFAC) Ethics Committee. 2005, June. Code of Ethics for Professional Accountants. IFAC Ethics Committee, New York, NY. Available at: www.ifac.org/Members/DownLoads/2005_Code_of_Ethics.pdf.

32. The Institute of Internal Auditors—UK and Ireland. 2004, March. Code of Ethics and International Standards for the Professional Practice of Internal Auditing. Implementation Standard 2130.A1, p. 19. Available at: www.internal-audit.ed.ac.uk/Standards2004.pdf.

33. Singer Lewak Greenbaum & Goldstein, LLP. 2006, September 19. Ethics & Compliance Officers Still Valued in American Corporations. Available at: www.bizactions.com/index.cfm/ba/e105/fa/51113080G288J975796P0P10028969T0/.

34. Defense Industry Initiative. 2004. The Defense Industry Initiatives on Business Ethics and Conduct. Available at: www.dii.org/Statement.htm.

35. The American Institute of Certified Public Accountants (AICPA). 2001. AT Section 9191. Attest Engagements: Attest Engagements Interpretations of Section 101. Available at: www.aicpa.org/download/members/div/auditstd/AT-00101_9.PDF.

36. The Institute of Chartered Accountants in England and Wales (ICAEW). n.d. Information for Better Markets: Reporting with Integrity. Available at: www.icaew.com/index.cfm?route=147468.

Part Two

Roles and Responsibilities of Corporate Governance Participants

Chapter 4

Board of Directors' Roles and Responsibilities

INTRODUCTION

Boards of directors are elected by shareholders to oversee the managerial function. Theoretically, boards of directors exist to resolve the agency problems associated with the separation of a company's ownership controls from decision controls. Intuitively, although directors are elected to align management's interests with those of shareholders, their close association with the company's senior executives can create conflicts of interest within the boardroom. Senior executives, particularly CEOs, are motivated to take over the board by influencing the election of directors and controlling their compensation, whereas directors have the fiduciary duty to maintain their independence, monitor the CEO, and discipline the CEO for poor performance. This chapter discusses the roles and responsibilities of the board of directors in advising management on its strategic decisions without micromanaging and overseeing its actions and performance.

Primary Objectives

The primary objectives of this chapter are to

- Identify the difference between decision management and decision control.
- Understand the role of the board of directors with regard to decision control and fiduciary duties.
- Understand that the board of directors is ultimately responsible for the business and its affairs.
- Provide an overview of what the oversight function entails.
- Identify and explain the fiduciary duties of the board of directors.
- Gain awareness of the variety of board models recommended in global corporate governance reforms.
- Identify the board attributes that affect the quality of monitoring and oversight functions performed by the company's board.
- Illustrate the importance of an independent board of directors.
- Become familiar with the best practices of determining directors' compensation.
- Identify and describe the determinants of an effective board of directors.
- Become familiar with board accountability, evaluation, and the legal obligations and liabilities facing outside directors of public companies.

ROLE OF THE BOARD OF DIRECTORS

Separation of ownership and control in public companies and resulting agency problems lead to the division of decision management and decision control. Decision management, which consists of initiation and implementation of strategies, is viewed as the management's responsibility, whereas decision control, which entails the ratification and monitoring of strategies, is viewed as the board of directors' fiduciary duty performed on behalf of the shareholders. In performing their oversight function, boards of directors should not involve themselves in managerial and operational decisions through micromanaging. They should oversee managerial strategies but not implement them. In today's ever-changing and challenging business environment, the traditional model of the board of directors in just overseeing financial activities and reporting may not be adequate as directors get involved more in corporate governance functions of ensuring their company is prepared to meet future challenges.

The board of directors is ultimately responsible for the company's business affairs and governance as stated in its governing documents, including the articles of incorporation, the bylaws, and shareholder agreements. Many state laws require corporations to form a board of directors to represent shareholders and make decisions on their behalf. The Delaware General Corporation Law Code states

> *The business and affairs of every corporation organized under this chapter shall be managed by or under the direction of a* board of directors*, except as may be otherwise provided in this chapter or in its certificate of incorporation.*[1] *(Emphasis added.)*

Almost all states have a similar statute authorizing and empowering the board of directors to direct, oversee, and control a company's business affairs, and to govern its activities. Shareholders have statutory rights to elect directors, to replace them, and in many states to approve major decisions or transactions such as mergers and acquisitions, the sale of major assets, or dissolution of the company. A vigilant board of directors proactively participates in strategic decisions; asks management tough questions; oversees management's plans, decisions, and actions; and monitors management's ethical conduct, financial reporting, and legal compliance. The primary oversight function of the board is the appointment of the CEO and concurrence with the CEO's selection of other senior executives to run the company. Corporations are legally required to have a board of directors, and many not-for-profit organizations (e.g., churches, universities) have a similar governing board. The success of the board of directors depends on the composition, structure, resources, diligence, and authority of the entire board, as well as their working relationships with other participants of corporate governance, including management, external auditors, internal auditors, legal counsel, professional advisors, regulators, standard-setting bodies, and investors. Traditionally, many companies' boardrooms are viewed as "gentleman's clubs" characterized by a tendency and desire to please the CEO and rubber-stamp the CEO's decisions rather than being the place for challenge and inquiry that adds value to corporate governance. The board, in overseeing management, should be able to influence the company's vision, mission, strategies, and goals as well as management's plans, decisions, and actions to achieve these goals without micromanaging.

The board may delegate its decision-making authority to the company's top management team, but it is still responsible and accountable for running the company. Boards of directors must realize that they not only are representing shareholders, but also all stakeholders who have direct or indirect human or physical capital interests in their corporations. This does not necessarily mean that all major stakeholders (investors, employers, suppliers, government, customers, creditors) must have representative or so-called constituency directors on the boards. Instead, both inside (executive) and outside (nonexecutive) directors must represent all stakeholders and protect their interests.

The board of directors is the cornerstone of the company's corporate governance structure with the primary role of safeguarding interests of shareholders and other stakeholders. In summary, roles and responsibilities of boards of directors are to

1. Represent shareholders and create shareholder value.
2. Align the interests of management with those of shareholders while protecting the interests of other stakeholders (customers, creditors, suppliers).
3. Define the company's mission and goals.
4. Establish or approve strategic plans and decisions to achieve these goals.

5. Appoint senior executives to manage the company in accordance with the established strategies, plans, policies, and procedures.

6. Oversee the company's performance by setting objectives, establishing short-term and long-term strategies to achieve these objectives, and assessing the performance of senior executives in fulfilling their responsibilities without micromanaging.

7. Approve major business transactions and corporate plans, decisions, and actions according to the bylaws.

8. Develop and approve executive compensation, pension, postretirement benefits plan, and other long-term benefits, including stock ownership and stock options.

9. Review financial reports, including audited annual financial statements, quarterly reviewed financial statements, and other important financial disclosures such as management discussion and analysis (MD&A) earnings releases and reports filed with regulators (SEC) or disseminated to the public.

10. Review management's report on the effectiveness of internal control over financial reporting.

11. Provide counsel to the company's senior executives, especially the CEO, on material strategic decisions and risk management.

12. Ensure the company's compliance with applicable laws, rules, and regulations.

13. Approve the company's major operating, investing, and financial activities.

14. Set the tone at the top by promoting legal and ethical conduct throughout the company.

15. Evaluate the performance of the board, its committees (e.g., audit, compensation, and nominating), and the members of each committee.

16. Hold the board, its committees, and directors accountable for the fulfillment of the assigned fiduciary duties and oversight functions.

17. Approve dividends, financing, capital changes, and other extraordinary corporate matters.

18. Oversee the sustainability of the company in creating long-term shareholder value and protecting interests of other stakeholders.

Table 4.1 compares roles and responsibilities of directors before and after corporate governance reforms. Boards of directors have experienced unprecedented challenges in the post-SOX era, and some still struggle to find the right balance between engaging in strategic decisions of directors advising management and monitoring its managerial decisions and actions. This is particularly important in light of landmark settlements by former directors of Enron and WorldCom agreeing to pay damages ($31 million) from their own pockets for their company's failures. Corporate boards are now under extensive scrutiny, and directors are concerned about their personal liability for questionable governance practices. One way to influence directors' ethical conduct is to hold them accountable and liable for poor performance and business misconduct. It is expected that boards of directors will engage more proactively in the oversight function in facing increasing business challenges.

Table 4.1   Comparison of Directors (Pre- and Postcorporate Governance Reforms)

Prereforms	Postreforms
• Personal ties to company management	• Oversight of the sustainability of the company in creating long-term shareholder value while protecting the interests of other stakeholders
• Economic ties to the corporation (consulting fees, generous ownership pensions)	• Representation of shareholders to protect their interests
• Infrequent and short meetings	• Appointment of the CEO and agreement with the CEO's appointment of other senior executives
• Less accountability	• Advising management in its strategic activities and monitoring its performance without micromanaging
• Lack of proper authority and resources	• The majority of directors should be independent (75 percent is suggested)
• Limited knowledge of business and financial expertise	• Separation of the positions of chairman of the board and CEO (suggested, but not mandated)
• Inadequate oversight of management	• Development of the knowledge and expertise to provide effective board oversight
	• Sufficient resources to hire advisors and independent staff support
	• A right "tone at the top" and a corporate culture that promotes ethical conduct
	• Periodic evaluation of the performance of the board of directors
	• More accountability and potential personal liability
	• Adequate knowledge of business and financial expertise
	• Executive sessions with external auditors

FIDUCIARY DUTIES OF THE BOARD OF DIRECTORS

Fiduciary duty means that, as shareholders' guardians, directors must be trustworthy, acting in the best interest of shareholders, and investors in turn have confidence in the directors' actions. Fiduciary duties of boards of directors are mandated by the laws of the state of incorporation, are generally specified in the company's charter and bylaws, and are often interpreted by courts when there are allegations of breach of fiduciary duties. Directors should realize that their primary duty is to be corporate gatekeepers by protecting investors and working toward the achievement of shareholder value creation and the protection of the interests of other stakeholders. Although directors' and officers' legal fiduciary duties are only extended to shareholders who, as investors in the company, have a residual claim to its assets, they may have many nonfiduciary duties to other stakeholders, including employees, creditors, customers, and suppliers, who also may have various interests in and claims to the company's welfare.

The corporate governance literature presents the following fiduciary duties of boards of directors.

Duty of Due Care

The duty of due care determines the manner in which directors should carry out their responsibilities. It pertains to both directors' decision-making authority of either routine business decisions or strategic decisions and their oversight responsibilities of monitoring managerial functions, internal control, financial reporting, and audit activities. To effectively fulfill the duty of due care, directors should (1) act in the best interest of the company and its shareholders; (2) act in good faith in a manner that is believed and perceived to be in the best interest of the company and its shareholders; (3) exercise the care that is expected of "a reasonable person" under the same circumstances; (4) be informed about the company's business affairs; (5) exercise a vigilant oversight function; (6) assure a reliable information reporting process; and (7) monitor compliance with applicable laws, rules, and regulations. Failure to uphold these stipulations may constitute a breach of the fiduciary duty of care expected of directors.

Duty of Loyalty

The duty of loyalty requires directors to refrain from pursuing their own interests over the interests of the company. The duty of loyalty prohibits directors from engaging in unfair self-dealing transactions that may cause conflicts of interest, competing with the company, or using the company's assets or confidential information for personal gain. Indeed, breach of loyalty can occur even in the absence of conflicts of interest if directors consciously disregard their duties to the company and its shareowners.

Duty of Good Faith

The duty of good faith is an important element of directors' fiduciary obligations, and any irresponsible, reckless, irrational, and disingenuous behavior or conduct by directors can breach this fiduciary duty. This duty is not well defined in the law and literature because state statutes address only the two duties of care and loyalty. Furthermore, intentional disregard (gross negligence) and a lack of exercising due diligence for the duties of care and loyalty and knowingly violating or allowing the violation of applicable laws, regulations, and rules are indicative of bad faith. Indeed, several former directors of Enron and WorldCom, in admitting breaching their fiduciary duties, have settled liability lawsuits brought against them by injured investors, which is explained later in this chapter. The only good thing that came out of the Enron bankruptcy and subsequent conviction of its executives is that directors and officers must be conscientious of their duty or eventually be held accountable for their actions.

Duty to Promote Success

Directors should act in good faith and promote the success of the company for the benefit of its shareholders and other stakeholders. The director's responsibilities include approving the establishment of strategic goals, objectives, and policies that promote enduring shareholder value and enhancement as well as other stakeholder value protection. Shareholder value creation can be achieved when the company engages in strategic decisions, activities, and sustainable performance that generate revenue and maximize shareholder wealth. Directors also have a duty to protect stakeholder value by promoting the interests of employees, fostering fair business relationships with the company's customers and suppliers, promoting ethical business conduct, and considering the impacts of the company's operations on the environment, community, and society.

Duty to Exercise Diligence, Independent Judgment, and Skill

The ultimate decision-making responsibilities rest with the company's board of directors. Thus, directors must exercise due diligence, skill, and independent judgment in making strategic decisions. Directors should be knowledgeable about the company's business and affairs, continuously update their understanding of the company's activities and performance, and use reasonable diligence and independent judgment in making decisions.

Duty to Avoid Conflicts of Interest

Directors must avoid any situation that may cause potential conflicts of interest that would jeopardize investor confidence in their oversight function or impair their independence in making strategic decisions. Potential conflicts of interest may occur when a director (1) receives material gifts or benefits from a third party that is doing business with the company, (2) either directly or indirectly enters into a transaction or arrangement with the company, (3) obtains substantial loans from the company, and (4) engages in backdated stock options.

Fiduciary Duties and Business Judgment Rules

Directors, in effectively fulfilling these fiduciary duties, operate under the legal doctrine of the so-called "business judgment rule." Under state law, directors are held responsible for fiduciary duties, and the standard of the business judgment rule applies in determining their liability. Under the business judgment rule commonly practiced in business, directors who make decisions in good faith, based on rational reasoning and an informed manner, can be protected from liability to the company's shareholders on the grounds that they have appropriately fulfilled their fiduciary duty of care. This implies that in the absence of evidence of gross negligence, business misconduct, and fraud, directors are typically provided with broad discretion to make decisions and carry out their fiduciary duties of due care, obedience, and loyalty without facing challenges of legal liability. Generally speaking, directors have a duty to the company to perform their oversight functions in good faith, in a manner that reasonably represents the best interests of the company, and with the care, skill, and diligence that a prudent person would use under similar circumstances. Directors are entitled to rely on information, reports, financial statements, and opinion provided to them by the company's management. A good faith presumption does not exist when a director relies on information that he or she knows is not reliable. The general perception is that directors will not usually be held liable for losses caused by their decisions, and courts often do not interfere with their activities.

Directors can be held liable under the the Securities Act of 1933 and the Securities Exchange Act of 1934 for engaging in the production and distribution of materially false, fraudulent, or misleading information to investors that influence the company's stock prices.

SOX also prohibits directors from fraudulently misleading investors or trading during the pension blackout periods. To effectively discharge their fiduciary duties, boards of directors must (1) review and approve the company's overall business strategy; (2) appoint, compensate, and, when necessary, dismiss the company's senior executives; (3) appoint, compensate, and oversee the work of the company's independent auditors and dismiss them when deemed warranted; (4) oversee the company's financial reports; (5) oversee the company's sustainable and enduring performance in creating and enhancing shareholder value while protecting stakeholder interests; and (6) evaluate the performance of the company's board of directors, its board committees, and individual members of committees.

BOARD COMMITTEES

The entire board of directors is responsible for fulfilling its fiduciary duty of acting in the best interest of the company's stakeholders, particularly shareholders. Operationally, the oversight function of corporate governance is typically performed by the company's board committees. Boards of directors perform their oversight function through well-structured, preplanned, and assigned committees in order to take advantage of the expertise of all the directors. Board committee formations and assignments depend on the size of the company, its board, and assumed responsibilities. Committee members address relevant issues and make recommendations to the entire board for final approval.

Board committees normally function independently from each other, are provided with sufficient resources and authority, and are evaluated by the board of directors. Thus, board committees are a subset of the board and perform specific functions that assist the board in discharging its advisory and oversight responsibilities. These committees are usually formed as a means of improving the effectiveness of the board in areas when more focused, specialized, and technically oriented committees are deemed necessary. Listing standards require listed companies form at least three board committees, including audit, compensation, and nominating/governance. Members of these committees should be independent directors. Corporate governance best practices recommend that public companies, if possible, establish at least four board committees, including (1) the audit committee composed of at least three independent directors; (2) the compensation committee composed of at least three independent directors; (3) the nominating committee composed of at least three independent directors; and (4) the governance committee composed of several executives and nonexecutive directors, with the majority being independent directors. Public companies may also form other special committees (e.g., finance, budget, mergers, acquisition) to address special board projects as needed.

The establishment of board committees can bring more focus to the board's oversight function, and by giving proper authority and demanding responsibility, these committees in particular and the entire board in general can be held accountable to shareholders. The board committee assignments enable the board to (1) clearly define the authority and responsibility of each committee, (2) fairly evaluate the performance of each committee and its members, (3) properly hold each committee accountable for its oversight activities, and (4) promote and possibly move toward a two-tiered structure consisting of a strategic board and an oversight board. The work of the board of directors or trustees is best performed in the committee form. The chair of each committee should present the committee's findings and recommendations to the entire board for approval and action.

Public companies usually have the following board committees:

- Audit committee
- Compensation committee
- Governance committee
- Nominating committee
- Disclosure committee
- Other standing or special committees

Board committees are briefly described here and are further examined in Chapter 5.

Audit Committee

An audit committee composed of at least three independent directors should be formed to implement and support the oversight function of the board, specifically in areas related to internal controls, risk management, financial reporting, and audit activities.

Compensation Committee

A compensation committee composed of at least three independent directors serves to design, review, and implement directors' and executives' compensation plans.

Governance Committee

A governance committee consisting of both executive and nonexecutive directors should be established to advise, review, and approve management strategic plans, decisions, and actions in effectively managing the company. The corporate governance committee can act as the executive committee to meet on an as-needed basis to discuss urgent business affairs between scheduled board meetings.

Nominating Committee

A nominating committee composed of at least three independent directors should be formed to monitor issues pertaining to the recommendation, nomination, and election activities of directors.

Disclosure Committees

Corporate governance reforms in the post-SOX period promote more reliable and transparent governance and financial reports. To comply with these reforms, companies have established the disclosure committee consisting of both directors and officers. This committee is usually led by corporate counsel, CFOs, or controllers. The disclosure committee is responsible for reviewing and monitoring the company's 10-K, 10-Q, and other SEC filings, earnings releases, materiality issues, conference call scripts, and presentations to investors by senior management. The disclosure committee typically meets as often as needed and between thirty days and one week in advance of a quarterly earnings release.

Special Committee

The board of directors may form special committees to assist the board in carrying out its strategic and oversight functions, including financing, budgeting, investment, mergers, and acquisitions. Special committees may consist of both executive and nonexecutive directors. The finance committee can be formed to (1) approve the company's major transactions with defined characteristics (e.g., mergers and acquisitions, research and development) or a specified threshold (e.g., above $100,000); (2) provide guidance on the company's financial decisions and policies; and (3) advise management on enterprise risk management activities. After September 11, 2001, corporate boards began to pay more attention to IT security and business continuity. Implementation of Section 404 on internal control over financial reporting underscores the importance of IT in financial reporting. Some companies have started to develop a separate IT board committee to address and oversee IT issues. Companies may also establish an executive committee to make decisions on behalf of the entire board of directors between regular board meetings. An outside directors committee can be established to secure director independence during the nomination process.

BOARD MODELS

A variety of board models have been suggested in the corporate governance literature, including one-tier, two-tier, and modern board models. A one-tier board model consisting of both executive and nonexecutive directors is similar to the structure in the United States and the UK. A two-tier board model composed of managing directors and supervisory directors is similar to the structure in Germany. The modern board consists of both the strategic board and the oversight board.

One-Tier Board Model

The one-tier board model consists of both inside (executive) directors and outside (nonexecutive) directors. Inside directors are perceived as the decision managers and outside directors are assumed to have the power and duty to monitor those decisions. Company boards that are composed of a majority of outside (independent) directors are considered to be able to monitor and control management, reduce agency costs, and create shareholder value. Furthermore, outside directors are more likely to act as expert directors, are more valued by shareholders, and are more willing to replace a poorly performing CEO.

Under the one-tier board model, the responsibilities of the board are to (1) act within its power under the company's article of incorporation and bylaws; (2) fulfill its fiduciary duties to shareholders as specified in corporate law and interpreted by the courts; (3) develop corporate strategies to generate sustainable performance; (4) appoint senior executives to run the company and its operations; (5) review and approve the appointment of other executives and key financial officers; (6) oversee management's plans, decisions, and actions; (7) form committees (audit, compensation, and nomination) to carry out the assigned oversight responsibilities; and (8) be accountable for board activities by annually evaluating the performance of the board, its committees, and their members.

Two-Tier Board Model

The two-tier board system, consisting of a supervisory board and a management board, better known as the German board model, establishes different authorities and responsibilities for members of each board.[2] The supervisory board, whose members are elected by the shareholders, is responsible for (1) appointing and dismissing members of the management board; (2) determining management's compensation; (3) overseeing the function of the management board; (4) reviewing and approving financial reports, including annual audited and quarterly reviewed financial statements; (5) appointing, retaining, compensating, and overseeing the work of external auditors; (6) establishing committees to carry out board oversight responsibilities; and (7) communicating with all stakeholders.

The management board is responsible for (1) managing the company for the benefit of a wide variety of stakeholders, (2) reporting to the supervisory board periodically on its strategic decisions and actions, (3) preparing financial statements and MD&A, (4) establishing and monitoring internal controls and reporting on their effectiveness, and (5) reporting the company's performance and future growth prospects to the supervisory board. This dual board approach is expected to create an appropriate system of checks and balances that promotes effective corporate governance.

Modern Board Model

Corporate governance reforms in the post-SOX era require that the company's board of directors be proactively engaged in both strategic and oversight activities. The board of directors is directly responsible for creating shareholder value and for overseeing the effective implementation of the company's strategic decisions in achieving sustainable performance. Thus, the structure of the modern board based on the two components of strategic board and oversight board is the natural offshoot of the emerging corporate governance reforms.

The suggested two-tier board structures of strategic board and oversight board are not similar to the two-tier board system in Germany, namely, management board and supervisory board, even though conceptually they sound similar. Under the German system, (1) the management board is charged with managing the company for the benefit of its stakeholders, (2) members of the supervisory board are elected by the shareholders at the annual meeting, (3) the supervisory board appoints, dismisses, and determines the compensation of the members of management board, (4) the supervisory board does not have the formal authority to give specific instructions to members of the management board, (5) the management board is required to give due consideration to the positions of the supervisory board by reporting to them at regular intervals, and (6) the supervisory board is expected to monitor the management board.

In contrast to the German two-tier board system, the strategic/oversight two-tier board structure has the following attributes: (1) all directors serving on both the strategic board and the oversight board are elected by shareholders in the annual shareholder meetings (as required by state statute); (2) the strategic board is charged with advising and approving management strategic plans, decisions, and actions; (3) the strategic board is composed of both executive and nonexecutive directors (preferably with a majority of independent, nonexecutive directors); (4) members of the strategic board may serve only on the governance or other special board committees; (5) the primary role of the oversight board is to monitor the operating and financial reporting of senior executives (e.g., CEO, CFO), determine compensation for directors and officers, evaluate board processes and performance, nominate potential directors, and oversee the company's business and affairs; (6) the audit, compensation, and nominating committees must be composed of members of the oversight board who are independent directors; (7) the two boards, strategic and oversight, are equally important and play a vital role in corporate governance; and (8) no corporate governance reforms (SOX, SEC rules, listing standards, state statutes) in the United States prevent public companies from considering this strategic/oversight two-tier board structure.

In the real world, inside directors serving on the strategic board are viewed as having too much influence over outside directors serving on the oversight board, and there is a possibility that the outsiders would collude with the insiders. Outside directors may be influenced by insiders (senior executives, CEO) because of (1) a lack of adequate knowledge and expertise to assess the quality of managerial decisions, and (2) a lack of proper incentives to challenge those decisions. Because of the possibility of asymmetric knowledge and information between executive directors (insiders) who have absolute knowledge of the business and nonexecutive directors (outsiders) who must rely on others to provide them with such knowledge, outside directors must be provided with advisors. In these circumstances, nonexecutive directors may feel more comfortable receiving information from these advisors than accepting executive directors' information on faith. Internal auditors can be a good source of advice to nonexecutive directors.

BOARD CHARACTERISTICS

The board of directors is the most essential component of corporate governance in providing advisory and oversight functions. Thus, the quality of the advising and oversight function of the board depends on its characteristics. Characteristics of the company's board of directors are defined by its articles of incorporation, bylaws, and other governing documents such as corporate governance policies and best practices as described in this section.

Board Leadership

Public companies are required to have a board of directors that is led by the chairperson. Companies often combine the positions of the chairperson and the CEO. This dual position allows the company's CEO to undertake the two most important functions of corporate governance, namely, the managerial and oversight functions, empowering the CEO to oversee the direction of the company as well as manage its operations. Both the chairperson of the board and the CEO should be leaders with vision, strategy, business acumen, motivation, and problem-solving skills. Ideally, two qualified individuals should assume these two separate positions. Thus, it is good to have an independent chairperson of the board to ensure maximum protection for investors. Many investor activists and organizations (The Conference Board, National Association of Corporate Directors [NACD]) have called for more independent board leadership through either the separation of the position of the CEO and the chairperson of the board or the establishment of a lead or presiding director position. Authoritative guidance (SOX, listing standards) in the United States does not directly address the responsibilities of the chair of the board by giving full flexibility to the board of directors to decide on the chair's responsibilities. The chair is directly responsible for developing a boardroom that facilitates individual director effectiveness.

The board of directors is required to meet regularly to discuss the company's business affairs and financial reports with and without the presence of management. The effectiveness of board meetings depends largely on the leadership ability of the chairperson to set an agenda and direct discussions. The chair's leadership style determines whether the meetings will be short or lengthy, formal or informal, friendly or adversarial, relaxed or tense, efficient or inefficient, productive or nonproductive, responsive or nonresponsive, relevant or irrelevant, decisive or indecisive, and predetermined or deliberative. The board agenda is usually prepared by the chairperson in close collaboration with the CEO (when the CEO is not also the chair) to ensure its appropriateness. In the case of CEO duality, the CEO should consult with the lead director or the chair of the committee of outside directors (if it exists) to ensure the agenda is relevant. The minutes of the board meeting should provide a brief description of issues discussed and the deliberation process, including voting, decisions, and actions taken by the board.

CEO Duality

CEO duality implies that the company's CEO holds both the position of chief executive and the chair of the board of directors. The separation of these offices has remained a challenge for many public companies even in the post-SOX era. Investors, in general, are in favor of the separation of the positions as a means of strengthening the board's independence and reducing the potential conflicts of interest, particularly when the company is perceived to be managed poorly. An example of a successful shareholder attempt is at the 2004 Disney annual meeting where shareholders, owning 43 percent of Disney's stock, cast their votes to separate the offices of the CEO and the chairperson of the board by stripping Michael Eisner's job as chair, although he stayed on as Disney's CEO.

The Conference Board, while acknowledging that no single board structure has yet demonstrated to be superior, recommends three alternatives for board structures. These alternatives are[3]

Alternative I: The offices of chairperson of the board and CEO should be separated.

Alternative II: Two separate individuals perform the roles of chairperson of the board and CEO. If the chairperson is not "independent," according to the definition provided in listing standards (e.g., NYSE), a lead independent director should be appointed.

Alternative III: A presiding director position should be established where boards choose not to separate the positions of the chairperson and CEO.

The Conference Board suggests that if companies choose not to employ any of the recommended three alternatives, they should explain their reasons and how their board structure achieves strong and independent board leadership. Regardless of which of these approaches is selected for the company's board structure, the chair of the board, lead independent director, or the presiding director should have the ultimate approval over board meetings, agendas, meeting schedules, transparency, and the information flow that goes to the board. The Conference Board also recommends that the company's board be composed of a "substantial" majority of independent directors who should effectively oversee the company's management, legal, and ethical compliance.

Proponents of the dual CEO position have argued that no gains will be achieved by separating the CEO and chairperson positions on the grounds that existing corporate governance reforms already address CEOs' potential conflicts of interest by requiring that (1) the independent compensation committee monitor CEO compensation; and (2) the board of directors control the CEO's power in situations where the CEO encounters conflicts of interest, the CEO is aggressive, and where there is a long-term and gradual failure of the company's business plan.[4] Thus, both the costs and the benefits of the separation of the CEO and chair positions must be evaluated on a case-by-case situation. The potential costs of the separation are (1) the likelihood of a reduction in the CEO's authority when power is shared with a nonexecutive director who is less informed and possibly less experienced in a leadership role; and (2) the introduction of a more complex and new relationship into the company's commitment to the unitary board, which may negatively affect the status and oversight responsibility of outside directors.

The potential benefits of the separation of the CEO and chair positions are (1) such separation aligns U.S. corporate governance with that of other countries, (2) CEO accountability is improved, (3) CEO potential conflicts of interest are reduced, (4) having two individuals in the corporate leadership role should improve corporate governance and operations, and (5) the board responsibility to oversee management for shareholders' benefit would be more effective when the chair of the board assumes no executive role.

Lead Director

Traditionally, public companies have appointed a lead director on an interim basis in crisis situations involving executive succession planning or CEO misconduct, which was subsequently eliminated once the crisis ended. In the postcorporate governance reforms era, the demand for an independent lead director has substantially increased, particularly in the presence of CEO duality positions, resulting from the growing concern that duality places too much power in the hands of the CEO, which may impede board independence. Thus, the need for the position of a lead or presiding director is gaining support to (1) manage and facilitate the board's governance process; (2) provide a measure of board independence from the CEO; (3) develop the board's agenda for meetings; (4) act as a liaison among the board, the CEO, and shareholders; (5) preside over executive sessions; (6) oversee governance-related activities and processes; and (7) oversee significant issues between board meetings and inform the entire board about these risks.

Best practices of corporate governance suggest that public companies' boards, in general, be chaired by an independent, nonexecutive director, and only under limited and unique circumstances should the two distinct roles of the CEO and the chair be combined. In circumstances of a combined role, the board should appoint an independent lead director who (1) is responsible for the board's operations (e.g., meetings, agendas, communications), (2) communicates via proxy materials the benefits of the combined role to shareholders, (3) chairs meetings of nonexecutive and independent directors, (4) serves as the liaison between the chair and the independent directors, (5) presides over board meetings in the absence of the chair, and (6) leads the board of directors and CEO performance evaluation process to prevent the chair/CEO from being placed in the conflicted position of evaluating his or her own performance.

Board Composition

Board composition in terms of the ratio of outside to inside directors and the number of directors influences the effectiveness of the board. The size of the board can affect the efficiency and effectiveness of the board of directors. Anecdotal evidence and the results of academic research regarding the size and the effectiveness of the board are inconclusive, and the direction is not clear. On the one hand, a small board size is considered to be efficient because the process of deliberation becomes time consuming and unwieldy with large boards. On the other hand, a large board can be more effective in monitoring managerial actions primarily because by increasing the number of directors involved with monitoring, the opportunity for wrongdoing is decreased and collusion becomes more difficult. A board size of nine to fifteen directors is considered to be adequately tailored to the number of board standing committees (audit, compensation, nomination, and governance), the size of the company, and the extent of its operations.

Board Authority

Decision-making authority of the board of directors is granted through shareholder election. The board of directors is authorized to hire, evaluate, compensate, and fire senior executives—including the CEO, CFO, and other key personnel—to manage the company's day-to-day operations. The board of directors exercises oversight of senior executives and advises many major plans, decisions, and actions of management to create shareholder value and protect stakeholder interests. Directors are elected by shareholders, and they have a fiduciary duty to act in the best interests of the shareholders. In practice, directors are nominated, and their election is significantly influenced by management, the very persons they are supposed to be monitoring. Also, some directors become beholden to the CEO because they enjoy the status, compensation, and other perquisites that go along with holding a public company board seat. Independent, outside directors may be influenced by insiders (senior executives, CEO) because of (1) a lack of adequate knowledge and expertise to assess the quality of managerial decisions, (2) a lack of proper incentives to challenge those decisions, and (3) the likelihood that management controls the flow of information to the board and influences the agenda.

SOX substantially expands the authority of directors, particularly audit committee members, as being directly responsible for hiring, firing, compensating, and overseeing the work of the company's independent auditor. This changed the balance of power sharing between management and the audit committee. Audit committees are also responsible for hiring and firing the chief audit executive (CAE) and overseeing the budget and audit plans of the company's internal audit function.

Responsibilities

The primary responsibility of the board of directors is to ensure that the company's assets are safeguarded and that managerial decisions and actions are made in a manner of maximizing shareholder wealth while protecting the interests of other stakeholders. In this context, the board of directors (1) identifies major stakeholders (investors, creditors, customers, suppliers, and others) who are affected by the company's business; (2) ensures proper stewardship of the company's resources; and (3) establishes an effective monitoring system and holds management accountable for performance. The board of directors is directly responsible for (1) defining the company's objectives; (2) establishing policies and procedures to ensure the achievement of defined objectives; (3) monitoring the established policies and procedures; (4) assuming ultimate accountability for the company's business and affairs; and (5) ensuring that the company is conducting its business in the utmost ethical, legal, and professional manner.

Resources

The board of directors should have adequate resources to effectively fulfill its oversight functions. Resources available to the board consist of legal, financial, and information resources. The board should have adequate financial resources to compensate the company's directors and officers and hire external auditors, legal counsel, and other advisors in assisting the entire board and its committees. Information resources are provided to the board from a variety of corporate governance participants, including management, internal auditors, external auditors, legal counsel, financial advisors, and investors. To ensure objectivity, independent consultants should be hired by and report to the company's board rather than getting their assignments from management.

The primary source of information for the board of directors comes from management, and may not always be relevant, complete, uncensored, and provided on a timely basis. Directors delegate decision-making authority to management, rely on information furnished to them, and are expected to be experts on every aspect of the company's business. Directors are expected to be diligent in identifying and considering facts based on the information they receive from management and others and make judgments about facts in which they have no expertise. Courts generally do not second-guess informed decision making, even if the decision turns out to be wrong later. Because of the possibility of asymmetric knowledge and information between executive directors (insiders) who have absolute knowledge of the business and nonexecutive directors (outsiders) who must rely on others to provide them with such knowledge, outside directors should be provided with advisors. Nonexecutive directors may feel more comfortable receiving information from these advisors than accepting executive directors' information on faith. Internal auditors can also be a good source of advice to independent, nonexecutive directors.

The board should have adequate staff support, internal or external advisors, and legal counsel to assist in preparing meetings, setting the agenda, identifying the relevant and important corporate governance issues that will be addressed in the meeting, assessing these issues, and suggesting possible recommendations. The corporate governance issues brought before the board for deliberation, whether initiated by management relevant to strategic plans and financial reporting by internal auditors pertaining to internal controls and risk assessment, or by external auditors regarding their audit findings, reports, and recommendations, should be submitted to the board prior to the meetings. The advance submission of meeting materials allows the directors to have sufficient time to study, analyze, and understand the issues, and also be prepared to ask relevant questions, discuss the issues, and deliberate them. Taking proper minutes of the board meetings is crucial in presenting different views on the deliberated issues, the consensus of the board, and the actions taken.

The corporate secretary may take the minutes of the meetings and, with the advice of the company's legal counsel, prepare the report and include it in the company's records. If the company's bylaws require the approval of minutes before they are official, the minutes should be approved at the next board meeting.

Board Independence

The independence of the company's board of directors is essential to the proper and objective functioning of the board. The wave of financial scandals in the early 2000s reinvigorated interest in corporate governance and encouraged national stock exchanges in the United States and abroad to address director's independence. National stock exchanges (NYSE, Nasdaq, and AMEX) required the majority of directors of a listed company to be independent. Several definitions of independent director are provided in the literature and by authoritative sources. The most comprehensive definition is given by the CII as follows:

> An independent director is someone whose only nontrivial professional, familial, or financial connection to the corporation, its chairman, CEO or any other executive officer is his or her directorship.[5]

This definition of independent director simply states that to be independent, a director should not have any other relationships with the company other than his or her directorship that may compromise the director's objectivity and loyalty to the company's shareholders. According to the guidance provided by the SEC, listing standards, and the CII, a director may not be independent if the director is, or in the past five years has been, or whose relative is, or in the past five years has been (1) employed by the company or employed by a director of an affiliate; (2) an employee, director, or greater than 20 percent owner of a company that is one of the corporation's or its affiliate's paid advisors or consultants; (3) a paid advisor or consultant to an executive officer of the company and receives at least $50,000 in revenue for the advisory services; (4) employed by, or has had a 5 percent or greater ownership interest in, a third-party that receives payments from or provides payments to the company (such payments must be equivalent to 1 percent of the annual consolidated gross revenues of the company or the third-party provider); and (5) an employee or director of a foundation, university, or other nonprofit organization that receives material grants or endowments ($100,000 or 1 percent of total grants) from the company or one of its affiliates or executive officers.[6]

The quality and quantity of independent directors on the company's board can play an important role in ensuring the board's effectiveness in representing and protecting shareholders. In terms of independent directors on the board, the general norm is no more than one-third of inside directors (executive directors) or a maximum of up to three nonindependent directors can serve on the board. However, the quality of directors' independence, influence, and ability to act independently as well as be an effective balance to executive directors is more important than the number of independent directors.

Director Compensation

Director compensation has recently received significant attention as companies complemented cash compensation for their directors as outside directors have also benefited from backdated stock options. There is no magic way of determining how to pay directors and how much to pay them. However, the general perception and best practices suggest that any

Table 4.2   Institutional Investors' Guidelines on Director Pay

California Public Employees' Retirement System (CalPERS)[a]	Council of Institutional Investors (CII)[b]	Teachers Insurance and Annuity Association—College Retirement Equities Fund (TIAA-CREF)[c]	Domini Social Investments[d]
1. Director compensation consists of a combination of cash and stock.	1. All directors should own stock in the company.	1. All unusual compensation should be reviewed by independent directors and disclosed in the proxy statement.	1. Directors should own stock in the company, but directorships should not be limited due to financial reasons.
2. Director's compensation should be examined on a case-by-case basis to ensure accountability to the shareholders.	2. Directors should be compensated only in cash and stock, with the majority being in stock.	2. The board should establish a fixed retirement policy for directors.	2. Outside directors should not receive pension plans.
3. Stock options for independent directors will be approved if reasonable, and are more favorable if they replace cash compensation.	3. Pay should be indexed to peer/market groups.	3. Directors must own a material amount of company stock, possibly equal to one year's compensation as a board member.	3. Outside directors should not receive more than $100,000 per year in compensation.
4. The company should refrain from providing pensions to nonemployees without shareholder approval.	4. Boards should consider options with forward contracts to align management and shareholders' interest.	4. Payment of directors should be at least partly in stock.	
5. Shareholders should analyze and approve directors' compensation.			
6. Retirement plans should only be for employee directors.			
7. At least half of a director's annual income should be from stock.			

[a]California Public Employees' Retirement System (CalPERS). 2005, April 6. Core Principles of Accountable Corporate Governance. Appendix B: Independent Chair/Lead-Director Position Duty Statement. Available at: www.calpers-governance.org/principles/domestic/us/page06.asp.
[b]Council of Institutional Investors (CII). 2005, September 30. Council Policies: Director Compensation: Nonemployee Director Compensation. CII, Washington, DC. Available at: www.cii.org/policies/dir_compensation.htm.
[c]Teachers Insurance and Annuity Association—College Retirement Equities Fund (TIAA-CREF). 2005. TIAA-CREF Policy Statement on Corporate Governance. TIAA-CREF, New York, NY. Available at: www.tiaa-cref.org/pubs/pdf/governance_policy.pdf.
[d]Domini Social Investments. 2007, May. Proxy Voting Guidelines & Procedures (12th Edition). Domini Social Investments, Providence, RI. Available at: www.domini.com/common/pdf/ProxyVotingGuidelines.pdf.

increases in stock ownership, reductions in cash payments, and changes in compensation should be aligned with shareholders' long-term interest determined by the board, approved by shareholders, and fully disclosed in public reporting. Traditionally, director compensation has consisted of a retainer for board membership and fees for being a committee chair and attending board and committee meetings. The ever-increasing amounts of time, commitment, and liability required of directors to fulfill their fiduciary duties in recent years have had positive effects on their compensation. Table 4.2 summarizes guidelines provided by several institutional investors relevant to director compensation. These guidelines suggest (1) director compensation consists of a combination of both cash and stock, (2) all directors should own stock in the company, (3) director pay should be comparable to the peer market groups, (4) all unusual compensation should be reviewed and approved by independent directors and disclosed in the proxy statement, (5) pensions and postretirement benefits should not be granted to outside directors, and (6) shareholders should approve director compensation.

Executives and directors should be given the opportunity or even be required to own a reasonable share of the company's common stock. The compensation committee should determine the amount and percentage of executive stock ownership that will motivate them to align their interests with those of shareholders. Academic research, however, finds a relationship between levels of directors, executive ownership, and firm performance, and therefore suggests that corporate performance could be improved by ownership as long as it is kept below 50 percent.[7] Target ownership plans are becoming a means of providing incentives for superior performance by encouraging directors and officers to hold a minimum specified level of equity (e.g., 10 percent) relative to their base salary (e.g., four times the base salary). Academic research also suggests that (1) poor firm performance is associated with low levels of managerial equity ownership, and (2) significant increases in executive ownership result in improvements in the company's future operating and stock market performance. Thus, companies should consider adopting a target ownership plan suitable to their corporate governance attributes and capital structure. It is perceived that stock options can cause directors to perversely use short-term incentives to artificially boost the company's stock price.

BOARD SELECTION

The election process of directors can also affect the board's effectiveness in the sense that the election process enables shareholders to replace unsatisfactory directors. A staggered board structure in which only a portion of the board is elected each year allows continuity of the board's monitoring function. Investors do not typically like staggered boards, and there are many shareholder proposals asking boards to declassify. This staggered structure makes the annual reelection of the entire board more difficult because under a typical staggered structure, only one-third of the board is elected each year for a three-year term. In the post-SOX era, the issue of increased shareholder involvement in the selection of directors has received a considerable amount of attention. Currently, the SEC's Rule 14a-8 is governing director election matters. Rule 14a-8, while permitting companies and their shareholders to address director selection matters, contains many exclusions that make its implementation difficult.

Traditionally, public companies have used a plurality vote system to elect corporate directors. Under a plurality vote system, directors can be elected by the vote of a single share unless they are opposed by a dissident director. It has been argued that a plurality vote system gives too much power to executive directors and management to influence the election of outside directors. Conversely, a majority vote system empowers shareholders to elect the most qualified outside directors. Although this issue is not a new phenomenon, recent corporate misconduct and related financial scandals have contributed to its importance and emerging momentum.

There have been moves toward requiring majority vote election procedures for corporate directors. Recently, the California Public Employees' Retirement System (CalPERs) board adopted a three-pronged plan to advocate majority vote requirements. According to CalPERs board president, Rob Feckner, "Majority vote will give shareholders the power to hold directors accountable for their actions and their performance, and elect the best person for the job."[8] CalPERs' majority vote plan recommends (1) implementing majority vote policies and procedures at public companies through the companies' bylaw and charter amendments, (2) making changes to state laws to implement majority vote where feasible, (3) implementing majority vote policies at the SEC and national stock exchanges, and (4) amending CalPERs Corporate Governance Core Principles and Guidelines to promote majority votes for corporate directors. In January 2006, Intel's board amended the company's bylaws to replace its plurality vote standard.[9] This move by Intel is viewed positively by its shareholders in holding its directors more accountable and in bringing democracy to its boardroom.

DIRECTOR EDUCATION AND EVALUATION

Corporate governance reforms and best practices issued by a number of organizations recommend continuous education and evaluation of the board of directors. Evaluation of the company's board should be performed formally and regularly (at least annually) through either self-evaluation, independent committee evaluation (audit, compensation, nominating), or outside consulting evaluations. Each approach has its own advantages and disadvantages. For example, self-evaluation of the board can be more in depth, whereas outside consultant evaluations can be perceived to be more independent. Assessment of individual directors' performance is very sensitive and often subjective, primarily because no generally accepted criteria are established for the evaluation. Directors are typically leery of making any of this information public to shareholders due to litigation concerns. However, some type of summary aggregate evaluation information to shareholders would be helpful.

Some of the generally accepted benchmarks for the entire board evaluation are (1) fulfillment of oversight functions, (2) transparency and accountability, (3) overseeing of conflicts of interest, (4) establishment of goals and strategies, and (5) assessment of management's performance. The committees of the board of directors should be evaluated according to their assigned oversight functions and the fulfillment of their responsibilities. The individual members of each board's committee should be evaluated based on their governing ability, integrity, financial literacy, strategic perspective, decision making and judgment, team work, communication, leadership, and business acumen. Table 4.3 provides several benchmarks and related criteria for an effective evaluation of board performance.

BOARD ACCOUNTABILITY

The board of directors' accountability can be classified into accountability to shareholders, accountability for the effectiveness of its operation, and accountability for its involvement in the company's strategic decisions to ensure sustainable performance.

1. Accountability to Shareholders. The company's board of directors is accountable to shareholders for protecting their rights and interests. To effectively discharge its accountability to shareholders, the board should (a) consider adopting shareholder proposals that received a majority of votes cast for or against; (b) take actions on recommendations

Table 4.3 Board Performance

Benchmarks	Criteria
Board independence	• There should be no more than two inside directors. • There should be no insiders on the audit, nominating, and compensation committees. • There should be no outside members who directly or indirectly draw consulting, legal, or other fees from the company. • There should be no interlocking directorships (CEOs who sit on each other's boards). • It is also desirable for outside directors to meet regularly without the CEO.
Board quality	• Fully employed directors should sit on no more than four corporate boards and retired directors on no more than seven. • More kudos are given if the board has at least one outside director experienced in the company's core business. • It is a plus if at least one director is a CEO of a company of similar size. • A higher rating was given if all directors attended 75 percent or more of meetings or if a board has no more than fifteen directors.
Board activism	• Boards should meet regularly without management present and should evaluate their own performance every year. • Audit committees should meet at least four times a year. • Boards should be frugal on executive pay. • Boards should be decisive when planning a CEO succession. • Boards should be diligent in oversight responsibilities. • Boards should be quick to act when trouble strikes.
Board accountability	• All board directors own a minimum of US$150,000 of stock, ensuring an alignment of their interests with those of investors. • More kudos are given if the company does not offer pension benefits to its directors—a benefit that many believe makes directors less likely to challenge the CEO. • Boards stand for election every year. • Boards that fail to evaluate their performance rate lower.

Source: Adapted from Ernst & Young. 2002. Corporate Governance Workshop: Board Performance.

approved by the majority of shareholders; (c) interact with large shareholders, respond to communications from shareholders, and consider their views, inputs, and insights on important governance and oversight functions; and (d) attend the annual shareholder's meeting and be willing to respond to shareholder questions.

On June 28, 2007, Pfizer announced that its board of directors will have face-to-face meetings with the company's institutional investors on corporate governance policies and practices.[10] Pfizer is the first public company to initiate such meetings in providing an opportunity to institutional investors to offer comments and perspectives on the company's governance policies and practices, including executive compensation. Other corporate governance best practices at Pfizer are (a) better shareholder access to the lead director and board committee chairs through e-mail; (b) the board's policy of regularly reviewing communications received from shareholders; (c) regular participation of directors in investor conferences relevant to governance practices; (d) the elimination of its poison pill; (e) declassification of the board; (f) the adoption of a majority voting policy; (g) additional disclosures on executive compensation above and beyond the SEC disclosure requirements; (h) the use of "plain English" rules to make disclosures more understandable to investors; (i) open and candid communications with shareholders; and (j) addressing of all stakeholders' viewpoints on governance, including shareholders, employees, customers, suppliers, and government.

2. Accountability for Board Operation. The company's board of directors should be accountable for its own operation to (a) ensure directors are working toward the achievement of the company's mission and strategic objectives; (b) perform regular evaluation of the board and its individual directors, including an assessment of the board's technical skills, financial expertise, experiences, and other qualifications; (c) require continuing professional development and education for directors; and (d) set high standards for attendance at board and committee meetings.

3. Accountability for Strategic Decisions and Performance. The company's board of directors should oversee the appropriateness and soundness of managerial strategic plans, decisions, actions, and performance to ensure sustainable performance in MBL activities of economic, governance, ethical, social, and environmental measures. The board should obtain necessary information about the company's operations and financial reporting process, and maintain familiarity with the company's business affairs and reporting requirements.

EFFECTIVE CORPORATE BOARDS

Corporate boards, through vigilant oversight of the company's governance, financial reporting, and audit activities, can ensure alignment of management's interests with those of shareholders. PricewaterhouseCoopers, in its 2007 publication *Global Best Practices*, discusses the following eight bonus attributes that assist directors in creating an appropriate balance between their role as compliance watchdogs and that of participating in managerial strategic planning[11]:

1. *Create an open and engaging boardroom atmosphere*—Effective boards are those whose directors work well in teams, possess good listening and problem-solving skills, have the diverse experience necessary to address relevant business and industry issues, and are independent minded. Directors should advise management in strategic planning without micromanaging, and oversee management operational, compliance, and reporting functions.

2. *Maximize the value of the board's time commitment by establishing clear roles and responsibilities within an appropriate structure*—To be effective, directors should focus their efforts on the most relevant and important issues that contribute to the achievement of sustainable performance in creating shareholder value.

3. *Determine the information the board needs and ensure it is delivered in a timely manner*—The company's board should receive the right information in the right format and at the right time to effectively fulfill its oversight function. In particular, the audit committee should receive adequate information about the company's internal control and financial reports, risk assessment, and compliance reports.

4. *Dedicate time to strategic issues*—The board of directors should be proactively engaged with management in establishing strategic planning, setting strategic priorities, and executing these priorities in a timely manner.

5. *Create a transparent, explicit, and accountable executive pay process*—Executive compensation should be linked to the company's long-term sustainable performance and aligned with the market and peer groups' benchmarks, pass the common-sense test in the public eye, and be fully transparent.

6. *Actively engage in the CEO succession process*—The board of directors should plan and be committed to the CEO succession process for replacement of a CEO in case of a crisis situation, and establish CEO selection criteria for a successor under normal circumstances.

7. *Assess the strength of the company's management talent*—The management team led by the CEO is crucial in ensuring the effectiveness of corporate governance and long-term sustainable shareholder value creation. The board of directors should ensure that the company has committed adequate resources to attract and train a competent and ethical management team.

8. *Monitor the company's enterprise risk management system*—The board of directors should oversee the adequacy and effectiveness of the company's risk management system. Some companies have established a position of chief risk officer (CRO) to coordinate risk management activities among the board of directors, management, and key personnel.

DIRECTOR LIABILITY

The separation of ownership and control cause a separation of decision management and decision control and the need for an oversight function by the board of directors to represent and protect the interests of all stakeholders, especially investors. Corporate boards are under extensive pressure in the post-SOX era to accept more oversight responsibility and accountability for the company's affairs. Directors are also concerned about their personal liability for questionable governance practices. Integrity and competence of the company's board minimize the potential for conflicts of interest.

The integrity of directors cannot be regulated or defined by corporate laws. It is entirely up to shareholders to elect the most competent and ethically motivated directors. However, state corporate laws define directors' obligations, because almost all corporations (except for some banks and federally regulated entities) are incorporated by states. One way to influence directors' ethical conduct and create more accountability for them is to increase their legal liability for poor performance and business misconduct. Federal laws and regulations (SOX, SEC rules) are also affecting business and the activities of corporations as well as the responsibilities of their board of directors, senior executives, and other key personnel. Directors are not reasonably expected to have first-hand knowledge of all company business affairs under their oversight capacity. Nevertheless, directors are responsible for ascertaining the validity, reliability, and quality of information provided to them. In most circumstances, directors make decisions by relying on information furnished by corporate officers, employees, and professionals, including legal counsel and accountants. Thus, the effectiveness of their performance depends on the validity and quality of the information provided to directors.

Until recently, it was very rare and almost nonexistent for outside directors of public companies to pay money from their own pocket to settle shareholder lawsuits relevant to their liability. In January 2005, former outside directors of Enron and WorldCom agreed to pay a total of $31 million ($18 million WorldCom and $13 million Enron) out of their own pockets, in addition to a total of $196 million paid by their directors and officers (D&O) insurance ($155 million Enron, $36 million WorldCom), to settle securities class action lawsuits. In the legal environment, outside directors are facing legal obligations and liabilities from a variety of sources. First, under federal securities laws (e.g., SOX, SEC rules), directors are potentially liable when the company discloses misleading public reports. Sections 305 and 1105 of SOX give the SEC authority to bar directors from serving on the board of public companies if they are deemed "unfit." Second, under corporate law, directors can be sued for breaching their fiduciary duties, loyalty, and due care as well as for failure to sufficiently oversee management. Third, under pension law, directors can be held liable if their company's retirement plan suffers significantly as a result of overinvestment in the company's own shares.

Prior to the WorldCom and Enron cases, the general understanding and perception was that outside directors never had to worry about paying out-of-pocket liability settlements unless there was significant evidence of director culpability, an insolvent company, inadequate D&O insurance, or outside directors who were wealthy enough to justify the risks to plaintiffs of taking a case to trial. Enron and WorldCom have changed the landscape of outside directors' liability in several ways: (1) outside directors' oversight responsibility was not adequately fulfilled; (2) even though they were not directly engaged in fraudulent activities, they sold their shares of the company during a time when share prices were high due to the fraud; (3) the potential liability cost exceeded available D&O insurance; (4) outside directors were collectively wealthy; and (5) plaintiffs were either motivated to force directors to disgorge profit gained from fraudulent financial activities they failed to prevent and detect, or they wanted to send the clear message to outside directors that they could be held personally liable for failing to effectively discharge their oversight responsibilities.

Lessons learned from the Enron and WorldCom director settlement cases are that (1) they are not immune to personal liability and resulting out-of-pocket costs, (2) they should thoroughly investigate the company's culture and management's integrity before accepting a directorship or continuing to serve on an existing board, (3) they should be vigilant and effectively discharge their fiduciary duties and oversight function, (4) they should not serve on many boards so as to ensure proper time, effort, and the commitment necessary to do the job right, (5) they should ensure that the company carries adequate D&O insurance, and (6) they should incorporate the likelihood of out-of-pocket liability costs into their director's fee or total compensation package.

Lessons learned by plaintiffs, particularly institutional investors, (1) do not create undue fear for qualified individuals to serve as outside directors; (2) go after the personal assets of outside directors only in cases of fraud involvement, deliberate self-dealing, or gross negligence in carrying out their oversight responsibilities; and (3) formulate a fair settlement strategy that demands no limit personal liability when directors are involved in fraud or self-dealing, and limited personal liability in the case of lax oversight function.

Under the business judgment rule commonly practiced in business, directors who make decisions in good faith, based on rational reasoning and an informed manner, can be protected from liability to the company's shareholders on the grounds that they have fulfilled their fiduciary duty of care. In a recent court case decided by the Delaware Chancery Court trial of the Walt Disney Company, (1) the plaintiffs claim that the directors breached their fiduciary duties of due care and good faith in failing to oversee generous compensation and severance packages for former Disney president, Michael Ovitz; and (2) the court's decision was that directors did not breach their fiduciary duties to shareholders in deciding to hire the Disney president and then fire him as the president 14 months later at a cost of $140 million. Krispy Kreme Donuts is a company whose seemingly high performance in terms of reported earnings was influenced by accounting errors.[12] The Krispy Kreme board authorized spending of money from the initial offering to reacquire franchises that were owned by the former wife of its CEO. In addition, senior executives paid $1 million more than the board authorized for the transaction, which was not apparently overseen by the board. The special committee investigated the board preformance and found the performance was far from exemplary in authorizing the questionable transaction without receiving an improper personal benefit.[13] The relevant question is to what extent outside directors can breach their fiduciary duties and how irresponsible they must be to face legal liability. In the Disney case, the Delaware judge had harsh criticism for Disney directors but concluded that they had acted legally, whereas at Krispy Kreme Doughnuts, the special committee strongly criticized the director's performance but recommended that the company should oppose suits against those directors.

The issue of a director's personal liability for breaching fiduciary duty is still unresolved because under the charter of most Delaware corporations, directors can be found personally liable for breaching their duty of loyalty, but are exculpated from liability for breaches of their duty of care, even if that breach occurred as a result of gross negligence. However, conduct that is lacking "in good faith" is not exculpable and may be the functional equivalent of a breach of the duty of loyalty for the purpose of finding directors personally liable (and subject to monetary damages) for their conduct. The general consensus in courts is that directors should not be held liable for ordinary negligence arising from honest mistakes, omission, or prudent risks as long as they act on a reasonably informed basis, in good faith, and free from conflicts of interest. Therefore, it is widely accepted under the business rule that directors cannot and should not be expected to guarantee corporate success and compliance.

SUMMARY

This chapter discusses the roles and responsibilities of boards of directors in fulfilling their oversight function. It appears that the only effective way to bring vigilance, objectivity, and independence to the boardroom is to ensure that directors understand that their reputation and personal wealth can be affected as a result of breaching their fiduciary duty. To improve oversight effectiveness, the board of directors should (1) engage in active, informed, independent oversight of the company's business and affairs; (2) adopt oversight corporate governance rules, standards, best practices, and other guidance presented in this chapter; (3) establish and preserve objectivity and independence of nonexecutive directors by avoiding conflicts of interest and undue influence by executive directors, particularly the CEO; (4) receive in a timely manner adequate strategic, operational, and financial information; (5) communicate with shareholders key issues affecting the company's sustainable performance and promote shareholder democracy; (6) form appropriate board committees to divide oversight authority and responsibilities and hold these committees and their members accountable for their performance; (7) perform an annual evaluation of the entire board of directors, its committees, and members of each committee; and (8) fulfill the fiduciary duties of due care, loyalty, and fair disclosures established in the general corporation laws of the states and court interpretations of these duties.

Directors' emerging issues are director liability, accountability, role in crisis management, and executive compensation. Establishing an appropriate executive compensation committee that aligns the interests of executives with those of shareholders and links executive pay with performance is perhaps the most profound challenge of many boards. Director accountability and related liability are the second most prevailing challenge for directors. Finally, directors' ability and willingness to deal with executive departures, succession planning, crisis management, and executive compensation are other important challenges.

The key points of this chapter are

- The ultimate responsibility of good corporate governance rests with the board of directors.

- Decision management, which consists of initiation and implementation of strategies, is viewed as the management's responsibility, whereas decision control, which entails the ratification and monitoring of strategies, is viewed as the board of directors' fiduciary duty.

- The board of directors is usually composed of both insiders (senior executives) and outsiders (independent directors). Nevertheless, the entire board of directors is considered representative of shareholders, that is, responsible for protecting shareholders' interests.

- One way to influence directors' performance and ethical conduct is to hold them accountable and liable for poor performance and business misconduct.

- The company's board of directors is ultimately responsible for its business and affairs. The board may delegate its decision-making authority to the company's top management team, but it is still responsible for running the company without micromanaging.

- The primary responsibilities of the board of directors are to (1) define the company's mission and goals; (2) establish or approve strategic plans and decisions to achieve these goals; (3) appoint senior executives to manage the company in accordance with the established strategies, plans, policies, and procedures; and (4) oversee managerial plans, decisions, and actions in achieving sustainable shareholder value while protecting the interests of other stakeholders.

- The business judgment rule provides directors with broad discretion to make good faith business decisions and implies that directors, when making business decisions, must be reasonably informed and rational in such a manner that a prudent person would concur with the decision.

- Investors, in general, are in favor of the separation of the positions of the CEO and the chairperson of the board of directors as a means of strengthening the board's independence and reducing the potential conflicts of interest, particularly when the company is perceived to be managed poorly.

- Corporate governance best practices suggest that companies designate one director to take the lead at executive sessions that do not include management.

- Board characteristics, including composition, authority, responsibilities, resources, independence, and compensation, significantly influence its effectiveness.

- To be independent, a director should not have any other relationships with the company other than his or her directorship that may compromise the director's objectivity and loyalty to the company's shareholders.

- The evaluation of board performance should be completed formally and regularly (at least annually) through either self-evaluation, independent committee evaluation (audit, compensation, nominating), or outside consulting evaluations.

- Board accountability can be classified into accountability to shareholders for protecting their rights and interests, accountability for the effectiveness of its operation, and accountability for its involvement in the company's strategic decisions to ensure enduring performance and success.

KEY TERMS

audit committee financial
   expert
business judgment rule
CEO duality
D&O insurance
duty of care

duty of fair disclosures
duty of loyalty
duty of obedience
fiduciary duty
independent director
lead director

National Association of
   Corporate Directors
   (NACD)
one-tier board model
staggered board
two-tier board model

REVIEW QUESTIONS

1. What is the difference between decision management and decision control?

2. Briefly explain the business judgment rule and the benefit it provides to directors.

3. What is the relationship between the supervisory and management boards of a two-tiered board system?

4. Why are investors in favor of separation of the positions of CEO and chairperson?

5. What are the requirements and criteria for being designated as an audit committee financial expert?

6. Why is it important for a company to have an appropriately sized board of directors?

7. Briefly discuss the benefits of small and large board sizes.

8. What are the direct responsibilities of the board of directors?

9. Board independence is essential for what purposes?

10. What responsibility does the compensation committee have toward the remuneration of board members?

11. How does the board of directors oversee corporate governance?

DISCUSSION QUESTIONS

1. Discuss the importance and objectives of directors' fiduciary duties to the company.

2. What are possible situations that could jeopardize a director's duty to avoid conflicts of interest?

3. Do you support CEO duality in a public company? Defend your response.

4. Why is it important for the members of the board of directors to have business knowledge and financial expertise?

5. In your opinion, who should be allowed to serve as a director of a public company?

6. Is a board that meets more often for shorter periods of time more effective and efficient than a board that meets less frequently but for a longer period of time? Explain.

7. Discuss the impact of the business judgment rule on directors' abilities to fulfill their fiduciary duties.

8. Compare and contrast the roles and responsibilities of executive and nonexecutive directors.

9. Describe both advantages and disadvantages of CEO duality.

10. Discuss how executive compensation should be determined.

NOTES

1. The State of Delaware. 2008. General Corporation Law. Title 8, Ch. 1, §141. Available at: delcode.delaware.gov/title8/c001/sc04/index.shtml.

2. Schmidt, R. H. 2003, August. Corporate Governance in Germany: An Economic Perspective. No. 2003/36. Center for Financial Studies, an der Johann Wolfgang Goethe Universität, Frankfurt, Germany. Available at: www.ifk-cfs.de/papers/03_36.pdf.

3. The Conference Board. 2003, January 9. The Conference Board Commission on Public Trust and Private Enterprise: Findings and Recommendations. Available at: www.ecgi.org/codes/documents/757.pdf.

4. Allen, W. T., and W. R. Berkley. 2003. In Defense of the CEO Chair. *Harvard Business Review* September: 24-25.

5. Council of Institutional Investors (CII). n.d. Independent Director Definition. Available at: www.cii.org/policies/ind_dir_defn.htm.

6. U.S. Securities and Exchange Commission (SEC). 2003, Strengthening the Commission's Requirements Regarding Auditor Independence. Available at: www.sec.gov/rules/final/33-8183.htm.

7. Core, J. E., and D. F. Larcker. 1999, December 7. Performance Consequences of Requiring Target Stock Ownership Levels. Revised working paper, The Wharton School, University of Pennsylvania, Philadelphia.

8. California Public Employees' Retirement System (CalPERS). 2005, March 14. CalPERS to Seek Majority Vote For Corporate Directors—Pension Fund to Use Public Company Accounting Oversight Board Auditor Independence Proposals as Guidelines for Proxy Votes. Press Release. Available at: www.calpers.ca.gov/index.jsp?bc=/about/press/pr-2005/march/majority-vote.xml.

9. Intel. 2006, January 19. Intel Board Adopts Majority Vote Standard for Election of Directors. Intel News Release. Available at: www.intel.com/pressroom/archive/releases/20060119corp.htm.

10. Pfizer. 2007, June 28. Pfizer Board of Directors to Initiate Face-to-Face Meetings with Company's Institutional Investors on Corporate Governance Policies and Practices. Available at: mediaroom.pfizer.com/portal/site/pfizer/index.jsp?ndmViewId=news_view&ndmConfigId=1006533&newsId=20070628005559&newsLang=en.

11. PricewaterhouseCoopers. n.d. Global Best Practices. Available at: www.globalbestpractices.com.

12. Norris, F. 2005, August 12. Inept Boards Need Have No Fear. *The New York Times*. Available at: events.nytimes.com/2005/08/12/business/12norris.html?8dpc.

13. Ibid.

Chapter 5

Board Committee Roles
and Responsibilities

INTRODUCTION

The oversight function of corporate governance is performed by the company's board of directors and its designated committees. Boards of directors perform their advisory and oversight function through well-structured, planned, and assigned committees to take advantage of the expertise of all the directors. Board committee formations and assignments depend on the size of the company, its board, and assumed responsibilities. Committee members address relevant issues and make recommendations to the entire board for final approval. Board committees normally function independently from each other and are provided with sufficient authority, resources, and assigned responsibilities in assisting the entire board.

Primary Objectives

The primary objectives of this chapter are to

- Provide an overview of the functions of board committees.
- Understand the roles and responsibilities of board committees.

- Be aware of the objectives of establishing board committees.
- Become familiar with the duties, responsibilities, and composition of the audit, compensation, nominating, governance, and special committees.
- Understand the process and emerging practices for the election of corporate directors.

RELEVANCE OF BOARD COMMITTEES

The establishment of board committees can bring more focus to the board's oversight function by giving proper authority and responsibilities and by demanding accountability for these committees. Listing standards of national stock exchanges require that listed companies form at least three board committees that must include audit, compensation, and nominating committees. Public companies often, in addition to these three mandatory committees, have governance and other committees such as finance, IT, and disclosure. The number and size of board committees depend on the number of directors on the company's board. The number of directors on the board of public companies normally ranges between nine and fifteen directors. A board with fewer than nine directors may be viewed as being dominated and controlled by a small group, and a board with more than fifteen directors is generally considered less effective and efficient. Regulators (SEC), professional organizations (The Conference Board, CII), and corporate governance activists have required or recommended a minimum of three members for board committees. Thus, to meet this minimum requirement and effectively use the time and expertise of their directors, companies sometimes combine some of the aforementioned board committees. For example, the nominating and governance committees are usually combined into one committee. The three mandatory committees for listed companies must be composed of at least three independent directors, making the total number of necessary independent directors nine. Of course, it is possible that an independent director could serve on more than one board committee, which frequently occurs at smaller companies.

AUDIT COMMITTEE

The analysis of the reported financial scandals of the late 1990s and early 2000s points to one consistent pattern of lapses in the audit committee oversight function. This raised the question, "Where was the audit committee?" Audit committees act as guardians of investor interests by assuming oversight responsibilities in the areas of corporate governance, financial reporting, audit activities, and compliance with applicable laws, regulations, and ethical standards. The audit committee has evolved from a debate over whether to voluntarily establish an audit committee to require the formation of audit committees, and now in light of emerging corporate governance reforms, how to integrate the audit committee into the company's corporate governance structure.[1]

Lawmakers (SOX), regulators (SEC rules), and listing standards of national stock exchanges (NYSE, Nasdaq, AMEX) generally require public committees to have an audit committee, which must be composed of independent directors with no personal, financial, or family ties to management. The audit committee has evolved from acting as a liaison between management and the independent auditor to preserve auditor independence to overseeing internal controls, financial reporting, and audit activities. The audit committee is now directly responsible for hiring, compensating, firing, and overseeing the work of the independent auditor. Independent auditors are ultimately accountable to the audit committee. The audit committee is responsible for overseeing responsible corporate governance, a reliable financial reporting process, and credible audit activities.

Recent developments in corporate governance reforms have boosted the relevance, importance, and public profiles of audit committees. Thus, the need for a better understanding of audit committees and their activities is becoming more acute as the corporate governance movement gains momentum. The audit committees must be mindful of emerging corporate governance reforms because these reforms are having a direct impact on the company's operations, business affairs, financial reporting, control environment, and audit activities. There is little doubt that new initiatives, regulatory changes, guiding principles, listing standards, and best practices have extended the role of audit committees, empowered their authority, provided more resources, shifted some traditionally perceived managerial responsibilities (hiring, firing, compensating auditors) to the audit committee, and required more quality time and effort.

On April 1, 2003, the SEC voted to adopt new rules and amendments to direct the national securities exchanges and associations to prohibit the listing of any security of an issuer that is not in compliance with the audit committee requirements established by SOX. SEC Release Nos. 33-8220 and 34-47654[2]: Standards Relating to Listed Company Audit Committees outline these requirements, which relate to (1) the independence of audit committee members, (2) the audit committee's responsibility to select and oversee the issuer's independent accountant, (3) procedures for handling complaints regarding the issuer's accounting practices, (4) the authority of the audit committee to engage advisors, and (5) funding for the independent auditor and any outside advisors engaged by the audit committee. Emerging corporate governance reforms, including SOX, SEC-related implementation rules, listing standards, and best practices, have had a positive impact on the overall audit committee oversight effectiveness. Infrequent meetings and audit committee meetings that lasted fewer than ten minutes have been replaced with frequent, longer, more constructive, and more productive committee meetings. Table 5.1 compares audit committee functions pre- and postcorporate governance reforms.

Definition of the Audit Committee

Several definitions of the audit committee are provided in authoritative reports, books, and articles. The Blue Ribbon Committee (BRC), although not providing any formal definition, states, "The [audit] committee's job is clearly one of oversight and monitoring, and in carrying out this job it acts in reliance on senior financial management and the outside auditors."[3] The audit committee has been narrowly defined as a standing committee of the company's board of directors to act as a liaison between management and the external auditor. The audit committee has also been broadly defined as acting as a representative of shareholders to protect their interests and rights.

The first legal definition of audit committee was provided in Section 205(a) of SOX, which defines the audit committee as

A committee (or equivalent body) established by and amongst the board of directors of an issuer for the purpose of overseeing the accounting and financial reporting processes of the

Table 5.1 Comparison of Audit Committees (Pre- and Postcorporate Governance Reforms)

Prereforms	Postreforms
• Voluntary audit committees	• Mandatory formation of audit committees
• Personal and economic ties to management and the corporation	• All committee members must be independent
• Liaison between management and independent auditors	• Financial expertise
	• Directly responsible for appointing, compensating, retaining, and overseeing independent auditors
• Limited knowledge of financial reporting	• Must establish procedures for receipt, retention, and treatment of complaints relating to accounting, auditing, and internal control matters
• Infrequent and short meetings	
• Lack of proper authority and resources	• Has authority to engage advisors
• Less accountability	• Given appropriate funding, as determined by the committee, for external auditors and advisors
• Inadequate oversight of financial reporting and audit activities	• Disclosure of existence of at least one audit committee financial expert, or if not, why
	• Name of the financial expert and whether independent from management
	• Oversees financial reporting, risk management, internal controls, and audit activities
	• Preapproves all audit and permissible nonaudit services
	• More accountability
	• Meets at least four times a year
	• Annual evaluation of the audit committee and its members

issuer and audits of the financial statements of the issuer; and if no such committee exists with respect to an issuer, the entire board of directors of the issuer.[4]

The audit committee has evolved as a representative of the board of directors to assisting the board in discharging its responsibilities in overseeing the financial reporting process, internal controls, and audit activities. Thus, in the context of the agency theory, the audit committee can be viewed as an internal corporate governance mechanism overseeing financial reporting to improve the quality of financial disclosures provided from agents (management) to principals (shareholders). The audit committee is also defined as

A committee composed of independent, nonexecutive directors charged with oversight functions of ensuring responsible corporate governance, a reliable financial reporting process, an effective internal control structure, a credible audit function, an informed whistleblower complaint process, and an appropriate code of business ethics with the purpose of creating long-term shareholder value while protecting the interests of other stakeholders.[5]

This definition is broad enough to address all important oversight functions, roles, and responsibilities of audit committees.

Audit Committee Relationships with Other
Corporate Governance Participants

1. **Relationships with the board of directors.** The audit committee is one of the major standing committees of the company's board of directors and, as such, works with the other board committees (compensation, nomination, and governance) to fulfill the board's fiduciary duties. The establishment of the audit committee as the standing committee of the board is based on the need for specialization within the board of directors. The board is ultimately accountable to investors for the company's performance, affairs, and business. The audit committee assists the board by bringing specialization and expertise in the areas of financial reporting, internal controls, risk management, and audit activities.

2. **Audit committee working relationships with management.** The audit committee should interact with management by asking appropriate questions pertaining to the company's corporate governance structure, internal controls, financial reporting, audit activities, risk assessment, codes of ethics, and whistleblower programs. Thus, audit committee members should have a sufficient understanding of the company's governance and operations and financial activities to efficiently interact with management. Senior executives should inform the audit committee of significant events and transactions that substantially affect the company's risk appetite. Management should communicate with the audit committee areas that pose financial risk and design controls to prevent and detect material financial misstatements. Management should also communicate with the committee important accounting policies and practices used in the preparation of reliable financial statements.

3. **Audit committee working relationships with external auditors.** The audit committee's relationship with the external auditor has changed since the passage of SOX and the issuance of auditing standards by the PCAOB. Under SOX, the audit committee has a direct responsibility to oversee the work of the independent auditor. The committee must be directly responsible for hiring, compensating, and firing external auditors, as well as overseeing their work. External auditors are held ultimately accountable to the audit committee and should submit their reports of the audit on ICFR and the audit of financial reporting to management via the audit committee. The audit committee should approve all audit and permissible nonaudit services, if any, provided by external auditors; review their audit scope, plan, and findings; and eventually evaluate their performance. External auditors, as part of their audit of internal control, evaluate the effectiveness of the audit committee and consider ineffective audit committees as material weaknesses in internal control.[6] Thus, dual evaluation of external auditor performance creates a check-and-balance communication process that should be guarded from potential conflicts of interest. The audit committee should have access and, when warranted, review all engagement letters signed by independent auditors and their clients for providing all preapproved audit and nonaudit services. In addition, the committee should receive from independent auditors a summary of each engagement describing the service involved, related fees, and justification that the services are compatible with independence rules.

4. **Audit committee working relationships with internal auditors.** The audit committee should be responsible for hiring, overseeing, compensating, and firing the head of the internal audit department (CAE), and internal auditors should report their audit findings directly to the audit committee, being ultimately accountable to that committee. This emerging working relationship between the audit committee and internal auditors requires (a) readily accessible and candid communication between the internal auditor and the audit committee; and (b) that the audit committee has a clear understanding of internal auditing policies, processes, practices, and findings.

Historical Perspectives on Audit Committees

Table 5.2 provides a historical perspective of the audit committee from its origin to its current oversight functions of corporate governance, internal controls, financial reporting, and audit activities. The origin of the committee can be traced back to the McKesson and Robbins financial scandal in the 1930s involving the fictitious reporting of inventories, overstatement of accounts, and audit failures in discovering these fraudulent financial activities.[7] This high-profile scandal, at the time, demonstrated the need for a special committee composed of outside directors to ensure the integrity of financial reporting.

The SEC issued in 1940 the Accounting Series Release (ASR), which recommended that outside directors elect the company's external auditor.[8] The NYSE set forth a similar recommendation that a special committee of outside directors be established to select external auditors.[9] Ultimately, the AICPA in 1967 recommended—but did not require—companies to establish audit committees composed of outside directors to act as a liaison between management and external auditors to preserve auditor independence.[10] In 1972, largely in response to the discovery of post-Watergate illegal political contributions, bribes, and slush funds from corporations, the SEC issued ASR 123, which endorsed the formation of audit committees composed of outside directors for all public companies to protect investors from misleading financial statements.[11] Ultimately, in 1974, the SEC issued ASR165, which required disclosures of the existence or nonexistence of audit committees in companies' filings with the SEC.

The first mandatory requirement for the establishment of audit committees composed solely of outside, nonexecutive directors was set forth by the NYSE in 1973.[12] This requirement received long-sought attention for the accounting profession and the business community in 1987, pursuant to the report of the COSO, which strongly recommended that the SEC issue the same mandate.[13] The COSO report, titled "Report of the National Commission on Fraudulent Financial Reporting," underscored the important role that the audit committee could play in preventing and detecting fraudulent financial reporting activities.

Many of the aforementioned recommendations were subsequently implemented by public companies and all national stock exchanges. These recommendations were also considered by the accounting profession when the AICPA issued its Statement on Auditing Standard (SAS) No. 61 titled Communication with Audit Committees, which requires, among other things, auditors to communicate material accounting and auditing matters, including any proposed or recorded audit adjustments, and any disagreements with management.[14] These recommendations were also addressed in SOX and subsequently became mandatory in the SEC rules concerning audit committees.

Table 5.2 Evolution of the Audit Committee

Year	Events influencing audit committee formation
1938	McKesson & Robbins fraud
1939	NYSE recommends the establishment of audit committees
1940	SEC recommends that companies form audit committees—Accounting Series Release (ASR) No. 19
1967	AICPA Executive Committee Statement on Audit Committees of Board of Directors recommends the establishment of audit committees
1970	Penn Central bankruptcy
1972	ASR Nos. 123 and 126
1973	NYSE White Paper opines that audit committees are a necessity
1974	ASR No. 165
	Committees chaired by Senator Lee Metcalf and Congressman John Moss complete their investigations into the accounting profession
	AICPA forms Commission on Auditors' Responsibilities (Cohen Commission)
1976	Metcalf Committee Staff Report, The Accounting Establishment, is issued.
1977	Foreign Corrupt Practices Act (FCPA)
1978	AICPA Cohen Commission issues Commission on Auditors' Responsibilities: Report, Conclusions, and Recommendations
	AICPA forms a special committee to consider the adoption of an audit committee requirement
	NYSE requires companies with common stock issues registered on NYSE to have an audit committee
1985	Congressman John D. Dingell convenes the first of a series of hearings into the effectiveness of independent auditors
1987	National Commission on Fraudulent Financial Reporting (NCFRR/the Treadway Commission)
1988	SEC's five commissioners, by a narrow vote, decide not to require all public companies to have audit committees, but encourage their formation
	Statement on Auditing Standards (SAS) No. 61, Communication with the Audit Committees
1989	The National Association of Securities Dealers (NASD) approves a requirement that National Market System companies (a subset of the over-the-counter market) must have audit committees
	Statement on Internal Auditing Standards No. 7 (SAIS No. 7) Communication with the Board of Directors
1991	Federal Deposit Insurance Corporation Improvement Act
1992	Committee of Sponsoring Organizations of the Treadway Commission (COSO) issues Internal Control-Integrated Framework
1993	Public Oversight Board of the AICPA's SEC Practices Section releases In the Public Interest
1994	Kirk Panel (Public Oversight Board of the AICPA's SEC Practices Section) releases Strengthening the Professionalism of the Independent Auditor
1995	Public Oversight Board of the AICPA's SEC Practices Section releases Allies in Protecting Shareholder Interests
1998	SEC Chairman Arthur Levitt delivers speech at the NYU Center for Business and Law in which he calls for the NYSE and Nasdaq to form a "blue ribbon committee" to study the role of the audit committee
1999	Report and Recommendations of the Blue Ribbon Committee on Improving the Effectiveness of Corporate Audit Committees
	SAS No. 90, Audit Committee Communications
	SEC Release No. 34-42266: Audit Committee Disclosure
	NYSE and Nasdaq adopt new listing requirements, mandating the existence, composition, director qualifications, and duties of an audit committee
2000	POB's Panel on Audit Effectiveness releases Report and Recommendations
2001	Arthur Levitt, SEC Chairman, issues letter to audit committee chairmen
2002	Sarbanes-Oxley Act
2003	SEC Release Nos. 33-8177 and 34-47235: Disclosure Required by Sections 406 and 407 of the Sarbanes-Oxley Act of 2002
	SEC Release Nos. 33-8220 and 34-47654: Standards Relating to Listed Company Audit Committees
	SEC approved amendments to NYSE and the Nasdaq corporate governance listing standards
2004	NYSE submitted to the SEC for approval amendments to its corporate governance listing standards

Congress passed the Federal Deposit Insurance Corporation Improvement Act (FDICIA) of 1991 in response to the savings and loan crisis.[15] In Section 112.36 of SOX, Congress identified needed improvements in financial management for insured depository institutions. The FDICIA requires that management of depository institutions issue a report on the effectiveness of internal controls over financial reporting and establish an independent audit committee entirely made up of outside directors. For banking institutions with more than $3 billion in assets, audit committees are required to "include members with banking or related financial management expertise." Although the FDIC is applicable only to depository institutions insured by the FDIC, SOX provisions became a guide for best practices for other corporations.

Audit Committee Principles

The following audit committee principles are derived from a variety of publications, rules, and regulations, including SOX, SEC-related rules, the BRC recommendations, and the KPMG audit committee institute publication.

Audit committee formation: Public companies should establish audit committees tailored to their corporate governance structure and unique corporate culture and characteristics—one size does not fit all.

Audit committee independence: Audit committees should be solely composed of independent directors.

Audit committee members' qualifications: At a minimum, all members of the audit committee should be financially literate with one member designated as the committee financial expert; members should also be knowledgeable, experienced, informed, vigilant, and diligent. Characteristics that make audit committee members effective are (1) a general understanding of the company's major economic, business, operating, and financial risk; (2) broad knowledge of the interrelationship of the company's operations and financial reporting; (3) a clear understanding of the difference between the company's decision-making function delegated to management and its oversight function assumed by the audit committee; (4) the ability to formulate and ask probing questions about the company's operations, business, internal control, financial reporting process, and audit activities; and (5) the courage to challenge management when necessary.

Audit committee authority: Audit committee authority should be delegated by the board of directors to carry out the assigned oversight responsibilities, including the authority to hire, compensate, and fire both the independent and internal auditors, the authority to engage independent counsel and other advisors, and the authority to conduct any investigations deemed necessary.

Audit committee funding: The audit committee should be provided with sufficient funding for payment and compensation to the independent auditor, the internal auditor (chief audit executive), legal counsel, and other advisors.

Audit committee oversight function: At a minimum, the audit committee should be responsible for overseeing corporate governance, internal control, financial reporting, risk assessments, internal auditing, codes of ethics, whistleblower programs, and external auditing.

Audit committee accountability: The audit committee should be ultimately accountable to the board of directors as representatives of all stakeholders, particularly shareholders. The committee should report quarterly to the board of directors, and annually to shareholders, about its activities, achievements, and performance. The audit committee should also be evaluated annually for the achievement of its objectives.

Audit committee charter: The audit committee should have a written charter tailored to the company that clearly describes its authority, resources, funding, duties, oversight responsibilities, structure, process, independence, membership qualifications and requirements, and relationship with management, the internal auditor, and the independent auditor.

Audit committee agenda: A comprehensive, written, and well-developed agenda helps the audit committee focus on its mission and fulfillment of its oversight responsibilities. The agenda should be prepared in advance with input from management, the internal auditor, the independent auditor, legal counsel, and other personnel involved, as well as effectively carried out and properly documented.

Audit committee orientation, training, and continued education: The evolving corporate governance reforms resulting from the passage of SOX, SEC-related implementation rules, and listing standards of national stock exchanges necessitate that audit committees find ways to carry out their assigned responsibilities and stay abreast of new regulations, standards, trends, and other requirements. Audit committees must be aware of emerging reforms and address their possible effects on their company's corporate governance structure. There should be an orientation program for newly appointed audit committee members, and all members should participate in annual training and continuing education programs to keep abreast of emerging initiatives.

Audit Committee Composition

Corporate governance reforms post-SOX have significantly improved the composition of audit committees by requiring that all members of the audit committee be independent and financially literate, with at least one member being designated as a financial expert, and have adequate resources and authority. Audit committee composition is discussed in terms of size, independence, qualifications, attributes, and resources.

Audit Committee Size

The audit committee should be composed of at least three members. The size of the committee usually ranges from three to six members, whereas the SEC rule and listing standards for public companies require at least three independent members.

Audit Committee Independence

The audit committee should be composed of independent, nonexecutive, outside directors. SEC rules and listing standards require members of the audit committee to be independent by (1) not receiving any compensation other than that that is determined as a board member; (2) not providing any advisory or consulting services to the company they serve, its affiliates, or other business ties; (3) not having been employed by the company or its affiliates within five years; and (4) not having been a member of the immediate family of the company's executives or its affiliates within the past five years.[16]

Recent corporate governance reforms have promoted director independence as the most important attribute to improve committee effectiveness. In the pre-SOX period, (1) audit committee members were not totally independent, with a significant portion of "grey" directors; (2) independent audit committee members were most likely to support the auditor's position; and (3) there was a positive relationship between audit committee independence and the proportion of outside directors, suggesting that the independence of committee members was largely affected by the independence of the board of directors. Audit committee independence can induce substantial benefits in terms of (1) improving the quality of financial reports by assisting in reducing financial reporting misstatements, (2) increasing interactions with internal auditors, and (3) improving the quality of financial statement audits by engaging higher-quality auditors.

The emerging corporate governance guidelines on audit committee independence should assist public companies in avoiding potential conflicts of interest due to committee members' excessive contractual or consulting ties to the company or its management. Yet, the conflict can occur when committee members' self-interest incites them to support management on controversial financial issues. For example, in the Enron debacle, one of the members of the audit committee was the wife of an influential senator who received substantial campaign donations from Enron. Another member was a university president whose medical research center received a significant endowment from Enron. These types of self-interest, which are not prohibited under listing standards and SEC regulations and may well create conflicts of interest, should also be considered when the audit committee is recruiting new members and evaluating their independence.

Member Qualifications

At least one member of the audit committee should be designated as a financial expert. The SEC defines the term "audit committee financial expert" and how that term applies to the audit committee, especially in relationship to required disclosures.[17] The final rules define an audit committee financial expert as a person who has all of the following attributes:

- An understanding of generally accepted accounting principles and financial statements
- The ability to assess the general application of such principles in connection with accounting for estimates, accruals, and reserves
- Experience preparing, auditing, analyzing, or evaluating financial statements that present a breadth and level of complexity of accounting issues that are generally comparable to issues that can be raised by the registrant's financial statements, or experience actively supervising one or more persons engaged in such activities
- An understanding of internal controls and procedures for financial reporting, and an understanding of audit committee functions

Under SEC rules, a person must have acquired such attributes through any one or more of the following:

1. Education and experience as a principal financial officer, principal accounting officer, controller, public accountant, or auditor, or experience in a position that involves similar functions

2. Experience actively supervising a principal financial officer, principal accounting officer, controller, public accountant, auditor, or person performing similar functions

3. Experience overseeing or assessing the performance of companies or public accountants with respect to the preparation, audit, or evaluation of financial statements

4. Other relevant experience

The company's board of directors should apply the SEC's definition and consider audit committee members' experience and knowledge in determining which members qualify as financial experts and, if none qualify, recruit at least one member who meets the required qualifications. The company must also disclose the expert's name and whether the designated financial expert is independent from management. If not, the company must disclose that there is no independent financial expert serving on its audit committee and explain why.

Audit Committee Authority/Resources

SOX, recognizing the increased responsibilities assigned to audit committees, authorizes them to engage independent counsel and other outside advisors as they determined necessary and requires the company to provide appropriate funding for such advisors. Given that at least one member of the audit committee is designated as a financial expert and the committee receives accounting advice from both internal and external auditors, should the audit committee be authorized to have an accounting advisor? Under normal circumstances, the audit committee should obtain financial and accounting assistance from the company's management, as well as internal and external auditors. In limited situations, where there are possible allegations of fraudulent financial activities involving management or possibly auditors, or in understanding complex accounting practices (derivatives, pensions, postretirement), the audit committee may retain an accounting advisor or forensic investigator.

Audit Committee Responsibility

The responsibility of the audit committee has evolved from acting as a liaison between management and external auditors in preserving auditor independence to overseeing the financial reporting process and internal controls. SOX extended audit committee responsibility and defines this responsibility as oversight of "the accounting and financial reporting processes of the issuer; and audits of the financial statements of the issuer."[18] Section 301 of SOX also holds the audit committee directly responsible for hiring, firing, compensating, and overseeing the audit work of external auditors. SEC rules require that the committee be directly responsible for preapproval of all services (audit and nonaudit) provided by the independent auditor to the company or its subsidiaries.[19]

The SEC rules are intended to reinforce the audit committee responsibility to improve objectivity and independence of external auditors, insulate the independent auditor from pressure that management may impose, and reduce potential conflicts of interest between management and external auditors. The SEC rule requires that all audit, review, and attestation services (1) be specifically preapproved by the audit committee on a case-by-case approach, or (2) meet the requirements of already established preapproval policies by the audit committee. Public companies are required to disclose the adopted preapproval policies for all audits and all permissible nonaudit services established by the audit committee, along with the two most recent years of all independent auditor fees in the four categories of audit, audit-related, tax, and all other services.

The audit committee, as the representative of the company's board of directors, should assume responsibility delegated to it by the board. Thus, the primary responsibility of the committee is to represent investors and other stakeholders and protect their investments. The board of directors, while delegating authority and responsibilities to the audit committee, should consider (1) the company's corporate governance structure; (2) that the delegated responsibilities are in compliance with applicable laws and regulations, including SOX, SEC-related rules, listing standards, and best practices; (3) the balance between authority and responsibilities delegated to the audit committee; and (4) the extent and nature of audit committee oversight functions in financial reporting, internal control, risk assessment, and audit activities.

Audit committee oversight responsibilities can be grouped into the following categories:

1. **Corporate governance.** The audit committee, as one of the crucial and influential participants of corporate governance, should participate with other board committees (compensation, nominating, governance) in overseeing the effectiveness of corporate governance without assuming a managerial responsibility.

2. **Internal controls.** The audit committee should oversee the company's internal control structure to assure (a) the efficiency and effectiveness of operations, (b) the reliability of financial reporting, and (c) compliance with applicable laws and regulations. The committee's oversight of Section 404 on internal control is becoming more important as public companies are required to certify their ICFR. The audit committee should (a) know the senior executive who is directly responsible and ultimately accountable for Section 404 compliance; (b) understand the process of establishing and maintaining adequate and effective internal control; (c) understand procedures for assessing both the design and the operation of ICFR; (d) understand the proper documentation of compliance with Section 404; (e) review the management report on the effectiveness of ICFR; (f) review auditor reports expressing an opinion on management's assessment of the effectiveness of ICFR; (g) evaluate the identified significant deficiencies and material weaknesses in internal control; (h) be satisfied with management and auditor efforts and reports on ICFR; and (i) ensure that management has properly addressed the identified material weaknesses.

3. **Financial reporting.** The audit committee should oversee the financial reporting process by reviewing annual and quarterly financial statements, including (a) MD&A; (b) accounting principles, practices, estimates, and reserves; and (c) independent auditors' suggestions, comments, adjusting, and classification entries. The audit committee is responsible for overseeing the integrity and transparency of the company's financial disclosures.

4. **Audit activities.** The audit committee is responsible for overseeing both internal and external audit activities. The committee has the direct responsibility for hiring, compensating, and firing the company's independent auditor and CAE (the head of the internal audit department). Sections 201 and 202 of SOX require the company's audit committee to preapprove all audit and permissible nonaudit services. This may be delegated to a member of the committee who must then present the preapproval of nonaudit services to the full audit committee in its regular meeting. Thus, the audit committee must (a) ensure understanding of all permissible nonaudit services, (b) evaluate the qualifications of providers of preapproved nonaudit services, and (c) select the best provider considering reinforcement of auditor independence from management. Although SOX and SEC-related implementation rules permit certain tax services to be performed by the company's independent auditor contemporaneously with audit services, the PCAOB in its Auditing Standard No. 4 limits the performance of certain tax services such as tax shelters.[20] Both the independent auditor and the CAE should ultimately be held accountable to the audit committee. The committee should review reports of the independent auditors on financial statements, ICFR, and other significant internal audit reports.

5. **Code of ethics conduct.** The audit committee is responsible for overseeing the establishment and enforcement of the company's code of ethical conduct to ensure that an appropriate "tone at the top" policy is implemented to promote ethical conduct throughout the company.

6. **Whistleblower program.** The audit committee is responsible for overseeing the establishment and enforcement of whistleblower programs in compliance with the requirements of SOX and SEC-related rules. SOX created the opportunity for confidential and anonymous submissions of complaints by requiring that the company's audit committee establish procedures for the collection and treatment of such complaints. The Occupational Safety and Health Administration (OSHA), a division of U.S. Department of Labor, is assigned the responsibility of hearing, investigating, and adjudicating charges of retaliation.[21] Pursuant to the passage of SOX, concerned employees are enabled to report financial and accounting irregularities as well as fraud without fear of suffering demotion, suspension, harassment, threats, loss of job, or any other form of retribution.

   To effectively implement provisions of SOX pertaining to whistleblowers, public companies should establish procedures that enable employees to anonymously report suspected incidents of misconduct. These programs and procedures encompass establishing an effective hotline with a toll-free number and the capability to accept collect calls, a fax number, a regular mail address or post office box, and a confidential Web site.

7. **Enterprise risk management.** The audit committee is responsible for overseeing the company's enterprise risk management and making sure it is suitable in identifying business events and transactions, their related risks, management risk tolerance, and actions taken to monitor and minimize risks threatening the integrity of financial reports.

8. **Financial statement fraud.** A 2003 KPMG Forensic Fraud Survey indicates that although financial statement fraud accounts for a small percentage (about 7 percent)

of total fraud occurrence, it constitutes a majority of the total costs.[22] Some of the factors that contribute to the occurrence of financial statement fraud are a lack of vigilant oversight by the board of directors, ineffective internal controls, and collusion between management and employees.

Audit Committee Meetings

Audit committee meetings should provide a forum for candid, open, and constructive dialogue between committee members, management, internal auditors, and external auditors. The committee's chair should set the tone for the nature, flow, agenda, frequency, and length of these meetings. The question of whether the company's CEO or CFO and the lead partner of its independent public accounting firm should attend every audit committee meeting has been extensively debated. The presence of the company's CEO or CFO at meetings can signal the commitment of senior executives to effective audit committee oversight functions as well as underscore the importance of those meetings. The presence of senior executives at all regular audit committee meetings, however, may prevent open and candid dialogue between the independent auditor and the audit committee or undermine the authority of the committee chair. Thus, the answer depends on the attitude of the company's audit committee and how the presence of senior executives is viewed.

A combination of formal audit committee meetings with the presence of senior executives and executive meetings with just internal and/or external auditors should improve the effectiveness of audit committee oversight functions. The perception of internal auditors as the "eyes and ears" of the audit committee suggests that the head of the internal audit department, also known as the CAE, should attend all formal audit committee meetings. The emergence of the integrated audit of financial statements and ICFR underscores the importance of the attendance of the company's lead partner in all important formal audit committee meetings, particularly those pertaining to the oversight function of financial risk, ICFR, and audit activities directly affecting the integrity and transparency of financial statements audited by independent public accountants.

The frequency of audit committee meetings and how members participate in those meetings depend on the extent of the committee's involvement in the company's oversight functions, responsibilities assigned to the audit committee, and activities undertaken by the committee. The audit committee should meet at least four times a year to review the company's quarterly financial reports and as needed to address other important issues. The quality and quantity of meetings can have a significant impact on the effectiveness of fulfilling its oversight responsibilities. Those individuals who should typically participate in meetings are all members of the audit committee, senior executives, internal auditors, external auditors, and others who can contribute to or be responsible for issues discussed in the meetings. The committee should also have private or executive meetings with both internal and external auditors as needed when there are major issues that would be better addressed without management's presence.

Audit Committee Agenda

The audit committee should have a well-defined, written agenda for all of its meetings. The agenda should cover (1) the minutes of the previous meeting; (2) a review of current financial statements, the related audit report, complex and unusual transactions, accounting policies, valuation of assets, determination of liabilities, and estimates of reserves; (3) a review of the current management, independent auditor reports on ICFR including identified material weaknesses in internal control, and the management responses to reported material weaknesses; (4) a review of the established whistleblower programs and the appropriate responses to those complaints; (5) a review of the company's enterprise risk management to ensure objectives are defined, risks are assessed, and procedures are designed to minimize risks; and (6) a review of internal auditors, external auditors, audit plans, scope, and findings. The effectiveness of audit committees is often impaired by focusing too much on administrative-type matters and too little on material critical accounting or related issues that affect strategic decisions, corporate governance, financial reporting, and audit functions.

Audit Committee Reporting

There are typically three audit committee reports. First, the audit committee should provide regular reports or minutes of its meetings to the company's board of directors describing the committee's agenda, activities, deliberations, and recommendations. Second, in addition to this regular report to the board, the committee should submit a formal annual report to the board of directors, summarizing its authorities, duties, oversight responsibilities, resources, funding, performance, recommendations, and deliberations for the past year and its agenda for the coming year. Third, the audit committee should prepare and submit a formal annual report to the shareholders, stating that (1) financial standards prepared in accordance with GAAP are included in the annual report on Form 10-K or Form 10-KSB, (2) the committee has adopted a charter and has satisfied its oversight responsibilities as specified in the proxy statement, (3) the committee has reviewed the audited financial statements with management, (4) the committee discussed with the independent auditor those matters required to be communicated to the committee in accordance with generally accepted auditing standards (GAAS), and (5) the committee received the independent disclosures from the independent auditor and discussed the matters relevant to auditor independence. Audit committee reports to shareholders further discuss (1) management and the independent auditor reports on ICFR; (2) the committee's oversight responsibility over internal controls; (3) preapproval policies and procedures for both audit and nonaudit services; (4) whistleblower programs; and (5) committee involvement in hiring, retaining, and overseeing the work of independent auditors, an overall assessment of audit quality, and the effectiveness of the independent audit of financial statements.

The audit committee's reporting responsibilities are primarily to the board of directors and shareholders, even though the committee should communicate with a variety of corporate governance participants, including management, internal auditors, legal counsel, financial advisors, and external auditors. The committee should report regularly to the company's board of directors regarding its activities, findings, recommendations, and meetings. The format and content of the audit committee report depends on the size of the audit committee, its assumed oversight responsibilities, the number of meetings during the year, and the number of designated financial experts (a minimum of one).

A typical report to shareholders consists of several paragraphs. The first paragraph describes the formation and composition of the audit committee. The second paragraph describes the responsibilities of the company's management, the independent auditor, and the audit committee pertaining to ICFR and the preparation of financial statements. Paragraph three states that the committee has met with both management and the independent auditor to discuss the preparation of financial statements in conformity with GAAP and the performance of a financial audit in accordance with GAAS. This paragraph also explains the committee's communication of accounting, auditing, and internal control issues with both management and the independent auditor. The fourth paragraph addresses auditor independence. This paragraph states that the independent auditor has provided to the committee the written disclosures required by the Independent Standard Board Standard No. 1 and has discussed auditor independence with the external auditor. This paragraph also describes provisions of nonaudit services that are compatible with maintaining auditor independence. The final paragraph states that, based on the audit committee's discussion with management and the independent auditor, the committee recommended that the board of directors include audited financial statements in its filings with the SEC on Form 10-K.

Legal Liability of Audit Committees

The enhanced oversight responsibility of the audit committee may create new legal exposures for the committee. In addition, audit committees are now under increased scrutiny by regulators, standard setters, shareholders, and corporate governance activists. This potential for increased legal exposure should (1) not adversely impact committee members' decision-making attitude and process in the sense that members should continue to base their decisions and actions on sound and justifiable professional standards, ethical behavior, and professional judgments; (2) encourage proper documentation of the committee's agenda; and (3) stress the retention of detailed meeting minutes and deliberation minutes of its oversight decisions and actions. It is expected that compliance with corporate governance reforms will enhance the effectiveness of audit committee oversight functions and thus reduce legal exposure. This compliance should also assist the committee in making informed decisions, which under the business judgment rule is regarded as fulfillment of fiduciary duty, in the absence of gross negligence, even if the decision is later proven to be incorrect.

Audit committees are expected to exercise due diligence in determining facts based on the information they receive from management and others and making judgments about events in which they have no expertise. Audit committee members can be held liable for breaking the fiduciary duty and be subject to litigation under state laws. They can also be held liable under the Securities Act of 1933 and the Securities Exchange Act of 1934 for the distribution of materially false or misleading information to investors. SOX prohibits directors from fraudulently misleading investors or trading during the pension blackout periods.

SEC rules provide the following safe harbors in addressing the concerns about the increased liability of an audit committee member designated as a financial expert:

1. An audit committee financial expert is not deemed to be an "expert" for the purpose of liability under Section 11 of the Securities Act of 1933.

2. The designation of a member as a financial expert does not impose liability, obligation, or duties above and beyond those of other members of the audit committee or the board of directors, nor does the designation affect the liability, obligations, or duties of other members of the committee or board.[23]

Evaluation of Audit Committee Effectiveness

Although SOX and SEC rules do not directly address audit committee performance evaluation, listing standards require that audit committees of listed companies complete an annual performance assessment, including a self-assessment by the full board. Listing standards of national stock exchanges require annual evaluation of the company's entire board of directors, each committee of the board of directors, and each committee member. In particular, the board of directors should evaluate audit committee effectiveness in fulfilling its oversight functions. The independent auditor assessment of the effectiveness of the audit committee oversight function of ICFR should include consideration of the following attributes of the audit committee: (1) committee members' independence from management; (2) the extent to which the committee oversight responsibilities are defined, articulated, and understood by all parties involved in the financial reporting process; (3) committee interactions; (4) the quality of issues that the committee discusses with management and the external auditor; and (5) responsiveness of the committee to issues and concerns raised by the independent auditor. The audit committee is also evaluated by management as part of its overall assessment of ICFR in compliance with Section 404. Thus, formal evaluation of audit committee oversight effectiveness is required by the company's board of directors, management, and the independent auditor. Informal evaluation of the committee's performance is often scrutinized by shareholders, corporate governance activists, rating agencies, and regulators.

Audit Committee Evaluation of External Auditors

Listing standards of national stock exchanges require audit committees of the listed companies to evaluate (at least annually) the independent auditor's qualifications, independence, and performance. The evaluation process includes a review of the auditor's quality control system, audit planning, staff assignments, the performance of the lead partner, an inspection or peer review reports, and the results of any investigation by authorities. The audit committee should pay particular attention to the nonpublic portion of reports in assessing independent audit performance and in making decisions to retain or dismiss the audit firm. This evaluation is intended to strengthen auditor independence, improve audit effectiveness, enhance audit credibility and quality, and protect investors from poor audit performance and audit failures.

COMPENSATION COMMITTEE

The compensation committee is usually formed to determine the compensation and benefits of directors and executives. To be effective and objective, the compensation committee should be composed of independent outside directors with sufficient human resources experience in compensation and related issues. This committee should hire outside compensation advisors that report directly to and are compensated by the committee to ensure objectivity. The recent debate over the reasonableness of executive compensations and the recognition of stock-based executive compensations as expenses has generated a considerable amount of interest in the formation and function of this committee.

The compensation committee is responsible for setting compensation plans that retain good directors and managers while motivating an optimal performance that creates shareholder value. Thus, to be effective, the committee should be independent from management. Furthermore, the IRS requires that the compensation committee must be composed entirely of two or more outside, independent directors for executive compensation to be considered tax deductible by the company.[24]

Listing standards of national stock exchanges require the compensation committee be composed of at least three independent directors with the primary responsibility of determining compensation for directors and senior executives.[25] The listing standards (1) provide guidance for companies in establishing their compensation policy and for shareholders in making their voting decisions; and (2) recommend that remuneration arrangements be determined based on financial performance (e.g., linking compensation to the company's business strategy and objectives). Furthermore, the NYSE prohibits cross-membership of compensation committees in the sense that an executive director of a company cannot serve on the compensation committee of another company, providing that reciprocity exists.

The compensation committee should be responsible for the development of executive pay, assessment of executive performance, and structure of the entire company's pay-for-performance programs subject to approval from the board of directors. The CII recommends the following principles and practices for ensuring the effectiveness of the compensation committee.[26]

Structure

The committee should be composed of all independent directors who rotate periodically, are knowledgeable or take responsibility to become knowledgeable regarding compensation and related issues, and can exercise due diligence and professional judgment in carrying out their assigned responsibilities.

Responsibilities

Committee responsibilities include (1) developing, approving, monitoring, and disclosing the company's executive pay philosophy, which considers the full range of pay components such as structure of programs, desired mix of cash and equity awards, relation of executive pay to compensation of other employees, policy regarding dilution, and the use of employment contracts; (2) vigilantly overseeing all aspects of compensation for top executives, including the company's CEO, CFO, and other highly paid executives of subsidiaries, special purpose entities, and other affiliates to ensure fair, nondiscriminatory, rewarding, and forward-looking pay; (3) implementing pay-for-performance executive compensation that rewards superior performance; (4) reviewing annually the performance of individuals in the oversight group (directors) and approving their bonuses, severance, equity-based award, death/disability, retirement, termination with or without cause, changes of control, and voluntary termination; (5) assuming accountability for the committee's operations, including attending all annual and special shareholder meetings, being available to respond directly to questions regarding executive compensation, reporting on its activities to the independent directors of the board, and preparing the compensation committee report included in the annual proxy materials; and (6) assuming the responsibilities for hiring, retaining, and firing outside independent experts, including legal counsel, financial advisors, and human resources consultants, when negotiating contracts with executives.

Proxy Statement Disclosure

The committee is directly responsible for ensuring that all aspects of executive compensation are fully and fairly disclosed in plain English in the annual proxy statement to enable shareholders to clearly understand how and how much directors and executives are paid, including salary and short- and long-term compensation incentives. The committee should properly disclose its philosophy that drives its policies. If the committee uses a criterion in determining compensation, such as the benchmarking of companies in peer groups, it should be properly disclosed. The committee should link executive compensation to the company's performance and provide transparency as to the extent of executive compensation, including the use of corporate airplanes, automobiles, and housing.

Compensation Committee Responsibilities

The role that the compensation committee plays in corporate governance is becoming more crucial as the issues concerning executive compensation are becoming more complicated and as the committee receives more advice from outside consultants. The relationship between the committee and its outside consultants is important, particularly when consultants provide advice to both the committee and management. Best practices recommend that the compensation committee (1) ensure that consultants are independent of management and provide objective and relevant advice to the committee; (2) retain and control all aspects and terms of the committee e-consultant relationship, including consultant appointment, retention, dismissal, scope of the work, and oversight and monitoring of work; and (3) allow, in rare cases, a consultant to perform limited services for management, as long as such services are properly disclosed in their reports to the compensation committee.

Responsibilities of the compensation committee can be generalized into four categories: (1) evaluating the performance of directors, (2) evaluating the performance of executives, (3) designing and implementing compensation plans for directors and executives, and (4) disclosing the work of the committee.

1. Evaluation of directors. Assessment of individual director performance is very sensitive and often subjective, primarily because of the lack of authoritative guidelines for the evaluation. Some of the generally accepted benchmarks for the entire board evaluation are (a) fulfillment of oversight functions, (b) transparency and accountability of oversight functions, (c) oversight of conflicts of interest, (d) establishment of goals and strategies, and (e) assessment of management's performance. The committees of the board of directors should be evaluated according to their assigned oversight functions and the fulfillment of their responsibilities. The compensation committee should use the following criteria in evaluating the performance of individual directors: (a) attendance at board or committee meetings; (b) the extent of preparation prior to meetings and participation in discussion at meetings; (c) availability and ability to provide advice and counsel to the company's senior executives, particularly, the CEO; (d) continuing professional education to keep abreast of corporate governance initiatives and reforms; and (e) level of commitment to the company in terms of time, effort, and financial interests (e.g., equity ownership). The individual members of each board committee should further be evaluated based on their governing ability, integrity, legal and financial literacy, strategic perspective, decision making and judgment, team work, communication, leadership, business acumen, and ability to ask probing, relevant questions.

Listing standards of national stock exchanges and best practices (e.g., CII, The Conference Board, NACD) require a formal annual evaluation process for the board of directors, each major committee of the board, and every committee member. A proper evaluation process can vary from company to company, depending on the independence of the board from the CEO, corporate governance structure, board composition, and executive power within the company. The purposes of evaluations are to (a) identify areas of concern and poor performance, (b) make constructive suggestions for improvements in the directors' oversight function, and (c) formulate a basis for determining directors' compensation.

2. Design and implementation of director compensation plans. The director compensation package should consist of both cash and stock ownership and is expected to increase in the post-SOX era as the time commitment required to carry out fiduciary duties also increases. The compensation committee should consider the following issues pertaining to the annual evaluation of the company's board of directors: (a) whether the evaluation should be a self-assessment or outside consultants should be hired, (b) whether the evaluation should be performed for each director in addition to the entire board and its committees, (c) who should oversee the evaluation, (d) what benchmark should be used to determine effective and successful evaluation, (e) how the board should document the evaluation, and (f) whether the evaluation or its synopsis should be disclosed to shareholders.

3. Evaluation of senior executives. Evaluation of senior executive performance is one of the most important functions of the compensation committee to ensure executives are working toward the achievement of the company's goal of creating shareholder value and protecting the interests of other stakeholders. The purposes of the executive evaluation are to (a) identify areas of concern and poor executive performance, (b) direct managerial activities toward achieving company goals, (c) align executive interests with those of shareholders, (d) ensure executive compliance with applicable regulations and ethical conduct, and (e) determine a basis for executive pay. Executives should be evaluated based on (a) motivation and desire to do the right thing, (b) professional accountability, (c) personal responsibility, (d) competence, (e) ethical leadership, (f) ability to represent shareholders' interests, (g) compliance with applicable laws and regulations, (h) personal integrity, (i) community outreach, (j) national recognition, and (k) other achievements.

To link CEO compensation to performance and bring it to today's business reality, the compensation committee should (a) calculate each component of compensation and tally it all up; (b) implement internal pay equity policies and ask internal audit or human resources departments to conduct internal pay equity audits; (c) use stock options as ownership incentives—not as components of current compensation—by preparing an accumulated gains and carried interest table to determine the total value of all options and other equity already delivered to the CEO and the incremental value of additional stock options; and (d) consider all components of CEO compensation, including retirement benefits in excess of that which would be payable under the company's retirement plan to all other employees, perks that the CEO may be receiving (e.g., jet usage), excessive severance, and termination payouts.[27]

4. Design and implementation of executive compensation plans. Proper design and implementation of fair and equitable executive compensation plans consisting of base salaries, annual bonuses, and long-term incentive packages can provide incentives and opportunities to retain competent and ethical executives and link their compensation to the company's sustainable performance. The compensation committee should determine whether executives are eligible for annual bonuses or benefits under long-term incentive plans. Annual executive bonuses should be based on relevant and rewarding criteria to improve the company's sustainable performance and to enhance shareholder value. Such bonuses are commonly paid in cash, but they can also be arranged for payment in the form of company shares to be held for a substantial period. These bonuses should have upper limits, be approved by shareholders, and be fully disclosed in the company's proxy statements. Long-term incentive plans can be in the form of shares granted, nonvested deferred remuneration, and nonexercisable options to be held for at least three years. The shares or options should be held for a significant period after vesting or exercise. These plans should be approved by shareholders, fully disclosed, and nonpensionable. As a general rule, only executives' basic salary should be pensionable.

Performance metrics typically used by the compensation committee include

a. **Earnings per share (EPS)**—EPS has been the most popular metric in both annual and long-term incentive plan (LTIP) bonus payouts. However, heavy reliance on the EPS metric can encourage share repurchases, is more subject to manipulation than cash flow, and may stimulate a greater risk appetite than is optimal.

b. **Cash flow**—Measures of cash flow, including free cash flow or operating cash flow, are relevant for inclusion in performance measurements. However, the use of earnings before interest, tax, depreciation, and amortization (EBITDA) as a proxy for cash flow is not a good performance metric, primarily because it can be easily manipulated through aggressive accounting practices. In general, measures of cash flow better reflect performance because they are less subject to manipulation.

c. **Total shareholder return (TSR)**—The use of TSR metrics in combination with other measures for evaluating long-term performance and LTIP payouts can be useful. However, TSR places too much emphasis on stock price, and as such, it may not be an appropriate performance measure for annual bonuses. Another limitation of the TSR measure is that it is more linked to board industry and market developments and less associated with the company's performance and its management. The relative TSR can be used, which is more industry specific. Any performance measure that is heavily dependent on share price performance thresholds tends to focus on stock price fluctuations that may not be associated with the company's performance or its directors and officers.

d. **Return metrics**—Return measures such as return on assets (ROA), return on equity (ROE), and even TSR are more appropriate if measured over the longer term for LTIP purposes and are used in combination with other performance metrics. Any executive pay based on return metrics can be subject to short-term fluctuations.

e. **Economic profit or economic value added (EVA)**—Economic profit metrics that incorporate cost of capital such as EVA, which is net operating profit minus the cost of capital, are rarely used in measuring the performance of directors and officers. These measures are designed to discipline capital allocation by discouraging growth strategies and spending programs that can erode a company's capital base.

f. **Revenue**—Reported revenue as a single performance metric can be designed to reward growth regardless of its merits and whether it is associated with the company's long-term growth strategies.

g. **Operational metrics**—Operational measures linked to operational goals and those specific to the industry can be a useful measure of directors and officers by focusing on the use of technology, promoting a total quality management approach, improving overall efficiency ratios, or maintaining strong asset quality. An example of an industry-specific operational goal is reserve replacement at oil and gas exploration and production companies, which could be important to the long-term health and credit quality of these companies.

h. **Qualitative factors**—Qualitative factors, such as the company's strategic goals and their incorporation into executive compensation structure, are regarded as valuable. However, companies usually do not disclose how qualitative factors are weighted into compensation schemes, making them harder for investors to understand and assess.

Public companies and their compensation committees should link performance metrics to their director and officer compensation structure, and tailor a combination of metrics discussed in this section to align directors' and officers' interests with long-term goals of their shareholders. In general, effective compensation performance metrics are those that are linked to the company's sustainable performance in shareholder value creation, are set at a reasonable maximum number of shares or options granted, and are in line with the company's long-term strategic decisions.

5. Compensation Committee Report. Compensation committees properly disclose in the compensation report, or include in the annual report, the following major aspects of the committee:

a. The composition of the committee, including the number of members, their names, qualifications, and independence

b. Committee policies and procedures

c. Compensation details of individual directors and officers, including salaries, bonuses, shares, and options

d. Shareholder approval of stock-based compensation plans and the costs of such plans

e. Accounting policies for the recognition and disclosure of expenses related to stock-based compensation

f. Means of contacting the company's board of directors, particularly compensation committee members

g. Shareholder advisory vote on executive compensation

SEC rules require proper disclosure of executive compensation without imposing or even assessing the nature and extent of the company's executive compensation. These rules are intended to assist investors in obtaining complete, accurate, and transparent information on executive compensation to make sound investment and voting decisions. SEC rules improve disclosure by requiring companies to (1) prepare and include the new compensation discussion and analysis (CD&A) in their proxy statements and annual reports on Form 10-K filed with the SEC; (2) refine their disclosure controls and procedures concerning executive compensation by gathering and analyzing the new, expanded compensation information; and (3) hold their compensation committee directly responsible for establishing executive compensation plans, getting the approval of the entire board regarding those plans, and disclosing the committee's authority, responsibility, roles, functions, and resources in its new Compensation Committee Report (CCR). The CCR, which is effectively modeled on the required Audit Committee Report (ACR), must be furnished—not filed—and should contain the following two statements: (1) whether the compensation committee has reviewed and discussed the CD&A with management; and (2) whether the compensation committee, based on its review and discussions, recommends to the board of directors that the CD&A be included in the company's annual report on Form 10-K and proxy statement.

SEC rules on executive compensation are intended to ensure shareholders and other users of financial statements receive complete, accurate, and transparent disclosures regarding related issues. These disclosure requirements pertain to executive and director compensation, related person transactions, security ownership of officers and directors, director independence, and other corporate governance matters. These rules do not suggest or regulate how much executives should be paid. Public companies are required to file the company's CD&A with the SEC. The guidelines on developing the CD&A are principles based, which should be tailored to the company's specifications and cover compensation for past fiscal years, including the objectives, elements, and implementation of compensation policies and practices. Table 5.3 compares current SEC rules on executive compensation with prior rules. The two primary objectives of the new compensation committee report are to state whether the compensation committee has (1) reviewed and discussed CD&A with management, and (2) recommended that the CD&A be included in Form 10-K. This report is "furnished to" not "filed with" the SEC and, as such, is not covered by executive certifications. The primary purpose of the CD&A is to accurately disclose the board's process of determining executive compensation and making it transparent to shareholders.

CORPORATE GOVERNANCE COMMITTEE

The corporate governance committee should be composed of both executive and nonexecutive directors and be responsible for developing and monitoring the company's governance principles, including the roles and responsibilities of directors and officers. The governance committee should ensure a proper power sharing balance between the board and management, the board and shareholders, and management and shareholders, as defined by state and federal statutes. The committee should describe job descriptions and responsibilities for the chairperson of the board or lead director, each of the board committees and their members, and the CEO. The committee should have executive sessions with and without the CEO present to discuss strategic decisions.

Table 5.3   Comparison of Prior Rules with New Rules on Executive Compensation

	Prior rules	New rules
Scope	CEO and the four other most highly compensated executive officers	Principal executive officer (PEO), principal financial officer (PFO), and the three other most highly compensated executive officers
Disclosures/tables	Disclosure of Board Compensation Committee Report on Executive Compensation	Older Compensation Committee Report eliminated; replaced by (1) new Compensation Committee Report, and (2) narrative Compensation Discussion and Analysis section
	Audit Committee Report required under Item 306 of Regulation S-K	No changes to format; moved to disclosure under Item 407(d) of Regulation S-K
	Performance graph required by Item 402 of Regulation S-K	No changes to format; moved to disclosure under Item 201 of Regulation S-K
Summary compensation table	• Salary and bonus • Other annual compensation • Dollar value of restricted stock awards • Securities underlying options/SARs • Long-term incentive plan payouts • All other compensation	• Salary and bonus • Dollar value of stock awards • Fair value of option/SAR awards • Nonequity incentive plan payouts • Change in pension value and nonqualified deferred compensation earnings • All other compensation (redefined) • Total compensation
Supplemental tables	• Long term incentive plan awards • Option and SAR grants • Ten-year report on repricing of options/SARs • Aggregated option/SAR exercises and FYE option/SAR value • Pension plan	• Grants of plan-based awards • Outstanding equity awards at fiscal year-end • Option exercises and stock vested • Pension benefits • Nonqualified deferred compensation • Director compensation
Severance benefits/change in control	Narrative disclosure of employment contracts and termination of employment and change-in-control arrangements	Narrative disclosure regarding potential payments on termination and change-in-control provisions
Other Director compensation	Narrative format	• New director compensation table • Narrative disclosures required
Related person transactions	• Disclosure threshold of $60,000 • Not required to disclose policies/procedures for approval	• Disclosure threshold of $120,000 • Disclose policies/procedures for approving related party transactions
Director independence/corporate governance	Various disclosures required by Items 306, 401, 402, and 404 of Regulation S-K	New and reorganized disclosure regarding corporate governance matters (i.e., independence of directors, compensation committee processes and procedures)

Source: PricewaterhouseCoopers. 2006. DataLine 2006-32: SEC Final Rule: Executive Compensation and Related Person Disclosure. Available at: www.pwc.com/extweb/pwcpublications.nsf/docid/A95E26B19C14026B85257245001342A3/$file/data_line_2006.pdf.

Responsibilities of the Corporate Governance Committee

The corporate governance committee should be in charge of establishing the agenda for the board of directors. Traditionally, management has controlled and dictated the board's agenda. The board has acted as a rubber stamp with inadequate discussion and often inevitably votes to ratify management's strategic recommendations. Many boards have not taken the initiative to direct management's strategic decisions. At many companies, the board's agenda is dictated by the CEO with inadequate information, shorter meetings, and less constructive discussion. The emerging corporate governance reforms require a higher level of board accountability. The committee should collaborate with the company's CEO in designing a mutually agreed-on agenda for board meetings. The governance committee can be formed to facilitate and coordinate the activities of the entire board and all other committees.

The corporate governance committee should (1) manage the agenda and the meeting by focusing on both long-term strategic and short-term performance issues, (2) review past agendas and minutes of meetings to ensure adequate time and discussion were devoted to each issue, (3) revise the agenda as necessary and set priorities for meetings, (4) ensure agenda topics are supported by relevant and timely documents, and (5) present briefing materials and supporting documents for the board agenda in advance. Each year, the committee, in collaboration with top-level management, should identify several top priorities for the board, including strategic direction, financing activities, investment opportunities, succession planning, and sustainable growth. These priorities should then be placed at the top of the agenda for board meetings. Management should submit recommendations for each priority, provide sufficient information and briefing materials in advance for each major issue, allow appropriate debate and discussion, and finally seek board approval on these major issues.

The corporate governance committee should also organize annual off-site meetings for directors to engage in face-to-face, one-on-one interaction with the CEO. Other board committees should coordinate their activities with the governance committee to provide continuity in governance, the nomination process, compensation schemes, financial reporting, and audit functions. Outside directors often have limited time to observe and comprehend the overwhelming information provided to them by senior management. Thus, it is the job of the corporate governance committee to ensure the right information is provided to the board by filtering excessive information or requesting more information when management attempts to disseminate too little information to the board. Management normally communicates with the board through CEO presentations or by providing briefing materials about corporate performance, operations, and legal and financial conditions. In either case, the committee should collaborate with management to ensure the right information is presented to the board at the right time.

The corporate governance committee should provide sufficient information to the board to enable it to effectively review the company's financial performance. The information should consist of both financial and nonfinancial measures of performance, its comparison with industry best practices, and the company's budget. Financial measures are (1) annual audit financial statements; (2) quarterly reviewed financial statements; (3) management certifications of financial statements and internal controls; (4) audit report on ICFR; (5) MD&A; (6) earnings releases; (7) management risk assessment; (8) budget performance;

and (9) other relevant financial information (e.g., mergers and acquisitions, research and development, related party transactions. Nonfinancial measures are (1) shareholders' and other major stakeholders' assessments of the business; (2) shareholder proposals and resolutions; (3) audit committee reports; (4) compensation committee reports and disclosures; (5) shareholder relations; (6) market share and positioning of key products, services, and brands; (7) customer satisfaction and retention; (8) supplier reliability and responsiveness; (9) employee satisfaction and turnover; (10) market share and proportion of the business attributable to new products and customers; (11) research and development investments and innovative measures; and (12) social, environmental, and ethical performance.

The corporate governance committee should be established to develop, assess, and continuously improve the company's governance structure, mechanisms, processes, and practices by (1) maintaining board independence; (2) ensuring directors receive relevant, reliable, and timely information to effectively carry out their oversight responsibilities; (3) working as a liaison between the board and management by providing opportunities for directors to express their concerns about the company's governance; (4) regularly reviewing the company's governance and recommending changes to the board of directors; (5) keeping the board updated on new corporate governance reforms, including legislations, regulatory developments, rules, listing standards, and industry best practices; (6) periodically speaking directly to employees other than senior executives; and (7) periodic evaluation of the company's social, ethical, and environmental performance.

Corporate Governance Reporting/Disclosures

1. Disclosures by public companies have traditionally provided little information about their corporate governance, including compensation of the senior management, CEO, CFO, directors, chairperson of the board, and corporate founders. Corporate governance committee should disclose more timely and transparent information about the company's governance, its board, top management team, and board committees.

2. The corporate governance committee should prepare an annual statement that discloses (a) the names of both executive and nonexecutive directors; (b) the designated audit committee financial expert(s); (c) shareholder election process, proposals, resolutions, and proxy access; (d) the strategic decisions that were made by the board in comparison with its planned agendas; (e) the board agendas for the upcoming year; (f) a brief description of the work of all board committees, including the number of meetings; (g) a statement from the audit committee regarding its recommendation that financial statements be disseminated to shareholders; (h) an explanation from management about its certifications of both ICFR and financial statements; (i) an explanation from management pertaining to material weaknesses in internal control and management's remediation actions; and (j) company initiatives on legal and risk management, including foreseeable risk factors and responses.

NOMINATING COMMITTEE

The nominating committee is usually responsible for evaluating and nominating a new director to the board, and it also facilitates the election of the new director by shareholders.

The committee may use staffing support provided by the CEO in identifying and recruiting the new members of the company's board of directors. An effective nominating committee can substantially reduce the traditional role played by the CEO in selecting new directors who may not be independent from management.

Responsibilities of the Nominating Committee

The nominating committee is responsible for (1) reviewing the performance of current directors; (2) assessing the need for new directors; (3) identifying and evaluating the skills, background, diversity, and knowledge of candidates; (4) having an objective nominating process for qualified candidates; and (5) assisting in the election of qualified new directors. The committee is also responsible for the proper composition of the board, including director's independence, skills, diversity, and commitment. The nominating committee should determine whether the entire board of directors meets the independence requirements set by listing standards in terms of the majority of directors (at least two-thirds) being independent. The committee should consider a well-balanced mixture of executive and nonexecutive directors. Both executive and nonexecutive directors should assume the oversight responsibility of exercising due care, loyalty, and diligence. However, in a real world board, the time devoted to the company's business and affairs, the knowledge of the company's governance and operations, the compensation received, and the liability assumed by executive directors are more than those of nonexecutive directors.

The board's nominating committee should lead the process for director election and evaluation of the balance of skills, knowledge, independence, diversity, and experience required for the election of new directors or reelection of incumbent directors. The committee should evaluate integrity and competency of the board of directors, its board committees, and individual directors. In addition to these attributes, personal characteristics of directors, including informed judgment, legal and financial literacy, high performance standards, and mature confidence, as well as the core competencies of the board, including accounting and finance, management, business judgment, crisis response, leadership, strategy and vision, industry knowledge, and international markets, should also be considered.

There should be an appropriate mix of personality types and experiences to generate proactive discussions of corporate issues and alternative courses of actions. Behavioral characteristics of a good director include the ability to (1) ask difficult questions; (2) work well with others; (3) use industry experience and awareness; (4) provide valuable input; (5) be available when needed; (6) be alert and inquisitive; (7) use business knowledge; (8) contribute to committee work; (9) attend meetings; (10) speak out appropriately at board meetings; (11) prepare for meeting; (12) make long-range planning contributions; (13) provide overall contribution; (14) assure responsibility and accountability; (15) learn about emerging corporate governance reforms and applicable regulations; (16) communicate effectively with all corporate stakeholders; and (17) support the company's economic, ethical, social, and environmental measures.[28]

Selection, Nomination, and Election of New Directors

The nominating committee should be responsible for selecting and nominating a new director. The company's CEO often serves on the nominating committee and thus can identify and recommend a new director. The nominating committee, with staff support from the

CEO or consultations with independent advisors, should annually determine the diversity, independence, expertise, knowledge, and other attributes needed on the board. Thus, a desired profile of the board should be used as a benchmark to compare with the existing board profile. The comparison of the desired board profile and the existing board profile determine the needed profile.

A pool of candidates who meet the needed profile should be selected, and their background, knowledge, expertise, diversity, and ethical status should be reviewed by the committee and their references checked thoroughly before being selected as potential nominees. The selected candidate should then be approved by the entire board before being finalized for election by shareholders at the company's annual meeting. The candidates should also be interviewed by the nominating committee to ensure that they are not only a good fit, but also have the time and interest to be an effective member of the board. Interviews of potential candidates with the nominating committee can be very helpful for the candidates to meet with existing directors, obtain greater understanding of the company's facilities and top management team, and better appreciate the opportunity to serve on the board. The company also benefits from this interview by providing an opportunity for management to assess the potential candidate and for other directors to get to know and finally try to convince the candidates to accept the directorship.

The candidates for directorship are normally introduced at the annual meeting of shareholders. The shareholders then vote to elect new directors who will assume the responsibility of representing and protecting their interests. The company's bylaws normally authorize the board to fill the interim vacancies on the board for the remainder of the unexpired terms, or until the next annual meeting of shareholders. Directors' terms usually begin and expire on the date of the annual meeting of shareholders and are specified for one to three years. Once a director is elected, the serving director often finishes the term, unless he or she is otherwise removed or forced to resign. Recent corporate governance reforms suggest that directors should be elected or reelected annually, with no staggered terms, to better represent shareholder interests.

Election of Directors

Election of directors is a vital role of shareholders in corporate governance because directors serve as agents. Under plurality voting, only one "for" vote will ensure the candidate seat on the board, regardless of the number of "withheld" or "against" votes. It may work fairly when there are more candidates than available board seats, and it can alternatively be ineffective when the candidate is ensured approval with as little as one vote. Majority voting empowers shareholders by requiring that the candidate be elected through approval from a majority of shareholders.

The issue of majority voting for directors' elections is receiving considerable attention and interest from shareholder activists. Although this issue is not a new phenomenon, recent corporate misconduct and related financial scandals have contributed to its importance and emerging momentum. Recently, the CalPERs board adopted a three-pronged plan to advocate majority vote requirements. According to CalPERs board president, Rob Feckner, "Majority vote will give shareowners the power to hold directors accountable for their actions and their performance, and elect the best person for the job."[29] CalPERs majority vote plan recommends (1) implementing majority vote policies at public companies through the company's bylaws and charter amendments, (2) making changes to state laws to implement majority vote where feasible, (3) implementing majority vote policies at the SEC and national stock exchanges, and (4) amending CalPERs Corporate Governance Core Principles and Guidelines to promote majority voting for corporate directors.

The currently practiced plurality standard allows directors to be elected if they cast one vote for themselves, even if the majority of shares are withheld from the nominee. The plurality standard is criticized for being undemocratic and unfair to average shareowners. The move toward majority voting for the election of directors has received a tremendous amount of attention and support from institutional investors on the grounds that it will (1) put real voting in the hands of shareowners; (2) democratize the corporate election process; (3) make the corporate board more accountable to and representative of shareholders; and (4) be in line with a majority voting standard of other developed countries such as the United Kingdom, Germany, Canada, Australia, and France. For example, the CII (e.g., American Federation of Labor and Congress of Industrial Organizations [AFL-CIO], American Federation of State, County, and Municipal Employees [AFSCME], Ohio Public Employees Retirement System [OPERS], TIAA-CREF, CalPERs) voiced their support for majority voting, whereas the Business Roundtable and others raised concerns about possible complications that could result.

Two types of amendments to the plurality voting system were proposed and voted on during the 2005 proxy season. The first type is to amend bylaws to switch from the plurality vote system to the majority vote system, which is referred to as the "majority vote standard." The second type is to amend the company's corporate governance principles by requiring that (1) directors who receive a majority of withhold votes submit their resignation to the company's board of directors, and (2) the board consider the resignation and make a recommendation. The latter type is regarded as "majority vote light," also referred to as "Pfizer-type majority withhold governance policy," and is criticized for failing to grant investors the right to vote "no," instead enabling the board to make the final decision.

Companies should integrate the majority vote system into their corporate governance structure by promoting shareholder democracy, empowering shareholders to vote "no" for nominees. Under the plurality voting system, directors encounter few, if any, challenges and little chance of losing an election.

Reelection of Incumbent Directors

Boards of directors have traditionally been staggered with no term limits. Although directors' positions are not tenured, there are usually no term limits in the bylaws. Thus, incumbent directors have traditionally been reelected unless they retire or are removed for some cause. The annual evaluation of directors should be the primary determinant of whether an incumbent director should be nominated for reelection. Several recommendations relevant to the proper and objective nomination of incumbent directors include

1. Having a mandatory retirement age for all directors. Currently, there are no laws, listing standards, or other external requirements mandating the standard retirement age for directors. Thus, public companies in following best practices should individually decide what mandatory retirement age works best for their directors (perhaps in the range of seventy to seventy-five years of age).

2. Using the annual board evaluation to assess the qualifications, knowledge, credentials, and changes in the status of existing directors and their eligibility to be nominated for reelection.

3. Using term limits for reelections of incumbent directors.

4. Requiring annual certification from directors to disclose any changes in their primary employment circumstances, potential conflicts of interest, and engagement in any illegal act or unethical behavior that could be embarrassing to the company.

5. Providing incentives and opportunities for directors to resign from the board prior to renomination and reelection in circumstances where the director performs ineffectively or engages in unethical conduct.

6. Encouraging shareholders, particularly institutional investors, to include their board nominees on the company's official ballot.

Succession Planning Process

The company's nominating committee should establish a routine succession planning process to ensure orderly succession to the company's board and other senior executive positions. The key features of an effective succession planning process include (1) a continuous process; (2) proper oversight and approval by the board; (3) CEO input, involvement, and collaboration as appropriate without dominating the committee; (4) an easily executable and adaptable procedure in the event of a crisis; (5) succession requirements aligned with the company's strategic plans; (6) aims to find the right leader at the right time; (7) the development of talent pools at lower levels; (8) a program in place to identify and professionally develop internal candidates; and (9) avoidance of a "horse race" mentality that may lead to loss of key deputies on the appointment of the new CEO.

The nominating committee in the post-SOX era has faced the challenges of establishing a more objective and transparent process of recruiting and nominating candidates who in turn are more carefully and thoroughly evaluating the time, commitment, risks, and rewards associated with directorship. The requirements that the majority of directors be independent and not have financial and personal ties to management make the nomination process more complex and time consuming. Thus, the nomination committee should give proper consideration to the skills, expertise, personality traits, and diversity needed on the board in light of the company's corporate culture, character, and strategic goals. The committee should be focused on a more effective and targeted recruitment process.

Nominating Committee Disclosures

Public companies should prepare a written charter for their nominating committee and make it available on the company's Web site or include a copy in the proxy statement. If the company does not have a charter for its nominating committee, it should state so in its proxy statement. If the company is listed on an exchange, it should disclose whether all members of its nominating committee are independent as defined in the listing standards. If the company is not listed, it should disclose whether each member of the committee is independent as determined by its board and consistent with the requirements of the listing standards. The nominating committee should establish policies for considering director candidates recommended by shareholders. If the committee does not have such procedures for considering director candidates recommended by shareholders, it should explain the board's justification and reasons in the proxy statement.

OTHER BOARD STANDING COMMITTEES

Public companies may form other standing or special committees to deal with issues requiring particular expertise. For example, a company may establish a finance committee to oversee its financing activities, capital structure, or strategic and planning activities. The board of directors may form a special committee to assist with special matters, transactions, or events. Special committees can also be established to deal with emerging issues such as environmental affairs, mergers, acquisitions, and investigation of alleged wrongdoing by directors and officers. Special committees normally dissolve on completion of their assigned tasks.

In a situation when the company's CEO is also serving as the chair of the board of directors, an outside directors' committee can be formed to maintain board independence. This committee should be composed solely of nonexecutive directors and should engage in advisory and oversight functions, whereas inside directors—including the CEO—assume the responsibility of managing the company. The chair of outside directors can be elected by the entire board, particularly by outside directors, and serve as the lead director.

Another example of a special committee is an executive committee that usually meets between board meetings to review and approve managerial decisions, plans, and actions on behalf of the entire board. The due process for a special committee is important as courts carefully scrutinize the process to ensure that the committee has a clear mandate, performs its responsibilities with due diligence, and is truly disinterested.

SUMMARY

New corporate governance reforms, complexity of business, globalization, and technological advances have encouraged the board to establish standing committees to best use the expertise, knowledge, and efforts of its directors. Several standing committees of the board have emerged; the most common being audit, nominating, corporate governance, and compensation. Other committees such as budget, finance, executive, outside, or investment may also be established by some companies. Listing standards require companies to have audit, nominating/governance, and compensation committees.

There has been increasing interest and demand for the formation of a diligent audit committee during the past several decades. An effective audit committee is an essential component of corporate governance in improving the company's financial reporting, internal control, and audit functions. The oversight function of audit committees has considerably expanded since the passage of SOX and SEC-related implementation rules. Thus, audit committees throughout the world are seeking guidelines and best practice benchmarks to effectively fulfill their oversight function in the areas of corporate governance, financial reporting, internal control, audit functions, and other activities.

The key points of this chapter are

- Listing standards require listed companies to form at least three board committees, including the audit, compensation, and nominating/governance committees.

- Board committees are usually formed as a means of improving the effectiveness of the board in areas where more focused, specialized, and technically oriented committees are deemed necessary.

- Audit committees act as guardians of investor interests by assuming oversight responsibilities in the areas of corporate governance, financial reporting, audit activities, and compliance with applicable regulations.

- The audit committee is one of the major standing committees of the company's board of directors and, as such, works with other board committees, company management, and external and internal auditors to effectively fulfill the board's fiduciary duties to all stakeholders.

- External and internal auditors are ultimately held accountable to the audit committee and should submit their reports to the audit committee.

- The determinants of an effective audit committee include diligence, independence, communication, responsibility, accountability, resources, working relationships, evaluation, functions, and legal liability.

- The composition of the audit committee, including size, independence, qualifications, and resources, can have a significant impact on its effectiveness.

- At least one of the members of the audit committee should be designated as a financial expert.

- Audit committee responsibilities may be grouped into the following categories: corporate governance, internal controls, financial reporting, audit activities, code of ethics conduct, whistleblower programs, enterprise risk management, and financial statement fraud.

- Audit committee reports to shareholders include, among other things, a description of audit committee responsibilities, its activities and accomplishments, and its self-assessment of how well it has discharged its assigned responsibilities.

- Responsibilities of the compensation committee can be generalized into three categories: (1) evaluating the performance of directors and senior executives, (2) designing and implementing compensation plans for directors and executives, and (3) disclosing the activities of the compensation committee.

- The compensation committee should be composed of independent outside directors with sufficient employment, compensation, retirement, and investment expertise.

- Listing standards of national stock exchanges and best practices require a formal annual evaluation process for the board of directors, each major committee of the board, and each member of the board committees.

- The compensation report should fully disclose the company's compensation policies in rewarding outstanding performance of directors and executives.

- The corporate governance committee should be composed of both executive and nonexecutive directors and be responsible for developing and monitoring the company's governance principles, including the roles and responsibilities of directors and officers.

- The corporate governance committee should be in charge of establishing the agenda for the company's board of directors to determine what the board should discuss with management and to what extent.

- The corporate governance committee should provide sufficient information to the board to enable it to effectively review the company's performance. The information should consist of both financial and nonfinancial measures of its performance, its comparison with the industry's best practices, and the company's budget.

- The nominating committee is responsible for the proper composition of the board, including director independence, skills, diversity, and commitment.

KEY TERMS

audit committee   nominating committee   succession planning
compensation committee   special committee   tone at the top
enterprise risk management   strategic board   whistleblower
governance committee

REVIEW QUESTIONS

1. What are the key functions of the nominating, audit, governance, and compensation committees?

2. What actions must be taken to make the compensation committee effective?

3. What are the key principles and best practices of an effective compensation committee?

4. What criteria or benchmarks are used by the compensation committee in the evaluation process?

5. What are the responsibilities of the corporate governance committee?

6. What issues should the nominating committee consider in the evaluation process?

7. What characteristics define a good director?

8. What are the key functions of the nominating, audit, governance, and compensation committees?

9. What is needed for the oversight function of audit committees to be effective?

10. Describe the relationship that should exist between the audit committee and management.

11. Members of the audit committee must be vigilant, effective, and informed. What are some characteristics that contribute to these traits?

12. What are some qualities or actions that can impede the effectiveness of an audit committee?

13. The text discusses the qualifications and characteristics of an audit committee financial expert. In your own words, define what a financial expert should be.

14. What are the positives and negatives of the CEO and executive management's attendance at audit committee meetings?

15. What disclosures must the audit committee make in its report to shareholders?

DISCUSSION QUESTIONS

1. To be effective, the compensation committee should be independent. Is the given statement true or false? Substantiate your answer.

2. Discuss the common-sense executive compensation program.

3. Explain the key features of an effective succession planning process.

4. Explain the views of executive compensation. Which one do you agree with? Why? Express your views on reasons for higher compensation for CEOs.

5. The text lists the characteristics that define a good director. Do you agree with these? Would you add any other characteristics? Defend your answer.

6. Search the library or Internet for the text of SOX. What does it require regarding the audit committee?

7. Briefly discuss the reasons that the audit committee needs effective working relationships with the board of directors, management, internal auditors, and the external auditors.

8. Listing standards require that audit committees be composed solely of independent directors. Do you agree or disagree with this? Why?

9. Best practices recommend ten audit committee principles. Identify five that you agree or disagree with, and explain your reasoning.

NOTES

1. Much of the discussion in this chapter comes from Rezaee, Z. 2006. *Audit Committee Oversight Effectiveness Post-Sarbanes-Oxley Act.* BNA Publications, Arlington, VA, Sections 1 and 2.

2. U.S. Securities and Exchange Commission (SEC). 2003. SEC Release Nos. 33-8220 and 34-47654: Standards Relating to Listed Company Audit Committees. U.S. Government Printing Office, Washington, DC.

3. Blue Ribbon Committee on Improving the Effectiveness of Corporate Audit Committees (BRC). 1999. Report and Recommendations of Blue Ribbon Committee on Improving the Effectiveness of Corporate Audit Committees. NYSE/Nasdaq, New York, NY/Washington, DC.

4. Sarbanes-Oxley Act of 2002 (SOX). Available at: www.sec.gov/about/laws/soa2002.pdf.

5. See note 1 above.

6. Public Company Accounting Oversight Board (PCAOB). 2004. Auditing Standard No. 2: An Audit of Internal Control over Financial Reporting Performed in Conjunction with an Audit of Financial Statements (Paragraph 17). Available at: www.pcaob.org/Standards/Standards_and_Related_Rules/Auditing_Standard_No.2.aspx.

7. Birkett, B. S. 1986. A Recent History of Corporate Audit Committees. *The Accounting Historians Journal* 13(2): 109–124.

8. U.S. Securities and Exchange Commission (SEC). 1940. In the Matter of McKesson & Robbins, Inc. Accounting Series Release No. 19. U.S. Government Printing Office, Washington, DC.

9. New York Stock Exchange (NYSE). 1940. Independent Audit and Audit Procedures. *Accountant* 102: 383–387.

10. American Institute of Certified Public Accountants (AICPA). 1967. Executive Committee Statement on Audit Committees of Board of Directors. *Journal of Accountancy* September: 10.

11. U.S. Securities and Exchange Commission (SEC). 1972. Accounting Series Release No. 123. U.S. Government Printing Office, Washington, DC.

12. New York Stock Exchange (NYSE). 1973. Response to the White Paper Questionnaire Concerning Recommendations to Shareholders and Related Matters. NYSE, New York, NY.

13. National Commission on Fraudulent Financial Reporting (NCFRR/Treadway Commission). 1987, October. Report of the National Commission on Fraudulent Financial Reporting. Government Printing Office, Washington, DC.

14. American Institute of Certified Public Accountants (AICPA). 1988. SAS No. 61. Communication with Audit Committees. AICPA, New York, NY.

15. Federal Deposit Insurance Corporation Improvement Act of 1991. Available at: www.fdic.gov/regulations/laws/rules/8000-2400.html#8549.

16. U.S. Securities and Exchange Commission (SEC). 2003. Strengthening the Commission's Requirements Regarding Auditor Independence. Available at: www.sec.gov/rules/final/33-8183.htm.

17. U.S. Securities and Exchange Commission (SEC). 2003. SEC Release Nos. 33-8177 and 34-47235: Disclosure Required by Sections 406 and 407 of the Sarbanes-Oxley Act of 2002. U.S. Government Printing Office, Washington, DC.

18. Sarbanes-Oxley Act of 2002 (SOX), Section 301.

19. See note 16 above.

20. Public Company Accounting Oversight Board (PCAOB). 2005, July 26. PCAOB Release No. 2005-015: Reporting on Whether a Previously Reported Material Weakness Continues to Exist. Available at: www.pcaobus.org/Rules/Docket_018/2005-07-26_Release_2005-015.pdf.

21. See note 4 above.

22. KPMG. 2004. KPMG Forensic Fraud Survey 2003. Available at: www.kpmg.com/aci/docs/Fraud%20Survey_040855_R5.pdf.

23. See note 2 above.

24. Internal Revenue Service (IRS). Code Section. Trade or Business Expenses. Section 162 (m)(c)(i).

25. New York Stock Exchange (NYSE). 2004. Listing Standards. Available at: www.nyse.com/regulation/listed/1022221392369.html.

26. Council of Institutional Investors (CII). 2005, August. Executive Compensation: Role of Compensation Committee. Available at: www.cii.org/policies/compensation/role_comp_committee.htm.

27. The Corporate Counsel. 2005, September–October. Highlights and Pitfalls: The New Standards for Compensation Committees—Our Updated Guidance. Vol. XXX, No. 5. Executive Press, San Francisco, CA. Available at: www.compensationstandards.com/Files/TCC/TCCSeptOct05.pdf.

28. Many of these characteristics are extracted from Brancato, C. K., and C. A. Plath, 2003, May. Corporate Governance Best Practices: A Blueprint for the Post-Enron Era. Report No. SR-03-05. The Conference Board. Available for purchase at: www.conference-board.org/publications/describe.cfm?id=674.

29. California Public Employees' Retirement System (CalPERs). 2005, March 14. CalPERS to Seek Majority Vote For Corporate Directors—Pension Fund to use Public Company Accounting Oversight Board Auditor Independence Proposals as Guidelines for Proxy Votes. Press Release. Available at: www.calpers.ca.gov/index.jsp?bc=/about/press/pr-2005/march/majority-vote.xml.

Chapter 6

Roles and Responsibilities of Management

INTRODUCTION

Management responsibilities are to ensure operational efficiency, financial reporting quality, and compliance with applicable laws, regulations, rules, and standards. Management responsibility in producing high-quality financial reports has received increasing attention pursuant to the rash of financial scandals by high-profile companies such as Enron, WorldCom, Tyco, Qwest, Global Crossing, Parmalat, and Refco. Laws and regulations including SOX emphasize the importance of an effective managerial function in corporate governance and financial reporting and the need for ethical and competent executives.

Primary Objectives

The primary objectives of this chapter are to

- Introduce the managerial function of corporate governance.
- Understand the roles, responsibilities, and duties of corporate senior executives, including the CEO and CFO.
- Identify the components of executive compensation and illustrate how each of these components relates to effective corporate governance.
- Identify the financial reporting requirements of public companies and SOX provisions that pertain to management certifications of financial reports and internal controls.
- Be aware of financial reporting challenges facing public companies including off balance sheet arrangements, aggregate contractual obligations, and critical accounting policies and practices.
- Discuss management's responsibilities for ICFR.
- Provide an overview of the costs and benefits resulting from Section 404 compliance.

MANAGEMENT RESPONSIBILITIES

Management, under the oversight direction of the board of directors, is fully responsible for acting in the best interests of shareholders for all managerial functions, including decision making, performance assessment, and fair presentation of financial reports. No corporate governance would be necessary if management acted in the best interests of shareholders and if corporate gatekeepers (board of directors, lawyers, and accountants) effectively discharged their fiduciary duties and professional responsibilities. Corporate governance is needed to avoid concentration of power in the hands of management and to create an effective system of checks and balances to appropriately balance power-sharing authority between shareholders, boards of directors, and management. The top management team, led by the CEO and supported by the CFO and other senior executives (controllers, treasurers, operating managers), manages the business and runs the day-to-day operations of the company.

Management is responsible for developing and executing the corporate strategies, safeguarding its financial resources, complying with applicable laws and regulations, achieving operational efficiency and effectiveness, and producing reliable and high-quality financial reports. Table 6.1 compares management functions pre- and postcorporate governance reforms. Management responsibilities described in this chapter are organized into the three areas of operating process, financial reporting process, and compliance process, with a keen focus on the financial reporting process.

Operating Process

The operating process involves the strategic decisions made by management to improve the efficiency and economy of operations, including developing visions, goals, and strategies to design, produce, and market the company's products and services. This process is considered as a value creation function that generates profit and thus enhances shareholder value. Management runs the operating process by analyzing the global markets and competition,

Table 6.1 Comparison of Management Functions (Pre- and Postcorporate Governance Reforms)

Prereforms	Postreforms
• Information asymmetry between management and shareholders • Focus on short-term performance at the expense of long-term and sustainable performance • Lack of transparency or timely disclosures in the financial reporting process • Lack of mandated disclosures on management's accounting policies and practices • Inadequate and ineffective disclosure controls and procedures • Misalignment of interests between management and shareholders • Imbalance of power sharing between the board of directors and management	• Public report on management's assessment of the effectiveness of internal control over financial reporting • Plan to comply with accelerated filing deadlines • Enhanced code of ethics for senior officers • Increased time and attention to corporate governance activities • Executive certifications of both internal controls and financial statements • Proper balance of power sharing between management, the board of directors, and external auditors • Improvements in MD&A • More timely financial information • More transparent disclosures of accounting policies and practices • Disclosures of executive compensations • Separation of the position of the chair of the board and the CEO

maximizing the utilization of essential and value-adding activities, minimizing the effects of nonessential and non–value-adding activities, and taking prudent business risks. The operating process entails (1) operating activities of designing products and services, marketing and delivering products, invoicing products, and servicing customers; (2) investing activities of investing in both human and capital resources; and (3) financing activities of funding investments and expenditures through internal growth, issuing stocks, or incurring debt.

Financial Reporting Process

Management is ultimately and directly responsible for the integrity, quality, reliability, relevance, and transparency of all internal and external financial and nonfinancial reports. Management understands that financial statements should be prepared from the perspective of shareholders who bear the ultimate financial risk. Thus, financial statements must report the true and fair presentation of the company's financial position and results of operations. There should be no earnings management to exaggerate earnings or misstate assets, liabilities, expenses, or revenues. Management should report both financial and nonfinancial KPIs that assist investors to predict the company's future cash flows from operating, investing, and financing activities.

Compliance Process

The compliance process involves compliance with all applicable rules, regulations, laws, and standards, including regulatory, legal, tax, environmental, social, and ethical standards and best practices. The interests and focus of the investing community and the financial markets have been and will continue to be on the company's economic and financial performance, but the company's social responsibility performance has received some recent attention. Management has been asked to provide sustainability reporting focusing on the company's compliance with social, ethical, and environmental (SEE) standards.

CORPORATE OFFICERS

The emerging corporate governance reforms create unprecedented and profound demand for competent and ethical corporate officers. The CEO, as an icon of the company's management team, plays a key role in the improvement of corporate governance. Many state corporate laws require a corporation to have a president and secretary. Corporations usually have a management team consisting of a CEO, CFO, controller, treasurer, and other key members, including chief compliance/governance officer, CRO, chief operating officer (COO), chief development officer (CDO), and corporate legal counsel. The role of the management team in the United States is to run the company and is generally vested by the board in the CEO. The managerial function in countries such as Germany is vested in the management board that operates collectively to carry out managerial responsibilities, where the supervisory board oversees the management board on behalf of the shareholders and employees.

Chief Executive Officer

The CEO is the heart of the managerial function of corporate governance. All other senior executives and managerial personnel look to the CEO for direction, guidance, and ethical conduct. The CEO sets the appropriate tone at the top by promoting effective functioning, ethical conduct, and professional behavior throughout the company. The long-term survival and success of the goal of sustainable and enduring stakeholder value creation are in the hands of the CEO. The CEO is in the driver's seat for taking the company on its long journey of success, growth, prosperity, failure, or bankruptcy. Thus, personal attributes, ethical values, and professional characteristics of the CEO should be in line with the company's board of directors' and shareholders' values, visions, and strategic plans. The wave of financial scandals and business misconduct raised serious concerns about the professional accountability, personal integrity, and competency of many CEOs.

Challenges Facing CEOs

This section presents key CEO challenges, including (1) fiduciary duties, (2) self-serving and self-dealing, (3) succession planning, (4) duality, and (5) financial knowledge and understanding.

Fiduciary Duties   Top management teams, including the CEO, CFO, chief accounting officers (CAOs), controllers, and other officers, are considered as agents of the company and its owners (shareholders). This agency relationship creates a fiduciary duty and relationship. One of these fiduciary duties is the duty of loyalty, which requires officers to act solely for the benefit of the company and its shareholders. This duty of loyalty obligates executives to not (1) act adversely to the best interest of the company and its shareholders, (2) compete with the company, or (3) use or wrongly communicate confidential information. Another duty is the duty of care, which requires the CEO to act in the best interest of shareholders. Breach of these duties entitles shareholders to a wide range of remedies, including a tort action against the agent for losses caused by the breach.

Self-Serving and Self-Dealing Several CEOs of high-profile companies have been indicted and, in some cases, convicted for self-serving, self-dealing, and engagement in fraud, conspiracy, and filing false financial reports. For example, Qwest's former finance chief, Robin Szeliga, pled guilty to insider trading. Former WorldCom CEO, Bernard Ebbers, got 25 years in prison for his involvement with overseeing the largest corporate fraud in U.S. history. John Rigas, the founder of Adelphia, received 15 years of prison time for his role in the fraud. Timothy Rigas, Adelphia's CFO, was sentenced to 20 years in prison. Calisto Tanzi, the founder and CEO of Parmalat, the Italian dairy and juice giant that collapsed in an $18 billion fraud, stands trial for the alleged market securities violations. Dennis Kozlowski, the former chairman and CEO of Tyco International was convicted of fraud, conspiracy, and grand larceny charges. Several executives of Enron, including Ken Lay (who later passed away) and Jeffrey Skilling, were convicted. These cases of executive indictments and convictions have greatly damaged the integrity and reputation of CEOs generally, while creating high demand for competent, ethical, and accountable CEOs.

Succession Planning There has been unprecedented CEO turnover in the post-SOX era as about 1,300 and 665 CEOs left their posts in 2005 and 2004, respectively. Given the recent high CEO turnovers, departures, and retirements, an effective succession plan is vital to the sustainability of many public companies. A 2006 survey of 1,330 directors conducted by Corporate Board Member and PricewaterhouseCoopers indicates that (1) 20 percent of the surveyed directors reported that their company did not have a succession plan, (2) about 23 percent believed that their CEO was uncomfortable with the topic of succession, and (3) more than 43 percent were dissatisfied with their company's succession plan.[1] The survey also indicates that the majority of surveyed directors (91 percent) believed that their CEO did not understand the value of such sessions, 7 percent reported executive sessions were not valuable to the board, and only 1 percent said that such sessions have started the board's relationship with their CEO. Effective CEO succession planning contributes to the sustainable performance of the company, the effectiveness of its corporate governance, better performance of the current CEO, smoother and seamless transition, and the success of the new CEO.

Duality The issue of CEO duality, where the CEO holds both positions of the chief executive and the chair of the company's board of directors, is extensively discussed in Chapter 4. CEO duality is still a challenge for many U.S. public companies attempting to establish a right power-sharing balance between executives, directors, and shareholders. It is expected that the trend toward the separation of the positions of the chairperson of the board and CEO will continue, eventually bringing the U.S. practice in line with that of European countries (e.g., the UK).

Financial Knowledge and Understanding CEOs in the post-SOX era are expected to have sufficient knowledge and understanding of their company's financial risks, internal controls, and financial reporting because they are responsible for the accuracy and completeness of both certifications of internal controls and financial statements. The fundamental issue relevant to the trials of several executives of high-profile scandals is the extent to which they had (or should have had) required knowledge of factors contributing to the scandals. Many CEOs of companies where accounting fraud has occurred have claimed that they knew nothing of the financial malfeasance that corrupted and bankrupted their companies. A defense of CEO ignorance about financial fraud did not prevail in the WorldCom trial when its former CEO Bernard J. Ebbers was found guilty of securities fraud, false regulatory filings, and conspiracy. This suggests that CEOs' pleas of innocence are not valid arguments of defense in cases involving financial statement fraud. In the post-SOX period, CEOs cannot plead ignorance of their company's financial reporting and finances because of new penalties for false filings and executive certification requirements of both internal controls and financial statements.

Chief Financial Officer

Traditionally, the role of CFOs has been defined as controllership, financial reporting, decisions support, and regulatory compliance. Emerging corporate governance reforms have refocused the role of CFOs in the new C-suite environment into both business and strategic corporate decision making. The role of the CFO has evolved from the traditional responsibility for the company's financial stewardship to a major corporate governance participant involved in internal control, financial reporting, and strategy execution.

The emerging role of the CFO in the post-SOX era consists of both strategic performance and reporting compliance activities. Users of financial reports demand high-quality, reliable, and transparent financial information and a comprehensive understanding of internal controls, financial reporting, strategic performance, risk assessment, and compliance reporting from the company's CFO. CFOs now are developing and assessing both financial and nonfinancial measures of the company's MBL performance of economic, governance, ethical, social, and environmental activities. CFOs in the post-SOX era step outside their accounting and financial role, participate in corporate governance, and assist the company's board in strategic decision making. Despite this current trend, the primary responsibility of CFOs is to ensure the effectiveness of ICFR, as well as the reliability, integrity, quality, and transparency of both internal and external financial reports.

Corporate Development Officer

Recent corporate governance reforms and increased investor scrutiny necessitate the establishment of a new position of the CDO, particularly for companies actively engaged in mergers and acquisitions. According to the Ernst & Young study, Striving for Transaction Excellence: The Emerging Role of the Corporate Development Officer, there is a need for another "C" in the C suites of corporate America: the CDO to assist the CFO to remain focused on financial reporting and compliance with applicable laws and regulations.[2] The study also presents several attributes of corporate development functions, including averting risk, meeting the emerging challenging transaction market, ensuring accountability, and improving performance.

Chief Risk Officer

Organizations of all sizes and types are facing a variety of risks concerning operating, financing, and investing issues. The enterprise risk management (ERM) framework has been used to identify and manage risks to minimize their detrimental effects. ERM enables organizations to implement a cost-effective and risk-based approach to achieve their objectives and foster accountability to their stakeholders, including shareholders. The CRO can significantly assist organizations with their ERM activities. ERM was originally used by organizations to identify and manage financial and litigation risks that impede production or negatively affect revenues. In the post-SOX period, ERM takes a broader strategic approach to promote corporate governance effectiveness of not only controlling risks but also identifying growth opportunities. A CRO can be appointed to oversee ERM overall strategies and proper implementation of their various policies related to financial risk, operational risk, internal audit, and compliance. The majority of financial service institutions are creating the position of CRO to manage their risks resulting from regulations, outsourcing, offshoring, mergers, and lending activities.[3] The number of financial institutions with CROs has increased about 30 percent since 2002. Public companies often combine the position of the CRO with the chief governance officer (CGO) position to ensure that their corporate governance policies are in line with the emerging reforms. The combined positions of the CRO and CGO can set a right tone at the top, promoting compliance with all applicable laws, regulations, rules, listing standards, and best practices of corporate governance, and ensure that noncompliance risks are managed.

Chief Internal Control Officer

A keen focus on internal control in the post-SOX period has necessitated companies to centralize their compliance efforts with internal control requirements. One way to synergize the compliance activities is to establish a new managerial position of the chief internal control officer (CICO) or to strengthen the existing position of CCO. In either case, the CICO or CCO should be primarily responsible for ongoing and periodic evaluation of internal controls. The roles and responsibilities of the CICO or CCO are to (1) provide the necessary standards and guidance to ensure actions taken by process owners (e.g., functional responsibilities) are adequate to support the year-end management assertion; (2) establish standardized documentation methods, including flowcharts, narratives, and control matrices to substantiate management certificates of financial statements and ICFR; (3) develop standards for ongoing development and approval of ICFR assessment and test plans; (4) develop protocols to consistently assess and fully understand control deficiencies; (5) facilitate the performance of the SOX compliance process; (6) take a central role in the identification and evaluation of change; (7) facilitate the comprehensive risk assessment process; (8) analyze business risk assessments; (9) oversee the SOX compliance process in identifying and assessing risks and related controls; (10) monitor test results on ICFR; (11) identify all testing exceptions and apply consistent guidelines to evaluate the scope and nature of deficiencies; (12) establish the most efficient and timely approach to remediation; (13) oversee remediation progress and retesting procedures; (14) analyze performance measurements and share performance benchmarks and achievements with the company's directors and senior executives; (15) establish tailored training programs for key stakeholders; (16) work with the IT function to use technology to manage the compliance process; and (17) work with all functional responsibilities to identify inefficiencies and plan improvements in the control environment.[4]

EXECUTIVE COMPENSATION

Executive compensation has been extensively and inconclusively debated in the literature and is now becoming an important aspect of corporate governance. Pay-for-performance decisions are an integral component of the monitoring function of corporate governance and an important way for shareholders to assess the performance of executives. The establishment of attainable, reasonable, and objective goals and proper structure of the company's pay-for-performance programs that reward executives for outstanding performance contribute to the effectiveness of corporate governance. There has been much discussion on the possible relationship between CEOs' performance and their compensation, and concerns about excessive pay. In 1992, CEOs were paid 82 times the average of blue-collar workers, whereas in 2004 they were paid more than 400 times the average. This excessive pay to CEOs, coupled with the perceived decline in their performance as measured by total shareholder return, has raised concerns about the equity and fairness of executive compensation

The extent, nature, and disclosure of executive compensation have been of great concern, have received extensive scrutiny, and are ultimately viewed as the directors' responsibility. Boards of directors have not adequately addressed excessive CEO compensation in the post-SOX era and thus encouraged regulatory initiatives. The board of directors and its representative, the compensation committee, should develop an effective, rewarding, and reasonable executive compensation program tailored to achieving the company's mission and strategic goals. The program should align with industry considerations and be subject to approval by shareholders through their advisory votes. Investors can obtain some information about companies' executive compensation by searching several documents filed with the SEC, including the company's annual proxy statement, the company's annual report on Form 10-K, and registration statements filed by the company to register securities for sale to the public.

Components of Executive Compensation

Executive compensation includes salary; annual incentive compensation (bonus); long-term incentive compensation; stock option awards; employment contracts, severance, and change-of-control payments; retirement arrangements; and stock ownership.[5]

1. **Salary:** Salary is the major component of executive compensation and should be set at a level that reflects responsibilities, tenure, and past performance yielding highest value for the company. Executive salaries should be comparable with the peer group—the compensation committee should publicly disclose its justification and rationale for paying any salaries above the median of the peer group.

2. **Annual incentive compensation (bonus):** The annual, short-term, cash-incentive compensation plans should be designed to (a) reward superior performance that meets or exceeds predetermined and disclosed performance targets, and (b) align

executive interests with the company's objectives and strategic goals. Section 304 of SOX requires that executives repay incentive compensation to the company when they engage in corporate scandals, malfeasance, or fraudulent financial activities that cause restatements of financial statements or significant harm to the company.

3. **Long-term incentive compensation:** Long-term compensation plans are designed to retain productive and highly qualified executives, align executives' financial interests with those of shareholders, and reward superior long-term performance. The compensation committee should thoroughly evaluate the costs and benefits of long-term compensation plans to ensure that they are effectively designed and are achieving their intended long-term strategic goals.

4. **Stock option awards:** Stock option awards are considered as long-term incentive plans granted to executives to reward superior performance. Stock options grant holders the right, but not the obligation, to buy stock in the future and thus have costs to the company that should be recognized as expense in the income statements according to the provisions of SFAS No. 123(R).

5. **Employment contracts, severance, and change-of-control payments:** These payment arrangements should be made on a limited basis. For example, employment contracts should be provided only to a newly hired or recently promoted executive and not exceed more than three years. Severance payments should be made only in noncontrol change situations in the event of wrongful termination, death, or disability—not for poor performance, failure to renew a contract, or resignation under pressure. Several provisions of SOX directly or indirectly affect executive compensation packages: (a) prohibition of personal loans to directors and executives (Section 404), (b) reporting insider trading (Section 403), (c) insider trading during pension fund blackout periods, and (d) forfeiture of certain bonuses and profits.

6. **Retirement arrangements:** Retirement arrangements consist of deferred compensation plans, supplemental retirement plans, retirement packages, and other retirement arrangements specially designed for high-paid executives. The compensation committee should review these special executive retirement arrangements to ensure that they are in the best interests of shareholders and consistent with benefits offered to the company's general workforce.

7. **Stock ownership:** Executive stock ownership is a useful incentive plan and an important component of executive pay. The agency theory suggests that the level of executive stock ownership in the company may provide incentives for management to align its interests with those of shareholders as it approaches high levels, but may have negative impacts on other corporate governance mechanisms as management becomes entrenched. Academic research suggests that earnings quality may be lower at entrenchment levels of between 30 percent and 50 percent of executive stock ownership.[5a] The board of directors and particularly the compensation committee can alleviate these concerns by restricting executive stock sales, requiring executive long vesting holding periods for shares obtained through exercise of stock options, or mandating strong executive stock ownership requirements. The SEC's amendments will require disclosure of the number of shares published by the

company's management as well as the inclusion of directors' qualifying shares in the total amount of securities owned.[5b]

Executive Compensation Disclosure

On July 26, 2006, the SEC approved comprehensive changes in the disclosure requirements for (1) the compensation of directors and officers, (2) related person transactions, (3) director independence, (4) ownership of securities by officers and directors, and (5) other corporate governance matters.[6] To comply with these requirements, companies should provide greater disclosure in their proxy statements, annual reports, and registration statements regarding total compensation of their directors, principal executive officer, principal financial officer, and three highest-paid officers. Other requirements pertain to disclosure of the grant-date fair value of the stocks options, changes in pension values and nonqualified deferred compensation earnings, and the company's CD&A section.

The SEC rules on executive compensation are intended to ensure shareholders and other users of financial statements receive complete, accurate, and transparent disclosures regarding executive compensation and related issues. These rules do not suggest or regulate how much executives should be paid. The guidelines on developing the CD&A are principles based, and should be tailored to the company's specifications and cover compensation for past fiscal years, including the objectives of compensation programs, elements of compensation, and implementation of executive compensation policies. SEC rules improve executive compensation disclosure by requiring companies to (1) prepare and include the new CD&A in their proxy statements and annual reports on Form 10-K filed with the SEC; (2) refine their disclosure controls and procedures by gathering and analyzing the new, expanded compensation information; and (3) hold their compensation committee directly responsible for establishing executive compensation plans, getting the approval of the entire board regarding those plans, and disclosing the committee's authority, responsibility, functions, and resources in its new CCR. The CCR, which is effectively modeled on the required ACR, must be furnished—not filed—and should contain the following two statements: (1) whether the compensation committee has reviewed and discussed the CD&A with management, and (2) whether the committee recommends to the board of directors that the CD&A be included in the company's annual report on Form 10-K and proxy statement. The primary purpose of the CD&A section is to disclose accurately and completely the board's process of determining executive compensation and making compensation transparent to shareholders. Outsized executive pay will continue to grow until shareholders are empowered to easily replace directors through a majority voting system and to approve executive compensation packages via their advisory votes.

FINANCIAL REPORTING REQUIREMENTS

Public companies with more than $10 million of assets whose shares are held by more than 500 investors are required to file auditor's annual reports (Form 10-K or 10-KSB) and quarterly reviewed reports (Form 10-Q or 10-QSB) with the SEC. The SEC's role in corporate financial reporting, according to the 1977 Report of the SEC Advisory Committee on Corporate Disclosure, is to assure public availability of all corporate-oriented information (including financial reports) to the investing public.[7] In addition to filings with the SEC, public companies also disseminate both annual and quarterly reports to their shareholders. The basic information in filings with the SEC and financial reports to shareholders is the same even though the format and the extent of details provided may differ. Financial reports submitted to shareholders usually contain, in addition to financial information, nonfinancial information about the company's markets, products, and people, whereas SEC filings are normally more detailed financial information.

The annual report of public companies normally contains the following financial information:

1. Audited financial statements, including their notes
2. MD&A of financial condition and results of operations
3. Management certifications of financial statements and internal controls
4. Management's assessment of the effectiveness of ICFR
5. ACR
6. Independent auditor's report on financial statements
7. Independent auditor's report on the effectiveness of ICFR
8. Five-year summary of selected financial data
9. Summary of selected quarterly financial data for the past two years
10. Quarterly market data for the past two years, including high and low stock prices for common stock, dividends paid, and price earnings ratio

Two provisions of SOX pertain to executive certifications of financial reports. Section 302 requires the principal executive and financial officers of the company to certify each periodic (quarterly and annual) report filed with the SEC. This is also referred to as civil certification because the certifying officers may face civil liability for false certifications. Under Section 906, each periodic report containing financial statements must be accompanied by a certification of the CEO and CFO of the company. Section 302 executive certification contains several statements that both officers certify that

1. Financial reports (quarterly and annual) are reviewed by them.
2. Financial reports are materially accurate and complete.
3. Based on their knowledge, financial statements, including footnotes and other information contained in the report, fairly present in all material respects the company's financial condition, results of operations, and cash flows. The fair presentation of financial reports, including financial statements and other financial information, is broader than fair presentation of financial statements under GAAP.
4. The certifying officers (a) are responsible for establishing and maintaining the company's "disclosure controls and procedures" and "internal control over financial reporting," (b) have assessed the effectiveness of the company's disclosure controls and procedures within 90 days prior to the filing of the report, and (c) have presented in the report their conclusions about the effectiveness of disclosure controls and procedures.

5. They have disclosed to the independent auditors and the audit committee of the board of directors (a) all significant deficiencies and material weaknesses in the design and operation of ICFR, and (b) any fraud that involves management or other employees with a significant role in ICFR.

In the post-SOX period, management provides integrated financial and internal control reporting (IFICR). IFICR includes (1) management report and certification of financial statements, (2) management report and certification of ICFR, (3) the independent auditor's opinion on fair and true presentation of financial statements, (4) independent auditor opinion on the effectiveness of ICFR, and (5) the audit committee's review of audited financial statements and both management and auditor reports on ICFR. The quality of financial reports can be improved significantly by focusing on both financial and nonfinancial forward-looking KPIs. To improve transparency management should (1) report to stakeholders clearly and candidly all relevant financial and nonfinancial information on a broad range of the company's business attributes, (2) focus on critical information used in managing the business of whether such information is relevant and needed by investors to assess investment risks and rewards in making sound investment decisions, and (3) provide more timely and user-friendly information using the eXtensible Business Reporting Language (XBRL) electronic financial reporting format.

Small Reporting Companies

The SEC proposed its principles-based rules for smaller companies for so-called nonaccelerated filers—those public companies with a public float (market capitalization) of $75 million or less.[8] When approved, the new SEC proposal would replace the use of the term "nonaccelerated filer" with "small reporting companies" to cover all companies below the $75 million market capitalization. The small reporting companies' requirements are intended to make SEC rules and disclosure requirements more scalable to smaller companies in several ways. First, the proposal would scale annual filing requirements for about 1,500 smaller companies to only the latest fiscal year's audited financial statements (balance sheet, income statement, statements of cash flow, and changes in shareholders' equity) for the past two fiscal years. The SEC's current annual filing rules require all public companies regardless of size to file the audited balance sheet for the past two fiscal years and audited income statements, statements of cash flow, and changes in stockholders' equity for the past three fiscal years.

Second, smaller companies could choose by item whether to comply with disclosure requirements designed for the smallest companies over those that are intended for their larger counterparts. This would give smaller companies the flexibility to determine the proper balance of a high level of disclosure on some items and a lower level for others while maintaining a baseline of required disclosure. This so-called "a la carte" allowance and flexibility enable smaller companies to customize their disclosure requirements and inform investors that they may receive different disclosures from smaller companies compared with large companies. This allowance is intended to scale disclosure requirements to the attributes of smaller companies and make the imposed costs of compliance with regulations proportional for smaller companies, yet commensurate with the induced benefits. This allowance should not by any means be interpreted as "lesser disclosure" to investors of smaller companies.

Third, the new proposal would allow about 5,000 smaller companies to limit their disclosures of executive compensation to only the three highest-paid executives, whereas larger companies must provide compensation disclosures for their top five executives, including the CEO and CFO. These changes are designed to make regulatory compliance more cost effective, efficient, and scalable for smaller companies and relax some rules for smaller companies to enable them to revise capital without compromising investor protection.

Finally, the proposal would exempt some compensatory employee stock option plans from registration. Under the current SEC rules, companies with 500 or more employees, directors, and consultants who receive compensatory stock options must register if they have more than $10 million in assets regardless of their status as private or public companies. The proposal would exempt such requirements for private companies that are not registered with the SEC.

FINANCIAL REPORTING CHALLENGES

It is expected that financial reports in the post-SOX era will be of better quality, improved transparency, and enhanced reliability. Public companies, their management, and directors, particularly audit committee members, should be aware of areas of financial reporting that are most susceptible to fraud, manipulation, and improper earnings management, and ask the company's independent auditor to pay special attention to these areas. SOX directed the SEC to examine the past five years of its accounting and auditing enforcement actions (AAEAs) to identify areas of financial reporting that are most susceptible to fraud, abuse, manipulation, and earnings management. The SEC conducted its study of the five-year period of 515 enforcement actions for financial reporting and disclosure violations.[9]

The SEC study reports the following prevalent problems associated with financial reporting of public companies: (1) many of the studied AAEAs (24.5 percent) were involved in improper revenue recognition, including recording fictitious sales, improper valuation of revenue, and improper timing of revenue recognition; (2) almost 20 percent were caused by improper expense recognition, including improper use of reserves, improper expense capitalization, or deferral and other understatement of expenses; (3) almost 5 percent were associated with improper accounting for business combinations; and (4) the remaining accounting violations (26.6 percent) involved improper use of off balance sheet arrangements, failure to properly disclose related party transactions, improper use of non-GAAP financial measures, or inadequate disclosure in MD&A and other financial documents.

The SEC report finds that members of senior management were mostly responsible for the majority of the accounting violations. In many cases, the independent auditors failed to obtain sufficient evidence to understand the nature of those accounting violations and discover related errors and fraud. The study made several recommendations to empower the SEC to more aggressively investigate accounting violations to reduce the likelihood of their further occurrence. SEC recommendations are to (1) improve the quality of MD&A disclosures, (2) require public companies to report financial restatements in a uniform manner, (3) allow public companies to provide privileged information to the SEC without waiving any privileges on other information, (4) give the SEC authority to serve subpoenas for civil actions, and (5) provide the SEC access to grand jury materials. This section of the chapter discusses these and other financial reporting challenges.

Off Balance Sheet Arrangements Disclosures

The SEC in January 2003 adopted amendments to its rules to require disclosure of off balance sheet arrangements as directed by Section 13(j) of the Securities Exchange Act of 1934 and added by Section 401(a) of SOX.[10] The amendments require a company to provide an explanation of its off balance sheet arrangements in a separately captioned subsection of the MD&A section of disclosure documents filed with the SEC. The SEC-released guidance on MD&A disclosures in financial statements addresses the MD&A information that should be presented and how it should be presented in financial statements filed with the SEC. The guidance emphasizes disclosures of critical accounting estimates, liquidity, and capital resources in the MD&A. Companies must include in their MD&A sections pertaining to (1) reasonable explanation of their off balance sheet arrangements, preferably in a separately captioned subsection; (2) a table summarizing certain contractual obligations; and (3) proper disclosure for critical accounting policies and estimates.

SEC rules broadly define an "off balance sheet transaction" as any transaction or contract with an unconsolidated entity under which the company has (1) any obligation associated with certain guarantee contracts; (2) a retained or contingent interest in assets transferred to an unconsolidated entity or similar arrangement made with that entity for such assets (e.g., credit, liquidity, market risk support); or (3) any obligation including a contingent obligation under a material variable interest held in an unconsolidated entity for the purpose of providing financing, liquidity, market risk, or credit risk support, or engaging in leasing, hedging, or research and development services. This definition of an "off balance sheet arrangement" is broad enough to cover a variety of ways that companies often structure their off balance sheet transactions or assume risks or losses that are not fully transparent to investors. This definition pertains to contractual arrangements, and thus, contingent liabilities resulting from litigation, arbitration, or regulatory actions are treated as off balance sheet arrangements.

Aggregate Contractual Commitments

Public companies, particularly accelerated filers (market capitalization of more than $75 million), are required to disclose their annual reports filed with the SEC in a table with their aggregate amounts of specified categories of contractual obligations shown on a yearly basis. This disclosure is intended to provide information about the timing and amount of contractual obligations to enable investors to evaluate a company's short- and long-term liquidity and capital resources needs. Companies may provide aggregated categories of contractual obligations tailored to their particular business.

Disclosure of Critical Accounting Policies

Section 204 of SOX requires that public accounting firms communicate on a timely basis with the audit committee regarding all critical accounting policies and practices used by the company's management. Section 204 also directs the SEC to issue implementation rules regarding the company's use of critical accounting policies. The SEC in 2003 issued its final rules, titled Strengthening the Commission's Requirements Regarding Auditor Independence,[11] requiring disclosure of the following two aspects of critical accounting practices:

1. Accounting estimates made by a company as part of its accounting policies, including quantitative analysis of sensitivity to different assumptions

2. The initial adoption of an accounting policy that has a material effect on the presentation of financial statements

Public companies are required to provide the following disclosures for each of the identifiable critical accounting estimates in the MD&A:

1. Description: an explanation identifying and describing the critical estimate, assumptions made, methodology used, and reasonably likely changes

2. Significance: a discussion of the relevance and significance of the identified accounting estimates to the company's financial position and results of operations, and whether material identification of the line items in the financial statements is affected by the accounting estimates

3. Sensitivity analysis: a quantitative analysis of changes in line items in the financial statements and overall financial reporting from changes in the accounting estimate

4. Historical changes: a qualitative and quantitative discussion of any material changes made to the identified accounting estimate during the past three years, the reasons for the changes, and the effect on line items in the financial statements and overall financial reporting

5. Communication to audit committee: a statement of whether management has disclosed to the audit committee the nature, selection, and possible effects of the accounting estimate and the related MD&A disclosure, and if not, the reason for this

6. Identification of segments: a statement identifying the segments of the company that are affected by the accounting estimate

7. Segment-specific effects: a discussion of the effect of the accounting estimate on a segment basis similar to the companywide basis to the extent that a failure to present segment information would result in an omission that causes a materially misleading overall disclosure

Initial Adoption of Accounting Policies

The initial adoption of accounting policies is required when economic events and business transactions (1) occur for the first time and have a significant effect on the company's financial presentation, (2) become material that were previously considered immaterial in their effect on the company's financial reporting, and (3) occur that are significantly different from previous events and transactions. Initially adopted accounting policies are regarded as value relevant to investors if their adoption results in a material effect on the company's financial position and results of operations. If no authoritative standards or literature exists governing the accounting for the particular events resulting in the initial adoption of a material accounting policy (e.g., nonrecurring, unusual, extraordinary transactions), the company must explain its choice of the selected accounting principle and the methods used for applying that principle.

Disclosure of Changes in Existing Accounting Policies

SEC rules and accounting standards require public companies to disclose changes in their existing accounting policies and practices. Management must justify that the selected accounting principle is preferable to the existing one under the circumstances, obtain a letter from the independent auditor to that effect, and properly disclose in the financial statements the change in accounting policy, reasons for the change, and explanations supporting the newly adopted policy.

Acceleration of Periodic Report Filing Dates and Real-Time Disclosures

Section 409 of SOX authorizes the SEC to issue rules requiring companies to make public disclosure of their financial information on a "rapid and current basis." The SEC adopted amendments to its rules and forms to accelerate the filing of quarterly reports on Form 10-Q and annual reports on Form 10-K for most U.S. public companies defined as "accelerated filers." These accelerated filers are companies that have a public float of at least $75 million, have been subject to the SEC periodic reporting requirement for at least 12 calendar months, have filed at least one annual report, and are not eligible to use the SEC's small business reporting forms. The rules also require accelerated filers to provide additional disclosure about the availability of their periodic and current reports on their Web sites, including information on whether the company provides Web access to its Form 10-K, 10-Q, and 8-K reports free of charge. Accelerated filers have been required to file with the SEC their management's assessment of the effectiveness of ICFR and the audit opinion on ICFR since 2004, while such requirements for nonaccelerated filers are postponed to their 2007 financial reports. Mandatory reports on ICFR by both management and auditors are discussed in the later part of this chapter.

Non-GAAP Financial Measures

SOX addresses the concerns over the aggressive use of non-GAAP financial measures. Sections 401 and 409 direct the SEC to issue rules regarding conditions for use of non-GAAP financial measures. The SEC in January 2003 issued rules and amendments to address public companies' disclosure or release of certain financial information that is presented on the basis of methodologies other than GAAP. The SEC adopted Regulation G, which requires public companies disclosing non-GAAP financial measures to include a presentation of the related GAAP financial measures and a reconciliation of the non-GAAP financial measures to the related GAAP financial measures.[12] Regulation G is not applicable to a non-GAAP measure included in a disclosure regarding a proposed business combination or written communications.

In the spirit of Regulation G, a non-GAAP financial measure is defined as "a numerical measure of a registrant's historical or future financial performance, financial position or cash flows that excludes amounts that are included in the most directly comparable measure calculated and presented in accordance with GAAP."[13] An example of a non-GAAP measure would be a measure of operating income that excludes one or more expense or revenue items that are identified as nonrecurring.

Voluntary Changes in Accounting Policies

SFAS No. 154 requires companies that make a voluntary change in their accounting policies to apply the change retrospectively by revising prior years' financial statements rather than showing the cumulative effect of accounting changes as one lump sum.[14] Retrospective application of voluntary accounting changes is intended to provide investors with more transparent information about year-to-year earnings information and bring U.S. GAAP closer to international accounting standards. These financial reporting restatements should be distinguished from those restatements caused by corrections of error or fraud. Retrospective application restatements occur when (1) the company voluntarily changes its accounting policies and practices (accounting for depreciation, inventory); and (2) the newly adopted accounting standards require the company to change its accounting policies unless the use of the "cumulative effect" approach is otherwise permitted under the new standards.

Accounting Pensions and Other Postemployment Benefits

Several prominent companies have announced that they would go out of business unless they were allowed to terminate their pension plans. One example is Pittsburgh Brewing, which informed the federal Pension Benefit Guaranty Corporation (PBGC) that unless its pension plan is terminated, it will not be able to continue in business.[15] The application of existing accounting standards for pension and other postemployment benefits (OPEBs) has created misleading and meaningless financial statements that often overstate reported total assets. For example, in 2004, the S&P 500 companies reported $99 billion in net pension assets on their balance sheet while their pension plans were underfunded by $165 billion, indicating a total overstatement of $265 billion.[16]

The recent rash of pension defaults among industries has raised serious concerns about the future of the PBGC. It is expected that defined benefit pension plans will continue to weaken because of insufficient returns on plan assets. In 2005, the FASB added a project to consider guidance in SFAS Nos. 87 and 106 Employers' Accounting for Pensions and Employers' Accounting for Postretirement Benefits Other Than Pensions, respectively. In a unanimous vote, the FASB decided to split the project into two parts. In September 2006, the FASB issued SFAS No. 158, Employers' Accounting for Defined Benefit Pension and Other Postretirement Plans, which requires companies to recognize on their balance sheet the funded status of their pension and OPEB plans as of December 31, 2006, for calendar-year companies.[17] SFAS No. 158 is intended to improve the accuracy, completeness, and transparency of financial statements by getting the balance sheet to better reflect the economics of the entity's pension and OPEB plans. The FASB is planning to move forward with Phase II of its project, which could result in a comprehensive overhaul of accounting standards for pension and OPEB plans. In the second phase, the FASB would address

(1) recognition and reporting in earnings and other comprehensive income the cost of providing pension and OPEB benefits to employees, (2) measurement of pension and OPEB obligations under plans with lump-sum settlement options, (3) guidance regarding measurement assumptions, and (4) whether OPEB trusts should be consolidated by the plan sponsor. The first phase is regarded as a temporary fix of pensions and OPEB disclosure problems because companies are required to book only the net difference between the fair value of their pension plan assets and estimated amount of their plans' future obligations to employees, whereas the second phase will provide accounting standards relevant to the measurement of plan assets and obligations.

Principles-Based versus Rules-Based Accounting Standards

Several factors have contributed to the complexity of accounting standards over time. These factors are the growing complexity of business transactions (off balance sheet), the ever-increasing litigious business environment, and too much focus on a theoretical and rules-based approach rather than a principles-based approach to accounting standards. Under a rules-based approach, the accounting practices were criticized for leaving too little room for judgment to improve the quality and transparency of financial reporting and encouraging management to find loopholes to manipulate financial information. Principles-based accounting standards are expected to be more understandable, allow the use of more professional judgment by auditors, make it more difficult to structure transactions, and facilitate convergence in financial reporting. The principles-based approach requires accountants, management, and auditors to consider the substance of business transactions and principles governing them rather than their form and rules that may apply to them. Principles-based accounting standards should be established to provide faithful presentation of economic reality, be responsive to needs of financial statement users for clarity, relevance and transparency, and be based on appropriately defined principles that reflect a broad area of accounting.

SOX requires the SEC to conduct a study on the adoption of a principles-based accounting system in the United States. In 2003, the SEC issued its study that suggests that U.S. generally accepted accounting standards are excessively rules based, which could produce financial information that is inconsistent with the underlying economic substance of events and transactions.[18] Nevertheless, the study concludes that the exclusive use of a principles-based set of standards could result in inconsistent accounting treatment of similar transactions, a lack of comparability of financial results of different companies, inadequate guidance or structure for exercising professional judgment by accountants, and implementation difficulties. The SEC's study recommends a hybrid of focusing on an "objectives-based" approach in establishing accounting standards. The objectives-based approach (1) enables accounting standards to be based on an improved and consistently applied conceptual framework, (2) clearly states the accounting objective of the standards, (3) provides sufficient structure and details to make the standard operational and applied on a consistent basis, (4) minimizes the use of exceptions from the standards, (5) avoids the use of percentage tests to prevent manipulations of standards by achieving technical compliance while evading the intent of the standards, (6) holds management responsible for capturing within the financial reports the economic substance of business events and transactions, and (7) establishes objectives and an accounting model for business transactions while providing sufficiently detailed guidance for management and auditors.

The SEC believes that the objectives-based approach would also hold management and auditors accountable for assuring the stated objectives of the standards are achieved. The use of this approach would also enable the FASB to react more quickly to emerging issues and trends because of less need to focus on complex rules and exceptions. The SEC states that the use of an objectives-oriented approach also facilitates the convergence of U.S. and international accounting standards.

Conceptual Framework for Financial Reporting

Both the existing FASB concepts statements and the International Accounting Standards Board (IASB) framework were developed mainly during the 1970s and 1980s, and they have well served the standard setters, preparers of financial statements, auditors, and users of financial statements. However, these concepts may be less relevant in the post–corporate governance reforms era that suggests the use of a principles-based approach, and thus, they should be refined, updated, completed, and converged. In May 2005, the FASB and the IASB undertook a new conceptual framework project.[19] The purpose of this joint project is to revisit both the FASB and IASB frameworks for financial accounting and reporting by converging the existing frameworks into a common, globally accepted framework. The new conceptual framework is expected to use the principles-based approach in the accounting standard-setting process.

The basic structure of the conceptual framework consists of objectives, qualitative characteristics of financial information, elements of financial statements (assets, liabilities, revenues, and expenses), criteria for recognition in financial statements, attributes and units of measurement, definition of reporting entity, display in financial statements, and disclosure in notes and other forms of financial reporting.

1. Objectives—The objective of financial reporting is to report financial information that is useful in making economic decisions by users, particularly investors and creditors, and in assessing cash flow, prospects about enterprise resources, claims to those resources, and changes in them.

2. Qualitative characteristics—Both the FASB and the IASB define fundamental qualitative characteristics of financial reporting as understandability, relevance, reliability, and comparability, as depicted in Figure 6.1. The only difference between the frameworks is in ranking these qualitative characteristics. The IASB ranks them equally, whereas the FASB places them in a hierarchy, and neither considers transparency as a key qualitative characteristic.

3. Elements of financial statements and their definitions—Both the FASB and IASB identify elements of financial statements as assets, liabilities, equity, revenues, and expenses, and they provide interrelated definitions of these elements.

4. Recognition in financial statements—Both the FASB and IASB specify that for an item to be recognized in the financial statements, it must (a) meet the definition of an element of financial statements, and (b) have a cost or value (measurement attribute) that can be reliably measured. However, there are some differences between both frameworks regarding the recognition criteria (e.g., relevancy), and neither addresses the issue of derecognition.

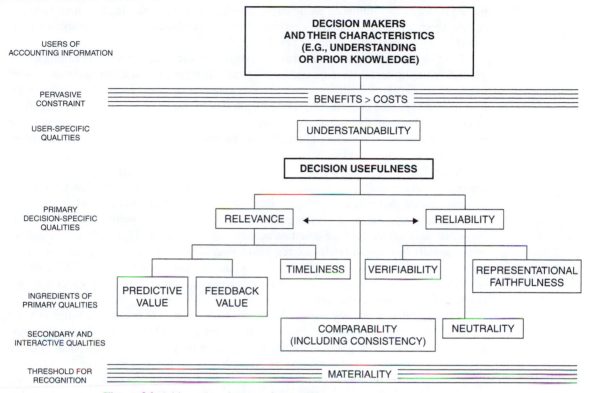

Figure 6.1 A hierarchy of accounting qualities.

Source: Reprinted with permission from Federal Accounting Standards Board (FASB). 1980, May. Statement of Financial Accounting Concepts No. 2, p. 20. FASB, Norwalk, CT. Available at: www.fasb.org/pdf/con2.pdf.

5. Measurement—One area in need of convergence between the FASB and IASB frameworks is the definition of measurement. The IASB focuses on monetary units of measurement, whereas the FASB emphasizes both the monetary unit and choice of attribute.

6. Reporting entity and control over other entities—There is a need for refinement and convergence in the definition of reporting entity as either an "economic unit" or a reporting enterprise.

7. Display and disclosure—Concepts of display (presentation) in financial statements and related disclosure in notes or other financial reports need significant refinements and convergence between the FASB and IASB frameworks.

Earnings Management

Management may have incentive to manage earnings and, when provided with the opportunity, may engage in illegitimate and fraudulent earnings management schemes. All corporate governance participants operate in a gamesmanship environment of continuous personal, financial, and political pressure. In the absence of a proper system of checks and balances, these pressures can influence participants' conduct. For example, management is under constant pressure to meet analyst's earnings forecasts, and management's compensation is based on improvements in earnings per share.

Earnings management is defined as a managerial discretionary practice of timing strategic and operating decisions (e.g., accelerating sales, postponing research and development) or choosing accrual estimates (excessive reserves) to manage short-term earnings. Earnings management is made possible and is often legitimately accomplished within the flexibility of GAAP rather than through noncompliance with GAAP. Earnings management with the purpose of creating misleading financial information or misrepresenting financial performance can constitute fraud.

Incentives for earnings management can be related to (1) market incentives for meeting or exceeding analyst's forecasts to prevent significant stock price declines following announcements that missed earnings estimates; (2) contractual incentives of maximizing managerial compensation or avoiding violation of debt covenants particularly when bonus plans and debt agreements are based on accounting information; (3) regulatory incentives of manipulated earnings to influence regulatory decisions (deflating earnings to avoid sanctions for potential antitrust violations); and (4) income smoothing incentives of reporting steadily increasing earnings to maximize stock prices, particularly when executives are compensated through stock options.

The capital markets may provide incentives to companies to manage earnings in order to meet or beat analysts' earnings forecasts to present a favorable picture of their prospects and thus influence stock prices. Earnings management may be perceived by some as being in the short-term interest of the company. Nevertheless, its pervasiveness can be detrimental to company value, ethical conduct, and managerial strategic decisions, and eventually cause regulatory enforcement actions. Management's conflicting incentives for manipulating earnings can be minimized by aligning management and investor interests and allowing management to own a significant portion of equity interests and by effective oversight of strategic decisions by the board of directors and the audit committee.

Management attempts to meet analysts' earnings projections have been viewed by many as one of the key incentives and causes of earnings manipulations and the resulting financial statement fraud. Management practices of providing forward-looking earnings numbers to analysts have also been under increasing scrutiny. Many prominent companies decided to no longer provide quarterly or annual earnings estimates because (1) earnings estimates distract management from long-term goals; (2) providing short-term earnings guidance prevents more meaningful focus on long-term, sustainable strategic intuitiveness and performance; (3) the current regulatory environment makes the practice of providing earnings guidance less wise or feasible; and (4) management's focus should be on sustainable shareholder value creation instead of meeting short-term expectations.[20] The use of quarterly earnings and other financial results can be detrimental to public companies' long-term prospects, the nation's economic growth, and the global competitiveness of the capital markets.

Financial Restatements

Financial restatements continue to be the major factor for the erosion of public trust in the quality of financial reports, particularly the quality of reported earnings. By addressing the factors that contribute to financial restatements (e.g., auditor independence, executive

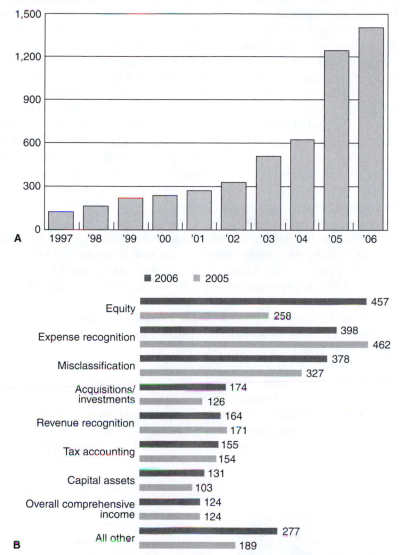

Figure 6.2 (Re)stating the case. **A:** The rapid rise in filings by U.S. public companies.
B: Restatements, by error category (reflects multiple categories in some cases).
Source: Glass Lewis & Co., 2003–2006, and Huron Consulting, 1997–2002.

compensation, management incentives, pressures), effective corporate governance can significantly reduce the number and magnitude of financial restatements. Figure 6.2 shows
almost a doubling in the number of financial restatements from 1997 to 2006, particularly
in the post-SOX period. Public companies in the United States made a record 1,420 restatements in 2006, with a substantial increase in the number of restatements by smaller
companies.[21] Figure 6.2 also reveals that the top three errors causing restatements in the
post-SOX era are related to equity, expense recognition, and misclassification, followed

by acquisitions/investments, revenue recognition, tax accounting, capital assets, and overall comprehensive income. More than half of these errors caused restatements related to misapplications of accounting standards, and books and records deficiencies. An overcomplexity in business transactions (e.g., derivatives, convertible debt) and related accounting standards and practices have also contributed to the occurrence of these errors.

Lawmakers, regulators, and standard-setting bodies have expressed great concern about increasing the number of financial restatements in recent years and the significant capital losses associated with them. The increasing trend in the number of financial restatements can be interpreted in several ways. First, corporate governance reforms created an unprecedented environment of extensive scrutiny that brings financial errors, irregularities, and fraud to light. Second, these reforms are a continuing process, and their full impact in preventing financial problems and improving the financial reporting process has not yet materialized. Third, for many public companies, 2004 was the first year of the mandatory internal control reporting under Section 404 of SOX, and more than 580 companies reported material weaknesses in their internal controls, suggesting ineffectiveness of their financial reporting process. Fourth, more public companies are now being audited by non–Big Four public accounting firms that have a greater restatement ratio (about 15 percent of audit clients) compared with Big Four accounting firms with restatement ratios of less than 7 percent of their audit clients.

About 10 percent of listed U.S. public companies restated their financial statements in 2006, which was up 13 percent compared to 2005.[22] This upward trend of financial restatements is worrisome, particularly if they are perceived as a sign of deficiencies in internal controls or unreliability of financial statements. Many of the reported restatements have resulted from corrections of accounting for leases, recognition of stock expenses under SFAS No. 123(R), and remedial actions taken to correct reported material weaknesses in ICFR. Figure 6.3 shows that the trend in the restatement rate for large companies that have implemented provisions of Section 404 is reversing. However, the restatement rate for smaller companies that have not yet implemented Section 404 appears to be an increasing

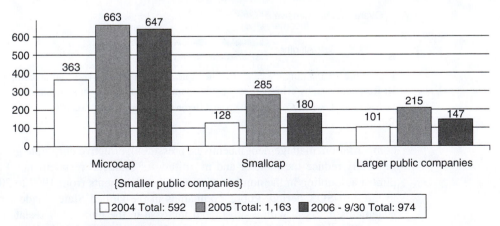

Figure 6.3 Number of companies that filed restatements, by company size.
Source: Glass Lewis & Co., 2006.

trend. This has been interpreted that Section 404 is working fine in reducing the number of financial restatements and thus improvement in financial reporting quality.

Convergence in Financial Reporting

Global competition and technological advances have played an important role in the move toward a single set of globally accepted accounting standards. In 2002, the European Parliament and the Council of the European Union adopted a regulation that requires all listed European Union (EU) companies to prepare their 2005 and succeeding consolidated financial statements in accordance with International Financial Reporting Standards (IFRS).[23] Regulation (EC) No. 1606/2002 was established to require the usage of a common set of accounting standards. The regulation intends to advance the efficiency and cost effectiveness of the capital market. Investors' rights and confidence are also at the core of this new regulation. The commission officially proposed the general adoption of international accounting standards (IAS) on June 13, 2000, in its publication "EU Financial Reporting Strategy: The Way Forward." Future IAS are to be known as IFRS, as established in April 2001 by the IASB. In addition to the naming change, IFRS were deemed the obligatory accounting standards that publicly traded EC companies should use. Adoption of IFRS into the EC requires that (1) it results in a true and fair view of the financial position and performance of an enterprise, (2) it is conducive to the European public good, and (3) it meets basic criteria as to the quality of information required for financial statements to be useful to users. The primary goal of the IASB is to improve transparency, quality, reliability, and comparability of global financial reports by issuing a single set of high-quality reporting standards for all companies throughout the world.

The EU Accounts Modernization Directive (EU AMD) requires companies to produce and enhance directors' reports in providing forward-looking information on KPIs, both financial and nonfinancial, including environmental and social strategies relevant to shareholders. EU AMD requires (1) proper changes to member states' national laws regarding the form and content of the company's accounts to conform with IAS; (2) a mandatory directors' enhanced review report; (3) an increase in the compatibility between European companies through a common reporting framework; (4) the use of common financial reporting standards that are transparent, fairly disclosed, properly audited, and effectively enforced; and (5) an analysis using both financial and nonfinancial KPIs pertaining to economic, social, employee, and environmental issues.

The ultimate convergence in financial reporting standards should benefit global investors and lenders when global consolidated financial statements are more comparable. The SEC, on April 12, 2005, amended Form 20-F to ease the transition by foreign companies (Australian and EU companies) to report under IFRS. The amendments provide a one-time accommodation for eligible foreign private issuers that adopt IFRS for their first fiscal year after January 1, 2007, to file two years rather than three years of financial statements prepared in accordance with IFRS. Two recent initiatives by the SEC move toward convergence in accounting standards. First, the SEC is exerting more control over the FASB by requiring a more formal role in FASB member nominations. Second, the SEC proposes to allow foreign private issuers to file financial reports using either U.S. GAAP issued by the FASB or IFRS issued by IASB. The SEC's proposal allows foreign firms to file their financial statements using IFRS without having to reconcile them to U.S. GAAP. This should reduce the regulatory compliance filing costs for foreign companies and encourage foreign companies to list in U.S. capital markets. It is expected that the SEC will eventually allow all listed companies in the United States (domestic and foreign) to use IFRS in place of U.S. GAAP. It is expected that the FASB standard-setting activities will significantly diminish or be limited to nonpublic companies on full convergence in accounting standards, which would produce a single, globally accepted set of accounting principles.

The SEC has recently taken two major initiatives to facilitate convergence toward IFRS. These initiatives are (1) a July 2, 2007, proposed rule that would allow foreign private issuers (FPIs) to file financial statements prepared using IFRS without reconciliation to U.S. GAAP, which was subsequently approved by the SEC in November 2007; and (2) an August 7, 2007, concept release discussing the possibility of providing the option to U.S. registrants, including investment companies, to prepare their financial statements in accordance with IFRS. It appears that U.S. GAAP will ultimately be replaced by IFRS as a single set of globally accepted accounting standards. During the past several years, more than one hundred countries have adopted IFRS as accounting standards for their financial reporting purposes. Some challenges that need to be addressed to facilitate convergence toward IFRS are (1) consistent interpretation and application of IFRS across jurisdictions, (2) the feasibility of adoption of IFRS by U.S. multinational companies in general and U.S. companies in particular, (3) the education of market participants regarding the differences between U.S. GAAP and IFRS, and (4) the effects of switching from national accounting standards to IFRS for regulatory filing purposes and auditing.

Complete convergence would enable countries worldwide to adopt IFRS in place of their domestic GAAP. The issue that remains to be resolved is the approach in adopting IFRS. Two general approaches are being suggested. The first approach is to require listed companies (both domestic and foreign) to use IFRS and thus bring financial statements, management assertions, and audit reports in conformity with IFRS. The second approach is to tailor all IFRS to the business, legal, and regulatory environments of the home country. Many countries have chosen, or are planning to choose, the second approach on the grounds that their legal and regulatory system requires conformity with national GAAP. The third approach is a hybrid approach of dual reporting in financial reports of stating conformity with the national GAAP and also compliance with IFRS. Countries currently requiring the third approach for their listing companies are Australia and New Zealand. Globalization and technological advances promote global investment and capital markets. Global capital markets demand reliable, transparent, and timely financial information generated under a single global accounting standard. Global financial reporting during the past two decades has transformed from the need for harmonization of accounting standards to reconciliation and now to full convergence in a single set of global accounting standards.

INTERNAL CONTROL REPORTING AND EXECUTIVE CERTIFICATIONS

SOX and SEC-related implementation rules require public companies to design and maintain effective internal controls and disclosures for assessment and reporting of their disclosure controls and procedures and ICFR. Disclosure controls and procedures defined in Rules 13a-15 and 15d-15 of the Exchange Act of 1934 are designed to ensure that information

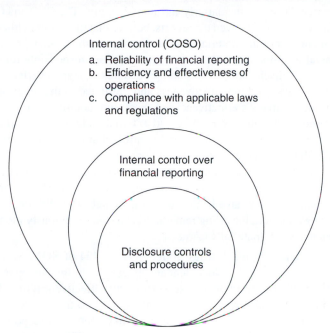

Figure 6.4 Internal control variations.

Source: Rezaee, Z. 2007. *Corporate Governance Post-Sarbanes-Oxley Act: Regulations, Requirements, & Integrated Processes.* John Wiley & Sons, Hoboken, NJ.

required to be disclosed in the company's Exchange Act reports is accurate and complete and is gathered, recorded, processed, summarized, and reported in the required time period.[24] ICFR is defined as a process designed to ensure that transactions are recorded properly in accordance with management's authorization and financial statements are prepared in accordance with GAAP.[25] Thus, the definition of ICFR is broader than that of disclosure controls and procedures in the sense that disclosure controls and procedures may include or exclude some components of ICFR, such as disposition and safeguarding assets.

The COSO report broadly defined internal control as "a process, effected by an entity's board of directors, management and other personnel, designed to provide reasonable assurance regarding the achievement of objectives in the following categories: (1) effectiveness and efficiency of operations; (2) reliability of financial reporting; and (3) compliance with applicable laws and regulations."[26] This definition is very comprehensive and addresses the four aspects of internal control as (1) the process, (2) individuals who affect internal control, (3) limitations, and (4) objectives. As is shown in Figure 6.4, the COSO definition of internal control is broader in the sense that it encompasses both ICFR and disclosure controls and procedures defined by SOX and related SEC rules.

Internal Control Over Financial Reporting

1. **Management responsibilities under Section 302 of SOX.** Section 302 of SOX requires management to assess and report on the effectiveness of disclosure controls

and procedures of both quarterly and annual reports. The CEO and CFO must certify that they (a) have reviewed the reports, believe that the report neither contains untrue statements nor omits material facts, and agree that the financial statements and other financial information are fairly presented; (b) are responsible for establishing and maintaining disclosure controls and procedures, designed such controls and procedures, and assessed the effectiveness and presented in the report their conclusions about the company's effectiveness of disclosure controls and procedures; (c) have disclosed to the audit committee and external auditors all significant deficiencies and material weaknesses in internal controls that could adversely affect the company's ability to record, process, summarize, and report financial information and also have disclosed any fraud, material or not, that involves management or other employees who have a significant role in the company's ICFR; and (d) have indicated whether there have been significant changes in ICFR subsequent to the date of their evaluation, including remediations of their previously identified significant deficiencies and material weaknesses.

2. **Management responsibilities under Section 404 of SOX.** Section 404 of SOX requires management to document and assess the design and operation of the company's ICFR and report on its assessment of the effectiveness of ICFR. This mandatory internal control report must be integrated into the company's annual reports and include the following assertions: (a) management's responsibility for establishing and maintaining adequate and effective ICFR, (b) the framework used by management in its assessment of the effectiveness of design and operation of ICFR, (c) management's assessment of the effectiveness of the design and operation of ICFR, (d) disclosure of any identified material weaknesses in the company's ICFR, (e) disclosure that the company's independent auditor has issued an attestation report on management's assessment of the effectiveness of ICFR, and (f) the inclusion in the company's annual report of the attestation report of the independent auditor.

The CEOs and CFOs of small- and medium-size and foreign companies still certify their ICFR under Section 302 of SOX for their 2004–2005 filings and onward. However, the SEC has postponed Section 404 compliance for smaller companies (market capitalization of less than $75 million) and foreign companies to their fiscal years ending on or after December 15, 2007. Quarterly and annual certifications of ICFR according to Section 302 present management assertions that there have been no material changes in internal controls, and any material weaknesses in ICFR have been properly disclosed. These certifications require proper documentation and assessment of internal controls by management and a justifiable basis for making such assertions. Section 404 requires management and auditors to test and report on the effectiveness of internal controls above and beyond the requirements of Section 302. Management's report on ICFR is presented here, and auditor reports on ICFR are discussed in Chapter 9.

Internal Control Evaluations

SEC rules do not specify the method or procedures that must be used by management in performing its evaluation of ICFR. Nevertheless, management evaluation should be supported by persuasive evidential matter consisting of adequate documentation of the design, operation, and review of internal control that provides a reasonable basis for the test procedures performed, the evaluation conducted, and conclusions reached. Management's annual assessment of ICFR must be conducted within 90 days of the end of the fiscal year and must be very thorough. Quarterly evaluations must also be performed; however, they do not have to be as extensive as the annual evaluation. Nevertheless, management must review and evaluate any significant changes in the company's ICFR that occurred pursuant to the annual assessment or during a fiscal quarter that has materially affected the company's ICFR, including corrections of material weaknesses identified by management or in the audit report.

SEC rules require public companies to identify the evaluation framework used by the company's management in assessing the effectiveness of ICFR. The selected framework must be established by a group exercising diligence or due process, and tailored to the company's circumstances. The framework must (1) be free from bias, (2) permit reasonably consistent qualitative and quantitative measures of ICFR, (3) be sufficiently complete by including all relevant factors that may influence the effectiveness of the company's ICFR, and (4) be relevant to a thorough evaluation of internal control. The internal control evaluation framework developed by COSO in 1992 meets the aforementioned criteria of the SEC for a suitable evaluation framework. Other frameworks are being developed in the United States and abroad.

Section 404 Costs

Two types of costs are associated with Section 404 compliance. The first category of costs is the cost of compliance of Section 404, SEC implementation rules, and PCAOB auditing standards to bring internal control effectiveness in line with these requirements. These costs are viewed as one-time start-up costs that have been significant for companies with inadequate and ineffective internal control structure, causing them to spend substantial financial and human resources in designing, implementing, and operating the required internal controls. The second category of costs relates to the initial assessment, documentation, attestation, and reporting on compliance with both Sections 302 and 404. The second category consists of costs pertaining to ongoing, year-after-year, continuous monitoring of both the design and operation of internal controls and the continuous documentation, assessment, testing, and reporting requirements.

A study shows that SOX has increased auditing costs by $1.4 billion for Fortune 1000 firms in 2004, which can be attributed largely to Section 404 compliance on internal controls.[27] The SEC previously estimated that the cost of auditing internal controls under Section 404 would be $91,000 on average; *however*, the actual cost of auditing ICFR is in the range of $1.5 million to $10 million, with an average of $2.6 million for Fortune 1000 companies. A 2006 survey of Financial Executives International (FEI) shows that the total average compliance cost of Section 404 during fiscal year 2006 was $2.9 million, which is down 23 (35) percent from 2005 (2004) totals.[28] The compliance costs have steadily decreased during the second and third years, which can be attributed to increased efficiencies in complying with Section 404. The substantial cost reductions resulted from significant decreases in both internal and external hours spent on compliance, while audit fees remained unchanged.

Benefits of Section 404 Compliance

The expected benefits of compliance with Section 404 are (1) more investor confidence in financial reports, (2) more accurate and reliable financial reports, (3) more financial fraud prevention and detection, (4) more effective ICFR that improves operating, investing, and financing activities, and (5) lower cost of capital.

The Institute of Internal Auditors Research Foundation conducted a survey of 171 prominent CAEs throughout the United States to determine costs and benefits associated with Section 404 of SOX compliance and ways in which the compliance can be improved.[29] The survey results indicate that Section 404 compliance has resulted in significant improvements in the "control identification, documentation, and testing process." The report lists the following "top 10" improvements that can be attributed to Section 404 compliance: (1) creation of a more engaged control environment resulting from active participation and commitment by the board of directors, the audit committee, and management; (2) recognition of continuous monitoring as an integral component of the control process with more thoughtful analysis of monitoring controls; (3) more structure brought to the year-end closing process and recording of journal entries; (4) implementation of antifraud programs and activities to prevent, detect, and correct errors, irregularities, and fraud, including responsibility for follow-up to resolve the issues; (5) better understanding of risks associated with electronics processing and related computer controls and the need to improve both controls and audit procedures to provide assurance that associated risks are properly managed; (6) improvements in documentation of controls and control process that can serve as a basis for continuous monitoring, training, and best practice guidance; (7) improvements in the concept and definition of internal controls and their relation to the organization with risk management; (8) better understanding of the internal controls concept at every operational level and reporting unit; (9) improvements in the sufficiency and competency of the audit trail as a basis to support operations and the assessment of the effectiveness of ICFR; and (10) new implementation of fundamental controls, including segregation of duties, authorization processes, and periodic reconciliation of accounts.

Sustainable Section 404 Compliance

It is obvious by now that SOX is here to stay, particularly in light of recent votes (April 2007) by the Senate against any amendments and revisions of provisions of SOX. The first two years of compliance with Section 404 have already passed for many public companies. The first year was viewed by many companies as the year of survival of a one-time project of compliance. PricewaterhouseCoopers states, "A sustainable approach to Sarbanes-Oxley requires a transition in both form and function—out of a 'one-time project' approach and into a mode in which compliance is well integrated into a company's daily operations."[30] In other words, companies should shift away from a project approach to a continuous process of integrating sustainable compliance into their corporate governance structure.

SEC Interpretive Guidance on ICFR

There is a general consensus that compliance costs of Section 404 are much higher than what was initially estimated by the SEC. After three years of costly compliance with SEC rules and auditing standards relevant to ICFR of Section 404, the SEC and PCAOB revised their rules and standards to make compliance more cost effective, efficient, and scalable. On May 27, 2007, the SEC unanimously approved its guidance on management's evaluation and assessment of ICFR as an interpretive release rather than a commission rule. The interpretive guidance enables the SEC to easily update or amend the guidance as needed and allows companies with effective ICFR processes to not have to change their procedures. The guidance is intended to preserve investor protection while improving cost effectiveness, efficiency, and scalability of compliance with Section 404. The guidance reconciles the differences between the SEC guidance and PCAOB AS No. 2 regarding the definition of material weakness, evaluation of control deficiencies, indicators of a material weakness, and the use of the term "entity-level" instead of "company-level" controls.

The SEC's interpretive guidance is designed to assist companies of all sizes in their evaluation efforts by allowing the flexibility necessary to tailor and scale the assessment processes to their company's facts and circumstances. This guidance is also intended to provide a cost-effective, efficient, and scalable approach to management's assessment of the effectiveness of ICFR by promoting the use of a top-down, risk-based approach to ICFR assessment, focusing on both materiality and risk considerations of financial reporting. The SEC's interpretive guidance centers around seven key themes of (1) management evaluation framework, (2) management's assessment of the effectiveness of ICFR, (3) safe harbor, (4) risk-based approach of focusing on significant risk, (5) top-down approach of focusing on materiality, (6) scalability of addressing flexibility to customize ICFR based on the company size and complexity, and (7) principles-based approach of offering very little prescriptive advice. The overriding principles of the guidance are adequacy, effectiveness, entity-level controls, ongoing monitoring, and fraud risk considerations.

Adequacy

The SEC's interpretive guidance requires management to assess the adequacy of ICFR by evaluating the design of the controls it has implemented to determine whether there is a reasonable possibility that a material misstatement would not be prevented or detected in a timely manner. This principle focuses on the adequacy of the design and implementation of ICFR by allowing management to focus only on those controls that are needed to prevent or detect material financial misstatements.

Effectiveness

Management should also assess the effectiveness of ICFR by gathering and analyzing evidence pertaining to the operation of the controls being evaluated based on its assessment of the risk related to those controls. This effectiveness principle allows management to align the nature and extent of its evaluation processes with those areas of financial reporting that pose the greater risks to reliable financial reporting.

Entity-Level Controls

The SEC's interpretive guidance provides adequate discussion of entity-level controls and their relation with financial reporting elements. Effective entity-level controls can have significant impacts on the nature, timing, and extent of testing. The guidance does not include extensive illustrative examples of entity-level controls in order to give flexibility to companies to tailor adequate controls in their IFCR.

Ongoing Monitoring

Management should consider the nature and effectiveness of ongoing monitoring controls on its assessment of ICFR. In a low-risk area, the evidence gathered on ongoing monitoring can be sufficient by itself and not necessarily demand periodic testing.

Fraud Risk Considerations

The SEC's interpretive guidance emphasizes the importance of fraud risk considerations by discussing that the risk of fraud exists in every company. Antifraud prevention and detection controls should be designed, and the possibility of management override of these controls, particularly in the period-end financial reporting closing process, should be considered.

Amendments to SEC Rules

The SEC approved three amendments to its rules pertaining to Section 404 compliance:

1. Elaborates that management's evaluation in accordance with the interpretive guidance satisfies the SEC's existing requirements for management reporting on ICFR.

2. Clarifies that the auditor reporting on ICFR expresses only one opinion on the effectiveness of internal controls. This eliminates the requirement for an auditor's opinion on management's assessment of the effectiveness of ICFR, which is regarded by many as having little, if any, incremental value to investors.

3. Codifies the definition of a "material weakness" to align with the PCAOB's definition. It is also expected that the SEC will adopt an amendment to codify the definition of "significant deficiency."

ENTERPRISE RISK MANAGEMENT

ERM has recently received considerable attention and interest from public companies, the business community, and the accounting profession. Financial scandals of the early 2000s and recent world events, including the September 11 terrorist attacks, have generated more interest in the issue of overall ERM including traditional risks. COSO defines enterprise risk management as

A process, effected by an entity's board of directors, management, and other personnel, applied in strategy setting and across the enterprise, designed to identify potential events that may affect the entity, and manage risks to be within its risk appetite, to provide reasonable assurance regarding the achievement of entity objectives.[31]

The relationship between ERM's objectives and its related components is depicted in Figure 6.5 in a three-dimensional matrix. The vertical column represents the four objectives of strategic, operations, reporting, and compliance. The horizontal rows depict the eight components of objective setting, event identification, risk assessment, risk response, control activities, information and communication, and monitoring. The third dimension of the cube

- The four objectives categories—strategic, operations, reporting, and compliance—are represented by the vertical columns.
- The eight components are represented by horizontal rows.
- The entity and its organizational units are depicted by the third dimension of the matrix.

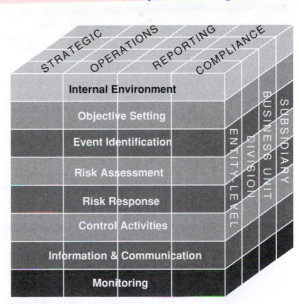

Figure 6.5 Relationship of objectives and components.

Source: Reprinted with permission from PricewaterhouseCoopers for Committee of Sponsoring Organizations of the Treadway Commission (COSO). COSO Enterprise Risk Management (ERM)—Integrated Framework (Downloadable PDF). AICPA, New York. Available at: www.cpa2biz.com/CS2000/Products/CPA2BIZ/Publications/COSO+Enterprise+Risk+Management+-+Integrated+Framework.htm.

shows ERM's ability to focus on the entire entity, its business subsidiaries, business units, divisions, or any other subunits.

ERM was originally used by organizations to identify and manage financial and litigation risks that impede production or negatively affect revenues. In the post-SOX period, ERM takes a broader strategic approach to promote corporate governance effectiveness of not only controlling risks but also revealing growth opportunities. A CRO can be appointed to oversee overall ERM strategies and proper implementation of their various policies related to financial risk, operational risk, internal audit, and compliance. The effectiveness of ERM depends on the adequate functioning of its components in achieving the entity's established objectives, as presented in Table 6.2. Entities in different industries, with different risk appetites and with different sizes, should tailor ERM objectives and components to their own specifications. Like any other system, the ERM framework is subject to limitations of mistakes, misjudgments, feasibility considerations, misapplications, breakdowns, collusions, and management overrides.

COSO's ERM framework enables management to achieve the entity's goal of creating stakeholder value by managing uncertainty and related risk and opportunity. The framework is developed based on six premises and capabilities of

1. Aligning risk appetite and strategy. An entity's risk appetite should be considered in assessing strategic alternatives, establishing objectives, and developing mechanisms to manage associated risks.

Table 6.2 Components of ERM

1. Internal environment	The foundation of ERM
2. Objective setting	Strategic goals and mission
3. Event identification	Internal and external factors affect objectives
4. Risk assessment	Likelihood and impact of potential events
5. Risk response	Risk tolerance
6. Control activities	Policies and procedures
7. Information and communication	From internal and external sources
8. Monitoring	Ongoing basis, periodic

Source: Adapted from PricewaterhouseCoopers for Committee of Sponsoring Organizations of the Treadway Commission (COSO). COSO Enterprise Risk Management (ERM)—Integrated Framework (Downloadable PDF). AICPA, New York. Available at: www.cpa2biz.com/CS2000/Products/CPA2BIZ/Publications/COSO+Enterprise+Risk+Management+-+Integrated+Framework.htm.

2. Enhancing risk response decisions. Management should identify and select risk responses (e.g., risk avoidance, reduction, sharing, acceptance) associated with the uncertainty its entity is facing.

3. Reducing operational surprises and losses. Management should minimize pitfalls and surprises that cause losses and expenses.

4. Identifying and managing multiple and cross-enterprise risks. Management should effectively identify and manage interrelated and integrated risks threatening the entity's operations and performance.

5. Seizing opportunities. Management should identify and proactively realize opportunities provided by uncertainties.

6. Improving deployment of capital. Management should assess overall capital needs and allocation of capital to manage risk.

The defined objectives are

1. Strategic—To support the entity's mission and achieve its related goals

2. Operations—To obtain effective and efficient use of the entity's resources

3. Reporting—To produce reliable reporting

4. Compliance—To ensure compliance with applicable laws and regulations

COSO also identifies eight components of ERM as follows:

1. Internal environment—Internal environment is the cornerstone of ERM that sets the tone of the entity's risk philosophy and appetite as well as integrity and ethical values.

2. Objective setting—An entity's established objectives should be aligned with its mission and consistent with its risk appetite.

3. Event identification—Both internal and external events affecting achievement of an entity's objectives should be identified and their related risk and opportunities assessed.

4. Risk assessment—Risks associated with an entity's events must be identified, and their likelihood of occurrence and possible effects must be easily analyzed on both an inherent and a residual basis.

5. Risk response—An entity's risk responses must be aligned with its risk appetite and tolerances.

6. Control activities—Control policies and procedures must be established to effectively implement selected risk responses.

7. Information and communication—Relevant information must be captured, processed, and communicated to personnel to fulfill their assigned responsibilities, and communications must flow across the entire entity.

8. Monitoring—Ongoing or separate monitoring of an entity's risk management must be performed to ensure its success.

ERM has received considerable attention due to its role in addressing challenges, opportunities, risks, and rewards facing organizations of all types, sizes, and complexities. As focus on the risk management concept is widening, it is important to clarify the roles and responsibilities of those who are directly involved with the organization's enterprisewide risk management process, including the audit committee, management, and internal auditors. Obviously, management is directly responsible for the adequate design and effective operation of the company's risk management process and appropriate assessment risk associated with the process. The audit committee is responsible for overseeing management policies, programs, procedures, and guidelines pertaining to corporate risk management activities. Internal auditors should report to the audit committee that (1) management has adequately identified and effectively controlled risk, (2) risk management policies and procedures are adequate and effective in addressing the related risk, and (3) objective assurance is provided regarding the effectiveness of the company's risk management process.

Regulators, standard setters, COSO, professional organizations, and public companies all work closely to implement guidelines provided in COSO's framework on ERM.

TAX ACCOUNTING

The aggressive use of corporate tax shelters has enabled organizations to avoid billions of dollars in their annual taxable income and payments as well as make financial disclosures more attractive to investors. The past two decades have witnessed a substantial decrease in corporate tax payments. Graham and Tucker report that S&P 500 companies paid federal taxes of 29 cents per dollar of reported earnings in 1994, while this figure fell to about 18 cents per dollar one decade later.[32] Tax shelters not only have detrimental effects on tax collections, but also the stock and the cost of debt prices can be affected. Accounting firms would be disqualified as a company's independent auditor when (1) the provided tax shelter services are included on the IRS's published list of abusive tax avoidance strategies or are similar to such strategies, (2) the auditor requires the client to sign a confidentiality agreement barring disclosure of the provided tax strategies, and (3) the auditor lacks a reasonable basis for believing that provided tax services will be challenged by the IRS and there is a 50-50 chance of not prevailing.

The Joint Committee on Taxation defines a tax shelter as a schema designed to avoid taxation without exposure to loss or economic risk.[33] Tax courts have established several judicial doctrines to curb corporate tax shelters, including (1) the sham transaction doctrine for transactions that either never occurred or occurred but absent tax considerations and lack economic substance or business purposes; (2) the economic substance doctrine on the grounds that a transaction must alter a taxpayer's economic position in a meaningful nontax manner for the IRS to recognize the transaction's tax treatment; (3) the business purpose doctrine in a sense that a transaction's tax treatment is not considered by the IRS as legitimate if the transaction does not have a nontax business purpose; (4) the substance-over-form doctrine, which permits the IRS to distinguish between economic form and formalistic, legal tax forms; and (5) the step transaction doctrine recognizing that each transaction is a series of related transactions (steps) that must have independent economic purpose; otherwise, the transaction can be stepped together for tax purposes.

SUMMARY

The managerial function is an important component of an effective corporate governance structure. The management team led by the CEO and supported by the CFO, controllers, treasurers, operating managers, and general counsel, under the oversight direction of the board of directors, is primarily responsible for operation efficiency, internal control effectiveness, soundness of the accounting information system, reliability of financial reports, and compliance with all applicable laws, rules, regulations, and standards. Globalization, technological advances, and emerging corporate governance reforms have created a new corporate environment saturated with new risks and opportunities. Management should consider these new challenges and move the company from the culture of mere compliance with laws to the culture of doing the right thing in creating shareholder value and protecting the stakeholders' interests.

The key points of this chapter are

- Management roles and responsibilities are to ensure operational efficiency; enhance the quality, reliability, integrity, and transparency of financial reports; and ensure compliance with applicable laws, regulations, rules, and standards.

- Management is responsible for all managerial functions, including decision making, performance assessment, fair presentation of financial reports, and the achievement of the goal of increasing shareholder value while protecting the interests of all stakeholders.

- The success and long-term survival of the company is in the hands of the CEO, and thus, the personal attributes, ethical values, and professional characteristics of the CEO should match and be in line with the company's values, visions, and strategic plans.

- Key challenges facing CEOs include (1) CEO fiduciary duties, (2) CEO succession planning, (3) CEO duality, (4) CEO financial knowledge and understanding, (5) CEO pay and skill, and (6) self-serving and self-dealing CEOs.

- Executive compensation includes salary, annual incentive compensation (bonus), long-term incentive compensation, stock option awards, stock award units, severance, change-of-control payments, retirement arrangements, and stock ownership.

- Several provisions of SOX directly or indirectly affect executive compensation packages, including (1) prohibition of personal loans to directors and executives, (2) reporting insider trading, (3) insider trading during pension fund blackout periods, and (4) forfeiture of certain bonuses and profits.

- Two provisions of SOX pertain to management certifications of financial reports. Section 302 of SOX requires the principle executive and financial officers of the company to certify each periodic report filed with the SEC. Under Section 906 of SOX, each periodic report containing financial statements filed by a reporting company must be accompanied by certification of the CEO and CFO of the company.

- Earnings management is defined as a managerial discretionary practice of timing strategic and operating decisions or choosing accrual estimates to manage short-term earnings. Any illegitimate earnings management can cause financial restatements.

- A high-quality financial report is defined in this book as a financial report that is relevant, useful, reliable, and transparent.

- Financial information is considered transparent when it provides shareholders and other stake-holders a clear understanding of the company's KPIs.

- Principles-based accounting standards are expected to be more understandable, allow the use of more judgment by auditors on the quality of financial information, make it more difficult to structure transactions, and facilitate convergence in financial reporting.

- Financial restatements continue to be the major factor in the erosion of investor confidence and public trust in the quality of financial reports, particularly the reliability of reported earnings.

- The development of IFRS is now considered one of the most commonly used accounting languages worldwide. Convergence of IFRS and U.S. GAAP should benefit the global capital market primarily because such convergence reduces the differences in global accounting policies and practices.

- The SEC requires that public companies design and maintain adequate and effective disclosure controls and procedures tailored to their management structure, industry, business processes, and supervisory practices.

- Section 302 of SOX requires the management of public companies to assess and report on the effectiveness of disclosure controls and the procedures of both quarterly and annual reports.

- Section 404 of SOX requires management to document and assess the design and operation of the company's ICFR and report on its assessment of the effectiveness of ICFR.

- Section 404 of SOX requires the independent auditor to attest to and report on management's assessment of the effectiveness of the company's ICFR.

KEY TERMS

chief audit executive (CAE)
chief risk officer (CRO)
corporate development
    officer (CDO)
enterprise risk management
    (ERM)
eXtensible Business
    Reporting Language
    (XBRL)

Financial Accounting
    Standards Board (FASB)
Institute of Internal Auditors
    Research Foundation
International Accounting
    Standards Board (IASB)
International Financial
    Reporting Standards
    (IFRS)

Joint Committee on Taxation
other postemployment
    benefits (OPEB)
tax shelter

REVIEW QUESTIONS

1. What are the advantages of having a former CFO as CEO?

2. What are the basic components of executive compensation?

3. What does transparency in context to the quality of the financial report mean?

4. What is an off balance sheet transaction?

5. What are the two aspects of critical accounting policies and practices required as disclosures by the SEC's Strengthening the Commission's Requirements Regarding Auditor Independence?

6. What is a non-GAAP financial measure?

7. What are the steps taken by public companies and internal auditors to fulfill their internal control requirements?

8. What are the types of costs associated with Section 404 compliance?

9. Explain the steps involved in continuous process of improving the effectiveness of corporate internal control over financial reporting.

10. Explain the term enterprise risk management (ERM).

11. What are the four objectives of ERM?

12. What are the major provisions of the Working Families Tax Relief Act?

13. What are the characteristics of abusive tax shelters?

14. What are the tax services provided for an audit client that can lead to an impairment of auditor independence?

15. What are the qualities of a CFO?

16. Explain the advantages of having a CFO with CPA certification.

DISCUSSION QUESTIONS

1. Discuss the possible relationship between CEO performance and compensation. Are CEOs overpaid or underpaid?

2. "Executives should be given proper motivation and be paid for their good performance to create sufficient incentives for outstanding performance, and not be paid excessively for poor or underperformance." Do you agree with this philosophy? Substantiate your answer.

3. Explain the importance of the determination of CEO compensation reasonableness and its link to the company's sustainable performance in the areas of economic, social, ethical, and environmental activities in general and creation of shareholder value in particular.

4. What, according to you, should be done to face the consequences of the retirement of the baby boom generation of financial executives?

5. Explain the role of management in the presentation of true financial statements in conformity with GAAP. Explain the advantages and disadvantages of incentives used by the management of any company.

6. Explain how disclosure of financial statements can affect shareholders' wealth.

7. Explain the importance of converging IFRS and GAAP.

8. Do you think ERM is gaining importance in today's economy?

9. What is meant by the term tax shelter? Can they help investors? Is it right on the part of the corporation to provide abusive tax shelters to corporations and individuals? Explain your point of view.

NOTES

1. Corporate Board Member & PricewaterhouseCoopers. 2006. What Directors Think: Annual Board of Directors' Survey: The 2006 Results. Available at: www.boardmember.com/media/files/research-pdfs/2006WDTResults.pdf.

2. Ernst & Young. 2004, October. Striving for Transaction Excellence: The Emerging Role of the Corporate Development Officer.

3. Deloitte & Touche. 2004/2005. *2004 Global Risk Management Survey.* Available at: www.deloitte.com/dtt/cda/doc/content/dtt_financialservices_GlobalRiskManagementSurvey2005_061204-v2.pdf.

4. PricewaterhouseCoopers. 2007. How to Move Your Company to Sustainable Sarbanes-Oxley Compliance—From Project to Process. Available at: www.pwc.com/Extweb/pwcpublications.nsf/docid/31F021B50359960 385256FF60056C4B6/$file/Sustainability_050605c_FINAL.pdf.

5. Much of the discussion in this section comes from the Council of Institutional Investors (CII). 2007, September 18. Council of Institutional Investors Corporate Governance Policies. Available at: www.cii.org/policies/Redesigned%20CII%20Corp%20Gov%20Policies%201-31-08.pdf. See also IBM. 2005. Report on Executive Compensation: 2006 Report of the Executive Compensation and Management Resources Committee of the Board of Directors. Available at: www.ibm.com/investor/corpgovernance/cgec.phtml#report; Poerio, M., and Keller, E. 2005. Executive Compensation 2005: Many Forces, One Direction. *Compensation Benefits Review* 37:4-6; CalPERS. Core Principles of Accountable Corporate Governance. Appendix C: Executive Compensation Policies. Available at: www.calpers-governance.org/principles/domestic/us/page07.asp#.

5a. Pergola, T.M. 2005. Management entrenchment: Can it negate the effectiveness of recently legislated governance reforms? *Journal of American Academy of Business* 6(2):177–185.

5b. U.S. Securities and Exchange Commission (SEC). 2006, July 26. SEC votes to adopt changes to disclosure requirements concerning executive compensation and related matters. Available at: www.sec.gov/news/press/2006/2006-123.htm.

6. U.S. Securities and Exchange Commission (SEC). 2006, July 26. SEC Votes to Adopt Changes to Disclosure Requirements Concerning Executive Compensation and Related Matters. Press release. Available at: www.sec.gov/news/press/2006/2006-123.htm.

7. U.S. Securities and Exchange Commission (SEC), Advisory Committee on Corporate Disclosure. 1977. *Report of the Advisory Committee on Corporate Disclosure to the Securities and Exchange Commission. Vol. 1.* U.S. Government Printing Office, Washington, DC.

8. *Federal Register.* 2007, July 19. Part II: Securities and Exchange Commission. 17 CFR Parts 210, 228, 229 et al. Smaller Reporting Company Regulatory Relief and Simplification; Proposed Rule. Vol. 72, No. 138. Available at: sec.gov/rules/proposed/2007/33-8819fr.pdf.

9. U.S. Securities and Exchange Commission (SEC). 2003. Report Pursuant to Section 704 of the Sarbanes-Oxley Act of 2002. Available at: www.sec.gov/news/studies/sox704report.pdf.

10. U.S. Securities and Exchange Commission (SEC). 2003, January 29. Disclosure in Management's Discussion and Analysis about Off-Balance Sheet Arrangements and Aggregate Contractual Obligation. Available at: www.sec.gov/rules/final/33-8182.htm.

11. U.S. Securities and Exchange Commission (SEC). 2003. Strengthening the Commission's Requirements Regarding Auditor Independence. Available at: www.sec.gov/rules/final/33-8183.htm.

12. U.S. Securities and Exchange Commission (SEC). 2003. Conditions for Use of Non-GAAP Financial Measures. Available at: www.sec.gov/rules/final/33-8176.htm.

13. Sarbanes-Oxley Financial and Accounting Disclosure Information. January 23, 2003. Available at: www.sarbanes-oxley.com/displaysection.php?level=2&pub_id=SEC-Rules&chap_id=SEC3&message_id=105.

14. Financial Accounting Standards Board (FASB). 2005, May. Summary of Statement No. 154: Accounting Changes and Error Corrections—A Replacement of APB Opinion No. 20 and FASB Statement No. 3. Available at: www.fasb.org/st/summary/stsum154.shtml.

15. Boselovic, L. 2005. Pittsburgh Brewing Says It's in Deep Trouble. *Pittsburgh Post Gazette* June 29.

16. Zion, D., and B. Carcache. 2005, November 11. Let the Games Begin: FASB to Tackle Pension and OPEB. *CSFB's Research and Analysis.*

17. Financial Accounting Standards Board of the Financial Accounting Foundation. 2006, September. Financial Accounting Series: Statement of Financial Accounting Standards No. 158. Employers' Accounting for Defined Benefit Pension and Other Postretirement Plans. No. 284-B. Available at: http://72.3.243.42/pdf/fas158.pdf.

18. U.S. Securities and Exchange Commission (SEC). 2003. Study Pursuant to Section 108(d) of the Sarbanes-Oxley Act of 2002 on the Adoption by the United States Financial Reporting System of a Principles-Based Accounting System. Available at: www.sec.gov/news/studies/principlesbasedstand.htm.

19. Bullen, H.G., and Crook, K. 2005, May. *Revising the Concepts: A New Conceptual Framework Project.* Financial Accounting Standards Board, Stamford, CT, pp. 1–18.

20. Kueppers, R., and G. Weaver. 2003, November. *Meeting the Street: A Discussion of Earnings and Other Guidance Provided to Investors.* Financial Executive Research Foundation, Inc., Florham Park, NJ.

21. Harris. R. 2007. Say Again? *CFO Magazine* April 1. Available at: www.cfo.com/article.cfm/8885662/c_8910395.

22. Glass Lewis & Co. 2007, February 27. Yellow Card Trend Alert. The Errors of Their Ways. Available at: www-tc.pbs.org/nbr/pdf/GlassLewis-Errors.pdf.

23. European Union (EC). 2002, July 19. Regulation (EC) No. 1606/2002 of the European Parliament and the Council: The Application of International Accounting Standards. *The Official Journal of the European Union.* Available at: http://eur-lex.europa.eu/smartapi/cgi/sga_doc?smartapi!celexapi!prod!CELEXnumdoc&lg=en&numdoc=32002R1606&model=guichett.

24. The Securities Exchange Act of 1934. Sections 13a-15, 15D-15, pp. 84-96, 154-155. Available at: www.sec.gov/about/laws/sea34.pdf.

25. U.S. Securities and Exchange Commission (SEC). 2003, June 11. Management's Report on Internal Control Over Financial Reporting and Certification of Disclosure in Exchange Act Periodic Reports. Available at: www.sec.gov/rules/final/33-8238.htm.

26. The Committee of Sponsoring Organizations of the Treadway Commission. (COSO). 2004. Internal Control—Integrated Framework (Executive Summary). Available at: www.coso.org/publications/executive_summary_integrated_framework.htm.

27. Accounting WEB.com. 2005. May 2. SOX Accounting Expensive for Fortune 1000 Companies. Available at: www.accountingweb.com/cgi-bin/item.cgi?id=100859.

28. Financial Executives International (FEI). 2006, April 7. FEI Survey on Sarbanes-Oxley Section 404 Implementation. Available at: www.insidesarbanesoxley.com/2006/04/fei-survey-on-sarbanes-oxley-section.asp.

29. Rittenberg, L. E., and Miller, P. K. 2005, January. Sarbanes-Oxley Section 404 Work: Looking at the Benefits. The IIA Research Foundation, Altamonte Springs, FL. Available at: www.theiia.org/download.cfm?file=343.

30. PricewaterhouseCoopers. 2005, May 2. How to Move Your Company to Sustainable Sarbanes-Oxley Compliance: From Project to Process. Available at: www.pwc.com/Extweb/pwcpublications.nsf/docid/31F021B50359960385256FF60056C4 B6/.

31. PricewaterhouseCoopers for Committee of Sponsoring Organizations of the Treadway Commission (COSO). COSO Enterprise Risk Management (ERM)—Integrated Framework (Downloadable PDF). AICPA, New York. Available at: www.cpa2biz.com/CS2000/Products/CPA2BIZ/Publications/COSO+Enterprise+Risk+Management+-+Integrated+Framework.htm.

32. Graham, J. R., and A. L. Tucker. 2005, January. Tax Shelters and Corporate Debt Policy. Working Paper, Duke University, Durham, NC.

33. U.S. Congress, Joint Committee on Taxation. 1999. Study of present-law penalty and interest provisions as required by section 3801 of the Internal Revenue Service Restructuring and Reform Act of 1998 (including provisions relating to corporate tax shelters). Volume I. JCS 3-99. US Government Printing Office, Washington, DC. Available at: frwebgate.access.gpo.gov/cgi-bin/getdoc.cgi?dbnane=1999_joint_committe_on_taxation&docid=f:57655.pdf.

Chapter 7

Regulatory Bodies, Standard Setters, and Best Practices

INTRODUCTION

Reported corporate and accounting scandals of the late 1990s and the 2000s suggest that market-based correction mechanisms have failed to prevent those scandals and properly penalize corporate wrongdoers. Therefore, regulations, rules, standards, and best practices established by governing bodies, standard setters, and professional organizations are important external mechanisms in creating an environment that promotes, monitors, and enforces responsible corporate governance, reliable financial reporting, and credible audit functions. Regulations are important external mechanisms of corporate governance intended to protect investors.

This chapter examines the role of regulatory bodies and standard setters that influences the structure, measures, and mechanisms of corporate governance in several ways through (1) regulation of the capital markets (legislation, SEC rules, listing standards); (2) regulation of corporate governance (SOX); (3) regulation of public companies' financial reporting process (accounting standards); and (4) regulation of public accounting firms (auditing standards). Compliance with applicable regulations and best practices is essential to the effectiveness of corporate governance, the reliability of financial reports, and the integrity of the capital markets.

Primary Objectives

The primary objectives of this chapter are to

- Understand the roles and responsibilities of regulators and standard setters in corporate governance.
- Provide an overview of fundamental provisions of SOX and their impacts on corporate governance, financial reporting, and auditing activities.
- Be aware that the provisions of SOX and SEC-related rules address the conduct of all gatekeepers, including directors, management, auditors, legal counsel, and financial advisors.
- Provide an overview of the evaluation of SOX and the costs and benefits of compliance.
- Understand why the SEC was established and provide an overview of its responsibilities and activities.
- Provide an overview of the primary functions of the PCAOB, including its responsibilities and activities.
- Become familiar with the role of the FASB and its activities.
- Provide an overview of the GASB.
- Understand the challenges facing the IFAC.
- Identify the primary responsibilities of the Committee of European Securities Regulators.
- Understand the role and authority of the state attorney general.
- Be aware of how state laws affect corporate governance.
- Be aware of the role of courts in corporate governance.
- Become familiar with corporate governance listing standards and best practices.

REGULATIONS

Regulations are aimed at protecting the investors and creating an environment for organizations to conduct their affairs in the utmost ethical, legal, and competent manner. The history of regulation in the United States appears to follow the pattern of lax regulation (early twentieth century) followed by corporate and accounting scandals (the stock market crash of 1929), responded to with more regulation (the Securities Act of 1933, the Securities Exchange Act of 1934), relaxed or compromised regulation (the end of the twentieth century), and yet another wave of financial scandals (the late 1990s and early 2000s), and then the resulting additional regulation. The intent of regulation has been to restore public trust and investor confidence in corporate America, its financial reports, and capital markets pursuant to the occurrences of massive financial scandals. It is expected that this endless cycle of financial scandals and government regulation will continue because regulation is often compromised, which leads to another wave of scandals. Regulations can generate positive externalities for investors in terms of rebuilding their confidence in public financial information and the capital markets. Regulations create an environment under which public companies can operate effectively in achieving sustainable performance, being held accountable for their activities, and providing protections for their investors.

During the early 1900s and prior to the establishment of the SEC in 1934, financial markets in the United States were primarily unregulated. Prior to the market crash of 1929, there was not much interest in federal regulation of the securities markets. The Securities Act of 1933 was passed by Congress with the primary purpose of requiring that investors receive adequate financial and other information regarding securities offered for public sale, prohibiting misinterpretations, deceit, and other fraud in the sale of securities. The Securities Exchange Act of 1934 provides protection for the investors who trade securities and created the SEC to oversee the securities industry. SOX was passed by Congress in July 2002 to further hold public companies accountable for their financial reports. Regulatory reforms in the United States are aimed at improving the integrity, safety, and efficiency of the capital markets while maintaining its global competitiveness. Regulations should strike the right balance of (1) not being so extensive as to discourage innovation, impose unnecessary costs on affected companies and their investors, or stifle competitiveness and job creation; and (2) not being so lax as to engage in a regulatory race to the bottom of eliminating necessary safeguards for investors. However, we should differentiate between underregulation, adequate regulation, and overregulation. Regulations are typically enacted in response to specific crises and concerns or protection needed due to the failure of market-based correction mechanisms. Adequate regulation creates a balance between reducing the likelihood of recurrence of the crisis and the imposed enforcement and compliance costs. Underregulation is when adequate rules are not in place to ensure long-term improvements and stability.

THE SARBANES-OXLEY ACT OF 2002

The economic downturn of the early 2000s, coupled with several years of steady decline in the capital markets and numerous high-profile financial scandals, paved the way for regulatory actions. Congress acted in July 2002 by passing the Public Company Accounting Reform and Investor Protection Act, better known as the Sarbanes-Oxley Act (SOX).[1] President George W. Bush, in signing SOX into law, praised it as "the most far-reaching reforms of American business practices since the time of Franklin Delano Roosevelt."[2] SOX creates new and unprecedented measures for public companies that affect all corporate governance functions discussed in this book. Its provisions are intended to address the conduct of boards of directors, audit committees, executives, internal and external auditors, financial analysts, legal counsel, investment banks and other groups, and individuals associated with financial reports.

The fundamental provisions of SOX can be categorized into the following five categories: (1) corporate governance; (2) financial reporting; (3) audit functions; (4) federal securities law enforcement; and (5) others (e.g., legal counsel, financial analysts). These provisions and related SOX sections are summarized in Table 7.1 and further discussed in the following sections.

Table 7.1 Sarbanes-Oxley Act of 2002 Provisions

Section	Provisions
I. Corporate governance provisions	
202	**Audit Committee Preapproval of Audit Services**
	All auditing services (which may entail providing comfort letters in connection with securities underwritings) and nonaudit services provided to an issuer by the auditor of the issuer shall be preapproved by the audit committee of the issuer.
205	**Amendments to the Securities Exchange Act of 1934**
	Defined audit committee and registered public accounting firm.
301	**Public Company Audit Committees**
	Each member of the audit committee shall be an independent member of the board of directors. The audit committee shall be directly responsible for the appointment, compensation, and oversight of the work of any registered public accounting firm associated by the issuer. The audit committee shall establish procedures for the receipt, retention, and treatment of complaints received by the issuer regarding accounting, internal accounting controls, or auditing matters and the confidential, anonymous submission by employees of the issuer or concerns regarding questionable accounting or auditing matters.
303	**Improper Influence on Conduct of Audits**
	It shall be unlawful for any officer or director of an issuer to take any action to fraudulently influence, coerce, manipulate, or mislead auditors in the performance of a financial audit of the financial statements.
304	**Forfeiture of Certain Bonuses and Profits**
	CEOs and CFOs who revise a company's financial statements for material noncompliance with any financial reporting requirements must pay back any bonuses or stock options awarded because of the misstatements.
305	**Amendments to the Securities Exchange Act of 1934**
	Adapted the phrase substantial unfitness to read unfitness.
306	**Insider Trades During Pension Fund Blackout Periods**
	It shall be unlawful for any directors or executive officers directly or indirectly to purchase, sell, or otherwise acquire or transfer any equity security of the issuer during any blackout periods. Any profits resulting from sales in violation of this section shall inure to and be recoverable by the issuer.
402	**Extended Conflict of Interest Provisions**
	It is unlawful for the issuer to extend credit or personal loans to any directors or executive officers.

(Continued)

Table 7.1   *(Continued)*

Section	Provisions
403	**Disclosures of Transactions Involving Management and Principal Stockholders** *Every person who is directly or indirectly the beneficial owner of more than ten percent of any class of any equity security (other than an exempted security) that is registered pursuant to Section 12, or who is a director or an officer of the issuer of such security, shall file the statements required by this subsection with the commission.*
406	**Code of Ethics for Senior Financial Officers** *The SEC shall issue rules to require each issuer to disclose whether it has adopted a code of ethics for its senior financial officers and the nature and content of such a code.*
407	**Disclosure of Audit Committee Financial Expert** *The SEC shall issue rules to require each issuer to disclose whether at least one member of its audit committee is a "financial" expert as defined by the commission.*
705	**Study on Investment Banks** *Directs the comptroller general to conduct a study and report the findings to Congress regarding the role of investment bankers and financial advisors assisting public companies in manipulating their earnings and obfuscating their true financial condition.*
806	**Whistleblower Protection** *Provides whistleblower protections for employees of any issuer who willingly provides evidence of fraud or violations of securities by that issuer.*
1105	**Authority of the SEC** *The commission may prohibit a person from serving as a director or officer of a publicly traded company if the person has committed securities fraud.*
1106	**Criminal Penalties for Violations of the 1934 Exchange Act** *Increases criminal penalties for violations of the 1934 Act from $1 million to $5 million for individuals; from 10 years to 20 years imprisonment for each violation; and from $2.5 million to $25 million for each entity.*

II. Financial reporting provisions

Section	Provisions
108	**Accounting Standards** 1. *The SEC may recognize as "generally accepted" any accounting principles that are established by a standard-setting body that meets the Act's criteria.* 2. *The SEC shall conduct a study on the adoption of a principles-based accounting system.*
302	**Corporate Responsibility for Financial Reports** *The signing officers (e.g., CEO, CFO) shall certify in each annual or quarterly report filed with the SEC that: (a) the report does not contain any untrue statement of a material fact or omitted material facts that cause the report to be misleading; and (b) financial statements and disclosures fairly present, in all material respects, the financial condition and results of operations of the issuer. The signing officers are responsible for establishing and maintaining adequate and effective controls to ensure reliability of financial statements and disclosures. The signing officers are responsible for proper design and periodic assessment of the disclosure of material deficiencies in internal controls to external auditors and the audit committee.*
401	**Disclosures in Periodic Reports** *Each financial report that is required to be prepared in accordance with GAAP shall reflect all material correcting adjustments that have been identified by the auditors. Each financial report (annual and quarterly) shall disclose all material off–balance sheet transactions and other relationships with unconsolidated entities that may have a material current or future effect on the financial conditions of the issuer.*

(Continued)

Table 7.1   *(Continued)*

Section	Provisions
404	**Management Assessments of Internal Controls** 1. *Each annual report filed with the SEC shall contain an internal control report, which shall: (a) state the responsibility of management for establishing and maintaining an adequate internal control structure and procedures for financial reporting; and (b) contain an assessment of the effectiveness of the internal control structure and procedures as of the end of the issuer's fiscal year.* 2. *Auditors shall attest to, and report on, the assessment of the adequacy and effectiveness of the issuer's internal control structure and procedures as part of an audit of financial reports in accordance with standards for attestation engagements.*
405	**Exemptions** *Nothing in Section 401, 402, or 404, the amendments made by those sections, or the rules of the commission under those sections shall apply to any investment company registered under Section 8 of the Investment Company Act of 1940.*
408	*The SEC must review disclosures made to the SEC on a regular and systemic basis for the protection of investors including a review of the issuer's financial statements.*
409	**Real-Time Issuer Disclosures** *Each issuer shall disclose information on material changes in the financial condition or operations of the issuer on a rapid and current basis.*
1001	**Corporate Tax Returns** *The federal income tax returns of public corporations should be signed by the CEO of the issuer.*

III. Audit function provisions

Section	Provisions
101	**Establishment of Public Company Accounting Oversight Board (PCAOB)** *The PCAOB is an independent, nongovernmental accounting oversight board that oversees the audits of publicly traded companies.*
102	**Registration with the PCAOB** *Registration of public accounting firms (foreign and domestic) that prepare audit reports for issuers.*
103	**Functions of the PCAOB** *The board shall establish, or adopt, by rule, auditing, quality control, ethics, independence, and other standards relating to the preparation of audit reports for issuers; conduct inspections of registered public accounting firms; conduct investigations and disciplinary proceedings and impose appropriate sections; enforce compliance with the Act; and establish the budget and manage the operations of the board and its staff.*
104	**PCAOB Inspections of Registered Public Accounting Firms** *The board shall conduct a continuing program of inspections to assess the degree of compliance of each registered public accounting firm and associated persons of that firm with this Act, the rules of the board, the rules of the commission, or professional standards, in connection with its performance of audits, issuance of audit reports, and related matters involving issuers.*
105	**PCAOB Investigations and Disciplinary Proceedings** *The board shall establish, by rule, subject to the requirements of this section, fair procedures for the investigation and disciplining of registered public accounting firms and associated persons of such firms.*
106	**Regulations of Foreign Public Accounting Firms** *Any foreign public accounting firm that prepares or furnishes an audit report with respect to any issuer shall be subject to this Act and the rules of the board and the commission issued under this Act, in the same manner and to the same extent as a public accounting firm that is organized and operates under the laws of the United States.*

(Continued)

Table 7.1   *(Continued)*

Section	Provisions
107	**Commission Oversight of the Board**
	The SEC shall have oversight and enforcement authority over the PCAOB.
109	**Funding of the PCAOB**
	The board shall establish, with the approval of the commission, a reasonable annual accounting support fee (or a formula for the computation thereof), as may be necessary or appropriate to establish and maintain the board.
201	**Auditor Independence: Services Outside the Scope of Practice of Auditors**
	Registered public accounting firms are prohibited from providing any nonaudit services to an issuer contemporaneously with the audit including but not limited to: (a) bookkeeping or other services related to the accounting record or financial statement of the audit client; (b) financial information systems design and implementation; (c) appraisal or valuation services; (d) actuarial services; (e) internal audit outsourcing services; (f) management functions or human resources; (g) broker or dealer, investment advisor, or investment banking; (h) legal services and expert services unrelated to the audit; or (i) any other services that the PCAOB determines, by regulation, are impermissible.
203	**Audit Partner Rotation**
	The lead audit or coordinating partner and reviewing partner of the registered accounting firm must rotate off of the audit every five years.
204	**Auditor Reports to Audit Committees**
	The registered accounting firm must report to the audit committee all critical accounting policies and practices to be used; all alternative treatments of financial information within generally accepted accounting principles, ramifications of the use of such alternative disclosures and treatments, and the preferred treatment; other material written communication between the auditor and management.
206	**Conflicts of Interest**
	The registered accounting firm is prohibited from performing an audit for an issuer who is CEO, CFO, controller, chief accounting officer or person in an equivalent position employed by the accounting firm during the one-year period preceding the audit.
207	**Study of Mandatory Rotation of Registered Public Accounting Firms**
	The Comptroller General of the United States will conduct a study on the potential effects of requiring the mandatory rotation of public accounting firms.
208	**Regulations and Independence Guidelines**
	The commission was given 180 days to implement final regulations regarding the Act. It shall be unlawful for any registered public accounting firm (or an associated person thereof, as applicable) to prepare or issue any audit report with respect to any issuer, if the firm or associated person engages in any activity with respect to that issuer prohibited by any of subsections (g) through (l) of Section 10A of the Securities Exchange Act of 1934, as added by this title, or any rule or regulation of the commission or of the board issued thereunder.
209	**Considerations by Appropriate State Regulatory Authorities**
	In supervising nonregistered public accounting firms and their associated persons, appropriate state regulatory authorities should make an independent determination of the proper standards applicable, particularly taking into consideration the size and nature of the business of the accounting firms they supervise and the size and nature of the business of the clients of those firms. The standards applied by the board under this Act should not be presumed to be applicable for purposes of this section for small- and medium-sized nonregistered public accounting firms.

(Continued)

Table 7.1   *(Continued)*

Section	Provisions
701	**GAO Study and Report Regarding Consolidation of Public Accounting Firms** *The GAO shall conduct a study regarding consolidation of public accounting firms since 1989 and determine the consequences of the consolidation, including the present and future impact and solutions to any problems that may result from the consolidation.*

IV. Securities law violations

Section	Provisions
601	**SEC Resource and Authority** *SEC appropriations for 2003 are increased to $776,000,000 from which $98 million shall be used to hire an additional 200 employees to provide enhanced oversight of audit services.*
602	**Practice before the Commission** **1.** *The SEC may censure any person or temporarily bar or deny any person the right to appear or practice before the SEC if the person does not possess the requisite qualifications to represent others, has willfully violated federal securities laws, or lacks character or integrity.* **2.** *The SEC shall conduct a study of "Securities of Professionals" (e.g., accountants, investment bankers, brokers, dealers, attorneys, investment advisors) who have been found to have aided and abetted a violation of federal securities laws.* **3.** *The SEC shall establish rules setting minimum standards for professional conduct for attorneys practicing before the commission.*
603	**Federal Court Authority to Impose Penny Stock Bars** *Amendment to the Securities Exchange Act of 1934 which allows the court to prohibit any person participating in, or, at the time of the alleged misconduct who was participating in, an offering of penny stock, from participating in an offering of penny stock, conditionally or unconditionally, and permanently or for such period of time as the court shall determine.*
703	**Study and Report on Violators and Violations** *The SEC is directed to conduct a study and report its findings to Congress regarding the proliferation of violations of securities laws and associated penalties.*
704	**Study of Enforcement Actions** *The SEC is directed to analyze all enforcement actions over the prior five-year period involving violations of reporting requirements and restatements of financial statements to identify areas of reporting that are most susceptible to fraud.*
802	**Criminal Penalties for Altering Documents** *Criminal penalties for document destruction, alteration, or concealment with the intent to impede federal investigations or in a federal bankruptcy case include fines and maximum imprisonment of 20 years.*
803	**No Discharge of Debts in a Bankruptcy Proceeding** *Liability for securities law or fraud violations may not be discharged under the U.S. Bankruptcy Code.*
804	**Statute of Limitations for Securities Fraud** *Statute of limitations to recover for a private action for securities fraud lengthened to the earlier of two years after the date of discovery or five years after the fraudulent activities.*
807	**Criminal Penalties for Defrauding Shareholders of Publicly Traded Companies** *Amended Chapter 63 of title 18, United States Code, by adding Sec. 1348. Securities fraud.*
902	**Attempts and Conspiracies to Commit Criminal Fraud Offenses** *Amended Chapter 63 of title 18, United States Code, by adding Sec. 1349. Attempt and conspiracy.*
903 **904**	**White-Collar Crime Penalty Enhancements** **1.** *Maximum penalty for mail and wire fraud is ten years.*

(Continued)

Table 7.1   *(Continued)*

Section	Provisions
906	2. *The SEC may prohibit anyone convicted of securities fraud from being a director or officer of any public company.* 3. *Financial reports filed with the SEC (annual, quarterly) must be certified by the CEO and CFO of the issuer. The certification must state that the financial statements and disclosures fully comply with provisions of the Securities Acts and they fairly present, in all material respects, financial results and conditions of the issuer. Maximum penalties for willful and knowing violations of these provisions of the Act are a fine of not more than $500,000 and/or imprisonment of up to five years.*
1102	**Tampering with a Record or Otherwise Impeding an Official Proceeding** *Whoever corruptly—(1) alters, destroys, mutilates, or conceals a record, document, or other object, or attempts to do so, with the intent to impair the object's integrity or availability for use in an official proceeding; or (2) otherwise obstructs, influences, or impedes any official proceeding, or attempts to do so; shall be fined under this title or imprisoned not more than ten years, or both.*
1103	**Temporary Freeze Authority for the Securities and Exchange Commission** *Whenever, during the course of a lawful investigation involving possible violations of the federal securities laws by an issuer of publicly traded securities or any of its directors, officers, partners, controlling persons, agents, or employees, it shall appear to the commission that it is likely that the issuer will make extraordinary payments (whether compensation or otherwise) to any of the foregoing persons, the commission may petition a federal district court for a temporary order requiring the issuer to escrow, subject to court supervision, those payments in an interest-bearing account for 45 days.*
1107	**Retaliation against Informants** *"Whoever knowingly, with the intent to retaliate, takes any action harmful to any person, including interference with the lawful employment or livelihood of any person, for providing to a law enforcement officer any truthful information relating to the commission or possible commission of any federal offense, shall be fined under this title or imprisoned not more than 10 years, or both."*

V. Other provisions not specifically related to the above categories.

Section	Provisions
307	**Rules of Professional Responsibility for Attorneys** *Attorneys who appear or practice before the SEC are required to report violations of securities laws to the CEO or chief legal counsel and if no action is taken, to the audit committee.*
308	**Fair Funds for Investors** *The SEC may impose civil penalties on disgorged executives for the compensation of victims.*
501	**Treatment of Securities Analysts** *Registered securities associations and national securities exchanges shall adopt rules designed to address conflicts of interest for research analysts who recommend equities in research reports.*
604	**Qualifications of Associated Persons of Brokers and Dealers** *Amends the Securities Exchange Act of 1934 and refines the Qualifications of Associated Persons of Brokers and Dealers.*
702	**Credit Rating Study and Report** *The SEC is directed to conduct a study and report its findings to Congress regarding the role, importance, and impact of rating agencies in the marketplace.*
805 **905** **1104**	**Review of Sentencing Guidelines** *The U.S. Sentencing Commission is authorized to review the sentencing guidelines for fraud, obstruction of justice, and other white-collar crimes and to propose changes to existing guidelines.*

Source: Adapted from Sarbanes-Oxley Act of 2002 (SOX). Available at: www.sec.gov/about/laws/soa2002.pdf.

Corporate Governance Provisions

Many provisions of SOX influence corporate governance through SEC-issued rules to implement the provisions and SEC requirements for national stock exchanges to establish listing standards pertaining to listed companies' directors, officers, and financial and internal control reporting. SOX provisions, SEC-related rules, and listing standards influence corporate governance structure in at least several ways. First, auditors, analysts, and legal counsel who were not traditionally considered as components of corporate governance are now brought into the realm of internal governance as the gatekeepers. Second, the legal status and fiduciary duties of directors and officers, particularly the audit committee and CEO, have been enhanced significantly. Third, certain aspects of state corporate law were preempted and federalized. For example, Section 404 of SOX prohibits loans to directors and officers, whereas state law permits such loans. Under Section 304, officers must reimburse certain compensation received if the company had to restate its financial statements as a result of fraud. Section 301 of SOX grants more direct statutory responsibilities to the audit committee than the state law (e.g., direct responsibility for hiring, compensating, and firing independent auditors). One of the most important objectives of SOX was to improve corporate governance of public companies by requiring companies to set an appropriate tone at the top of promoting ethical behavior.

Finally, SOX is considered a process whose impact on improving the effectiveness of corporate governance will continue for years to come. In its infancy, SOX was viewed as a compliance document that often caused complications and substantial compliance costs for many companies regardless of size. As SOX is approaching its maturity stage, it will encourage (1) public companies to move away from their practice of a checklist compliance mentality and move toward incorporating its provisions into their sustainable business strategies and governance practices; (2) regulators and standard setters to establish more effective, efficient, and scalable related implementation rules, accounting and auditing standards, and corporate governance guiding standards to ease the complexities and compliance costs of adopting its provisions; and (3) global adoption of many of its key provisions, which are considered worldwide as cost justified.

Financial Reporting Provisions

The primary focus of SOX was to improve the quality, reliability, and transparency of public financial reports. High-quality financial information can significantly contribute to the integrity and efficiency of the capital markets. Financial reporting provisions of SOX and SEC-related rules are

1. Certification of financial statements and internal controls by CEOs and CFOs
2. Disclosure of off balance sheet transactions
3. Disclosure pertaining to the use of non-GAAP financial measures
4. Disclosure of material current events affecting companies
5. Mandatory internal control reporting by management
6. A study of principles-based accounting standards

7. Convergence of accounting standards
8. Recognition of an adequate funding for the FASB as an accounting standard-setting body
9. Oversight function of the FASB by the SEC

Audit Function Provisions

A fundamental objective of SOX was to enhance the reliability and integrity of audit functions and the audit process as well as the credibility of audit reports. SOX has caused significant changes in both audit fees and types of services performed by independent auditors, including (1) a 345 percent increase in audit fees from an average of $1.4 million in 2001 to $2.7 million in 2006, (2) a substantial reduction in consulting services, (3) audits of ICFR, (4) a significant shift in auditor fees from nonaudit services to audit and audit-related fees; (5) changes in market share of non–Big Four firms from 1.97 percent in 2002 to 5.5 percent in 2006.[3] Provisions of SOX and SEC-related rules addressing audit functions are

1. Creation of the PCAOB to regulate public accounting firms' practice before the SEC
2. Adoption of new rules related to auditor independence
3. Establishment of auditing standards in guiding auditors to improve audit quality
4. Issuance of new rules related to improper influence on auditors
5. Issuance of new rules pertaining to retention of records and audit evidence relevant to reviews and audits of financial statements
6. Establishment of quality control standards to protect investors from receiving misleading financial information
7. Oversight function of the PCAOB by the SEC
8. Attestation of and report on ICFR

Enforcement of Federal Securities Laws

SOX empowered the SEC to better enforce federal securities laws to improve public trust and investor confidence in the capital markets. SOX enabled the SEC to use various means to bring enforcement actions against corporate wrongdoers, sanction them, obtain penalties and disgorgement, and compensate injured investors. SOX strengthened the SEC efforts to conduct more thorough, effective, flexible, transparent, and fair investigations of corporate and auditing wrongdoers. The Fair Funds Provision of SOX empowers the SEC to obtain civil penalties resulting from enforcement cases and add them to disgorgement funds to compensate investors who suffer losses due to securities law violations. Prior to the passage of SOX, any collected civil penalties were given to the U.S. Treasury. Section 1103 of SOX authorizes the SEC to (1) obtain a temporary order to escrow extraordinary payments by the company to its directors, officers, partners, agents, controlling persons, or employees; and (2) prevent the payment of extraordinary rewards to executives and others while the company is under investigation by the commission.

Provisions Addressing Conduct of Other Individuals

Several provisions of SOX address the conduct of all corporate governance participants in the financial reporting supply chain, including the board of directors, the audit committee, management, internal auditors, external auditors, investment banks, legal counsel, and financial analysts. The following SEC-related rules address the conduct of gatekeepers other than directors, management, and auditors:

1. Rules governing research analysts' potential conflicts of interest
2. Rules regarding standards of conduct for attorneys practicing before the SEC
3. Rules pertaining to rating agencies
4. Rules concerning mutual and hedge funds
5. Rules pertaining to investment banks

Evaluation of the Sarbanes-Oxley Act

SOX is being broadly viewed as (1) measures and reforms to identify, assess, manage, and mitigate potential conflicts of interest among different participants in financial reporting supply chains; (2) the mechanics of creating, retaining, and protecting records (certifications of financial statements and internal controls); and (3) measures to promote professional accountability and personal integrity (director independence, audit committee financial expert, auditor independence). The debate over the possible impacts of new corporate governance reforms, including SOX and their compliance costs on U.S. capital market global competitiveness, centers around two key views. The first view is that SOX and its implementation costs have contributed significantly to the loss of U.S. capital market global competitiveness as the majority of IPOs have recently been listed on capital markets abroad. This view is supported by those who believe some provisions of SOX should be revised and their implementation rules should be relaxed, particularly for smaller companies. However, exemptions of certain companies (smaller companies) or the allowance of voluntary compliance with Section 404 of SOX can result in the following four negative consequences: (1) noncompliant companies will continue to produce financial reports that are inferior to those of compliant companies; (2) investors in the long term will adjust the cost of capital to reflect the discrepancy in the quality of financial information of compliant versus noncompliant firms; (3) audit costs, insurance costs, and litigation costs will increase for noncompliant companies to compensate for the increased level of risk; and (4) as investors in noncompliant companies start to lose money, litigation will increase for the companies and their boards, management, and auditors. The other view is that SOX and its implementation rules have significantly improved the accountability of corporate America, the quality and reliability of its financial reporting, and the integrity and efficiency of its capital markets. This view is supported by those who believe that SOX rebuilt investor confidence in U.S. capital markets, and investors are willing to pay a premium for more protection provided by tougher regulations. Yet, there is a middle-ground view that although SOX has had positive impacts on corporate America, its implementation has not been cost effective, efficient, or scalable, and thus, its implementation rules should be relaxed. This view is gaining momentum and is supported by (1) lawmakers, as Congress voted to not roll back provisions of SOX; (2) regulators, as the SEC and PCAOB are currently relaxing some of the rigorous rules concerning Section 404 compliance; and (3) the business and investment community, as they reap the benefit and incur the cost of regulation.

Global Reach of SOX

In its inception, SOX was not received positively by the global business community. This initial perception toward SOX has gradually changed with the onset of more global financial scandals such as Parmalat, ABB, and Royal Ahold. Regulators worldwide now realize that financial scandals are not limited to U.S. businesses, and corporate malfeasance is a global phenomenon that can be addressed and prevented through effective corporate governance and efficient regulations. Countries worldwide either revised or established corporate governance best practices or codes. For example, the SOX provision on executive certification of financial statements is now required in countries such as Australia, Canada, China, and Mexico. The creation of an independent standard-setting body similar to the PCAOB for the auditing profession has now been adopted by the EU and Canada. Other examples are the move toward independent directors serving on the corporate board, more disclosures of executive compensation, and rotation of audit partners.

Several provisions of SOX have been adopted in countries worldwide, which lends credibility to SOX and its intended purpose of protecting investors. Voluntary adoption of SOX's provisions can be interpreted as an indication of the cost effectiveness and efficiency of some of its provisions. Adopted provisions by other countries, including Australia, Canada, China, India, and Mexico, are executive certification of financial statements, mandatory audit committees consisting of all independent directors, creation of standard-setting bodies similar to the PCAOB in regulating the auditing profession, the rotation of audit partners and audit firms, and executive certification of ICFR without requiring an audit opinion. The EU has also strengthened the robustness of financial reporting and corporate governance practices through the European Parliament and the European Council from the founding EC in modernizing corporate governance and company law both in short-term and long-term horizons by addressing board structure, shareholder voting, company structure, and investor disclosures. The EU has focused on the following corporate governance issues: (1) establishing a framework to enable shareholders to exercise their rights, (2) strengthening rules pertaining to director compensation, (3) developing the European Corporate Governance Forum to promote the integration of national codes, (4) implementing annual corporate governance statements, and (5) enhancing the responsibility and involvement of nonexecutive directors.

The Asian crisis and Japanese banking difficulties prompted regulators in Asia to improve their corporate governance. For example, the Code of Corporate Governance for listed companies in China was developed by the China Security Regulatory Commission to (1) strengthen shareholder rights, (2) decrease governmental power, (3) incorporate independent board members into the board structure, (4) require boards to evaluate management activities, (5) develop a foundation for executive and director remuneration, (6) mandate systems of ICFR, and (7) strengthen external auditor independence. China's Code, like the UK Combined Code, is based on the approach of "comply and explain." Some perceive the ability of the government to intervene, as well as the lack of proper measures to prevent and detect corporate corruption and fraud, as continuing obstacles that China faces in its attempt to reform its corporate governance. South Africa also adopted the King Report on corporate governance, in 2002, which is similar to the UK Combined Code and the approach of "comply or explain."

SECURITIES AND EXCHANGE COMMISSION

The twentieth century is regarded as the era of the industrial revolution, the creation of corporations as separate legal entities distinct from their owners, and the formation of capital markets. The separation of ownership and control in corporations created the potential for opportunistic management behavior and the need for an independent audit to verify management performance. The stock market collapse of 1929 was attributed to the lack of reliable financial information and meaningful reporting requirements to protect investors. Congress responded by passing the Securities Act of 1933 and the Securities Exchange Act of 1934 to improve investor confidence. These acts were intended to protect investors from receiving false and misleading financial information relevant to public companies' stocks (e.g., financial statements) and to maintain the integrity and efficiency of the capital markets.[4] Congress also established the SEC to enforce provisions of the acts in protecting investors. The SEC has five commissioners, including the chairman, who are appointed by the president with the advice and consent of the Senate, where no more than three commissioners belong to the same political party. Commissioners' responsibilities are to (1) interpret federal securities laws, (2) amend existing rules, (3) propose new rules, and (4) enforce rules and laws.

The SEC is the federal agency in charge of administering and enforcing the federal laws governing securities markets in the United States with its vision of strengthening the integrity and soundness of securities markets and the mission of protecting investors; maintaining fair, orderly, and efficient markets; and facilitating capital formation.[5] The goals of the SEC are to (1) enforce compliance with federal securities laws by detecting problems in the markets, preventing and deterring violations of the laws, alerting investors to possible wrongdoing, sanctioning wrongdoers, and returning funds to harmed investors; (2) promote healthy capital markets through an effective and flexible regulatory environment that facilitates innovation, competition, and capital formation, and improves investor confidence in the capital markets; (3) foster informed investment decision making by ensuring that investors receive complete, accurate, and transparent financial information and implementing a variety of investor education initiatives; and (4) maximize the use of SEC resources through improvements in its organizational and internal controls effectiveness and sound investments in human capital and new technologies. Achievement of these goals contributes to improvements in public companies' governance, the integrity and efficiency of the securities markets, economic growth, and prosperity for the nation.

The SEC has four divisions: (1) the Division of Corporate Finance, which oversees corporate disclosure of public information by reviewing registration statements for newly offered securities, annually audited and quarterly reviewed filings (Forms 10-K and 10-Q), proxy materials sent to shareholders before an annual meeting, annual reports to shareholders, documents pertaining to tender offers, and mergers and acquisitions filings; (2) the

Division of Market Regulation, which establishes and maintains standards for fair, orderly, and efficient capital markets by regulating the major securities market participants, including broker/dealer firms and self-regulatory organizations (SROs) such as stock exchanges and the NASD; (3) the Division of Investment Management, which oversees and regulates the investment management industry and administers securities laws relevant to investment companies (e.g., mutual funds) and investment advisors; and (4) the Division of Enforcement, which investigates possible violations of securities laws, recommends actions either in a federal court or before an administrative law judge, negotiates settlements on behalf of the commission, and publishes accounting and auditing enforcement releases (AAERs).

The SEC's leadership consists of a bipartisan five-member commission including the chairman and four commissioners. The SEC has twenty offices, which include the office of the chairman who serves as the CEO and nineteen functional offices. The SEC's nineteen officers carry out the commission's oversight function of public companies. These offices are (1) administrative law judges, (2) human resources, (3) chief accountant, (4) compliance inspections and examinations, (5) financial management, (6) economic analysis, (7) equal employment opportunity, (8) the executive director, (9) filings and information services, (10) information technology, (11) inspector general, (12) international affairs, (13) investor education and assistance, (14) legislative affairs, (15) public affairs, (16) secretary, (17) general counsel, (18) risk assessment, and (19) administrative services. The SEC's headquarters are in Washington, DC, with eleven regional and district offices throughout the United States.

Table 7.2 summarizes the laws that govern the securities industry. Public companies have been required by the Securities Act of 1933 and the Securities Exchange Act of 1934 to provide "full and fair disclosure" of financial reports in connection with the public offer and sale of their securities. The intention was to establish a continuous disclosure system to protect investors and ensure the integrity of securities markets. The requirements of these acts have shaped and continue to influence the corporate governance of public companies. Among these requirements are periodic filings of the company's annual audited and quarterly reviewed financial statements with the SEC; the maintenance of books, records, and accounts that fairly reflect transactions; and maintenance of an adequate and effective internal control system. These acts provide the SEC with broad powers for the administration and enforcement of violations of securities laws, including bringing either administrative proceedings or civil injunctive actions against individuals who violate the laws. Section 14 of the 1934 act authorizes the SEC to regulate the proxies of public companies, and Rule 2(6) gives the SEC power to suspend, or permanently bar from practicing, any person who willfully violates, or aids and abets in the violation of, the securities laws.

The SEC has issued more than twenty rules in implementing various provisions of SOX. SOX, by creating the PCAOB, established new responsibilities for the SEC. Section 107 of SOX authorizes the SEC to have oversight and enforcement authority over the PCAOB by stating that (1) PCAOB adopted rules and standards should be approved by the SEC before they become effective; (2) the PCAOB's disciplinary actions must be communicated through the SEC on final judgment; and (3) the SEC has censure authority to rescind PCAOB authority, limit its activities, functions, and operations, and remove from office the PCAOB's board members who are deemed to violate prescribed authority.

Table 7.2 Laws That Govern the Securities Industry

Securities Act of 1933	Securities Exchange Act of 1934	Public Utility Holding Company Act of 1935	Trust Indenture Act of 1939	Investment Company Act of 1940	Investment Advisers Act of 1940	Sarbanes-Oxley Act of 2002
• "Truth in Securities Law." • Requires all securities in the U.S. to be registered. • Registration is designed to help investors make informed decisions before purchasing securities.	• Created the U.S. Securities and Exchange Commission (SEC). • Gives the SEC powers to register, regulate, and oversee the securities markets.	• Regulates holding companies operating in the electric utility industry or in the retail distribution of natural or manufactured gas. • Utility holding companies are required to submit reports providing detailed information concerning their organization, financial structure, and operation.	• Applies to bonds, debentures, notes, and other debt securities that are offered for public sale. • Securities may not be offered for sale to public investors until full disclosure of the bond issue details are released through a Trust Indenture, or agreement between the issuer of bonds and bondholder. • Requires that a trustee be selected for all bond issues, so that the rights of bondholders are not compromised.	• Regulates the organization of companies, including mutual funds, that engage primarily in investing, reinvesting, and trading in securities, and whose own securities are offered to the investing public. • Purpose is "to mitigate and … eliminate the conditions … which adversely affect the national public interest and the interest of investors." • Objective of this act is to improve disclosure of relevant information and investment goals of funds to investors.	• States that companies or individuals that are compensated for advising others about securities investments must register with the SEC and are subject to regulations intended to protect investors. • Amendment in 1996 decreases the scope by requiring only advisers who have at least $25 million of assets or advise a registered investment company must register with the commission.	• "The most far reaching reforms of American business practices since the time of Franklin Delano Roosevelt." • Dictated a broad spectrum of reforms to boost corporate responsibility, improve financial disclosures, and fight corporate and accounting fraud. • Established the Public Company Accounting Oversight Board (PCAOB) to oversee the activities of the auditing profession.

Source: Adapted from the U.S. Securities and Exchange Commission (SEC). n.d. The Laws That Govern the Securities Industry. Available at: sec.gov/about/laws.shtml.

SEC Activities

The SEC is regarded as an independent agency created by Congress to protect investor interests. Two important sources of federal laws are the Securities Act of 1933 and the Securities Exchange Act of 1934, both designed to protect investors by ensuring an efficient and transparent securities market, promoting market stability, mitigating the risk of misleading financial information, and enforcing securities laws. Public companies registered with the SEC must adhere to these laws and file annual and quarterly reports. The SEC is empowered to (1) establish rules, including accounting and auditing standards for public companies under its jurisdiction; (2) bring civil enforcement actions against the individuals who violate its rules and securities laws; (3) review periodic financial reports filed with the commission in Forms 10-K and 10-Q; and (4) review appeals from sanctions imposed by national stock exchanges or other professional organizations on their members. ASRs issued by the SEC from 1937 through 1982 document rulings regarding accounting and auditing as well as enforcement actions for violations of Rules 2(6) and 10(b)-5 of the 1934 act. The SEC has documented its enforcement actions since 1982 in its AAERs.

The SEC has also addressed the governance of SROs in response to concerns raised about the adequacy of SRO governance practices. The SEC requires each SRO, including the NYSE and Nasdaq, to review the adequacy of their governance practices. SROs are being criticized for not exercising the high corporate governance standards usually applied to business corporations and not being held to that high level. The SEC has issued rules to improve the governance and financial transparency of all SROs that play an important role as standard setters for public companies and operators of trading markets. The SEC has approved mutual fund reform initiatives to strengthen the governance structure of mutual funds, including the requirements for certain mutual funds to have an independent, nonexecutive chairman of the board and at least 75 percent of their board members to be independent.

The SEC has also established a new Office of Risk Assessment (ORA) to assist the commission in better anticipating, finding, and mitigating areas of significant financial risk and potential fraud. The ORA works closely with the SEC's field staff to identify and prevent corporate malfeasance. Section 306(a) of SOX prohibits any director or executive officer of a public company from directly or indirectly purchasing, selling, or otherwise acquiring or transferring any equity security of the company during a pension plan blackout period. This provision of SOX temporarily prevents plan participants or beneficiaries from engaging in equity securities transactions through their plan accounts, if they acquired the equity security in connection with their service to or employment in the company as directors and executive officers.

The SEC should improve the fairness of its enforcement program in pursuing civil and criminal actions against corporate wrongdoers and in preventing, detecting, and correcting securities law violations that cause corporate malfeasance and scandals. The SEC, in continuing its strong and vigorous enforcement actions, should be mindful of the devastating consequences of the financial scandals of Enron, WorldCom, Global Crossing, Qwest, Adelphia, Tyco, Parmalat, Ahold, Fannie Mae, AIG, and others, caused by securities law violations, and, at the same time, be aware of the unintended consequences of excessive enforcement that may have burned good companies that contribute to the efficiency, health, and

Table 7.3 SEC Enforcement Actions By Year

	2000	2001	2002	2003	2004	2005	2006
Financial disclosure	103	112	163	199	179	185	128
Securities offering	125	95	119	109	99	60	61
Broker/dealer	72	65	82	137	140	94	75
Inside trading	40	57	59	50	42	50	46
Investment advisor/company	44	40	52	72	90	95	95
Civil contempt	36	31	47	42	21	23	
Market manipulation	48	40	42	32	39	46	27
Other	35	44	34	38	29	44	27
Delinquent filings	N/A	N/A	N/A	N/A	N/A	33	91
Total	**503**	**484**	**598**	**679**	**639**	**630**	**574**

Source: Johnson, S. 2006, November 3. SEC Enforcement Declines 8.9 percent. Available at: www.cfo.com/article.cfm/8127167/c_2984409/?f=archives.

competitiveness of the capital markets. Table 7.3 shows SEC enforcement actions brought against public companies from 2000 to 2005.

PUBLIC COMPANY ACCOUNTING OVERSIGHT BOARD

Section 101 of SOX authorizes the establishment of the PCAOB to oversee the audit of public companies under the SEC jurisdiction. Congress authorized the PCAOB to fund its expenses by imposing a fee on all public companies determined in proportion to their market capitalizations and registration fees received from public accounting firms. Some criticized the rapid growth of the PCAOB's budget and employment levels, and even suggested that the PCAOB's basic role of registering and inspecting public accounting firms and standard-setting activities should be transferred to the SEC. The PCAOB has also appointed a standing advisory group (SAG) of thirty members with expertise in accounting, auditing, corporate governance, investments, and corporate finance to assist in carrying out its standard-setting responsibilities. Table 7.4 summarizes the PCAOB structure, including its composition and responsibilities.

PCAOB Responsibilities

This section highlights some of the PCAOB's responsibilities that are discussed in depth in Chapter 9. These responsibilities are to

1. Prepare its budget and manage its operation. The PCAOB gets its budget from fees paid by public companies and mutual funds, and registration fees paid by public accounting firms that audit public companies. PCAOB governance, budget, and operations are designed in such a manner to maintain its independence from public accounting firms and the federal government.

2. Register both U.S. and non-U.S. public accounting firms auditing U.S. public companies. Both domestic and foreign public accounting firms that prepare or issue audit

Table 7.4   Public Company Accounting Oversight Board Structure

Composition	Responsibilities

1. A private, not-for-profit organization registered in the District of Columbia.
2. A nongovernmental authoritative organization funded by the SEC registrants and registered public accounting firms.
3. Consists of five members, two of which are CPAs.
4. Members serve full time for a five-year staggered term, with a two-term limit.
5. The chair may be held by a CPA who has not been in practice for at least five years prior to the appointment.
6. The first group of members consists of
  a. William J. McDonough (chair)
  b. Charles D. Niemeier
  c. Kayla J. Gillan
  d. Daniel L. Goelzer
  e. Willis D. Gradison, Jr.
  f. Douglas R. Carmichael (Chief Auditor and Director of Professional Standards)
  g. Thomas Ray (Deputy Chief Auditor)
7. The Standing Advisory Group consists of thirty members to advise the PCAOB in its standard-setting process.
	1. Regulate the auditing profession.
	2. Restore investor confidence and public trust in the auditing profession.
	3. Prepare its budget and manage its operations.
	4. Register and inspect public accounting firms that audit public companies (registered firms).
	5. Establish, adopt, and modify auditing, independence, quality control, ethics, and other standards for registered firms.
	6. Enforce compliance with applicable laws and regulations, including securities laws, professional standards, SEC rules, and PCAOB standards by registered firms.
	7. Investigate registered firms for potential violations of applicable laws, regulations, and rules.
	8. Impose sanctions for violations.
	9. Perform other duties or functions as deemed necessary.
	10. Hire necessary staff to conduct inspections; perform operating activities; and develop auditing, independence, quality control, ethics, and other professional standards.
	11. File an annual report with the SEC.

Source: PCAOB. Adapted from pcaob.org/about_the_pcaob/index.aspx.

    reports must register with the PCAOB. Public accounting firms that play a role in the preparation or furnishing of an audit report are covered by this registration requirement.

3. Inspect registered public accounting firms. The PCAOB ended several decades of self-regulation and peer reviews for registered public accounting firms. Firms that audit more than one hundred public companies are annually inspected by the PCAOB, whereas other firms are inspected triennially.

4. Establish auditing, quality control, and ethics standards for registered public accounting firms.

5. Enforce compliance with applicable laws and regulations. The PCAOB is authorized to enforce compliance of registered accounting firms with securities laws, professional standards, SEC rules, and PCAOB professional standards.

6. Investigate registered public accounting firms. The PCAOB is also authorized to investigate registered public accounting firms and their personnel for potential violations of applicable laws, rules, and regulations.

7. Impose sanctions for violations. The PCAOB is empowered to discipline errant firms and their personnel by revoking registration or imposing monetary penalties of up to $15 million.

8. Hold roundtables addressing emerging issues affecting the functions and performance of registered public accounting firms to obtain the views of interested parties, including accounting firms, public companies, investor groups, standard setters, and academicians.

9. Take initiatives in addressing auditing in a small business environment. The PCAOB also launched the Forum on Auditing in a Small Business Environment to discuss the PCAOB's standard-setting processes and inspections that may be affected by the PCAOB's oversight actions. The SEC has also established the advisory committee for smaller public companies.

10. Perform other duties or functions as deemed necessary.

PCAOB Standard-Setting Process

The PCOAB standard-setting process, as presented in Figure 7.1, is an open and deliberate process consisting of the following systematic processes:

1. Encouraging participation by the accounting profession, including academicians, the preparers of financial statements, the investor community, and others

2. Reviewing existing GAAS, and adopting, changing, or establishing new GAAS

3. Seeking advice and input of a standing advisory group and other ad hoc task forces

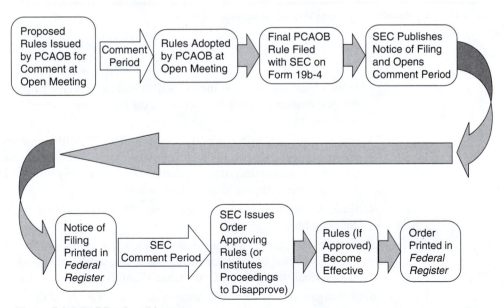

Figure 7.1 PCAOB rulemaking process.

Source: Adapted from the PCAOB. Available at: pcaob.org/standards/standards_setting.aspx.

4. Releasing proposed standards for public comment

5. Adopting standards by the board

6. Submitting the adopted standards to the SEC for approval, as required by SOX, which then have the effect of federal laws

FEDERAL SENTENCING GUIDELINES FOR ORGANIZATIONS

In 1984, Congress created the U.S. Sentencing Commission (USSC) with the authority to issue guidelines for punishing organizations, including companies that have committed federal crimes.[6] The USSC's guidelines have been used by companies as a benchmark for reducing the risk of significant penalties if a violation occurs. Pursuant to the passage of SOX, the USSC revised its guidelines by focusing on a compliance program to ensure companies' compliance with all applicable laws and regulations.[7] The revised guidelines, as summarized in Table 7.5, are expected to have a significant impact on the effectiveness of corporate governance by requiring (1) companies to establish and maintain an effective compliance program; (2) boards of directors to accept accountability to ensure compliance throughout the company; and (3) companies to assign high-level individuals (e.g., executives) to oversee the company's compliance program.

AMERICAN INSTITUTE OF CERTIFIED PUBLIC ACCOUNTANTS

The AICPA is a national professional association of more than 330,000 CPAs in public practice, industry, government, and academia. Prior to the creation of the PCAOB, the Auditing Standards Board (ASB) of the AICPA was responsible for issuing GAAS and their interpretations of Statements on Auditing Standards (SAS) in providing guidance for external auditors to conduct their audits of both public and private companies as well as not-for-profit organizations. The ASB also promulgated quality control standards to assess the quality of auditors' performance.

More than a century old, the AICPA, the accounting profession's trade organization and its auditing standard-setting board, has been criticized for not responding properly to accounting scandals and related audit failures. The passage of SOX created the PCAOB, which has practically replaced the AICPA in its standard-setting process and the monitoring and disciplining of registered public accounting firms that audit financial statements of public companies. In the post-Enron and SOX era, the AICPA has tried to stay relevant in providing a variety of professional services to its members engaging in audits of private companies and not-for-profit organizations.

AICPA Roles in the Post-SOX Era

The AICPA has introduced some initiatives in the post-SOX era to improve public trust in the accounting profession and public accounting firms. AICPA standards issued after April 2003, are relevant and applicable to nonpublic companies and their independent auditors. A few months after the passage of SOX, the AICPA launched its new accounting culture presenting the six leadership roles of the AICPA as (1) a standard-setting role of obtaining greater involvement of users of financial statements in setting auditing standards

Table 7.5   Federal Sentencing Guidelines

To have an effective compliance and ethics program, organizations should	The minimum requirements an organization should have for the program are
1. Exercise due diligence to prevent and detect criminal conduct. 2. Promote an organizational culture that encourages ethical conduct and compliance with the law. 3. Reasonably design, implement, and enforce the program. 4. Consider that the failure to prevent/detect an instant offence does not necessarily mean the program is not effective.	1. The organization should establish standards and procedures to prevent and detect criminal conduct. 2. The governing authority should be knowledgeable about the content and operation of the program. 3. The governing authority should exercise reasonable oversight of the implementation and effectiveness of the program. 4. Individuals with operational responsibility should periodically report to management and when appropriate to the governing authority on the effectiveness of the program. 5. The organization should to the best of its ability not hire anyone to a position of authority who is known to have committed illegal or unethical acts. 6. The organization should inform their employees of the program and conduct periodic training sessions on the employees' responsibility and role with the regard to the program. 7. The organization should take reasonable steps to ensure the program is followed, and to periodically evaluate the effectiveness of the program. 8. The organization should have and publicize a system for employees to report potential or actual criminal conduct without fear of reprisal. 9. The organization should have appropriate incentives for compliance and disciplinary action for noncompliance. 10. Once criminal conduct is detected the organization should take reasonable steps to prevent similar conduct, including modifying the program. 11. The organization should periodically assess the risk of criminal conduct and take steps to reduce that risk.

Source: U.S. Sentencing Commission. 2005. 2005 Federal Sentencing Guidelines. §8B2.1. Available at: www.ussc.gov/2005guid/8b2_1.htm.

and establishing new guidance on issues affecting the profession, such as auditor rotation requirements and compensation policies for audit partners; (2) a fraud prevention and detection liaison role of assisting market institutions and corporations in designing and communicating antifraud controls and programs to the public and assisting corporations to implement them; (3) a research role of promoting academic research in areas such as corporate fraud prevention, how investors can help protect themselves against fraud, and the strengthening of undergraduate antifraud education through cooperation with universities and the Association of Certified Fraud Examiners by establishing an Institute of Fraud Studies; (4) an educational role of developing training programs aimed at combating fraud, changing the continuing education rules for CPAs to include more credits on fraud detection, and integrating antifraud education into college courses and textbooks for accounting students and antifraud training materials into courses for management and directors; (5) a financial reporting role of working with other standard setters to improve the quality, reliability, and transparency of business and financial reporting and initiating debates on such topics as big GAAP versus little GAAP; and (6) a corporate governance role of improving corporate governance and internal control systems by revising auditing standards so the public will be put on notice when the auditor communicates internal control weaknesses to the audit committee.[8]

In 2002, the AICPA issued SAS No. 99 titled Consideration of Fraud in a Financial Statement Audit. SAS No. 99 supersedes SAS No. 82, providing risk factors broken into the fraud pyramid of incentives/pressures, opportunities, and attitudes/rationalizations. However, SAS No. 99 states that "absolute assurance is not attainable and thus even a properly planned and performed audit may not detect a material misstatement resulting from fraud." SAS No. 99 requires auditors to (1) approach every audit with professional skepticism; (2) discuss among the audit team members the risks of material misstatement due to fraud; (3) identify fraud risk and management incentives, opportunities, and ability to rationalize occurrence of fraud; and (4) design audit tests responsive to the risks of fraud. SAS No. 99 requires that auditors place an increased emphasis on discovering financial statement fraud.

The AICPA has issued several other SASs pertaining to risk assessment and auditor communication. The ASB, in February 2006, approved eight new standards, collectively referred to as the Risk Assessment Standards. The new SAS Nos. 104–111 provide guidance regarding the auditor's assessment of risks of material misstatement, design and performance of tailored audit procedures to address assessed risks, audit risk and materiality, planning and supervision, and audit evidence. These standards were established to provide (1) a more in-depth understanding of the audited entity and its environment, including internal control; (2) a more rigorous assessment of the risk of where and how the financial statements could be materially misstated; and (3) improved linkage between the auditor's assessed risks of material misstatements and the nature, timing, and extent of audit procedures performed in addressing those issues.[9]

FINANCIAL ACCOUNTING STANDARDS BOARD

The FASB has been the designated private sector not-for-profit organization for promulgating standards of financial accounting and reporting since 1973. The SEC has delegated its accounting standard-setting authority to the FASB to issue authoritative Statements of Financial Accounting Standards (SFAS) for the measurement, recognition, and reporting of business transactions and economic events and the preparation of their financial statements. SFAS are generally accepted as authoritative guidelines in the financial reporting process primarily because the SEC, the accounting profession, and the investing public rely on SFAS in facilitating credible, reliable, comparable, and transparent financial information. The FASB develops broad accounting concepts as well as standards for financial reporting. It also provides guidance on the implementation of the standards.

The FASB has been criticized for being too slow to respond to emerging changes in the business environment. Standard-setting bodies such as the FASB and the IASB can improve the quality and transparency of financial information by establishing principles-based standards that encourage companies to portray the economic reality of their transactions and reflect the underlying economic performance rather than issuing accounting rules that can be easily circumvented. The FASB has also been criticized for being too influenced by corporations and auditors and not enough by investors in its standard-setting process.[10] This influence is being exerted on the FASB because (1) corporations, their executives, auditors, and professional associates are continuously in contact with the FASB in expressing their opinions and influencing the deliberative process; (2) corporate executives and auditors are more engaged in the standard-setting process; and (3) the composition of the FASB's seven board members consists of three former auditors and two former executives with no members from institutional investors.

Traditional financial statements, providing historical financial information concerning an entity's financial condition and results of operations as a proxy for future business performance, may not provide relevant information to investors. Investors demand forward-looking financial and nonfinancial information on KPIs concerning the entity's governance, economic, ethical, social, and environmental activities. Standard setters worldwide are considering overhauling financial reporting and restructuring financial statements by focusing on KPIs and providing information concerning how businesses are actually run. The SEC has already approved rules to allow foreign companies to file their statements using IFRS without reconciliation to U.S. GAAP. This is an important step by the SEC toward the adoption of a single set of GAAP because many U.S. companies may choose to use IFRS for their financial reporting. This move toward full convergence in accounting standards may make the FASB less relevant for issuing accounting standards for public companies and refocus its standard-setting process on establishing accounting standards for private and not-for-profit organizations.

GOVERNMENT ACCOUNTING STANDARDS BOARD

The GASB, since 1984, has issued accounting standards for state and local governments to improve the quality of their financial reporting. GASB, in April 2005, issued its Concept Statement No. 3, Communication Methods in General Purpose External Financial Reports That Contain Basic Financial Statements. Concept Statement No. 3 provides (1) a conceptual framework for determining communication methods for improving the presentation of financial reports of governmental entities, (2) criteria for each communication method, and (3) a hierarchy for their use.[11] The major required communication methods include recognition in basic financial statements, disclosures in notes to basic financial statements, and presentation as supplementary information. Concept Statement No. 3 addresses the necessary elements for the communication of reliable and relevant messages within financial reports, including the description of roles and responsibilities of those who prepare, use, and analyze the information.

INTERNATIONAL FEDERATION OF ACCOUNTANTS

Challenges facing IFAC are finding ways to improve the credibility of the accounting profession worldwide, establishing globally accepted accounting and auditing standards, and developing global corporate governance guiding principles. These challenges require IFAC to quickly move toward the global convergence of both accounting and auditing standards issued by a variety of standard-setting bodies such as the FASB, AICPA, PCAOB, and IASB.

In February 2005, the International Organization of Securities Commissions (IOSCO), the Basel Committee on Banking Supervision (BCBS), the International Association of Insurance Supervisors (IAIS), the World Bank, and the Financial Stability Forum created the Public Interest Oversight Board (PIOB) to oversee the public interest activities of IFAC.[12]

COMMITTEE OF EUROPEAN SECURITIES REGULATORS

The EC established the Committee of European Securities Regulators (CESR) to ensure efficient functioning of the European capital market. CESR's membership consists of the national securities regulators in the twenty-five member states and the securities authorities of Norway and Iceland. As an enforcement arm of the EC, CESR has observer status on several other regulatory bodies, including the European Securities Committee (ESC), the Accounting Regulatory Committee (ARC), and the European Financial Reporting Advisory Group (EFRAG). The primary responsibilities of CESR are to (1) issue standards and guidance to national securities regulators for implementation by member states, (2) promulgate standards for the enforcement of financial reporting while allowing member states to take enforcement actions, and (3) issue implementation guidance on some of the key capital market directives. Unlike its U.S. counterpart, the SEC, CESR does not currently have enforcement powers over EU securities issuers. Regulators in individual member states have enforcement authority, while CESR coordinates their enforcement authority.

In May 2004, the SEC and CESR released a joint statement that specifies the terms of reference for future cooperation and coordination between the two bodies.[13] The primary objectives of such cooperation are to (1) identify and address emerging risks in the EU and U.S. markets at an early stage; (2) discuss potential regulatory projects to facilitate converging ways of addressing common issues; and (3) set priorities for discussion and collaboration between the two bodies, including market structure issues, the role and responsibility of credit rating agencies and analysts, and mutual fund regulation.

STATE INFLUENCE ON CORPORATE GOVERNANCE

State laws generally affect corporate governance by setting requirements for companies' directors and officers. State laws are aimed at protecting shareholder rights by allowing them to (1) inspect and copy the company's stock ledger, its list of shareholders, and certain books and records; (2) approve certain business transactions (e.g., mergers and acquisitions); (3) receive proxy materials; and (4) obtain significant disclosures for related party transactions. There is no uniform body of corporate law in the United States because each state is allowed to establish its own model. The state of Delaware has been prominent in shaping corporate law because more than half of public companies are incorporated in Delaware. The differences in company law between states can encourage "company law shopping" by companies and promote states to compete for company incorporation.

The Committee on Capital Markets Regulation recommends limiting how and when state law can pursue enforcement actions against auditing firms and financial institutions by suggesting that (1) the U.S. Department of Justice (DoJ) have the ability to sign off on all state indictments only in cases when the SEC chose not to take enforcement actions, and (2) the SEC have the final say on any settlement cases of national importance.[14] The committee proposes that state attorneys general coordinate prosecutions of companies with federal agencies. The DoJ should only pursue corporate criminal indictments as a last resort, with the rare possibility that a company would waive its attorney–client privilege. The committee basically recommends that lawmakers and regulators should not be tough on the gatekeepers (management, directors, legal counsel, and auditors) who violate securities laws by relaxing some of the measures designed to protect investors from corporate malfeasance and wrongdoers, and by promoting less aggressive civil and criminal investigations.

CORPORATE GOVERNANCE AND COURTS

The role of courts in corporate governance and corporate internal affairs has been debated in the law literature. The debate centers around two important aspects of corporations. The contractarianists view the corporations as a nexus of contracts that establishes a set of private contractual relationships among all corporate governance participants, including providers of capital and services.[15] This suggests that a corporation is brought into being, is subject to extensive regulation by the state of incorporation and federal agencies, and does not exist apart from the contracts among its participants. Anticontractarianists, in contrast, argue that a corporation is not a typical contract subject to extensive government regulation and view the corporation as a concession of the state.[16] Regardless of acceptance of either the contractarian or concession view of corporations, the state and federal governments as well as judicial process (courts) play an important role in today's corporate governance in determining and interpreting the fiduciary duties of its participants.

Emerging corporate governance reforms have been established through legislation, regulations, standards, and voluntary best practices, yet there is still room for improvement. One argument is that when these reforms do not function well and do not properly address corporate governance issues (e.g., executive compensation), the courts should step in and interpret the applicability of these reforms. For example, when shareholders raise concerns about the potential lack of director independence and whether independence rules have been observed, the court can determine whether the director is acting independently according to the rules and the good faith concept. Thus, courts play a role in corporate governance by interpreting implications and applicability of corporate governance measures, rules, and regulations in a disputed circumstance.

The judicial process and court decisions in several landmark cases have affected the structure of corporate governance in the United States. Many of the court cases have led to increased accountability and liability for a company's board of directors. For example, in *Escott v. Barrchris Construction Corp.* (1968), directors were held liable for misleading financial statements in the registration statements, whereas in *Gould v. American-Hawaiian Steamship Co.* (1972), directors were held liable for information in the proxy statement. The U.S. District Court in *SEC v. Mattel* ruled that Mattel must restructure its board to include a majority of outside auditors and establish an audit committee.

CORPORATE GOVERNANCE AND SELF-REGULATORY ORGANIZATIONS

An SRO is a nongovernmental entity that represents registrants and is organized for the purpose of regulating the operations and standards of practice and business conduct. The

Table 7.6   Listed Self-Regulatory Organizations

- American Stock Exchange (AMEX)
- Boston Stock Exchange (BSE)
- Chicago Board Options Exchange (CBOE)
- CBOE Futures Exchange, LLC (CFE)
- Chicago Mercantile Exchange (CME)
- Chicago Stock Exchange (CHX)
- Depository Trust Company (DTC)
- Emerging Markets Clearing Corporation (EMCC)
- Fixed Income Clearing Corporation (FICC)
- International Securities Exchange (ISE)
- Municipal Securities Rulemaking Board (MSRB)
- National Association of Securities Dealers (NASD)
- National Futures Association (NFA)
- National Securities Clearing Corporation (NSCC)
- National Stock Exchange (NSX)
- New York Stock Exchange (NYSE)
- National Market System Plans (NMS)
- NQLX (NQLX)
- OneChicago LLC (OC)
- Options Clearing Corporation (OCC)
- Pacific Exchange, Inc. (PCX)
- Philadelphia Stock Exchange (PHLX)
- Stock Clearing Corporation of Philadelphia (SCCP)

Source: U.S. Securities and Exchange Commission. n.d. Self-Regulatory Organization (SRO) Rulemaking and National Market System (NMS) Plans. Available at: sec.gov/rules/sro.shtml.

main objective of an SRO is to promote the protection of investors and the public interest based on a foundation of firm ethics and equality.[17] Table 7.6 provides a list of SROs listed with the SEC. Although defined as self-regulatory, an SRO is regulated in part by the SEC. Recently, new rules have been proposed relating to the governance, administration, transparency, and ownership of SROs registered with the SEC.[18] Specifically, one item proposed would require that the board of directors of registered organizations comprise a majority of independent members. Other items seek to amend existing reporting requirements of the Securities Exchange Act of 1934, with the stipulation that an SRO file and disclose on a frequent basis information relating to the governance, regulatory programs, finances, ownership structure, and other items deemed essential. To improve SEC oversight and surveillance of SROs, the SEC has also proposed that quarterly and annual reports be filed that outline and detail the particular areas of regulatory programs.

By establishing listing standards for their listed companies, SROs including stock exchanges can also influence corporate governance. For example, the NYSE has long been an advocate of the formation of an independent audit committee. The rash of financial scandals of 2001 encouraged SROs to revise their listing standards and address additional corporate governance measures to prevent further scandals. Pursuant to the passage of SOX, SROs proposed and adopted new corporate governance measures specified in SOX in their listing standards. The listing standards of the SROs govern the structure, composition, and independence of listed companies' boards of directors, formation and functions of board committees, and communication with their shareholders. The requirements of listing standards appear to go beyond the SEC's SOX implementation rules regarding director independence and oversight functions. Listing standards require that the majority of directors be independent; the board hold executive sessions; and the board form independent audit, compensation, and nomination committees.

National stock exchanges originally established criteria for the admission of stocks to their listings to ensure that investors receive adequate information about listed companies. To properly and continuously monitor stocks, national stock exchanges require periodic disclosures of business activities, financial reports, and future plans of listed companies. Exchanges also establish corporate governance listing standards to ensure investors are protected from corporate malfeasance and abuse and provide enforcement mechanisms to promote compliance with their standards. Furthermore, exchanges establish trading processes designed to enhance the efficiency of capital markets. Listing standards adopted by national stock exchanges "are designed to promote liquidity and transferability of shares by increasing investor confidence in both the markets and listed issuers."[19] These listing standards consist of (1) qualification requirements related to listed companies' annual revenues, assets, cash flow, public float, or market capitalization; and (2) corporate governance measures relevant to listed companies' internal structure and conduct that are designed to promote high standards of corporate democracy and responsibility, as well as integrity and accountability to shareholders. These listing standards are intended to (1) promote liquidity and transferability, (2) lend stability to the capital markets by permitting access only to listed companies with good corporate governance practices, and (3) improve investor confidence by monitoring companies' corporate governance practices.

Listing standards of national stock exchanges are reasonably uniform among the exchanges. The SEC has attempted to create convergence in these standards, and they are, to a large extent, still a matter of private contract between national stock exchanges and their listing companies. Nonetheless, noncompliance with these listing standards may result in delisting that can be very costly and detrimental to the delisted company's survival. Recent reported financial scandals by high-profile companies have resulted in delisting from national stock exchanges. Although there are many similarities between the listing standards of the NYSE and Nasdaq, some differences remain. It is desirable that these listing standards be consolidated with a keen focus on convergence toward more principles-based listing standards.

U.S. capital markets have traditionally operated under a system of self-regulation. Congress, in 1934, authorized the SEC to oversee securities exchanges, issue rules and regulations, and monitor exchange activities. SROs initially organized as not-for-profit entities have played an essential role in (1) facilitating an entry point to the capital markets, (2) providing a forum for investors to trade securities, (3) promoting market liquidity, (4) strengthening the integrity and efficiency of the capital markets, and (5) enforcing their members' compliance with exchange rules and securities laws. Recent years have witnessed several significant changes in securities markets in the United States and abroad. First, many SROs have transformed from not-for-profit status to shareholder-owned entities that operate as for-profit enterprises driven primarily by electronic trading systems. Exchanges transformed to a for-profit structure to raise the needed capital to finance their infrastructure expenditures of offering cheaper and more efficient electronic trading services. National stock exchanges have demutualized and converted into for-profit entities through public listing of their shares on exchanges. Second, SROs have encountered competition for market share and the need for balancing their members' interests with fiduciary duties to investors. Third, like listed public companies, SROs are expected to improve their governance, oversight, and transparency in the post-SOX period. As exchanges have become public companies themselves, their own governance and governance requirements of their listed companies that trade on exchanges have been scrutinized by regulators and the investing public.

The new structure of exchanges as for-profit entities has raised several governance issues. First, exchanges have traditionally been SROs that establish listing standards for their listed companies. These standards have also been subject to approval by the SEC. The standard-setting function of exchanges as SROs and for-profit entities has not been properly addressed. Second, emerging corporate governance reforms affect all public companies, including demutualized exchanges. Third, demutualized exchanges are better candidates for cross-border mergers (e.g., NYSE Euronext), which raises legitimate questions concerning regulations of these global exchanges.

BEST PRACTICES

The effectiveness of corporate governance depends on compliance with state and federal statutes and listing standards, as well as best practices recommended by investor activists and professional organizations. Public companies are required to comply with state and federal statutes and listing standards of national stock exchanges. Nevertheless, mere compliance with corporate governance through rules, regulations, laws, and standards will not guarantee effective corporate governance, and companies should integrate best practices into their governance structure. Best practices can be used as benchmarks to determine the best way to improve business processes and corporate governance by following the means by which leading organizations achieve excellence performance. Best practices should be viewed as sources of high achievement and creative insights for improvements, not substituted for solutions to business problems. In addition, companies may be penalized by investors if they fail to consider best practices. Best practices of corporate governance discussed in the following sections are these of The Conference Board, American Law Institute (ALI), American Bar Association (ABA), and institutional investors.

The Conference Board

In the wake of the financial scandals of 2000–2002, The Conference Board established a Commission on Public Trust and Private Enterprise, which issued a three-part report relevant to executive compensation, corporate governance, audit, and accounting. Some examples of recommendations pertaining to executive compensation are (1) performance-based compensation should be linked to specific goals, (2) the compensation committee should be responsible for all aspects of executive pay, and (3) fixed-price stock options should be expensed. Corporate governance recommendations are (1) the board of directors should develop a structure that establishes an appropriate balance of power sharing between the CEO and the independent directors; (2) the board should be composed of a substantial majority of independent directors; (3) the board should establish a nominating/governance committee; (4) the board should establish a three-tier director evaluation mechanism to assess the performance of the entire board of directors, each committee of the board, and each member of the board committees; and (5) shareholders, particularly in the long term, should be more active in the governance of their companies. Auditing and accounting recommendations address audit committees' oversight responsibilities relevant to financial reporting and auditing, including (1) the audit committee should be vigorous in complying with provisions of SOX, (2) all companies should have an internal audit function, (3) public accounting firms should limit their nonaudit services to their audit clients, and (4) the auditing profession should establish a model to improve audit quality.

American Law Institute

In 1994, the ALI published *Principles of Corporate Governance: Analysis and Recommendations*, which was intended to clarify fiduciary duties of corporate directors and officers, and suggest guidelines for fulfillment of these responsibilities.[20] This document has not been revised in the post-SOX era. ALI's principles address the objective and conduct of the company and its structure, directors' and officers' duty of care, the business judgment rule, and the duty of fair dealing. ALI's *Principles of Corporate Governance* is organized into seven parts, with each part consisting of one or more recommended rules or principles, comments on the rule or principle, and comments on the related notes. The seven parts are

- Part 1, which presents precise definitions for the essential terms used in the analysis and recommendations
- Part 2, which defines the fundamental objective of the business corporation as enhancing corporate profit and shareholder gain
- Part 3, which discusses the legal functions and powers of the directors and officers, and the composition of the board of directors and its committees
- Part 4, which elaborates on the directors' and officers' duty of care
- Part 5, which presents the duty imposed on directors, officers, and controlling shareholders to deal fairly with the company
- Part 6, which covers the role of directors and shareholders regarding transactions in control and tender offers
- Part 7, which deals with corporate remedies

American Bar Association

The ABA issued its first Model Business Corporation Act in 1950 and has issued several editions of the *Corporate Director's Guidebook*.[21] The *Corporate Director's Guidebook* is a valuable source for directors to better understand their duties, and how to effectively fulfill their responsibilities, and it also provides guidelines for board structure, its committees, leadership, meetings, size, and quality of information. The fourth edition of the book addresses recent developments affecting corporate governance in the post-SOX era and the basic legal duties and responsibilities of directors. The ABA formed a Task Force on Corporate Responsibility to examine the many corporate governance concerns that contributed to the bankruptcy of Enron and WorldCom and make suggestions for governance improvements.[22] The recommendations of the ABA task force relating to the professional conduct of lawyers and board structure, composition, leadership, and committees were adopted as ABA policy in August 2003.

Institutional Investors

The diversity in shareholder base of public companies, inability of the average investors to exercise control over management decisions and actions, reported managerial aggressive and unethical conduct, and the ever-increasing agency problems have strengthened shareholder activism. Shareholder activism can assist in reducing agency costs by promoting corporate governance principles and monitoring compliance with corporate governance best practices. For example, CalPERS has been an active institutional investor in promoting vigilant corporate governance. As a shareholder activist, CalPERS has published its focus list since 1992. The focus list is a list of public companies with poor corporate governance practices and poor financial performance that should be closely monitored for their underperformance by regulators and the investment community.

Institutional investors have long been advocates for strengthening corporate governance of companies in which they invest. CalPERS; OPERS; TIAA-CREF; the CII; and the AFL-CIO have suggested guidelines for corporate governance principles and best practices, and use their guidelines for making voting decisions. Institutional investors often rely on proxy voting advisory services of others, including Glass Lewis & Co. and ISS, to make voting recommendations, vote their shares in electing directors, or participate in other matters at companies' annual and special meetings.[23] In some cases, corporate governance best practices suggested by institutional investors go beyond the requirements of state and federal statutes and even listing standards (e.g., definition of director independence). It is expected that individuals would also consider proxy voting advisory services provided to them by Glass Lewis & Co. and ISS in closely monitoring their companies' governance practices, financial reporting process, and audit activities.

Generally speaking, institutional investors have both incentives and opportunities to actively engage in corporate governance and monitor managerial actions to ensure better performance for their investment. Nevertheless, they may not fully exercise their corporate governance oversight function and monitoring controls for several reasons. First, pension fund managers are not typically the ultimate beneficiaries of the wealth generated by corporations, and they may not have strong incentives to monitor a company's affairs. Second, such monitoring engagements are not without cost, and fund managers may be reluctant to incur these costs, particularly when other investors will benefit costlessly from such monitoring (the free-rider problem). Finally, institutional investors are often not long-term investors and may not be motivated to engage in long-term costly monitoring, instead choosing to divest in poorly performing stocks. Nevertheless, the equity holdings of institutional investors are becoming more indexed and diversified, which create fewer opportunities for an easy exit for divesting poorly performing stocks. This indexing and diversification may result in an alignment of the fund with the public interest and market performance as opposed to alignment with a specific company. In this capacity, institutional investors play an important role in improving investor confidence in corporate governance through their presence and active participation in monitoring public companies' governance structures. Conceptually, institutional investors represent small shareholders such as pensioners or beneficiaries. To ensure that they protect the interests of their beneficiaries or trustees, they should disclose their corporate governance and voting policies as well as potential conflicts of interest and how they manage them.

Council of Institutional Investors

The CII was founded in 1985 in response to takeover activities that threatened the financial interests of pension fund beneficiaries for the purpose of encouraging member funds to take an active role in protecting plan assets and to increase return on investment for its members.[24] The CII started with twenty members, and in 2005 had more than 140 pension fund members with total assets of more than $3 trillion and more than 130 educational sustainers. The CII is a significant voice for institutional shareholder interests and encourages every company to have written, transparent, and disclosed governance policies and procedures; an ethics code that is applicable to directors, officers, and employees; and provisions for the strict enforcement of these.

National Association of Corporate Directors

Since 1996, the NACD has established several BRCs on issues related to corporate governance, including the commissions on (1) executive compensation and the role of the compensation committee, (2) audit committees, (3) board evaluation, (4) CEO succession, (5) risk oversight, and (6) the role of the board in corporate strategy.

Business Roundtable

The Business Roundtable is an association of CEOs of leading U.S. companies and has addressed issues relevant to corporate governance. The Business Roundtable has several reports, including (1) Principles of Corporate Governance, (2) Executive Compensation: Principles and Commentary, and (3) The Nominating Process and Corporate Governance Committees: Principles and Commentary. These publications have addressed many corporate governance matters and established several best practices.[25]

Public Pension Funds

According to the U.S. Census Bureau, there are more than 2,656 public pension funds that hold more than 20 percent of publicly traded U.S. equity and, as such, are considered as major shareowners of the U.S. capital markets.[26] Many public pension funds, including CalPERS and the State Board of Administration (SBA) of Florida, have received considerable attention in the post-SOX era for their participation in corporate governance. These pension funds have improved the investor monitoring function through shareholder proposals, support of regulations to enhance shareholder democracy, and participation in securities fraud actions. However, smaller pension funds are not expected to be actively involved in corporate governance primarily because of substantial monitoring costs. For example, the negative impacts of backdating practices on corporate governance and financial reporting at UnitedHealth Group have encouraged CalPERS to demand governance reforms at UnitedHealth Group by sending letters to thousands of shareholders asking for effective proxy access to the director nomination process. The purpose of this is to promote board accountability and support proposals designed to allow shareholders who have held at least 3 percent of the company's shares for at least two years to nominate two directors to management election ballots.

SUMMARY

This chapter examines the roles and responsibilities of state and federal statutes, regulators, and standard setters in the corporate governance structure. Public companies are required to comply with federal and state statutes, SEC rules and regulations, standards of standard-setting bodies, and listing standards of national stock exchanges. Best practices of professional organizations and investor activists have also provided benchmarks for improving corporate governance. The move toward globalization of corporate governance, financial reporting, and auditing practices requires that regulators and standard setters in the United States work closely with their counterparts worldwide to make ultimate convergence possible.

The key points of this chapter are

- Compliance with applicable laws, regulations, rules, and standards is essential to the efficiency and integrity of the capital markets, the effectiveness of corporate governance, and the reliability of financial reports.

- The fundamental provisions of SOX can be categorized into the following five categories: (1) corporate governance; (2) financial reporting; (3) audit functions; (4) federal securities law enforcement; and (5) others (e.g., legal counsel, financial analysts).

- The SEC was established to protect investor interests and was given the responsibility for issuing financial reporting standards.

- SOX directs the SEC to issue rules in implementing its provisions pertaining to corporate governance, financial reporting, audit activities, and others.

- Section 101 of SOX authorizes the establishment of the PCAOB as an independent, non-governmental, not-for-profit organization to oversee the audits of public companies under SEC jurisdiction.

- The PCAOB's primary functions are to (1) register public accounting firms that audit public companies; (2) inspect the registered public accounting firms on a regular basis; (3) establish auditing, attestation, ethics, quality control, and independence standards; and (4) conduct investigations and disciplinary proceedings.

- The PCAOB ended several decades of self-regulation and peer reviews for registered public accounting firms because both domestic and foreign public accounting firms that prepare or issue audit reports must now register with the PCAOB.

- The AICPA has introduced many initiatives in the post-SOX era to improve public trust in the accounting profession and public accounting firms.

- FASB has been the designated private sector not-for-profit organization for promulgating standards of financial accounting and reporting since 1973.

- The state attorney general can play an important role in enforcing compliance with applicable regulations and corporate governance standards to protect investors.

KEY TERMS

Accounting and Auditing
  Enforcement Releases
  (AAERS)
Accounting Regulatory
  Committee (ARC)
administrative law judges
American Bar Association
  (ABA)
American Institute of
  Certified Public
  Accountants
  (AICPA)
anticontractarianists
blackout period

California Public Employees'
  Retirement System
  (CalPERS)
Committee of European
  Securities Regulators
  (CESR)
contractarianists
Council of Institutional
  Investors (CII)
European Financial Reporting
  Advisory Group
  (EFRAG)
generally accepted accounting
  principles (GAAP)

generally accepted accounting
  standards (GAAS)
Government Accounting
  Standards Board (GASB)
International Accounting
  Standards Board (IASB)
investment protection
  principles (IPPs)
Investor Task Force
Office of Risk Assessment
self-regulatory organization
  (SRO)
U.S. Sentencing Commission
  (USSC)

REVIEW QUESTIONS

1. Explain the categories of the fundamental provisions of SOX.

2. Explain the financial reporting provisions of SOX and SEC-related rules.

3. What is one fundamental objective of SOX?

4. Explain the Fair Funds Provision of SOX.

5. What are the four divisions of the SEC?

6. Explain the blackout period.

7. Explain the composition of the PCAOB.

8. What is SAS No. 99, and what are its requirements?

9. What are some of the advantages of complying with SOX?

10. What is the objective behind cooperation and coordination of the SEC and CESR?

11. Explain the role of courts in corporate governance. Also explain the two views on the role of courts.

DISCUSSION QUESTIONS

1. What do you think about this perception that the majority of corporate executives believe that the emerging corporate governance reforms, including SOX, provide standards and measures for corporate compliance, but there is no adequate training, education, or standards for individuals who carry out compliance? Substantiate your answer.

2. "The recent wave of financial scandals indicates that regulators are often slow in responding to those scandals, bringing enforcement actions against corporate wrongdoers, and preventing widespread effects of aversion towards the scandal." Do you agree with the given statement? Why?

3. Do you feel the concept of best practices helps the effectiveness of corporate governance? Explain how.

4. Can SOX and other corporate governance provisions be beneficial for nonpublic companies even though they are not obligated to comply with such provisions? Explain your answer.

5. How do companies encourage compliance with rules and regulations established by regulatory bodies within the corporate governance structure?

6. How does the regulatory and legal environment of a country shape the corporate governance structure?

7. Describe the impact of regulatory conflicts and overload on the long-term attractiveness and global competitiveness of the U.S. capital markets.

NOTES

1. Sarbanes-Oxley Act of 2002 (SOX). Available at: www.sec.gov/about/laws/soa2002.pdf.

2. Allen, M. 2002. Bush Signs Corporate Reforms into Law: President Says Era of "False Profits" Is Over. *Washington Post* July 31, p. A04.

3. The Corporate Library. 2007, September. Big Four Audit Firms Feel the Effects of Post SOX Inroads as Audit Fees Skyrocket. Available at: findarticles.com/p/articles/mi_pwwi/is_200709/ai_n19525842.

4. Much of the discussion in this section is from the U.S. Securities and Exchange Commission (SEC). 2005. The Investor's Advocate: How the SEC Protects Investors, Maintains Market Integrity, and Facilitates Capital Formation. Available at: www.sec.gov/about/whatwedo.shtml.

5. U.S. Securities and Exchange Commission (SEC). 2005. 2005 Performance and Accountability Report. Available at: www.sec.gov/about/secpar/secpar2005.pdf.

6. U.S. Sentencing Commission. n.d. An Overview of the United States Sentencing Commission and the Organizational Guidelines. Available at: www.ussc.gov/training/corpover.pdf.

7. U.S. Sentencing Commission. 2004, May 10. Amendments to the Sentencing Guidelines. Available at: www.ussc.gov/2004guid/RFMay04.pdf.

8. Melancon, B. C. 2002, September 4. Worth Repeating: A New Accounting Culture. Available at: www.aicpa.org/pubs/jofa/oct2002/melancon.htm.

9. The American Institute of Certified Public Accountants (AICPA). n.d. Auditing Standards. Available at: www.aicpa.org/Professional+Resources/Accounting+and+Auditing/Authoritative+Standards/auditing_standards.htm.

10. Henry, O. 2006. Generally Improvable Accounting Principles. *BusinessWeek* November 20. Available at: www.businessweek.com/magazine/content/06_47/b4010075.htm.

11. Governmental Accounting Standards Board (GASB) 2005, April. Summary of Concept Statement No. 3: Communication Methods in General Purpose External Financial Reports That Contain Basic Financial Statements. Available at: www.gasb.org/st/concepts/gconsum3.html.

12. Public Interest Oversight Board (PIOB) Web site. Available at: www.ipiob.org/.

13. U.S. Securities and Exchange Commission (SEC). 2004, June 4. SEC-CESR Set Out the Shape of Future Collaboration. Press Release. Available at: www.sec.gov/news/press/2004-75.htm.

14. Committee on Capital Markets Regulation. 2006, November 30. Interim Report of the Committee on Capital Markets Regulation. Available at: www.capmktsreg.org/research.html.

15. Jensen, M., and W. Meckling. 1976. Theory of the Firm: Managerial Behavior. Agency Costs and Ownership Structure. *Journal of Financial Analysis* 3:305-311.

16. Henssen, R. 1979. *In Defense of the Corporation.* Stanford, CA: Hoover Institution.

17. Investopedia.com. 2005. Self-Regulatory Organization (SRO). Available at: investopedia.com/terms/s/sro.asp.

18. U.S. Securities and Exchange Commission (SEC). 2005. Fair Administration and Governance of Self-Regulatory Organizations; Disclosure and Regulatory Reporting by Self-Regulatory Organizations; Recordkeeping Requirements for Self-Regulatory Organizations; Ownership and Voting Limitations for Members of Self-Regulatory Organizations; Ownership Reporting Requirements for Members of Self-Regulatory Organizations; Listing and Trading of Affiliated Securities by a Self-Regulatory Organization. Available at: sec.gov/rules/proposed/34-50699.htm.

19. American Bar Association (ABA). 2002, August. Special Study on Market Structure Listing Standards and Corporate Governance. A Special Study Group of the Committee on Federal Regulation of Securities, ABA, Section of Business Law. 57 Bus. Law. 1487.

20. American Law Institute (ALI). 1994. *Principles of Corporate Governance: Analysis and Recommendations* (2 vols.). West Publishing, Philadelphia.

21. American Bar Association (ABA). 2004. *Corporate Director's Guidebook* (4th Edition). National Book Network, Chicago.

22. American Bar Association (ABA). 2003, March 31. Report of the American Bar Association Task Force on Corporate Responsibility. Available at: www.abanet.org/buslaw/corporateresponsibility/final_report.pdf.

23. Goodman. A., and B. Schwartz. 2004. *Corporate Governance: Law and Practice.* Matthew Bender & Co.

24. The Council of Institutional Investors (CII). 2005. About the Council: Who We Are. Available at: www.cii.org/about.

25. Business Roundtable. 2005, November. Principles of Corporate Governance 2005. Available at: 64.203.97.43/pdf/CorporateGovPrinciples.pdf; Business Roundtable. 2007, January. Executive Compensation: Principles and Commentary. Available at: http://64.203.97.43/pdf/ExecutiveCompensationPrinciples.pdf; Business Roundtable. 2004, April. The Nominating Process and Corporate Governance Committees: Principles and Commentary. Available at: http://64.203.97.43/pdf/20040421002CorpGovComm.pdf.

26. U.S. Census Bureau. 2005. Federal, State, and Local Governments: 2005 State and Local Government Employee-Retirement Systems. Available at: www.census.gov/govs/www/retire05view.html.

Chapter 8

Internal Auditors' Roles and Responsibilities

INTRODUCTION

Internal auditing has evolved from a traditional appraisal activity to an objective, assurance, and consulting activity. Internal auditing is viewed as a value-added service that improves the organization's operations, risk management, internal controls, and financial reporting. Internal auditors' roles changed from merely providing input and objective feedback to management, to directly participating in corporate governance, and thus, in the decision-making function. The CAE is primarily responsible for managing, directing, and overseeing the internal audit function. The company's audit committee is directly responsible for hiring, compensating, firing, and overseeing the work of the CAE. This chapter discusses the role of internal auditors in corporate governance.

Primary Objectives

The primary objectives of this chapter are to

- Understand the importance and value-added nature of the internal audit function.
- Review the qualities of an effective internal audit department.
- Discuss the role of internal auditors as assurance providers and consultants.
- Review the trends of the internal auditing profession.
- Discuss the relationship of internal audits and the audit committee.
- Analyze the determinants of an effective internal audit.
- Discuss the professional practices framework (PPF) adopted by The Institute of Internal Auditors (IIA).
- Promote the best practices and internal audit framework.

INTERNAL AUDITING FUNCTION AND CORPORATE GOVERNANCE

Recent corporate governance reforms require an effective corporate governance structure based on a vigilant board of directors; diligent, competent, and ethical management; a credible independent audit function; and an effective internal audit function. As an integral component of corporate governance, the internal audit function should provide objective and independent assurance and consulting services for all of the company's activities, including risk management, internal controls, financial reporting, and other corporate governance functions. Listing standards of national stock exchanges require that listed companies establish an internal audit function. Although privately held companies and not-for-profit organizations are not mandated to have an internal audit function, best practices suggest that every organization can benefit from assurance and consulting services provided by their internal auditors.

Corporate governance reforms have significantly strengthened the role and responsibility of internal auditors because they are assuming a much higher organizational profile, and the board of directors is expecting them to play a more active role in corporate governance. A 2007 PricewaterhouseCoopers survey reveals that 79 percent of responding internal auditors reported that their internal audit functions have (1) assessed the effectiveness of their company's corporate governance structure and practices, and (2) made specific recommendations to improve their company's governance processes and activities.[1] Furthermore, internal auditors are well trained and positioned to (1) assess and ensure effective performance management and accountability; (2) identify and communicate risks and related controls to the company's board of directors, audit committee, and management; (3) promote appropriate ethical behavior and conduct throughout the company; (4) assess both internal and external corporate governance mechanisms and procedures; (5) assist in the preparation of corporate governance reports and providing assurance on the effectiveness of the corporate governance structure; and (6) review the company's quality assurance programs and procedures.

In the bankrupted WorldCom, the internal audit department was ineffective as evidenced by the following: (1) the director of internal audit reported to the company's CFO rather than to the audit committee, with no executive sessions between the audit committee and

Table 8.1 Comparison of Internal Audit (Pre- and Postcorporate Governance Reforms)

Prereforms	Postreforms
• Voluntary internal audit functions	• Mandatory internal audit functions
• Outsourcing of internal audit functions	• Objective internal auditors
• Auditing services to management	• Oversight function by audit committee
• Inadequate resources and organization	• Reporting responsibility to the audit committee
• Improper oversight of internal audit functions	• Provide assurance and consulting services in the areas of risk management, internal control, financial reporting, and corporate governance
• Lack of cooperation with external auditors	• Adequate resources and authority
• Regarded as the "eyes and ears" of management	• Better cooperation with external auditors
	• Regarded as the "eyes and ears" of the audit committee

internal auditors; (2) the internal audit's budgets, staffing, compensation, and bonuses were controlled by the company's CEO; (3) the internal audit department failed to review and monitor ICFR; and (4) internal auditors focused primarily on operation and efficiency audits of cost savings and finding additional revenues to gain management acceptance.[2]

Table 8.1 compares internal audits pre- and post corporate governance reforms. Internal auditors' services can be viewed as value added in improving the effectiveness of their organization's governance by assisting management in assessing internal controls and ERM, identifying their material weaknesses, and making suggestions for improvement. Internal auditors are now participating in both the internal corporate governance processes, such as internal controls and ERM, and the external corporate governance process, which includes (1) assisting the board of directors and the audit committee in their oversight function, (2) cooperating with independent auditors in their integrated reports on audits of ICFR and financial statements, and (3) participating in environmental audits and the preparation of corporate governance and sustainability reports.

To ensure that the internal auditing role is viewed as a value-added function contributing to the improvement of both internal and external aspects of corporate governance, internal auditors should (1) be independent by reporting directly to the board of directors or the board's representative, the audit committee; (2) have adequate financial and human resources; and (3) participate in almost all corporate governance functions by assisting all participants, including the board of directors, the audit committee, management, external auditors, and legal counsel in effectively fulfilling their responsibilities.

The IIA, in its 2002 position paper presented to the U.S. Congress, states, "Internal auditors, the board of directors, senior management, and external auditors are the cornerstones of the foundation on which effective corporate governance must be built."[3] The IIA promotes the role of the internal auditor as not only an active participant in the corporate governance process, but also an independent observer. The role of internal auditors has evolved from performing traditional appraisal activities and audit functions of evaluating internal controls to being considered an important component of corporate governance by improving operations. Internal auditors now focus on adding value to their organizations in performing a variety of assurance-related functions by providing assistance to (1) the audit committee in effectively discharging its oversight responsibilities; (2) management in making business decisions, assessing ERM, certifying internal controls and financial statements, and identifying and preventing problems and potential risks; and (3) the independent auditor in performing the integrated audit of both internal control and financial statements.

Internal Auditors as Assurance Providers

Internal auditors are well trained and positioned to provide numerous assurance services. The emerging trend toward more emphasis on MBL of governance, economic, ethical, social, and environmental performance requires organizations to provide assurance on a variety of their performance measures and achievements. Assurance reports on these measures are currently voluntary, except for the audit report on economic measures (four basis financial statements), and should be performed by the organization's internal auditors. The objectivity and credibility of these voluntary assurance services depend on the independence and competence of the individual providing the services (internal auditors). Assurance services described in this section relate to (1) corporate governance, (2) ethical considerations, (3) social responsibilities, and (4) environmental matters.

Internal auditors, in addition to these voluntary assurance services, can assist external auditors in their integrated audit of internal controls and financial statements. The PCAOB in its Auditing Standard (AS) No. 2, as superseded by AS No. 5, encourages external auditors to use testing results performed by others (internal auditors) in determining the nature, extent, and timing of tests of controls in an integrated audit.[4] The extent of reliance on the work of internal auditors in an integrated audit depends on their objectivity, independence, and competence.

Internal auditors may assist management in complying with Section 302 and 404 requirements of SOX by reviewing management's certifications on internal controls and financial statements or providing some type of assurance on the accuracy of those certifications. Internal auditors should confirm that their assurance services are in compliance with their professional standards and are based on and supported by sufficient and competent audit evidence. Internal auditors are focusing more on risk assessments and the use of a risk-based approach in their audit coverage by (1) adopting a process approach to risk assessment and planning, (2) supplementing annual risk assessments with quarterly or more frequent updates, (3) leveraging prior assessment results, (4) aligning risk assessments, (5) obtaining the needed specialized talent, and (6) coordinating with other risk management groups.[5]

Internal Auditors as Consultants

Internal auditors can provide a variety of consulting services to the company's board of directors, the audit committee, management, and other personnel at all levels.

1. **Consulting services to the board of directors and audit committee.** Section 301 of SOX requires that public companies establish funding for and provide resources to their audit committees, including funding to retain and compensate independent

counsel and other advisors as the committee deems necessary. One means to achieve audit committee oversight effectiveness is to ask internal auditors to provide consulting services to the committee in overseeing financial reports, internal controls, risk assessment, whistleblower programs, and codes of business ethics. Indeed, internal auditors are well trained to provide consulting services to the entire board of directors and all board committees, particularly audit committees, to effectively discharge their fiduciary duties and oversight functions.

2. **Consulting services to management.** The internal auditor role has been defined as providing consulting services to management at all levels to assess the efficiency, effectiveness, and economy of managerial performance. Traditional consulting services to management have been in the areas of operational effectiveness and efficiency, internal controls assessment, risk management, financial reporting, safeguarding assets, and compliance with applicable laws, rules, regulations, and standards. To maintain their independence and objectivity, internal auditors should ensure that they refrain from making decisions on behalf of management.

3. **Internal auditor training services.** Internal auditors provide numerous training services to all personnel within their organizations, including training on IT, internal control procedures and assessment, risk management, financial reporting, and compliance with applicable regulations and other activities without impairment of objectivity and independence. As the organization's training and educational experts, internal auditors bring more knowledge to the entire organization and assist all personnel in carrying out their assigned responsibilities.

TREND AND RELEVANCE OF INTERNAL AUDITORS

Internal auditing has transformed over the past several decades from its beginnings as a financial enforcer and service function to a value-added function as an important component of corporate governance. This transformation is far from over in light of emerging reforms requiring the establishment of internal audit functions for listed companies. The Foreign Corrupt Practices Act (FCPA) of 1977 requires that public companies establish an internal accounting control system to provide reasonable assurance for achieving control objectives.[6] Indeed, the FCPA was labeled as the "Internal Auditors Full Employment Act of 1977."[7]

COSO, in its Report of the National Commission on Fraudulent Financial Reporting, underscored the important role that the internal auditing function can play in preventing and detecting fraudulent financial reporting. The COSO report in 1987 stressed the need for an internal audit function and made several recommendations for enhancing the role of internal auditors by stating, "it is the general belief of our Commission that the internal audit function is far too hidden from public view."[8] The COSO report recognizes that an effective internal audit function enables management and audit committees to monitor the integrity of the financial reporting process. The report made the following recommendations for internal auditing:

1. Public companies should establish an effective internal audit function, with sufficient qualified personnel, tailored to their size and the nature of their business.

2. The company's established internal audit function should be objective.

3. Management and the audit committee should determine whether the internal auditor's involvement in the audit of financial reports is appropriate and properly coordinated with the independent auditor.

The IIA redefined internal auditing in 1999 as follows:

> *Internal auditing is an independent, objective* assurance and consulting activity *designed to* add value *and improve an organization's operations. It helps an organization accomplish its objectives by bringing a systematic, disciplined approach to evaluate and improve the effectiveness of risk management, control, and* governance processes.[9]

(Emphasis added.)

This definition of internal auditing promotes the role of internal auditors in corporate governance and their contributions to the emerging corporate governance reforms worldwide, particularly those in the United States. SOX does not directly address internal auditor responsibilities or the internal audit function. However, several provisions of SOX implicitly address that internal auditors can be of a great assistance to (1) management (executive certifications of financial reports and internal control); (2) the audit committee (establishing whistleblower programs, corporate codes of business and conduct); and (3) the independent auditor (audit of financial statements and internal control).[10] Nevertheless, listing standards of national stock exchanges require listing companies to have an internal audit function. The PCAOB has encouraged independent auditors to rely on the work of others, particularly internal auditors, in their auditing and reporting on ICFR. The PCAOB in its AS No. 2 states that "internal auditors normally are expected to have greater competence with regard to internal control over financial reporting and objectivity than other company personnel."[11] Thus, internal auditors have been of a great assistance to management in compliance with both Sections 302 and 404 of SOX and the registered independent auditor's audit and report on internal controls. However, PricewaterhouseCoopers' 2005 study indicates that in the few years after the passage of SOX (2003–2004), internal auditors had been so consumed by SOX compliance that their other priorities suffered and their primary focus on risk-based auditing was diverted.[12]

AUTHORITIES AND RESPONSIBILITIES OF INTERNAL AUDITORS

Authority

The internal audit function and the CAE in particular should have (1) full and free access to the company's audit committee; (2) unrestricted access to the company's records, documents, property, and personnel; (3) authority to determine the scope, nature, extent, and timing of internal audit activities; (4) plans that have already been approved by the audit committee; (5) authority to review risk assessment, internal controls, compliance, financial reporting, and governance processes; (6) authority to provide consulting services to corporate governance participants, including directors, executives, and key financial personnel; (7) authority to assist the audit committee in its oversight responsibilities relevant to financial reporting and audit activities; and (8) authority to discuss initiatives, policies, and procedures regarding risk assessment, internal controls, compliance, financial reporting, and governance processes with management and other corporate governance participants.

Figure 8.1 presents a sample internal audit department charter as suggested by the IIA. This sample charter describes the mission and scope of the work of internal auditors, their accountability, independence, authority, and responsibilities. The charter should be approved by the audit committee and senior management, and then be signed by the CAE, CEO, and audit committee chair.

Sample Internal Audit Department Charter

MISSION AND SCOPE OF WORK

The mission of the internal audit department is to provide independent, objective assurance and consulting services designed to add value and improve the organization's operations. It helps the organization accomplish its objectives by bringing a systematic, disciplined approach to evaluate and improve the effectiveness of risk management, control, and governance processes.

The scope of work of the internal audit department is to determine whether the organization's network of risk management, control, and governance processes, as designed and represented by management, is adequate and functioning in a manner to ensure

- Risks are appropriately identified and managed.
- Interaction with the various governance groups occurs as needed.
- Significant financial, managerial, and operating information is accurate, reliable, and timely.
- Employees' actions are in compliance with policies, standards, procedures, and applicable laws and regulations.
- Resources are acquired economically, used efficiently, and adequately protected.
- Programs, plans, and objectives are achieved.
- Quality and continuous improvement are fostered in the organization's control process.
- Significant legislative or regulatory issues impacting the organization are recognized and addressed appropriately.

Opportunities for improving management control, profitability, and the organization's image may be identified during audits. They will be communicated to the appropriate level of management.

ACCOUNTABILITY

The chief audit executive, in the discharge of his or her duties, shall be accountable to management and the audit committee to

- Provide annually an assessment on the adequacy and effectiveness of the organization's processes for controlling its activities and managing its risks in the areas set forth under the mission and scope of work.
- Report significant issues related to the processes for controlling the activities of the organization and its affiliates, including potential improvements to those processes, and provide information concerning such issues through resolution.
- Periodically provide information on the status and results of the annual audit plan and the sufficiency of department resources.

- Coordinate with and provide oversight of other control and monitoring functions (risk management, compliance, security, legal, ethics, environmental, external audit).

INDEPENDENCE

To provide for the independence of the internal auditing department, its personnel report to the chief audit executive, who reports functionally to the audit committee and administratively to the chief executive officer in a manner outlined in the above section on accountability. It will include as part of its reports to the audit committee a regular report on internal audit personnel.

RESPONSIBILITY

The chief audit executive and staff of the internal audit department have the responsibility to

- Develop a flexible annual audit plan using an appropriate risk-based methodology, including any risks or control concerns identified by management, and submit that plan to the audit committee for review and approval as well as periodic updates.
- Implement the annual audit plan, as approved, including as appropriate any special tasks or projects requested by management and the audit committee.
- Maintain a professional audit staff with sufficient knowledge, skills, experience, and professional certifications to meet the requirements of this charter.
- Evaluate and assess significant merging/consolidating functions and new or changing services, processes, operations, and control processes coincident with their development, implementation, and/or expansion.
- Issue periodic reports to the audit committee and management summarizing results of audit activities.
- Keep the audit committee informed of emerging trends and successful practices in internal auditing.
- Provide a list of significant measurement goals and results to the audit committee.
- Assist in the investigation of significant suspected fraudulent activities within the organization and notify management and the audit committee of the results.
- Consider the scope of work of the external auditors and regulators, as appropriate, for the purpose of providing optimal audit coverage to the organization at a reasonable overall cost.

AUTHORITY

The chief audit executive and staff of the internal audit department are authorized to

- Have unrestricted access to all functions, records, property, and personnel.
- Have full and free access to the audit committee.
- Allocate resources, set frequencies, select subjects, determine scopes of work, and apply the techniques required to accomplish audit objectives.
- Obtain the necessary assistance of personnel in units of the organization where they perform audits, as well as other specialized services from within or outside of the organization.

The chief audit executive and staff of the internal audit department are not authorized to

- Perform any operational duties for the organization or its affiliates.
- Initiate or approve accounting transactions external to the internal auditing department.
- Direct the activities of any employee not employed by the internal auditing department, except to the extent such employees have been appropriately assigned to auditing teams or to otherwise assist the internal auditors.

STANDARDS OF AUDIT PRACTICE

The internal audit department will meet or exceed the Standards for the Professional Practice of Internal Auditing of the Institute of Internal Auditors.

_____
Chief Audit Executive

_____
Chief Executive Officer

_____
Audit Committee Chair

Dated _____

Figure 8.1 Internal auditing charter.

Source: Adapted from the Institute of Internal Auditors. Available at: www.theiia.org./guidance/standards-and-practices/additional-resources/audit-committees-board-of-directors/internal-audit-department-charter/.

Responsibility

The internal audit function under the direct oversight of the audit committee is responsible for providing assurance that (1) management operations are efficient; (2) both operational and financial risks are identified, managed, and monitored; (3) proper communication and interactions exist between all corporate governance participants; (4) key operational, managerial, and financial information is accurate, timely, and reliable; (5) the company is in compliance with applicable laws, regulations, rules, and standards; (6) employees adhere to both internal policies and external regulations; (7) resources are safeguarded and used efficiently; (8) managerial programs, plans, and objectives are effectively achieved; (9) the internal audit function uses appropriate risk-based audit methodology; (10) the established annual audit plan is effectively implemented; (11) a professional internal audit staff is maintained with adequate skills, knowledge, education, certification, and experience; (12) an appropriate quality assurance program is established to assess the effectiveness of the internal audit function; (13) a continuous improvement process is implemented; (14) external and internal audit activities are properly coordinated to ensure adequate coverage and prevent duplication; (15) codes of corporate ethics are complied with; and (16) the audit committee receives periodic reports on internal audit activities and significant financial and internal control processes.

INTERNAL AUDIT OUTSOURCING

SOX, SEC-related rules, listing standards, and professional organizations (the IIA, PCAOB) all directly or indirectly recognize the important role that internal auditors can play by adding value and improving organizations' governance. Thus, the internal audit function is crucial to the effectiveness of a company's corporate governance in achieving its goal of creating stakeholder value and protecting stakeholder interest. However, the issue of whether an internal audit function should be established internally or outsourced has not been properly addressed by regulators and standard-setting bodies. The Conference Board recommends that all public companies have an internal audit function.[13] The established internal audit function can be either an "in-house" function or an "outsource" function performed by a public accounting firm. To improve the internal audit function and its independence, internal auditors should have a direct line of communication with and reporting responsibility to the audit committee.

The decision of whether to establish and maintain an internal audit function or outsource the function should be made by the company's board of directors and its representatives—the audit committee, management, legal counsel, and the independent auditor. A variety of factors, including the company's size in terms of total assets, sales, and number of employees; complexity of its operation; financial reporting process; geographic diversity of its operations; ERM; governance process; and availability of required financial and human capital, should be considered in deciding whether to outsource the internal audit function.

SOX prohibits independent auditors from providing certain internal auditing outsourcing services to public companies contemporaneously with audit services. This does not mean that public accounting firms are not permitted to provide internal audit outsourcing services to public companies. It simply means they cannot perform audit services on financial statements and internal audit outsourcing to the same public client for the same fiscal year. Independent auditors are not prohibited from performing internal auditing outsourcing services for non–public company audit clients. The SEC, in implementing the provisions of internal audit outsourcing of SOX, in January 2003, issued its release Nos. 33-8183 and 34-47265 to clarify the types of internal audit services that are prohibited.[14] In general, SEC rules prohibit services that may be subject to audit procedures throughout the audit of a client's financial statements, such as the audit client's internal control, accounting system, auditing systems, or financial statements. The SEC rule permits internal audit outsourcing to the client's independent auditor in the following areas:

1. Operational internal audits that are not related to internal accounting controls, financial systems, or financial statements.

2. Nonrecurring assessment of discrete items or other programs unrelated to outsourcing of the internal audit function.

AUDIT COMMITTEE RELATIONSHIP WITH INTERNAL AUDITOR

The internal audit function as an integral part of corporate governance has received well-deserved and long-awaited attention in the post-SOX era. Under the emerging corporate governance reforms, internal auditors are responsible for serving their entire organization and are accountable to the audit committee. Listing standards of national stock exchanges have substantially improved the stature of internal auditors by requiring that listed companies have an internal audit function to assist the company's audit committee and management with continuous assessments of internal controls and ERM. These initiatives should encourage companies to invest in competent and objective internal audit functions.

A close working relationship between the audit committee and internal auditors can improve the effectiveness of corporate governance. First, the independence and objectivity of internal auditors can be enhanced when they report their findings directly to the audit committee. The internal audit function should be independent in the sense that auditors maintain their (1) planning independence in determining scope and audit planning, (2) investigating independence in conducting the audit and performing audit procedures, and (3) reporting independence in communicating audit findings to senior management and the audit committee. Second, the prestige and status of internal auditors can be strengthened when they work with management at all levels. Third, internal auditors have the potential to be a significant source of assistance to the audit committee to effectively fulfill their oversight responsibilities in functions such as financial reporting, internal controls, risk management, external audit, whistleblowing, ethics, and taxes.

The audit committee can contribute to the success of internal auditors and the achievement of their value-added activities by ensuring that they have

1. Sufficient independence from management by reporting to and being held accountable to the audit committee
2. Adequate resources, competence, and focus to assess the company's operational efficiency, internal control effectiveness, ERM, and reliability of financial reports
3. Proper knowledge of the company's corporate governance, internal control, financial reporting, and audit activities
4. The mechanisms and confidence to bring forward controversial financial reporting issues
5. A process for communicating directly with the company's audit committee on a regular and timely basis
6. Access to the audit committee to discuss concerns related to management activities, financial reporting risk, and fraudulent financial reporting
7. Audit committee approval of the budget and staffing of the internal audit function

To improve the stature of the company's internal audit function, the CAE should report directly to, be evaluated and compensated by, and ultimately be held accountable by and directly responsible to the audit committee. Emerging corporate governance reforms hold the company's internal audit function primarily responsible and give ultimate accountability to the audit committee. The audit committee oversight function of the internal audit department requires the committee to approve the budget, audit plan, and policies of internal auditors. Specifically, the committee should hire, evaluate, fire, or transfer key internal audit personnel. The committee should meet regularly in executive sessions with the company's CAE to discuss important business, financial reporting, internal controls, and audit issues. In this regard, internal auditors are viewed as the "eyes and ears" of the audit committee. Internal auditors should regularly assess the likelihood of financial statement fraud or violations of security laws and inform the audit committee of significant alleged fraud, particularly if it involves management.

INTERNAL AUDITORS' ROLE IN INTERNAL CONTROL

Section 302 of SOX requires management quarterly certifications of both financial statements and financial reporting controls, whereas Section 404 requires annual management assessment of the effectiveness of both the design and operation of ICFR. Although management's responsibilities for compliance with both Sections 302 and 404 cannot be delegated or abdicated, internal auditors can considerably assist management in fulfilling their compliance responsibilities. Internal auditors in assisting management should maintain their objectivity and independence according to their charter and properly communicate with the audit committee. The CAE should consult with the audit committee in devoting internal audit resources to Sections 302 and 404 without compartmentalizing their other internal audit activities in adding value to their organization's performance. Management is primarily responsible for the design, implementation, and maintenance of ICFR, and internal auditors provide assurance and consulting services.

The IIA's 2004 position paper presents the Section 404 compliance process, several phases of this process, activities within each phase, accountability for each activity, individual(s) responsible for carrying out each activity, and recommendations for the

Table 8.2   Section 404 Compliance

Phase/activity	Lead responsibility	Recommended internal auditor roles
Planning		
Plan	Project sponsor	Provide advice and recommendations. Participate in project team planning.
Scope	Project team	Provide advice and recommendations. Participate in project team planning.
Execution		
Document	Line managers, project team, or specialists	Advise management regarding processes to be used. Perform quality assurance reviews.
Evaluation and testing	Line managers, project team, or specialists	Independently assess management's documentation and testing. Perform effectiveness testing (for highest reliance by external auditors).
Issues	Project team and line managers	Identify control gaps. Facilitate management discussions.
Corrective action	Line managers	Perform follow-up reviews.
Monitoring systems	Senior management	Perform follow-up reviews.
Reporting		
Management reporting	Senior management and line managers	Facilitate determinations (to report). Provide advice.
External audit reporting	External auditor	Act as a coordinator between management and the external auditor.
Monitoring		
Ongoing monitoring	Senior management	Perform follow-up services.
Periodic assessment	Project team or line managers	Perform periodic audits.

Source: Adapted from The Institute of Internal Auditors (IIA). 2004, May 26. Internal Auditing's Role in Sections 302 and 404 of the U.S. Sarbanes-Oxley Act of 2002. IIA, Altamonte Springs, FL. Available at: www.theiia.org/iia/download.cfm?file=1655.

Table 8.3   Internal Auditors' Activities Pertaining to Sections 302 and 404

Project oversight	Consulting and project support	Ongoing monitoring and testing	Project audit
1. Participate on project steering committee, providing advice and recommendations to the project team and monitoring progress and direction of the project. 2. Act as facilitator between external auditor and management.	1. Provide existing internal audit documentation for control processes. 2. Advise on best practices—documentation standards, tools, and test strategies. 3. Support management and process owner training on project, risk, and control awareness. 4. Perform quality assurance review of process documentation and key controls prior to handoff to the external auditor.	1. Advise management regarding the design, scope, and frequency of tests to be performed. 2. Independently assess of management and testing and assessment processes. 3. Perform tests of management's basis for assertions. 4. Perform effectiveness testing (for highest reliance by external auditors). 5. Aid in identifying control gaps and review management plans for correcting control gaps. 6. Perform follow-up reviews to ascertain whether control gaps have been adequately addressed. 7. Act as coordinator between management and the external auditor as to discussions of scope and testing plans. 8. Participate in disclosure committee to ensure that results of ongoing internal audit activities and other examination activities, such as external regulatory examinations, are brought to the committee for disclosure consideration.	1. Assist in ensuring that corporate initiatives are well managed and have a positive impact on an organization. Their assurance role supports senior management, the audit committee, the board of directors, and other stakeholders. 2. Use a risk-based approach in planning the many possible activities regarding project audits. Audit best practices suggest internal auditors should be involved throughout a project's life cycle—not just in postimplementation audits.

Source: Adapted from The Institute of Internal Auditors (IIA). 2004, May 26. Internal Auditing's Role in Sections 302 and 404 of the U.S. Sarbanes-Oxley Act of 2002. IIA, Altamonte Springs, FL. Available at: www.theiia.org/iia/download.cfm?file=1655.

internal auditor's role for each activity. Table 8.2 provides a summary of Section 404 compliance efforts and recommended internal auditor roles. Table 8.3 summarizes internal auditors' involvements with Sections 302 and 404. The position paper specifies that services performed by the company's internal audit function in assisting management compliance with Sections 302 and 404 of SOX are consistent with internal auditors' professional standards and should not interfere with their professional obligations to maintain their independence and objectivity. It also recommends (1) project oversight, (2) consulting and project support, (3) ongoing monitoring and testing, and (4) project audit.

The extent of internal auditors' involvement with Sections 302 and 404 depends on the company's internal auditing function, resources, funding, personnel qualifications, and charter. Any activities performed by internal auditors should be in compliance with their charter, professional standards, and the mission of adding value to their organization's operations. The IIA's 2004 position paper suggests the following factors be considered: (1) consulting management on internal control activities compliance does not impair the internal auditor's independence and objectivity; (2) making key management decisions in the compliance process impairs the internal auditor's objectivity and independence; (3) having responsibility for specific operations or participation in directing key management decisions impairs the internal auditor's objectivity and independence; (4) the design, implementation, and drafting procedures for internal controls to comply with Sections 302 and 404 impair the internal auditor's independence and objectivity; (5) recommendation of standards for internal controls or review of internal control procedures does not impair the internal auditor's objectivity and independence; and (6) devoting a significant amount of effort to consult with management on Sections 302 and 404 compliance can deplete internal auditors' resources and deviate their attention from other value-adding activities.

INSTITUTE OF INTERNAL AUDITORS

The IIA is a well-recognized organization representing more than 102,000 members throughout the world from which about 46,000 are in 133 chapters established in the United States. The IIA is viewed as the global voice of internal auditors through its issuance of the international Standards for the Professional Practice of internal Auditing (SPPIA). Since its inception in 1941, the IIA has played an important role in improving corporate governance, internal control, and financial reporting.

The IIA has adopted a PPF that includes new and updated internal auditing standards. The PPF provides a definition of internal auditing, its code of ethics, SPPIA, practice advisories, and development and practice aids.[15] The IIA Code of Ethics consists of two components of principles and rules of conduct. The four principles are integrity, objectivity, confidentiality, and competency, whereas rules of conduct describe these principles and related ethical conduct. The IIA's attribute standards, performance standards, practice advisories, and code of ethics are summarized in Tables 8.4 to 8.6, respectively.

The SPPIA are composed of three sets of mandatory standards: (1) attribute standards specifying appropriate features of individual auditors or audit functions performing internal auditing, (2) performance standards regarding the performance of internal audit engagements, and (3) implementation standards describing the attribute and performance standards and how they can be applied to specific types of audits. Internal auditors are required to apply attribute, performance, and implementation standards when performing both the assurance and consulting engagements. In an assurance engagement, auditors provide an independent assessment of the effectiveness of risk management, internal control, or corporate governance, whereas in a consulting engagement they work with audit clients as to the nature and scope of their consulting services in the same areas. In either consulting or assurance services, internal auditors add value to their organization's performance by

Table 8.4 IIA's Attribute Standards

Purpose, authority, and responsibility	• The purpose, authority, and responsibility of the internal audit activity should be formally defined in a charter, consistent with the standards, and approved by the board.
Independence and objectivity	• The internal audit activity should be independent, and internal auditors should be objective in performing their work.
Proficiency and due professional care	• Engagements should be performed with proficiency and due professional care.
Quality assurance and improvement program	• The chief audit executive should develop and maintain a quality assurance and improvement program that covers all aspects of the internal audit activity and continuously monitors its effectiveness. This program includes periodic internal and external quality assessments and ongoing internal monitoring.

Source: Adapted from The Institute of Internal Auditors. Available at: www.theiia.org/guidance/standards-and-practices/professional-practices-framework/standards/standards-resources/?C=189.

Table 8.5 IIA's Performance Standards

Managing the internal audit activity	• The chief audit executive should effectively manage the internal audit activity to ensure it adds value to the organization.
Nature of work	• The internal audit activity should evaluate and contribute to the improvement of risk management, control, and governance processes using a systematic and disciplined approach.
Engagement planning	• Internal auditors should develop and record a plan for each engagement, including the scope, objectives, timing, and resource allocations.
Performing the engagement	• Internal auditors should identify, analyze, evaluate, and record sufficient information to achieve the engagement's objectives.
Communicating results	• Internal auditors should communicate the engagement results. • Communications should include the engagement's objectives and scope as well as applicable conclusions, recommendations, and action plans.
Monitoring progress	• The chief audit executive should establish and maintain a system to monitor the disposition of results communicated to management.
Resolution of management's acceptance of risks	• When the chief audit executive believes that senior management has accepted a level of residual risk that may be unacceptable to the organization, he or she should discuss the matter with senior management. If the decision regarding residual risk is not resolved, the chief audit executive and senior management should report the matter to the board for resolution.

Source: Adapted from The Institute of Internal Auditors. Available at: www.theiia.org/guidance/standards-and-practices/professional-practices-framework/standards/standards-resources/?C=820.

Table 8.6 Code of Ethics

Principles	
Integrity	• The integrity of internal auditors establishes trust and thus provides the basis for reliance on their judgment.
Objectivity	• Internal auditors exhibit the highest level of professional objectivity in gathering, evaluating, and communicating information about the activity or process being examined. Internal auditors make a balanced assessment of all the relevant circumstances and are not unduly influenced by their own interests or by others in forming judgments.
Confidentiality	• Internal auditors respect the value and ownership of information they receive and do not disclose information without appropriate authority unless there is a legal or professional obligation to do so.
Competency	• Internal auditors apply the knowledge, skills, and experience needed in the performance of internal auditing services.

Rules of Conduct	
Integrity	• Shall perform their work with honesty, diligence, and responsibility.
	• Shall observe the law and make disclosures expected by the law and the profession.
	• Shall not knowingly be a party to any illegal activity, or engage in acts that are discreditable to the profession of internal auditing or to the organization.
	• Shall respect and contribute to the legitimate and ethical objectives of the organization.
Objectivity	• Shall not participate in any activity or relationship that may impair or be presumed to impair their unbiased assessment. This participation includes those activities or relationships that may be in conflict with the interests of the organization.
	• Shall not accept anything that may impair or be presumed to impair their professional judgment.
	• Shall disclose all material facts known to them that, if not disclosed, may distort the reporting of activities under review.
Confidentiality	• Shall be prudent in the use and protection of information acquired in the course of their duties.
	• Shall not use information for any personal gain or in any manner that would be contrary to the law or detrimental to the legitimate and ethical objectives of the organization.
Competency	• Shall engage only in those services for which they have the necessary knowledge, skills, and experience.
	• Shall perform internal auditing services in accordance with the Standards for the Professional Practice of Internal Auditing.
	• Shall continually improve their proficiency and the effectiveness and quality of their services.

Source: Reprinted with permission from The Institute of Internal Auditors (IIA). 2000. Code of Ethics IIA, Altamonte Springs, FL. Available at: www.theiia.org/guidance/standards-and-practices/professional-practices-framework/code-of-ethics/code-of-ethics–english/.

assisting its units, departments, and management to fulfill their responsibilities. Practice advisories are intended to provide best practices and are typically endorsed but not required by the IIA to be used in performing both assurance and consulting services. Development and practice aids usually offer training and education on emerging developments in internal auditing, consisting of courses, research reports, and continuing education seminars.

The IIA has supported the emerging corporate governance, worked with the SEC and PCAOB to find ways to most effectively implement these reforms, and gathered information from a survey of more than 1,900 CAEs regarding SOX implementation. Based on the findings of this survey, the IIA has made several recommendations to the SEC and PCAOB to improve Section 404 compliance.[16] Recommendations to the SEC are (1) consideration of the importance of enterprisewide risk management in improving corporate governance rather than just ICFR; (2) more detailed guidance regarding management's assessment of internal controls; (3) more detailed guidance on the quarterly Section 302 management assessment process and reporting on management corrections of reported material weaknesses; (4) clarification of "principal evidence" and additional guidance regarding key issues such as a vigilant board of directors and management overrides; (5) increasing the cost effectiveness of compliance with provisions of SOX by clarifying SEC implementation rules and providing better communication between the audit committee, external auditors, and management; and (6) creation of appropriate balance between the focus on compliance with Section 404 and other enterprisewide risks affecting all aspects of corporate governance.

IIA's recommendations to the PCAOB are (1) increasing reliance on the work of others (internal auditors) in the testing of management's assessment of the effectiveness of ICFR, and (2) consideration of partial reliance on the results of the internal control tests from prior years, particularly if there have not been significant changes in the design and operation of ICFR. The proposed redrafted IIA 610 titled The Auditor's Consideration of the Internal Audit Function specifies (1) the relevance of the internal audit function to the external auditor, (2) the extent to which the external auditor should use the work of the internal audit function in an integrated audit, (3) the risk assessment procedures that should be done to obtain sufficient understanding of the role of internal audit in the entity's internal control, and (4) the audit procedures necessary to decide to use the work of the internal audit function as audit evidence.[17] The independent auditor should determine how the work of the internal audit function could affect the nature, timing, and extent of audit procedures performed otherwise in gathering sufficient competent evidence.

DETERMINANTS OF EFFECTIVE INTERNAL AUDIT

In the postcorporate governance reforms, internal auditors are viewed as the eyes and ears of the audit committee in providing consulting and assurance services to improve corporate governance, risk management, internal controls, financial reporting, and audit functions. Internal auditors are striving to effectively fulfill their responsibility by using the best practices.

Best Practices

PricewaterhouseCoopers suggests that internal auditors' best practices should include the following:

1. *Build an adequate internal audit staff to support the needs of business.* Internal audit activities should be viewed as value-added functions with sufficient resources to carry out their assigned responsibilities.

2. *Structure the internal audit function on a fluid and flexible framework.* Adjust to dynamic changes in both internal and external forces that influence internal audit plans, strategies, and operations.

3. *Design an enterprisewide risk-based audit program.* Develop and use an enterprisewide risk-based internal audit function that focuses on high-risk financial and operational activities and allows for a degree of flexibility to adjust to unexpected events and shifting priorities.

4. *Broaden audit scope to address third-party and vendor risk.* Apply proactive risk strategies that prevent or immediately respond to potential problems, including outsourcing, supplier agreements, mergers and acquisitions, and joint ventures.

5. *Combat fraud by advocating ethical conduct throughout the organization.* The board of directors and senior executives should set an appropriate tone at the top, promoting ethical conduct throughout the organization. Internal auditors should assist in preventing, detecting, and correcting fraudulent financial activities, including asset misappropriation (theft of cash or other assets), corruption (bribes, kickbacks), and financial statement fraud.

6. *Manage information systems risk proactively.* Use capabilities offered by IT in internal audit strategies, planning, and procedures while addressing the potential risk associated with the use of IT capabilities.[18]

The following steps are suggested for the establishment or improvement of an effective internal audit function:

1. *Appoint the right person to be the CAE.* The audit committee of the board of directors is directly responsible for the appointment, compensation, and, when necessary, the dismissal of the company's CAE. The committee should also oversee the work of the CAE by approving the internal audit function's budget, audit plan, and scope, and by receiving internal audit reports. The CAE's responsibilities are to provide assurance, counsel, and advice to management regarding operations efficiency, risk management, financial reporting, internal controls, and governance processes under the oversight function of the audit committee. To effectively fulfill these responsibilities, the CAE should be regarded as part of a top management team; participate in relevant management meetings; and provide comments, input, and insight on managerial decisions. Administratively, the CAE is accountable and reports to the CEO, but functionally, he or she is accountable and reports to the audit committee. As the head of the company's internal audit function, the CAE should be competent and knowledgeable in internal auditing standards, tools, methodology, and practices; supervise the internal audit function; communicate with the audit committee, management, and internal audit staff; and demand productive performance and ethical conduct from internal audit staff.

2. *Establish a written audit charter*. The internal audit charter should specify the purpose, authority, and responsibility of the internal audit function as an integral component of corporate governance in adding value to the company's sustainable performance. The purpose of the internal audit function should be clearly described in the charter, as stated by the IIA, in providing assurance and consulting services in risk management, financial reporting, internal controls, and governance processes. The authority of the internal audit function is granted by the company's board of directors, particularly the audit committee, to have sufficient resources to carry out its responsibilities, and to have access to all records, personnel, and property required to conduct internal audits.

3. *Develop an audit strategy*. The internal audit function should have a sound audit strategy that adds value to the company's operations in risk management, financial reporting, internal controls, and governance processes. The internal audit strategy should be developed by the CAE in collaboration with management and should be approved by the audit committee. The strategy should specify audit plans, scope, nature, procedures, and timing of all internal audit activities.

4. *Implement the audit strategy*. Effective implementation of the internal audit strategy requires proper audit plans; sufficient resources, including ethical, highly specialized, and competent staff; commitment from senior management; and approval of the audit committee. Internal auditors should have proficiency in accounting practices, internal auditing standards, corporate governance reforms, and management principles, and a knowledge base in accounting, economics, taxation, business law, finance, IT, and quantitative methods.

5. *Establish quality assurance and performance evaluation*. To ensure a high-quality internal audit function, it should be evaluated annually. The performance of the internal audit staff should be evaluated by the CAE based on predetermined evaluation benchmarks. The performance of the CAE should be evaluated by management and reviewed by the audit committee. The purpose of this evaluation is to improve the quality of the internal audit function and provide a basis for promotion, advancement, and compensation.[19]

Internal Audit Performance

To appropriately assess internal audit quality and effectiveness, PricewaterhouseCoopers suggests an approach consisting of the following four-phase plan:

Phase 1: Project planning consisting of establishing specific internal audit objectives in line with stakeholder expectations.

Phase 2: Value-driver identification, including gathering information about value drivers of internal audit.

Phase 3: Current state assessment consisting of reviews and analysis of internal audit core processes, benchmarks, and best practices.

Phase 4: Solution development of preparing report findings, observations, and recommendations for improvement in performance.[20]

Internal Audit Framework

PricewaterhouseCoopers suggests a six-step framework to assist organizations in achieving a balance between demands, priorities, and resources of their internal audit function to align their efforts with shareholder expectations:

Step 1: Reevaluate the risk assessment.

Focus on the traditional risk-based internal audit plans of (1) evaluating the entire risk profile of the organization, including risks related to financial reporting, operations, strategy, and IT; (2) ranking or prioritizing risk categories; (3) facilitating a common understanding of risk by involving senior management and the audit committee in the assessment process to provide transparency about a comprehensive internal audit plan with stakeholders; and (4) developing a risk-based internal audit plan based on an enterprisewide risk assessment.

Step 2: Prevalidate stakeholder expectations.

Revisit stakeholder expectations by (1) clearly defining internal audit services of stakeholder value protection and value enhancement activities, and (2) focusing on independent assurance pertaining to financial and compliance controls as well as internal audit plans.

Step 3: Align the internal audit plan.

Prepare and present the annual overall internal audit plan to the audit committee that (1) provides a right balance between value protection (compliance reporting) and value enhancement (efficiency and effectiveness) projects and services, and (2) aligns the plan with the organization's strategic and operational objectives.

Step 4: Align resources, budget, and staff skills.

Determine the necessary resources, budget, and staff skills to carry out the approved internal audit plans by (1) identifying gaps between current resources and capabilities and those required to perform internal audit activities according to the plan; (2) identifying and reducing inefficiencies in core internal audit activities; and (3) using technology to improve the efficiency, quality, and value of internal audit processes, including data analysis software, best practices, knowledge base, and internal audit infrastructure software.

Step 5: Rearticulate the internal audit charter.

Ensure that the internal audit charter is current and aligned with stakeholder value drivers and expectations, and if deemed necessary, revise the charter to clearly define the role of internal auditors in the SOX compliance process.

Step 6: Measure results.

Develop a comprehensive and relevant set of performance metrics to measure the achievement of internal audit objectives by using balanced scorecards for measuring internal audit performance and value.[21]

Internal Auditing Education

The Institute of Internal Auditors Research Foundation (IIARF) is in the process of establishing the Common Body of Knowledge (CBOK) for internal auditors, which is intended to broaden the understanding of internal auditing practices and the state of the internal auditing profession worldwide. The CBOK will include (1) the knowledge and skills of internal auditors, (2) the organization and skills of practicing internal auditors, (3) the actual duties performed and responsibilities assumed by internal auditors, (4) the structure of internal audit organizations, (5) the types of industries that practice internal auditing, and (6) the regulatory environment of various countries that affect internal auditing.[22] The IIA will refine its CBOK every three years to provide up-to-date and relevant guidance for practicing internal auditors worldwide. The CBOK promotes interauditing practices and enables internal auditors to remain relevant and vibrant and add value to their organizations in the areas of risk management and organizational governance.

The IIA has established the Internal Auditing Education Partnership (IAEP) program to promote internal auditing in colleges and universities in educating the next generation of auditors. The IAEP program offers business schools three levels of promoting internal auditing education through participation in an entry level, partner level, and advanced level at a Center for Internal Auditing Excellence (CIAE).[23] The entry level requires a minimum of six hours of internal auditing–related subjects covering internal auditing and risk management and control. The partner level requires a minimum of three core course equivalents per year in internal auditing–related subjects. The advanced level requires the establishment of a CIAE with an undergraduate or graduate formal concentration or minor in internal auditing.

The Internal Audit Opinion on Internal Controls

It has been suggested that the CAEs provide an annual summary opinion about their organization's internal controls in general and ICFR in particular. In expressing an opinion on internal controls, internal auditors should assess the current status of ICFR, possible challenges and opportunities in ICFR, recommendations and remediation actions to improve ICFR, management's willingness and commitment to implement remedial actions, and internal auditors' understanding of objectives and limitations of ICFR. The quality and reliability of internal auditor opinions on ICFR depend on transparency, constructive recommendations, and the objectivity, independence, and organizational status of the CAE signing the report. To be relevant, internal auditor opinions and recommendations should be related to identified risks and intended controls to address risks, and be constructive, reliable, clear, concise, and relevant in making recommendations and remediation actions to improve the effectiveness of the design and operation of ICFR. In expressing an opinion on ICFR, internal auditors should carefully consider and follow the guidance issued by the IIA, *Practical Considerations Regarding Internal Auditing Expressing an Opinion on Internal Control.*[24]

SUMMARY

The internal audit function of corporate governance provides objective and independent assurance and consulting services designed to add value and improve the company's sustainable performance in the areas of operations, risk management, internal controls, financial reporting, and government processes. The audit committee should be directly responsible for the appointment, compensation, promotion, or dismissal of the company's internal audit directors, commonly referred to as the CAE.

The CAE should have unrestricted access to the audit committee and ultimately be held accountable to the committee. The audit committee should participate in the development of the internal audit department's goals and mission, and oversee the work of internal auditors and how management is responding to their recommendations. Public companies should (1) consider whether the internal audit function is adding value to the company's success, (2) review the goals and mission of the internal audit function, (3) assess the adequacy of resources (budget and personnel) for the internal audit function to achieve its objectives, and (4) monitor the performance of the internal audit function.

The key points of this chapter are

- The internal audit function of corporate governance provides objective and independent assurance and consulting services designed to add value and improve the company's sustainable performance in the areas of operations, risk management, internal controls, financial reporting, and government processes.

- Internal auditors are well trained and positioned to provide numerous assurance services to their organization. The emerging trend toward more emphasis on MBL of governance, economic, ethical, social, and environmental performance requires organizations to provide assurance on a variety of their performance measures and achievements.

- SOX does not directly address internal auditor responsibilities or internal audit function.

- The internal audit function should have (1) full and free access to the company's audit committee; (2) unrestricted access to the company's records, documents, property, and personnel; and (3) authority to discuss initiatives, policies, and procedures regarding risk assessment, internal controls, compliance, financial reporting, and governance processes with management and other corporate governance participants.

- A close working relationship between the audit committee and internal auditors can improve the effectiveness of corporate governance.

- Internal auditors, as an integral component of the organization's governance, should continue to improve their internal audit quality and effectiveness to secure their position in the corporate governance continuum.

- The IIA has promoted the role of internal auditors in corporate governance as providing objective and independent assurance and consulting services to their organizations.

- The IIA has established a PPF, which provides a definition of internal audits, its code of ethics, SPPIA, and development and practice aids.

KEY TERMS

chief audit executive (CAE)
Committee of Sponsoring
   Organizations of the
   Treadway Commission
   (COSO)

Foreign Corrupt Practices
   Act (FCPA) of 1977
Institute of Internal
   Auditors (IIA)

Standards for the Professional
   Practice of Internal
   Auditing (SPPIA)

REVIEW QUESTIONS

1.   What are the recommendations made by the IIA to the SEC and PCAOB in improving the effectiveness of Section 404 compliance?

2. What does The Conference Board recommend regarding the establishment of an internal audit function in an organization?

3. Why is the establishment and maintenance of an internal audit function crucial to the effectiveness of a company's corporate governance in achieving its goal of creating shareholder value and protecting stakeholder interests?

4. What are the areas in which SEC rules permit internal audit outsourcing to the client's independent auditor?

5. What are the factors to be considered by the internal auditors when supporting and consulting management to comply with Sections 302 and 404?

6. Explain the steps involved for the establishment or improvement of an effective internal audit function.

7. Discuss the responsibilities of the internal audit function.

8. Explain the three sets of mandatory SPPIA.

9. What are the best practices that should be implemented by organizations according to PricewaterhouseCoopers?

10. What purpose does the written audit charter serve for the company?

11. What authoritative rights should be granted to the internal audit function and the CAE?

DISCUSSION QUESTIONS

1. A close working relationship between the audit committee and internal auditors can improve the effectiveness of corporate governance. Do you agree with this statement? Substantiate your answer.

2. How can an audit committee contribute to the success and effectiveness of internal auditors and the achievement of their value-adding activities?

3. In your opinion, why are there no regulations that require internal audit assurance reports?

4. In what ways does the internal audit department add value to an organization?

5. What factors have led to the transformation of the IIA's definition of "internal auditing"? Research your answer.

6. What are the benefits and negative results of outsourcing the internal audit function?

7. The role of internal auditors has evolved from performing traditional appraisal activities and audit functions of evaluating internal controls to being considered an important component of corporate governance by adding value to organizations by improving operations. Is the given statement true or false? Substantiate your answer.

8. Explain how internal auditors' expertise in internal control can ensure effectiveness of the corporate governance structure.

NOTES

1. PricewaterhouseCoopers. 2007, May. PricewaterhouseCoopers 2007 State of the Internal Audit Profession Study: Pressures Build for Continual Focus on Risk. Available at: www.theiia.org/download.cfm?file=41088.

2. Beresford, D. R., N. deB. Katzenbach, and C. B. Rogers, Jr. 2003, March 31. Report of Investigation by the Special Investigative Committee of the Board of Directors of WorldCom, Inc. Available at: news.findlaw.com/hdocs/docs/worldcom/bdspconim60903rpt.pdf.

3. The Institute of Internal Auditors (IIA). 2002, April 8. Recommendations for Improving Corporate Governance: A Position Paper Presented by the Institute of Internal Auditors to the U.S. Congress. IIA, Altamonte Springs, FL. Available at: www.theiia.org/download.cfm?file=1609.

4. Public Company Accounting Oversight Board (PCAOB). 2004. Auditing Standard No. 2: An Audit of Internal Control over Financial Reporting Performed in Conjunction with an Audit of Financial Statements (Paragraph 17). Available at: www.pcaob.org/Standards/Standards_and_Related_Rules/Auditing_Standard_No.2.aspx.

5. See note 1 above.

6. U.S. Department of Justice (D.J). 1977. Foreign Corrupt Practices Act (FCPA). Available at: www.usdoj.gov/criminal/fraud/fcpa/.

7. Rezaee, Z., and G. H. Lander. 1991. The Internal Auditor-Education and Training: The Partnership Concept. *Managerial Auditing Journal* 6(2): 4-8.

8. The Committee of Sponsoring Organizations of the Treadway Commission (COSO). 1987. Report of the National Commission on Fraudulent Financial Reporting. Washington, D.C: U.S. Government Printing Office.

9. The Committee of Sponsoring Organizations of the Treadway Commission (COSO). 1999. Report of the National Commission on Fraudulent Financial Reporting. U.S. Government Printing Office, Washington, DC.

10. Sarbanes-Oxley Act of 2002 (SOX). Available at: www.law.uc.edu/CCL/SOact/soact.pdf.

11. Public Company Accounting Oversight Board (PCAOB). 2004, March 9. PCAOB Auditing Standard No. 2. An Audit of Internal Control over Financial Reporting Performed in Conjunction with an Audit of Financial Statements. Available at: www.pcaob.org/Rules/Rules_of_the_Board/Auditing_Standard_2.pdf.

12. PricewaterhouseCoopers. 2005, May 25. How to Rebalance Internal Audit Priorities in the Sarbanes-Oxley Era. Available at: www.pwc.com/extweb/pwcpublications.nsf/docid/07d11e01f3a2d1c785256fd30004a331.

13. The Conference Board. 2003, January. The Conference Board Commission on Public Trust and Private Enterprise: Findings and Recommendations. Part 3: Audit and Accounting. SR-03-04. Available at: www.conference-board.org/pdf_free/SR-03-04.pdf.

14. U.S. Securities and Exchange Commission (SEC). 2003, January 28. Strengthening the Commission's Requirements Regarding Auditor Independence. Available at: www.sec.gov/rules/final/33-8183.htm.

15. The Institute of Internal Auditors (IIA). 2007, July. Professional Practices Framework. Available at: www.theiia.org/guidance/standards-and-practices/professional-practices-framework/?search=professional%20practices%20framework.

16. The Institute of Internal Auditors (IIA). 2005, March 31. Re: Implementation of U.S. Sarbanes-Oxley Act Internal Control Provisions [Letter]. IIA, Altamonte Springs, FL. Available at: www.theiia.org/download.cfm?file=73806.

17. International Auditing and Assurance Standards Board (IAASB). 2006, December 22. Proposed Redrafted International Standard on Auditing: ISA 610 (Redrafted), The Auditor's Consideration of the Internal Audit Function. Available at: www.ifac.org/Guidance/EXD-Details.php?EDID=0073.

18. PricewaterhouseCoopers. n.d. Global Best Practices. Available at: www.globalbestpractices.com.

19. Tarr, R. 2002. Built to Last. *Internal Auditor* December: 29-33.

20. PricewaterhouseCoopers. 2005. Assessing Quality. Available at: www.pwc.com/extweb/service.nsf/docid/A166C151774183FB85256F8D0076B2FB.

21. Ibid.

22. The Institute of Internal Auditors (IIA). n.d. The IIA Research Foundation Common Body of Knowledge (CBOK). IIA, Altamonte Springs, FL. Available at: www.theiia.org/research/common-body-of-knowledge/.

23. The Institute of Internal Auditors (IIA). n.d. Academic Relations Program. IIA, Altamonte Springs, FL. Available at: www.theiia.org/academic.

24. The Institute of Internal Auditors (IIA). 2005, June 10. *Practical Considerations Regarding Internal Auditing Expressing an Opinion on Internal Control*. Available at: www.theiia.org/download.cfm?file=25663.

Chapter 9

External Auditors' Roles and Responsibilities

INTRODUCTION

External auditors are responsible for auditing the company's financial statements and providing reasonable assurance that they are presented fairly and in conformity with GAAP and that they reflect true representation of the company's financial position and results of operations. Auditors are also required to express an opinion on the effectiveness of the design and operation of ICFR. The external audit function is intended to lend credibility to financial reports and reduce information risk that financial reports are biased, misleading, inaccurate, incomplete, and contain material misstatements that were not prevented or detected by the ICFR system.

Primary Objectives

The primary objectives of this chapter are to

- Recognize the role independent auditors play in achieving effective corporate governance and reliable financial reports.
- Understand the history of auditing, the traditional roles of auditors, and regulations recently placed on them.
- Address the expectation gap regarding what auditors can provide in the way of reasonable assurance and the expectations of investors for a higher level of assurance.
- Identify the roles and responsibilities of the PCAOB, and discuss the auditing standards published by the PCAOB.
- Demonstrate the importance of auditor independence both in fact and in appearance.
- Discuss an integrated audit of both financial statements and ICFR.
- Address the issue of a liability cap for independent auditors and understand the rationale on both sides of the issue.

EXTERNAL AUDITING AND CORPORATE GOVERNANCE

The audit function performed by external auditors can play an important role in achieving effective corporate governance. The external audit function can be viewed as a value-added function when lending credibility to published financial reports. However, audit failures at the turn of the twenty-first century that caused the demise of Andersen, one of the Big Five public accounting firms, raised serious concerns as to whether the audit function has a positive impact on the effectiveness of corporate governance. Flesher, Previts, and Samson trace the origin of auditing to a governance procedure by Pilgrims and Puritans. They argue that auditing was developed long before the establishment of the accounting profession and regulations requiring financial statements of public companies to be audited by independent auditors.[1] They provide evidence that traces auditing to the corporate governance practices of early business enterprises. Accounting has evolved from number crunching to a service activity for management, and now in light of emerging corporate governance reforms, a function that lends credibility, dependability, and objectivity to the preparation of reliable, useful, and transparent financial reports and effective internal controls.

The Securities Exchange Act of 1934 set the requirement that companies that offer stock to the public in raising capital must have their financial statements audited by an independent public accountant. Thus, the auditor role in corporate governance and the financial reporting process is to provide independent assurance to shareholders regarding fair presentation, in all material respects, of the company's financial statements in conformity with GAAP. In the late 1900s, public accounting firms expanded their services from the grassroots, prestigious, and conspicuous product of audit services to the performance of a wide range of nonaudit services. Indeed, during the 1980s and 1990s, the audit was considered a low margin activity and a means of generating revenues for other nonaudit services (e.g., consulting, tax, accounts, internal control outsourcing, IT supports). The concept of one-stop shopping for all audit and nonaudit services became a common practice for many public accounting firms and their clients. This concept and its practice impaired both auditor independence and public trust. The phrase "public accounting firm" was replaced with "professional services firm" by almost all the Big Five (now Big Four) accounting firms, and eventually they became market-driven service firms rather than firms to serve public interests.

SOX drastically changed these characteristics of the accounting profession by (1) creating the PCAOB to regulate the auditing profession; (2) connecting the audit function to the corporate governance structure; and (3) requiring that the audit committee be directly responsible for not only hiring, compensating, and firing external auditors but also overseeing their work and monitoring their independence. Table 9.1 compares external audit pre- and postcorporate governance reforms. An auditor's responsibility is to express an opinion on the true and fair presentation of financial statements in conformity

Table 9.1   Comparison of Independent Audit (Pre- and Postcorporate Governance Reforms)

Prereforms	Postreforms
• Auditor dependency on nonaudit fees from major clients	• More restricted auditor independence
• Performance of nonaudit services	• Auditors not immune from economic pressures
• Auditors influenced by economic pressures	• Regulatory framework for the auditing profession
• Management hires, compensates, and fires auditors	• A five-member Public Company Accounting Oversight Board (PCAOB)
• No proper communication with audit committees	• PCAOB empowered to register, inspect, and review registered public accounting firms and impose disciplinary actions
• Do the minimum to meet GAAS	• PCAOB responsible for issuing auditing, quality controls, and ethics standards
• Reduce the cost of audit	• More effective communication with the audit committee
• Employment relationship	• Nine nonaudit services prohibited (bookkeeping, financial information system design and implementation, actuarial services, appraisal, management function, broker/dealer and investment advising, legal services, expert witness services)
• Self-regulation of auditing profession	
• Ineffective public oversight board	
• Inadequate and ineffective disciplinary and monitoring process of the auditing profession	
	• Audit of internal control over financial reporting (ICFR)
	• Report on management's assessment of the effectiveness of ICFR
	• Promotion of an integrated audit approach for audit of internal controls and financial statements
	• Shareholder vote on the ratification of the auditor
	• Rotation of the lead and reviewing auditor every five years

with GAAP and to assess the quality of the financial reports and effectiveness of ICFR.

The six largest global accounting networks state the following three benefits of audits for the global economy and capital markets: (1) audits improve the allocation of capital among global companies regardless of their location by facilitating investors' decisions to channel funds to global companies that offer the highest risk-adjusted returns, (2) audits help insulate the global financial system against systemic risk by providing transparency of the financial status of companies in their home economy, and (3) audits facilitate good corporate governance by empowering global investors with the right information.[2] CEOs of the six largest global audit networks believe these benefits can be achieved when (1) there are global accounting and auditing standards that guide the preparation and audit of financial statements, (2) regulators that oversee audits are formally coordinated and globally established, (3) audit quality is improved, and (4) consistency of audits across different countries within the global audit networks is observed.

EXTERNAL AUDITOR RESPONSIBILITIES

The agency problems associated with the separation of ownership and control in the corporate structure, along with information asymmetry, created the need for independent auditors to verify management assertions concerning financial statements. The passage of the Securities Act of 1933 and the Securities Exchange Act of 1934 established the demand for independent audits of financial reports of public companies filed with the SEC. Auditors were viewed as gatekeepers to protect investors from receiving misleading financial information. By the mid-1980s, the investor protection value-adding audit services were turned into a revenue-generating commodity.

Current auditing standards require that independent auditors provide *reasonable assurance* that the financial statements are free from material misstatements, whether caused by error or fraud, to render an unqualified opinion on the financial statements. This level of reasonable assurance is regarded as a high level of assurance, but not absolute assurance. Reasonable assurance may mean different levels of assurance to different groups. Investors, in the post-Enron era, expect that independent auditors discover and report on all material misstatements, including errors, irregularities, and fraud. Independent auditors, however, in complying with their professional standards have provided reasonable assurance that financial statements are free from material misstatements.

The discussion of a reasonable or high level of assurance is the classic expectation gap argument that has been a controversial and unresolved issue casting doubt on the value relevance of external audits. In the auditing profession, the so-called expectation gap is the difference between (1) what the investing public and other users of audited financial statements believe the responsibilities of auditors are, and (2) what auditors are willing to assume as responsibilities according to their professional standards. For example, the public desires to hold auditors responsible for all fraudulent activities involved in public companies' financial reports, whereas auditors only provide reasonable assurance that financial statements are free from material misstatements. To narrow this perceived expectative gap and to clarify what reasonable assurance means, the PCAOB states in its AS No. 2: "Reasonable assurance includes the understanding that there is a remote likelihood that material misstatements will not be prevented or detected on a timely basis. Although not absolute assurance, reasonable assurance is, nevertheless, a high level of assurance."[3] The International Auditing and Assurance Standards Board also defines reasonable assurance to be a high, but not absolute, level of assurance in an assurance audit engagement.[4] Both reasonable assurance and high level of assurance are subject to professional interpretation. Independent auditors are required to document their assessment of reasonable assurance through (1) the use of the materiality concept, and (2) the audit risk model. Materiality guides independent auditors in the amount of evidence they should gather to form an opinion on the financial statements, whereas the audit risk model justifies the means of gathering sufficient competent evidence through tests of controls and substantive tests.

External auditors are not and should not be expected to provide absolute assurance regarding reliability of financial statements primarily because of (1) the nature and limitation of evidence-gathering procedures that are conducted on selective testing; (2) management assertions and financial representations that include accounting estimates that are not certain by nature; (3) the use of judgments in the preparation and audit of financial statements; and (4) the possibility of collusion, false documentation, management override, or engagement in fraud. The yet-to-be-resolved issue is what type and level of assurance the public desires and whether auditors are willing and able to provide such a level of assurance. The public currently desires a high level of assurance—not just reasonable assurance—about fair and true presentation of financial statements. Users of audited financial statements generally expect external auditors to detect financial statement fraud and employees' illegal acts and fraud, which affects the integrity of financial reports. External auditors, however, are more concerned with material misstatements in the audited financial statements.

AUDITOR COMPETENCY

Auditors' competencies in providing reasonable assurance that financial statements are free from material misstatements, whether caused by errors or fraud, can be classified into professional competencies, technical competencies, process competencies, and reporting competencies.

1. *Professional competencies.* The first general standard of the so-called ten GAAS requires that auditors have professional training and proficiency to conduct the audit. This means auditors should have education, experience, and certification in performing financial statement audits. To audit public companies, auditors should register with the PCAOB and meet all registration and inspection requirements.

2. *Technical competencies.* Technical competencies refer to auditor knowledge of relevant professional standards, rules, laws and regulations, and the technical understanding of their clients' industry and business, corporate governance, financial reporting process, and internal controls in effectively conducting the audit.

3. *Process competencies.* Process competencies pertain to auditors' ability to choose appropriate evidence-gathering procedures (tests of controls, substantive tests) and execute auditing procedures. Many auditors use a risk-based approach of focusing their audit procedures on risk areas threatening the effectiveness of ICFR, and the reliability and integrity of financial statements. An integrated audit approach

should be used to ensure process competencies in auditing both internal controls and financial statements.

4. *Reporting competencies*. Reporting competencies refer to auditors' ability and willingness to discover and report material misstatements. Auditors have been criticized for failing to detect errors, irregularities, and fraud as well as failing to report discovered misstatements. There are many cases of auditors' failures to report discovered misstatements in the financial statements. For example, Arthur Andersen, then the auditor of Qwest, warned the company and its directors that the SEC would challenge the company's accounting policies and practices concerning revenue recognition and then signed off on its financial statements. The auditor at Adelphia urged management to provide additional disclosures on its related party loans and then rendered a clean, unqualified opinion on its financial statements, despite management refusal to provide such disclosures to investors. Xerox's auditor was warned about accounting problems at the company; however, the auditor chose to ignore them and then issued a clean, unqualified opinion on its financial statements. Auditors at HealthSouth were alerted to potential financial fraud, but they ignored such warnings and issued a clean, unqualified opinion on its financial statements. At Raytheon, auditors issued a clean, unqualified opinion when, in fact, financial statements were misleading. These cases of egregious behavior by auditors and obvious audit failures contributed to the loss of investor confidence as many investors asked the question, "Where were the auditors?" Despite substantial losses to investors resulting from these audit failures, public accounting firms are attempting to reform the U.S. securities litigation environment or establish a liability cap to reduce their cost of litigation, which is discussed in depth later in this chapter.

AUDIT FAILURES AND AUDIT QUALITY

Audit failure occurs when a company with reported unqualified financial statements discloses low-quality and misleading financial information or has to restate previously audited financial statements. Audit failure can be separated into two categories of audit process failure and independent audit failure. This distinction is important because (1) reported financial scandals and related audit failures provide evidence of impairments in auditor independence; (2) regulations and auditing standards are more concerned with and address the incidence of independent audit failure rather than audit process failure; (3) the audit process has often discovered misstatements, but auditors failed to disclose them due to financial and personal ties to their clients; (4) audit process failures are often unintentional, resulting from a lack of exercising due professional care and the imperfection in audit methodology, whereas independent audit failure is caused by auditors intentionally compromising their professional responsibilities; and (5) auditors are more likely to benefit directly by compromising their independence to secure continuity of their contract with their clients.

The bubble economy and technology stocks of the late 1990s encouraged management to make aggressive accounting assumptions and estimates in measuring, recognizing, and reporting business transactions to meet analysts' unrealistic earnings forecasts. The capital market rewarded companies that were able to report a steady increase in their earnings and meet analysts' expectations. Auditors were not skeptical of management's aggressive accounting policies and practices, and sometimes auditors assisted their clients in designing financial products (e.g., tax shelters) based on overly aggressive accounting policies and practices. Investors placed a high degree of confidence in audited financial statements in truly and fairly reflecting the companies' financial condition and results of operations.

Financial scandals and related audit failures called into question the ability of the accounting profession to self-police, and SOX effectively ended the self-regulatory environment. SOX created the PCAOB, which assumed responsibility for issuing auditing standards and overseeing auditing practices. Several initiatives have been suggested to improve audit quality as well as the transparency of the audit process and report. These initiatives are

1. Publication of audit engagement letters—The public disclosure of the content of audit engagement letters should improve transparency of the audit process and enable investors to better understand the scope and terms of the audit, including the presence of auditor limitation of liability provisions. Auditor limited liability agreements' (LLAs') so-called liability cap is discussed later in this chapter.

2. Shareholders' rights to question auditors—Shareholders should be given the opportunity to question the auditor in advance of the company's annual meeting by communicating with the auditor via the company regarding the conduct of the audit and the content of the audit report.

3. Publication of auditor resignation statements—Comprehensive and public disclosure of information in auditors' resignation letters could provide relevant information about the reasons for the resignation and their impacts on the company's corporate governance, financial reporting, and audit process to investors. Auditor changes and their consequences for investors are discussed later in this chapter.

4. Lead audit partner's signature on audit reports—Currently, the lead partner signs the audit report in the name of the company's public accounting firm. The requirement of the printed name and signature of the lead partner, along with the name of the company's public accounting firm, will bring auditor accountability in line with other professionals and is expected to encourage further personal responsibility for the audit conduct.[5]

5. Active audit committee participation in evaluating the scope and results of the integrated audit of both ICFR and financial statements by comparing provisions of the engagement letter with what the auditor actually did and reviewing the PCAOB's inspection reports of the audit firms and any enforcement actions against the firms.

6. Mandatory rotation of the audit firm every seven to twelve years in the context of the quality of audit work performed by the firm and the audit efficacy.

7. Mandatory shareholder vote on the ratification of the independent auditor each year.

PUBLIC COMPANY ACCOUNTING OVERSIGHT BOARD

The PCAOB was created by SOX to regulate the auditing profession. The PCAOB ended several decades of self-regulation for public accounting firms that audit public companies that was clearly not working as originally intended. The PCAOB is a not-for-profit organization that functions under the SEC oversight, consisting of five members where two of them are CPAs, and chaired by a member who has not practiced as a CPA for at least five years prior to appointment. The PCAOB's primary functions are to

1. Register public accounting firms that audit public companies.
2. Inspect the registered public accounting firms on a regular basis.
3. Establish auditing, attestation, ethics, quality control, and independence standards.
4. Conduct investigations and disciplinary proceedings.

Registration and Inspection of Public Accounting Firms

The PCAOB is authorized to register both domestic (U.S.) and non-U.S. public accounting firms that audit public companies under the SEC's jurisdiction. As of the end of 2003, only 735 public accounting firms were registered with the PCAOB. The number of firms registered with the PCAOB has substantially increased as 1,423, 1,591, 1,738, and 1,805 firms have registered in 2004, 2005, 2006, and at the end of the third quarter of 2007, respectively. More than half of the registered firms are domestic firms, from which about 65 percent are subject to triennial inspection. Registered public accounting firms that audit more than one hundred public companies are annually inspected by the PCAOB, whereas other firms are inspected triennially. The PCAOB is authorized to refer violations of its professional standards, SEC rules, quality controls, ethics, independence, or other applicable rules, regulations, and standards to the SEC and appropriate state regulatory authorities, along with inspection reports and audit firms' letters of response. The PCAOB inspection process is designed to be evenhanded in investigating audit failures resulting from inadequate auditing or excessive audits.

There are two parts to PCAOB inspection reports. Part 1, which is the public information of an overview of inspection reports, is typically posted on the PCAOB Web site, and Part 2 is communicated to public accounting firms regarding the inspected audit failures and remediation suggested for correcting the discovered problems. Inspection reports including violations may be made available to the public if concerns presented in the report are not properly addressed by the accounting firm within twelve months. The PCAOB, in 2004, conducted its first inspection of the Big Four public accounting firms by reviewing firms' quality control policies and procedures, audit working papers, methodologies, audit plans, programs, and procedures, and it visited certain practice offices. The PCAOB's first inspection of the Big Four firms raised several concerns related to audit independence, quality control, and audit effectiveness. The PCAOB performed 497 inspections of U.S. triennial public accounting firms between 2004 and 2006.[6] More than 56 percent (248 reports) identified audit performance issues ranging from a single audit deficiency to multiple and serious deficiencies in one or more audits, 28 percent did not identify any audit performance deficiencies, and more than 15 percent identified concerns about potential defects in the firm's quality control system. The identified audit performance deficiencies are related to auditing of revenues, auditing of related parties, auditing of losses incurred on uncollectible loans and receivables, and valuation of stock given as compensation. These audit deficiencies raise questions of whether proper measures are being taken by regulators of the audits of private companies governed by the state board of accountancy to ensure audit quality.

The inspection reports serve the five primary purposes of (1) improving audit effectiveness by identifying and requiring resolution of audit failures; (2) identifying and properly addressing the emerging and common accounting and auditing issues; (3) improving the audit firm's system of quality control and evidence-gathering procedures; (4) assisting the PCAOB in establishing appropriate auditing, quality control, and ethics standards; and (5) enhancing public trust in the auditing profession. The 120 inspection reports released by the PCAOB indicate serious audit problems with the Big Eight public accounting firms and more severe problems with audits of smaller firms. The continuous existence of these audit problems does not help instill investor confidence in the quality of the audit and the evidence that audits are conducted in accordance with the required standards. Nonetheless, it appears that PCAOB inspections are much more thorough and in-depth than under the previous self-regulatory and peer review regime. On May 1, 2006, the PCAOB released statements regarding its approach to inspections of audits of ICFR for the 2006 inspection cycle.[7] The PCAOB combines reviews of audits of ICFR with financial statement audit procedures. Inspections will focus on how efficiently the public accounting firms perform audits pursuant to AS No. 2 by evaluating (1) the degree of integration between the audit of ICFR and financial statement audits; (2) the use of a top-down approach to the integrated audit; (3) the use of a risk-based approach in properly evaluating and responding to identified risk; and (4) reliance on the work of others. The inspection process is conducted at three levels of (1) meeting with senior firm leadership to determine the firm's strategies in achieving efficiencies in light of four given guidelines (integrated audit, risk-based and top-down approaches, and reliance on the work of others); (2) national office inspection procedures to assess how well the firms' guidance and audit tools address the four areas of efficiency; and (3) engagement inspection procedures in which at least one of the four areas of efficiency will be selected for inspection for each accelerated filer audit that is reviewed.

PCAOB Auditing Standards

SOX authorized the PCAOB to adopt or revise the existing auditing standards or issue new auditing standards. The PCAOB initially adopted as its interim standards the AICPA's SASs, which existed on April 16, 2003. The PCAOB has decided to take on the responsibility of issuing auditing, attestation, ethics, and independent standards for registered public accounting firms that audit financial statements of public companies. Meanwhile, the PCAOB is reviewing all adopted interim standards and deciding whether to modify, repeal, or permanently adopt them as its own standards. The PCAOB has issued five auditing standards as of September 2007.

PCAOB Auditing Standard No. 1

The first PCAOB auditing standard addresses the audit report by making two minor changes in the language of the AICPA standard unqualified audit report. The first change is in the scope paragraph of the report by replacing the phrase "audit is conducted in accordance with generally accepted auditing standards (GAAS)" to "audit is conducted in accordance with auditing standards of PCAOBUS." Second, AS No. 1 added the state and city in which the public accounting firm prepared the audit report.[8] Figure 9.1 presents the standard audit report format adopted by the PCAOB.

We have audited the accompanying balance sheets of X Company as of December 31, 20X3 and 20X2, and the related statements of operations, stockholders' equity, and cash flows for each of the three years in the period ended December 31, 20X3. These financial statements are the responsibility of the Company's management. Our responsibility is to express an opinion on these financial statements based on our audits.

We conducted our audits in accordance with the standards of the Public Company Accounting Oversight Board (United States). Those standards require that we plan and perform the audit to obtain reasonable assurance about whether the financial statements are free of material misstatement. An audit includes examining, on a test basis, evidence supporting the amounts and disclosures in the financial statements. An audit also includes assessing the accounting principles used and significant estimates made by management, as well as evaluating the overall financial statement presentation. We believe that our audits provide a reasonable basis for our opinion.

In our opinion, the financial statements referred to above present fairly. In all material respects, the financial position of the Company as of [at] December 31, 20X3 and 20X2, and the results of its operations and its cash flows for each of the three years in the period ended December 31, 20X3, in conformity with U.S. generally accepted accounting principles.

[*Signature*]

[City and State or Country]

[*Date*]

Figure 9.1 Report of independent registered public accounting firms.

Source: PCAOB. Auditing Standard No. 1. Available at: www.pcaobus.org/Rules/Rules_of_the_Board/Auditing_Standard_1.pdf.

The current audit reporting model has been criticized for not reflecting auditors' assurance on the quality of financial statements by focusing on a pass/fail approach to audit reporting. The pass/fail approach states whether financial statements are presented fairly in conformity with GAAP (pass) or not (fail). The advantages of this approach are (1) the audit report is standard pass/fail language that provides uniformity and improves comparability, and (2) this approach is commonly accepted by the investing public. The disadvantages are (1) the pass/fail approach does not reflect the quality of the financial statements, (2) this approach does not provide useful information to investors regarding the quality of the company as investment or credit risks, and (3) this approach focuses on fair presentation rather than true and accurate presentation of financial position and results of operations. The current audit report approach "on or off," "comply/do not comply," "black and white," "pass or fail" audit opinion is not value relevant to investors. Users of financial statements may demand that auditors express their opinion on overall financial health and future prospects of the company. Auditors should express their judgment on both financial and nonfinancial information in a more customized audit report.

PCAOB Auditing Standards No. 2 and 5

In June 2004, the PCAOB issued its AS No. 2, An Audit of Internal Control over Financial Reporting Performed in Conjunction with an Audit of Financial Statements.[9] AS No. 2

requires the independent auditor to express an opinion on management's assessment of the effectiveness of ICFR. The independent auditor must also audit and express an opinion on the effectiveness of ICFR. In performing tests of controls, the independent auditor must assess (1) the nature and extent of management's documentation of internal controls in providing reasonable support for management's assessment, and (2) factors pertaining to the effectiveness of the audit committee in overseeing the company's external financial reporting and its ICFR.

On May 24, 2007, the PCAOB voted to adopt its AS No. 5, An Audit of Internal Control over Financial Reporting That Is Integrated with an Audit of Financial Statements.[10] AS No. 5, which was subsequently approved by the SEC in July 2007 and supersedes controversial AS No. 2, is a principles-based approach in providing guidance for registered auditors to detect material weaknesses in ICFR that may result in material misstatement of financial statements. AS No. 5 focuses audit attention on the procedures necessary to perform a high-quality audit tailored to the client's facts and circumstances, and promotes risk-based and scalable audit procedures to satisfy the needs of public companies and their shareholders. Key themes of AS No. 5 are (1) audit opinion on only the effectiveness of ICFR, (2) consideration of the work of previous audits, (3) reliance on the work of others, (4) use of risk-based approach of focusing on risk areas, (5) use of a top-down approach of focusing on materiality and what does matter, (6) consideration of size and complexity, (7) a principles-based approach of reducing unnecessary prescriptive audit standards, and (8) more congruence with SEC interpretive guidance. AS No. 2 was criticized for escalating Section 404 compliance costs by (1) promoting bottom-up and control-based approach to testing of ICFR, and (2) requiring extensive control documentation of the process level controls and less focus on the entity-level control and assessment of risk related to significant controls. The top-down, risk-based approach promoted in both SEC's interpretive guidance and AS No. 5 is designed to refocus both management and auditors on controls that matter and risks that threaten the integrity and reliability of financial reports. Both AS No. 5 and SEC's interpretive guidance are intended to bring down the compliance costs of Section 404.

Specifically, AS No. 5 is intended to achieve the following four objectives:

1. Focus ICFR on the most important matters—AS No. 5 is designed to draw auditors' attention and focus their audits on those areas that present the greatest risk by identifying material weaknesses in ICFR before they result in material misstatements. Auditors should address both higher risk areas that cause financial statement fraud and lower risk areas that may cause errors. The risk assessment should be considered in determining the extent, nature, and timing of tests of controls. The auditors' knowledge and experience accumulated in previous years' audits of ICFR and work performed by the client's personnel, including internal audit function, should be factored into risk assessment and audit procedures.

2. Eliminate unnecessary audit procedures—AS No. 5 does not require auditors to (a) assess management's own evaluation process, (b) opine on the adequacy of management's process, or (c) test a large portion of the client's company operations or financial position.

3. Make audit of ICFR scalable and tailored to fit the size and complexity of the company being audited—AS No. 5, by promoting a principles-based approach, provides guidance on how to apply the standard to smaller, less complex companies.

4. Simplify the text of the standard—AS No. 5 is shorter, more focused, better organized, easier to read, and more fine-tuned and collaborated with SEC rules and management guidance.

Improvements made in AS No. 5 compared with AS No. 2 are (1) alignment of terms and concepts used in AS No. 5 with those of SEC rules and guidance, (2) more focus on fraud risk and antifraud controls and their importance in assessing risk of ICFR, (3) using the term entity-level controls and their effects on risk assessment and tests of controls, (4) performance of walk-through tests in documenting the complete and accurate understanding of ICFR rather than creating a checklist approach to ICFR, (5) focusing on identifying material weaknesses that may result in material misstatements rather than focusing on individual control deficiencies that may collectively constitute significant deficiencies, (6) assessment of all identified control deficiencies, (7) better use of the work of the client's internal audit function in the audit of ICFR, and (8) focus on a top-down approach in identifying controls assertions that need to be tested.

1. Identification of internal control deficiencies. PCAOB AS Nos. 2 and 5 provide a list of circumstances that may result in a significant deficiency indicating a material weakness in ICFR, including

    a. Restatement of previously issued financial statements reflecting the correction of a misstatement

    b. Identification of a material misstatement in the current period financial statements that were undetected by the company's ICFR

    c. Ineffective oversight functions of the company's audit committee regarding its financial reporting and ICFR

    d. Ineffective internal control or risk assessment function to monitor the company's risk assessment related to complex business events or transactions

    e. Ineffective regulatory compliance function to ensure compliance with applicable laws and regulations, particularly for complex companies in highly regulated industries

    f. Identification of any financial statement fraud

    g. Uncorrected significant deficiencies that were previously communicated to the company's management and the audit committee by the independent auditor and remain uncorrected after a reasonable period of time

    h. An ineffective control environment that creates opportunities for the occurrence of significant deficiencies or material weaknesses in the company's ICFR

2. Classification of internal control deficiencies. PCAOB AS No. 5 slightly changes the definition of significant deficiencies and material weaknesses as follows:

A significant deficiency is a deficiency, or a combination of deficiencies, in internal control over financial reporting that is less severe than a material weakness, yet important enough to merit attention by those responsible for oversight of the company's financial reporting.

A material weakness is a deficiency, or a combination of deficiencies, in internal control over financial reporting, such that there is a reasonable possibility that a material misstatement of the company's annual or interim financial statements will not be prevented or detected on a timely basis.[11]

3. The independent auditor's opinion on internal controls. The independent audit report on ICFR can be a separate report or be combined with the audit report on financial statements. Figure 9.2 shows the format and content of a combined report of both a financial statement audit and an internal control audit according to AS No. 5. It is expected that the auditing profession will eventually move toward an integrated audit approach that is the combined audit of both ICFR and financial statements, necessitating the use of an integrated

---

[Introductory paragraph]

We have audited the accompanying balance sheets of W Company as of December 31, 20X8 and 20X7, and the related statements of income, stockholders' equity and comprehensive income, and cash flows for each of the years in the three-year period ended December 31, 20X8. We also have audited W Company's internal control over financial reporting as of December 31, 20X8, based on [*Identify control criteria, for example, "criteria established in Internal Control — Integrated Framework issued by the Committee of Sponsoring Organizations of the Treadway Commission (COSO)."*]. W Company's management is responsible for these financial statements, for maintaining effective internal control over financial reporting, and for its assessment of the effectiveness of internal control over financial reporting, included in the accompanying [title of management's report]. Our responsibility is to express an opinion on these financial statements and an opinion on the company's internal control over financial reporting based on our audits.

[Scope paragraph]

We conducted our audits in accordance with the standards of the Public Company Accounting Oversight Board (United States). Those standards require that we plan and perform the audits to obtain reasonable assurance about whether the financial statements are free of material misstatement and whether effective internal control over financial reporting was maintained in all material respects. Our audits of the financial statements included examining, on a test basis, evidence supporting the amounts and disclosures in the financial statements, assessing the accounting principles used and significant estimates made by management, and evaluating the overall financial statement presentation. Our audit of internal control over financial reporting included obtaining an understanding of internal control over financial reporting, assessing the risk that a material weakness exists, and testing and evaluating the design and operating effectiveness of internal control based on the assessed risk. Our audits also included performing such other procedures as we considered necessary in the circumstances. We believe that our audits provide a reasonable basis for our opinions.

[Definition paragraph]

A company's internal control over financial reporting is a process designed to provide reasonable assurance regarding the reliability of financial reporting and the preparation of financial statements for external purposes in accordance with generally accepted accounting principles. A company's internal control over financial reporting includes those policies and procedures that (1) pertain to the maintenance of records that, in reasonable detail, accurately and fairly reflect the transactions and dispositions of the assets of the company; (2) provide reasonable assurance that transactions are recorded as necessary to permit preparation of financial statements in accordance with generally accepted accounting principles, and that receipts and expenditures of the company are being made only in accordance with authorizations of management and directors of the company; and (3) provide reasonable assurance regarding prevention or timely detection of unauthorized acquisition, use, or disposition of the company's assets that could have a material effect on the financial statements.

[*Inherent limitations paragraph*]

Because of its inherent limitations, internal control over financial reporting may not prevent or detect misstatements. Also, projections of any evaluation of effectiveness to future periods are subject to the risk that controls may become inadequate because of changes in conditions, or that the degree of compliance with the policies or procedures may deteriorate.

[*Opinion paragraph*]

In our opinion, the financial statements referred to above present fairly, in all material respects, the financial position of W Company as of December 31, 20X8 and 20X7, and the results of its operations and its cash flows for each of the years in the three-year period ended December 31, 20X8 in conformity with accounting principles generally accepted in the United States of America. Also in our opinion, W Company maintained, in all material respects, effective internal control over financial reporting as of December 31, 20X8, based on [*Identify control criteria, for example, "criteria established in Internal Control – Integrated Framework issued by the Committee of Sponsoring Organizations of the Treadway Commission (COSO)."*].

[*Signature*]

[*City and State or Country*]

[*Date*]

Figure 9.2 Integrated audit report of independent registered public accounting firm.
Source: Excerpt from PCAOB. 2007, June 12. Auditing Standard No. 5—An Audit of Internal Control Over Financial Reporting That Is Integrated with An Audit of Financial Statements. Available at: www.pcaobus.org/Rules/Rules_of_the_Board/Auditing_Standard_5.pdf.

audit report. An integrated audit report should be issued particularly when the independent audit issues an unqualified opinion on both financial statements and ICFR. Nevertheless, management's report on internal control should be a separate report and should be placed right after the MD&A section of Form 10-K and immediately before the financial statements section.

In accordance with PCAOB AS No. 5, the independent auditor should only opine on the client's effectiveness of ICFR, not management's assessment of ICFR, either as a separate report or as a combined report with an opinion on the financial statements. There are three possible types of audit opinions on ICFR:

- a. **Unqualified opinion.** The unqualified opinion can be rendered when there are no identified material weaknesses in ICFR and no scope limitations. In this case, the audit report states, "In our opinion, the company maintained, in all material respects, effective internal control over financial reporting."
- b. **Adverse opinion.** The adverse opinion should be rendered when there are significant deficiencies in the company's ICFR that result in one or more material weaknesses. In this case, the audit report states, "In our opinion, the company did not maintain, in all material respects, effective internal control over financial reporting."

      c. **Qualified/disclaimer opinion.** The disclaimer opinion should be given when there is a scope limitation and the auditor cannot express an opinion on the effectiveness of the company's ICFR.

PCAOB Auditing Standard No. 3

The SEC in January 2003 issued rules requiring public accounting firms to retain for seven years certain records relevant to their audits and reviews of a company's financial statements.[12] Records to be retained include work papers and other audit documents that contain conclusions, analyses, financial data, and opinions pertaining to the review or audit of the client company's financial statements. Section 802 of SOX addresses fines and imprisonment for anyone who knowingly alters, mutilates, conceals, covers up, destroys, or falsifies documents or records with the intent to influence or obstruct an investigation conducted by regulators. Section 1520(a) requires an auditor who performs financial statement audits in compliance with SEC requirements to maintain all audit papers for a period of five years pursuant to the audit. The SEC rule extended the retention period to seven years after the auditor concludes the audit. AS No. 3 (1) establishes general requirements for documentation that the auditor should prepare and retain in an audit of financial statements, and (2) requires auditors to prepare and maintain—for at least seven years—audit documentation in sufficient detail to support the conclusion reached in their reports.[13]

PCAOB Auditing Standard No. 4

PCAOB AS No. 4 establishes a voluntary engagement for the auditor's report on the company's elimination of previously reported material weaknesses in its ICFR.[14] The proposed standards would apply when

1. The auditor has already issued an adverse opinion indicating material weakness in ICFR

2. The company, subsequent to audit, eliminated a material weakness

3. There is a voluntary, stand-alone audit engagement to provide assurance about the reliability and effectiveness of internal controls

PCAOB Auditor Independence

The PCAOB adopted ethics and independent rules in 2005 that identify circumstances that would be considered as impairing auditor independence. These rules treat an auditor as not independent of the client if the audit firm (1) provided any service or product to the client for a contingent fee or commission; (2) received from the client, directly or indirectly, a contingent fee or commission; (3) provided assistance in planning or provided tax advice on certain types of potentially abusive tax transactions (e.g., a transaction that the Treasury Department considers as a listed or confidential transaction); or (4) provided tax services to certain persons employed by the client.[15] In addition, these rules require auditors to provide certain information to the client's audit committee relevant to preapproval to render nonprohibited tax services.

    The new rules restrict public accounting firms in performing a variety of tax services to their audit clients. The rules are intended to prevent the selling of abusive tax shelters by accounting firms, investment banks, and law firms that began during the 1990s and cost the U.S. Treasury billions of dollars. These abusive tax shelters involve transactions that lack economic substance and are designed to create bookkeeping losses or deductions. PCAOB standards prevent public accounting firms from providing tax shelter services to their audit clients that impair their independence because auditors subsequently opine on proper disclosures of provided tax strategies in the financial statements.

There is no standard or law defining the term "tax shelter" or differentiating between "tax planning," which is a legitimate means of reducing tax liability, and "abusive tax shelter," which is illegal. Nonetheless, abusive tax shelters are characterized as "transactions in which a significant purpose is the avoidance or evasion of Federal, state or local tax in a manner not intended by the law."[16] The Senate Report finds that (1) a variety of professional groups, including public accounting firms, law firms, banks, and investment advisory firms, were heavily involved in the design and marketing of tax shelters; (2) during the period 1998 to 2003, KPMG devoted significant resources to producing and selling illegal or potentially abusive tax shelters; (3) KPMG took steps to conceal its tax services from tax authorities; and (4) other Big Four public accounting firms were involved in providing aggressive tax services to their audit clients and have subsequently committed to cultural, structural, and institutional changes to dismantle their tax shelter activities.

PCAOB Enforcement Investigations

The PCAOB initiated its enforcement actions against several registered auditors who were alleged to have concealed information requested by the PCAOB through its inspection process. The PCAOB investigation process is very similar to SEC enforcement investigations. This process starts with the staff of the Enforcement and Investigation Division issuing document requests, also called "accounting board demands" (ABDs), and subsequently requests for testimony from partners and managers of the alleged audit firms.[17] The staff then proceeds pursuant to a board "formal order" of investigation. PCAOB enforcement investigations pertain to any financial statement that is included within statements that are filed with the SEC after the audit firm registered with the PCAOB in 2003. PCAOB enforcement investigations are often coordinated with those of the SEC in the sense that (1) the PCAOB staff meets frequently with the SEC staff, (2) the PCAOB staff attends the SEC testimony of auditors, and (3) the SEC staff sits in on PCAOB testimony without asking questions.

AUDIT COMMITTEE OVERSIGHT OF EXTERNAL AUDITORS

The emerging corporate governance reforms have expanded audit committee oversight responsibility over the external audit function. These extended responsibilities make the independent auditor responsible to the audit committee, not management. These reforms hold the audit committee directly responsible for overseeing the external audit function, and the external auditor is ultimately accountable to the audit committee. The extended oversight responsibilities for the audit committee are

1. Appointment, compensation, and retention of registered public accounting firms
2. Preapproval of audit services and permissible nonaudit services

3. Review of the independent auditor's plan for an integrated audit of both ICFR and annual financial statements

4. Review and discussion of financial statements audited or reviewed by the independent auditor

5. Monitoring the auditor's independence

6. Auditor rotation requirement

Appointment, Compensation, and Retention of Auditors

Section 301(2) of SOX states that the audit committee is directly responsible for hiring, compensating, and firing the company's independent auditor. The audit committee is also directly responsible for overseeing the work of the company's independent auditor in performing all audit and nonaudit services, including audit of financial statements, audit of ICFR, review of interim financial statements, and performance of permissible nonaudit services such as tax services. These provisions are intended to reduce potential conflicts of interest between the company's management and its independent auditor.

SOX provides the audit committee with the authority to obtain funding for compensation of the independent auditor. Management has traditionally negotiated the fees in the context of reducing the cost of both audit and nonaudit services. The audit committee now directly participates in the negotiation process for determining the audit fees and in approving fees for both audit and permissible nonaudit services. It is expected that the audit committee will place more emphasis on audit quality in light of recent substantial increases in audit fees due to an extended audit scope, which includes an audit of ICFR. As the audit of financial reports moves toward an integrated audit of the financial statements and ICFR, we expect that the cost of the audit will substantially increase and the audit committee will be directly responsible for compensating auditors. The Audit Landscape reports companies' auditor fees between 2001 and 2006 and concludes that (1) the Big Four continue to dominate more than 95 percent of the market for large accelerated filers (companies with more than $750 million in market capitalizations), (2) the demise of Arthur Andersen benefited the Big Four firms equally, (3) the median increase in audit fees between 2001 and 2006 was 345.68 percent, (4) the median total auditor costs rose from $1,420,000 in 2001 to $2,741,087 in 2006, and (5) total fees paid to auditors for the matched sample of companies (more than 3,000 public companies) were $6.8 billion in 2006 compared to $5.8 billion in 2001.[18]

Preapproval of Audit Services and Permissible Nonaudit Services

Sections 201 and 202 of SOX require that all audit and permissible nonaudit services to be performed by the company's independent auditor must be approved by the audit committee. The preapproval process can be based on engagement by engagement, or the company can establish preapproval policies for all audit and permissible nonaudit services. The preapproval of permissible nonaudit services may be delegated to a member of the company's audit committee. However, such a decision by a member of the audit committee must be presented to the audit committee at its next meeting and should be approved by the company's board of directors.

Review of Independent Auditor Plan for the Integrated Audit

SOX has substantially increased audit committee involvement and the quality and quantity of working relations with independent auditors. A typical once-a-year short meeting between external auditors and the audit committee is replaced with more frequent and more extensive discussion regarding audit work. Independent auditors obtain more information from the audit committee regarding the company's financial reporting process, internal controls, and ERM. Audit committees gather information regarding audit scope, complex accounting policies and practices, alternative accounting treatments, accounting estimates and reserves, and other significant accounting and auditing discussed with management. In conducting the audit, auditors interact with management, which includes gathering evidence, evaluating evidence, making decisions, and establishing a cooperative working relationship with management. Nevertheless, independent auditors should understand that under recent corporate governance reforms and the regulatory environment, they are ultimately accountable and professionally responsible to the audit committee as representatives and guardians of the company's investors and other stakeholders.

The audit committee should review the independent auditor's plan for performing audit services, including audit of the company's annual financial statements and ICFR. The audit committee, after approving the audit services, should discuss the audit plan, including audit scope, supervision, staffing, review process, audit sites to be visited, reporting date, areas that require special audit attention (special purpose entities, related party transactions, fraud risk), and any arrangements for audit of the company's subsidiaries, particularly foreign affiliates.

Review and Discussion of Financial Reports

The audit committee should review annual audited financial statements and interim reviewed financial statements with the company's independent auditor. The purpose of this discussion is for the committee to obtain an understanding of the financial reports; assurance provided by auditors on the financial reports; resolution of any disagreements between management regarding the content, format, and presentation of financial reports; and, finally, recommendations to the company's board of directors for the filing and distribution of financial reports. The audit committee should meet with the company's CFO, internal auditor, independent auditor, and legal counsel to discuss the integrated audit of annual financial statements, including management's assessment of the effectiveness of ICFR and the auditor's report on management's assessment and audit of annual financial statements to evaluate the overall integrity and quality of financial reports before they are filed or distributed. Issues that should be addressed in this meeting include

1. The quality and integrity of financial reports in terms of their content, format and disclosure, and presentation in conformity with GAAP

2. All critical accounting policies and practices used by management in measuring and recognizing the company's transactions and events as well as the preparation of financial statements

3. All alternative treatments within GAAP for accounting policies and practices related to material financial items used by management and approved by the independent auditor

4. Disagreements between management and the independent auditor regarding accounting and internal control issues and presentation of financial statements

5. All material communications (oral and written) between management and the independent auditor, including audit adjustments, fraud risk factors, significant deficiencies, and material weaknesses in ICFR

6. All material unusual transactions, significant fluctuations, accounting estimates and reserves, and significant internal control issues

7. The independent auditor disagreements with management about the scope of the integrated audit, material weaknesses in ICFR, and the wording of the audit (reports)

8. Any difficulties or lack of cooperation and coordination by management during the audit engagement, including any delays in providing requested information, schedules, records, or documents

9. Substantial changes in the audit fee resulting from departures from the initial integrated audit plan

10. Any suspected fraud by management, or material employee fraud affecting the reliability and integrity of financial statements or illegal acts by senior management, including violations of applicable laws and regulations

Monitoring the Auditor's Independence

Auditor independence is the backbone of the auditing profession, affecting the auditor's planning, evidence-gathering procedures, findings, judgment, credibility, and public trust in the auditor's opinion. Thus, it is essential that the audit committee monitor auditor independence in fact and in appearance during (1) the planning of the audit to ensure that management is not influencing the audit plan or scope of the audit; (2) the evidence-gathering phase of the audit to ensure that the auditor has access to all information, records, schedules, and financial statements, and the scope of the audit was not limited; and (3) the reporting of audit findings to ensure the auditor's judgment and opinion were not influenced by management or a sense of loyalty to the company. The SEC requires that the audit committee indicate in its annual report whether the committee has received disclosures about auditor independence and discussed it with the independent auditor. To ensure proper disclosures of auditor independence, the committee should receive an auditor independence confirmation from the company's independent auditor prior to the filing and distribution of audited financial statements. Auditor independence is further discussed in the next section of this chapter.

Auditor Rotation Requirement

Section 203 of SOX and SEC-related rules require the lead and concurring partners to rotate off the company's audit after five years and stay off for five years (five years on, five years off). Audit partners other than the lead and concurring partners involved in an engagement must rotate off after no more than seven years and are subject to a two-year time-out. The audit committee should monitor auditor rotation requirements for audit partners prior to an audit engagement. In addition, the committee should ensure that no employee of the company with a financial reporting oversight role, including the CEO, CFO, controller, or CAO, was a member of the current audit engagement team at any time within a one-year period (the cooling-off period).

The issue of audit firm rotation is extensively and yet inconclusively debated in the literature. The general perception is that audit firm rotation can be very costly, complex, and ineffective without adding much to the objectivity and independence of financial statement audits. More than 50 percent of public companies changed their auditors in the post-SOX period, which accounts for a more than 60 percent auditor turnover rate.[19] Such a high auditor turnover rate justifies the possibility of audit firm rotation every several years. These auditor changes are also linked to financial restatements and disclosure of material weaknesses in internal controls, as they occurred more frequently (three times as often) within one year of auditor changes. Figure 9.3 shows the number of companies that changed auditors and the number of auditor changes.

Corporate governance reforms do not require, although they are suggested in special circumstances, audit firm rotations. However, the upward trend in audit firm switches and their consequences in the post-SOX era have received the attention of regulators, the accounting profession, and the investing community. Auditor changes can occur as a result of auditor dismissal by the company or the auditor's resignation. In either case, the SEC must be notified of auditor changes by filing Form 8-K. Auditors usually resign when there is an unresolved dispute with their client or when their client's financial health deteriorates, which increases the likelihood of litigation risk. Auditor dismissals often result from disagreements about key issues pertaining to financial reporting, internal controls, and audit fees. The Conference Board recommends that the company's audit committee consider rotating the company's public accounting firm when its independence from management is severely in doubt.[20] It specifically states that the existence of some or all of the following circumstances merits consideration of audit firm rotations: (1) one or more former partners or managers of the audit firm hold key financial positions in the company; (2) the audit firm has been performing audit and assurance services to the company for a substantial period of time (e.g., more than ten years); and (3) the audit firm has performed significant nonaudit services for the company. In the context of the current trend in auditor changes, it is reasonable to suggest that the audit firm should be rotated every seven to twelve years.

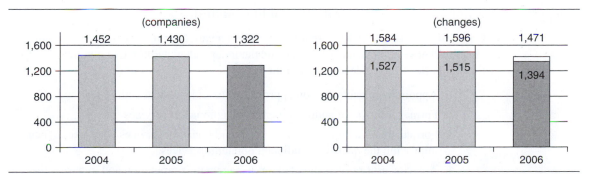

Figure 9.3 The number of companies that changed auditors, and number of auditor changes.
Source: Glass Lewis, company filings.

The audit committee is now directly responsible for the appointment, compensation, and retention of the company's independent auditor. In selecting the company's public accounting firm, the committee should pay particular attention to auditor independence (e.g., not engaging in prohibited nonaudit services), industry specialization, reputation, reasonableness of the audit fee, and requirement for rotation of the lead partner. If the committee at any time becomes aware of a violation of auditor independence, inappropriateness of audit services, significant damages to auditor reputation, or substantial difficulties between management and the independent auditor, the committee should consider changing the company's independent auditor.

When the audit committee determines there is a need for a change of the company's public accounting firm, it should seek audit engagement proposals from other firms. In receiving and evaluating proposals, the committee should investigate the potential public accounting firm's industry specialization; professional qualifications; personal integrity; reputation of lead auditor; latest PCAOB inspections, particularly nonpublic portions of the inspection report; and other relevant information provided by the firm. The audit committee should then prepare a short list of potential independent auditors, interview the potential candidates (the CFO and the director of the internal audit department may participate in the interview process), and then select at least two independent auditors to submit the formal proposal and advise other auditors that they are no longer being considered.

The two selected public accounting firms should be given the opportunity to investigate the company, the integrity of its management, and its financial solvency, business risk, financial records, books, and filing requirements; visit the company's important plants and office, including key personnel; contact the company's current and past business associates; and communicate with the preceding auditor. The two potential independent auditors should show their intent and interest by submitting a formal proposal indicating the proposed audit fee or method of determining the audit fee and other important issues (auditor independence, rotation requirements). Based on the information provided, the company selects one public accounting firm and asks them to prepare and sign a written contract (engagement letter). The appointed independent auditor then signs the contract to perform the audit. The selected audit firms should provide adequate information about how they are planning to conduct the audit. They should also present their past three years of inspection reports conducted by the PCAOB, along with any enforcement actions, if any, against the firms.

Independent Auditor Communication with the Audit Committee

Corporate governance reforms require or suggest a variety of formal and informal communications between the audit committee and the independent auditor. Communications from the committee to the independent auditor include

1. Appointment and retention approval of the independent auditor
2. Formal approval of audit and permissible nonaudit services
3. Formal approval of fees for both audit and nonaudit services with a keen focus on improving the quality of audit and nonaudit services
4. Any concerns or risks threatening management's reputation and integrity, the reliability of financial reporting, or the effectiveness of internal controls known to the

audit committee that could possibly affect audit activities and the quality of audit services

5. Allegations of financial statement fraud known to the audit committee that affect the integrity and reliability of financial statements and the effectiveness of a related audit

Communications from the independent auditor to the audit committee include

1. Seeking committee preapproval of all audit and nonaudit services in a timely manner

2. The critical accounting policies and practices used by management in the preparation of financial statements

3. All alternative treatments of financial information within GAAP that have already been discussed with management, the ramifications of the use of such alternative accounting treatments, and the treatment preferred by the auditor

4. Any accounting disagreements between the independent auditor and the company's management

5. Any material written communications between the independent auditor and the company's management throughout the course of the audit

6. Significant deficiencies and material weaknesses of ICFR

7. The audit report on annual financial statements

8. The review report on quarterly financial statements

9. The audit report on management's assessment of the effectiveness of ICFR

10. The audit report on the effectiveness of ICFR

11. Financial risks associated with financial reports

AUDITOR INDEPENDENCE

Auditor independence is the cornerstone of the auditing profession and one of the fundamental aspects that makes audit functions value-adding services to society and the investing community. External auditors are outside, independent contractors hired to independently assess and lend credibility to the accuracy of the financial statements. Thus, auditor independence in both fact and appearance is important in assessing the value of audit services provided to clients.

Auditor independence is influenced by the entire audit process—from the selection and appointment of auditors to financial reporting audit findings and opinions. Auditor independence also affects the entire audit process of accepting a client and planning the engagement, evidence-gathering phase, and final reporting phase. Auditor independence in this book is defined as a process that is affected by the appointment of auditors, services provided by auditors, and the manner in which services are provided. This process also affects the acceptance of clients, planning of the audit engagement, conducting of the audit, and reporting of audit findings and opinion. It is derived from the three basic independence

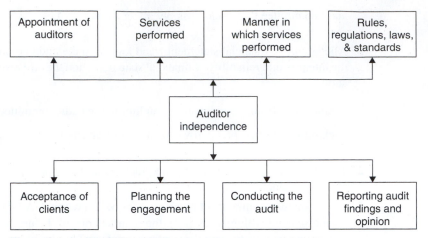

Figure 9.4 Auditor independence.

Source: Rezaee, Z. 2007. *Corporate Governance Post-Sarbanes-Oxley Act: Regulations, Requirements, & Integrated Processes.* John Wiley & Sons, Hoboken, NJ.

principles of (1) auditors cannot be part of management or its team, (2) auditors cannot audit their own works, and (3) auditors cannot serve in advocacy roles as specified by the SEC and as depicted in Figure 9.4.[21]

1. The appointment of auditors. Traditionally, auditors had been appointed by management to perform a variety of audit and nonaudit services. However, management could have influenced the selection of services provided by auditors. Corporate governance reforms have changed the process of selection of the auditors by requiring the audit committee to be directly responsible for the appointment, retention, and compensation of auditors. Selection, appointment, and retention decisions made by the audit committee should be approved by the entire board and be put forth for final approval by shareholders in the form of acceptance or rejection at the shareholder annual meetings.

2. Services performed. Traditionally, auditors have performed a variety of audit and nonaudit services for their clients. The fundamental element of auditor independence is the separation of audit and nonaudit services and economic independence from sources of revenue (consulting) other than audit services. Section 201 of SOX and SEC-related rules prohibit auditors from performing nine different types of nonaudit services contemporaneously with audit services. Prohibited nonaudit services are (a) bookkeeping or other related accounting services; (b) financial information systems design and implementation; (c) appraisal or valuation services; (d) actuarial services; (e) internal audit outsourcing services; (f) management functions or human resources; (g) broker/dealer, investment advisor, or investment banking services; (h) legal services; and (i) expert services unrelated to the audit.[22] The nonaudit services that are prohibited for reasons of independence can still be provided by auditors for nonaudit clients. The PCAOB proposed standard on auditor independence also prohibits registered auditors from performing certain tax services (aggressive tax shelters) to their audit clients.

3. Manner in which services are performed. The manner in which audit services are performed can influence the objectivity and independence of auditors. For example, the reported financial scandals of the late 1990s (e.g., Cendant, Sunbeam, McKesson HBOC) and the early 2000s (e.g., Informix, MicroStrategy, Rite Aid, Waste Management, Enron, Global Crossing, WorldCom) have prompted lawmakers, regulators, and the accounting profession to address earnings management schemes and the perceived audit failures associated with these schemes. Particularly, the SEC improved auditor independence rules. The SEC suggests that increased auditor independence leads to higher-quality financial reporting by reduced earnings management schemes.

4. Independence rules. Several regulators and professional organizations have issued authoritative guidelines to assist in preserving their independence. Authoritative guidelines focus on two concepts of auditor independence: independence in fact and independence in appearance. Independence in fact states that external auditors should be intellectually honest, impartial, objective, and unbiased, and have an objective state of mind. Independence in appearance suggests that external auditors should be perceived as being independent in the public mind. Independence in appearance can be assessed through observation of external facts, whereas independence in fact requires direct evidence of the auditor's mental state.

SOX addresses auditor independence in several of its provisions: (a) Section 206 prohibits auditors from performing an audit for a company whose CEO, CFO, controller, CAO, or equivalent was employed by the accounting firm during the one-year period preceding the audit (the "cooling-off period"); (b) Section 201 prohibits auditors from providing any nonaudit services to the company contemporaneously with audit services; (c) Section 203 requires the lead audit or coordinating partner and reviewing partner to rotate off the audit every five years; (d) Section 204 requires auditors to report to the audit committee all critical accounting policies and practices used, all alternative treatments of financial information within GAAP, ramifications of the use of such alternative disclosures and treatments, the preferred treatment, and other material written communication between the auditor and management; (e) Section 103 requires a second partner to review and approve each public company audit report; and (f) Section 204 prohibits registered auditors from setting compensation or allocation of partnership based on the revenue generated by providing nonaudit services to clients.[23] These provisions of SOX were intended to strengthen auditor independence. Thus, public companies should establish proper policies and procedures for the implementation of these provisions, and the company's audit committee should oversee the effectiveness of the established policies and procedures to ensure auditor independence. Listing standards of national stock exchanges require the listing company's audit committee to establish hiring policies for employees or former employees of the company's public accounting firm.[24]

The SEC, as directed by SOX, issued its rules on auditor independence in January 2003, which (a) define several nonaudit services that would impair auditor independence if provided simultaneously to an audit client, (b) require lead and review partner rotation every five years, (c) require audit partner compensation to be based on audit quality rather than selling engagements to an audit client for nonaudit services, (d) indicate that auditor independence is impaired if the client company's principal financial officers had been members of the audit engagement team within a one-year period before the start of the audit, (e) require proxy statement disclosures of fees billed by the auditor for nonaudit and audit services, and (f) require proper disclosures related to the audit committee's preapproval process for audit and permissible nonaudit services.[25]

The SEC staff has provided additional guidance regarding the application of auditor independence roles in certain areas of (a) employee benefit plans, (b) FIN 46(R), and (c) the "not subject to audit" provision. First, it is addressed whether the auditor of an employee benefit plan can provide certain nonaudit services to the plan sponsor without violating auditor independence rules. SEC staff guidance suggests that the independence of the auditor of the 11-k filer would not be impaired if the auditor performed certain nonaudit services for the sponsor provided that (a) the auditor does not perform any services that would affect the benefit plan audit, and (b) such provided services are within the scope of the "not subject to audit" provision.[26] Second, as a general rule, the auditor should be independent of all entities that are required to be consolidated under FIN 46(R), regardless of whether a variable interest entity (VIE) is consolidated or not consolidated due to materiality or other considerations. Third, six of the prohibited nonaudit services (bookkeeping, financial information system design and implementation, actuarial services, internal audit outsourcing, appraisal, or valuation) have an exception clause, "unless it is reasonable to conclude that the results of these services will not be subject to audit procedures during an audit of the audit client's financial statements," the so-called "not subject to audit" provision.[27] The SEC's staff perception is that a successor auditor's independence would not be impaired if the successor auditor performed such prohibited nonaudit services in the current audit period and he or she (a) relates primarily to the prior period that was audited by a preceding auditor, (b) does not perform management functions, and (c) will not be subject to audit procedures by the successor auditor.

CONSOLIDATION AND COMPETITION IN PUBLIC ACCOUNTING FIRMS

SOX directs the General Accounting Office (GAO) to study public accounting firm consolidation and competition. Section 701 of SOX specifically mandated that the GAO consider (1) factors contributing to mergers in public accounting firms in the 1980s and 1990s; (2) the implications of consolidation on competition, client selection, auditor independence, audit quality, and audit fees; (3) the effects of consolidation on capital formation and securities markets; and (4) any barriers to entry for obtaining large public company clients by smaller public accounting firms.

The GAO conducted its study and submitted the results in 2003 in a 147-page report to the Senate Committee on Banking, Housing, and Urban Affairs and to the House Committee on Financial Services.[28] The results indicate that (1) the Big Four public accounting firms (Deloitte & Touche, Ernst & Young, KPMG, and PricewaterhouseCoopers) audit more than 78 percent of U.S. public companies and 99 percent of all public company revenues, which has already raised several concerns regarding audit fee, audit quality, and client selection; (2) although there is no evidence of impaired competition today, the emerging significant changes in the audit profession may have implications for competition and client selection in certain industries; (3) there is no evidence of direct association between audit fees and consolidation; (4) audit fees have already started to increase and are expected to continue increasing as the audit environment responds to emerging changes in the audit market; (5) there is no conclusive evidence of association between consolidation and audit quality and independence; (6) the biggest challenge to many large public companies will be the limited number of auditor choices if they voluntarily switch and are required to switch through mandatory firm rotation, industry specialization, or a new independence rule; (7) the majority of surveyed public companies reported that they would not consider using a smaller (non–Big Four) firm for their audit and attestation services; (8) smaller public accounting firms faced a significant barrier to entry into the large public company audit market due to a lack of adequate staff, capital formation, reputation, and global reach; increased litigation risk and insurance costs; and a lack of industry and technical experience; and (9) certain factors and conditions could cause a further reduction in the number of major public accounting firms, whereas market forces are not likely to result in the expansion of the current Big Four accounting firms.

SEC rules require public companies that change their public accounting firms to file a Form 8-K, Item 4.01, to disclose changes within four days, whereas auditors are required to provide standard letters within ten days stating whether they agree with the company's disclosure without specifying any reasons. The public filings of auditor changes should reveal whether certain items occurred within the previous two years, including (1) whether the former accountant resigned or was dismissed; (2) whether the auditor's opinion on the company's financial statements was other than unqualified; (3) whether there were any disagreements with the former auditor regarding accounting principles and practices, audit scope, or financial statements disclosures; or (4) whether there was any advice from the auditors regarding the effectiveness of ICFR, lack of reliance on management's representations, or new information that materially affected the fairness or reliability of previously issued financial statements (e.g., restatement of financial statements).[29]

INTEGRATED AUDIT APPROACH

Auditing standards issued by the PCAOB recommend the use of an integrated audit approach consisting of an audit of internal controls and financial statements. The integrated audit requires independent auditors to express an opinion on (1) management's assessment of the effectiveness of ICFR, (2) the effectiveness of both design and operation of ICFR based on control criteria, and (3) fair presentation of financial statements in conformity with GAAP. A review of a sample of 2005 audit engagement letters of Big Four public accounting firms reveals that the letters were prepared based on the performance of integrated audits. An integrated audit requires auditors to change their audit strategy.

Audit Strategy

Independent auditors have traditionally performed a combination of tests of controls and substantive tests to provide reasonable assurance that financial statements are free of material misstatements. This level of assurance requires auditors to reduce the risk of material misstatements to an appropriately low level. The level of tests performed is not sufficient to opine on internal controls. Tests of controls must be broadened to include understanding of ICFR and provide reasonable assurance about the effectiveness of both the design and operation of internal controls. Auditors have often performed limited tests of controls, used a cycle rotation approach to test controls, or conducted dual tests of internal controls and substantive audit procedures. These audit approaches are less relevant to an integrated audit.

1. **No limited tests of controls.** The second standard of fieldwork requires auditors to obtain a sufficient understanding of internal controls to plan the audit and to determine the nature, timing, and extent of audit procedures (mainly substantive tests) to be performed. This standard requires only an understanding of internal control and does not require the performance of tests of controls. Independent auditors in complying with this standard have performed limited tests of controls only when (1) adequate controls exist (built in the internal control system), and (2) it is cost justifiable/feasible to perform some limited tests of controls to possibly reduce the extent of substantive tests. This approach is no longer acceptable in integrated audits of public companies in accordance with PCAOB AS No. 2.

2. **No use of cycle rotation in tests of controls.** To comply with the second standard of fieldwork, in the past auditors have used cycle rotation in tests of controls. The cycle rotation approach involves: (a) identifying and classifying the client's transactions into groups of interrelated transactions (cycles), depending on the nature of the client's business and industry [e.g., for manufacturing companies, typical transaction cycles are (i) revenue and collection cycle; (ii) acquisition and payment cycle; (iii) conversion cycle; (iv) payroll and personnel cycle; and (v) finance and investment cycle]; (b) obtaining an understanding of internal controls of all relevant transaction cycles; and (c) performing tests of controls on several of these transaction cycles while conducting a walk-through test to ensure the absence of control changes in the remaining transaction cycles previously tested. Auditors conducting an integrated audit should express opinions on the effectiveness of both the design and operation of ICFR on an annual basis.

3. **Dual testing of controls and substantive audit procedures.** Independent auditors, in performing dual tests of internal controls and substantive audit procedures, have in the past primarily focused on transaction-level prevention, detection, and correction controls as well as transactions and account balance substantive tests. Under the integrated audit approach, auditors should test controls at both the company level and the transaction level. Company-level controls are relevant to the effectiveness of the company's governance, the vigilance of its board of directors, the integrity and reputation of its management, the possibility of management overriding the control system, and its overall corporate culture. The effectiveness of the company-level controls is important in expressing an opinion on ICFR under an integrated audit approach.

Auditors should focus on prevention, detection, and correction of controls at both the company level and the transaction level. Auditors should use evidence gathered by performing tests of controls in determining the nature, timing, and extent of substantive tests of details and analytical procedures for classes of transactions and account balances. Auditors should perform tests of controls as a basis for forming an opinion on the effectiveness of ICFR. Auditors should also perform substantive tests as a basis for expressing an opinion on the fair presentation of financial statements, regardless of the identified significant deficiencies and material weaknesses in internal controls.

AUDIT OF DEFINED BENEFIT PENSIONS

Recent large corporate bankruptcies and the related transfer of unfunded pension liabilities to the PBGC have caused both the U.S. administration and Congress to focus on the minimum funding rules relevant to private sector–defined benefit pension plans. In 2005, the administration issued a proposal to strengthen the annual funding requirements for pension plans, and Congress subsequently introduced bills for such plans. Employer-defined benefit pension reforms, as proposed by the administration and introduced by both the House and the Senate, would require plan sponsors to make minimum funding contributions equal to the greater of (1) the contributions required under the plan's funding standard account estimated based on the plan's actuarial accrued liability, or (2) deficient reduction contributions calculated under current liability rules. These reforms would replace the current law's "double-barrel" system with a single measure of assets and liabilities and required funding method.

Auditor engagement to audit the employee benefit plans is receiving a considerable amount of attention in the post-SOX era. Public companies are required to file an 11-K report regarding their employee benefit plans.[30] The report requires an audit report on a plan financial statement filed with the SEC. Sections 404 and 906 of SOX may also apply to employee benefit plans. Many companies have included Sections 404 and 906 certifications with Forms 11-K filed in light of uncertainties and lack of needed guidance from the SEC regarding the statutory language. The general understanding is that Sections 404 and 906 certifications do not apply to SEC Form 11-K. Nonetheless, the company's audit committee should pay attention to any developments in 11-K reporting.

AUDITOR LIABILITY LIMITATION AGREEMENTS

Independent auditors are subject to both civil and criminal liabilities for their audit failures under common and statutory laws. Auditors usually obtain malpractice liability insurance to protect themselves from exposure to legal claims. Auditors have also entered into agreements with their clients to limit their liability to a percentage of total losses from audit failure. In many cases, in the aftermath of business failures and resulting bankruptcy, injured investors have found it more feasible to bring lawsuits against auditors as having the "deepest pockets," even though they may not be fully responsible for the business failure. Thus, auditors have been exposed to high-risk, large claims for alleged negligence in performing audit services. The ever-increasing liability and exposure to lawsuits have been detrimental to the financial solvency of public accounting firms.

The issue of auditor liability has been extensively and inconclusively debated in the literature. The general perceptions are (1) the number of lawsuits against public accounting firms is increasing; (2) in many cases, the amount of settlements or incurred liabilities are disproportional to the audit fees; (3) auditor liability insurance may provide incentives to injured parties to bring lawsuits against auditors rather than insolvent or bankrupt companies based on the "deep pocket concept," although in many cases (e.g., Enron, WorldCom, tax shelters) other professionals such as investment banks and legal counsel have been also charged; and (4) investor losses have risen more rapidly than settlements during the period from 1991 to 2005.

Opponents of liability caps or auditor liability limitation agreements (LLAs) provide the following arguments for not limiting auditor liability:

1. Unlimited auditor liability is a quality driver in the sense that auditor liability exposure can be substantially decreased if auditors deliver high-quality audits. In other words, there is a positive association between audit failures and auditor liability.

2. Legal liability measures are intended to protect individuals who suffered damages, not for the convenience of those who may be at fault.

3. Increased auditor liability is to some extent a self-created problem by public accounting firms that are willing to settle their suits easily out of court to prevent further damages to their reputation or the brand name. Furthermore, an audit failure in a local office can potentially ruin the reputation of the whole firm. Examples are aggressive tax shelter services provided by several partners of KPMG or the demise of Arthur Andersen caused largely by the actions of several partners.

4. Audits are conducted for the benefit of investors and public interest, and auditors' responsibility is to protect investors from receiving misleading financial information that adversely affects their investment and voting decisions. Thus, investors should have the confidence to rely on audited financial statements and be in a position to recover damages in case of fraudulent financial reporting.

In February 2006, the Federal Financial Regulatory Agencies issued an interagency advisory that raised concerns regarding the negative impacts on the quality and reliability of audits when financial institutions agree to limit their independent auditors' liability.[31] The advisory, while observing an increase in the types and extent of provisions in financial institutions' external audit engagement letters that limit auditor liability, informs financial institutions that they should not enter into an audit engagement that includes unsafe and unsound limitation of liability provisions relevant to an integrated audit of their financial statements and ICFR. Unsafe and unsound auditor limited liability provisions include the practices of (1) indemnifying the independent auditor against claims made by third parties, including punitive damages; (2) holding harmless or releasing auditors from liability for claims or potential claims that might be asserted by the client's financial institution; or (3) limiting remedies available to the client's financial institution. Table 9.2 provides a summary comparison of provisions of auditor LLA as proposed by the AICPA, the Federal Financial Institution Examination Council (FFIEC), and the Federal Financial Regulatory Agencies (FFRA). In summary, the advisory requires that financial institutions not enter into any agreement that limits external auditor liability in an integrated audit and document their business rationale for agreeing to any other provisions that limit their legal rights to sue external auditors. Financial institutions should take appropriate supervisory action if unsafe and unsound limitation of liability provisions are included in external audit engagement letters on or after February 3, 2006.

Any auditor limited liability arrangements may create incentives and opportunities for auditors to engage in conflict of interest situations that may adversely affect audit reliability, effectiveness, and quality, as well as auditor judgment, professional skepticism, and accountability. Furthermore, limited liability provisions may impair auditor independence as set forth in independence rules of the SEC, PCAOB, and AICPA. The potential impairment of auditor independence, in fact or even in appearance, will adversely affect investor

Table 9.2   Auditor Limited Liability Arrangements

Type of clause*	AICPA proposed interpretation*	FFIEC proposed advisory*	2006 interagency advisory**
Auditor indemnified against claims based on auditor's negligence	Impairs independence	Unsafe and unsound practice	Unsafe and unsound practice
Auditor indemnified against claims based on knowing misrepresentation by audit client's management	Does not impair independence	Unsafe and unsound practice	Unsafe and unsound practice
Auditor indemnified against claims based on audit client's negligence	Impairs independence	Unsafe and unsound practice	Unsafe and unsound practice
Auditor's liability limited to the amount of fees paid	May impair independence	Unsafe and unsound practice	Unsafe and unsound practice
Limitation of period during which audit client could otherwise file claim	Impairs independence	Unsafe and unsound practice	Unsafe and unsound practice
Limitation on audit client's right to assign or transfer claim	Impairs independence	Unsafe and unsound practice	Unsafe and unsound practice
Exclusion of punitive damages	Does not impair independence	Unsafe and unsound practice	Does not impair independence as long as fully disclosed
Agreement to use ADR	Impairs independence only if it also limits the auditor's liability for actual damages or incorporates a provision that would impair independence	Presents safety and soundness concerns if it incorporates additional limitations of liability or if ADR rules may limit auditor liability	Does not present a threat to safety and soundness given that such arrangements do not constitute auditor limitation of liability provisions.
Unsuccessful party to pay adversary's legal fees	Does not impair independence	Silent	Silent
Auditor's liability limited to the amount of losses occurring during periods audited	May impair independence	Unsafe and unsound practice	Unsafe and unsound practice

Sources: *Public Company Accounting Oversight Board (PCAOB). 2006, February 9. Briefing materials provided to the Standing Advisory Group. Available at: www.pcaobus.org/Standards/Standing_Advisory_Group/Meetings/2006/02-09/Indemnification.pdf.

**Department of Treasury. 2006, February 1. Interagency Advisory on the Unsafe and Unsound Use of Limitation of Liability Provisions in External Audit Engagement Letters. No. 2006–04. Available at: www.federalreserve.gov/newsevents/press/bcreg/bcreg20060203a1.pdf.

confidence and public trust in audits and raise safety and soundness concerns regarding auditor objectivity, impartiality, and performance. On the other hand, the absence of such arrangements may increase the costs of integrated audits and restrict the ability of the audit parties to allocate the audit risk. However, the advisory did not consider the provision of waiving the right of financial institutions to seek punitive damages from their external auditors to be an unsafe and unsound practice provided that such a waiver audit's nature is properly disclosed in annual proxy statements or public reports. In addition, the advisory does not consider alternative dispute resolution (ADR) or waiver of jury trial provisions as a threat to safety and soundness, given that such arrangements do not constitute auditor limitation of liability provisions and, as such, do not encourage or discourage the use of ADR in audit engagement letters.

Public accounting firms, particularly the Big Four, argue that these agreements are a standard part of their contracts with their clients that have been in practice for a long time and thus do not impair their independence. In particular, ADR is a widely accepted process by other professionals in resolving disputes. The six largest global public accounting firms, in November 2006, issued a report titled Global Capital Markets and the Global Economy.[32] The report calls for (1) relaxed liability standards for public accounting firms; (2) efforts to standardize accounting and auditing standards worldwide; (3) creation of a new business reporting model that more rapidly provides more relevant and reliable financial and nonfinancial information; (4) establishment of forensic audits in addition to financial audits to thoroughly investigate the occurrences of financial statement fraud and ways to prevent, deter, detect, and correct such fraud; and (5) development of an effective recruiting process to attract outstanding individuals and train them for the new audit environment in multiple disciplines (e.g., accounting, tax, finance, IT) to ensure delivery of consistent, high-quality audit services.

The SEC may support the idea of shielding public accounting firms from liability if they fail to detect fraud on the grounds that the loss of another Big Four accounting firm would be devastating to the U.S. capital market competitiveness and investor protection.[33] Obviously, auditor liability is an important risk management issue for auditing firms because many of their audit failures concerning high-profile scandalized companies have been settled recently. In many of these cases, auditors discovered misstatements due to error or fraud, but failed to report them to investors. Federal security lawsuits brought against public accounting firms in the post-SOX era have substantially decreased; five new lawsuits were filed in 2005 and only one in 2006. Thus, the large liabilities that public accounting firms are currently facing, which are proportionately the smaller of losses incurred by investors, pertain to the pre-SOX period and are due in large part to audits conducted during the market bubble and scandal period. In the pre-SOX period, public accounting firms operated under an ineffective self-regulatory oversight function, and unfortunately in the post-SOX period, these firms are permitted to operate without many of the governance measures and financial reporting requirements mandated of public companies, such as an independent board of directors or trustees and periodic filing of financial statements. Such requirements would increase the oversight and transparency of public accounting firms and allow markets to assess their liability exposures.

The Big Four and other public accounting firms, while enjoying a substantial increase in their revenue in the post-SOX period, seek a liability cap or protection from lawsuits that investors filed against them for flawed audits. Two influential groups, the committee studying the competitiveness of U.S. financial markets and the U.S. Chamber of Commerce, are considering recommending that the government enact the new protections for auditors concerning their liability limitations.[34] It is difficult to assess the risk public accounting firms are facing resulting from the threat of lawsuits and other liabilities and whether their revenues are adequate to ensure substantial growth, profitability, and coverage of malpractice suits for several reasons. First, public accounting firms are private partnerships (limited liability partnership or limited liability corporations) that usually do not disclose their financial condition and results of operation, and thus, their financial information is not transparent. Second, public accounting firms typically annually distribute their profit among their partners and ask them to give back money as needed, and thus the actual capital of their firm is unknown. Finally, public accounting firms have grown in size and profitability in the post-SOX era as their audit authority and fees substantially increased, while changes in their level of profitability and even insurance are not known. Thus, it is difficult to assess whether auditor liability is in proportion to their capital, profitability, or participation in any problem or audit fortune.

SUMMARY

External auditors play an important role in corporate governance by lending credibility to published financial reports. The emerging integrated audit of both internal controls and financial statements is expected to improve audit quality, enhance the reliability of financial reports, strengthen the effectiveness of the design and operations of ICFR, restore investor confidence in public financial information, and contribute to the efficiency and integrity of the financial markets. Recent corporate governance reforms (1) reaffirm the importance of the external audit function in the corporate governance context, (2) mandate that external auditors must be independent of their client's management, (3) require external auditors to report directly to the company's audit committee, (4) limit the scope of services (nonaudit services) that external auditors may provide to their audit clients, and (5) require an integrated audit approach by expanding auditors' reporting responsibilities to express opinions on both internal control and financial statements. Regulation of the auditing profession by the PCAOB is expected to improve audit quality, efficiency, and effectiveness. Unresolved challenges facing the auditing profession are its ability to attract ethical and competent individuals to the profession, concentration and competition in the auditing profession, auditor changes, auditor independence, and auditor liability caps. Any indemnification, limitation of liability, or ADR clause in audit engagement letters, while reducing audit costs, may impair auditor independence and reduce audit quality and objectivity.

The key points of this chapter are

- The audit function should be regarded as an external corporate governance mechanism that serves to protect investors from receiving incomplete, inaccurate, or misleading financial information and thus adds value to the effectiveness of corporate governance.

- SOX drastically changed the characteristics of the accounting profession by connecting the audit function to the corporate governance structure by requiring that the audit committee be directly responsible for not only hiring, compensating, and firing external auditors, but also overseeing their work, monitoring their independence, and avoiding potential conflicts of interest.

- In the auditing profession, the so-called expectation gap is referred to as the difference between (1) what the investing public and other users of audited financial statements believe the responsibilities of auditors are, and (2) what auditors are willing to assume as responsibilities according to their professional standards.

- New PCAOB AS No. 5 superseded AS No. 2 and requires the independent audit to opine only on the effectiveness of ICFR, not the management processes and assessments concerning ICFR.

- Sections 201 and 202 of SOX require that all audit and permissible nonaudit services to be performed by the company's independent auditor be approved by the audit committee.

- Auditor independence is the backbone of the auditing profession, affecting the auditor's planning, evidence-gathering procedures, findings, judgment, and credibility, and public trust in the auditor's opinion.

- Auditor independence is derived and guided by the three principles of (1) independent auditors may not audit their own work, (2) independent auditors may not function in the role of their client's management, and (3) independent auditors may not serve in an advocacy role for their audit clients.

- Tests of controls must be broadened to include understanding of ICFR, and provide reasonable assurance about the effectiveness of both the design and operation of internal controls.

- Any contractual provisions that limit the external auditor's liability or require waiving the right to a jury trial may have detrimental effects on auditor impartiality, objectivity, and quality.

KEY TERMS

The Accountancy Investigation & Discipline Board (AIDB)
audit quality
audit risk
audit strategy
auditor independence
control risk

detection risk
expectation gap
inherent risk
integrated audit approach
Internal Revenue Service (IRS)
International Standards on Auditing (ISAs)

PCAOB-US
Professional Ethics Executive Committee (PEEC)
Standing Advisory Group (SAG)
Statements on Auditing Standards

REVIEW QUESTIONS

1. How can an effective audit function be achieved?

2. Explain the term "expectation gap" in auditing.

3. Explain the initiatives taken to improve audit quality as well as the transparency of the audit process and report.

4. What are the structural factors of accounting that provide opportunities for bias to influence judgment?

5. What is the underlying basis of audit firm rotation?

6. Explain the "pass/fail" approach used in current audit reports.

7. What are the three categories in which internal control deficiencies are classified according to AS No. 2?

8. Explain the different types of opinions on internal control over financial reporting.

9. What are the four tests used to classify tax planning as aggressive?

10. Explain several of the steps followed by the PCAOB for its inspection process.

11. Explain the importance of the inspection report.

12. How are PCAOB enforcement investigations coordinated with those of the SEC?

13. When does the audit committee monitor auditor independence and why?

14. How can the audit committee ensure proper disclosures of auditor independence?

15. Explain the term auditor independence and the principles on which it is based.

16. Explain the dual testing of controls and substantive tests.

17. What are the four aspects of the financial reporting process that are targeted by SOX as needing improvement?

18. What are the six steps for the effective assessment of company-level controls?

19. Explain AS No. 3, Audit Documentation.

20. What is the PCAOB proposed standard on auditor independence, and what circumstances consider auditor independence impairment?

DISCUSSION QUESTIONS

1. "The public trust in auditors' judgments and reputation is vital in regarding the audit function as value-added services that lend credibility to published financial reports." Do you agree or disagree with the given statement? Explain your answer.

2. Do you believe that auditors' responsibilities should be extended beyond opining on fair presentation of financial statements in conformity with GAAP to assessing the quality of financial information?

3. Confidence and public trust in auditors have been reduced due to the concern that auditors serve the interests of management who write their checks rather than the shareholders who eventually pay their fees. Do you agree or disagree? Explain your answer.

4. Explain the importance of public accounting firms in a capital market.

5. Do you think it is right to eliminate incentives that cause auditor self-serving biases in order to improve the quality of the audit? Substantiate your answer.

6. Is there any difference between tax planning and abusive tax shelters? Explain your point of view.

7. Explain why auditor independence is the backbone of the auditing profession.

8. Explain how internal auditors are important in performing the integrated audit.

9. Do you think auditors are solely responsible for any audit failure? What steps would you, as an auditor, take to ensure that you are minimally blamed for a business failure?

10. "Critics argue that any contractual provisions that limit the external auditor's liability or require waiving the right to a jury trial may have detrimental effects on auditor impartiality, objectivity, and quality." Express your views on the given statement.

11. Discuss briefly the steps established by the PCAOB for its inspection process.

12. Explain the importance of auditor independence in the auditing profession and to society and the investing community.

13. How do external auditors lend credibility to public financial information and the effectiveness of the corporate governance structure?

NOTES

1. Flesher, D. L., G. J. Previts, and W. D. Samson. 2005. Auditing in the United States: A Historical Perspective. *Abacus* 41(1): 21–39.

2. International Audit Networks. 2006, November. Global Capital Markets and the Global Economy: A Vision from the CEOs of the International Audit Networks. Available at: www.deloitte.com/dtt/cda/doc/content/dtt_CEOVision110806(2).pdf.

3. Public Company Accounting Oversight Board (PCAOB). 2004. Auditing Standard No. 2: An Audit of Internal Control over Financial Reporting Performed in Conjunction with an Audit of Financial Statements (Paragraph 17). Available at: www.pcaob.org/Rules/Rules_of_the_Board/Auditing_Standard_2.pdf.

4. International Auditing and Assurance Standards Board (IAASB). 2005. Handbook of International Auditing, Assurance, and Ethics Pronouncements. 2005 Edition. Available at: www.riigikontroll.ee/upload/failid/2005_iaasb_handbook.pdf.

5. U.K. House of Lords. 2005, November 1. HL Bill 34: Company Law Reform Bill. The Stationery Office Limited, London. Available at: www.publications.parliament.uk/pa/ld200506/ldbills/034/2006034.pdf.

6. Public Company Accounting Oversight Board (PCAOB). 2007, October 22. Report on the PCAOB's 2004, 2005, and 2006 Inspections of Domestic Triennially Inspected Firms. PCAOB Release No. 2007-010. Available at: www.pcaobus.org/Inspections/Other/2007/10-22_4010_Report.pdf.

7. Public Company Accounting Oversight Board (PCAOB). 2006, May 1. Statement Regarding the Public Company Accounting Oversight Board's Approach to Inspections of Internal Control Audits in the 2006 Inspection Cycle. PCAOB Release No. 104-2006-105. Available at: www.pcaobus.org/Inspections/2006-05-01_Release_104-2006-105.pdf.

8. Public Company Accounting Oversight Board (PCAOB). 2004, May 14. Auditing Standard No. 1: References in Auditors' Reports to the Standards of the Public Company Accounting Oversight Board. Available at: www.pcaob.org/Standards/Standards_and_Related_Rules/Auditing_Standard_No.1.aspx.

9. Public Company Accounting Oversight Board (PCAOB). 2004. Auditing Standard No. 2: An Audit of Internal Control over Financial Reporting Performed in Conjunction with an Audit of Financial Statements (Paragraph 17). Available at: www.pcaob.org/Rules/Rules_of_the_Board/Auditing_Standard_2.pdf.

10. Public Company Accounting Oversight Board (PCAOB). 2007, May 24. Auditing Standard No. 5. An Audit of Internal Control over Financial Reporting That Is Integrated with an Audit of Financial Statements. Available at: www.pcaob.org/Rules/Rules_of_the_Board/Auditing_Standard_5.pdf.

11. Ibid.

12. U.S. Securities and Exchange Commission (SEC). 2003, January 24. Retention of Records Relevant to Audits and Review. Available at: www.sec.gov/rules/final/33-8180.htm.

13. Public Company Accounting Oversight Board (PCAOB). 2005. Auditing Standard No. 3: Audit Documentation. Available at: www.pcaob.org/Standards/Standards_and_Related_Rules/Auditing_Standard_No.3.aspx.

14. Public Company Accounting Oversight Board (PCAOB). 2006, February 6. Auditing Standard No. 4—Reporting on Whether a Previously Reported Material Weakness Continues to Exist. Available at: www.pcaobus.org/Rules/Rules_of_the_Board/Auditing_Standard_4.pdf.

15. Public Company Accounting Oversight Board (PCAOB). 2005. Ethics and Independence Rules Concerning Independence, Tax Services and Contingent Fees. Available at: www.pcaobus.org/Rules/Docket_017/2005-07-26_Release_2005-014.pdf.

16. U.S. Senate Permanent Subcommittee on Investigations, Committee on Homeland Security and Governmental Affairs. 2005, February 8. The Role of Professional Firms in the U.S. Tax Shelter Industry Report. Available at: www.lawprofessorblogs.com/taxprof/linkdocs/FINALTAXSHELTERREPORT.pdf.

17. Gibson Dunn Update. 2005. PCAOB Initiates Enforcement Investigations (June). Available at: www.gibsondunn.com/practices/publications/detail/id/766/?pubItemId=7794.

18. The Corporate Library. 2007, September. Big Four Audit Firms Feel the Effects of Post SOX Inroads as Audit Fees Skyrocket. Available at: findarticles.com/p/articles/mi_pwwi/is_200709/ai_n19525842.

19. Grothe. M., and B. Post. 2007, May 21. Yellow Card Trend Alert. Speak No Evil. Glass Lewis & Co.

20. The Conference Board. 2003, January. The Conference Board Commission on Public Trust and Private Enterprise. Part 3: Auditing and Accounting. Available at: www.conference-board.org/pdf_free/SR-03-04.pdf.

21. U.S. Securities and Exchange Commission (SEC). 2003, January 22. Commission Adopts Rules Strengthening Auditor Independence. Press Release. Available at: www.sec.gov/news/press/2003-9.htm.

22. Sarbanes-Oxley Act of 2002 (SOX), Section 201: Services Outside the Scope of Practice of Auditors. Available at: www.openpages.com/solutions/sarbanes-oxley/sarbanes-oxley-sec201.asp.

23. Ibid.

24. New York Stock Exchange (NYSE). 2004. Final NYSE Corporate Governance Rules. Available at: www.nyse.com/pdfs/finalcorpgovrules.pdf.

25. U.S. Securities and Exchange Commission (SEC). 2003, January 22. Commission Adopts Rules Strengthening Auditor Independence. Press Release. Available at: www.sec.gov/news/press/2003-9.htm.

26. Husich, M. W. 2006, December 11. Speech by SEC Staff: Remarks before the 2006 AICPA National Conference on Current SEC and PCAOB Developments. Available at: www.sec.gov/news/speech/2006/spch121106mwh.htm.

27. U.S. Securities and Exchange Commission (SEC). 2003, January 22. Commission Adopts Rules Strengthening Auditor Independence. Press Release. Available at: www.sec.gov/news/press/2003-9.htm.

28. U.S. General Accounting Office (GAO). 2003, September. Accounting Firm Consolidation: Selected Large Public Company Views on Audit Fees, Quality, Independence, and Choice. Report to the Senate Committee on Banking, Housing, and Urban Affairs and the House Committee on Financial Services. Report No. GAO-03-1158. Available at: www.gao.gov/new.items/d031158.pdf.

29. Glass Lewis & Co. 2006, July 27. Yellow Card Trend Alert: Mum's the Word.

30. U.S. Securities and Exchange Commission (SEC). 2002, September 25. Annual Report Pursuant to Section 13 or 15(d) of the Securities Exchange Act of 1934. Available at: www.sec.gov/Archives/edgar/data/357001/000101968703000058/0001019687-03-000058.txt.

31. U.S. Department of Treasury. 2006, February 3. Federal Financial Regulatory Agencies Issue Interagency Advisory on External Auditor Limitation of Liability Provisions. Press Release. Available at: www.federalreserve.gov/boarddocs/press/bcreg/2006/20060203/attachment.pdf.

32. See note 2 above.

33. Anand, V. 2007, January 11. SEC Accountant Backs Shielding Auditors from Lawsuits. *Bloomberg News*.

34. Reilly. D. 2006. Booming Audit Firms Seek Shield from Suits. *The Wall Street Journal* November 1, p. C1. Available at: online.wsj.com/article/SB116235111161209823.html?mod=todays_us_money_and_investing.

Chapter 10

Stakeholders' Roles and Responsibilities

INTRODUCTION

Shareholders and other stakeholders, including employees, customers, creditors, suppliers, and society, by being attentive and engaged, play an important role in corporate governance. The discussion in this chapter is based on the modern model of corporate governance presented in Chapter 2, which suggests that the primary goal of corporate governance is to provide appropriate mechanisms for ensuring shareholder value creation while protecting the interests of other stakeholders. The monitoring function of corporate governance can be achieved through the direct participation of investors in business and financial affairs of corporations or through intermediaries such as securities analysts, institutional investors, and investment bankers. Institutional investors are regarded as important monitors of public companies, their corporate governance, and their financial disclosures because they own more than half of all U.S. public securities. Large public pension funds (PPFs) are also expected to be actively involved in monitoring public companies because they hold about 10 percent of the total U.S. equity market. This chapter presents the important role that investors and other stakeholders can play in improving corporate governance effectiveness.

Primary Objectives

The primary objectives of this chapter are to

- Discuss shareholder responsibilities in monitoring the effectiveness and validity of corporate governance.
- Provide insight for strengthening shareholder rights.
- Discuss the role institutional investors play in ensuring effective and responsible corporate governance.
- Provide methods employees can use to participate in the monitoring of corporate governance.
- Examine activities by investor activists to strengthen corporate governance reforms.

SHAREHOLDERS

Corporate governance reforms aimed at protecting investors have made the United States: (1) a nation of share owners, with about 57 million households either directly or indirectly owning shares through mutual funds or stocks; and (2) a nation whose capital markets are the deepest, most liquid, and most efficient worldwide. The second wave of financial scandals of stock option backdating practices reported in 2006 proves that even four years after the passage of SOX, investors still need protections and safeguards from corporate malfeasance. Recent corporate governance reforms have raised investor expectations for corporate governance, and any attempt to relax or roll back these reforms would be disappointing to investors and adversely affect their confidence in public financial reports and the capital markets.

The direct ownership of stocks by American households has decreased substantially in the past several decades from 91 percent in 1950 to just 32 percent in 2004, whereas stock ownership for financial institutions has increased substantially from 9 percent in 1950 to more than 68 percent in 2004.[1] Factors contributing to this change are the move toward institutionalization of financial markets through financial institutions, privatization of pension plans, and individual investors' preference toward long-term investments. These changes in the ownership structure from individual investors to institutional investors have several profound effects on corporate governance. The formation of institutional shareholders, including mutual funds and pension funds, has changed the traditional agency concept of the separation of ownership control from decision control. Under the emerging agency-dominated investment society, the majority of individual investors indirectly participate in the capital markets by investing in pension plans and mutual funds, and then financial institutions acquire stocks of public companies.

Corporate ownership and types of owners of public companies have significantly changed during the past several decades. The capital markets are more liquid than before, which makes stock ownership more liquid. Both individual and institutional investors can influence the structure of corporate governance. Regulation of the capital markets and financial reporting is intended to protect the rights and interests of investors. Active investors, particularly institutional investors, can play an important role in the efficiency of the capital markets. Monitoring of managerial decisions by large shareholders is an effective and direct corporate governance mechanism that can reduce agency costs. Small individual investors are not effective in directly monitoring management because (1) the substantial costs of monitoring usually outweigh the small fraction of benefits (the free-rider problem), and (2) the ultimate decision of small investors to sell their shares will not possibly have any impact on the company's stock prices due to the liquidity and efficiency of the capital markets. For large investors, however, who own a substantial portion of the company's outstanding shares, the free-rider problem is mitigated, and their decision to sell their shares can have a substantial impact on the value of the company's shares, which may force its management to change course. Nevertheless, monitoring by large investors is not without its costs. Large investors' incentives and interests may be different from small investors, and they may face the same free-rider problem as small shareholders.

The division of internal and external equity securities can influence the shape of the corporate governance structure and the extent of monitoring control within the company. Management can exert more control over the company's affairs when ownership is concentrated in the hands of directors and officers, and thus create fewer opportunities for outsiders (shareholders) to exert control. The absence of adequate monitoring by outsiders can result in an entrenchment effect, which is detrimental to the company because managerial actions are not properly monitored by outsiders. Significant ownership by insiders, however, may provide more incentive for management attempts to increase its own wealth through maximizing the company value and thus decreasing agency costs. Blockholdings by outsiders (typically, the ownership of more than 5 percent of the company's outstanding shares) can shape the corporate governance structure by determining the level of monitoring exerted by outsiders (e.g., the opportunity to nominate directors). The level of blockholdings by outsiders, particularly institutional investors, provides them with both incentives and opportunities to effectively monitor management actions.

Outside shareholders own the majority of corporations' outstanding shares. Typically, individual shareholders own very small fractions of the corporation's share, which may not give shareholders much incentive or opportunity to participate actively in monitoring managerial actions and decisions. However, shareholders with significant ownership positions have more incentives and opportunities to engage in the monitoring function. Shareowners should be attentive through their participation in the nomination and election process and approval of major business decisions. Shareholders of public companies with dispersed ownership have little, if any, incentives and opportunities to monitor their company's business affairs and managerial activities. The prevailing plurality voting system also makes it difficult for shareholders to monitor their companies. State statutes have traditionally limited shareholder monitoring other than through electing directors and voting on major corporate issues (e.g., mergers and acquisitions). Federal statutes have improved shareholder monitoring through the proxy rules, which allow shareholders to include their proposals in the company's proxy materials.

Investors should also share some of the blame for reported financial scandals for their lack of monitoring of their companies' governance. The publicized financial scandals of the early 2000s originated from the use of aggressive accounting and earnings management practices of the late 1990s. Financial irregularities and earnings management practices of many companies such as Waste Management, Sunbeam, Cendant, Lucent, Xerox, and McKesson definitely sent strong signals of forthcoming financial scandals. Nonetheless, investors either did not want to ask tough questions about their governance or did not care as long as the stock prices were going up. Earnings management practices of prominent companies such as Tyco, General Electric, and Cisco were reported in the press, but investors did not raise many concerns about the irregularities of these companies that were making profit for them. The economic downturn; stock market plunges of 2000 and 2001; failures of Enron, WorldCom, Adelphia, Global Crossing, and others; and ineffectiveness of their corporate governance made investors angry when the roots of these problems traced back to the capital market inefficiency of the 1990s. The two biggest corporate bankruptcies in U.S. history, Enron and WorldCom, and the failures of other high-profile companies primarily caused by fraud, which cost investors and pensioners more than $500 billion, made investors take notice and demand corporate accountability.

Shareholder Monitoring

Shareholders of public companies with dispersed ownership have few, if any, incentives or opportunities to monitor their company's business affairs and managerial activities. The prevailing plurality voting system also makes it difficult for shareholders to monitor their companies. State statutes have traditionally limited shareholder monitoring other than through electing directors and voting on major corporate issues (e.g., mergers and acquisitions). Federal statutes have improved shareholder monitoring through the proxy rules, which allow shareholders to include their proposals in the company's proxy materials. The effectiveness of the monitoring and control function by investors is determined based on the interrelation factors of (1) property rights established by law or contractual agreement that define the relations between a company's investors and its management, as well as the existence of such relations between different types of investors; (2) financial systems facilitating the supply of finances between households, financial intermediaries, and corporations; and (3) networks of intercorporate competition and cooperation establishing relations between corporations in the marketplace.

1. **Property rights.** Investors' influence, monitoring, and control are significantly affected by the rights set forth by corporate law, articles of incorporation, and contractual agreements. Property rights establish the legal relations between a company's investors and management as well as the relations among different types of investors (e.g., equity owners, debt holders). Effective property rights create a well-balanced and proper division of powers between investors and management in the sense that investors are provided with adequate control while management autonomy is preserved. Property rights, particularly corporate law, specifically define how shareholder rights translate into voting rights in corporations, including voting rights of shares, rules on proxy votes, voting thresholds for particular decisions, and investor meeting quorums. Corporate laws, including state and federal statutes, also establish the fiduciary duty, structure, role, and composition of the company's board of directors.

2. **Financial system.** The financial system provides a means of financing of corporate ownership that fundamentally constitutes the supply side of capital markets. The supply side of financial markets is significantly influenced by regulatory measures, pension plans, and labor rules.[2] Financial systems provide two alternative modes of financial mediation between households (investors) and corporations.[3] The first mode is bank-based finance, where banks take deposits from households and channel

this savings into loans made to companies. The second mode is market-based finance in which households, directly or indirectly through retirement plans, invest in equity or debt securities issued by corporations. Household savings level, time horizons (short term, long term), and types (regular, retirement) affect the incentives and investment policies of financial institutions, including pension funds and mutual funds, which in return can impact corporate governance by providing different types of financing requiring different reforms of financial and corporate governance systems.

3. **Intercorporate networks.** Investor influence in corporate governance is affected by the patterns of intercorporate networks.[4] Intercorporate networks determine (a) the relation between the company and other corporations or organizations; (b) the structure of power and opportunity; and (c) access to critical resources, information, and strategic decisions. These relations, by creating a coalition of power and opportunities, can influence corporate governance and the ways these intercorporate networks are managed. The nature and extent of corporate control within networks is affected by state regulation of market competition and antitrust law. For example, market competition regulations discourage capital ties between competing corporations, which may force them to merge. These mergers may reduce the concentration of ownership within large corporations and strategic interests within corporate governance.

Strengthening Shareholders' Rights

Shareholders have been inattentive and have not effectively participated in corporate governance by letting their preferences or voice be heard by the company's board. The lack of transparency, accountability, and proper communication between shareholders and the board of directors is perhaps the most detrimental factor to the effectiveness of corporate governance. Inattentive shareholders allow the CEO to have significant influence on the election of directors, their compensation, and their role on the board. When the CEO is given such an opportunity to shape the board structure, the likelihood of directors challenging the CEO's preferences or effectively overseeing the managerial function can be substantially reduced. This perceived compromised boardroom culture can adversely impact corporate governance.

Access to Information

State and federal laws are aimed at protecting shareholder rights by allowing shareholders to (1) inspect and copy the company's stock ledger, its list of shareholders, and certain books and records; (2) approve certain business transactions (e.g., mergers and acquisitions); (3) receive proxy materials; and (4) obtain significant disclosures for related party transactions. Shareholders hold the board of directors accountable for business strategies, performance, and investment decisions. In the era of IT and the Internet, shareholders should be provided with timely electronic access to all relevant information in advance of shareholders' annual meetings. Shareholders should be able to communicate regularly with corporate directors. Companies are required to provide the following disclosures with regard to their processes for security holder communications with board members (1) if there is a process by which shareholders can send communications to board members, and if not why; (2) if there is a process, a description of that process and any filters used; and (3) the company's policy on board members attending annual meetings.

Shareholder Democracy

The relationship between the board of directors and shareholders has received a considerable amount of attention in the post-Enron era. Accountability and transparency between the board and shareholders have not been effective in the sense that the board was not informed of what shareholders were expecting of it, and shareholders were not aware of the board's activities or its effectiveness. Shareholders have voting rights to elect directors as their agents; however, individual directors have no direct responsibility or accountability to shareholders. Traditionally, public companies have used a plurality vote system to elect corporate directors. Under a plurality vote system, directors can be elected by the vote of a single share unless they are opposed by a dissident director. Conversely, a majority vote system empowers shareholders to elect the most qualified outside directors. The nominating committee can play an important role in promoting majority voting and developing an efficient mechanism for shareholders to nominate or endorse director candidates.

Shareholder Nomination

The process of nominating and electing directors should be fair, candid, and transparent to ensure the right of every shareowner to meaningfully participate in corporate governance. Shareowners are empowered under state corporate statutes to elect directors to oversee management, but in reality, they have no real voice in the nomination and election process. The real election appears to be cast in the boardroom due to the fact that even if the majority of shareholders oppose a corporate-sponsored nominee, that person will still be elected as a director. Thus, the extent of shareholders' participation in the election of directors is limited to the rubber-stamp process of affirmation. The requirement for the establishment of a nominating committee composed solely of independent directors has provided some structure to the nomination and election process, even though in many cases independent directors still serve at the will of the CEOs and other executive directors.

Directors should be elected annually by a majority of the votes cast when state law, the company's charter, and bylaws permit majority voting. Alternatively, when state law requires plurality voting for director election, the board can adopt policies requiring that directors tender their resignation if the number of votes withheld from the director exceeds the number of votes for the director. If such a director decides not to tender resignation, he or she should not be renominated after the expiration of his or her current term. The board should consider shareholder proposals that receive a majority of votes cast for and against. The nominating committee should establish procedures to (1) receive shareholders' nominations for board candidates and proposals for significant strategic decisions, (2) consider nominees and proposals received from small individual investors, and (3) communicate with shareowners.

The existing SEC rules allow companies to reject any proposal pertaining to director election. The U.S. Second Circuit Court of Appeals, on September 5, 2006, issued a ruling that enabled shareholders in its jurisdiction (New York, Connecticut, Vermont) to nominate corporate directors.[5] The SEC has considered amending its rule governing shareholder nomination of directors in light of this recent court ruling. Public companies usually send proxy ballots to shareholders, including the names of directors up for election. A director candidate can be nominated by a board committee and placed on the ballot. Shareholders, of course, can nominate their own candidate through separate ballots, which are often a complicated and costly process. The court ruled that under the existing SEC rules, shareholders should have access to the proxy for purposes of nominating their choice of candidate for director.

The SEC issued a proposal, in October 2003, to give shareholders access to the proxy, but no action has been taken by the SEC to finalize the proposal. Pursuant to the court decision, the SEC announced that it will recommend an amendment to Rule 14a-8 under the Securities Exchange Act of 1934 pertaining to director nominations by shareholders. The decision by the Second Circuit Court of Appeals is important because (1) it states that shareholders should be able to access the proxy for the purpose of nominating their choice of candidate for director, which disagrees with the SEC staff's long-standing interpretation of the proxy rules; (2) a large number of public companies are subject to the jurisdiction of the Second Circuit Court of Appeals; and (3) the SEC is expected to revise its proxy rules to ensure consistent rational application to shareholder proposals. It is highly possible that the SEC will adopt the rule to allow companies to keep shareholders' director nominees off corporate ballots. The shareholders' basic ownership rights of having unrestricted access to company proxies for board elections are not aligned with other developed countries, which undermines the effectiveness of corporate governance in U.S. and shareholder democracy.

Shareholder resolutions in 2007 contain several important proposals, including (1) an advisory vote on executive compensation packages, (2) say-on-pay resolutions that pressure companies to link their compensation policies to executive performance, (3) proposals to allow shareholders to run opposing board candidates, (4) majority votes for nominations and elections of directors, and (5) monitoring of the company's executive pay and related compensation expenses. Indeed, shareholder proposals during the 2007 proxy season received majority votes in favor of "say on pay," requiring shareholder advisory votes on executive compensation at several high-profile companies (e.g., Verizon Communications, Inc.; Blockbuster, Inc.).

Shareholder Proxy Process

In July 2007, the SEC approved two proposals addressing the shareholder proxy process. The first proposed rule would require public companies to allow shareholder access to the company's proxy statements.[6] The second proposed rule would facilitate electronic shareholder forums. Proxy access proposals are shareholder proposals that enable shareholders to nominate director candidates who would be named in the company's proxy statement. The SEC has traditionally allowed companies to exclude such shareholder proposals from their proxy statements under its Rule 14a-8(i)(8) to avoid contested elections. The U.S. Court of Appeals for the Second Circuit in *AFSCME v. AIG,* in September 2006, questioned the SEC staff's interpretation of Rule 14a-8(i)(8) that suggests that all proxy access shareholder proposals are excludable from the company's proxy materials. On July 25, 2007, the SEC reaffirmed its historical interpretation of Rule 14a-8 and approved a proposed rule that would allow the inclusion of certain proxy access shareholder proposals and would require additional disclosures by companies and proponents when such proposals are included. The proposed rule indicates that a proxy access shareholder proposal is not excludable under

Rule 14a-8(i)(8) if (1) the shareholder proposal seeks to amend the company's bylaws, (2) the shareholder proposal is binding, (3) the shareholder(s) submitting the proposal held at least 5 percent of the company's outstanding shares for at least one year, and (4) the shareholder(s) submitting the proposal are eligible to and have filed a Schedule 13G with respect to the company. Unlike a proxy access rule proposed by the SEC in 2003 that was never adopted, the new proposed rule does not dictate the terms of proxy access shareholder proposals that should comply with state law and with the company's charter and bylaws.

The new SEC proposed rule enables companies and shareholders to communicate in electronic shareholder forums by eliminating possible impediments to such forums under the SEC's proxy rules. The proposed rule would provide that (1) public companies and others who set up electronic shareholder forums are not liable under the federal proxy rules for false and misleading statements electronically posted by others on such forums, and (2) individuals who post communications on electronic shareholder forums at least 60 days in advance of a shareholder meeting who are not seeking a solicitation will not be considered to be engaged in a solicitation for purposes of the proxy rules. This proposal permits companies and others to develop their own format, content, and methods of electronic shareholder forums.

Security Class Actions

Private lawsuits are vital mechanisms for enforcing securities laws, compensating defrauded investors, and improving corporate governance to be used effectively by institutional investors, particularly public pension funds. The Private Securities Litigation Reform Act (PSRLA) of 1995 was passed to bring more focus to private lawsuits by (1) providing more client control of shareholder litigation, (2) ensuring lawsuits were meritorious and well prosecuted, and (3) encouraging institutional investors to take charge of private lawsuits regarding securities litigation. Indeed, shareholder recoveries have significantly increased and attorneys' fees have substantially decreased since institutional investors have taken the lead on securities litigation in the post-PSRLA period. Institutional investors often participate as lead plaintiffs in class action securities lawsuits under the PSRLA, and as part of negotiated settlements, try to influence corporate governance. For example, the California State Teacher's Retirement System (CalSTRS) brought a class action suit against Homestore, an Internet real estate company, and then settled the suit by (1) obtaining $64 million in cash and stock for shareholders; (2) demanding that the company agree to appoint a shareholder-nominated director to the board; and (3) asking the company to ban the use of stock options in compensating directors, gradually eliminate staggered terms for directors, and increase the number of independent directors and board committees.[7]

INSTITUTIONAL INVESTORS

Institutional investors consisting of insurance companies, pension funds, investment trusts, mutual funds, and investment management groups often hold substantial outstanding shares of public companies. Institutional investments in the United States have grown significantly in the past five decades and will continue to grow as more employees participate in pension funds. Table 10.1 provides types and definitions of investment funds. Institutional investors

Table 10.1 Investment Funds and Their Definitions

Term	Definition
Hedge fund	High-risk, aggressively managed fund that uses short selling, swaps, derivatives, and arbitrage techniques to get a maximum rate of return
Mutual fund	Collective investment plan managed by an investment firm that allows its participants to invest in a portfolio that is diversified into different bonds, stocks, and other securities
Pension fund	Fund established by an organization for the investment of member pension contributions, and the payment of pension benefits to those members who have retired

Source: Global Investor. 2007. Glossary. Available at: www.finance-glossary.com.

may not fully exercise their corporate governance oversight function and monitoring controls for several reasons. First, pension fund managers are not typically the ultimate beneficiaries of the wealth generated by corporations, and they may not have strong incentives to engage in monitoring of the company's affairs. Second, fund managers may be reluctant to incur monitoring costs, particularly when other investors will benefit from such monitoring (the free-rider problem). Finally, institutional investors are often not long-term investors and may not be motivated to engage in long-term costly monitoring, instead choosing to divest poorly performing stocks. Nevertheless, the equity holdings of institutional investors are becoming more indexed and diversified, diminishing opportunities for an easy exit to divest poorly performing stocks. This indexing and diversification may result in alignment of the fund with public interest and market performance as opposed to alignment with a specific company. In this capacity, institutional investors play an important role in improving investor confidence and public trust in corporate governance through their presence and active participation in monitoring public companies' corporate governance structure.

Corporate governance structure is affected by large blockholders because they often have representation on the company's board of directors. Blockholders may have more incentives than small shareholders to monitor management actions, primarily because of (1) the size of their holdings, (2) more opportunity for insider trading, and (3) the greater possibility of presenting a credible takeover threat. The involvement of large shareholders has the potential to limit agency problems associated with the separation of ownership and control in public companies. Institutional investors can play an important role of reducing information asymmetry between management and shareholders by obtaining private information from management and conveying that to shareholders and, thus, the capital markets. The integrity and credibility of such information should be verified in order to be relevant and useful to investors.

Institutional Investors' Monitoring

The company's board of directors should become familiar with each of their key institutional investors. Institutional shareholders normally monitor their holdings by using a screening system based on financial performance (e.g., benchmarks), identifying problem areas and concerns, and determining causes and effects of the problems. Although they often do not micromanage their investments, they monitor their holdings by ensuring that the investee company is well managed and has a clear and attainable strategy. Institutional investors do not regularly intervene in the investee company except in rare circumstances. Intervention may occur in situations where there are concerns about strategy, operational performance, mergers and acquisitions strategy, inadequate oversight function by independent directors, reported material weaknesses in internal controls, inadequate succession planning, noncompliance with corporate governance reforms, inappropriate executive compensation plans, lack of commitment to SEE issues, material financial restatements, and corporate malfeasance and fraud.[8] Institutional investors may intervene by (1) having additional meetings with management; (2) expressing concerns through the company's advisors; (3) meeting with directors, particularly independent directors, lead directors, or the chairperson of the board; (4) collaborating their intervening activities with other institutions; (5) making a public statement in advance of annual shareholder meetings; (6) submitting resolutions at shareholders' meetings; (7) requisitioning an additional general meeting, possibly to change the company's board; and (8) meeting with individual board committees (e.g., audit, compensation, nominating/governance).

The Commission of the European Communities requires institutional investors to (1) disclose their investment policy and their policy relevant to the exercise of voting rights in companies in which they invest, and (2) disclose to their beneficial holders at their request how those rights have been used in a particular case.[9] These requirements are designed to improve both the internal governance of institutional investors and their participation in the business and affairs of the companies in which they invest. The commission believes that institutional investors play an important role in the governance of public companies and fostering this role will require amendments to a series of European legal texts pertaining to insurance companies, pension funds, and mutual and other investment funds. Nonetheless, the commission does not believe that a requirement for institutional investors to systematically exercise their voting rights is desirable, and thus, institutional investors may vote in favor of any proposed resolution to fulfill the requirement.

Institutional shareholders play an important role in corporate governance by (1) exercising their right to elect directors, (2) raising their concerns about the company's governance by either selling their shares or voicing their dissatisfaction, (3) improving the efficiency of the capital markets by transmitting private information they obtain from management to the financial markets, and (4) reducing agency problems by possessing resources and expertise to monitor the managerial and oversight functions as well as reduce information asymmetry between management and investors. The ever-increasing presence of institutional investors in the capital markets empowers them to influence corporate governance. For example, institutional investors claim that they have played an important role in increasing board independence and through close monitoring encouraged management to focus more on the company's sustainable performance rather than short-term profit maximization. Institutional investors are not only seeking a more active role in the nomination process but are also trying to influence the process. Opponents to institutional investor activism argue that (1) institutional shareholders' primary role is to manage pension functions on behalf of their beneficiaries and their monitoring activities detract them from their main responsibilities; and (2) to credibly perform the monitoring function, institutional investors should maintain the investment for a sufficiently long period of time and hold ample shares to reduce the free-rider problem.[10]

Governance of Institutional Investors

America's one hundred largest money managers now hold about 58 percent of stocks of public companies in the United States. It is expected that these giant financial institutions will get actively involved in monitoring public companies' governance, business, and affairs. These financial institutions, on the one hand, are agents of individual shareholders with the fiduciary duty of managing these funds for the best interest of their individual investors (principals). Financial institutions, on the other hand, own and manage public companies' stocks, which make them responsible for monitoring public companies' governance. This dual responsibility of institutional investors as agents of individual investors and principals of public companies may create conflicts of interest. This real or potential conflict of interest has, in many cases, caused institutional investors to refrain from active monitoring of corporate affairs and governance. These conflicts of interest will continue to exist as long as the ownership society is diminishing and the agency (intermediate) society is effectively monitoring public companies' governance, affairs, and business.

Lack of effective monitoring by institutional investors can be attributed to and explained by several reasons. First, institutional investors, with the exception of a few (e.g., state and local pension funds, unions, TIAA-CREF), have their own interests to serve aside from the interests of their investor-principals. For example, corporate pension plans are often controlled by the company's executives whose compensation is linked to the reported earnings, and mutual fund managers' compensation is often not based on the return-on-funds assets. Second, financial institutions have a tendency and motivation to focus on short-term speculation of stock price changes rather than long-term investing based on sustainable intrinsic corporate value. Third, managers of mutual funds and pension plans are less likely to support a proxy proposal that is opposed by the management of a corporate client. Conceptually, institutional investors represent small shareholders as pensioners or beneficiaries. To ensure that institutional investors protect the interests of their beneficiaries or trustees, they should disclose their corporate governance and voting policies as well as potential conflicts of interest and how they manage them.

MUTUAL FUNDS

According to the U.S. Census Bureau, there are more than 2,656 public pension funds that hold more than 20 percent of publicly traded U.S. equity and, as such, are considered major shareowners of U.S. capital markets. Many public pension funds, including CalPERS and the SBA of Florida have received considerable attention in the post-SOX era for their participation in corporate governance. These funds have improved the investor monitoring function through shareholder proposals, support of regulations to enhance shareholder democracy, and participation in securities fraud actions. Smaller pension funds are not expected to be actively involved in corporate governance primarily because of substantial monitoring costs.

Congress passed the Investment Company Act in 1940 to set requirements for prohibiting investment companies (mutual funds) from engaging in certain transactions that may create conflicts of interest.[11] The Investment Company Act also requires that a fund's board of directors provide oversight over management to align management interests with those of shareholders while granting broad authority to the SEC to provide exemptions to this act (conditionally or unconditionally) when the exemptions are in the public interest and provide protections for investors. More than 95 million Americans invest and entrust their savings in mutual funds, an industry with more than $7 trillion in assets. The rash of mutual fund scandals in 2003 indicates significant ineffectiveness in fund governance structures that eroded investor confidence in the mutual fund industry. In response to those scandals, the SEC has brought enforcement actions against troubled mutual funds and obtained more than $2.2 billion in disgorgements and civil penalties, which is being used to compensate injured investors.[12] To improve independent director oversight of mutual funds, the SEC requires mutual funds to have independent chairs.

The SEC has taken several mutual fund initiatives designed to (1) address late trading, market timing, and revenue sharing that create conflicts of interest between management of mutual funds and their shareholders; (2) improve transparency of disclosures to fund investors; and (3) strengthen the oversight function of mutual funds by improving their governance, ethical standards, compliance, and internal controls.

Improving the Oversight Function

In July 2004, the SEC, in a close 3-2 vote, adopted mutual fund governance reforms that require mutual funds to have an independent chairman (nonexecutive director) and 75 percent of board members to be independent. The independent directors must have the authority to hire staff to support their oversight function, engage in an annual self-assessment, and hold separate executive sessions with the presence of fund management. On June 29, 2005, one day before William Donaldson stepped down as the chairman, the SEC preapproved its rule requiring mutual fund boards to have at least 75 percent of their directors be independent, including the chairman of their board. The SEC initially approved this rule in 2004, the U.S. Chamber of Commerce brought a lawsuit against the rule, and the U.S. Court of Appeals in the last week of June 2005 nullified the rule on the grounds that the SEC failed to consider the cost to mutual fund companies in complying with the rule. The four horsemen of mutual fund governance as promoted by the SBA of Florida are (1) no more than one management company on the fund's board, (2) independent chairman of the board, (3) dedicated fund staff, and (4) federal statute of fiduciary duty.[13]

Chief Compliance Officer

The SEC, in December 2003, adopted initiatives that require mutual funds and their advisors to have comprehensive compliance procedures and to appoint a CCO to assist the board in improving the governance structure. The CCO is accountable to the fund's board and can only be terminated by a board decision.

Code of Ethics

The SEC, in July 2004, issued rules that require registered investment advisors to adopt a code of ethics that sets forth the standards of ethical conduct for each employee to reinforce ethical behavior and integrity in the investment management industry. Mutual funds and their advisors should comply with the requirements of code of ethics.

HEDGE FUNDS

Hedge funds are expected to grow significantly as (1) pension plans and other large institutions are expected to invest about $4,300 billion in hedge funds by 2008, (2) large companies such as Weyerhaeuser and Eli Lilly are investing a significant portion (up to 39 percent) of their pension fund's assets in hedge funds, and (3) Congress is considering changing the definition of "plan assets" and relaxing the pension law for hedge funds by raising the limit (up to 50 percent) on how much pension money a hedge fund can have before it is considered a fiduciary under the pension law.[14]

Hedge funds and other private equity investors play an important role in influencing corporate governance issues by promoting investor protection as their primary goal. Investors in general, and hedge and mutual funds in particular, can influence corporate governance by demanding that boards of directors act independently from management, holding boards accountable for their decisions, and holding the compensation committee accountable for approving excessive executive pay. The hedge fund industry accounts for trillions of investment assets. The SEC rule requires that hedge fund advisors managing more than $25 million for more than fifteen clients register with the SEC. Some hedge funds have a suit against the SEC on the grounds that the commission has overstepped its jurisdiction. The SEC has filed numerous enforcement cases against hedge funds in connection with their inappropriate fund valuation schemes, insider trading violations, and failures to supervise the hedge funds. These cases are significantly associated with violations of rules related to market timing and late trading, which have victimized both investors and the capital markets. The SEC has recently aggressively enforced the insider trading laws for insider trading abuses by both individual investors and market professionals (e.g., a UBS research executive, a Morgan Stanley attorney).

INVESTOR ACTIVISTS

The monitoring function led, to a great extent, by large and proactive institutional shareholders has played an important role in improving corporate governance. Investor activists generally claim that recent corporate governance reforms are not adequate, whereas others believe these reforms are unfair to those public companies (e.g., utilities) that are highly regulated and have been in compliance with applicable laws, rules, and regulations. The rash of financial scandals of high-profile companies caused investors to be more active in monitoring companies in which they invested, and they have begun to consider corporate governance effectiveness in their investment decisions. This well-deserved, long-awaited investor focus on corporate governance generated a demand for and interest in the development of ratings metrics or systems that gather, analyze, rank, and compare corporate governance practices of public companies. National and international organizations, including ISS, The Corporate Library, Standard & Poor's, Moody's Investment Service, CoreRatings, and GMI have all developed and published variations of corporate governance ratings that are often used by shareholders in assessing their stock returns and by bondholders in determining the costs of lending.

EMPLOYEE MONITORING

The agency theory aspect of corporate governance focuses primarily on the relation between investors and management with shareholders considered the only bearers of residual risk.

In modern corporations, particularly in the era of technological advances, labor resources are becoming an important part of corporate governance as capital resources. The balance of power and association between property rights (investor protection), managerial control (management prerogative), and employee participation rights (labor management and employee protection) can play an important role in the effectiveness of corporate governance. Employee participation in corporate governance can influence managerial control and authority, and can influence employee cooperation in the implementation of decisions. The shape and extent of employees' participation in corporate governance is a function of the employee level of investment in the company's stock through retirement plans and whether their skills are firm specific. In a situation in which employees invest in skills specific to their company and their retirement funds and pensions are tied to the company's stock, their incentives to participate in corporate governance are greater. Alternatively, when employees' skills are portable across companies and their investments in the company are insignificant, they may prefer strategies of exit over voice in response to dissatisfaction and grievances. Thus, employees' interests in corporate governance are shaped by their economic, investment, and employment ties to the company, as well as their participation in managerial decisions.

Employees' participation rights can be defined by employment contracts, employer action, labor law, ownership, or collective bargaining. First, employee participation may be established by the employment contract in terms of involvement in decision making. Second, participation may be determined through decisions made by the employer. Labor law, or statutory law, may also establish participation rights. Finally, collective bargaining can be an important vehicle for establishing contractual participation rights. Employee participation can also be established by direct ownership as shareholders, or through employee share ownership plans (ESOPs). Employee stock options and other performance-related incentives may shape employee participation. The financial scandals and bankruptcies of Enron and WorldCom, which caused significant loss of jobs and employee pension funds, underscore the importance of employee participation in corporate governance.

Employee Ownership

Employees are one of the important stakeholders of corporations whose productivity and efficiency contribute to the bottom line of increasing firm value. Employees are usually paid fixed salaries or wages regardless of the company's performance (unless there is a threat of bankruptcy or job loss). One way to get employees more engaged in corporate governance is to link their pay to company performance through equity ownership plans such as ESOPs. Theoretically, combining labor capital and equity capital by ultimately moving to employee-owned corporations can substantially reduce agency costs by empowering employees and protecting both labor and equity capital. Nonetheless, employees often (1) do not have the incentive to sustain physical capital, which may cause inefficiency in the use of both human and physical capital; (2) are motivated to maximize net revenues per worker rather than to maximize profit, which results in the inefficient use of resources and production levels; and (3) are risk averse, prefer a fixed wage, and may be unable to diversify their risks efficiently as opposed to investors who are more risk neutral and able to diversify their portfolios. The Enron debacle indicates that employees are motivated to invest in their company, and when given the incentives and opportunity, they invest to their maximum financial capacity without diversifying their investment portfolio.

The possible effects of employee ownership on corporate governance depend on the type and extent of the ownership. First, employee ownership may result in improved performance by employees and thus increase firm value. Second, in some industries (e.g., steel, air travel, trucking) employee ownership facilitated employee or union representation on the board of directors. Nevertheless, employee stock ownership quite often enables employees to have neither board representations, nor voting control of their shares, nor the right to decide whether to tender their shares in the event of a takeover board of directors. Stock held in profit-sharing trusts, ESOPs, and pension funds are controlled by the trustees, which entitle them to mirror voting according to employees' wishes.

Employee ownership has significantly increased. Employees can be turned into shareholders in several ways: (1) buying their company stock as part of a pension fund or 401(k), (2) participating in an ESOP, or (3) obtaining stock through an individual reward package. Employee ownership causes employees to feel some loyalty to the company and may result in a better alignment of their interests with those of shareholders.

Employee Roles in Corporate Governance

Employees contribute to company value creation through the utilization of their human skills. Employees are often motivated to do the minimum to sustain continuation of their employment rather than make improvements in their performance that would result in the maximization of company value. This goal of company value maximization can be achieved when employees own the company's shares. Senior executives and skilled employees should be provided with incentives through compensation plans consisting of restricted stock and stock options. The employees' total compensation should be divided into (1) performance of the assigned job, and (2) performance of firm-specific skills. Performance of the assigned job should be compensated through salary-based pay, whereas performance of firm-specific skills should be compensated through stock ownership to encourage employees to devote these skills to the company.

Employees play important roles in corporate governance in a variety of ways. First, employees, as the most important human capital in the company, work toward the achievement of sustainable and enduring performance. Second, employees are regarded as investors by owning corporate shares through their retirement plan, savings plan, 401(k) plan, or a separate ESOP. Although employees do not have the legal right of participating in the oversight of retirement plans, they rely on plan trustees to exercise oversight functions on their behalf. Thus, employees, through retirement plan administrators, indirectly engage in monitoring their company's corporate governance. Third, recent reforms empower employees to participate in the monitoring function by requiring the company's board or its audit committee to establish whistleblower programs encouraging employees to report corporate misconducts, fraudulent financial activities, or violations of applicable laws, rules, and regulations without the fear of retaliation. An effective whistleblower program should improve corporate governance.

There are several advantages of employee participation in corporate governance. First, through ownership of company shares, employees have more incentives to align their interests with those of shareholders. Second, employee involvement in corporate governance is a learning process for employees to advance their position and improve the company's operational efficiency. Third, employee participation in corporate governance can be regarded as an internal mechanism to monitor managerial performance and prevent management opportunistic conduct. The only concern is whether employee governance and monitoring conflict with shareholder governance and monitoring. Academic research suggests that these two forms of governance are indeed complementary and mutually beneficial in the sense that cooperative monitoring by both employees and shareholders provides more incentives for management to align its interests with those of employees and shareholders.[15]

Employee Class Actions

Financial scandals of the early 2000s resulted in several major bankruptcies of high-profile corporations, including Enron and WorldCom, which caused employees not only to lose their jobs but also their retirement and savings plans. Enron employees subsequently brought a class action lawsuit that covers all 20,000 former Enron employees who were participants in or beneficiaries of Enron Corporate Savings Plan [401(k) plan] from January 20, 1998 through December 2, 2001, and who held investments in Enron stock, as well as participants of the Enron stock ownership plan or cash balance plan. Enron employees sued the board of directors, board committees, executive and nonexecutive directors, and officers of Enron on the grounds that they failed to disclose the company's true financial condition.

In many cases, the settlement of employee class actions suits causes changes in corporate governance mechanisms to protect employee rights. In 2004, Board Analyst Alert tracked the association between corporate governance effectiveness (board effectiveness) and securities claim action suits and found that (1) most securities class actions were triggered by substantial drops in stock prices or one or more significant financial restatements by the defendant firm, (2) strong relationships exist between board effectiveness ratings and the incidence of class action suits, and (3) high-risk companies were about three times more likely to become the subject of a class action filing than low-risk companies.[16]

SUMMARY

In the post-SOX era, institutional investors have continued their monitoring of public companies and attempted to influence governance of companies in which they invested by putting forth many proposals intended to improve corporate governance effectiveness. In summary, an effective monitoring function can be achieved when shareholders are allowed to (1) vote their shares by proxy regardless of whether they attend the meetings in person, (2) cast their votes confidentially, (3) cast the cumulative number of votes allotted to their shares for one or a limited number of board nominees, (4) approve changes in corporate policies and practices that may alter their relationship with the company, (5) nominate directors for election to the board, (6) submit proposals for consideration at the company's annual meetings, and (7) take legal or seek regulatory action to protect and enforce their ownership rights. Shareholders have the ultimate power to exercise control of a company to ensure value creation and enhancement.

The key points of this chapter are

- The monitoring function of corporate governance is the direct responsibility of shareholders and other stakeholders, and can be achieved through direct participation of investors in business and financial affairs of corporations.

- Shareholders play an important role in monitoring public companies to ensure the effectiveness of their corporate governance and strengthen shareholder rights by (1) providing timely access to information, (2) enhancing shareholders' rights, and (3) promoting shareholder democracy.

- Institutional investors can play an important role in reducing information asymmetry between management and shareholders by obtaining private information from management and conveying that to shareholders and, thus, the capital markets.

- Employee participation in corporate governance can influence managerial control and authority, and can influence employee participation in decision making and cooperation in the implementation of decisions.

- Institutional investors influence the governance of public companies in which they invested by putting forth proposals intended to improve corporate governance effectiveness.

KEY TERMS

blockholding	institutional shareholder	security class actions
employee class actions	intercorporate networks	shareholder democracy
free-rider problem	property rights	

REVIEW QUESTIONS

1. What are the interrelation factors on which the effectiveness of the monitoring and control function by investors is based?

2. Explain the two alternative modes of financial mediation between households (investors) and corporations.

3. Discuss the five rules that the Business Roundtable recommends for fair and respectful treatment of shareowners and their views.

4. What are the policies and procedures that should be established by the nominating committee to better enhance the viability of shareholders' nominations?

5. What situations can lead to institutional investor intervention with the invested company?

6. How can institutional investors participate in the corporate governance of the company?

7. Explain the advantages of employee participation in corporate governance.

DISCUSSION QUESTIONS

1. What factors and opportunities have led to the movement of direct individual ownership of stocks to a more institutional ownership structure?

2. Should investors share some of the blame for reported financial scandals for their lack of monitoring of their companies' governance? Why?

3. Traditionally, the accountability and transparency between the board and shareholders have not been effective in the sense that the board was not informed of what shareholders were expecting of it, and shareholders were not aware of the board's activities and its effectiveness. What should be done about this communication gap? Substantiate your answer.

4. Describe the importance of shareholders' proactive participation in the nomination and election of corporate directors.

5. Do you believe that the extent of shareholders' participation in the election of directors is limited to the rubber-stamp process of affirmation? Explain the given statement.

6. Elaborate on the following statement: "In modern corporations, particularly in the era of technological advances, labor resources are becoming an important part of corporate governance as capital resources."

7. Describe shareholder voting rights and effective ways to exercise those rights.

8. Discuss shareholders' participation in monitoring their companies' affairs, decisions, and corporate governance.

9. Describe how shareholder proposals can influence corporate governance.

NOTES

1. Bogle, J. C. 2005, October 3. Individual Stockholder, R.I.P. [Opinion]. *The Wall Street Journal* October 3. Available at: online.wsj.com/article/SB112829417598858002.html.

2. Jackson, G., and S. Vitols. 2001. Between Financial Commitment, Market Liquidity and Corporate Governance: Occupational Pensions in Britain, Germany, Japan and the USA. In *Comparing Welfare Capitalism: Social Policy and Political Economy in Europe, Japan and the USA*, edited by B. Ebbinghaus and P. Manow. Routledge, London.

3. Zysman, J. 1983. *Governments, Markets and Growth: Finance and the Politics of Industrial Change.* Cornell University Press, Ithaca, NY.

4. Windolf, P., and J. Beyer. 1996. Co-operative Capitalism: Corporate Networks in Germany and Britain. *British Journal of Sociology* 47(2): 205-231.

5. Pender, K. 2006. Board Drama in East. *San Francisco Chronicle* September 10, p. F-1. Available at: www.sfgate.com/cgibin/article.cgi?file=Chronicle/archive/2006/09/10/BUGJ9L1IPA1.DTL.

6. U.S. Securities and Exchange Commission (SEC). 2007, July 27. Shareholder Proposals and. Releases 34-56160 and 34-56161. Available at: www.sec.gov/rules/proposed/2007/34-56160.pdf; U.S. Securities and Exchange Commission (SEC). 2007, July 27. Shareholder Proposals Relating to the Election of Directors. Available at: www.sec.gov/rules/proposed/2007/34-56161.pdf.

7. CalSTRs' Ethical Victory. 2003. *Financial Times* August 25.

8. London Stock Exchange. 2004, July. Corporate Governance: A Practical Guide. London Stock Exchange, London. Available at: www.londonstockexchange.com/NR/rdonlyres/C450E4FC-89C2-4042-804A-685855FF217B/0/PracticalGuidetoCorporateGovernance.pdf.

9. Commission of the European Communities. 2003, May 21. Communication from the Commission to the Council and the European Parliament: Modernising Company Law and Enhancing Corporate Governance in the European Union—A Plan to Move Forward. Available at: europa.eu.int/eurlex/lex/LexUriServ/site/en/com/2003/com2003_0284en01.pdf.

10. Gillan, S. L., and Starks, L. T. 2003, August. Corporate Governance, Corporate Ownership, and the Role of Institutional Investors: A Global Perspective. Weinberg Center for Corporate Governance Working Paper No. 2003-01. Available at: ssrn.com/abstract=439500.

11. U.S. Congress. 1940. Investment Company Act of 1940. Available at: www.sec.gov/about/laws/ica40.pdf.

12. U.S. Securities and Exchange Commission (SEC). 2005, April. Exemptive Rule Amendments of 2004: The Independent Chair Condition. A Report in Accordance with the Consolidated Appropriateness Act, 2005. Available at: www.sec.gov/news/studies/indchair.pdf.

13. State Board of Administration (SBA) of Florida. 2006. Corporate Governance: Annual Report 2006. Available at: www.sbafla.com/pdf%5Cinvestment%5CCorpGovReport.pdf.

14. Atlas, R. D., and Walsh, M. W. 2005. Pension Officers Putting Billions Into Hedge Funds. *The New York Times* November 27. Available at: www.nytimes.com/2005/11/27/business/yourmoney/27hedge.html.

15. Boatright, J. R. 2004. Employee Governance and the Ownership of the Firm. *Business Ethics Quarterly* 14(1): 1–21.

16. Marshall, R. 2005, April 12. Research Highlights: Board Effectiveness & Securities Class Action Suits. Available at: www.boardanalyst.com/alerts/alert_classaction_041205.html.

Chapter 11

Roles and Responsibilities of Other Corporate Governance Participants

INTRODUCTION

Roles and responsibilities of corporate officers, directors, and gatekeepers, including independent auditors, are discussed in previous chapters. This chapter presents the advisory function of corporate governance that is typically assumed by professional advisors, including legal counsel, financial analysts, and investment bankers. These corporate governance participants assist companies in evaluating legal and financial consequences of business transactions. Professional advisors participate in corporate governance by providing advisory services to the company's board of directors and management. Management has traditionally engaged professional advisors for the structure, measurement, recognition, and disclosure of business transactions. SOX requires that the audit committee be provided with funding to hire advisors as deemed necessary. This funding should be provided to the entire board of directors.

Primary Objectives

The primary objectives of this chapter are to

- Understand the advisory function of corporate governance normally provided by legal counsel, financial advisors, and investment banks.

- Recognize the traditional role of legal counsel and how it has changed, as well as the lines of communication between legal counsel, the company, and its board of directors.

- Identify the rules and regulations implemented by the SEC for corporate attornies representing public companies, specifically the up-the-ladder approach for reporting violations.

- Understand the roles and responsibilities of financial advisors, specifically securities analysts.

- Recognize the need for independence in research conducted by securities analysts and the inherent bias in any research.

- Comprehend the five standards of best practices governing the relationship between corporations and their analysts.

LEGAL COUNSEL

The legal counsel role in corporate governance has traditionally been to stand outside the corporate structure and provide legal advice to ensure compliance with applicable laws, rules, and regulations and to keep the company's conduct within the boundaries of the law. Thus, a lawyer's role in corporate governance has been as the outside gatekeeper to promote legal corporate behavior and to protect the interest of the company. Although lawyers (in-house or outside legal counsel) are hired to represent their client's (company) interests, they work with and for client's executives and may be subject to pressure to conform their advice and behavior to the interests of executives. To the extent that corporate executives engage in fraudulent activities, the lawyer's role as gatekeeper can be weakened. SOX addresses lawyers' potential conflicts of interest and SEC-issued rules requiring legal counsel practicing before the commission or representing public companies to report violations of securities laws. Thus, SOX makes legal counsel an integral component of the internal processes of the corporate governance structure to monitor corporate misconduct.

The issue of attorney–client privilege as it applies to corporate lawyers representing their client companies before the SEC has been controversial and unresolved in the post-SOX period. Corporate attorneys have been pressured to waive the privilege in connection with government (SEC) investigations. It should be noted that attorneys are generally viewed as advocates for those they represent as opposed to being representatives of investors. The roles of the other two gatekeepers (the board of directors and the independent auditor) are legally and conceptually regarded as being representatives of investors with the keen purpose of protecting investor interests. Legal counsel plays an important role in presenting and analyzing relevant information, as well as providing valuable advice to the company's board of directors, committees, officers, and employees in effectively discharging their assigned responsibilities. Corporate legal counsel should coordinate their activities and serve as (1) counselors to the board, its committees, and directors in carrying out their oversight responsibilities and fiduciary duty; (2) advisors to management in participating in the negotiation, development, process, documentation, and restoration of material business transactions; (3) gatekeepers to ensure compliance with all applicable regulations; and (4) enforcement agents to evaluate risks associated with legal issues and to prevent violation of securities laws and engagement in corporate malfeasance, misconduct, and fraudulent activities.

To effectively promote a culture of compliance within the company, a major role of lawyers is to bring legal compliance issues to the attention of the appropriate authorities in the company, including management, general counsel, the CCO or its equivalent, the audit committee, or a committee of independent directors. The Task Force of the ABA suggests that (1) the board of directors should establish a practice of regular and executive session meetings between the general counsel and a committee of independent directors, and (2) the retained outside lawyers should communicate with the employed inside lawyers or general counsel and advise them of material or potential violations of applicable laws or duties.[1] This requires proper communication between general counsel and independent directors as well as communication between outside counsel and general counsel.

Former SEC Chairman, William Donaldson, raised concerns regarding lawyers not performing their duties as gatekeepers by stating, "This is an area where I have been disappointed by the contribution of some lawyers, who appear in at least some cases to devise their own narrow interpretations of the rules while disclosing as little as possible, rather than to seek helpful disclosure for investors."[2] Legal counsel (chief in-house attorneys and general counsel) at Apple, Inc.; Monster Worldwide, Inc.; and more than twelve other companies who are responsible for ensuring the legality of business transactions resigned or were dismissed as a result of their involvement with alleged option backdating practices.[3] The SEC position is that "Any lawyer who works at a public company should do everything possible to thwart fraud—not participate in it."[4] As rightly stated by Fred Krebs, president of the Association of Corporate Counsel, "If something goes wrong in an organisation, the Securities and Exchange Commission looks at the general counsel and says if you didn't stop it, you're at fault."[5]

Communication with Legal Counsel

1. Communication between general counsel and independent directors. Legal counsel plays an important role in corporate governance by providing professional advice to the company's directors, officers, and other key employees, and ensuring that the company is in compliance with all applicable regulations. As an important gatekeeper, legal counsel adds value to the companies' sustainable performance. Thus, the appointment, retention, and compensation of the company's general counsel should be approved by the board of directors. General counsel should coordinate the activities of internal and outside lawyers, require continuous reporting of material or potential violations of law, and meet regularly in executive sessions with independent directors or a committee of independent directors to discuss legal matters and concerns about violations of laws or breaches of fiduciary duties.

The general counsel usually works with senior management and reports to the CEO or other senior executives. Although this interaction with management is administratively and functionally necessary, general counsel is hired by the company, and as such, the company is the general counsel's client. Nonetheless, where the general counsel concludes that the action or inaction of an officer or employee is in violation of applicable laws or is breaching the fiduciary duty to the company, counsel should discuss the legal issues and their ramifications with the appropriate authorities in the company. When the alleged violating individuals are senior executives or the CEO, the general counsel should communicate the matter to an independent committee of the board of directors.

Practically, the casual communication of legal issues to the board of directors may adversely affect the relationship between the company's directors and its officers (senior executives) as well as the relationship between general counsel and senior executives. Thus, the Task Force of the ABA recommends that public companies adopt a routine practice of having regular and periodic executive session meetings with their general counsel and an independent committee of the board of directors to discuss real and potential violations of laws and the actual or potential breach of fiduciary duties. This established practice should require the general counsel to (1) thoroughly investigate relevant legal issues; (2) determine actual or potential violations of laws or breaches of duty by the company or its directors, officers, employees, or agents; (3) communicate these legal matters to the individuals involved; (4) take appropriate steps to correct the violations and prevent their recurrences; and (5) proceed up the corporate ladder to a committee of independent directors or the entire board of directors in instances in which the resolution could not previously be achieved.

2. Communication between outside counsel and general counsel. Public companies usually retain numerous outside lawyers who are either selected by or work with the company's directors, officers, and employees in providing them with legal advice relevant to their activities. These outside lawyers may not directly interact with or report to senior officers and directors. They usually establish working relationships with their contact person within the company. In the case of violation of laws or breach of duties by the contact person and in the absence of proper mechanisms to report the violations to proper authorities in the company, outside counsel may either be pressured to silence or not have appropriate resources and authority to further investigate the alleged violations. The Task Force of the ABA recommends that the general counsel (1) establish policies and procedures for outside lawyers to communicate with the general counsel facts and cases where an officer or employee is engaged in material violations of law or fiduciary duty, and (2) require outside lawyers provide important information and analysis of legal matters to the general counsel where appropriate action can be taken.[6]

SEC Rules of Professional Conduct for Lawyers

Section 307 of SOX directs the SEC to establish rules of professional conduct for lawyers appearing and practicing before the commission. SEC rules for attorneys, established in August 2003, require corporate attorneys to report suspicions of fraud and violations of securities laws.[7] SEC rules apply to any lawyer who is appearing and practicing before the Commission in the representation of an issuer. When the lawyer becomes aware of evidence of a material violation by the company or its directors, officers, employees, or agents, the lawyer is responsible for reporting such violation to the company's chief legal or executive officer. Unless the attorney reasonably believes that the individual seemingly in violation has provided an appropriate response within a reasonable time, the lawyer must report the evidence to the audit committee. SEC rules basically require the up-the-ladder approach in reporting violations of securities laws by the issuer. SOX, by engaging lawyers in policing corporate malfeasance and requiring reporting of such misconduct, makes the lawyer an important gatekeeper within the corporate governance structure. Legal counsel as advisors to management and the board plays an important role in identifying financial reporting risks for management and any noncompliance with regulations in financial disclosures to investors.

It is expected that SEC rules will lead to more ethical lawyers who contribute to the achievement of business ethics. Lawyers played a role in reported financial scandals by either facilitating management impropriety or not detecting and preventing management misconduct. Indeed, the Powers report of Enron's internal investigation states, "There was an absence of forceful and effective oversight by ... in-house counsel, and objective and critical professional advice by outside counsel...."[8] The general understanding is that when management and accountants are attempting to break the law, it is the professional responsibility of legal counsel to detect and prevent the wrongdoing rather than act as facilitators or enablers of wrongdoings.

Responsibilities of Legal Counsel

Legal counsel normally provides legal advice to the company's board of directors and management. The role of legal counsel in corporate governance has received significant attention in the post-Enron era. The primary roles of corporate legal counsel are to (1) ensure compliance with all applicable laws, regulations, and rules; (2) provide legal advice and analysis regarding legal compliance issues; and (3) communicate material potential or ongoing violations of law and breaches of fiduciary duties to the general counsel and independent directors or a committee of independent directors.

Legal counsel, either an in-house or outside lawyer, should (1) serve the integrity of the company aside from the personal interests of its directors, officers, employees, shareholders, or other stakeholders; (2) be responsible for implementing an effective legal compliance system under the oversight of the company's board of directors to ensure compliance with all applicable regulations; (3) advise the board of directors or a board committee on special investigations and report directly to the board or the board committee; (4) have appropriate rules of conduct in conformity with SEC and state attorney requirements and enforce these rules; and (5) be aware of adherence to their professional codes of ethics and responsibilities in their representation of public companies. When an attorney becomes aware of violations, the attorney must immediately report the matter to the chief legal officer (CLO), both CLO and CEO, or qualified legal compliance committee (if it exists). The reporting attorney may ultimately report the violations to the audit committee or another committee consisting solely of independent directors on unsatisfactory responses from either the CEO or the CLO.

The CLO must make necessary inquiries to determine if the alleged material violation has occurred or is likely to occur, take appropriate actions on further evidence concerning such violations, or otherwise advise the reporting attorney that such violations did not occur. No further action is required by the reporting attorney on receiving an appropriate response within a reasonable time period. If the reporting attorney does not receive a satisfactory response within a reasonable time period, then the attorney must explain the concerns to the CLO and CFO, or their equivalents, and then take the matter up the ladder as follows: (1) the audit committee; (2) if there is no audit committee, to another committee of the board of directors that is composed solely of independent directors; (3) if there is no such committee, to the board of directors; and (4) if the reporting attorney was discharged from employment or a retainer as a result of making such a report, the attorney may notify the board of directors or its representative in the audit committee.

If the company designates a qualified legal compliance committee (QLCC), usually composed of solely independent directors, the reporting attorney's only responsibility is to report the alleged material violations to this committee with further follow-up. Alternatively, the reporting attorney can initially report the violations to the company's chief legal counsel, and the chief legal counsel can forward that report to the preestablished qualified legal compliance committee and notify the reporting attorney without further obligation to pursue the matter.

To meet the regulatory definition of a QLCC, such a committee must also have been established by the issuer's board of directors, with the authority and responsibility to (1) inform the issuer's CLO and CEO of any report of evidence of a material violation [see 17 CFR Section 205.2(k)(3)(i) 2005]; (2) determine whether an investigation is necessary regarding any report of evidence of a material violation by the issuer (or its officers, directors, employees, or agents) and, if it determines an investigation is necessary or appropriate, to (a) notify the audit committee or full board of directors; (b) initiate an investigation, which may be conducted either by the CLO or outside attorneys; and (c) retain such additional expert personnel as the committee deems necessary [see 17 CFR Section 205.2(k)(3)(ii) 2005]; (3) at the conclusion of any such investigation to (a) recommend, by majority vote, that the issuer implement an appropriate response to evidence of a material violation; and (b) inform the CLO, CEO, and board of directors of the results of any such investigation and the appropriate remedial measures to be adopted [see 17 CFR Section 205.2(k)(3)(iii) 2005]; and (4) act by majority vote to take all other appropriate action, including notifying the SEC in the event that the issuer fails in any material respect to implement an appropriate response that the QLCC has recommended [see CFR Section 205.2(k)(4) 2005].

SEC Chairman William H. Donaldson, in a speech before the Practicing Law Institute in Washington, DC, criticized the actions of some attorneys in mutual fund scandals and urged corporate legal counsel "to identify today's issues and prevent them from blossoming into tomorrow's scandals."[9] Donaldson further states that

> *Some will pursue questionable activity right up to technical conformity with the letter of the law or accounting standards, and some will step over the red line, perhaps with the help of a lawyer or accountant.... Think how much anguish we could have avoided if a few more lawyers had pointed out to their hedge-fund clients that late trading of mutual fund shares is illegal, as are duplicitous market timing and quid pro quo "sticky asset" arrangements.*[10]

Outside legal counsel and the CLO can play an important role in assisting directors and officers in understanding new corporate governance measures, implications for the company, and compliance with these measures. Regarding the importance of participation of legal counsel in corporate governance, the Federal Reserve Governor Schmidt Bies states, "In today's environment, regulators, lawmakers and shareholders are looking for providers of legal services to be vigilant on behalf of their clients and to ensure that clients receive the best possible assistance in meeting the standards for corporate governance, compliance, internal controls, and legal and reputational risk management."[11]

FINANCIAL ADVISORS

The impact of SOX and SEC rules on attorney–client privilege communication has recently received considerable attention. On December 12, 2006, Deputy Attorney General Paul J. McNulty, of the U.S. D.J, issued new guidelines for prosecutors to consider when charging corporations.[12] The new guidelines promote the preservation of corporate legal privileges and establish new requirements for prosecutors who seek privileged information from companies. Prosecutors must obtain approval from the U.S. Attorney and prove a legitimate need before requesting waivers of corporate privileged information, unless the company voluntarily waives such privileges. Prosecutors also refrain from considering in their charging decision whether a company advances legal fees to former or current employees who are subjects of an investigation. Thus, prosecutors are restricted but not prohibited from seeking corporate privilege waivers. This includes request waivers of attorney–client or work product protections when there is a legitimate need for the privileged information. The new guidelines, however, provide greater protection for the attorney–client privileged communication.

Financial advisors, through their discretionary authority to manage investments on behalf of their clients (investors) and participate in proxy voting, play an important role in corporate governance. Investment advisors are required to exercise due diligence, maintain objectivity, and service their clients to the best of their ability. Conflicts of interest may arise when the investment advisors have personal or business relationships with the company, its directors, or participants in proxy contents. The SEC, in addressing this potential conflict of interest, has adopted a rule that requires investment advisors to (1) establish policies and procedures to guide their proxy voting in the best interest of their clients, (2) disclose adequate information regarding the established policies and procedures and how they have voted their proxies, and (3) maintain proper records regarding proxy voting.[13]

Securities Analysts

Unlike other professionals, such as accountants and lawyers who are either hired or retained by companies, securities analysts are hired by brokerage firms to analyze financial performance of the corporations they follow, assess the quality of the company as an investment, and make recommendations for investment opportunities based on their analysis. In this regard, securities analysts, by influencing investors' investment decisions, can directly or indirectly affect the quality and quantity of financial information dissemination to the public by companies. Analysts are regulated by the NASD, whose rules are designed to prevent bad practices, and they are also subject to the broker-dealer rules issued by the SEC and national stock exchanges. Nonetheless, like accountants and lawyers, securities analysts have been subject to pressures and incentives to be biased toward corporations they follow, particularly when they are associated with firms that also do investment banking. During the economic downturn of 2001, when the capital market was already well into a downward spiral, for the total 26,000 analysts' recommendations about 30 percent were strong buy, 38 percent buy, 31 percent hold, and only 1 percent either sale or strong sale.[14]

Securities analysts play an important role in recommending stock. During the economic and market boom of the 1990s, analysts' objectives and skeptical attitudes became irrelevant. The prudent, objective, skeptical, and diligent analysts who predicted reasonable earnings growth and stock appreciation were unheard. The perception was that the analysts' research was not influenced by investment banking concerns. Recent reported financial scandals (e.g., Enron, Global Crossing, Qwest, WorldCom) raised concerns regarding the conflicts faced by research analysts. Popular press and academic research allude to analysts' conflicts of interest in the sense that (1) although the Nasdaq Composite Index was dropping by more than 60 percent, less than 1 percent of analysts' recommendations were to "sell";

(2) about 99 percent of all research sell-side analysts' recommendations in 2000 were to "hold," "buy," or "strong buy"; and (3) companies often withheld business from firms whose analysts issued unfavorable reports.[15] Lawmakers and regulators' concerns have been that investors may not know about research analysts' conflicts of interest in situations where (1) analysts' compensation and other payments may be determined based on the promotion of investment banking businesses, and (2) favorable analyst research reports could be used to market investment banking services. Thus, activities of research departments have come under increasing scrutiny and accordingly, in May 2002, the SEC approved the proposed NASD Rule 2711 and the amended NYSE Rule 472 designed to manage, monitor, and disclose research analysts' conflicts of interest in connection with research reports on equity securities and public appearance.

Section 501 of SOX directs the SEC to issue rules addressing securities analyst conflicts of interest issues. The SEC, on February 20, 2003, adopted its final rule Regulation Analyst Certification (Regulation AC).[16] SOX and Regulation AC address concerns regarding the independence of research from investment banking and the analysts' perceived conflicts of interest. Regulation AC requires brokers, dealers, and certain other associated persons to incorporate into their research reports certification by the research analyst that includes (1) that the views expressed in the research reports accurately reflect the analyst's personal views; and (2) whether the analyst received any compensation in connection with the expressed recommendations or views, and if so, the source, amount, and purpose of such compensation along with its possible influence. The distribution by a broker-dealer of any report that does not contain such certifications is a violation of Regulation AC. Furthermore, Regulation AC requires that brokers, dealers, and certain other associated persons obtain research analyst certifications to ensure that (1) the views expressed in all public appearances during the prior calendar quarter accurately reflect the analyst's personal views, and (2) no part of such analyst compensation is connected to any specific recommendations or views expressed in any public appearances during the prior calendar quarter. Research analysts who are not able to provide these required certifications must present notice of such failure to their examining authorities. Brokers and dealers must (1) disclose such failures in any research reports provided by the analysts for 120 days following notification, and (2) maintain proper related records for a period of at least three years.

Requirements of Regulation AC are consistent with and complement other rules governing conflicts of interest disclosure by research analysts mandated by the NASD and the NYSE. NASD Rule 2711 and NYSE Rule 472 (1) require analysts' disclosure of any possible conflicts of interest between the given stock advice and their own financial interests; (2) reinforce the "Chinese wall" between research and investment banking; (3) prohibit analysts from receiving compensation directly tied to investment banking services and related fees; (4) require analysts to disclose (both in research reports and public appearances) any financial relationship with companies they analyze; and (5) prohibit a firm's investment banking department from interfering, supervising, or controlling any member of the research department. Section 501 of SOX, amended NYSE Rule 472, NASD Rule 2711, and Regulation AC are collectively addressing research analysts' conduct, the perceived conflicts of interest, and the development of standards to improve research analysts' objectivity and independence.

Regulation AC was issued with the intent to improve the objectivity of analysts' forecasts and forecast revisions. If Regulation AC increases the objectivity and credibility of analyst reports and forecasts, then we expect a higher consensus among analysts and lower forecast dispersion in the post-AC period relative to the pre-AC period. In addition, if analysts are now more skeptical and objective, and spend more time researching a firm, then the average number of analysts following a firm will decrease in the post-AC era. Several factors may contribute to the improvement of the information environment after the implementation of Regulation AC. First, Regulation AC may have improved the credibility and integrity of analyst research reports by reducing potential conflicts of interest. Second, investor confidence in analyst research reports may have improved because of mere certifications of those reports. Finally, companies may have increased the quality and quantity of information provided to analysts or disseminated through public disclosures.

Securities analysts can be an important communication channel between public companies and investors in promoting the transparency of financial disclosures. Securities analysts, by covering public companies, conducting research, asking hard questions, exercising due diligence, performing fair and objective analysis, and making impartial and unbiased research conclusions and recommendations, can provide valuable information to investors and identify potential risks to investors.

The global Association for Investment Management and Research (AIMR) and the National Investor Relations Institute have jointly proposed ethical guidelines governing the relationship between public companies and their securities analysts.[17] The proposed guidelines require analysts to refrain from any conflicts of interest with companies they cover, conduct thorough and diligent research, and be objective and unbiased in their research reports. Corporations, on the other hand, must not (1) discriminate among analysts based on their research and recommendations; (2) withhold relevant information from analysts or deny access to the company's representatives to influence their research; or (3) exert pressure on analysts via other business relationships, including investment banking.

The proposed guidelines address that analyst-compensated research is appropriate when (1) companies engage qualified, competent, and objective analysts; and (2) analysts fully disclose in their research report the nature and extent of the compensation received. The guidelines provide five standards of best practices governing the relationship between corporations and their analysts. These standards are summarized as follows.

Standard I: Information Flow

Analysts, investors, and public companies must not disrupt or threaten to disrupt the free flow of information between corporations, investors, and analysts in any manners that inappropriately influence the behavior of those with whom they are communicating.

Standard II: Analyst Conduct

Analysts must conduct their research and recommendations with utmost objectivity, independence, fairness, and unbiased opinion by (1) issuing objective research and recommendations that have a reasonable bias and sufficient evidence supported by thorough, diligent, and appropriate investigation; (2) differentiating between fact and opinion; (3) ensuring the transparency and completeness of the information presented in their reports; and (4) engaging in no bias or threat to use their research reports or recommendations to improve their relationship with the corporations they cover.

Standard III: Corporate Communication and Access

Corporations must not (1) discriminate among recipients of information disclosed based on the recipient's prior research, recommendations, earnings estimates, conclusions, or opinions; (2) deny or threaten to deny information or access to company representatives to influence the research recommendations or actions of investment professionals and analysts; or (3) influence the research, recommendations, or actions of analysts or investment professionals by exerting pressure through other business relationships.

Corporations must (1) provide access to the company's management, officers, and other knowledgeable officials to qualified persons or entities, including analysts and investors; and (2) establish and adhere to policies that address how the company defines access, prioritizes requests for access or information, and responds to each request, and under what circumstances and to whom different types or levels of access will be granted.

Standard IV: Reviewing Analyst Reports or Models

Analysts, prior to the publication of their reports, may request that corporations review for factual accuracy only those portions of the research report that do not contain analysts' conclusions, recommendations, valuations, or price targets. Corporations may also comment on historical or forward-looking information that is already in the public domain.

Standard V: Issuer-Paid Research Reports

Analysts who engage in research paid by corporations must (1) only accept cash compensation for their work; (2) not accept any compensation contingent on the contract or conclusions of the research or the potential effect on share price; (3) disclose in the report (a) the nature and extent of compensation received from drafting the report; (b) the nature and extent of any personal, professional, or financial relationship they, their firm or its parent, subsidiaries, agents, or trading entities may have with the company; (c) their credentials, including professional designations and experience; and (d) any matters that could reasonably be perceived to impair their objectivity; and (4) certify that the analysis or recommendations in the report represent the true opinion of the author or authors.

The company that hires analysts to produce research must (1) engage analysts who are qualified and committed to produce objective and thorough research, including disclosure of any matters that could reasonably be expected to impair their objectivity; (2) pay for the research in cash and only in a manner that does not influence the content and conclusions of the research; (3) not attempt explicitly or implicitly to influence the research, recommendations, or behavior of analysts to produce research or recommendations favorable to the company; and (4) ensure that all disclosures required by the analyst are fully included in the research report that is published or distributed by the company.

INVESTMENT BANKS

Investment banks have been criticized for their involvement in reported financial scandals. Several investment banks that were once the major players in providing financial advice and financing Enron's operations, including J.P. Morgan Chase & Co.; Toronto-Dominion Bank; Citigroup, Inc.; Deutsche Bank AG; Merrill Lynch & Co.; Barclays Bank PLC; and Credit

Suisse Group are now being sued by Enron for helping it hide liabilities and inflate earnings. Enron filed lawsuits against these banks, contending that the banks could have prevented the company's collapse if they had not aided and abetted fraud, and is now settling its lawsuits with them. Enron shareholders are seeking damages from Merrill Lynch & Co. on the grounds that investment banks played key roles in Enron's scheme to defraud.[18] For example, J.P. Morgan Chase & Co. paid $350 million in cash and dropped $660 million in claims against the company, whereas Toronto-Dominion paid $60 million in cash and dropped $60 million of its claims. These investment banks also settled for several billion dollars with Enron shareholders. Several investment banks had lawsuits settled against them alleging their engagement in the Enron debacle. Table 11.1 shows investment banks involved, the

Table 11.1   Investment Banks in Enron Settlements

Investment banks	Date	Settlement amounts	Description
J.P. Morgan	August 2005	$350 million	Paid Enron to settle claims for helping the company's former management commit fraud
Toronto-Dominion Bank	August 2005	$130 million ($70 million to Enron)	Paid Enron to settle a lawsuit alleging it helped Enron's former management defraud stockholders and creditors
Canadian Imperial Bank of Commerce	July 2005	$2.4 billion, $274 million	Paid Enron to settle a lawsuit alleging its involvement in helping company management to defraud stockholders and creditors
J.P. Morgan	June 2005	$2.2 billion	Agreed to this amount to settle a class action lawsuit filed by investors of Enron
Citigroup	June 2005	$2 billion	With an unprecedentedly large settlement at that time, Citigroup agreed to pay this amount for the sale of stock and bonds before the collapse of Enron
Lehman Brothers	November 2004	$222.5 million	Paid to investors to acknowledge Lehman's involvement in the sale of Enron notes shortly before the company's bankruptcy proceedings
Bank of America	July 2004	$69 million	Paid to investors who lost billions of dollars as a result of the collapse of Enron
Canadian Imperial Bank of Commerce	December 2003	$80 million	Paid in response to SEC civil charges that some CIBC employees helped Enron manipulate its financial statements
Citigroup, J.P. Morgan	July 2003	$305 million	Banks agreed to pay this amount and change their vetting process for financial deals over actions related to loans and trades the firms made with Enron and Dynegy
Merrill Lynch	February 2003	$80 million	The first financial services firm to settle with regulators paid to resolve civil charges that it aided Enron in fraudulently overstating earnings

Source: Extracted from Smith, R. 2005, August 3. CIBC to Pay $2.4 Billion Over Enron; Canadian Bank Is Settling Investors' Fraud Claims; Spotlight on Merrill, CSFB. *Wall Street Journal*, p. A3. Available at: ABI/INFORM Global database. (Document ID: 876699911).

settlement date, the amount of the settlement, and a description of the settlement. In the post-SOX era, investment banks and the major brokerage firms have grown rapidly and generated record revenue.

SUMMARY

Professional advisors such as legal counsel and financial advisors assist public companies in the determination and execution of business transactions and in the assessment of their risks and financial consequences. Professional advisors by virtue of their association with public companies can influence corporate governance and financial reports. Legal counsel assists companies to comply with applicable laws, rules, and regulations, and often advises them in structuring business transactions to ensure full disclosures and compliance with accounting standards. Financial analysts and investment bankers, by virtue of providing financial advice to corporations, their directors, officers, and other key personnel, and by providing coverage and stock recommendations, can influence corporate governance.

The key points of this chapter are

- The advisory function of corporate governance is assumed by professional advisors, including legal counsel, financial analysts, and investment bankers who normally assist companies in evaluating legal and financial consequences of business transactions.

- Traditionally, a lawyer's role in corporate governance has been as the outside gatekeeper to promote legal compliance and to protect the interest of the company.

- SOX makes legal counsel an integral component of the internal processes of the corporate governance structure to monitor corporate misconduct.

- The board of directors should approve the appointment, retention, and compensation of the company's general counsel.

- General counsel should coordinate the activities of internal and outside lawyers, require continuous reporting of material or potential violations of law, and meet regularly in executive sessions with independent directors or a committee of independent directors to discuss legal matters and concerns about violations of laws or breaches of fiduciary duties.

- Conflicts of interest may arise when investment advisors have personal or business relationships with the company, its directors, or participants in proxy contents.

- Like accountants and lawyers, securities analysts have been subject to pressures and incentives to be biased toward corporations they follow, particularly when they are associated with firms that also do investment banking.

- SOX and Regulation AC are intended to promote the integrity of research reports and investor confidence in those reports by properly disclosing conflicts of interest that are known or should have been known by securities analysts, brokers, or dealers to exist at the time of the appearance or the date of distribution of the report.

- Professional advisors by virtue of their associations with public companies can influence corporate governance and financial reports.

KEY TERMS

Association of Investment
   Management and
   Research (AIMR)
investment bank

National Association of
   Securities Dealers (NASD)
National Investor Relations
   Institute (NIRI)

Regulation Analyst
   Certification (Regulation
   AC)

REVIEW QUESTIONS

1. How does legal counsel play an important role in corporate governance?

2. What is the purpose of the legal counsel serving as advisors to management?

3. Why is reliable and transparent information a necessity to operate an efficient market?

4. What is "Regulation AC"?

5. What are the standards of best practices governing the relationship between corporations and their analysts?

DISCUSSION QUESTIONS

1. List external participants in corporate governance who help monitor the corporate governance structure and provide advice to internal participants.

2. Should attorney–client privileges be waived in certain situations for corporate attornies representing public companies before the SEC for violations of securities laws? Explain.

3. With respect to attorneys, will the imposition of SEC rules relating to ethics positively impact behavior?

4. What has contributed to the improvement of information since the SEC implemented "Regulation Analyst Certification" (Regulation AC)?

NOTES

1. American Bar Association (ABA). 2003, August 11–12. Report on the Task Force on Corporate Responsibility. Available at: www.abanet.org/leadership/2003/journal/119a.pdf.

2. Donaldson, W. H. 2005, March 4. Speech by SEC Chairman: Remarks before SEC Speaks Conference. Available at: www.sec.gov/news/speech/spch030405whd.htm.

3. O'Reilly, C. 2007, February 16. Options-Toll Rises as Corporate Lawyers Retire, Quit. *Bloomberg*. Available at: www.sddt.com/news/article.cfm?SourceCode=20070216fp.

4. U.S. Securities and Exchange Commission (SEC). 2007, February 15. SEC Charges Former General Counsel of Monster Worldwide, Inc. for Backdating Options. Available at: www.sec.gov/news/press/2007/2007-23.htm.

5. Masters, B. 2006. General Counsels Feel Stock Options Heat. *Financial Times* November 27. Available at: www.ft.com/cms/s/0/d404737a-7e47-11db-84bb-0000779e2340.html?nclick_check=1.

6. Ibid.

7. U.S. Securities and Exchange Commission (SEC). 2003, August 5. Implementation of Standards of Professional Conduct for Attorneys. Available at: ww.sec.gov/rules/final/33-8185.htm.

8. Powers, W. C. 2002, February 1. Report of Investigation by the Special Investigative Committee of the Board of Directors of Enron Corp. Available at: news.findlaw.com/wp/docs/enron/specinv020102rpt1.pdf.

9. Donaldson, W. H. 2005, March 4. Speech by SEC Chairman: Remarks before SEC Speaks Conference, Washington, DC. Available at: www.sec.gov/news/speech/spch030405whd.htm.

10. Ibid.

11. The Federal Reserve Board. 2003, August 10. Remarks by Governor Susan Schmidt Bies: Effective Corporate Governance and the Role of Counsel. Speech presented at the annual meeting of the American Bar Association, San Francisco, CA. Available at: www.federalreserve.gov/BoardDocs/speeches/2003/20030810/default.htm.

12. U.S. Department of Justice (DoJ). 2006. Memorandum from Paul J. McNulty, Deputy Attorney General, to Heads of Department Components, United States Attorneys. Available at: www.abanet.org/poladv/priorities/ privilegewaiver/2006dec 12_privwaiv_dojmcnulty.pdf.

13. U.S. Securities and Exchange Commission (SEC). 2003, January 13. Disclosure of Proxy Voting Policies and Proxy Voting Records by Registered Management Investment Companies. Available at: www.sec.gov/rules/final/ 33-8188.htm.

14. Coffee, J. C. 2001. Virtue of the Securities Analysts. *New York Law Journal* July 19.

15. Arkin, S. S. 2002. Analysts' Conflicts of Interest: Where's the Crime. *New York Law Journal* February, 3.

16. U.S. Securities and Exchange Commission (SEC). 2003, February 20. Regulation Analyst Certification. Available at: www.sec.gov/rules/final/33-8193.htm.

17. Chartered Financial Analysts (CFA) Institutes. 2004, March 11. Securities Analysts and Investor Relations Association Jointly Forge Guidelines for Ethical Conduct in the Analyst-Corporate Relationship. Press Release. Available at: www.cfainstitute.org/aboutus/press/release/04releases/20040311_01.html.

18. CantonRep.com. 2006, December 22. SEC Considering Taking Side of Merrill Lynch in Enron Damages Case. Available at: www.cantonrep.com/printable.php?ID=326211.

Part Three

Contemporary Issues in Business Ethics and Corporate Governance

Chapter 12

Technology and Corporate Governance

INTRODUCTION

Technology plays an important role in corporate governance, particularly in improving and automating the compliance process in the post–corporate governance reforms era. Section 404 compliance of SOX reveals significant control deficiencies in the use of IT. The proper use of technology to automate controls and the financial reporting process enables companies to improve the quality of both financial and nonfinancial information on their KPIs, strengthen accountability of functional responsibilities (e.g., production, sales, marketing, accounting), and ensure compliance processes are performed in accordance with sustainable strategies. The effectiveness of all corporate governance functions depends on the quality of support received from the IT function. The IT function enables other corporate governance functions to operate in real-time, online processes facilitating simultaneous decision making, continuous monitoring, instantaneous assessment electronic reporting, and continuous auditing. This chapter discusses the use of IT in improving corporate governance effectiveness.

Primary Objectives

The primary objectives of this chapter are to

- Address the broad influence of technology in twenty-first-century corporate governance.

- Introduce a theoretical "cybercompany model" to promote the use of information technology in areas of shareholder communication, electronic commerce, electronic financial reporting, and continuous auditing.
- Recognize the factors that help build a firm information infrastructure.
- Present electronic financial reporting using XBRL format.
- Discuss continuous auditing.

INFORMATION TECHNOLOGY

Corporate governance should be responsive to the emerging challenges and opportunities of the twenty-first century. These challenges are the Internet, globalization, and regulations. IT can play an important role in corporate governance as a tool to improve the efficiency and effectiveness of corporate governance. IT serves as an effective means of delivering timely and accurate information for planning, monitoring, and reporting purposes. The IT manager is an important senior executive working with other senior executives (CEO, CFO, controllers) as part of the managerial function of corporate governance. The CIO or IT manager is responsible for management and operation of the IT function to support other corporate governance functions. Compliance with Sections 404 (real-time disclosures) and 802 (criminal penalties for altering documents) of SOX necessitates the use of IT solutions for timely access to secure and complete business documents.

The important role that IT can play in improving the effectiveness of corporate governance, particularly with regard to financial reporting and disclosure, is not yet well recognized in the business literature or the financial reporting process. IT, specifically the use of the Internet and e-commerce, has had a significant impact on the way companies operate and, accordingly, on the governance of companies. A 2006 survey of the CEOs of 312 of the fastest growing companies indicates that (1) their company's total operating budget devoted to IT development averaged 8.14 percent in 2005, which is up 24 percent compared with 6.56 percent reported in 2002; and (2) several areas of IT development, including security applications, wireless networks, faster data transactions, Internet technology, and data convergence, continue to have significant impacts on their business.[1]

The SEC has recently accepted, on a voluntary basis, filing of financial reports in XBRL format, along with statutory filings under the Electronic Data Gathering, Analysis, and Retrieval (EDGAR) system. Technology solutions and software packages are being developed to document compliance with provisions of SOX, particularly Section 404 compliance on ICFR. After September 11, 2001, corporate boards began to pay more attention to IT security and business continuity. Implementation of Section 404 on ICFR underscores the importance of IT in financial reporting. In fact, some companies have started to develop a separate IT board committee to address and oversee IT issues.

Modern video conferencing, or "web cam" technology, enables companies to conduct their meetings electronically without requiring everyone to be physically present. In the future, shareholders' annual meetings can be arranged at a specified physical location, date, and time, where the means of participation may be either physical or electronic. A more advanced electronic shareholder annual meeting would be a "virtual" meeting in which there is no chosen physical location for the meeting, but discussions are organized through the use of an electronic bulletin board that shareholders can access and where the discussion can be managed effectively.

CYBERCOMPANY MODEL

The future extensive use of IT in the areas of shareholder communication, electronic commerce, electronic financial reporting, and electronic continuous auditing would eventually move companies toward the "cybercompany" model. The emerging cybercompany model would require changes in many components of the corporate governance structure presented in Chapter 2. Corporate governance aspects of shareholder value creation and enhancement as well as other stakeholder value protection would remain the same. Corporate governance principles of fairness, honesty, transparency, responsiveness, accountability, and resilience would also be applicable to the cybercompany model. However, the corporate governance structure, including internal and external mechanisms, would change to some extent. Corporate governance objectives, principles, and functions would be the same, but the manner in which these functions operate (oversight, managerial, internal audit, compliance, external audit, advisory, and monitoring) would differ. Thus, the full and effective use of IT may shape and improve corporate governance functions.

Electronic Communication with Shareholders

Shareholder voting can be done electronically by using the same technologies used in local and national elections. Thus, it is expected that in the future, the majority, if not all, of companies' communications will be conducted in electronic form. The UK 2005 proposed Corporate Law Reform recommends, subject to shareholder approval, companies use electronic means such as Web sites and e-mail to communicate with their shareholders.[2] The use of electronic communication in lieu of traditional communications on paper can be beneficial to both companies and their shareholders by (1) saving substantial costs of paper-based production and dissemination of annual proxy and financial statements, and (2) improving the timeliness and transparency of communications with shareholders. Shareholders can also benefit by participating in meetings that might otherwise be inaccessible or difficult to attend because of time or location constraints. Nevertheless, the existing corporate laws require the use of paper-based means of shareholder communications, which prevents both companies and their shareholders from reaping the benefits of electronic communication.

On September 25, 2006, the SEC announced that it awarded three separate contracts totaling $54 million to transform its filing disclosure system from a form-based electronic filing cabinet to a dynamic real-time system with interactive capabilities.[3] The move toward an interactive data system is being viewed as the commission's commitment to widening acceptance of interactive data filing by computers through the XBRL computer language. The three contracts are intended to (1) modernize the EDGAR database to use interactive data using the XBRL language, (2) complete writing of XBRL code for U.S. GAAP financial statements by preparing XBRL taxonomies that can be used by all companies in all industries, and (3) develop interactive data tools for investors on the SEC's Web site to enable investors to view and analyze companies' financial data that are filed in XBRL. It is expected that the SEC will require large public companies to file audited XBRL financial statements in the near future to make them more comparable, easily researchable, and interactive documents.

Electronic Commerce

The global economy during the past several decades has changed from an industrial economy to an information economy, and recently, with the Internet, it has transformed into a digital economy. The digital economy is significantly changing the way businesses, governments, and individuals interact and exchange goods and services. IT, in general, and the Internet, in particular, enabled the establishment of cybercompanies such as Google, Yahoo, eBay, CNET, E-cost, and Amazon.com. Almost all traditional retailers have established online trades. Electronic commerce (e-commerce) has become an integral component of business strategies and has altered the way organizations conduct their daily operations. The business framework has transformed from "brick-and-mortar" to "brick-and-click" infrastructure. E-commerce can be broadly defined as conducting business affairs, transactions, and communications over the Internet or through private online networks.

E-commerce strategies are classified into (1) business to business, the online exchanges of products, services, and business transactions between businesses and suppliers; (2) business to consumer, conducting business online with consumers; (3) consumer to consumer, where consumers trade among themselves; (4) business to government, exchanging transactions between business and governmental entities; (5) government to government, consisting of online programs and activities between governmental agencies; and (6) government to consumers, where online transactions are exchanged between governmental entities and consumers.[4] E-commerce transactions have grown from about $100 billion in 1999 to more than $8 trillion in 2004 and are expected to grow at about 20 percent compound annual growth over the next five years. This exponential growth in e-commerce activities significantly affects the way companies are operated, managed, and monitored. E-commerce has had profound implications for corporate governance and raised several policy, legal, and business issues that need to be addressed.

Electronic Financial Reporting

The effectiveness of corporate governance and the efficiency of the capital markets are greatly influenced by the amount, timeliness, accuracy, and completeness of public financial information produced by companies. Accurate and reliable financial information enables investors to monitor companies' governance and assess their operating, financing, and investment performance. High-quality financial information can be produced only under effective accounting and internal control systems guided by sound accounting practices and audited by competent and independent auditors.

1. **Information infrastructure.** Information infrastructure determines the way financial information is generated, processed, analyzed, audited, and used in making business and investment decisions, and is affected by the company's (1) directors in overseeing the financial reporting process, internal controls, and audit activities; (2) top management team in designing sound accounting and internal control systems and in certifying its financial statements and ICFR; (3) independent auditors by providing opinions on both financial statements and ICFR; (4) legal counsel in

assisting management with financial disclosures; (5) financial analysts in accurately and objectively forecasting their earnings; and (6) standard-setting bodies in promulgating accounting and auditing standards to be used in financial reporting and audit activities.

2. **Internal controls.** Several sections of SOX require the use of IT solutions to comply with its provisions. The use of IT solutions can be more effective in complying with Sections 302, 404, 409, and 802. Sections 302 and 404 require public companies to provide disclosure controls and management assessment and reporting on ICFR. Section 409 regarding real-time issuer disclosures requires companies to rapidly report events that could affect their performance. Section 802 on criminal penalties for altering documents requires companies to provide complete, secure, and timely access to documents. Timely compliance with provisions of SOX, particularly Sections 302, 404, 409, and 802, requires companies to use their IT resources or obtain IT solutions required to access and process the data. A 2007 Ernst & Young survey reveals that (1) only 49 percent of respondents believe their internal controls for IT activities were effective; (2) IT systems were initially developed on a piecemeal basis, which makes IT controls more challenging; and (3) critical issues in IT systems that demand more effective controls are in security, user access, program change management, and application control, as only 54 percent of respondents reported their internal controls in these areas were effective.[5]

3. **Information security.** Technological advances have substantially altered the business environment and the need for information security because business communications have evolved from real space to virtual space (e.g., eBay, Google). Information security involves protecting the integrity, availability, and confidentiality of both financial and nonfinancial information and consists of both manual and computer-based systems security. Although SOX does not explicitly address information security, Sections 302 and 404, along with related SEC implementation rules, require management to assess and document IT controls, including information security, to ensure the realiability of financial statements.

Information security and privacy of technology companies have received significant attention. Technology company executives worldwide are facing intense competition and changes in their corporate governance. The global convergence to digital services and worldwide economic expansions in China, Europe, and India encourage technology companies to be flexible. A survey conducted by PricewaterhouseCoopers of 126 technology executives in thirty-four countries reveals that technology companies should (1) properly manage their business risks by remaining flexible in their governance, strategies, business models, and culture; (2) develop partnerships and alliances with other technology companies to profit from technological changes; (3) pay close attention to customers' needs and changes in products and markets; and (4) become more adaptable and better able to assess and manage risks and opportunities.[6]

EXTENSIBLE BUSINESS REPORTING LANGUAGE

The emerging regulatory and corporate governance reforms demand more reliable, timely, and transparent financial information. Currently, many companies post their financial statements on their Web sites. The Web-based financial reports are basically electronic reproductions of the printed annual reports with no value added except that they are readily available. The use of the Internet in the electronic financial reporting process should make financial information easily accessible and readable by a wide variety of applications. Electronically published financial information is often integrated through hyperlinks, which makes separation of financial information from other information quite difficult. The XBRL enables business reporting information to be transferred automatically between different computer platforms and applications. XBRL allows the selection, analysis, storage, and exchange of tagged data that can be displayed automatically in various formats.

In XBRL, an electronically readable tag (bar code) is assigned to each financial statement item that provides additional context, including definition of the item, accounting standards used, time period, and company. These electronic tags are standardized, are defined according to commonly accepted taxonomies, and remain unchanged when they move from one computer platform to another. They are accompanied by a tagging tool that retrieves the tags from the standard taxonomies and applies them to the software being used (e.g., Microsoft Word or Excel). XBRL intends to enhance existing business reporting practices. A PricewaterhouseCoopers publication titled *XBRL: Improving Business Reporting Through Standardization* briefly discusses the concept and benefits behind the electronic innovation. Currently,

> *Business information is created and consumed at many points in the enterprise that often are not connected to one another. The management and reporting of business information does not follow an agreed-upon vocabulary, and its dispersion limits an organization's ability to reuse and share information. All organizations are required to summarize, consolidate, prepare, analyze, and often share this information within and outside their boundaries.*[7]

XBRL is an XML-based (Extensible Markup Language) platform for the analysis, exchange, and reporting of financial information with the purpose of integrating business reports and technology solutions. XBRL International currently freely licenses the XBRL standard and framework.[8] The current methodology lacks the ability to meet the demand. Available technology provides users with connectivity, shareability, and reusability that will meet the demand and provide the opportunity to realize lower costs in the process. XBRL intends to remove the bottlenecks in reporting and provide a more reliable system. Presently, XBRL is under development by a number of interested partners all sharing the same desire: to produce, consume, and exchange business information in a simplified manner. Development of the appropriate taxonomy is the key to the application of XBRL in financial reporting simply because XBRL is not dependent on any particular hardware platform, software system, programming language, or application standards (accounting, tax, or regulatory).

The standardized XBRL format allows all market and corporate governance participants to electronically share financial information to the extent that investors have access to the same information as analysts. XBRL provides a computer-readable identifying tag for each individual item of financial reports rather than treating those items as a block of computer text or printed documents. The XBRL tags are prepared according to applicable taxonomies such as GAAP for financial reporting, tax rules for tax purposes, or specific regulatory definitions for regulatory filings. The XBRL tagging process can handle financial information in different accounting standards and languages to serve a wide range of users.

IT and its integration across all corporate governance functions ensure more timely financial information, more effective regulatory compliance (SOX), more efficient use of IT systems, and more effective use of software applications. Many companies are still using IT infrastructures based on stand-alone systems to achieve their goals. The emerging issue in IT infrastructures is integrating IT services and business processes based on Web services. XML tags unstructured data from applications, servers, and databases. XML-tagged data can be sent across the Internet in a universal, platform-independent language. XBRL-GL is the specific XBRL general ledger that has a hierarchical structure that collects and communicates financial information. The use of Web-based programs such as XML, XBRL, and XBRL-GL enables companies to (1) eliminate manual processes and their related costs; (2) integrate their automated operational and financial activities; (3) improve their control environment; (4) enhance the accuracy and timeliness of financial reports; (5) enable convergences in global financial reporting by identifying, automating, and tagging financial information in any language or financial standards used by the company; (6) link to other sources of authoritative guidance such as IFRS; and (7) shorten turnaround between events and decisions by automating inefficient manual information gathering and analysis. Mike Willis, founding chairman of XBRL International, states that "XBRL enables CFOs to tell their own story to investors and other market stakeholders, precisely and clearly, without concerns about their tale becoming distorted by a third-party storyteller."[9]

XBRL makes it easier to generate, compile, validate, and analyze business and financial information. These features of XBRL improve the quality, completeness, comparability, and timeliness of business and financial information in making decisions. XBRL has developed an international public consortium of about 2,500 organizations from twenty-seven countries worldwide. Since the fall of 2005, more than 8,200 financial institutions in the United States have submitted their quarterly call reports, also known as risk-oriented filings, in XBRL format to federal banking regulators. These institutions have substantially reduced their filing compliance costs and provided higher-quality data, better analytical procedures (ratios), and more relevant benchmarking data. In addition, about twenty-five public companies (e.g., Ford, General Electric, Microsoft, PepsiCo, Bristol-Myers Squibb, United Technologies) have filed their annual (10-K) and quarterly (10-Q) reports in XBRL as part of a voluntary SEC pilot program. Other countries (e.g., Australia, Canada, China, the EU, India, Japan) are following suit.

Costs and Benefits of XBRL

Providing supplementary XBRL-related documents as in Exhibit 100 to the SEC's EDGAR system yields potential costs. There are also costs associated with the initial adoption of the XBRL-tagged data system, including the costs of testing and evaluating the XBRL format. Nevertheless, XBRL holds significant potential for the future of electronic financial reporting with the following perceived benefits: (1) XBRL can be used on any operating system or computer hardware to store data that can be easily shared without being rekeyed, which reduces error and results in productivity improvements for all users; (2) XBRL data does not change from the time and place of origination to their eventual designation and use, which results in more transparency in financial reporting; (3) the XBRL format can provide time and cost savings for users of financial statements by enabling them to analyze key financial ratios, compare companies to peers or indices, and perform other financial analysis without having to rekey or reformat financial information; (4) the use of XBRL might result in improvements in ICFR by enabling the use of continuous monitoring and automatically checking electronic information and its related internal controls; (5) improvements in internal controls might decrease the cost of compliance with Section 404; (6) the consistency and comparability provided by the use of XBRL might result in more efficient and effective filings and analysis of financial information by the SEC; and (7) XBRL improves the transparency of financial information by allowing organizations to respond much more quickly to changes in business conditions, regulatory requirements, and economic developments.[10]

The incompatibility among information formatting is negated through XBRL. XBRL provides cost savings through usage; such savings occurred at the FDIC and Deutsche Bank. Not only are the primary users finding benefits through XBRL, but secondary users such as investors will be able to search and locate information in a more timely fashion. XBRL allows for information to be searched and gathered on a need basis. Information can be linked through the XML Linking Language (XLink).

XBRL Application

The SEC, in September 2004, proposed a voluntary plan for all public companies to submit their financial statements using XBRL beginning with the 2004 calendar year-end report filings.[11] The SEC's intent in adopting voluntary XBRL filings was to (1) enhance users' ability to search the filings database, (2) extract and analyze financial information, (3) perform financial comparisons within industries, and (4) facilitate the SEC's review of filings. The SEC issued a release in February 2005 adopting amendments to establish a voluntary program relating to XBRL.[12] The program began with the 2004 calendar year-end reporting when registrants could voluntarily furnish XBRL data in an exhibit to specified EDGAR filings. The XBRL data tag is gaining prominence as a platform and data format for enhancing the quality and availability of financial reporting information.

The SEC permits voluntary XBRL financial reporting filings with the SEC as a way of supplementing required filings on the EDGAR system. The supplemental data would be submitted as Exhibit 100 to the filings under EDGAR. The SEC rule indicates that (1) no preapproval is required to submit the XBRL data; (2) one submission will not commit a registrant to future XBRL supplemental submissions; (3) the use of XBRL for the notes to financial statements is optional; (4) the XBRL data on Exhibit 100 should provide the same information that the registrant includes in its filing under the Exchange Act of 1934 or the Investment Company Act of 1940; (5) cautionary language must be exercised to advise investors that the XBRL protocol is still in the testing stages, and accordingly, they should not rely on the XBRL data to make investment decisions; (6) the XBRL-related documents must be labeled as "unaudited for annual filings" and "unreviewed for quarterly financial statements"; and (7) submitted XBRL-related documents that provide information related to a different filing must reference the official filing from which the XBRL data were derived.

The SEC XBRL program, as of now, is a voluntary program giving opportunities to public companies to participate in the program and start, as well as stop, their participation as they desire. XBRL documents can be submitted simultaneously with the official filings with the SEC or subsequent to official filings. The XBRL-submitted documents are viewed as furnished in addition to the official filings, with some flexibility in the tagged data being submitted. The SEC strongly encourages companies to participate in the voluntary filing program and submit XBRL documents on EDGAR. On October 9, 2007, the SEC announced the establishment of a new office to lead the transformation to interactive financial report by public companies. The new Interactive Disclosure office will work with all financial reporting participants worldwide, including preparers of financial statements, investor groups, analysts, journalists, and others to advance the use of interactive data in financial reporting. The SEC's intent is to improve the efficiency of capital markets by making financial information more suitable, less costly, and more timely.

The first mandatory e-filing using XBRL format is now implemented under the call report modernization project for about 8,400 financial institutions.[13] The call report uses the central data repository (CDR), a secure, shared database of the quarterly schedules of the nation's commercial banks. The call report modernization project is designed to simplify and increase the transparency of the call report process to supervise and evaluate financial conditions and results of operations of financial institutions. Call report filings are used to compile and verify institutional reports used by the FDIC, the Federal Reserve Bank (FRB), the Office of the Comptroller of the Currency (OCC), and the public.

Future of XBRL

The widespread application of the XBRL format depends on the acceptance of XBRL-tagged data for financial reporting and tax purposes by regulators and standard setters as well as the development of appropriate XBRL taxonomies for all industry segments. Taxonomy is "the mechanism for describing, naming, and classifying items of business information in a document."[14] Taxonomies are to be developed for various instances. Currently, XBRL has instituted taxonomy for internal business reporting of an organization. XBRL-GL, the journal taxonomy, provides for basic accounting needs such as general ledger postings, chart of accounts creation, customer and vendor master files maintenance, and operations of accounts receivable and payable.

Basic taxonomy frameworks can be used within individual business and expanded to meet specific needs. Regulators, standard setters, and tax authorities are still taking a hard look at XBRL capabilities to produce reliable and transparent financial information in the most feasible and effective manner. The SEC may decide to make XBRL filing mandatory, and thus, the PCAOB may require auditors to use continuous auditing to attest to and report on the accuracy and completeness of the tagged data. The FASB has already appointed an XBRL fellow and is in the process of testing the XBRL taxonomy developed for U.S. GAAP. Furthermore, the IRS will require corporations with $50 million or more in assets to file some of their tax return forms electronically. The taxonomy for U.S. GAAP financial reporting provides coverage for information in both the financial statements and the notes to the financial statements. The taxonomy also provides references to the authoritative literature relevant to various elements of financial statements, including captions on financial statements (current assets) or line items (cash and cash equivalents, deferred tax assets). Convergence to international accounting standards and other initiatives taken by the EC support the development and adoption of XBRL in the EU. Other countries are considering proposals for adopting XBRL reporting, including Japan, South Africa, Australia, Canada, Korea, and Singapore.

XBRL International, in July 2005, released the latest version of XBRL-GL, which is the general ledger taxonomy of XBRL. XBRL-GL enables more information handling of financial transactions, including the information found in a chart of accounts, journal entries, and transactions. XBRL-GL enables the development of a standardized vocabulary for (1) efficient communication between accountants; (2) expression of information from business documents that flow into financial reports; and (3) moving information between accounting systems, spreadsheets, and service providers.[15] XBRL-GL is expected to provide the following advantages:

1. *Reporting independence*. Business and financial information can be compiled, verified, and represented through flexible links to XBRL.
2. *System independence*. A simple import/export routine can be developed for converting information to XBRL-GL.
3. *Consolidation*. Business and financial information can be easily moved between systems or combined.
4. *Flexibility*. The entire business reporting supply chain from the recognition of business transactions to the preparation of financial reports can be standardized and improved.

PricewaterhouseCoopers suggests the following four-step implementation process to successfully adopt an XBRL-based financial reporting system:

1. *Assessing*. Companies should first evaluate the potential costs and benefits of adopting an XBRL-based reporting system; the current way financial data are collected, analyzed, recognized, and reported; and how data will be presented in XBRL format.
2. *Designing*. In designing a suitable XBRL-based reporting system, companies should choose appropriate XBRL taxonomies (U.S. GAAP, IFRS).
3. *Constructing*. Companies should build and test the appropriate infrastructure to link with legacy systems and convert them to the XBRL-based reporting systems.
4. *Implementing*. In this final stage, companies implement the selected XBRL-based reporting system for a variety of purposes, including financial reporting, tax, and regulatory filing purposes, and provide training for all personnel involved in the process.[16]

In summary, XBRL is expected to substantially reduce manual effort in the preparation of financial statements, strengthen ICFR, improve financial statement comparability, and level the playing field for investors to gain access to real-time, online financial information. Despite the perceived benefits of XBRL, less than 100 of the 10,000 public companies have submitted an XBRL filing under the SEC's voluntary filing program as of June 2007. This low acceptance of XBRL can be explained by (1) a lack of knowledge or understanding of XBRL; (2) common misconceptions about costs, resources required, and technical proficiency; and (3) unrealized benefits.[17]

CONTINUOUS AUDITING

Technological advances enable corporations to conduct material portions of their transactions online, prepare their financial statements electronically, and eventually prepare statements on a real-time basis using the XBRL format. In a real-time accounting system using XBRL taxonomies, the traditional source documents such as purchase orders, sales inventories, and checks are replaced with electronic messages, and much of the financial information and related audit evidence are available only in electronic form for a certain time period. The use of an electronic, real-time, XBRL-format financial reporting process by clients necessitates that auditors use a continuous auditing approach. Continuous auditing is defined as "a comprehensive electronic audit process that enables auditors to provide some degree of assurance on continuous information simultaneously with, or shortly after, the disclosure of the information."[18] This definition is comprehensive and covers all professional services provided by auditors to their clients, including review, attestation, and audit services. Continuous auditing enables auditors to use the integrated audit approach of both an audit of ICFR and an audit of financial statements, offering the following benefits:

1. Reduction of the cost of an audit engagement by enabling auditors to test a larger sample of client's transactions

2. Reduction of the amount of audit resources needed to manually perform tests of controls and substantive tests

3. Increase in the quality of financial statement audits by allowing auditors to use the integrated audit approach of understanding the entity-level control environment

4. Specification of transaction selection criteria to choose transactions or transaction cycles and perform integrated audits

Continuous auditing by shortening audit cycle times can provide more timely risk and control assessment and assurance. Continuous auditing enables auditors to audit a significant portion of the transaction population—up to 100 percent rather than just transaction samples. A 2006 PricewaterhouseCoopers survey reveals that (1) about 81 percent of respondents reported that they either had a continuous auditing or monitoring process or were planning to establish one; (2) more than 50 percent said they had some form of continuous auditing or monitoring process in place in 2006 compared with only 35 percent in 2005; (3) more than 56 percent said their continuous auditing processes include both manual and automated elements, whereas 41 percent reported their processes are entirely manual and about 3 percent indicated having fully automated processes; (4) the majority of the continuous auditing cycle (57 percent) is quarterly, while 34 percent focus on monthly monitoring activities and only 9 percent perform daily applications; (5) more than 52 percent reported having a formal quality assurance and improvement program in place; and (6) more than 79 percent routinely include an overall rating or conclusion in their reports to reflect their audit results.[19] Perceived benefits of continuous auditing are (1) making the audit process faster and more cost effective, efficient, and scalable; (2) facilitating shortening audit cycle times to provide more timely risk and control assurance; (3) achieving greater audit coverage of up to 100 percent of transactions in the population without the need to expand audit resources; (4) conducting audits on a daily, monthly, or quarterly basis; (5) automating periodic audit testing and improving audit cycle times; and (6) improving assurance quality.

On May 25, 2005, the PCAOB released staff questions and answers regarding XBRL attest engagements based on data furnished to the SEC under the XBRL voluntary financial reporting program on the EDGAR system.[20] PCAOB's guidance addresses the audit report on whether XBRL data accurately reflects the corresponding financial information. The voluntary XBRL program does not currently require companies to obtain auditor assurance on XBRL data. However, the PCAOB's staff questions and answers provide guidance on the application of PCAOB's attestation standards to auditors engaged in performing attestations to XBRL data for companies seeking to obtain assurances. The AICPA in its AT 101 Interpretation Attest Engagements of Financial Information Included in XBRL Instance Documents addresses practitioner considerations when they are engaged to examine and report on XBRL data.[21]

An XBRL instance document is a stand-alone document in a machine-readable format of financial information consisting of numerous data points and their corresponding XBRL tags that may be published using e-mail, a Web site, or other electronic distribution means. Practitioners (CPAs) may be engaged to examine and report on whether the XBRL instance document accurately reflects the financial information provided through the XBRL tag process, which also may include reference to other financial items in a PDF format.

The AICPA position is that because the existing XBRL taxonomies have yet to go through due process procedures, practitioners should perform the following necessary procedures to gather sufficient evidence to form an opinion on the accuracy and reliability

---

We have examined the accompanying XBRL Instance Document of XYZ Company, which reflects the data presented in the financial statements of XYZ Company as of December 31, 20XX, and for the year then ended [*optional to include the location of the financial statements, such as "included in the Company's Form 10-K for the year ended December 31, 20XX"*]. XYZ Company's management is responsible for the XBRL Instance Document. Our responsibility is to express an opinion based on our examination.

We have also audited, in accordance with auditing standards generally accepted in the United States of America, the financial statements of XYZ Company as of December 31, 20XX, and for the year then ended, and in our report dated [*Month*] XX, 20XX, we expressed an unqualified opinion on those financial statements.

Our examination was conducted in accordance with attestation standards established by the American Institute of Certified Public Accountants and, accordingly, included examining, on a test basis, evidence supporting the XBRL Instance Document and performing such other procedures as we considered necessary in the circumstances. We believe that our examination provides a reasonable basis for our opinion.

In our opinion, the XBRL Instance Document of XYZ Company referred to above accurately reflects, in all material respects, the data presented in the financial statements in conformity with [*identify the criteria—for example, specific XBRL taxonomy, such as the "XBRL U.S. Consumer and Industrial Taxonomy," and where applicable, the company extension taxonomy, such as "XYZ Company's extension taxonomy," and the XBRL International Technical Specifications 2.0*].

[*Signature*]

[*Date*]

Figure 12.1 Independent accountant's report on financial statements.

Source: Adapted from AICPA'sStatementson Standards for Attestation Engagements, AT § 9101.54. 2003. AICPA.

of instance documents: (1) compare the rendered instance document to the financial information, (2) trace and reconcile the instance document's tagged information to financial information, (3) test that the financial information is appropriately tagged and included in the instance document, (4) test for consistency of tagging to ensure that the financial information from one year to another is tagged consistently, and (5) test that the entity extension or custom taxonomy is in compliance with the XBRL International Technical Specification.[22] The practitioner should obtain a written assertion from management regarding the accuracy and reliability of the rendered instance document. An example of such a written assertion is as follows:

> *We [client's management] assert that the accompanying XBRL Instance Document accounting reflects the data presented in the financial statements of XYZ Company as of December 31, 20XX and for the year then ended in conformity with [identified criteria, for example, XBRL U.S. Consumer and Industrial Taxonomy, the XBRL International Technical Specifications].*

The AICPA also provides an example of reporting on the subject matter of the instance document. Figure 12.1 provides an example of such a report adapted from AT § 9101.54 of the AICPA's *Statements on Standards for Attestation Engagements*, and Figure 12.2 presents reporting on the related management assertions.

We have examined management's assertion that [*identify the assertion—for example, the accompanying XBRL Instance Document accurately reflects the data presented in the financial statements of XYZ Company as of December 31, 20XX, and for the year then ended in conformity with (identify the criteria—for example, specific XBRL taxonomy, such as the "XBRL U.S. Consumer and Industrial Taxonomy," and where applicable, the company extension taxonomy, such as "XYZ Company's extension taxonomy," and the XBRL International Technical Specifications 2.0)*]. XYZ Company's management is responsible for the assertion]. Our responsibility is to express an opinion on the assertion based on our examination.

We have also audited, in accordance with auditing standards generally accepted in the United States of America, the financial statements of XYZ Company as of December 31, 20XX, and for the year then ended, and in our report dated [*Month*] XX, 20XX, we expressed an unqualified opinion on those financial statements.

Our examination was conducted in accordance with attestation standards established by the American Institute of Certified Public Accountants and, accordingly, included examining, on a test basis, evidence supporting the XBRL Instance Document and performing such other procedures as we considered necessary in the circumstances. We believe that our examination provides a reasonable basis for our opinion.

In our opinion, management's assertion referred to above is fairly stated, in all material respects, in conformity with [*identify the criteria—for example, specific XBRL taxonomy, such as the "XBRL U.S. Consumer and Industrial Taxonomy," and where applicable, the company extension taxonomy, such as "XYZ Company's extension taxonomy," and the XBRL International Technical Specifications 2.0*].

[*Signature*]

[*Date*]

[Issue Date: September 2003.]

Figure 12.2 Independent accountant's report on management's assertions.

Source: Adapted from AICPA'sStatementson Standards for Attestation Engagements, AT § 9101.54. 2003. AICPA.

Technology Solutions

In the post-SOX era, companies, their accountants, and their auditors are searching for any technology solutions or tools to assist them in complying with provisions of SOX. Among the recently developed technology solutions is business assurance analytics software designed by ACL Services Ltd. to alert company executives when questionable transactions occur. Analytics software continuously monitors business activities, drawing attention to any suspicious or fraudulent activities.

Several solutions have been suggested or developed to improve and simplify the use of XBRL in business and financial reporting. First, a PDF document containing embedded XBRL for U.S. GAAP or any other taxonomy enables organizations to create a single document that makes compliance and regulatory filing possible through system-to-system filings simultaneously. Second, the Microsoft Office tool for XBRL is now available to be used with Microsoft Office Professional Edition 2003,[23] particularly Word 2003 and Excel 2003, to create and analyze documents in XBRL format.

Third, Financial Reporting and Auditing Agent with New Knowledge (FRAANK) has been developed to provide integrated and automated access to financial information available on the Internet.[24] FRAANK enables organizations to (1) extract accounting numbers from natural-text financial statements available from the SEC EDGAR system; (2) develop an understanding of financial information and accounting numbers by matching the line item labels to synonyms of tags in an XBRL taxonomy; (3) convert the consolidated financial statements, including the balance sheet, income statement, and statement of cash flows, into XBRL-tagged format; and (4) integrate the accounting numbers with other financial information publicly available on the Internet, including stock quotes and analysts' earnings forecasts.

SUMMARY

Technological advances have leveled the playing field by enabling corporations, organizations, and individuals worldwide to conduct their business electronically using the Internet. The ever-increasing use of e-commerce encourages (1) companies to use electronic financial reporting such as XBRL to produce and disseminate financial reports, and (2) independent auditors to employ continuous auditing methodologies in conducting audits. XBRL is a business reporting language that enables financial information to be readily exchanged within and among organizations and on the Internet. Financial statements are tagged, which allows them to be processed automatically in different platforms, by different users, for different purposes. XBRL is currently administered by XBRL International, a not-for-profit consortium of about 450 high-profile companies, governmental agencies, and organizations worldwide. The perceived benefits of XBRL are (1) financial information is entered once and can be used for a variety of purposes, reducing the potential for data entry errors and saving time; and (2) financial information can be accessed easily and used over the Internet, enabling investors and analysts to make more timely decisions. Potential XBRL costs are associated with the development of XBRL software, taxonomies, education, and training to use specific software and taxonomies.

The key points of this chapter are

- IT can play an important role in corporate governance as a tool to improve the efficiency and effectiveness of corporate governance. IT is an essential component of corporate governance as a means of delivering timely and accurate information for planning, monitoring, and reporting purposes.

- The cybercompany model presented in this chapter is characterized by (1) electronic communication with shareholders, (2) e-commerce, (3) electronic financial reporting, and (4) electronic continuous auditing.

- E-commerce has become an integral component of business strategies and has altered the way organizations conduct their daily operations. The business framework has transformed from "brick-and-mortar" to a "brick-and-click" infrastructure.

- XBRL enables business reporting information to be transferred automatically between different computer platforms and applications. XBRL allows the selection, analysis, storage, and exchange of tagged data that can be automatically displayed in various formats.

- The SEC XBRL program, as of now, is a voluntary program giving opportunities to public companies to participate in the program and start, as well as stop, their participation as they desire. The SEC strongly encourages companies to participate in the voluntary filing program and submit XBRL documents on EDGAR.

- XBRL-GL is expected to provide the following advantages: reporting independence, system independence, consolidation, and flexibility.

- Continuous auditing can offer the following benefits:
  - Reduction of the cost of an audit engagement by enabling auditors to test a larger sample of client's transactions
  - Reduction of the amount of audit resources needed to manually perform tests of controls and substantive tests
  - Increase in the quality of financial statement audits
  - Specification of transaction selection criteria to choose transactions or transaction cycles and perform integrated audits

KEY TERMS

chief information officer (CIO)	Electronic Data Gathering, Analysis, and Retrieval (EDGAR)	Financial Reporting and Auditing Agent with New Knowledge (FRAANK)
continuous auditing	eXtensible Business Reporting Language (XBRL)	information infrastructure
cybercompany model		reporting independence
digital economy	eXtensible Markup Language (XML)	system independence
e-commerce		taxonomy

REVIEW QUESTIONS

1. How does IT serve as a benefit and tool for the overall objectives of corporate governance?

2. How do public companies benefit from electronic communication? How do shareholders benefit from electronic communication?

3. What is e-commerce? What are the different e-commerce strategies?

4. What is information infrastructure? Explain how it is influenced by the board of directors and top management.

5. What are XBRL taxonomies and what role do they play in the promotion and application of the XBRL format for financial reporting?

6. Explain the function of the XBRL.

7. What are the intended purposes of XBRL?

8. What are the purposes of the XBRL-GL technology?

9. What are the advantages of XBRL-GL?

10. What is continuous auditing? Explain the benefits of continuous auditing.

11. What is an XBRL instance document?

DISCUSSION QUESTIONS

1. Discuss the impact that the Internet, globalization, and regulations are having on corporate governance reforms.

2. How have modern video conferencing and other methods of telecommunications impacted the corporate governance of public companies?

3. Research current business literature or the Internet for examples of the six e-commerce strategies.

4. "The business framework has transformed from 'brick-and-mortar' to a 'brick-and-click' infrastructure." Compare this statement with your views and cite some examples.

5. Discuss the future of financial reporting and the emergence of XBRL format financial reports.

6. Describe the need for the use of continuous auditing of online and real-time financial reports.

NOTES

1. PricewaterhouseCoopers. 2006, October 10. Trendsetter Barometer: Security Applications, Wireless Networks and Faster Data Transactions Are Hottest Areas of IT Development for Next Three Years. Available at: www.barometersurveys.com/production/barsurv.nsf/89343582e94adb6185256b84006c8ffe/10ed4733b6409b2d85257 20200559a27?OpenDocument.

2. U UK Department of Trade and Industry. 2005, March. Company Law Reform. Available at: www.berr.gov.uk/files/file13958.pdf.

3. U.S. Securities and Exchange Commission (SEC). 2006, September 25. SEC to Rebuild Public Disclosure System to Make It Interactive. Press Release. Available at: www.sec.gov/news/press/2006/2006-158.htm.

4. Rezaee, Z. 2002. Fraud in a digital environment. In: *Financial Statement Fraud: Prevention and Detection.* John Wiley & Sons, New York, pp. 275–301.

5. Ernst & Young. 2007, May. From Compliance to Competitive Edge: New Thinking on Internal Control. Available at: www.ey.com/Global/assets.nsf/International/AABS_InternalControl2007/$file/InternalControlsSurvey 2007_online.pdf.

6. PricewaterhouseCoopers. 2005. Technology Executive Connections: Volume 1: Embracing Change in the Technology Industries. Available at: www.pwc.com/extweb/pwcpublications.nsf/docid/F5DBAFA7B3F4501D85257 0830007AD84/$FILE/EmbracingChange.pdf.

7. PricewaterhouseCoopers. 2004. XBRL: Improving Business Reporting Through Standardization. Available at: www.pwc.com/techforecast/pdfs/XBRL_web_X.pdf.

8. XBRL International Web site. Available at: www.xbrl.org.

9. Ibid.

10. Organizations interested in the emerging developments of XBRL taxonomies, tools, and solutions should visit the XBRL Web site at www.xbrl.org.

11. U.S. Securities and Exchange Commission (SEC). n.d. Comments on Proposed Rule: XBRL Voluntary Financial Reporting Program on the Edgar System. Available at: www.sec.gov/rules/proposed/s73504.shtml.

12. U.S. Securities and Exchange Commission (SEC). 2005, February 3. XBRL Voluntary Financial Reporting Program on the EDGAR System. Available at: www.sec.gov/rules/final/33-8529.htm.

13. AccountingWeb.com. 2005, September 1. A Closer Look at the First Mandatory E-Filing System Using XBRL. Available at: www.xbrlspy.org/XBRL_A_Closer_Look.

14. See note 7 above.

15. AccountingWeb.com. 2005, September 2. XBRL GL: More than Reporting. Available at: www.xbrlspy.org/xbrl_gl_more_than_reporting.

16. PricewaterhouseCoopers. 2005. Predicting the Un-Predictable: Protecting Utilities against Fraud, Reputation & Misconduct Risk. Available at: www.pwc.com/extweb/challenges.nsf/docid/f6d685397da561d3802571550031332a/$file/utilities_predicting_unpredictable.pdf.

17. Stantial, J. 2007, June. ROI on XBRL. *Journal of Accountancy Online*. AICPA. Available at: www.cpa2biz.com/News/Journal+of+Accountancy/2007/June+2007/XBRL.htm.

18. Rezaee, Z., A. Sharbatoghlic, R. Elam, and P. L. McMickle. 2002. Continuous Auditing: Building Automated Auditing Capability. *Auditing: A Journal of Practice and Theory* 21(1):147, 163.

19. PricewaterhouseCoopers. 2006. 2006 State of the Internal Audit Profession Study: Continuous Auditing Gains Momentum. Available at: www.pwc.com/extweb/pwcpublications.nsf/docid/1981a92e13dee3cf8525718b006de802.

20. Public Company Oversight Accounting Board (PCAOB). 2005, May 25. Staff Questions and Answers: Attest Engagements Regarding XBRL Financial Information Furnished under the XBRL Voluntary Financial Reporting Program on the EDGAR System. Available at: pcaobus.org/Standards/Staff_Questions_and_Answers/2005/05-25%20.pdf.

21. American Institute of Certified Public Accountants (AICPA). 2003. Attest Engagements: Attest Engagements Interpretations of Section 101, Interpretation No. 5. Attest Engagements on Financial Information Included in XBRL Instance Documents. AT Section 9101. AICPA, New York.

22. American Institute of Certified Public Accountants (AICPA). 2004. Attest Engagements on Financial Information Included in XBRL Instance Documents. Statements on Standards for Attestation Engagements. AT § 9101.47.

23. Microsoft Office Online. n.d. Improving Financial Analysis and Reporting Using XBRL and the Microsoft Office System. Available at: www.microsoft.com/office/solutions/xbrl/default.mspx.

24. Bovee, M., A. Kogan, K. Nelson, R. P. Srivastava, and M. A. Versarhelyi. 2005. Financial Reporting and Auditing Agent with Net Knowledge (FRAANK) and Extensible Business Reporting Language (XBRL). *Journal of Information Systems* 19(1):1–18.

Chapter 13

Corporate Governance in Private and Not-for-Profit Organizations

INTRODUCTION

Not-for-profit organizations (NPOs) are usually established to achieve philanthropic purposes rather than maximize the wealth of their stakeholders. The emerging corporate governance reforms discussed in the previous chapters are normally aimed at improving corporate governance of for-profit organizations (FPOs), particularly public companies. However, private companies and NPOs such as government entities, health care organizations, colleges and universities, and charitable organizations have been under scrutiny for their governance. In the context of corporate governance and accountability, NPOs have the same stewardship responsibilities as business corporations. NPOs have a fundamental difference with business corporations with respect to their relationship with their stakeholders in that NPOs receive grants, which are funds from their constituencies, to provide services to the community. This chapter discusses corporate governance in private companies, state and local government entities, health care, colleges and universities, and other NPOs.

Primary Objectives

The primary objectives of this chapter are to

- Discuss the purpose and roles of NPOs.
- Evaluate SOX and its potential application to private companies and NPOs.
- Present the corporate governance principles, mechanisms, and functions found in public companies in a comparable structure for use in private companies and NPOs.
- Elaborate on the duties of the audit committee of NPOs.
- Reiterate the importance of an effective internal control structure for entities of all types and sizes.

TYPES OF NPOs

There are a variety of NPOs created for philanthropic purposes.

State and Local Governments

State and local governments have received more attention in the era of increased security on financial reporting. Like their counterparts in public companies, state and local governmental entities are improving their stewardship and the effectiveness of their governance and financial reporting oversight functions.

Health Care Organizations

The emerging corporate governance reforms are affecting the formation, structure, role, accountability, and responsibility of health care organizations. The improved oversight functions of health care are in the areas of stewardship, managerial and financial reporting, and risk assessment functions.

Colleges and Universities

Institutions of higher education have evolved from first being funded by the state government, then being supported by the state, and now being only assisted by the state. This means that the majority of colleges and universities are generating a greater portion of their annual budget through tuition and fundraising. In this era of an increasingly self-supporting environment, the stewardship of the board of trustees, or its equivalent, becomes more important to improving governance. Academic research shows that colleges and universities in the United States are experiencing substantial demands for stronger stewardship and accountability that could be achieved through the use of vigilant audit committees.[1]

Charitable Organizations

Recent financial and ethical scandals of charitable organizations underscore the important role that organized governance can play to increase stewardship and improve the managerial function, financial reporting, and ethical oversight functions.

PURPOSE AND ROLE OF NPOs

The primary purpose of NPOs is to serve the public rather than earn profit. Characteristics of NPOs are (1) they do not attempt to make a profit and are often exempt from income taxes; (2) they are owned collectively by their constituents, where ownership is not evidenced by equity shares that can be sold or traded; and (3) their policy and operating decisions are normally made by majority vote of an elected or appointed governing body. However, there are some similarities and differences between FPOs and NPOs. Similarities between NPOs and FPOs are

1. Both are integral parts of the same economic system and use financial, capital, and human resources to achieve their objectives.

2. Both obtain and convert scarce resources into goods and services.

3. Both are required to have a reliable accounting system and effective internal control system.

Differences are

1. Organization objectives. FPOs seek to create shareholder value, whereas NPOs seek to expend their financial resources for the benefit of their constituencies.

2. Evaluating performances and operating results. FPOs are typically evaluated based on their sustainable earnings quality and quantity. In an NPO, the budget authorizes and limits the amount that may be expended for specified purposes.

3. The SEC regulates public companies to protect investors and the capital markets. The IRS regulates NPOs for compliance with laws regarding tax exemption in order to protect constituencies.

Governance of NPOs is very crucial in managing and monitoring their activities and balancing their budgets. NPOs receive their budgets through grants, contributions from their stakeholders, or fees or membership dues charged for their services or memberships. Thus, NPOs' activities for generating funds are similar to profit-oriented business firms' activities for generating revenues. Section 501(c) of the IRS code defines tax-exempt organizations as those that are operated for philanthropic purposes. The organization must serve the public good and not benefit a private shareholder or individual. The organization cannot be a lobbying organization attempting to influence legislation by propaganda or otherwise, or an organization participating in a political campaign.[2] NPOs that want to obtain federal tax-exempt status file the request with the IRS and, on approval, receive the exemption. Tax-exempt organizations can be subject to tax on revenue generated from engagement in a trade or business unrelated to their philanthropic purposes. Tax-exempt organizations must file an annual return with the IRS to maintain their tax-exempt status. Donations to tax-exempt organizations classified by the IRS as a 501(c) entity are tax deductible by donors.

The Panel on the Nonprofit Sector was organized, in 2005, to demonstrate the role of charitable organizations in American life and strengthen NPOs' accountability, transparency, and governance.[3] The panel developed eight principles regarding the role of charitable organizations, the responsibilities of the charitable community, and the need for balanced government oversight. The panel's suggested principles regarding the charitable sector are (1) a vibrant charitable community is vital for a strong America; (2) the sector's effectiveness depends on its independence; (3) the sector's success depends on its integrity and credibility; (4) comprehensive and accurate information must be available to the public; (5) a viable system of self-regulation and education is needed; (6) government should ensure effective enforcement of the law; (7) government regulation should deter abuse without discouraging legitimate charitable activities; and (8) compliance with applicable laws and high standards of ethical conduct should be required and commensurate with the size, scale, and resources of the organization.

The panel made recommendations calling for improvement within the nonprofit sector, more effective oversight, and changes in the law. The panel's recommendations are (1) effective oversight requires vigorous enforcement of federal and state law; (2) annual information returns filed to the IRS (Forms 990, 990-EZ, and 990-PF) should be improved; (3) Congress should implement a new periodic review system to verify that charitable organizations continue to meet the qualifications for tax exemption; (4) Congress should require charitable organizations with annual revenues of between $250,000 and $1 million to have annual financial statement audits and those with more than $1 million to have their financial statements reviewed quarterly and audited annually by independent auditors; (5) charitable organizations should provide more detailed information about their operations and performance to the public through annual reports, a Web site, or other means; (6) regulations governing donor-advised funds should be strengthened to ensure that donors and related parties do not receive inappropriate benefits from those funds; (7) every supporting organization should be required to reveal on its Form 990, whether it is operating as a type I, II, or III supporting organization, with particular limitations for activities of type II organizations; (8) tax-exempt organizations are subject to the same requirements as taxable entities with regard to reporting their participation in potentially abusive "listed" or other "reportable" tax shelter transactions, with applicable penalties for engaging in aggressive tax shelters; (9) Congress should strengthen the rules for the appraisals taxpayers can use to substantiate deductions claimed or property donated to charitable organizations and for the violation of these rules; (10) charitable organizations should be discouraged from providing compensation to their board members, and when such compensation is provided, the amount, reason, and the method of determination should be fully disclosed; (11) charitable organizations should be required to disclose clearly the compensation paid to their CEO, other "disqualified persons" as determined by the IRS, and the five highest-compensated employees; (12) charitable organizations should establish and enforce appropriate travel expense policies to pay for or reimburse travel expenses of board members, officers, employees, consultants, volunteers, or others traveling to conduct the business of the organization; (13) charitable organizations should have a minimum of three members on its governing board to be qualified as a 501(c)(3) tax-exempt organization, and at least one-third of the governing board members should be independent to qualify as a public charity rather than a private foundation; (14) charitable organizations should include individuals with some financial literacy on their boards of directors, and those whose financial statements are audited should consider establishing a separate audit committee of the board; and (15) charitable organizations should adopt and enforce a conflict of interest policy, and the IRS should require them to disclose on their Form 990 series whether they have such a policy.

PUBLIC TRUST IN NPOs

NPOs, particularly charities, have been under extensive scrutiny regarding their governance, financial integrity, stewardship of resources, and appropriateness of their compensation schemes. The IRS has also increased its efforts in reviewing about four hundred foundations regarding their tax-exempt status and compensation decisions. Some states such as California now require charities reporting more than $2 million in revenue to have audit committees and their financial reports audited.[4] California's Nonprofit Integrity Act of 2004 was effective as of January 1, 2005, and applies to charities, commercial fundraisers, fundraising counsels, unincorporated associations, and trusts. This act requires that (1) charitable organizations register and file their Articles of Incorporation with the Attorney General's Registry of Charitable Trust within 30 days; (2) charities with gross revenues of $2 million or more have their financial statements audited by independent auditors; (3) charities with gross revenues of $2 million or more establish and maintain an audit committee whose members are not members of the governing board; (4) executive compensation be reviewed and approved by charities' governing boards or authorized board committee; (5) commercial fundraisers notify the Attorney General before starting a solicitation campaign; (6) commercial fundraisers have written contracts with the charitable organizations for whom they work; (7) charitable organizations void contracts with unregistered commercial fundraisers; (8) fundraising counsel notify the Attorney General before starting a solicitation campaign; (9) fundraising counsel have written contracts with charitable organizations; (10) charitable organizations cancel contracts with commercial fundraisers; (11) charitable organizations and commercial fundraisers for charitable purposes have specific obligations (e.g., exercise control over fundraising, do not misrepresent when fundraising); (12) charitable organizations and commercial fundraisers for charitable purposes are prohibited from engaging in misrepresentation and certain other acts (e.g., unfair, deceptive, fraudulent conduct) when soliciting donations; and (13) commercial fundraisers keep records of solicitation campaigns for at least ten years. It is expected that other states will follow suit and make such requirements for NPOs. Lawmakers are now paying more attention to NPOs because Iowa Senator Charles E. Grassley suggested more accountability and public disclosure from NPOs.[5]

A study shows that NPOs are practicing good governance and focusing on their accountability in the post-SOX era.[6] For example, a strong majority of 247 surveyed boards (1) are highly or significantly involved in the major strategic oversight functions; (2) set organizational missions and objectives; (3) are involved in the approval of significant monetary functions, including organizational budgets and finances; (4) review accounting and auditing standards and practices; (5) engage in establishing executive compensation; (6) are involved in setting ethical standards; and (7) have undergone an independent audit within the past two years and distributed their financial reports to the boards.

Other survey studies indicate some skepticism among donors and the public at large regarding governance and the accountability of large national charitable organizations.[7,8] These surveys suggest that (1) there is some evidence of scandal and waste in charitable organizations; (2) there are concerns that charitable organizations are becoming too business-like and not focusing on passion and commitment to their mission; (3) the majority (about 60 percent) of surveyed participants who regularly donate to charity had a great deal or some confidence in charities, whereas about half expressed concern about waste; (4) public confidence in charities depends on whether they have done a good job helping people and allocating money; (5) timely, accurate, and accessible financial disclosures improve public confidence in charitable organizations; (6) charitable organizations should adopt standards for best governance practices to prevent possible increases in federal regulation of NPOs; (7) honest and credible communication plays an important role in improving public confidence in NPOs; and (8) rebuilding public confidence in charitable organizations requires sustained investment in strengthening their capability to achieve measurable impacts toward their mission.

To regain public confidence, NPOs should improve their governance by demonstrating integrity, honesty, ethics, and transparency. William H. Donaldson, then the chairman of the SEC, in his remarks before the Annual Conference of Independent Sector in November 2004, stated that the lack of public confidence in NPOs is very serious. Donaldson suggests some type of self-regulation for NPOs by stating that "the goal should be not simply to avoid unwanted legislation, but rather to advance a regime of self-regulation that produces better results than any congressional proposal or regulatory overseer can achieve. The ultimate goal of a self-regulatory approach should be for leaders throughout the nonprofit sector to mobilize in support of improved governance standards, greater accountability, and a higher ethical code."[9] To regain public trust, NPOs should educate their board about the importance of effective corporate governance (e.g., financial expertise for audit committee members) and establish a set of best practices of corporate governance as a minimum eligibility requirement for tax exemption.

It is expected that the IRS will start distinguishing between good governance and eligibility for tax exemption (e.g., conflict of interest policy). Persistence of ineffective governance and lack of self-policing and self-regulatory approach may encourage enactment of federal regulations similar to SOX for NPOs.

GOVERNANCE OF NPOs

In the business environment, the board of directors represents the owners (shareholders) of the company. NPOs are typically owned by their members (e.g., trade associations, professional societies), their communities (e.g., social services, education, hospitals), or their constituencies (e.g., state, local governments). Thus, the board of directors or its equivalent, the board of trustees, represents its members, communities, or constituencies in an NPO. Regardless of the type of NPOs and the nature of their ownership, the board has total authority over the organization, is directly responsible for its activities, is ultimately accountable to its ownership, and delegates its authority to others to carry out the organization's activities. In the business sector, the CEO manages the company, whereas in NPOs the CEO may be called executive director, president, general manager, superintendent, or director-general. The board grants its authority to the CEO. Emerging corporate reforms, rules, and regulations are having significant implications for the governance and accountability of NPOs such as higher education institutions, charities, and churches. Many provisions of SOX are applicable to NPOs, even though these provisions were intended for public companies.

Governance of Institutions of Higher Education

Several governance models for institutions of higher education are suggested, including bureaucratic, collegial, cultural, and political models.[10,11] Institutions of higher education may use any one model or a combination of models relevant to their mission, size, history, and unique needs. The bureaucratic model focuses on formal structures rather than informal processes and is driven by adherence to regulations. The collegial model emphasizes the satisfaction of its members and is shaped by consensus interaction and communication within the group. The cultural model is determined by cultural symbols that give identity to the organization. The political model is shaped based on influence and conflict resolution by encouraging the involvement of differing groups in the decision-making process. The factors that determine which model(s) is more appropriate depends on the type of institution, its culture, goals, resources, professional relationships, personnel structure, administrative philosophy, visions, types (public vs. private), and functional areas.

Some scholars suggest that institutions of higher education are unique organizations and do not share the same characteristics as corporations in the sense that their governance is usually shared by their members, including students, faculty, and administration.[12] Others, however, argued that the administrative functions of such institutions are similar to business functions, and thus, corporate governance best practices of corporations can be adapted, revised, and used in colleges and universities.[13] The four distinct cultures of the academy that shape its governance infrastructure are collegial, managerial, developmental, and negotiating.[14] The collegial culture is shaped by different disciplines presented by the faculty. The managerial culture focuses on the organization's missions and goals, along with fiscal responsibility and accountability for achievements of established goals. The developmental culture emphasizes the development of programs that promote personal and professional achievements for all members of the university. The negotiating culture focuses on confrontation and fair bargaining among faculty administration and staff for the fair and equal distribution of resources and benefits. These cultures determine the type of governance and leadership at colleges and universities.

Ethics in Institutions of Higher Education

Financial scandals of the twenty-first century have renewed interest in business ethics and academic programs because investors are now more educated about the impacts of unethical behavior and business schools realize the importance of training ethical business leaders. Several incidents of ethical violations and cheating have been reported in highly rated business schools where future business leaders are trained (e.g., Duke, Texas A&M). These and other cases call for business schools to (1) adopt *zero tolerance* ethics and honor codes, (2) establish appropriate policies and procedures to implement honor codes, (3) properly communicate the honor code and related policies to students, (4) require business students to certify their understanding of honor codes, and (5) establish a due diligence process for the strict enforcement of honor codes.

The honor code should describe (1) the purpose of the code in creating a culture of integrity, fairness, honesty, respect for others, and trustworthiness; (2) policies in determining the scope of the honor code measures taken to assure the achievement of its objectives and details of its violations, including lying, cheating, and stealing; (3) enforcement procedures and actions determining due judicial process and penalties; and (4) an appeal process. Academic integrity and ethical conduct by students and faculty are important to sustainable well-being and reputation. This integrity can be achieved when (1) there is an effective and fairly enforceable academic honor code; (2) faculty are willing to take proper actions against suspected cheaters; (3) adequate research is conducted to identify factors that affect academic integrity, including fundamental ethical values; and (4) ethics is integrated into the business curriculum, and pedagogies are developed to teach and encourage adherence to ethical values and conduct.

Reactions to student cheating at Duke, Texas A&M, and other reputable universities can be threefold. First, business students justify their cheating by rationalizing their actions in light of financial scandals and political unethical behavior in our intensively competitive workplace environment, which provides incentives and opportunities for cheaters to get ahead as a justifiable means of succeeding. Second, technological advances (wireless Internet access in classrooms, cell phones, online term paper mills) create more opportunities for cheating, and thus, carelessness on the part of professors giving unmonitored take-home exams and unsupervised exams contributes to student cheating. Third, lack of understanding of the university honor codes and ineffective enforcement of such codes can also contribute to student cheating. Business schools should provide ethical education and training for students and require them to behave ethically and be academically honest. Ethical training is important in setting a tone for ethical behavior in the workplace because studies show students who engaged in academic dishonesty in college were more likely to commit unethical acts in the workplace environment.

The evidence of cheating in colleges and universities is indicated in a survey showing (1) more than 21 percent of undergraduates engage in cheating; (2) about 33 percent of undergraduate students obtained unauthorized information prior to an exam; (3) undergraduate business majors were more engaged in acts of academic dishonesty than nonbusiness majors; (4) about 40 percent of undergraduates committed some form of plagiarism (e.g., using materials without attribution); and (5) students in colleges and universities with honor codes committed fewer acts of academic dishonesty.[15] Corporate governance reforms, including SOX, provide stiff penalties for corporate executives engaging in white-collar crime. Perhaps it is about time that colleges and universities impose strong penalties for students who engage in academic dishonesty.

Applicability of Corporate Governance Reforms to Private Companies and NPOs

Congress, in passing SOX, intended to bring more accountability to the financial reporting process and corporate governance of public companies. However, private companies are experiencing the impacts of SOX in the following areas of their business practices, listed in order of importance: (1) improving control documentation and testing, (2) refining corporate governance policies and procedures, (3) strengthening the code of business conduct/ethics, (4) adopting public company best practices, (5) establishing and updating whistleblower programs and policies, (6) creating an independent audit committee, and (7) establishing an independent and vigilant board of directors. Surveyed companies that did not believe that the benefits of SOX compliance outweigh its compliance costs still will adopt some of its provisions (1) to achieve a best business practice, (2) to address potential or future problems, (3) to respond to recommendations of outside constituents, (4) to consider the future sale of the business to another company, (5) to resolve present business problems, and (6) to consider going public (IPO).[16]

Some private companies will eventually enter the capital markets through either IPOs or as candidates for public company acquisition, yet others may have dispersed share-owners. These private companies can benefit tremendously from best practices of SOX, and the extent of their compliance with SOX requirements can have substantial impact on their valuation or readiness to enter the public markets. For private companies ready to enter the capital markets, compliance with Section 404 of SOX on internal control is mandatory. However, for private companies that are considering becoming IPO candidates, early establishment of Section 404 readiness is vital. This is essential particularly for preacquisition companies in the sense that if their internal control is ineffective, it would cause significant problems for potential acquisitions. Acquiring companies are typically unwilling to risk an adverse opinion on their ICFR caused by an acquired company's material weaknesses in its internal controls. Other provisions of SOX that can be beneficial to private companies are the requirement that the majority of directors are independent, the establishment of an audit committee composed of independent directors, and the adoption of codes of business conduct and ethics.

Many NPOs are adopting some of the provisions of SOX to improve their corporate governance, financial reporting, internal control, and audit activities, even though they are not required to comply. Provisions of SOX that would be appropriate for NPOs are (1) establishing an audit committee composed solely of independent directors, (2) prohibiting the shredding of records, (3) establishing whistleblower programs, and (4) establishing codes of ethical conduct.[17] Specifically, provisions of SOX that are more applicable to private companies and even NPOs are requirements for

1. *More vigilant and independent directors.* Private companies and NPOs can greatly benefit from effective corporate governance. More vigilant and independent directors on the board of trustees can improve board effectiveness.

2. *Audit committees.* The audit committees of public companies in the post-SOX era are an important component of corporate governance in overseeing financial reporting, internal control, risk management, and audit activities. It is expected that private companies and NPOs will establish or revise their audit committee charter by adopting requirements of SOX regarding the independence and financial expertise of audit committees.

3. *Improvements in the financial reporting process.* Private companies and NPOs can significantly benefit from the provisions of SOX requiring more transparent and timely financial reports in the areas of contingent liabilities and prevention of fraudulent financial activities.

4. *Risk management and internal controls.* Risk management assessment and internal controls are vital to the sustainable success of private companies and NPOs. Provisions of SOX, SEC rules, and PCAOB standards pertaining to ICFR are applicable and beneficial to both private companies and NPOs.

5. *Audit quality.* Recent corporate governance reforms are intended to improve audit quality and strengthen the audit independence of public companies. The requirements for an integrated audit approach of audits of both internal controls and financial

statements are well suited to private companies and NPOs. More independent and better quality audits are also essential to the integrity, relevance, and transparency of financial reports.

6. *Codes of conduct.* Public companies are required to establish codes of conduct and business ethics for their employees in general and financial officers in particular. There is no doubt that every organization, whether private, public, or NPO, would benefit from promoting ethical conduct.

7. *Whistleblower programs.* Public companies are now required to establish proper whistleblower programs to facilitate employees voicing their concerns and reporting corporate wrongdoing to authorities without the risk of retaliation or losing their job.

8. *Prohibition of document destruction.* Sections 802 and 1102 of SOX make it illegal to knowingly alter, destroy, conceal, mutilate, cover up, or falsify any record, document, or other object to impair the integrity or availability for use in official proceedings. PCAOB auditing standards also require retention of audit evidence for at least seven years.

Congress intended SOX for public companies; however, many nonprofit advisors and trade groups urged voluntary compliance with best practices of SOX. Examples include

1. Independent Sector and Board Source, in a 2003 report, called SOX "a wake-up call for the entire nonprofit community" and asked for voluntary compliance with best practices of SOX, even if not required by law.

2. The National Association of College and University Business Officers (NACUBO) issued its 2003 advisory recommendation that colleges and universities look to SOX as a framework.

3. The Coordinating Committee on Nonprofit Governance of the ABA published a *Guide on Nonprofit Corporate Governance in the Wake of SOX.*

4. In 2003, New York Attorney General Eliot Spitzer released a draft to apply certain provisions of SOX to New York charities.

5. In 2004, California passed the Nonprofit Integrity Act, requiring audits and audit committees for charities with gross revenues of more than $2 million.

6. The Pension Protection Act of 2006 requires some charitable reforms, including addressing matters of corporate governance.

7. The Senate Finance Committee White Paper, in 2004, addressed corporate governance issues of NPOs, including the CEO signing Form 990, which is similar to executive certification of financial statements and internal controls for public companies under Sections 302 and 404.

A 2004 survey conducted by Foley & Lardner indicates that more than 40 percent of the private and nonprofit surveyed organizations have voluntarily adopted the following provisions of SOX: (1) executive certifications of financial statements, particularly CEO/CFO financial statement attestation; (2) whistleblower initiatives; (3) board approval of nonaudit services provided by external auditors; and (4) adoption of corporate governance policy guidelines.[18]

GOVERNANCE STRUCTURE OF NPOs

Previous chapters presented various components of corporate governance of public companies, including principles and mechanisms. These two components of the corporate governance structure are also applicable to NPOs with some exceptions.

Governance Principles

The Society of Corporate Secretaries and Governance Professionals has issued *Organizational Governance Principles and Resources for Directors of NPOs,* which states, "Service on a nonprofit board is not merely an honor . . . it entails legal obligations and an important responsibility for stewardship. . . ."[19] NPOs should make their fiscal and operational oversight an integral component of their governance by selecting directors to oversee fiscal and operational performance, recruit management to run the operation, and hire legal counsel to ensure compliance with applicable laws, regulations, and rules.

Corporate governance principles are as important and relevant to NPOs as to business firms. Specifically, some NPOs often use public funds, contributions, and grants, and are tax exempt. They must be monitored closely to ensure their budgets are spent on the intended philanthropic purposes. Thus, the principles of fairness, transparency, responsiveness, accountability, resilience, communication, and disclosure discussed in Chapter 2 for public companies are also relevant to NPOs. Governance of NPOs depends on the mission and culture of the organization and is designed to protect the organization's constituents and reputation. Recent reforms for public companies have also affected governance principles for NPOs.

Governance Mechanisms

The corporate governance mechanisms of NPOs are different from those of corporations discussed in the previous chapters. Unlike business firms, NPOs do not have the external corporate governance mechanisms of the capital markets, the market for corporate takeovers, or product market competitions. Thus, NPOs must rely primarily on internal governance mechanisms to assess performance, reward good performance, and discipline poor performance. The primary governance mechanisms of NPOs are their governing and advisory boards. The governing board is directly responsible and ultimately accountable for the organization's affairs. In a large NPO with sufficient, competent staff, the governing board provides more of an oversight function while allowing staff to assume the managerial role of making day-to-day decisions. However, in a small NPO, the governing board may perform both managerial and oversight functions.

The advisory board of an NPO typically provides advice and gives counsel rather than engages in governing the organization. The advisory board often comprises volunteers rather than elected or appointed members. For example, in a state-supported university, the governing board is usually appointed by the state at the university level, whereas the voluntary advisory board for all colleges and departments within the university (law, business, medical, engineering, and education schools) is composed of members of the community and the student body. Unlike business firms, NPOs' boards are often composed of volunteers. The volunteers serve on the board by committing their time, effort, and even money because of their dedication, beliefs, and interests for a good cause unlike their counterparts in business firms, who are largely motivated by substantial compensation. Furthermore, the boards of NPOs often do not have the resources to hire advisors and rely on the commitment, dedication, and competence of its members for giving counsel.

NPO directors or trustees must avoid conflicts of interest such as engaging in significant transactions with the NPO, serving as an attorney, or providing other services for substantial fees. Like business firms, NPOs should have an effective internal control system to ensure (1) the organization is performing efficiently within given resources and budgets; (2) the organization is achieving its program results; (3) the organization's financial reports are reliable and transparent; and (4) the organization is in compliance with applicable laws and regulations, particularly the IRS tax-exempt statutes.

For-profit entities must have their annual financial statements audited and their quarterly financial statements reviewed by an independent auditor and filed with the SEC. These audited or reviewed financial statements are used as mechanisms for accountability, whereas there are no similar mechanisms for accountability among NPOs. Instead, there is Form 990 filed by all charities that are registered with the IRS.[20] Although Form 990 provides financial information regarding assets, liabilities, revenue, and compensation of the five most highly paid employees of charitable entities, it is not subject to audit and thus is regarded as a weak accountability mechanism.

The NPO's internal control structure should also prevent and detect errors, irregularities, and fraud, particularly employee embezzlements. Fraudsters steal money even from an NPO. It is not uncommon that donated funds, grants, or contributions to an NPO are appropriated and restricted for activities for achieving the intended philanthropic purposes. Thus, the NPO's internal control system should ensure that appropriated funds are spent on the designated programs. The directors or trustees of NPOs are typically volunteers or are appointed by the sponsoring organization to oversee the organization's activities and affairs. The chairperson of the board is also selected by the sponsoring organization or directors for a limited number of terms and often the chair is rotated among the members of the board or trustees. NPOs, like business firms, organize their work through the establishment of committees. The type, structure, and membership of committees depend on the size of the organization and the size of its board of trustees. The most commonly structured committees of NPOs are governance or nominating; development or fundraising; finance, budget, or audit; and operations, programs, personnel, or executive. The organization is managed through the committee assignments. The committees often make decisions, take action, and report their activities to the board of trustees.

OVERSIGHT FUNCTION OF NPOs

NPOs are typically organized as nonprofit corporations with either a board of directors or board of trustees, or as trustees or foundations with a board of trustees. Boards of directors or trustees are regarded as governing bodies primarily responsible for the affairs of the organization. In an NPO, there are multiple constituencies or stakeholders who have interests in the organization, yet no one owns the organization in the sense of ownership by shareholders. Members of boards of directors/trustees, depending on the organization's size and activities, may provide oversight functions or, in the case of smaller organizations, engage in both oversight and managerial functions. This section examines the duties and responsibilities of boards of directors, composition of the board, qualification of its members, and board committees.[21]

Duties of the Board of Directors/Trustees

Directors and trustees of NPOs have three major fiduciary duties:

1. *Duty of obedience,* which requires directors and trustees to carry out their assigned responsibilities in accordance with the organization's rules, standards, and procedures as specified in its articles of incorporation, bylaws, and mission statements

2. *Duty of care,* which requires directors and trustees to exercise due care, diligence, and skill that an ordinary, prudent person would exercise under similar circumstances

3. *Duty of loyalty,* which requires directors and trustees to carry out their activities in pursuing the best interests of the organization by avoiding self-dealing and self-serving activities

Board Committees

The work of the board of directors or trustees is most effectively performed in committee form. The chair of each committee should present the committee's findings and recommendations to the entire board for approval and action. The following board committees are relevant to NPOs:

1. *Audit committee,* composed only of independent directors or trustees responsible for overseeing financial reporting, internal control, audit activities, and compliance with applicable regulations

2. *Executive committee,* composed of officers and committee chairs that can act on behalf of the entire board between board meetings if circumstances require

3. *Development/fundraising committee,* which organizes and oversees fundraising events and capital campaigns

4. *Finance committee,* which oversees financing and investments, including budget, tax, and investment activities

5. *Nominating committee,* which identifies the board membership needs and makes recommendations to the board about vacant board positions

6. *Program committee,* which is responsible for the organization's programs, activities, and future initiatives

7. *Personnel committee,* which develops compensation and benefit plans for the organization's paid staff

Responsibilities of the Board of Directors/Trustees

The primary responsibilities of the board of directors/trustees of NPOs are to

1. Establish the organization's mission and goals.
2. Develop strategies to achieve these goals.

3. Establish appropriate board committees (e.g., audit, development, finance, fundraising, nominating, program) to oversee the organization's activities.

4. Appoint officers and executives to run the organization.

5. Determine the compensation of executives, oversee their work, and evaluate their performance.

6. Review the organization's programs and services.

7. Oversee financial reporting, internal controls, and audit activities.

8. Oversee compliance with applicable laws, rules, and regulations, particularly tax rules.

9. Promote ethical behavior and accountability throughout the organization.

10. Ensure adequacy and effective use of resources.

11. Evaluate the board's performance.

12. Approve director/trustee compensation, if any.

13. Assess board vacancy and recruit new board members.

14. Ensure executives and staff provide the board with relevant and timely information to effectively carry out its fiduciary duties.

15. Set an appropriate "tone at the top" promoting ethical conduct throughout the organization.

16. Ensure that all board members participate in orientation and continuing education programs.

17. Establish fair whistleblowing policies to encourage employees to come forward in reporting wrongdoing without the fear of retaliation.

Attributes of Board Members

The effectiveness of the organization's board depends on the attributes, personal integrity, competence, dedication, insight, and professional qualifications of its members. Important qualities of an effective board member are

1. *Vision*: the ability to see the big picture and establish the organization's mission

2. *Leadership*: the ability and courage to set direction to achieve the organization's mission and related goals

3. *Stewardship*: the sense of accountability and integrity to pursue the organization's goals and serve the interests of the organization, its intended beneficiaries, its constituents, and the public

4. *Skill*: the knowledge and skill to provide effective oversight of the organization's operations, programs, activities, and performance

5. *Diligence*: the ability to exercise due care, dedication, and commitment to carry out oversight responsibilities in achieving the organization's goals

6. *Collegiality*: the teamwork and respect of colleagues and their views

Audit Committees of NPOs

The AICPA has developed a toolkit to improve audit committee effectiveness of NPOs, covering a wide range of governance topics, including audit committee charter, evaluation of independent auditors, and the hiring of the CAE.[22] This toolkit provides an audit committee charter matrix to assist NPOs in tailoring their audit committee charter to their own specifications and size by using best practices. Some of the most important attributes of audit committees for NPOs provided in the toolkit are (1) all members of the committee should be independent; (2) the chair of the committee should be a member of the board of directors in good standing; (3) the committee should have access to financial expertise; (4) the committee's charter should be reviewed annually; (5) the committee should meet as needed to address matters on its agenda, but not less frequently than twice a year; (6) the committee should conduct executive sessions with external auditors, internal auditors, and CFOs; (7) the committees should be authorized to hire independent auditors, counsel, or other consultants as deemed necessary; (8) the committee should review and approve the appointment, replacement, reassignment, or dismissal of the CAE or the director of the organization's internal audit function; (9) committees should appoint the independent auditors, approve their audit fees, and preapprove nonaudit services to be provided by independent auditors; (10) management policies and procedures should be reviewed by the committee; (11) committees should review with management and independent auditors the audit findings and auditors' judgments about the quality, not just acceptability, of accounting policies and practices; (12) committees should review the organization's code of conduct and ethics; (13) committees should review the organization's whistleblower policies; (14) committees should review the organization's compliance with applicable regulations; and (15) committees should annually evaluate their own performance as well as the performance of independent and internal auditors.

The AICPA has also developed a toolkit for audit committees of government organizations.[23] This toolkit is designed to provide guidance and best practices for audit committee oversight functions. The following attributes are specified in the AICPA's audit committee charter matrix for government organizations: (1) committee members should be appointed by the governing body; (2) at least one member of the committee should have financial experience; (3) the committee charter should be reviewed annually to ensure its adequacy, effectiveness, and compliance with all applicable regulations, including government auditing standards (yellow book); (4) the committee should meet at least four times per year or more as deemed necessary; (5) committees should have executive sessions with the CEO, CFO, independent auditor, internal auditor, legal counsel, and other key personnel involved in the financial reporting process; (6) committees should have authority to hire professional consultants as necessary; (7) committees should review and approve the appointment, replacement, reassignment, or dismissal of the CAE; (8) committees should oversee the appointment of the independent auditors to be engaged for external reporting; (9) when the use of a particular independent auditor is not specified by law or regulation, the committee should establish related audit fees and a regular schedule for periodically rebidding the audit contract with public accounting firms; (10) the committee should review with management the policies and procedures relevant to the use of expense accounts, public monies, and public property by management, key personnel, and public officials; (11) the committee should review with management the organization's risks and steps taken to minimize risks; (12) the committee should periodically review the audit plan, scope, and findings of both internal and external auditors; (13) the committee should inquire with management about the financial health of the organization, including financial status in relation to its adopted budget; (14) the committee should review with management and the independent auditor the effects of regulatory and accounting initiatives on the organization's financial reporting process; (15) the committee should periodically review the code of conduct to ensure its adequacy and effectiveness; (16) the committee should review the organization's whistleblower policies for the receipt, retention, and treatment of complaints received by the organization; (17) the committee should annually evaluate independent and internal auditors as well as the committee oversight effectiveness; and (18) the committee should review and approve the audit committee's agenda.

Best Practices

In the previous chapters, four sources of corporate governance were discussed for for-profit entities. These sources are corporate law, federal law, listing standards, and best practices. Except for best practices, these sources of corporate governance are not relevant to NPOs. Thus, the only source of corporate governance applicable to NPOs is best practices. The suggested corporate governance best practices for NPOs consists of the following checklist of elements for good governance[24]:

1. *Make ethical behavior central to a board's culture*. The board of directors or trustees should set a right tone at the top by establishing and enforcing an ethical code of conduct for board members, officers, staff members, and volunteers.

2. *Strengthen internal controls*. Effective internal controls can provide a vital mechanism of checks and balances to ensure that gifts and donations are properly accounted for; restricted gifts are properly administered; expenditures are properly authorized and recorded; board minutes are properly kept; and report filings of the annual application for a property tax exemption, Form 990, and other applicable regulatory reports are submitted in a timely manner.

3. *Review bylaws*. Bylaws should be revisited and revised periodically to ensure they reflect emerging corporate governance best practices, changes in the nonprofit sector, growth in the organization, and the experiences of peer groups.

4. *Use board committees*. One or more of the following board committees should be established to ensure fulfillment of a board's fiduciary duties: audit, investment, nominating, and finance.

5. *Use the Internet to inform the public*. NPOs should use the Internet to communicate efficiently with their constituencies by posting their core governing documents, filing reports, and information about their mission, governing board, staff, and volunteers.

6. *Review investment and spending policies*. NPOs should periodically assess their investment and spending policies and practices to ensure they are in compliance with their mission.

7. *Perform board training and evaluation*. NPOs should require annual evaluation of their directors and officers.

8. *Monitor compensation.* Excessive executive compensation has been a controversial issue for both FPOs and NPOs. Excessive compensation of directors, officers, and staff of NPOs can adversely affect contributions of both existing and potential donors and volunteers.

INTERNAL CONTROL IN NPOs

Mandatory internal control reporting for large public companies in the post-SOX era has been controversial and evolving. Almost five years after the passage of SOX, its Section 404 efficacy on internal controls has been addressed by (1) lawmakers (Congress) in a symbolic voting of not making Section 404 compliance optional for smaller companies; (2) regulators (SEC) by issuing its interpretive guidance intended to preserve investor protection while making management reporting on ICFR more cost effective, efficient, and scalable; and (3) standard setters (PCAOB) in issuing its AS No. 5 to encourage independent auditors to conduct cost-effective, principles-based, top-down, and risk-based approach audits of ICFR with a keen focus on expressing an opinion on only the effectiveness of ICFR. Private companies and NPOs can benefit significantly from best practices of ICFR offered by these reforms.

ICFR, operations, and compliance with applicable laws and regulations, particularly the tax-exempt status of many NPOs, are important internal governance mechanisms. Internal controls over fundraising and operations are important to ensure donations, grants, and other financial support are properly accounted for and assets are safeguarded against misappropriation. ICFR of NPOs is designed to prevent, detect, and correct misstatements to improve the reliability, integrity, and quality of financial reports. Internal controls pertaining to compliance with applicable regulations are essential in an NPO to ensure continuation of tax-exempt status.

Governance documents of NPOs consist of four major documents: two organization documents (mission statement and code of conduct) and two legal documents (charter and bylaws)[25]:

1. *Mission statement*: A mission statement defining an organization's vision, mission, and goals is regarded as the most important document, setting an appropriate tone for directors, management, and volunteers to act toward achieving the organization's objectives. A mission statement is not a legal document per se, but it is an important document describing an organization's reasons for existence and its goals.

2. *Code of conduct*: A code of conduct is currently required by law for NPOs, whereas SOX requires public companies to establish a code of conduct for their financial executives. Codes of conduct set an "appropriate tone at the top" and related guidance for directors, management, employees, and volunteers to follow in carrying out their responsibilities in dealing with sensitive information and avoiding conflicts of interest.

3. *Charter*: An organization's charter, which is also referred to as "articles of organization" or "certification of incorporation," is a legal document that should be filed with the secretary of state. This charter serves as the constitution of NPOs and a prerequisite for official status as a nonprofit organization. For nonprofit groups established as trusts, the official governance document is often called a "declaration

of trust" or the "trust instrument," which also requires periodic filings or reporting obligations.

4. *Bylaws*: Bylaws spell out the basic operating procedures and the way an organization is structured and governed. Bylaws establish rules and procedures for the selection of directors, the appointment of officers, meetings, voting, and indemnification.

SUMMARY

The corporate governance structure of private companies and NPOs plays an important role in their governance, financial reporting, and audit functions. Many private companies will eventually enter the public markets through either an IPO or acquisition by a public company. These private companies can benefit significantly from best practices of corporate governance presented in this chapter. NPOs are expected to improve their stewardship and accountability, which can be achieved through effective corporate governance. Important attributes of corporate governance of NPOs are independence of members of the board of trustees, written charters, and regular meetings of the board with management, officials, internal auditors, and external auditors. In the absence of the regulatory requirements for NPOs to reform their governance practices, they should voluntarily adopt strong governance and accountability principles, guidance, and practices to (1) improve the performance of their board by requiring board members to be independent and establish an audit committee, (2) enhance the reliability and transparency of their financial information and public disclosures, (3) manage their organization efficiently, and (4) protect the interests of their constituencies and maintain public trust.

The key points of this chapter are

- Many private companies will eventually enter the public markets, and thus, their corporate governance practices will be publicly scrutinized.

- There are a variety of NPOs for philanthropic purposes, namely, state and local governments, health care organizations, colleges and universities, and charitable organizations.

- The primary purpose of NPOs is to serve the public rather than maximize shareholder wealth through earning profits.

- The Panel on the Nonprofit Sector was organized to demonstrate the role of charitable organizations in American life and to strengthen NPOs' accountability, transparency, and governance.

- Many provisions of SOX are very applicable to private companies and NPOs, including requirements for (1) more vigilant and independent directors, (2) audit committees, (3) improvements in the financial reporting process, (4) risk management and internal controls, (5) audit quality, (6) codes of conduct, (7) whistleblower programs, and (8) prohibition of document destruction.

- Corporate governance measures are as important and relevant to NPOs as to business firms. Specifically, some NPOs often use public funds, contributions, and grants, and are tax exempt. They must be monitored closely to ensure their budgets are spent on the intended philanthropic purposes.

- Corporate governance principles of fairness, transparency, responsiveness, accountability, resilience, communication, and disclosures discussed in Chapter 2 for public companies are also relevant to private companies and NPOs.

- NPOs must rely primarily on internal governance mechanisms to assess performance, reward good performance, and discipline poor performance. The primary governance mechanisms of NPOs are their governing and advisory boards.

- Directors and trustees of NPOs have three major fiduciary duties: duty of obedience, duty of care, and duty of loyalty.

- The important qualities of an effective board member are vision, leadership, stewardship, skill, diligence, and collegiality.

- ICFR, operations, and compliance with applicable laws and regulations, particularly the tax-exempt status of many NPOs, are important internal governance mechanisms.

KEY TERMS

Articles of Incorporation
charter
development/fundraising
   committee
executive committee

finance committee
Nonprofit Integrity Act
   of 2004
not-for-profit organization
personnel committee

program committee
Society of Corporate
   Secretaries and Governance
   Professionals
whistleblower programs

REVIEW QUESTIONS

1. What are the different types of NPOs?

2. What is the primary purpose of an NPO?

3. Discuss the role of NPOs in our society.

4. What are the corporate governance principles of NPOs?

5. Explain how whistleblower programs help NPOs.

6. Explain the role of the governing board in an NPO.

7. Explain the role of internal governance in an NPO.

8. How can NPO directors or trustees avoid conflicts of interest?

9. Explain the three major fiduciary duties of the board of directors of NPOs.

10. What are the qualities of an effective board member of an NPO?

11. What are the governance documents of NPOs?

DISCUSSION QUESTIONS

1. The Panel on the Nonprofit Sector has made a long list of recommendations calling for improvement within the nonprofit sector, more effective oversight, and changes in the law. Review the recommendations and discuss the recommendations with which you agree or disagree.

2. Compare and contrast California's Nonprofit Integrity Act of 2004 to SOX.

3. Several provisions of SOX should be applicable to private companies and nonprofit organizations. Which of these do you most agree with? Why?

4. There are fifteen primary responsibilities of the board of directors/trustees of NPOs. Which of those do you believe are the most effective, efficient, and necessary?

5. "Not-for-profit organizations are created to serve the public—often individuals other than organizations." Do you agree or disagree with this statement? Support your answer with points regarding transparency, governance, and accountability of charitable organizations.

6. Discuss the skepticism among donors and the public at large with respect to the governance and accountability of NPOs, keeping in mind the following two statements:

   (a) "There are concerns that charitable organizations are becoming too business-like and not focusing on passion and commitment to their mission."

   (b) "Public confidence in charities depends on whether they have done a good job helping people and spending money."

7. Explain how the role of CEO in a company is related to role of president in an NPO. Substantiate your answer with examples.

NOTES

1. Rezaee, Z., R. C. Elmore, and J. Z. Szendi. 2000. The Relevance of Audit Committees for Colleges and Universities. *Research in Accounting Regulation* 14: 39–60.

2. Internal Revenue Service (IRS). n.d. Section 501(c) Organizations. Available at: www.irs.gov/publications/p557/ch03.html.

3. Panel on the Nonprofit Sector. 2005, June. Strengthening Transparency, Governance, and Accountability of Charitable Organizations: A Final Report to Congress and the Nonprofit Sector. Available at: www.nonprofitpanel.org/report/final/panel_final_report.pdf.

4. California Registry of Charitable Trusts. 2004, October. Nonprofit Integrity Act of 2004. Available at: ag.ca.gov/charities/publications/nonprofit_integrity_act_nov04.pdf.

5. U.S. Senate Committee on Finance. 2004, June 22. Opening Statement of Senator Chuck Grassley, Hearing on Charitable Giving. Available at: www.senate.gov/~finance/hearings/statements/062204cg.pdf.

6. Salamon, L. M., and S. L. Geller. 2005, October. Nonprofit Governance and Accountability. The John Hopkins Nonprofit Listening Post Project, Communique No. 4. Available at: www.jhu.edu/listeningpost/news/pdf/comm04.pdf.

7. Public Agenda. 2005. The Charitable Impulse: Those Who Give to Charities—and Those Who Run Them—Talk About What's Needed to Keep the Public's Trust. Available at: www.publicagenda.org/research/pdfs/charitable_impulse.pdf.

8. Light, P. C. 2005, October. Rebuilding Public Confidence in Charitable Organizations. Public Service Brief, Brief #1. NYU Robert F. Wagner Graduate School of Public Service. Available at: www.wagner.nyu.edu/news/wpb1_light.pdf.

9. Donaldson, W. H. 2004, November 8. Speech by SEC Chairman: Remarks before the Annual Conference of Independent Sector. U.S. Securities and Exchange Commission. Available at: www.sec.gov/news/speech/spch110804whd.htm.

10. Barr, M. L. 1993. Organizational and Administrative Models. In: *The Handbook of Student Affairs Administration.* Jossey-Bass, San Francisco, CA.

11. Bergquist, W. 1992. *The Four Cultures of the Academy: Insights and Strategies for Improving Leadership in Collegiate Organizations.* Jossey-Bass, San Francisco, CA.

12. Trow, M. A. 1985. Comparative Reflections on Leadership in Higher Education. *European Journal of Education* 20(2–3): 143–159.

13. McLan, E. H. 1993. Quality Improvement in Higher Education: TQM in Administrative Functions. *College and University Personnel Association* 44(3): 7–18.

14. See note 11 above.

15. Burke, J., R. S. Polimeni, and N. S. Slavin. 2007. Academic Dishonesty: A Crisis on Campus Forging Ethical Professionals Begins in the Classroom. *The CPA Journal* May.

16. PricewaterhouseCoopers. 2005, June 21. Trendsetter Barometer: 30% of Fast-Growth Private Companies Applying Sarbanes-Oxley Principles. Available at: www.barometersurveys.com/production/barsurv.nsf/vwAllNewsByDocID/834B5ECEF36C79C685257026006F2DC7.

17. Foley & Lardner LLP. 2004, May 19. What Private Companies and Non-Profits Need to Know About SOX. Report presented at Foley & Lardner's 2004 National Directors Institute (NDI), Chicago. Available at: www.foley.com/files/tbl_s31Publications/FileUpload137/2250/KnowaboutSOX.pdf.

18. Ibid.

19. Society of Corporate Secretaries & Governance Professionals, 2007. Governance for Nonprofits: From Little Leagues to Big Universities: A Summary of Organizational Governance Issues and Principles for Directors of Nonprofit Organizations. Society of Corporate Secretaries & Governance Professionals, New York. Available at: www.governanceprofessionals.org/nfp/governance-for-nonprofits-2007.pdf.

20. Internal Revenue Service (IRS). 2007. Instructions for Form 990 and Form 990-EZ: Return of Organization Exempt From Income Tax and Short Form Return of Organization Exempt From Income Tax. Available at: www.irs.gov/pub/irs-pdf/i990-ez.pdf.

21. See note 19 above.

22. The American Institute of Certified Public Accountants (AICPA). n.d. The AICPA Audit Committee Toolkit: Not-for-Profit Organizations. AICPA, New York. Available at: www.aicpa.org/Audcommctr/toolkitsnpo/homepage.htm.

23. The American Institute of Certified Public Accountants (AICPA). n.d. The AICPA Audit Committee Toolkit: Government Organizations. AICPA, New York. Available at: www.aicpa.org/Audcommctr/toolkitsgovt/homepage.htm.

24. Delucia, M. S. 2004. Sarbanes-Oxley and the Impact upon New Hampshire Nonprofit Organizations. *New Hampshire Bar Journal* 45.

25. See note 19 above.

Chapter 14

Corporate Governance in Transition

INTRODUCTION

Corporate governance has evolved from its role in reducing agency costs to maximizing shareholder wealth and now to the emerging role of creating shareholder value and protecting the interests of all stakeholders. The twenty-first century is viewed as the era of corporate governance in transition from a compliance requirement to a business imperative. The corporate governance structure in different countries is also influenced by the country's cultural, political, and historical factors as well as the legal and regulatory environment. This chapter presents both historical and global perspectives of corporate governance.

Primary Objectives

The primary objectives of this chapter are to

- Realize that corporate governance is evolving and the structure varies across countries, industries, and companies.
- Understand the history of corporate governance.
- Identify and list the cross-country factors that differentiate corporate governance structure across different countries.

- Identify the challenges of the global business and financial markets.
- Provide an overview of corporate governance worldwide.
- Recognize the initiatives taken during the past decade to improve corporate governance worldwide.
- Identify the issues to be addressed to promote convergence in global corporate governance.
- Provide an overview of corporate governance issues related to multinational corporations.

HISTORICAL PERSPECTIVE OF CORPORATE GOVERNANCE

Traditionally, discussion of the corporate governance concept was introduced in the three-book series by Berle and Means during the time of the formation of the SEC in 1933. During that period, the primary corporate governance issue centered around the requirement of public companies to establish infrastructures to address the need for a separation of powers between the company's management (agent) and its shareholders (principals).[1] According to Tricker, early American businesses were formed without limited liability provisions for shareholders, which exposed shareholders to personal bankruptcy caused by poor management performance.[2]

The creation of limited liability provisions for corporations, driven by significant growth in the number of shareholders investing in public companies in the early 1900s, caused more distance between shareholders and management in terms of location, knowledge, and access to the company's day-to-day operations. These developments demand an oversight role of the board of directors, as representative of shareholders, without much attention being given to corporate governance. Early references to the term "corporate governance" are documented in a speech by Clifford C. Nelson, the president of the American Assembly in 1978, who defined corporate governance as "a fancy term for the various influences that determine what a corporation does and does not do or should and should not do."[3] These influences at that time were commonly referred to as corporate infrastructures to separate power between management and shareholders.

The legal view of corporate governance initially appeared in the report of ALI in 1984 titled "Principles of Corporate Governance."[4] Jensen and Meckling in their well-cited paper titled, "Theory of the Firm: Managerial Behavior, Agency Costs and Ownership Structure," address the potential for struggle and conflict of interest between management and owners, and the need for maintaining equilibrium between these parties.[5] The ultimate responsibility for maintaining an appropriate balance between management and the owners rests with the board of directors to oversee managerial functions and ensure protection of investors' interests. To maintain such equilibrium, it is important to ensure the independence of the board of directors from management and to improve the board of directors' oversight function through effective corporate governance.

CORPORATE GOVERNANCE: A GLOBAL PERSPECTIVE

Corporate governance has evolved from its role in reducing agency costs that arise from the separation of ownership and control in public companies to maximize shareholder wealth to the emerging role of creating stakeholder value. Nevertheless, corporate governance structure varies across countries, industries, and even companies. Corporate governance structure can be differentiated across countries in terms of the degree of ownership and control. For example, the corporate governance structure in the United States, the UK, and Canada is characterized by widespread ownership, and thus, the fundamental conflict of interest is between decision control (management) and ownership control (widespread shareholders). In other countries such as Germany and Japan, the ownership is concentrated in the hands of a few blockholders (e.g., banks, organizations), and thus, the potential conflict of interest is between controlling shareholders and minority shareholders. The corporate governance structures in different countries are also influenced by the country's cultural and historical factors as well as the legal, regulatory, and institutional environments. All industrial countries have established corporate governance standards, guidelines, and best practices, including listing standards (United States), the TSX and Dey Commission (Canada), The King Report (South Africa), the Cadbury Commission and the Combined Code (UK), and the OECD (Europe).

Global corporate governance ineffectiveness can be traced to the 1980s and 1990s in several industrialized countries. In the United States, the financial scandals of several prominent companies such as ZZZZ Best, Webtech, Waste Management, Sunbeam, and Cendant, as well as the savings and loan debacle, raised concerns about the credibility of corporate governance. In the UK, the corporate failures of BCCI, Maxwell, and Polly Peck and Barings were reported. Canada endured the business failures of Canadian Commercial Bank and Caster Holdings and Roman Corporation. Other European countries had their share of business failures such as Credit Lyonnais, Metalgesellschaft, and Schneider. The East Asian financial crisis in 1997 also raised concerns about the effectiveness of corporate governance, the reliability of financial reports, and the credibility of audit functions in Asian countries. Corporate scandals at the turn of the twenty-first century further increased the emergence of corporate governance reforms and interest in aspects of corporate governance. Today, corporate governance stands at the forefront of organizational thought, influencing such areas as business ethics, auditing, executive compensation, and director independence. Corporate scandals worldwide have ensured that corporate governance interest and reforms are a global issue and are not confined to the borders of the United States.

Cross-country factors that differentiate corporate governance structures across different countries can be classified into (1) legal infrastructure, (2) regulatory environment, (3) information infrastructure, and (4) market infrastructure.[6] A country's legal infrastructure can significantly influence the corporate governance structure including its principles, internal and external mechanisms, and functions. It provides legal protection for investors with the right to elect corporate boards, appoint management, vote on important corporate decisions, demand reliable and transparent financial information, and hold directors and officers accountable for corporate affairs. The legal infrastructure defines the legal rights of corporations and fiduciary duties of their directors and officers. In the United States, state and federal statutes constitute the legal infrastructure for corporate governance. The rule of law and order is vital to the effectiveness of corporate governance. Academic studies indicate various types of national laws that shape the structure of corporate governance, including corporate law, tort law, and bankruptcy law.[7] Corporate law plays a vital role in corporate governance by determining how companies are established, and in defining the rights of shareholders and fiduciary duties of directors and officers.

Securities law, determined by federal statutes, is also important in protecting investor interests and rights by setting minimum requirements for companies offering securities to the public and presenting investors with accurate, relevant, and useful financial information. Although bankruptcy law may not play an important role in the way the company is governed, it defines the rights of creditors, investors, and other stakeholders and any settlement procedures in deciding whether to liquidate or restructure an insolvent company. Corporate governance in crisis situations, including hostile takeovers and bankruptcy, is vital in protecting the interests of both equity holders and debt holders. Vigorous enforcement of corporate law significantly influences the effectiveness of corporate governance and the context to which internal and external mechanisms are implemented and the legal rights of shareholders are protected. Examples of corporate governance attributes affected by corporate law are the company's formation, rights of its shareholders, fiduciary duties of its directors and officers, financial reporting and disclosures, proxy rights at its annual shareholder meetings, voting procedures, rights of its foreign creditors and shareholders, and rights of its minority shareholders.

The market infrastructure consists of rules, regulations, and best practices of determining how capital markets function. Market infrastructure can influence corporate governance structure and practices; listing standards of organized stock exchanges; governing independence of a company's directors, its board committees, and their responsibilities; shareholder voting process; and financial reporting requirements. In an active competitive market, corporations strive to survive by adopting the most effective corporate governance mechanisms to maximize their value, and those corporations with poor performance and ineffectual corporate governance would be replaced. In this context, market competition is viewed as significantly influential and shapes corporate governance with no justification for public or governmental intervention. Market correction mechanisms resolve corporate governance problems by monitoring and disciplining corporations' performance and behavior in a competitive market. Examples of these market correction mechanisms are the capital markets, the managerial labor market, and the market for corporate control. For example, if investors are not satisfied with the company's performance, they can sell their shares, and when many investors follow suit, the company's stock price drops and forces management to change course. In another example, in a competitive labor market, managerial performance is affected by management reputation and tenure in the labor market. Inefficient and poor-performing corporations will be a target for takeover.

Globalization and IT enable the development of the global business and financial market with profound challenges for businesses and regulators to protect investors worldwide. The speed with which financial transactions can be conducted and money can be moved around the world encourages regulators to establish a global financial infrastructure. The International Monetary Fund, the World Bank, the Basel Committee for Banking Supervision, the OECD, IOSCO, and U.S. regulations have taken initiatives to improve global corporate governance and provide guidance and sources of supervisory standards for national and international business and financial markets. Thus, countries and their companies that conduct business in global markets have to comply with global standards of regulations and guidance provided by those organizations. However, global best practices in corporate governance are emerging.

The corporate governance structure is shaped by the availability, efficiency, and effectiveness of both internal and external mechanisms. These governance mechanisms and their collective functions differ from one company to another, one industry to another, and one country to another. Specifically, each country has its own corporate governance structure tailored to and suitable for its legal, political, cultural, and regulatory environment, business practices, financial systems, and patterns of business performance successes. A review of industrial countries suggests four distinct global corporate governance structures of the United States, the UK, Germany, and Japan. Others are seemingly derivatives of these four structures. For example, the Canadian corporate governance structure is similar to the UK's structure, whereas Dutch and Swiss corporate governance structures are closely modeled after the German structure.

Corporate Governance in the United States

Under the free enterprise system in the United States, the capital markets, including bond and equity markets, are an important source of funds for corporations and play a significant role in their corporate governance. There is a two-way relationship between corporations and the capital markets. On the one hand, the capital markets provide funds to corporations and thus monitor their corporate governance to align the interests of management with the interests of investors. On the other hand, corporations provide relevant financial information to the capital markets, which facilitates the efficiency and liquidity of the capital markets. Thus, applicable rules and regulations are designed to ensure the protection of investors and facilitate the liquidity and efficiency of the capital markets. These rules, regulations, and laws have become an integrated component of corporate governance in the United States, which under Regulation Fair Disclosure requires full and fair disclosure of financial information to all investors, levels the playing field for all capital market participants, and prohibits insider trading by using proprietary insider information about company affairs. The SEC was created in 1934 in the United States to protect investor rights by requiring public companies to provide fair and full disclosures of their financial conditions and results of operations.

The market for corporate control through friendly and hostile takeovers in the United States has shaped corporate governance as a disciplinary mechanism, and improved the corporate governance structure of target companies by disciplining underperforming managers. The wave of hostile takeovers in the 1980s raised serious concerns about the possibility of the concentration of financial power in the hands of major corporations, which caused state and antitakeover legislators to respond to the mass of takeover activities.[8] Furthermore, public companies have implemented various antitakeover charter provisions, such as poison pill provisions, to prevent aggressive hostile takeovers.

The boards of directors in public companies in the United States are considered as the essential overseers that have fiduciary duties of overseeing and monitoring corporations' affairs as well as representing and protecting shareholder's interests. The effectiveness of the boards of directors in their advisory and oversight functions is highly debated and adequately addressed in recent developments and initiatives of corporate governance reforms in the post-Enron era in the United States. The majority of CEOs of public companies in the United States also serve as the chairman of their board, which creates both incentives and opportunities for them to (1) actively dominate the selection of outside directors, (2) exert influence over outside directors, (3) set an agenda for their board meetings, (4) manage their board activities, and (5) entrench management by facilitating inside directors' influence over outside directors.

CEOs and other senior executives in the United States usually have a more autocratic management style than their counterparts in other countries, particularly Germany and Japan, in the sense that they have more power over decision making, decision control, and information.[9] This makes the monitoring of senior executives by the board of directors more difficult and less effective in the United States than in other countries. Executives in the United States also typically own shares in their companies and receive compensation packages designed to relate their pay more closely to their performance and to align their interests with those of shareholders. That is, executive ownership and contingent compensation plans (stock options) are intended to establish bonding devices to create shareholder value.

The basic premise underlying the U.S. capital markets has been that the integrity, liquidity, and efficiency of the market depends on the reliability, transparency, and accuracy of financial information disseminated to the market by corporations. The capital markets are efficient in sorting out bad financial information from good information. Corporate management is required to provide fair and full financial disclosures. If management is not fulfilling its financial reporting requirements, dissatisfied shareholders start selling the company's shares. When many investors flow this path, the company's stock price will fall, and management would be forced to change course. However, this premise may not work in reality because (1) individual investors do not own a substantial portion of a corporation's outstanding equity; (2) individual investors are not actively involved in managing their investment portfolios and monitoring the corporation's affairs; and (3) institutional investors' equity holdings are often indexed, which would not give them the incentives or opportunities to discipline underperforming companies in a timely fashion.

Concerns about the responsibilities and effectiveness of corporate governance of public companies in conducting legitimate transactions and producing reliable financial reports grew in the 1970s and 1980s, with the increased incidence of business failures and disclosure of questionable and illegal payments. Congress responded to concerns over incidents of misleading financial reports, bribes, and business failures in the 1970s by passing the FCPA in 1977. The FCPA requires public companies registered with the SEC to have sufficient internal controls to ensure that transactions are authorized by management, and financial statements are prepared in conformity with GAAP. The FCPA was one of the first pieces of legislation that significantly affected the structure of corporate governance by requiring the establishment and maintenance of internal accounting controls.

A number of bank failures in the 1980s received the attention of Congress to improve the corporate governance system at banks and savings and loan associations. The GAO (now Government Accountability Office) reported that insider abuse and fraud contributed to bank failures and that a lack of effective corporate governance provided opportunities for fraud and abuse.[10] Thus, Congress responded by enacting the FDICIA. The FDICIA requires that management and independent auditors of depository institutions report on the adequacy and effectiveness of their ICFR. The FDICIA also sets forth requirements for the existence, composition, responsibilities, and functions of audit committees in large banks and savings and loan associations. Under the FDICIA, boards of directors of large financial institutions are responsible for determining when their audit committee is in compliance with the independent requirements and whether members of the committee have the necessary qualifications, experience, financial literacy in banking, and related financial management to discharge their responsibilities. Although the requirements and provisions of the FDICIA were designed to improve corporate governance at large financial institutions, they set standards and benchmarks for all public companies, many of which are later addressed in SOX. SEC rules on corporate governance have primarily addressed its role in protecting investors through the requirements of proxy statement disclosures of information to shareholders, including the company's board of directors' composition, responsibility, executive compensation, and relationship with its independent public accountants.

Corporate governance in the United States has traditionally been shaped by state law as determined in the company's article of incorporation, charter, and bylaws in defining fiduciary duties of its directors. Federal government through its legislation (e.g., the Securities Act of 1933 and the Securities Exchange Act of 1934) aimed at financial disclosures and processes also influences corporate governance. The passage of SOX has significantly increased the role of the federal government, although some of the provisions of SOX could have been implemented through market-based mechanisms (auditor independence, director independence, executive compensation). Market-based mechanisms failed to correct the corporate malfeasance and misconduct of the early 2000s. As a result, investors lost confidence, and Congress passed SOX to restore investor confidence in corporate America, its governance, and financial disclosures. In summary, the corporate governance structure in the United States is influenced by (1) state statutes defining shareholder rights and fiduciary duties of directors and officers, (2) federal statutes establishing financial reporting and proxy statements, (3) court decisions in interpreting state and federal statutes, (4) listing standards of national stock exchanges, and (5) best practices. U.S. corporate governance, its structure, and its functions are thoroughly examined in Chapters 1 to 13.

An important question, have recent corporate governance reforms including SOX caused a capital shift from U.S. capital markets to non-U.S. capital markets?, has been recently raised. High compliance costs of SOX have promoted companies to decide whether their capital financing should come from U.S. capital markets or from capital markets abroad with a possibly lower degree of strictness and disclosure requirements. Globalization and technological advances have promoted tight competition among the world's leading capital markets (e.g., NYSE, LSE, Hong Kong, Shanghai, Dubai) and thus regulations governing these markets can have a considerable impact on the balance of capital worldwide.

There are more than fifty stock exchanges worldwide that assist companies to conduct their IPOs. Stock exchanges in India, Italy, and South Korea have recently attracted many domestic IPOs, and many state-owned enterprises in China and France have done their fundraising domestically and have listed their IPOs on their home exchanges. Companies have traditionally listed on their domestic stock exchanges, and only about 10 percent of companies have chosen to list abroad.[11] Indeed, in the first half of 2006, only 8 of the 110 IPOs in the United States listed abroad, of which 6 listed on London's Alternative Investment Market (AIM), raising $323 million in total. Thus, this perception that the high compliance cost of SOX has forced U.S. companies to list their IPOs overseas is not warranted, and the fact that smaller foreign companies choose to go public in their domestic exchanges provides no justifiable evidence about the global competitiveness of U.S. capital markets. Nonetheless, best practices of corporate governance in the U.S. suggest that

1. Investors pay a premium for companies with effective corporate governance.
2. Companies with effective corporate governance and shareholder rights marginally outperform those companies with weak corporate governance and investor rights.

3. Companies with effective corporate governance tend to benefit more from regulations and rules than those with weak governance primarily because of compliance costs.

4. Effective corporate governance improves market liquidity and reduces share price volatility.

Technological advances and global competition have enabled companies and their investors to "largely meet in the jurisdiction of their choosing.... [They] have choices about where to invest, where to raise capital and where secondary trading is to occur."[12] Thus, companies can choose the regulatory regime they desire to operate under, and investors have a choice of safeguards and protections provided under different regulatory reforms. Effective regulatory reform creates an environment under which companies can achieve sustainable performance, be held accountable for their activities, and provide protections for their investors. Regulatory reforms in terms of their effectiveness and context can be classified into three concepts of (1) a race to the bottom, (2) a race to the top, and (3) a race to optimality. The "race to the bottom" concept suggests that global securities regulators, in an effort to attract issuers, deregulate the points that provide issuers with maximum flexibility for their operations at the expense of not providing adequate protections for investors. The "race to the top" concept suggests that global securities regulators provide maximum protection for investors through rigid regulations and highly scrutinized enforcement at the expense of putting companies in the global competition at a disadvantage with non–cost-justified regulations. The "race to optimality" concept is a hybrid of the first two concepts, in which both issuers and investors prefer a regulatory regime and jurisdiction that provide cost-justified investor protection.

In real-world global competition, a combination of these three concepts may work best because many provisions of SOX have been globally adopted, particularly those pertaining to strengthening auditor independence, assessment of ICFR, the creation of an independent board to oversee the accounting profession, and the strengthening of audit committee requirements. Table 14.1 presents major provisions of SOX that have reinvigorated regulatory reforms in other countries, suggesting that regulations around the world are converging toward the key provisions of SOX. These globally adopted provisions of SOX should promote integrity and efficiency in cross-border financial markets rather than cause competition disadvantage for U.S. financial markets and U.S. companies.

Corporate Governance in the United Kingdom

The BCCI debacle in the late 1980s in the United Kingdom encouraged the Cadbury Committee to examine accountability of boards of directors of public companies to their shareholders and society.[13] The committee issued its report in 1992, titled "Report of the Committee on the Financial Aspects of Corporate Governance." The Cadbury Report and related Code of Best Practices made recommendations for improving corporate governance, the oversight function of the board of directors, corporate accountability, and financial reporting. Subsequently, the Greenbury report in 1995 addressed director remuneration and its disclosure in companies' annual reports, and the Hempel Report in 1998 examined corporate governance for UK companies. The work of these three committees was collaborated in the Combined Code on Corporate Governance (Combined Code) in 2003 and adopted

Table 14.1 SOX Global Reach

Country/ global entity	Provision			
	Audit oversight bodies	Auditor independence	Audit committee requirements	Internal controls
United States	The Public Company Accounting Oversight Board (PCAOB) was established as a nonprofit, private sector corporation subject to the SEC and is designed to provide autonomous oversight of the audit profession. Main functions of the PCAOB include enforcing auditing standards, inspecting public accounting firms registered with the PCAOB, disseminating auditing standards, and registering public accounting firms.	• Independence of PCAOB from auditing profession, as PCAOB members must not have practiced auditing for at least one year. • Independence of auditors, in that certain nonaudit services provided by an audit firm contemporaneously with an audit are prohibited, audit partners must rotate off the client every five years, and temporary restrictions exist on auditing a client whose management consists of previous employees of the firm.	The audit committee is charged with • Appointing, compensating, and overseeing the audit firm • Approving all services performed by the auditor • Receiving auditor reports regarding important financial issues • Establishing procedures for the handling of complaints regarding auditing, internal controls, or accounting issues • Maintaining independence from the company	• Management must explicitly acknowledge in their annual report their responsibility for creating and maintaining a sufficient internal control system. • Management must assess in their annual report the effectiveness of the system of internal control. • The audit firm auditing the annual report must report on and attest to the assessment of internal control by management.
United Kingdom	The Financial Reporting Council (FRC) is an independent body that regulates the audit profession. Unlike the PCAOB, the FRC does not register audit firms (professional entities are left with this task).	• Disclosure of nonaudit services provided contemporaneously with the audit is required. • Audit partner rotation is required. • The audit firm is temporarily restricted from performing an audit of a client whose key employees are previous employees of the firm.	The audit committee is charged with • Maintaining independence from the company • Disclosing whether a financial expert exists on the audit committee • Providing oversight over auditor independence and the performance of nonaudit services • Recommending audit firms to the board of directors • Compensating the audit firm	• Organizations must either comply with corporate governance code provisions or explain their noncompliance with those provisions. • Auditors report, under the comply-or-explain method, only assessments of internal control by management that are deemed to be inappropriate or unsupportable given the auditor's perception of the organization's process of internal control.

(Continued)

Table 14.1 *(Continued)*

Country/ global entity		Provision		
	Audit oversight bodies	Auditor independence	Audit committee requirements	Internal controls
Canada	The Auditing and Assurance Standards Oversight Council is an independent body charged with overseeing standard setting by professional entities, while the functions of registration, enforcement, and inspection are carried out by the independent Canadian Public Accountability Board.	• Specific services provided contemporaneously with the audit are prohibited. Audit partner rotation is required. • The audit firm is temporarily restricted from performing an audit of a client whose key employees are previous employees of the firm.	The audit committee is charged with • Maintaining independence from the company • Approving nonaudit services proposed by the audit firm (which are not prohibited to begin with) • Recommending audit firms to the board of directors	• Canadian Securities Administrators (CSA) are introducing regulations that are moving Canada to a more rules-based approach. • The CSA will require the CFO and the CEO to take responsibility for implementing a system of internal control. • Management must report on the framework to which the system of internal control is being compared. • The CSA has chosen not to implement an earlier provision on auditors conducting an evaluation of the assessment of internal control by management.
France	Accounting and professional auditing entities are self-regulated at this time, while a statutory body oversees self-regulation. Governmental agencies intervene in the case of serious audit irregularities.	• Specific services provided contemporaneously with the audit are prohibited. Audit partner rotation is required. • A previous member of the auditing firm is temporarily restricted from joining the management of a firm's client.	The audit committee is charged with • Maintaining independence by making sure that a majority of members are independent of the company • Approving nonaudit services proposed by the audit firm (which are not prohibited to begin with), as suggested by The French Corporate Governance of Listed Corporations • Recommending audit firms to the board of directors	• Internal control requirements are rules based, closely resembling those of SOX. • An assessment of the system of internal control by management is required, with responsibility for those controls implied. • The AMF issued guidance on reporting that contains standards of content for reports of internal control systems, proposing that the evaluations of management concentrate on disclosing relevant information (as far as business risk is concerned). • Auditors are required to report on the assessment of internal control by management, although no prescribed manner of conducting such audit evaluations exists.

Germany	Accounting and professional auditing entities are self-regulated at this time, while a statutory body oversees self-regulation. Governmental agencies intervene in cases of serious audit irregularities.	There is independence of the oversight authority in that its members cannot have practiced auditing for at least five years. Specific services provided contemporaneously with the audit are prohibited.	The audit committee is charged with • Maintaining independence by making sure that the chairperson is independent of the company • Disclosing whether a financial expert exists on the audit committee • Providing oversight over auditor independence and the performance of nonaudit services • Compensating the audit firm	• Organizations must either comply with corporate governance code provisions, or explain their noncompliance with those provisions according to German Company Law. • Germany's Stock Corporation Law, however, requires organizations to have a sufficient internal control system. • Under the comply-or-explain method, corporate governance codes propose that auditors release a public report on the assessment of internal control by management.
European Union	Members of the EU appoint capable authorities tasked with registration, inspection, approval, quality assurance, and discipline in accordance with the directive. All member authorities must cooperate with other member authorities, and they are required to organize themselves to the extent that conflicts of interest are prevented.	• Audit partner rotation is required. • A previous member of the auditing firm is temporarily restricted from joining the management of a firm's client.	The audit committee is charged with • Maintaining independence by making sure that one member is independent of the company • Disclosing whether a financial expert exists on the audit committee • Recommending audit firms to the board of directors • Providing oversight over auditor independence and the performance of nonaudit services	• The EU Company Directives are tilting to a method of comply-or-explain, in which organizations would either comply with corporate governance code provisions or explain their noncompliance. The European Corporate Governance Forum is requiring considerable disclosures in order to maintain an effective method of comply-or-explain concerning the reporting of internal control. • The revised EU Company Directives do not mandate an assessment of the internal control system, but do require management to describe the system of internal control in their annual report.
Mexico	The accounting and auditing profession is self-regulated, with standard setting left to nongovernmental agencies. Governmental authorities exercise regulatory functions.	• Specific services provided contemporaneously with the audit are prohibited. • Audit partner rotation is required.	The audit committee is charged with • Maintaining independence from the company • Approving nonaudit services proposed by the audit firm (which are not prohibited to begin with)	• An internal control system report is not required at this time, and is voluntary. A code of corporate governance is published by the stock exchange or securities regulator that urges listed companies to abide by internal control guidelines established within the code. • The Securities Market Law is expected to mandate that boards of companies approve the guidelines for their system of internal control, and that management apply those guidelines.

(Continued)

Table 14.1 (*Continued*)

Country/ global entity	Audit oversight bodies	Auditor independence	Provision — Audit committee requirements	Internal controls
Brazil	The accounting and auditing profession is self-regulated, with standard setting left to nongovernmental agencies. Governmental authorities exercise regulatory functions.	Audit firm rotation is required.	The audit committee is charged with • Maintaining independence from the company • Disclosing whether a financial expert exists on the audit committee • Compensating the audit firm	• Under the comply-or-explain method, corporate governance codes propose that auditors release a public report on the assessment of internal control by management. The Brazilian Institute of Corporate Governance (IBGC) issued a code with which compliance is voluntary.
China	Governmental agencies have the sole authority to set standards and regulate public accounting firms.	• Specific services provided contemporaneously with the audit are prohibited. • Audit partner rotation is required.	The audit committee is charged with • Maintaining independence by making sure that a majority of members are independent of the company • Disclosing whether a financial expert exists on the audit committee • Recommending audit firms to the board of directors	• The China Securities Regulatory Commission (CSRC) is currently working on revising the Security Law, and will introduce internal control requirements before revision is complete. • The revised Security Law requires organizations to have a sufficient internal control system. • Auditors are required to report on the assessment of internal control by management.
Japan	Accounting and professional auditing entities are self-regulated at this time, while a statutory body oversees the self-regulation. Governmental agencies intervene in the case of serious audit irregularities.	• Specific services provided contemporaneously with the audit are prohibited. • Audit partner rotation is required. • A previous member of the auditing firm is temporarily restricted from joining the management of a firm's client.	The audit committee is charged with • Maintaining independence by making sure that a majority of members are independent of the company • Recommending audit firms to the board of directors • Compensating the audit firm	• Internal control requirements are rules based, closely resembling those of SOX. • An organization is required to have a sufficient internal control system (the Financial Instruments and Exchange Bill and the revised Company Law contain the initial framework for management to create and maintain a system of internal control).

Hong Kong	The Hong Kong Financial Reporting Council is an entity designed to investigate audit irregularities. The Hong Kong Institute of Certified Public Accountants is charged with setting and enforcing standards, registering firms, and performing other regulatory functions.	• Disclosure of nonaudit services provided contemporaneously with the audit is required. • Audit partner rotation is required. • The audit firm is temporarily restricted from performing an audit of a client whose key employees are previous employees of the firm.	The audit committee is charged with • Maintaining independence from the company • Disclosing whether a financial expert exists on the audit committee • Providing oversight over auditor independence and the performance of nonaudit services • Recommending audit firms to the board of directors • Compensating the audit firm	• Auditors are required to report on the assessment of internal control by management, while referencing the framework presented by COSO. • Organizations must either comply with corporate governance code provisions or explain (by way of a content standard used for disclosures) their noncompliance with those provisions. • Boards of companies are urged, under the comply-or-explain method, to notify shareholders that they have finished the yearly review of internal control system effectiveness and that the review has been placed in the section on corporate governance of the company's annual report.
Australia	The Australian Auditing and Assurance Standards Board is an independent body under the Financial Reporting Council, charged with setting standards. The Australian Securities and Investments Commission is a governmental agency charged with registering and investigating audit firms. The Companies Auditors and Liquidators Disciplinary Board is designed to discipline auditors.	• Specific services provided contemporaneously with the audit are prohibited. • Audit partner rotation is required. • A previous member of the auditing firm is temporarily restricted from joining the management of a firm's client. Also, a previous member of the auditing firm is prohibited from joining the management of the firm's client whose management already consists of a previous member of the same firm.	The audit committee is charged with • Maintaining independence from the company • Disclosing whether a financial expert exists on the audit committee • Providing oversight over auditor independence and the performance of nonaudit services • Recommending audit firms to the board of directors	• Organizations must either comply with corporate governance code provisions or explain their noncompliance. • The recommendation of the Australian Corporate Governance Code is to have the board make internal control system policies, while management implements the internal control system based on those system policies. • Management, under the comply-or-explain method, is urged to publish internal control system descriptions and internal control system policies on their organization's Web site.

Sources: Tafara, E. 2006, September. Statement by SEC Staff: A Race to the Top: International Regulatory Reform Post Sarbanes-Oxley. *International Financial Law Review.* Available at: www.sec.gov/news/speech/2006/spch091106et.htm; Downes, D. Revised 8th Directive, approved by Council of the EU. *Accountancy Ireland* 38.3 (June 2006): 28(2).

by the LSE and incorporated into its *Corporate Governance: A Practical Guide* in 2004.[14] The 2003 Combined Code made recommendations for improving the corporate governance of UK public companies and their financial reporting process. The Combined Code recommends, and the LSE requires, that the annual reports of UK-listed companies contain a report from the remuneration committee and a statement of corporate governance, directors' responsibilities, internal controls, and going-concern status.

The Financial Reporting Council (FRC) in the UK released a revised Combined Code on Corporate Governance by incorporating many recommendations of previous reports issued by Derek Higgs and Sir Robert Smith.[15] All companies incorporated in the UK and listed on the LSE are required to report on whether and how they are applying the Combined Code. The Combined Code is composed of both principles and provisions that should be complied with by listed companies. The Combined Code as of July 2003 contains the code, its principles and provisions, and related guidance, including the Turnbull guidance on internal control, the Smith guidance on audit committees, and the Higgs report on best practices. The Combined Code is composed of fourteen main principles, twenty-one supporting principles, and forty-eight detailed provisions.

Companies listed on the LSE must include in their annual report (1) a narrative statement of how they have applied the principles of the Combined Code; (2) a statement as to the extent to which companies have complied during the reporting period with the provisions of the Combined Code; and (3) for companies that have not complied with any provisions of the Combined Code, complied with only some of the provisions, or complied with the provisions for only part of the reporting period, a report specifying the Combined Code provisions with which they have not complied, if applicable for what part of the reporting period, and reasons for any noncompliance. The 2003 UK Combined Code and the LSE listing rules do not prescribe any form or content for the annual statement of how the listed companies have complied with various provisions of the code to provide flexibility to companies to tailor the code provisions into their corporate governance policies and processes.

The UK Combined Code describes the responsibilities of the companies' boards of directors which are to

1. Provide entrepreneurial leadership to the company in the context of adequate and effective controls to assess and manage prudent business risk.

2. Establish the company's strategic activities relevant to its financial and human resources and ensure the company's objectives are met and its management performance is reviewed.

3. Set the company's values and standards and ensure its obligations to shareholders and other stakeholders are understood and met.

The role of independent, nonexecutive directors, regardless of the type of corporate governance system (unitary, two tier, or oversight), is to oversee the development of the company's strategy and monitor executives' activities. There should be a balance between these two roles of independent directors in the sense that placing too much emphasis on strategic development makes nonexecutive, independent directors closer to executive directors at the risk of undermining stakeholder confidence in the effectiveness of the board. Overemphasizing the monitoring role may result in resistance and resentment from executive directors, causing a lack of cohesiveness and camaraderie.

Outside directors may assume the following responsibilities:

1. Develop, or participate in the development of, strategies.
2. Monitor the performance of management in achieving the company's goals and objectives.
3. Oversee the integrity, reliability, quality, and transparency of financial reporting as well as the adequacy and effectiveness of ICFR.
4. Determine the level of remuneration of inside directors and senior executives, and appoint and remove inside directors.

The major provisions of the Combined Code are

1. The board should meet regularly to effectively fulfill its duties.
2. Directors should release accurate, timely, and clear information. Although management should provide such information, directors should seek clarification and amplification.
3. The chair of the board should ensure that directors continuously update their knowledge, skills, and familiarity with the company.
4. The chairperson should discuss governance and strategy with major shareholders and ensure that their views are communicated to the board.
5. The chairperson should meet with nonexecutive directors in executive sessions without the executives present.
6. The board should annually evaluate its own performance, its committees, and individual directors.
7. The positions of the chair of the board and the CEO should be separated.
8. Directors' concerns about the running of the company or unresolved proposed actions should be recorded in the board minutes.

The LSE *Practical Guide to Corporate Governance* requires listed companies to include a statement in their annual report indicating their compliance with the Combined Code. Such a statement must include

1. Types of decisions that are to be taken by the board and those that are to be delegated to management
2. Reporting responsibilities of the board regarding the preparation of accounts
3. The number of meetings of the board and its committees and the individual attendance of directors
4. The board responsibilities for conducting a review of the effectiveness of the group's system of internal controls
5. Performance evaluation of the board, its committees, and individual directors
6. Proper justifications when the offices of the chair of the board and the CEO are not separated

7. Major board committees (e.g., audit, nominating, compensation) and their roles and responsibilities

8. The terms and conditions of appointment of nonexecutive directors

9. Remuneration consultants' other connections with the company

10. Explanations of how external auditor objectivity and independence is safeguarded when the auditor provides nonaudit services

11. When the board does not accept the audit committee's recommendation on the appointment, reappointment, or removal of the external auditor, a statement from the committee explaining its recommendation and the reasons why the board has taken a different position

12. The steps taken by the board to ensure its directors, particularly nonexecutive directors, develop a sufficient understanding of the views of major shareholders about the company[16]

U.S. corporate governance reforms clearly separate the board's oversight function from management's managerial functions, whereas under the UK Combined Code directors are responsible for preparation of financial statements and review of internal controls. Unlike the board of directors of public companies in the United States, the board of UK companies is usually composed of independent, nonexecutive directors, and the CEO does not typically assume the position as the chairman of the board. Like CEOs in the United States, CEOs in UK corporations possess the ultimate power over information flow, which may cause a concentration of decision making in the hands of CEOs. Senior executives, including CEOs, can own shares in their companies, which in turn can provide incentives for them to align their interests with those of shareholders. In UK companies, contingent executive compensation plans (performance bonuses, stock options) are often used to link executive incentives with company performance. These plans, however, are established and administered under the control of senior executives, which makes it difficult to assess the effectiveness of compensation plans in contributing to the creation of long-term shareholder value.

The UK approach to corporate governance reforms is more principles based, which requires companies to "comply or explain why not." This flexible approach to corporate governance, coupled with the fact that UK shareholders are in a much stronger position than their U.S. shareholders to nominate directors and forward their resolutions, has recently made the UK capital market more attractive to global IPOs. Different types of corporate governance structure are exposed to different financial misconduct and scandals. For example, a dispersed ownership system of governance in the United States is prone to earnings management schemes (e.g., Enron, WorldCom), whereas concentrated ownership systems are more vulnerable to the appropriation of private benefits of control (e.g., Parmalat).[17]

UK convergence measures that are usually more stringent than U.S. reforms are the requirements for (1) nonexecutive directors to meet at least once per year to evaluate their performance; (2) independent nonexecutive directors to compose at least 50 percent of the board, not including the chair; (3) shareholders' approval of new corporate arrangements and changes; (4) mandatory preparation of a corporate governance report, along with a statement of compliance with provisions of the Combined Code; (5) an executive session of the chair of the board with the company's nonexecutive directors, without the company's executive directors present; (6) the separation of the positions of CEO and chair of the board; (7) the availability of a senior independent director to any shareholders to express concerns not addressed by the company's officers; (8) directors' responsibility for the preparation of financial statements and the review of ICFR; (9) a shareholder advisory vote on executive compensation; and (10) annual ratification of the independent audit form by shareholders.

Corporate Governance in Germany

German corporate governance is influenced by its legal environment, the perception that corporations should act in the best interests of their shareholders and other stakeholders, and the importance of internal mechanisms and relationships to ensure corporate governance effectiveness.[18] Employees play an important role in German corporate governance by actively participating and representing in the corporate boardroom. German corporate governance is characterized by the two-tier board of director system, which creates different rights and obligations for directors of each board as specified in the German Stock Corporation Act and the German Corporate Governance Code.

The German two-tier board of directors system consists of the management board and the supervisory board. The management board is responsible for managing the company for the benefit of a variety of stakeholders, whereas the supervisory board oversees the management board. Directors of the supervisory board are elected by the shareholders at the annual meeting, and the supervisory board then appoints the directors of the management board. The three major oversight functions of the supervisory board are to (1) appoint and, when necessary, dismiss the directors of the management board; (2) determine remuneration of members of the management board; and (3) oversee the work and performance of the management board by regularly receiving reports from the management board without giving specific instructions to its members on how to run the company.

The supervisory board consists of representatives from the following four groups of influential stakeholders: (1) shareholders—both individuals and other corporations that typically own large blocks of stock and often have the power to veto important decisions; (2) wealthy families, typically relatives of the company's founder; (3) financial institutions, mostly large commercial banks (e.g., Comerz Bank, Deutsche Bank, Dresdner Bank, Hypo Vereinsbank); and (4) employees, who often make up half of the representatives of the supervisory board. The dual responsibilities of members of the supervisory board to act in the best interests of the company while securing the interests of their own constituencies may create conflicts of interest within the supervisory board that can potentially influence its oversight effectiveness of the management board.

The market for corporate control in Germany is not as effective as it is in the United States in the sense that although friendly takeovers are often practiced, the occurrences of hostile takeovers are rare. There are several reasons for the inactive market for corporate control in Germany, particularly as it relates to hostile takeovers. First, German banks usually own or control a large portion of the outstanding shares of public companies, and by nature, they stand against hostile takeover bids. Second, voting limitations in corporations' bylaws discourage hostile takeovers. Finally, inadequate financial disclosures and a lack of transparent financial reports make the assessment of the actual and potential values of target companies difficult and inaccurate, which reduces opportunities for hostile takeovers.

In Germany, there has been a lack of equity capital in the sense that capital is provided in the form of debt from large banks. Banks are actually involved in investing in and monitoring public companies, and laws are established to provide protection for banks. Thus, the lack of active participation by the capital markets in monitoring and disciplining public companies is largely compensated by the monitoring exercised by banks. German banks also provide long-term lending to corporations and, through the lending process, perform consulting services. German banks can often influence public companies' corporate governance in three different ways: (1) as shareholders, by owning a substantial portion of corporations' outstanding shares; (2) as lenders, by lending long-term funds to corporations; and (3) by participating in the so-called deposited share voting right by banks assisting shareholders who deposited their shares in banks on how to vote.

Managerial share ownership and contingent compensation plans are rarely used in the German corporate governance structure as a motivation or bonding device to align management interests with those of shareholders. Internal labor markets in Germany play an important role in monitoring managerial decisions because, for large companies, half of their supervisory directors are employees. Nevertheless, the external labor market in Germany is not as effective as it is in the United States and UK. The German Corporate Governance Code adopted in February 2002, allows duality of the board in German companies, commonly referred to as the two-tier board structure.[19]

The German code of corporate governance has traditionally provided protection to creditors, particularly banks, controlling families, and labor. There has been a lack of protection for investors, and the supervisory board has not been very effective in providing adequate oversight of the management board. However, two recent laws, namely, UMAG and Kap-MuG, were established to promote protection for German shareholders. KapMuG is aimed at penalizing companies that mislead investors by allowing groups of ten shareholders to collectively bring class action damages claims against companies that have provided false, misleading, or incomplete financial information.[20] UMAG is a broader law that makes it easier for shareholders to vote their shares by eliminating the previous requirement that shares be deposited when shareholders register for a company's annual meetings, and instead only requiring that they own shares on a specified date before the annual meeting. The two laws are intended to enhance shareholder democracy in Germany and provide protection for investors.

Corporate Governance in Japan

In Japan, the business structure is shaped and business practice is dominated by networks of organizations called *keiretsu*. Banks in Japan play an important role in the *keiretsu* system by (1) investing up to 5 percent allowed under the law in the group companies (practically in each of the individual companies and in the group companies), (2) lending to all companies within the group, and (3) assisting nonfinancial companies in obtaining and providing substantial amounts of trade credit to the group companies.[21] Because the majority of outstanding shares (up to 90 percent) are in the possession of *keiretsu*-affiliated financial institutions or *keiretsu*-affiliated nonfinancial companies, the individual investors do not have much of a voice in corporate governance. Furthermore, the major shares owned by the *keiretsu* group are considered stable shareholdings, which make takeovers almost impossible unless engineered by the *keiretsu*-affiliated financial institutions to discipline or prevent poor performance by an affiliated company.

The cultural and political environment in Japan today encourages individual investors to place their savings in banks rather than to directly invest in the capital markets by owning shares of a company's stock. This pattern has allowed for the enlargement of banks and for banks to become the main suppliers of capital for Japanese corporations. Lack of public policy support for the capital markets, more stable shareholdings, less liquidity in the capital markets, a lack of insider trading laws, and a lack of full financial disclosures discourage investing in the Japanese capital markets by individual investors; thus, there is no active role for the capital markets to monitor corporations' governance. However, extensive monitoring by *keiretsu*-affiliated institutions compensates for the lack of monitoring by the capital markets and the market for corporate control. A well-established relation between banks and corporations has been an important corporate governance mechanism to improve company value. This relation encourages management to observe guidelines established by *keiretsu*-affiliated banks and banks to not interfere directly in the management of the group corporations as long as their performance is satisfactory.

Boards of directors in Japanese corporations are primarily composed of insiders who are usually top executives of companies with no outside directors representing small individual investors.[22] That is, boards of directors do not typically have a monitoring function. The president of a Japanese company is equivalent to the CEO of a U.S. company with managerial power to make decisions, whereas the position of the chairman of the board is more or less symbolic, with not much decision management or decision control. Managerial decision making in Japanese corporations is more of a participative decision process, where lower managers provide input through a consensus-building process. This consensus decision-making process creates a collegial environment with a high potential for mutual monitoring. Thus, consensus building, a collegial atmosphere, and mutual monitoring are important corporate governance mechanisms in Japanese corporations. Stock ownership and contingent compensation plans (stock or stock options) are not commonly used as incentive plans for top Japanese executives, whereas bonuses linked to performance are effectively used to motivate higher performance by executives.

External labor markets, similar to U.S. capital markets, do not play a significant role in the corporate governance of Japanese corporations. Nevertheless, the internal labor markets are efficient because employees tend to stay in one corporation throughout their working life. Corporations reward and promote high-performance employees, and employees are viewed as important stakeholders who are also entitled to the residual value created by the company. The participation of employees in profit sharing, decision making, and lifelong employment in the company have been effective corporate governance mechanisms in reducing the potential conflicts of interest between employees, management, and shareholders. In 2006, Japan took several initiatives to improve the infrastructure of its capital markets by (1) establishing a cross-sectional framework of a wide range of financial instruments and services (e.g., broadening the definitions of investment schemes, including financial instruments); (2) strengthening the quality of independent audits of financial statements; (3) enhancing protections for investors; (4) improving disclosures through quarterly reporting; (5) reporting to management and auditors on internal controls; (6) providing for self-regulatory structures; and (7) increasing penalties against market fraud.[23]

Corporate Governance in Other Countries

Corporate governance worldwide has recently made significant progress. After many decades of European and American domination of global markets, trades and investments are now flowing between the Middle East and Asia. With oil prices riding high, Middle Eastern countries and their investors and companies have funds to invest, and Asian countries have the capability to attract such investments. It is inevitable that governments in both Asia and the Middle East will create a more hospitable business and investment climate for investments to reach their global potential. The following pages discuss corporate governance in other countries, including Canada, Singapore, and Australia, which have more worldwide relevance.

1. **Corporate governance in Canada.** In Canada, in 1994, the Dey Committee recommended fourteen best practice guidelines for corporate governance, including the suggestions that the majority of directors be independent and that there be a separation of the roles of chairman of the board and CEO.[24] The Dey Committee, in 2003, urged that the voluntary corporate governance guidelines be made mandatory for companies listed on the TSX.[25] The Joint Committee on Corporate Governance was established by the Canadian Institute of Chartered Accountants, the TSX, and the Canadian Venture Exchange to conduct an ongoing examination of corporate governance issues in Canada. The Joint Committee, in November 2001, issued its final report titled, "Beyond Compliance: Building a Governance Culture," which recommends changes to several TSX guidelines for corporate governance, and requires additional disclosure requirements.[26] The TSX requires that its listed companies incorporated in Canada to disclose on an annual basis a Statement of Corporate Governance Practices, which describes the company's system of corporate governance, its comparison with each of the TSX guidelines, and proper explanation of any differences or their inapplicability. Thus, there is no formal requirement that a company's governance procedures conform to the TSX corporate governance guidelines, only the description of the system and any discrepancies. Unlike U.S. public companies whose ownership is widely held and significantly dispersed across a large number of investors, Canadian companies' ownership is less widely held and less widely dispersed.

2. **Singapore code of corporate governance.** The Singapore code of corporate governance (the Code) was developed in March 2001 by a private sector committee appointed by the government and the corporate governance committee, and was issued by the Ministry of Finance in July 2005. All listed companies on the Singapore Exchange are required to describe in their annual reports corporate governance practices in compliance with the Code or any deviations from the Code.[27] Like the UK Combined Code, the Singapore code of corporate governance has a unitary board system that requires all directors to share responsibility for both the direction and the control of the company. That is, the company's board of directors and management are the same, as opposed to the board of directors in the United States that has oversight responsibility or to a two-tier board system in Europe where the supervisory board has oversight of a management board. Similar to UK Corporate Governance Combined Code, the Singapore code has fifteen "principles" and

fifty-five "guidance notes" in four major categories of board matters, remuneration matters, accountability audit, and communication with shareholders. Compared to the UK Combined Code, the Singapore code has "guidance notes" instead of "provisions." The Singapore code is considered a voluntary code in the sense that the listed companies are required to comply with the code or explain noncompliance.

CONVERGENCE IN CORPORATE GOVERNANCE

The word "convergence" as used in the literature means the process of moving toward a set of common objectives and principles.[28] In accounting, it has been used as the process of minimizing differences between the national accounting standards, for example, U.S. GAAP and IFRS, in an attempt to adopt a set of global uniformly accepted accounting principles (GUAAP). Financial scandals of the early 2000s were not unique to U.S. companies. The revelation of global financial scandals encouraged regulators worldwide to recognize the need to address global corporate governance deficiencies and work together to improve the quality, reliability, and transparency of global financial reports.

Several initiatives have been taken during the past decade to improve corporate governance worldwide. Many of these initiatives are primarily national. There is no globally accepted set of corporate governance principles or global regulatory framework that governs corporations, global financial institutions, or capital markets worldwide. Regulators in the United States, the SEC, IOSCO, and the World Federation of Exchanges (WFE) have yet to agree on a global regulatory framework or a global corporate governance structure. The OECD's international standards of corporate governance have not achieved global acceptance to be included in the global regulatory framework.

The corporate governance debate in the United States started in the 1970s and received broader acceptance on the publication of the ALI's *Principles of Corporate Governance* in 1994.[29] Corporate governance became part of the UK business process pursuant to the issuance of the Cadbury Report on the financial aspects of corporate governance.[30] The Cadbury Report provided guidance only on the financial elements of corporate governance and applied to companies listed on the LSE. The Commission of European Communities suggests that the EU should actively coordinate the corporate governance efforts and reforms of its member states. This coordination should require each member state to (1) identify its corporate laws, securities laws, listing rules, codes of conduct, and best practices; (2) make progress toward designating a code of corporate governance, intended for use at the national level, with which listed companies should comply or disclose noncompliance; (3) coordinate its code or corporate governance with other member states; and (4) participate in the coordination process established by the EU.[31] European corporate governance initiators require separation of the positions of chairperson of the board and the CEO. U.S. corporate governance reforms, however, do not require the separation of the positions.

Many countries have established corporate governance reforms to improve the quality of public information and the integrity of their capital markets. A review of global corporate governance reforms suggests three distinct governance reforms. First, corporate governance reforms in the United States and Canada are shaped primarily by market mechanisms and best practices with adequate oversight regulatory roles taken by governmental agencies (both state and federal). Second, corporate governance reforms in the

UK and Australia are influenced primarily by market participants with some regulatory compliance. Finally, corporate governance reforms in France, Germany, and Japan are shaped primarily by the regulatory framework designed by the central government. Several issues need to be addressed to promote convergence in global corporate governance. The first and most important issue is whether corporate governance principles and provisions should be mandatory as a set of rules that all companies must comply with as opposed to recommendations and disclosure practices that require companies to disclose whether and how they complied with recommendations. This issue should be addressed in determining what approach will prevail in global corporate governance. In the United States, emerging corporate governance reforms are regulated either by Congress and regulators or mandated by national stock exchanges. Corporate governance reforms in other countries (the Cadbury Report and the Combined Code in the UK) are mostly in the context of recommendations for best practices encouraging compliance rather than being imposed on corporations.

The second issue is the rules- versus principles-based approach to corporate governance convergence. The United States uses a rules-based approach, whereas other countries, such as the UK, promote the principles-based approach. The American approach is viewed as rules based in the sense that SOX and SEC-related rules, as well as requirements of national stock exchanges and best practices of corporate governance advocated by professional organizations, all provide quantitative corporate governance measures. These quantitative measures are designed to legislate and standardize proper business conduct and business ethics. Although these measures are necessary to provide guidance for promoting effective corporate governance, they may not be adequate to achieve the intellectual honesty needed to restore public trust and investor confidence in corporate America. Thus, the principles-based corporate governance approach of focusing on more qualitative measures is needed to ensure corporate governance participants are acting in the best interests of the company and its shareholders. In the case of Enron, its corporate governance met many of the quantitative corporate governance measures (e.g., audit committee, outside directors, internal audit function, independent auditors); however, it lacked the qualitative measures of intellectual honesty, ethical corporate culture, due diligence, good faith, and transparency.

U.S. corporate governance is traditionally geared toward increasing shareholder value with little focus on protecting the interests of other stakeholders. Thus, until recently, there was no guidance as to how the board should treat stakeholders other than shareholders. Modern corporate governance emphasizes both financial aspects of governance in increasing shareholder value and an integrated approach that considers the rights and interests of all stakeholders. Corporate governance should be viewed as a dynamic and integrated approach of addressing financial, social, environmental, and economic concerns of all stakeholders.

The principles-based approach to corporate governance is viewed by many to be more effective than the rules-based approach for several reasons. First, the principles-based approach is more flexible and relies on the professional judgments and professionalism of corporate governance participants to preserve the integrity, effectiveness, and quality of the system. Second, global corporate governance mechanisms are moving toward the principles-based approach of corporate governance and focus more on both qualitative measures (due care, due diligence, good faith, ethical conduct, straight thinking) and quantitative measures (independence, outside directorships, financial experts, inside ownerships, number of directors, rules, requirements) than a rules-based approach. As rightly stated by SEC Chairman William Donaldson, "[A] 'check the box' [rules-based] approach to good corporate governance will not inspire a true sense of ethical obligation. It could merely lead to an array of inhibiting, 'politically correct' dictates."[32] These principles-based approaches are very broad and comprehensive without specifying rules in terms of the number of independent nonexecutive directors and their term limits, but they are steps in the right direction in improving accountability and reinforcing investors' rights. It appears that convergence would be more feasible when countries agree on the principles-based approach rather than having to reconcile voluminous and often irreconcilable rules.

The third issue is the consensus on the primary purposes of global corporate governance. The primary goal and focus of corporate governance in the United States is on the creation and enhancement of shareholder value, whereas in some other countries the protection of interests of all stakeholders is the main goal. Convergence would be possible if all nations agreed on the primary purpose of corporate governance as the enhancement of shareholder value while protecting the interests of other stakeholders.

One should not expect that convergence in corporate governance will be possible for all provisions of corporate governance. Some provisions that have already been converged or are good candidates for convergence are (1) director independence where the majority of directors should be independent; (2) the audit committee financial expertise requirement; (3) the oversight responsibility of the audit committee to appoint, compensate, dismiss, and monitor the work of independent auditors; and (4) board committees and their oversight responsibilities (audit, compensation, and nomination).[33] Major differences that make convergence more difficult are (1) CEO duality, where in many countries the position of the CEO and the chairperson of the board are required to be separated, whereas there is no such requirement in the United States; and (2) the independence requirement for the majority or all members of various board committees.

The commission encourages the coordination and convergence of national codes of corporate governance through high-level meetings of the European Corporate Governance Forum typically chaired by the commission and participation of representatives from all member states, European regulators, investors, issuers, and academics. Technological advances and globalization have developed to the point that, as pointed out by Tom Friedman, the world is made "flat."[34] In a flat world, cross-border investments are common as investors consider global markets in making investment decisions. Regulators worldwide have collaborated to improve the effectiveness of global corporate governance. First, the SEC has been very active in developing financial dialogue with its counterparts in the EU. The United States and EU should establish better cooperative efforts in promoting the development of a principles-based regulatory framework that is sensitive and responsive to different cultures, histories, political and legal regimes, economic systems, and regulatory philosophies. Second, economic developments in Asia, particularly China and India, will soon have unprecedented effects on the global economy, financial markets, and cross-border investments. The SEC and the Japanese Financial Service Agency have had continuous dialogue to enhance the quality of regulatory discussions and participation in the U.S.-Japan Financial Services Working Group to discuss financial sector developments in both countries.[35] Third, SEC Chairman Cox, along with Treasury Secretary John Snow and Federal Reserve Chairman Alan Greenspan, have participated in a U.S.-China Joint Economic Committee to discuss with their counterparts a range of policy issues and regulatory matters relevant to financial markets in both countries and possible collaboration initiatives. Table 14.2 shows the diversity of corporate governance attributes across

Table 14.2 Corporate Governance Attributes Across Countries

	Australia[a]	Canada[b,c]	Germany[d,e]	Japan[f]	United Kingdom[g,h]	Singapore[i]
Regulatory oversight	• Australian Securities and Investments Commission (ASIC). • Australian Stock Exchange (ASX).	• No federal regulatory body • Ontario and Quebec Securities Commissions are unofficial standard setters	• BAFin • Ministry of Finance • Frankfurt Stock Exchange	• No SEC equivalent • Responsibilities divided between Ministry of Finance and the Securities and Exchange Surveillance Committee	• No SEC equivalent • Federal Services Authority (FSA) • London Stock Exchange (LSE) • Department of Trade and Industry	
Proxy voting	Voting is by choice and management is not authorized to vote for shareholders due to absenteeism	Regulations require that each shareholder be represented; however, company officer's may vote on their behalf	If shareholders do not provide absentee instructions, custodian banks are authorized to vote as they see fit	Shareholder votes default to a "for" vote if desires are not communicated	Voting is by choice	
Shareholder organizations	• Investment and Financial Services Association • Australian Shareholders Association	• Canadian Coalition for Good Governance	• Deutsche Schutzvereinigung für Wertpapierbesitz	• Association of Life Insurers • Commercial Law Center	• United Kingdom Shareholders Association	
Types of shares	Predominantly a one-share/one-vote system	One-share/one-vote, nonvoting, multiple voting, and special shares	One-share/one-vote and nonvoting	One-share/one-vote and nonvoting	Predominantly a one-share/one-vote system	
Board setup	One-third of the board is eligible for election each year	• Full board election each year • Board should appoint a nominating committee composed entirely of independent directors to identify qualified individuals and recommending them to the board	• Two-tiered board setup: supervisory and management boards • Elections to supervisory board made on an individual basis • Supervisory board appoints and dismisses members of the management board	Two-tiered/two-year election cycle	• One-third of the board is eligible for election each year • Shareholders are permitted to vote "against" • Selection process should be formal, rigorous, and transparent • All directors should be submitted for reelection at regular intervals, subject to continued satisfactory performance	Selection process should be formal and transparent

Disclosure issues	ASX requires disclosures of corporate governance practices	Comparable to U.S. disclosure rules with few exceptions	Shareholders granted access to reports no less than four weeks prior to annual meetings	Viewed as a weak regulator by U.S. SEC	• Toughest disclosure requirements outside the United States • First to require independent audit committees • Company position and prospects should be presented by the board	Remuneration, company performance, position, and prospects should be disclosed
Accounting standards	Australian Accounting Standards (AASB)		International Accounting Standards (IAS)		Set by the Accounting Standards Board and its Urgent Issues Task Force	
Executive compensation disclosure	Required to report the aggregate compensation of executives and directors	Listed companies must publish the compensation packages of the top five highest paid executives	Proposal for the disclosure of all elements of executive pay pending	Japanese companies are not required to release information regarding executive pay	• LSE governs what salary information is disclosed • Currently all elements of executive pay are required	Remuneration policy, level and mix of remuneration, and procedure for setting remuneration should be disclosed in the annual report
Independence requirements	Majority of boards are composed of a majority of nonexecutive directors	• Majority of boards are composed of a majority of nonexecutive directors • Board should have a majority of independent directors • Chair of the board should be an independent director (and when not appropriate, an independent director should be appointed to act as "lead director")	• Management board is responsible for independently managing the enterprise • External auditors must disclose potential impairments of independence prior to being elected for the audit • Supervisory board should be adequately independent from the management board	Independent directors are encouraged but not required	Majority of boards are composed of a majority of nonexecutive directors	An element of independence should exist on the board

(Continued)

Table 14.2 (*Continued*)

	Australia[a]	Canada[b,c]	Germany[d,e]	Japan[f]	United Kingdom[g,h]	Singapore[i]
Audit committees	The 500 largest listed companies are required to have an audit committee		• Audit committee is set up by the supervisory committee • Audit committee may not be chaired by the chair of the supervisory board nor may a former member of management board sit on the audit committee	Companies receive regulatory benefits for utilizing an audit committee but not a requirement	Audit committees must be composed of a minimum three independent members	Audit committees should be established by the board, with written terms of reference which clearly set out its authority and duties
Chairman/CEO segregation	Advised to segregate the roles of chairperson and CEO to enhance oversight and independence	Advised to segregate the roles of chair and CEO to enhance oversight and independence	Required segregation of chair and CEO	Nonexecutive chairmen do not exist in most cases	Advised to segregate the roles of chairperson and CEO to enhance oversight and independence	There should be a clear division of responsibilities at the top of the company between the working of the board and the executive responsibility of the company's business
Board information access					Board should be supplied in a timely manner with information in a form and of a quality appropriate to enable it to discharge its duties	To fulfill their responsibilities, board members should be provided with complete, adequate, and timely information prior to board meetings and on an ongoing basis
Communication		Board roles, responsibilities, code of business conduct and ethics, and contribution to the board should be communicated with the members of the board	• Open discussion between and among the members of the supervisory and management boards should be used • Both boards of a target company in a takeover situation should present a statement of reasoned position		• Board as a whole has responsibility for ensuring that a satisfactory dialogue with shareholders takes place • AGMs should be used to communicate with shareholders	• Companies should engage in regular, effective, and fair communication with shareholders • Shareholder participation at AGMs should be encouraged

Category				
	• Management board should disclose conflicts of interest to the supervisory board, and also disclose insider information to the public • Auditor communicates audit results to the supervisory board			
Assessment of the board	The board, its committees, and each individual director should be regularly assessed regarding effectiveness and contribution		Board should undertake a formal and rigorous annual evaluation of its own performance and that of its committees and individual directors	There should be a formal assessment of the effectiveness of the board as a whole and the contribution by each director to the effectiveness of the board
Level of remuneration		• Overall compensation of the members of the management board will comprise a fixed salary and variable components • Supervisory board members received both fixed and performance-based compensation	Levels of remuneration should be sufficient to attract, retain, and motivate quality directors, but should not be excessive	Levels of remuneration should be sufficient to attract, retain, and motivate quality directors, but should not be excessive
Remuneration procedure	The board should appoint a compensation committee composed of independent directors, responsible for reviewing and approving corporate goals relevant to CEO compensation, making non-CEO compensation recommendations, and reviewing executive compensation disclosures before publicly available	• At the proposal of the committee dealing with management board contracts, the full supervisory board will discuss and regularly review the structure of the management board compensation system • Compensation of the members of the management board is determined by the supervisory board at an appropriate amount based on a performance assessment in considering any payments by group companies	• There should be a formal and transparent procedure for developing policy on executive remuneration and for fixing the remuneration packages of individual directors • No director should be involved in deciding his or her own remuneration	• There should be a formal and transparent procedure for developing policy on executive remuneration and for fixing the remuneration packages of individual directors • No director should be involved in deciding his or her own remuneration

(Continued)

Table 14.2 *(Continued)*

	Australia[a]	Canada[b,c]	Germany[d,e]	Japan[f]	United Kingdom[g,h]	Singapore[i]
Board requirement					Every company should be headed by an effective board, which is collectively responsible for the success of the company	Every company should be headed by an effective board to lead and control the company
Internal control requirement					Board should maintain a sound system of internal control to safeguard shareholders' investment and the company's assets	Board should ensure that the management maintains a sound system of internal controls to safeguard the shareholders' investments and the company's assets

Sources: [a]Investor Responsibility Research Center. 2005. Governance Research Service 2004 Proxy Voting Guide: Australia.

[b]Investor Responsibility Research Center. 2005. Governance Research Service 2005 Proxy Voting Guide: Canada.

[c]Adapted from the Toronto Stock Exchange. 2005, April. National Policy 58–201. Corporate Governance Guidelines. Available at: tsx.com/en/pdf/NP58-201_CGGuidelines_Apr15-05.pdf.

[d]Investor Responsibility Research Center. 2005. Governance Research Service 2005 Proxy Voting Guide: Germany.

[e]Adapted from the Government Commission on the German Corporate Governance Code. 2002, February 26. German Corporate Governance Code. Available at: www.ifac.org/Credibility/ViewPoints_PubDL.php?PubID=00052.

[f]Investor Responsibility Research Center. 2005. Governance Research Service 2005 Proxy Voting Guide: Japan.

[g]Investor Responsibility Research Center. 2005. Governance Research Service 2005 Proxy Voting Guide: United Kingdom.

[h]Adapted from Financial Services Authority (FSA). 2003, July. The Combined Code on Corporate Governance. Available at: www.fsa.gov.uk/pubs/ukla/lr_comcode2003.pdf.

[i]Singapore Code of Corporate Governance 2005 (issued by the Ministry of Finance in July 2005).

countries. The following issues should be resolved to facilitate global convergence in corporate governance:

1. **The Board System**
   a. Unitary board system where the board of directors and management are the same (e.g., Singapore board system).
   b. Two-tier board system where there are two boards, supervisory and management, and the supervisory board has oversight over the management board. The European two-tiered model of corporate governance consists of an executive board and a supervisory board. The executive board is composed of senior executives and inside directors, and is primarily responsible for managing the company. The supervisory board, however, is typically composed of outside directors who represent shareholders, employers, and lenders, and, appoints and oversees the activities of the executive board.
   c. Oversight board system where the board of directors appoints management and oversees its activities (United States).

2. **Compliance with the Code**
   a. Voluntary compliance where the listed companies are required to comply with the code or explain noncompliance. That is, one size does not fit all, no single model for all listed companies. The listed companies should tailor their corporate governance practices to their circumstances and choose the best-suited practices. The company should view the code as benchmarks and suggestions for good governance practices and justify noncompliance, whereas unjustifiable deviations from the code are penalized by the capital markets (Singapore Code).
   b. Compulsory compliance where the listed companies are required to comply with the code and noncompliance will be penalized. The U.S. compulsory compliance approach permits no flexibility, which presents a one-size-fits-all approach to corporate governance.

3. **Corporate Governance Approach**
   a. Rules-based approach to corporate governance where corporate governance reforms and listing standards are very rigid and applicable to all listed companies, detailing requirements for compliance and prescribed to a set of rules.
   b. Principles-based approach to corporate governance where corporate governance principles establish benchmarks and norms for good governance practices but companies establish their own corporate governance rules tailored to their circumstances with adequate flexibility to set their own rules. This approach may create more room for manipulation and even noncompliance with minimum standards.

4. **Director Independence**
   a. At least one-third of the board should be composed of independent directors (Singapore code).
   b. The majority of the board must consist of independent directors (U.S. listing standards).
   c. At least half of the board, excluding the chairman, must consist of independent directors, whereas for smaller companies at least two independent directors should be on the board (UK Code).

5. Tenure and Time Commitment Two three-year terms as a norm for outside directors and any term beyond six years subject to extensive reviews.

Convergence in corporate governance is possible when all nations agree on (1) a common goal of corporate governance to create long-term shareholder value while protecting the interests of other stakeholders, and (2) a set of mandatory corporate governance principles where consensus and reconciliation are feasible. Reconcilable corporate governance principles are (1) the majority of directors must be independent, nonexecutive directors; (2) members of the audit, compensation, and nomination committees must be independent; (3) nonexecutive, independent directors do not receive compensation or fees other than their director fees; (4) the audit committee, composed of truly independent directors, oversees financial reporting, internal controls, and audit activities; and (5) the audit committee is directly responsible for the appointment, retention, and compensation of the external auditor. The most important step in the convergence process is the statutory power to implement and enforce the globally accepted corporate governance principles, rules, or best practices. Table 14.2 presents attributes of corporate governance across countries. Different nations have different enforcement processes, statutory powers, and criminal sanctions for the violation of corporate governance principles.

CORPORATE GOVERNANCE IN MULTINATIONAL CORPORATIONS

Multinational corporations (MNCs) play an important role in the world economy and in trade. As the number of MNCs increases and they continue to be more important to the world economy and trade, their corporate governance becomes essential in aligning the interests of their headquarters with those of subsidiaries, which usually have divergent political, economical, cultural, and environmental interests. IAS No. 27 states that a parent–subsidiary relationship arises when one enterprise (the parent) is able to control another enterprise (the subsidiary) in which control is defined as the power to govern the operating and financial policies of the subsidiary, or the ability to influence substantially the subsidiary's decisions.[36]

In purely domestic corporations, corporate governance mechanisms are designed to align the interests of management and shareholders that arise from the separation of ownership and control. In a multinational corporation, corporate governance mechanisms are designed not only to align the interests of subsidiaries with those of the parent company, but also to align the interests of the management of the parent company with the interests of both its majority and minority shareholders. Thus, the potential conflicts of interest between the subsidiaries and the parent company and the parent company and its shareholders create agency costs. In an MNC, a parent company can be both an agent and a principal: an agent in relation to its own shareholders, and a principal in relation to its subsidiaries, with shareholders of the parent company being the ultimate residual risk–bearing owners (principals). Thus, the agents should be monitored, controlled, and bonded through a set of contracts that are costly to write and enforce in order to align their interests with the interests of shareholders.

In the absence of interest alignment, the management of subsidiaries may make decisions to maximize their own interests, which may be detrimental to the long-term performance of the parent company. Likewise, the management of the parent company may make decisions that result in reducing shareholder value. Thus, the nexus of contracts to reduce agency costs constitutes the corporate governance structure between the parent company and its subsidiaries, and between shareholders of the parent company and its management. Both internal and external corporate governance mechanisms of the company have evolved over time to monitor, bond, and control management. These mechanisms are the capital markets, the managerial labor markets, regulations, investors (particularly institutional investors), and the board of directors, which may act independently, substitutionally, and complementarily to align the interests of stockholders and management. The parent-subsidiary corporate governance structure is designed to align the interests of subsidiaries with those of the multinational corporation's headquarters.

The parent-subsidiary corporate governance structure is shaped by both the host and home countries' legal, political, cultural, and regulatory systems; the business practices and historical patterns of countries; the global capital, labor, and managerial markets; global institutional investors; and the boards of directors. Other influential factors are the international strategy of MNCs and the subsidiary's industry, size, and relative importance to the entire system of MNCs. Particularly, when the subsidiary is wholly owned by the parent company and is managed automatically (independently) by a management who has little if any ownership interest in the MNC or the subsidiary, then the effectiveness of parent-subsidiary corporate governance becomes more crucial in monitoring and controlling managerial actions of the subsidiary.

SUMMARY

Corporate governance has transformed from minimizing agency costs to maximizing shareholder value and in the post-SOX era a compliance requirement to a business imperative. Globalization and IT have made cross-border investments possible and attractive to investors who consider the global financial markets for their investment decisions. Effective corporate governance can improve the attractiveness and efficiency of the global financial markets. This chapter presented corporate governance in transition, including historical and global perspectives of corporate governance.

The key points of this chapter are

- The corporate governance structure can be differentiated across countries in terms of the degree of ownership and control.

- Corporate law plays a vital role in corporate governance by determining how companies are established and in defining the rights of shareholders and the fiduciary duties of directors and officers.

- For companies listed on the LSE, the UK has established annual reporting requirements on whether and how they are complying with the Combined Code.

- The German board system is a two-tiered system that consists of a management board and a supervisory board.

- The Japanese business structure is dominated by networks of organizations called *keiretsu* that significantly influence the corporate governance structure in Japan.

- Convergence of global corporate governance would be possible if all nations would agree that the primary purpose of corporate governance is the enhancement of shareholder value while protecting the interests of other stakeholders.

- The most important step in the convergence process is the statutory power to implement and enforce the globally accepted corporate governance principles, rules, or best practices.

- In a multinational corporation, corporate governance mechanisms are designed not only to align the interests of subsidiaries with those of the parent company, but also to align the interests of the management of the parent company with the interests of both its majority and minority shareholders.

KEY TERMS

information infrastructure	Regulation Fair	U.S. Goverment
keiretsu	Disclosure	Accountability Office
legal infrastructure	UK Financial Reporting	(GAO)
market infrastructure	Council (FRC)	unitary board

REVIEW QUESTIONS

1. What are the primary responsibilities of the supervisory board in the German board structure?

2. Briefly describe the board structure in Japanese corporations.

3. What are the four factors that can differentiate the corporate governance structure from one country to another?

4. What factors help shape the corporate governance structure of multinational corporations?

DISCUSSION QUESTIONS

1. Discuss the global corporate governance structure.

2. Explain the three commonly used approaches to regulatory reforms in terms of their effectiveness and context.

3. Discuss the primary aspects of corporate governance in the UK.

4. Describe the new initiatives taken in Japan to improve the infrastructure of its capital markets.

5. Are you expecting many changes in corporate governance reforms in the Middle East and Asia?

6. Explain the types of board systems worldwide.

7. Compare and contrast rules-based versus principles-based approaches of corporate governance.

NOTES

1. Berle, A. A., Jr., and G. C. Means. 1932. *The Modern Corporation and Private Property.* MacMillan, New York.

2. Tricker, R. I. 2000. *Corporate Governance.* History of Management Thought Series. Ashcroft, Aldershot, UK.

3. Ocasio, W., and J. Joseph, 2005. Cultural Adaptation and Institutional Change: The Evolution of Vocabularies of Corporate Governance, 1972–2003. *Poetics* 33(3–4): 163–178. Available at: linkinghub.elsevier.com/retrieve/pii/S0304422X05000458.

4. See note 2 above.

5. Jensen, M., and W. Meckling, 1976. Theory of the Firm: Managerial Behavior, Agency Costs and Ownership Structure. *Journal of Financial Economics* 3: 305–311.

6. These four factors are used in Standard and Poor's Corporate Governance Scores in ranking corporate governance both at a country and at a company level. See Standard & Poor's Governance Services. 2002, July. Standard and Poor's Corporate Governance Scores: Criteria, Methodology and Definitions. Standard & Poor's Governance Services, New York. Available at: www2.standardandpoors.com/spf/pdf/products/CGSCriteria.pdf.

7. LaPorta, R., F. Lopez-de-Silanes, A. Shleifer, and R. Vishny, 1997. Legal Determinants of External Finance. *Journal of Finance* (52): 113–1150.

8. Schleifer, A., and R. W. Vishny, 1997. A Survey of Corporate Governance. *Journal of Finance* 52(2): 737–783.

9. Charkham, J. 1994. *Keeping Good Company: A Study of Corporate Governance in Five Countries.* Oxford, UK: Oxford University Press.

10. U.S. General Accounting Office (GAO), 1991, April. Failed Banks: Accounting and Auditing Reforms Urgently Needed. Report to Congressional Committees. GAO/AFMD-91-43. Available at: archive.gao.gov/d20t9/143697.pdf.

11. Ernst & Young. 2007, January. Global Capital Market Trends. Available at: www.ey.com.archive.gao.gov/d20t9/143697.pdf

12. Tafara, E. 2006, September. Statement by SEC Staff: A Race to the Top: International Regulatory Reform Post Sarbanes-Oxley. *International Financial Law Review.* Available at: www.sec.gov/news/speech/2006/spch091106et.htm.

13. The Committee on the Financial Aspects of Corporate Governance. 1992. Cadbury Report on the Financial Aspects of Corporate Governance. Gee, London.

14. London Stock Exchange. 2004, July. Corporate Governance: A Practical Guide. Published by the London Stock Exchange and RSM Robson Rhodes. Available at: www.ecgi.org/codes/documents/rsmi_lse_guide2004.pdf.

15. Financial Reporting Council (FRC). 2003, July. The Combined Code on Corporate Governance. Available at: www.frc.org.uk/documents/pagemanager/frc/combinedcodefinal.pdf.

16. Ibid.

17. Coffee, J. C., Jr. 2005. A Theory of Corporate Scandals: Why the USA and Europe Differ. *Oxford Review of Economic Policy* 21(2): 198–211. Available at: oxrep.oxfordjournals.org/cgi/content/short/21/2/198.

18. Schmidt, R. H. 2003, August. Corporate Governance in Germany: An Economic Perspective. CFS Working Paper No. 2003/36. Center for Financial Studies, an der Johann Wolfgang Goethe-Universität, Frankfurt am Main, Germany. Available at: www.ifk-cfs.de/fileadmin/downloads/publications/wp/03_36.pdf.

19. Government Commission. 2003, May 21. German Corporate Governance Code. Available at: www.corporate-governance-code.de/eng/download/DCG_K_E200305.pdf.

20. Jenkins, P. 2005, October 31. Bigger Powers For Big Shareholders: New Regulation To Promote Investor Protection Has Something For Management As Well. *Financial Times.* Excerpt available at: securities.stanford.edu/news-archive/2005/20051031_Headline100998_Times.html. Full article available through lexisnexis.com (membership required).

21. Rose, N. 1993. *Lesson Learning in Public Policy: A Guide to Learning across Time and Space.* Chatham: Chatham House.

22. Anderson, C. A. 1984. Corporate Directors in Japan. *Harvard Business Review* 62(3): 30–38.

23. Financial Services Agency, Japan. 2006, September. New Legislative Framework for Investor Protection: "Financial Instruments and Exchange Law." Available at: www.fsa.go.jp/en/policy/fiel/20061010.pdf.

24. Toronto Stock Exchange (TSX). 1994. Guidelines for Improved Corporate Governance (Excerpt). In: The Dey Report: Where Were the Directors? Available at: www.ecgi.org/codes/documents/dey.pdf.

25. Toronto Stock Exchange (TSX). n.d. Corporate Governance: A Guide to Good Disclosure. Available at: www.ecgi.org/codes/documents/tsx_gtgd.pdf.

26. Joint Committee on Corporate Governance. 2001, November. Beyond Compliance: Building a Governance Culture: Final Report. Joint Committee on Corporate Governance, Toronto, Canada. Available at: www.goodgovernance-bappenas.go.id/publikasi_CD/cd_penerapan/ref_cd_penerapan/download/unfolder/Building%20a%20%20Governance%20Culture.pdf.

27. Ernst & Young. 2003, October 7. Corporate Governance Workshop—Achieving Business Objectives: A Record. Assurance & Advisory Business Services. Available at: www.ey.com/global/download.nsf/Singapore/ CG_Workshop_Achieving_Business_Objectives_A_Record/$file/CG%20Workshop_ Achieving%20Business%20Objectives.pdf.

28. Ugeux, G. 2004. Toward Global Convergence in Corporate Governance: An Assessment of the Current Situation. *International Journal of Disclosure and Governance* 1(4): 339–355.

29. American Law Institute. 1994. *Principles of Corporate Governance*. Philadelphia.

30. See note 13 above.

31. Commission of the European Communities. 2003. May 21. Communication from the Commission to the Council and the European Parliament: Modernising Company Law and Enhancing Corporate Governance in the European Union—A Plan to Move Forward. Available at: europa.eu.int/eurlex/lex/LexUriServ/site/en/com/2003/ com2003_0284en01.pdf.

32. Donaldson, W. H. 2003, March 24. Speech by SEC Chairman: Remarks at the 2003 Washington Economic Policy Conference. Available at: www.sec.gov/news/speech/spch032403whd.htm.

33. See note 31 above.

34. Friedman, T. L. 2005. *The World is Flat: A Brief History of the Twenty-First Century*. Farrar, Straus & Giroux, New York.

35. Glassman, C. A. 2005, October 7. Speech by SEC Commissioner: Remarks before the Center for the Study of International Business Law Breakfast Roundtable Series. New York. Available at: www.sec.gov/news/speech/ spch100705cag.htm.

36. International Accounting Standards Board Foundation. 2005. Technical Summary: IAS 27. Consolidated and Separate Financial Statements. Available at: www.iasb.org/NR/rdonlyres/51A969A8-CC91-4C2C-97D7- BF6ACD8466DA/0/IAS27.pdf.

Chapter 15

Emerging Issues in Corporate Governance

INTRODUCTION

This chapter presents corporate governance emerging issues, including challenges, opportunities, and improvements. These issues are classified into sections pertaining to (1) global market and investor confidence; (2) the corporate governance structure, including shareholder democracy and director independence; (3) internal controls and risk management, including Section 404 compliance; (4) financial reporting, including convergence in standards and stock option expensing, pension liability recognition, electronic financial reporting, and financial reporting disclosure; and (5) audit function, including an integrated audit approach, liability caps, and auditing for fraud. These emerging issues are classified into governance, financial reporting, audit, and other categories.

Primary Objectives

The primary objectives of this chapter are to

- Understand emerging issues and the challenges, opportunities, and improvement they present to corporate governance.
- Realize the importance of maintaining investor confidence worldwide and illustrate how different countries are trying to reestablish investor confidence.
- Understand the initiatives being taken toward convergence in corporate governance.
- Recognize the importance of SEE performance on sustainable shareholder value creation activities.
- Understand the emerging shareholder issues pertaining to the nomination process, voting system, proxy statements, and regulations, and possible improvements to these processes.
- Illustrate the challenges to director independence, nomination, compensation, composition, and evaluation, and how those challenges can be met.
- Show the challenges that arise from unresolved financial reporting issues, including financial restatements, enhanced business reporting, forward-looking financial reports, and stock option accounting, and how they can be addressed.
- Understand antifraud programs and controls designed to strengthen the reliability of financial reports.
- Define the emerging audit issues in the post-SOX era and solutions to these issues.

INVESTOR CONFIDENCE AND GLOBAL FINANCIAL MARKETS

Investor confidence in the global financial markets is the key driver of economic growth, global competition, and financial stability in the sense that when confidence increases, consumers buy more goods and investors are willing to invest at prevailing prices. Investor confidence in the global financial markets is complex, and there is no worldwide well-established indicator of investor confidence. Generally speaking, investors are considered to be confident when stock prices are on an upward trend and the news about future stock performance is optimistic. Erosion in investor confidence worldwide has been attributed to the fear of terrorist attacks, the economic downturn in many countries, instability in the governments of some countries, and the bad news of pervasive global financial scandals. Accurate and reliable financial information assists investors to make informed and sound investment decisions, whereas inaccurate financial information is likely to mislead them into making wrong decisions.

The wave of financial scandals of the late 1990s and early 2000s motivated IFAC, in October 2002, to commission the Task Force on Rebuilding Public Confidence in Financial Reporting to examine the causes, determinants, and effects of the global loss of public trust in financial reporting and ways to restore credibility of financial reports.[1] The task force includes knowledgeable and experienced members from six countries: Australia, Canada, France, Japan, the UK, and the United States. The task force addressed (1) the causes of the loss of financial reporting credibility; (2) ways to restore such credibility; and (3) best practice recommendations in the areas of corporate governance, financial reporting, and audit functions.

The report of the task force was issued in July 2003, and it confirms that the loss of confidence in financial reporting is a serious global issue that should receive proper attention from all corporate governance participants, including boards of directors, executives, auditors, and regulatory bodies. The task force made the following recommendations toward the restoration of investor confidence in financial reports:

1. Establishing, enforcing, and monitoring effective corporate codes of ethics in promoting ethical conduct throughout the organization and assisting in the resolution of ethical dilemma.

2. Designing and maintaining an adequate and effective internal control system with firm commitment from the audit committee and top executives to ensure proper functioning of the system.

3. Identifying, managing, and reducing incentives to misstate financial information by focusing on the terms and conditions of employment and compensation of senior management.

4. Improving the effectiveness of the oversight function of boards of directors by requiring mandatory audit committees and periodic evaluation of the board's performance.

5. Improving the objectivity and independence of external auditors by identifying the threats to auditor independence and preapproving both audit and nonaudit services.

6. Promoting audit effectiveness and audit quality by focusing on client acceptance and retention policies and processes as well as proper supervision and review of audit engagements.

7. Requiring codes of conduct for all participants in the financial reporting supply chain.

8. Strengthening audit standards and regulation by adopting International Standards on Auditing (ISAs) as worldwide standards and encouraging the International Auditing and Assurance Standards Board (IAASB) to issue standards pertaining to the assessment of risk and fraud.

9. Strengthening accounting and reporting standards and practices by supporting IFRS to become the worldwide standard and convergence between international and national accounting standards and practices.

10. Improving the regulation standards of issuers by supporting implementation of national regulations in conforming to the IOSCO Principles of Securities Regulation.

Many of these recommendations such as convergence to IFRS and corporate codes of ethics have already been implemented or are in the process of being implemented.

Global Financial Markets

The speed with which financial transactions can be conducted and money can be moved around the world encourages regulators to establish a global financial infrastructure. The

EU is now the world's second largest economic power composed of the French, German, and other EU capital markets. The formation of a single European capital market was first initiated in the Financial Services Action Plan (FSAP), which was published in 1999 by the EC with the keen objective of establishing a single EU securities market.[2] The U.S. free enterprise system has transformed from large ownership of corporations by a small number of investors to small stock ownership by more than 100 million investors. This widespread investor participation requires proper investor protection through regulations, listing standards, and best practices. Different types of corporate governance structure are exposed to different financial misconduct and scandals. For example, the dispersed ownership system of governance in the United States is prone to earnings management schemes (e.g., Enron, WorldCom), whereas concentrated ownership systems are more vulnerable to the appropriation of private benefits of control (e.g., Parmalat). It is vital that U.S. regulators and their counterparts in Europe and other continents work together to assess the feasibility of convergence in global capital markets to improve integrity and prevent a global crisis that would eventually affect the economies of countries worldwide.

Stock exchanges in the UK and United States are the most liquid in the world. In the UK, the LSE is primarily for established companies and the Alternative Investment Market (AIM) for smaller companies. In the United States, the NYSE comprises the large-cap company market, while Nasdaq is typically the home for high-tech and growing companies and AMEX usually lists smaller companies. The other active stock exchanges worldwide are the TSX, Euronext, and Deutsche Börse. Although listing standards in the United States and UK are similar in terms of share ownership, market requirements, information disclosures, and board models, there are some differences with respect to shareholders' and directors' roles and responsibilities. Technological advances and globalization, including cross-border share ownership, necessitate that many global companies observe a variety of corporate governance reforms and guidelines—at least the listing standards of the country in which they are incorporated and the country in which they are listed. These listing standards and corporate governance guidelines are often in conflict, reflecting differences in regulatory, legal, and cultural traditions.

The merged NYSE/Euronext is moving into the global market, including China. This merger created the first transatlantic exchange with about $28.5 trillion total market capitalization, which is greater than the combined total of its counterparts worldwide. One reason for this merger was to provide global companies with the flexibility of listing on either the most liquid, deepest U.S. stock exchange, which was currently affected by SOX, or the less-rigid Euronext exchange. NYSE Euronext has established a strategic alliance in Japan with the TSX, has about 5 percent ownership in the National Stock Exchange of India, and is moving into the Chinese Shanghai Stock Exchange. The U.S. Treasury Department is also taking initiatives to promote consolidation of some regulators with overlapping responsibilities in governing the capital markets as the first step in changing the regulatory system in the United States.

Global Corporate Governance

Corporate governance models throughout the world can be classified into three general categories of "close," "open," and "hybrid." The close model of corporate governance is characterized by (1) concentration of ownership of both equity capital and debt capital;

(2) a long-term financing relationship with a few borrowers and lenders; (3) less dependence on capital markets for financing activities; (4) more direct control and management by a few major investors such as banks, insurance, or individuals; (5) more direct and close oversight function by monitoring bodies such as supervisory boards; (6) a well-balanced distribution of control rights and information rights; (7) less information asymmetry between management, the supervisory board, and major investors; and (8) more focus on internal information flows and controls. An example of a close model, which is also referred to as "insider control," is German corporate governance.[3]

The open model of corporate governance, better known as the "market-based" or "outsider" model, is characterized by (1) total reliance on capital markets for sources of financing activities (both equity capital and debt capital); (2) less concentration of ownership in the hands of a few major investors; (3) an oversight function by the board of directors; (4) less regulation of corporate governance and corporate activities; (5) total separation of the managerial function and oversight function; (6) existence of a market-based system of checks and balances; (7) information asymmetry between management, the board of directors, and investors; and (8) more focus on external information flows and controls. A purely market-based corporate governance model does not exist from a practical perspective or in a real-world environment. The hybrid model encompasses a combination of market-based mechanisms, internal mechanisms, and regulatory mechanisms. The closest to the market-based model is the corporate governance model in the United States. In reality, the U.S. corporate governance model is a hybrid model based on market-based mechanisms, with proper monitoring by governmental regulations.

The hybrid model is a set of both internal and external mechanisms designed to manage, monitor, control, reward, and discipline arrangements among all stakeholders to create sustainable and enduring value and to protect their interests. Stakeholders are broadly defined as those who have contractual relationships with the company, such as investors, creditors, suppliers, customers, employees, and those who affect or are affected by the company's business affairs, including social constituents; the community; society at large; local, state, and federal governments; and environmental interests. Companies that do not adopt an effective corporate governance structure would presumably be inefficient and, in the long term, would be disciplined by the capital markets. Thus, there is no need for policy or governmental interventions because market mechanisms correct any corporate governance inefficiencies. However, recent financial scandals demonstrate that market correction mechanisms were not adequate by themselves to solve the market failure arising from asymmetric information and potential conflicts of interest among corporate governance participants. Market failures and resulting financial scandals provide justifiable grounds for policy intervention to prevent management from adopting a suboptimal level of corporate governance. Thus, an effective corporate governance structure depends on a well-balanced relation between internal mechanisms; external mechanisms; and policy, regulatory, and legal requirements.

The pervasiveness of global financial scandals has encouraged policy members and regulators to respond by adopting laws and regulations to mitigate problems. The costs and benefits of these laws and regulations are often not assessed in considering their appropriateness on regulatory measures and the international impact of such measures. SOX's impact on foreign registrants is an example of the global reach of regulations and challenges associated with establishing national regulatory reforms. In response to the global reach and extraterritorial effects of national regulations, the OECD published the *OECD*

Principles of Corporate Governance in 1999, subsequently revised in 2004, and already adopted by the ICGN. These principles provide a framework and a platform for all countries in developing their own corporate governance structure.

Several initiatives have been taken during the past decade to improve corporate governance worldwide. Many of these initiatives are primarily national. Regulators in the United States, the SEC and IOSCO, the OECD, and the WFE have yet to agree on a global regulatory framework or a global corporate governance structure. The ICGN was founded in 1995 as a collaboration of institutional investors, companies, financial intermediaries, academics, and other parties interested in the establishment of global corporate governance practices.[4] The ICGN adopted corporate governance principles developed by the OECD as minimum acceptable standards for companies and investors worldwide. The ICGN highly recommends that companies use the adopted OECD corporate governance principles as best practices to improve their governance. The ICGN's principles of corporate governance are comprehensive enough to be applicable to corporations throughout the world. However, companies should establish their own corporate governance code comparable to ICGN principles and tailored to their own political, cultural, economic, legal, and regulatory environment. Figure 15.1 provides a framework for the future corporate governance continuum. The corporate governance continuum consists of postulates, principles, structures, and functions of corporate governance discussed in Chapters 2 to 10. The functions are classified into value creation and accountability as depicted in Figure 15.2.

Corporate Governance Reporting

Corporate governance reporting is a new phenomenon that has emerged since the passage of SOX. Methodologies and standards are yet to be established. The framework of corporate governance reporting and assurance that can be used is the AA 1000 Framework and its Global Reporting Initiative (GRI) guidelines, which promote accountability reports. GRI guidelines consist of five components: (1) the introduction, which describes the motivation for and benefits of sustainability reporting; (2) part two, which provides basic information regarding the nature of the guidelines, their documentation, design, and reporting expectations; (3) part three, consisting of reporting principles that describe the principle of sustainability performance; (4) part four, consisting of reporting content, providing detailed information about the content of a GRI report; and (5) the final part, consisting of glossary and annexes, giving background information about the GRI and supplemental information pertaining to the preparation of GRI reports and assurance provided on such reports.[5]

The GRI Sustainability Reporting Guidelines can also be used to provide relevant and credible information on the organization's economic, governance, ethical, social, and environmental performance. Many companies are disclosing information about their SEE performance in their annual reports to their shareholders. However, there are no generally accepted standards and guidelines for properly measuring and reporting such nonfinancial indicators. Thus, these sustainability reports are not uniform, and no assurance is provided on their completeness and reliability. Corporate governance reporting entails the assessment of the quality of the organization's corporate governance and reporting findings to interested stakeholders. Corporate governance standards should be developed to assess, attest to, and report on the effectiveness of corporate governance. Corporate governance reporting should (1) disclose all relevant information about the company's corporate governance, (2) focus

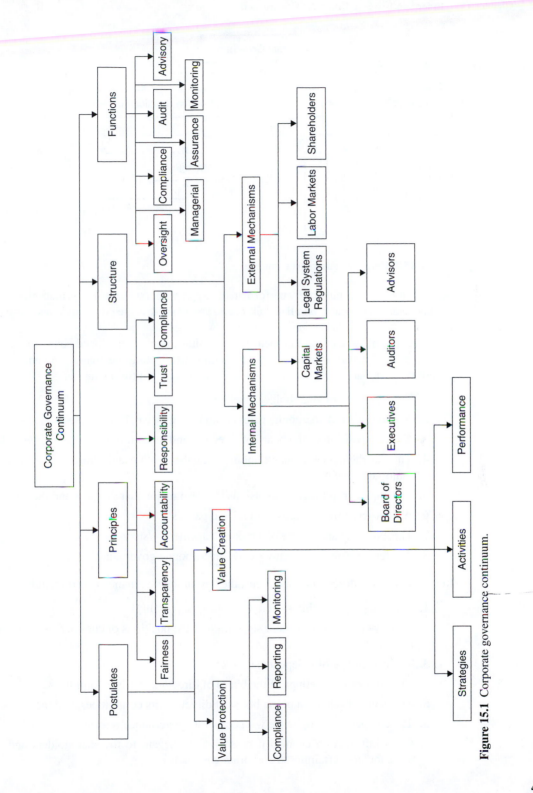

Figure 15.1 Corporate governance continuum.

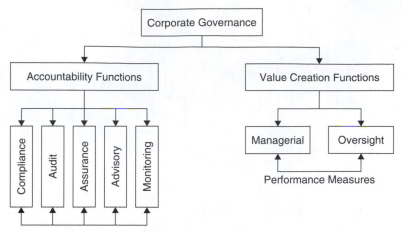

Figure 15.2 Corporate governance function.

on the company's sustainability performance, (3) provide transparent information about performance and its impacts on all stakeholders, and (4) assess the company's responsiveness to the needs of its stakeholders.

The Commission of the European Communities requires that listed companies include in their annual report a comprehensive statement reflecting the major elements of their corporate governance structure and practices, including the following items:

1. The operation of shareholder meetings
2. A description of shareholder rights and how they can be exercised
3. The composition of the board of directors and its committees
4. The shareholders with major holdings and their voting and control rights and related major agreements
5. Any direct or indirect relationships between major shareholders and the company
6. Any material transactions with related parties
7. The existence and nature of a risk management system
8. A reference to the company's code on corporate governance[6]

In addition to the aforementioned items, the corporate governance report includes

1. The company's voting system (majority vs. plurality)
2. Duality of CEO positions or separation of the positions of chairperson of the board and CEO
3. The percentage of independent directors
4. The number of meetings of the board of directors and its committees
5. The annual evaluation of the board of directors, its committees, and members
6. The company's compliance with corporate governance reforms
7. Other information deemed necessary and relevant to the shareholders and other stakeholders pertaining to corporate governance

8. The company's objectives and management visions to achieve these objectives

9. Major share ownership and voting rights

10. Summary of financial position and results of operations

11. Compensation policy for directors and officers

12. Significant issues relevant to employees and other stakeholders

13. Corporate governance structure, including aspects principles and functions

14. Material information on MBL sustainability performance

15. Initiatives on risk management, including foreseeable risk factors and responses

Corporate governance reporting changes one-dimensional financial reporting to multidimensional bottom lines. MBL reporting entails reporting on multiple dimensions of governance: ESEE performance to disclose the company's commitment to accountability to its stakeholders. MBL reporting goes one step beyond the corporate sustainability reporting prepared according to the guidelines of the GRI. The GRI focuses on the three sustainability dimensions of SEE performance, whereas corporate governance reporting emphasizes multidimensional sustainability of governance, economic, ethical, social, and environmental performance.

ACCOUNTABILITY: THE NEW BUSINESS IMPERATIVE

In today's business environment, global businesses are under close scrutiny and profound pressures from lawmakers, regulators, the investment community, and their diverse stakeholders to accept accountability and responsibilities for their MBL of governance, economic, ethical, social, and environmental performance. Corporations worldwide should establish total corporate governance structure (TCGS) to fulfill their accountability for MBL performance. Figure 15.3 presents a framework for such a corporate accountability model. Chapter 5 presents economic performance and reporting, corporate governance performance and reporting is discussed in the previous section, and the following section presents other aspects of MBL performance and reporting.

Accountability is the cornerstone of corporate governance in continuously monitoring best practices and being accountable to shareholders. Main drivers of accountability are the acceptance of responsibility, ethical decision making, transparency, and candor, which results in trust and a mutually beneficial working relationship between the company and its shareholders. Accountability suggests that companies worldwide focus on their MBL performance relevant to their economic, ethical, environmental, governance, and social activities. Although the primary focus and goal of accountability reporting in the foreseeable future will continue to be an economic issue to create sustainable long-term shareholder value, the issues of SEE performance of companies will gain momentum.

SOCIAL, ENVIRONMENTAL, AND ETHICS PERFORMANCE

Interest in public companies' SEE measures and performance in addition to economic performance is growing. Companies have begun to recognize the importance of SEE performance on their sustainable shareholder value creation activities. The 2003 World Economic

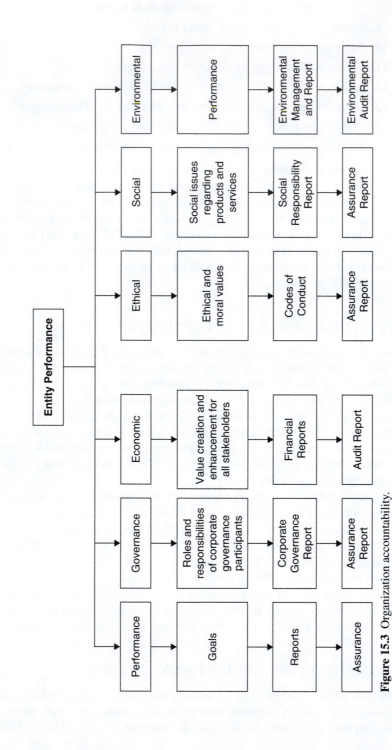

Figure 15.3 Organization accountability.

Forum Survey of business leaders indicated that corporations can reap the following benefits of supporting corporate social responsibilities: (1) promoting brand, reputation, equity, and trust; (2) attracting, motivating, and maintaining talent; (3) managing and mitigating risk; (4) enhancing operational and cost efficiency; (5) developing new business opportunities, products, and services; and (6) creating a more secure and sustainable operating environment.[7]

The effectiveness of a company's SEE performance is influenced significantly by firm commitments from its board of directors and senior executives, and their strong support for SEE measures. A survey conducted by the Association of British Insurers (ABI) indicates that less than half of listed companies in the UK have provided full or even moderate disclosures on their SEE issues. ABI has established disclosure guidelines on socially responsible investment for public companies that suggest that the company's annual disclosures reveal whether its board (1) has recognized the significance of SEE matters, (2) has considered the significant risks and opportunities provided by appropriate responses to SEE matters, (3) has obtained adequate information to assess the importance of SEE matters, (4) has established appropriate policies to manage risks to short- and long-term value resulting from SEE issues, and (5) has provided sufficient measure of the company's SEE performance.

Corporate Social Responsibility

A new report indicates that total assets managed by a socially responsible investing (SRI) portfolio have increased more than fiftyfold in the past two decades in the United States, and an increasing number of mutual funds fall under the SRI definition.[8] ABP, the world's biggest pension fund, takes into consideration corporate social responsibility (CSR) among the companies it invests in by treating the CSR factor as a risk element in the sense that a poor CSR company is at a greater risk. ABP also uses GMI for corporate governance performance ratings. The trend toward emphasis on SEE issues will continue to increase as more shareholders show concern about these issues, file proposals, and bring these proposals to a vote.

Environmental Performance

Environmental matters, particularly climate change, are receiving a considerable amount of attention from the SRI community. Goldman Sachs, a leading global financial institution, regards a healthy environment as a necessary factor for the well-being of society, the success of business, and a sustainable and strong economy, and as such plays a constructive role to address the challenges facing the environment.[9] Goldman Sachs' environmental policy framework is designed to address environmental matters and promote policy measures with a keen focus on providing real solutions to environmental problems. Goldman Sachs' environmental initiatives are (1) working with government and private sectors in establishing policies that guide environmental public policy development based on market-based mechanisms, mandatory actions, and global solutions to mitigate environmental problems; (2) reporting its own environmental performance to ensure that its facilities and business practices adopt leading-edge environmental safeguards; (3) acting as a market maker by seeking investment opportunities and investing in the environmental markets; (4) increasing its commitment to systematically incorporate governance, social, and environmental criteria into fundamental analysis of companies; (5) establishing and funding a Center for

Environmental Markets to conduct independent research with partners in academia and other research organizations to develop appropriate environmental public policies; (6) taking into consideration environmental issues, policies, and practices in business selection decisions; and (7) applying its environmental policy to the Goldman Sachs Group, Inc., and its majority-owned subsidiaries. Risks and opportunities of focusing on environmental issues should be considered by boards of directors as the investing community values companies' environmental initiatives and responses in developing new "green" products.

Institutional investors, including the nation's largest public pension plans such as CalPERS and CalSTRS, gathered in New York City in May 2005 to address the climate change, including an assessment of the associated risks and opportunities.[10] The 2005 Investor Summit on Climate Risk was hosted by the United Nations with more than 300 participants, including representatives of both domestic and foreign pension programs. These pension programs have traditionally supported initiatives to ensure that companies in their portfolios provide adequate disclosures of their environmental liabilities. Investors value the company's environmental considerations in making their investment decisions. Several companies have announced that they seek to increase their profit by focusing on the environment and offering environmentally friendlier products and services. Some insurance companies such as Swiss Re are providing coverage for environmental liabilities and have established procedures to assess and consider environmental risk.

Ethics Performance

Emerging reforms require public companies to adopt a code of conduct for key financial officers. Companies have adopted codes of conduct, offered employee training programs in ethics, and often appointed chief ethics officers to oversee ethics programs. The established codes of conduct and ethics programs address the following:

1. Avoidance and resolution of conflicts of interest between the company and employees
2. Compliance with all applicable laws, rules, regulations, standards, and policies
3. Emphasis on customer relations to enhance the company's reputation
4. Proper use of confidential information
5. Encouragement of whistleblowers to reveal dishonesty and wrongdoings

SHAREHOLDER CHALLENGING ISSUES

Several emerging shareholder issues pertaining to the nomination process, voting system, proxy statements, and regulations, along with suggested improvements in these areas are presented in this section.

Nomination Process

Regulations in the United States, including SEC rules, do not grant shareholders the right to place the names of director-nominees or even resolutions regarding the election process on the corporate ballot, whereas management is using the company's assets (shareholder residual claims) to distribute those ballots to campaign for its candidates. Of course, shareholders can access management's proxy card by filing a shareholder resolution that is difficult to place on the corporate proxy. Existing SEC rules allow companies to reject any proposal pertaining to director election. The U.S. Court of Appeals for the Second Circuit, on September 5, 2006, issued a ruling that enables shareholders in its jurisdiction (New York, Connecticut, Vermont) to nominate corporate directors.[11] Public companies usually send proxy ballots to shareholders, including the names of directors up for election. A director candidate can get nominated by a board committee and placed on the ballot. Shareholders, of course, can nominate their own candidate through separate ballots, often a complicated and costly process. The court ruled that under the existing SEC rules, shareholders should have access to the proxy for purposes of nominating their choice of candidate for director. The decision by the U.S. Court of Appeals for the Second Circuit is important because (1) it states that shareholders should be able to access the proxy for the purpose of nominating their choice of candidate for director, which contradicts the SEC staff's long-standing interpretation of the proxy rules; and (2) a large number of public companies are subject to the jurisdiction of the U.S. Court of Appeals for the Second Circuit.

In July 2007, the SEC approved two proposals addressing the shareholder proxy process. The first proposed rule would require public companies to allow shareholder access to the company's proxy statements.[12] The second proposed rule would facilitate electronic shareholder forums. Proxy access proposals are shareholder proposals that enable shareholders to nominate director candidates who would be named in the company's proxy statement. The SEC has traditionally allowed companies to exclude such shareholder proposals from their proxy statements under its Rule 14a-8(i)(8) to avoid contested elections. The U.S. Court of Appeals for the Second Circuit in *AFSCME v. AIG*, in September 2006, questioned the SEC staff's interpretation of Rule 14a-8(i)(8) that suggests that all proxy access shareholder proposals are excludable from the company's proxy materials. On July 25, 2007, the SEC reaffirmed its historical interpretation of Rule 14a-8 and approved a proposed rule that would allow the inclusion of certain proxy access shareholder proposals and would require additional disclosures by companies and proponents when such proposals are included. The proposed rule indicates that a proxy access shareholder proposal is not excludable under Rule 14a-8(i)(8) if (1) the shareholder proposal seeks to amend the company's bylaws, (2) the shareholder proposal is binding, (3) the shareholder(s) submitting the proposal held at least 5 percent of the company's outstanding shares for at least one year, and (4) the shareholder(s) submitting the proposal are eligible and have filed a Schedule 13G with respect to the company. Unlike a proxy access rule proposed by the SEC in 2003 that was never adopted, the new proposed rule does not dictate the terms of proxy access shareholder proposals that should comply with state law and with the company's charter and bylaws.

The new proposed rule enables companies and shareholders to communicate in electronic shareholder forums by eliminating possible impediments to such forums under the SEC's proxy rules. The proposed rule would provide that (1) public companies and others who set up electronic shareholder forums are not liable under the federal proxy rules for false and misleading statements electronically posted by others on shareholder forums, and (2) individuals who post communications on electronic shareholder forums at least 60 days in advance of a shareholder meeting who are not seeking a solicitation will not be considered to be engaged in a solicitation for purposes of the proxy rules. This proposal permits companies and others to develop their own format, content, and methods of electronic shareholder forums.

Voting System

The election of directors is a vital role of shareholders in corporate governance, as directors serve as agents. Under plurality voting, only one "for" vote will ensure the candidate's seat on the board, regardless of the number of "withheld" or "against" votes. It may work fairly when there are more candidates than available board seats, but it can be alternatively ineffective when the candidate is ensured approval with as little as one vote. Majority voting empowers shareholders by requiring that the candidate be elected through approval from a majority of shareholders.

Under the commonly practiced plurality voting, (1) nominated candidates can vote for themselves; (2) a single affirmative vote, even by the candidate, is sufficient for a director to be elected, regardless of how many (majority) shareholders oppose the candidate; (3) the nominating committee provides shareholders with the option of voting for nominees or choosing not to vote at all; and (4) the majority of shareholders, up to 99 percent, can vote against a nominee and he or she can still be elected. Two types of amendments to the plurality voting system were proposed and voted on during the 2005 proxy season. The first type amends bylaws to switch from the plurality vote system to the majority vote system, which is referred to as the majority vote standard. The second type amends the company's corporate governance principles by requiring that (1) directors who receive a majority of withheld votes submit their resignation to the company's board of directors, and (2) the board consider the resignation and make a recommendation. The latter type, referred to as "Pfizer-type majority withhold governance policy," is criticized for failing to grant investors the right to vote "no," enabling the board to make the final decision on director selections. Shareholder resolutions are less likely to induce changes in the nominating and election process as SEC rules allow companies to omit resolutions that would permit shareholders to list candidates for directors. SEC rules should empower shareholders to replace underperforming directors and provide them with incentives to spend more time and effort in monitoring corporate activities and performance. More effective shareholder democracy is likely to increase market mechanisms for corporate control, reduce management entrenchment devices, and elect independent directors who focus on long-term sustainable shareholder value creation and enhancement.

Proxy Statements

Shareholders of public companies with dispersed ownership have few, if any, incentives or opportunities to monitor their company's business affairs and managerial activities. The prevailing plurality voting system also makes it difficult for shareholders to monitor their companies. State statutes traditionally have limited shareholder monitoring other than through electing directors and voting on major corporate issues. Federal statutes have improved shareholder monitoring through proxy rules, which allow shareholders to include their proposals in the company's proxy materials. In July 2007, the SEC issued its rule to provide investors with Internet availability of proxy materials.[13] The SEC's amendments to the proxy rules permit public companies and other persons to use the Internet to satisfy requirements relevant to the delivery of proxy materials and enable shareholders to choose the means by which they access proxy materials. Under the existing SEC rules (Rule 14a-3), the proxy statement and annual report must be delivered on paper unless demanded by shareholders to be delivered electronically. These amendments provide two significant benefits of (1) substantially reducing the cost of complying with proxy rules, and (2) enabling persons other than the company with more cost-effective means to undertake their own proxy solicitations.

These amendments are effective as of January 1, 2008, and are expected to reduce the $1 billion of annual costs of printing and mailing proxy statements to shareholders who often do not exercise their right to vote. The amendments (1) allow the solicitation of proxy votes by simply mailing a postcard-type notice informing shareholders of the Internet location of the company's proxy statement, (2) include on the postcard the information on shareholder meetings required by the state statute, (3) include a notice of proxy ballots and voting instructions on the postcard, (4) permit shareholders to request a paper copy of the proxy statement if they desire, (5) make it less expensive and easier for institutional investors who are dissatisfied with incumbent directors to waive proxy contents for board representation, (6) apply equally to public companies and others such as dissident shareholders in a proxy contest, and (7) provide options to companies to either mail proxy material to shareholders or post them on their Web site.

The SEC rules on e-proxy allow public companies to routinely disclose proxy materials on the Web rather than in hard copy, along with a postcard combining a ballot and summary agenda by mail. Institutional investors should support e-proxy because it would make challenging nomination campaigns more feasible and affordable. The goal of the SEC in allowing the use of e-proxy is to simplify the process, save on costs relevant to printing and making proxy materials, and make the process less tedious and more flexible for investors. Nonetheless, several issues pertaining to e-proxy deserve further consideration.[14] First, the possible impacts of e-proxy on investor preference and behavior may result in lower response rates by individual investors. The majority of individual/retail investors do not want e-proxy because of (1) security concerns of financial information over the Internet, (2) the difficulty of reading materials on a computer screen, and (3) not having Internet access at all times. Second, e-proxy delivery may not be successful in the long term if the majority of individual investors decide to opt back into printed proxy materials. Third, e-proxy may not result in lower costs for investor-to-investor communications and may shift the cost of printing proxy materials from companies to investors. Fourth, e-proxy may further complicate compliance with NYSE Rule 452, the so-called broker vote or 10-day rule.

The only shortcoming of simple postcards is that any promanagement summary postcard has the potential of driving down turnout or encouraging automatic "yes" voting in contentious annual general meetings. SEC rules allowing online proxy statements (1) bring U.S. proxy rules in line with rules in other countries (e.g., UK); (2) enable dissidents seeking board seats to level the playing field with incumbent directors who usually use corporate funds to support their candidacies; and (3) make it easier and less costly for institutional investors by offering them the option of proposing their own slate of directors. It is, however, important that (1) e-proxy rules be flexible by allowing investors to "opt-in" by selecting electronic delivery rather than requiring electronic proxy voting and material distribution, and (2) the voting card not be separated from proxy materials.

CHALLENGES FACING DIRECTORS

Corporate governance reforms have increased significantly the roles and responsibilities of boards of directors. Roles of boards are expanding to both advisory and oversight functions.

The advisory role requires boards to mentor and guide management in business strategic decisions designed to create shareholder value without micromanaging. The oversight role requires boards to monitor management plans, decisions, actions, and performance to ensure the protection of interests of all stakeholders, particularly shareholders. The boardroom climate of "country club board," a "too cozy" relationship with management, and a few-hours job has also changed to a "fiduciary board," a collegial relationship with management, and an average of 200 hours-per-year job. Yet the future challenges for boards of directors are in the areas of executive compensation, CEO succession, strategic planning, risk management and assessment, and corporate sustainable performance on economic, social, governance, ethical, and environmental matters. Corporate governance reforms have also addressed many important issues pertaining to directors, including director independence, nomination, compensation, board composition, and evaluation. Nonetheless, several prevailing challenges facing directors remain unresolved: (1) director accountability and personal liability, (2) the separation of chair and CEO roles, (3) director stock ownership, (4) board diversity, (5) director interlocks, (6) director performance scorecard, and (7) rotation of audit committee members.

Director Accountability and Personal Liability

Recent corporate governance reforms have not adequately tackled director liability or accountability because directors in rare cases are paying out of their pockets for their breach of fiduciary duties and shareholder class action lawsuits are often settled before trial. Settlements are usually paid by companies or their D&O insurance, and ultimately, shareholders bear the costs of director litigation, which eventually dilutes the value of their shares. Ten former Enron directors agreed to pay $13 million out of their own pockets as part of a $168 million settlement of a shareholder-filed lawsuit, with the remainder of the settlement being paid out of D&O insurance policies.[15] In this settlement agreement, Eighteen of twenty-nine former directors who were named in a 2002 lawsuit agreed to settle civil claims against them. Former directors of WorldCom also agreed to pay from their personal money to settle allegations of federal securities laws violations for allowing disclosure of misleading financial information. These settlements are viewed by many as the start of a new litigation strategy, even though the settlement amounts are far less than the losses to investors resulting from corporate failures.

Separation of the Chairperson of the Board and CEO Roles

One of the most controversial and unresolved issues in corporate governance worldwide, particularly in the United States, has been CEO duality. There are no rules, regulations, or standards in the United States that require the separation of functions of the CEO and the chairperson of the board. However, corporate governance reforms in other countries (e.g., UK) promote the separation of the two positions. Best practices recommend the separation of the positions where (1) the CEO can influence the nomination of independent directors, and (2) the CEO has the ability and the tendency to dominate the board leadership and process. In cases where CEO duality exists, the lead director should be in charge of managing and running the board.

Director Compensation and Stock Ownership

Director compensation has recently received significant attention as companies have complemented cash compensation with stock, stock options, and restricted stock for their directors and integrated director pay into their corporate governance structure. Recent reforms have promoted more active engagement of outside directors in the company's affairs and more involvement in the strategic decision-making and oversight functions. Thus, investors have questioned whether director compensation packages are in line with this renewed emphasis on directors' activities or if they might cause a focus on short- rather than long-term sustainable shareholder value creation. To increase accountability in the boardroom and improve the effectiveness of board committees, companies are changing their compensation policies by (1) paying per meeting fees to members of board committees, and (2) increasing the use of restricted and deferred stock.

The issues of whether the presence and magnitude of directors' stock ownership can align director and shareholder interests and whether it is a critical factor to improving directors' oversight functions have been extensively debated in the accounting profession and the academic community. One may expect that a higher percentage of stock ownership by outside directors provides more incentive for them to be more effective in their oversight functions, particularly the monitoring of financial reporting. There are two distinct relations between shareholdings of directors and earnings management schemes. First, there is a positive association between the extent of shareholdings by directors and earnings management. That is, higher shareholdings by directors provide more incentives for the directors to participate in gamesmanship schemes with top management in managing earnings. Second, there is a negative relation between the extent of shareholdings by directors and the earnings management activities of top management. This suggests that the higher the shareholdings of directors are, the more incentives they have to monitor management activities to protect their own interests as well as the interests of other shareholders.

The director's stock ownership reward and other financial incentives have proven to be an ineffective way of aligning directors' interests with shareholder interests as directors are often motivated by other factors (e.g., prestige, popularity). Perhaps the fear of negative consequences in terms of increased liability or severe penalties (e.g., disgorgement) would be a better way to increase director vigilance in carrying out their fiduciary responsibilities. Emerging corporate governance reforms have addressed the issue of director independence in reducing potential conflicts of interest. Yet, independent directors can be ineffective and biased if the corporate governance structure is flawed. Best practices recommend that (1) director compensation plans consist of both cash and restricted stocks; and (2) directors, over time, obtain a meaningful position in the company's common stock.

Executive Compensation

Design and approval of executive compensation remain a challenge for the board of directors in the post-SOX era. The SEC rules on executive compensation are intended to ensure that shareholders and other users of financial statements receive complete, accurate, and transparent disclosures regarding companies' executive compensation, related person transactions, security ownership of officers and directors, director independence, and other corporate governance matters. These rules do not suggest or regulate how much executives should be paid, but rather require proper disclosure of such pay. Public companies are required to file a CD&A with the SEC. The guidelines on developing the CD&A are principles based, should be tailored to the company's specifications, and should cover compensation for the past three fiscal years, including the objectives of compensation programs, elements of compensation, and implementation of executive compensation policies and practices. Public companies failing to comply with these rules will be prosecuted by the SEC as it has filed cases (e.g., Buca, Inc.) against companies and their executives for failing to disclose properly their director and executive compensation. The Corporate Library analyzes the link between executive compensation and company performance and finds that many public companies paid their top executives some of the highest salaries in 2006, while long-term shareholder value significantly decreased.[16]

Best practices of executive compensation disclosures are emerging as high-profile companies, including GE and Pfizer, disclose information above and beyond SEC requirements regarding their compensation consultant services. These companies in their 2006 proxy material disclosed (1) names of compensation consultants, (2) what they are engaged for, (3) other work done for the company and service fees, (4) the responsibility of the compensation committee to engage compensation consultants, and (5) consultants' involvement with compensation committee meetings. These best practices could be improved by companies providing the total fees paid to their compensation consultants along with the breakdown of the fees for consulting and other services. This would bring transparency to the same level as is currently required for independent auditors.

Unresolved Director Issues

Directors' emerging issues are director liability, accountability, role in crisis management, and executive compensation. Establishing appropriate executive compensation that aligns interests of executives with those of shareholders and links executive pay with performance is perhaps the most profound challenge of many boards of directors. Directors should obtain shareholder advisory votes on executive compensation and assume the ultimate responsibility for approving executive compensation packages. Director accountability and related liability are the second most prevailing challenge for directors. Finally, directors' ability and willingness to deal effectively with executive departures, succession planning, and crisis management are also important challenges. Given the recent high CEO turnovers, departures, and retirements, an effective succession plan is vital to sustainability of many public companies.

Some best practices of UK corporate governance pertaining to directors can also be relevant to their counterparts in the United States. The primary aspects of corporate governance in the UK pertaining to the board of directors are (1) a single board that is collectively responsible for the success of the company, (2) separation of the position of the CEO and the chairperson of the board, (3) a proper balance of executive and nonexecutive directors, (4) strong independent audit and remuneration committees, (5) emphasis on objectivity of directors in the interests of the company, (6) transparency on appointments and remuneration, (7) annual evaluation by the board of its performance, and (8) effective rights for shareholders.[17]

Corporate governance areas in which progress has been made in the post-SOX era are (1) many boards have moved beyond mere compliance with applicable regulations and now engage more proactively in independent stewardship and accountability, (2) the overall makeup of boards is more independent, (3) all mandatory board committees are composed of independent directors, (4) the supermajority of boards have designated an independent lead or presiding director to improve the independence of board leadership, (5) the lead or presiding director has made independent directors more accountable for and invested in oversight functions, (6) CEO succession has been more proactively addressed by boards of directors, (7) institutional investors are more engaged in monitoring of corporations by approaching the board directly to voice their governance concerns, and (8) some boards implement best practices of corporate governance above and beyond mere compliance with rules and regulations.

Corporate governance practices that need much more improvement are (1) the separation of the chairperson and the CEO; (2) higher quality of financial expertise to be considered a financial expert on the audit committee; (3) board diversity in terms of expertise, race, and gender; (4) a trend toward boards with fewer directors; and (5) ambiguous definition of director liability as director compensation continues in double-digit increases and equity compensation constitutes a significant component of director compensation.

SOX COMPLIANCE CHALLENGES

It has been argued that the emerging corporate governance reforms, including SOX, SEC-related implementation rules, and listing standards, have caused smaller companies to (1) incur compliance costs that are disproportionate to the induced incremental benefits, and (2) divert the attention of company management away from strategic decisions and operational activities. In October 2005, COSO issued its report titled "Guidance for Smaller Public Companies Reporting on Internal Control over Financial Reporting."[18] The report is designed for companies that do not have an in-house, in-depth, and adequate internal audit function. The framework is a principles-based approach to internal control effectiveness for small public companies, nonpublic entities, and not-for-profit organizations of all sizes. The framework consists of twenty-six control principles regarding the five components of internal control environment, risk assessment, control activities, information and communication, and monitoring. The draft offers alternative solutions for small companies for the segregation of duties by having senior executives perform the monitoring of the effectiveness of internal controls, establishing a more vigilant audit committee, outsourcing the internal audit function, and communicating strong ethical values on financial reporting. The report emphasizes that the hands-on approach of management at smaller companies can result in less formal controls without compromising quality. The new guidance is intended to assist small companies to implement, assess, and report on ICFR in compliance with Section 404 of SOX and PCAOB AS No. 2.

SOX was intended to have positive impacts on the capital markets through improvement of investor confidence and enhancement in the integrity and efficiency of the capital markets. Academic research finds positive capital market reactions to several congressional events leading up to the passage of SOX.[19] However, anecdotal evidence suggests costs of compliance with SOX's provisions and SEC-related rules exceed the benefit gained by listing on U.S. capital markets as (1) one out of ten IPOs since the passage of SOX occurred on Wall Street; (2) $9 out of $10 raised by foreign companies through new stock offerings were done in oversees capital markets in the post-SOX era where a reverse trend was observed in the pre-SOX period; and (3) foreign companies listed on merged megaexchanges (e.g., NYSE/Euronext) are being exempted from compliance with SOX rules.[20]

It has been argued that SOX is not the problem because its provisions were intended to restore investor confidence through improving corporate governance, internal controls, audits, and financial practices of public companies. SOX authorizes the SEC to issue rules to implement its provisions. Some of these rules, for example, rules concerning internal controls of Section 404, cost at least one hundred times more than what was originally estimated by the SEC (e.g., estimated cost of $91,000 per company to the first-year actual cost of, on average, $9.8 million). Thus, while rolling back provisions of SOX aimed at protecting investors is not an appropriate action, making SEC-related implementation rules more effective, efficient, and scalable is a step in the right direction in ensuring sustainable efficacy of SOX.

Best practices recommend that (1) management use the integrated compliance approach according to Sections 302, 404, and 906 of SOX in providing certifications of both ICFR and financial statements; (2) management report on ICFR annually and assess both the design and operating effectiveness of internal controls over all relevant financial statement assertions on an annual basis, using the suggested COSO internal control framework for smaller companies; (3) independent auditors audit and report on the effectiveness of both design and operation of ICFR by performing walk-through tests of controls and an assessment of the control environment, while relying on the work of others (e.g., internal auditors) in determining the extent, timing, and nature of other tests of controls; (4) smaller companies not be exempted from compliance with Section 404, even though their compliance costs may be disproportionately high; (5) as long as smaller companies generate their financing through public investments and funds, they are subjected to compliance with all provisions of SOX; (6) there be only one set of financial reporting standards, namely, GAAP; (7) listing standards of national stock exchanges regarding director independence, formulation of board committees, and designated audit committee financial experts be uniformly and consistently applied to both small and large companies; (8) the SEC not differentiate in its application of financial reporting and disclosure requirements between small and large companies; and (9) standard setters issue accounting and auditing standards that are applicable to companies of all sizes and complexity, with proper consideration being given to smaller companies.

FINANCIAL REPORTING CHALLENGES

In the post-SOX era, there are several unresolved financial reporting issues. This section addresses some of these issues.

Financial Restatements

Financial restatements typically occur when material misstatement—whether caused by errors or fraud—are found in previously published financial statements. About 10 percent of listed U.S. public companies restated their financial statements in 2006. Financial restatements hit a new record in 2006 as 1,356 public companies filed 1,538 restatements, which was up 13 percent compared to 2005.[21] In the post-SOX period, (1) about 2,931 U.S. companies filed at least one restatement and 683 restated two or more times; (2) restatements by accelerated companies required to comply with SOX declined by

14 percent, whereas non–Section 404 compliance companies rose 40 percent; (3) about one-third of large companies (accelerated) and two-thirds of smaller companies that restated claimed they have effective ICFR; (4) restatements by large companies with $75 million or more in revenue are down 20 percent, whereas for smaller companies, they are up 49 percent; (5) restatements by companies audited by Big Four accounting firms are down 32 percent, whereas, for non–Big Four audit clients, they are up 76 percent; and (6) restatements for companies listed on national stock exchanges are down 20 percent, whereas for companies listed on the over-the-counter stock markets, restatements are up 76 percent.

The substantial decline in the number of restatements by large public companies suggests that Section 404 is working well in reducing the number of financial restatements and thus improving financial reporting quality. The persistence of financial restatements adversely affects investor confidence in public information and thus should be properly addressed by policymakers, regulators, and standard setters. The business community and the accounting profession should also strive to substantially reduce the number of restatements reported by public companies. The PCAOB, in its October 2007 Standing Advisory Group meeting, addressed the possible impacts of reported restatements on investor confidence and their audit implications. The SEC Advisory Committee recommends that the number of unnesessory restatements be reduced because they are costly to companies and auditors and may reduce investor confidence in financial reports.

Enhanced Business Reporting

The value relevance and information content of historical financial statements are being questioned as many investors and other users of financial reports do not use financial statements in making financial decisions. Enhanced business reporting (EBR) focusing on both financial and nonfinancial information about current and future KPIs is suggested as an alternative to improve the quality, transparency, and integrity of financial reporting.[22] The Enhanced Business Reporting Consortium (EBRC) was established through the cooperative efforts of several professional organizations, including the AICPA, Business Roundtable, Confederation of British Industry, International Chamber of Commerce, Nasdaq, National Association of Corporate Directors, National Investor Relations Institute, Open Compliance and Ethics Group, and XBRL International.

The EBRC is in the process of trying to develop a voluntary, global disclosure framework for EBR that will provide structure for the presentation of nonfinancial components of business reports. This framework will integrate financial and nonfinancial components of business reporting, including performance indicators on an industry-by-industry basis that will better reflect the company's opportunities and risks, complexities of modern business, and the quality of both earnings and cash flows. The improved transparency provided by the EBR framework will ensure the effectiveness of the company's corporate governance process.

The AICPA's Special Committee on Enhanced Business Reporting formed both the Public Company and Private Company EBR Task Forces to develop EBR frameworks, including the scope of EBR and the range of alternatives for reporting on particular components, sample disclosures for numerous industries, performance measures, and applications of XBRL in the EBR process. The Public Company Task Force is also developing guiding principles for EBR disclosures, and eventually, ways regulators and standard setters can simplify business reporting to improve transparency.

Stock Options Accounting

Stock options have been used as a part of compensation plans to provide long-term incentive measures for directors, officers, and key personnel. Accounting for the recognition and pricing of stock options has been controversial and recently under increasing scrutiny by lawmakers, regulators, and standard setters. The FASB, in its SFAS No. 123 (SFAS No. 123R), requires recognition of employee stock options as an expense. SFAS No. 123R provides guidance on how companies recognize outstanding options as expenses on their financial reports. Implementation of provisions of SFAS No. 123R is expected to affect companies of all sizes that provide stock options to their employees as part of their incentive plans. The two pricing models commonly used in determining the real value of a stock option are Black-Scholes and indexing of similar publicly traded companies. However, the current pricing models are being criticized for not properly determining the value of stock options.

Investors may have the perception that options are awarded on fixed dates and the exercise price of options equals the market value of the underlying stock on the same date. This perception may not hold true in the case of backdated options granted at below-market prices. Backdating or preemptive timing of options can cause a substantial increase in the value of backdated options. Option backdating practices enable companies to issue discounted so-called "in-the-money" options without shareholder approval and proper disclosure, which have already resulted in internal investigation probes by federal authorities, late filings, financial restatements, internal deficiencies, shareholder lawsuits, and executive departures. These detrimental effects of option backdating, along with the opportunity for executives to benefit at the expense of investors, can have negative effects on shareholder wealth. The other two schemes of managing the timing of option grants are spring loading and bullet dodging. The spring-loading scheme involves setting the grant date shortly before disclosing good news or withholding good news until after options are granted. The bullet-dodging scheme involves setting the option grant date shortly after bad news is reported. Best practices recommend that companies adopt fixed grant date schedules (e.g., quarterly or annual meetings) for granting options; establish option policies that are approved by their board and have received shareholder advisory votes; and provide full disclosures of option grant policies, practices, and schedules.

Antifraud Program and Practices

Corporate malfeasance, executive misconduct, and fraudulent financial activities have contributed to the reported financial scandals of the past several years. Entities of all sizes are susceptible to both employee fraud (e.g., theft, embezzlement) and management fraud (e.g., manipulation of financial reports). Effective antifraud programs of focusing on fraud awareness and education in the workplace environment, whistleblowing policies and procedures of encouraging and protecting employees to report suspicious behavior, adequate internal control procedures designed to prevent and detect fraud, and conducting surprise audits can significantly reduce fraud. Lawmakers, regulators, and standard setters have responded to the pervasiveness of fraudulent financial activities that have eroded investor confidence and public trust in corporate America and its financial reports. Public companies in compliance with SOX are required to implement several measures designed to prevent and detect financial statement fraud. Examples of these measures are (1) a more independent and vigilant board of directors, (2) effective audit committee oversight, (3) whistleblower programs for communicating fraud to the audit committee and independent auditors, and (4) a fraud risk assessment.

SEC rules pertaining to SOX Sections 302, 404, and 906 address controls relevant to prevention and detection of fraud by requiring management to assess the effectiveness of the design and operation of internal controls in general and antifraud controls in particular on an annual basis. PCAOB AS No. 2 requires independent auditors to test and report on managements' assessment of the effectiveness of antifraud controls. PCAOB's new AS No. 5 promotes auditors to control testing toward prevention and detection of financial statement fraud. Any discovered deficiencies in antifraud controls should be evaluated, reported to the audit committee, and considered in issuing an opinion on ICFR.

Antifraud prevention and detection controls and assessments addressed by SOX, SEC rules, and PCAOB auditing standards are relevant only to financial statement fraud. Fraud is a broad concept that covers both financial statement fraud and occupational fraud. The Association of Certified Fraud Examiners (ACFE) estimates that fraud can cost U.S. companies up to 6 percent of their revenues.[23] The 2005 Global Economic Crime Survey conducted by PricewaterhouseCoopers indicates that the threat of fraud in the post-SOX era is more prominent than ever with companies that do not have an adequate antifraud program to assess the scale of the problem.[24] The primary findings of the survey are (1) more than 45 percent of the surveyed companies experienced fraud in the two years after the passage of SOX; (2) the number of companies that reported cases of corruption and bribery in 2004 and 2005 increased more than 71 percent, whereas money laundering increased by 133 percent; (3) the number of companies reporting financial misrepresentation increased by about 140 percent in the post-SOX period; and (4) fraud costs companies, on average, more than $1.7 million, whereas 40 percent suffered significant loss of reputation, damaged business relations, and decreased staff motivation. A 2007 survey conducted by Ernst & Young indicates that the majority of respondents (more than 68 percent) do not have any antifraud prevention program and did not consider their fraud controls to be effective.[25] These results suggest that companies of all sizes should identify and assess fraud risks and design-related antifraud controls, and incorporate antifraud measures into their business operations.

PricewaterhouseCoopers, in discussing the limitations of SOX, SEC rules, and PCAOB audit standards in addressing antifraud programs and controls beyond financial statement fraud, recommends a five-step antifraud program applicable to all sorts of fraud consisting of (1) establishing a baseline from a project team to assess existing antifraud programs and controls, develop a remediation plan, and communicate with the audit committee and independent auditors; (2) conducting a fraud risk assessment independently or integrated with the overall risk assessment process to identify the company's risks and strengthen its effectiveness in preventing and detecting fraud; (3) assessing and testing the design and operating effectiveness of internal controls to prevent and detect fraud; (4) assigning the internal audit function to address residual risks that are not adequate or mitigated by antifraud programs or controls; and (5) standardizing a process for fraud incident investigation and remediation and prompt responses to allegations or suspicions of fraud.[26] These steps cover antifraud programs and controls relevant to both financial statement fraud and occupational fraud. Companies should use these five steps and integrate them into their corporate governance structure to promote that fraud prevention and detection are everyone's responsibility from directors to all personnel. The PCAOB should establish further guidance and auditing standards on auditor responsibility for detecting financial statement fraud.

Antifraud programs should be designed and maintained to deter, prevent, and detect all types and sizes of fraud from misrepresentation of financial information to misappropriation of assets and employee fraud. An effective antifraud program should address corporate culture, control structure, and fraud procedures:

1. *Corporate culture*—Corporate culture should create an environment that sets an appropriate tone at the top, promoting ethical behavior, reinforcing antifraud conduct, and demanding "doing the right thing always." The corporate culture provides incentives for everyone in the company, from directors to officers and employees, to act competently and ethically.

2. *Control structure*—An effective control structure should eliminate opportunities for individuals to engage in fraudulent activities. Section 404 of SOX, SEC rules, and PCAOB AS No. 5 underscore the importance of internal controls in preventing and detecting fraud.

3. *Antifraud procedures*—Adequate fraud procedures should be developed and performed to ensure prevention and detection of potential fraud.

Global Financial Reporting Standards

Convergence of accounting principles and auditing standards should enhance comparability of global financial reporting, which in turn should make the global capital market more transparent, efficient, and fair. The following benefits of convergence of accounting principles and auditing standards can be argued:

1. Facilitating comparability of financial reports of companies in different countries and thus providing greater opportunity for investment and diversification

2. Mitigating the risk that global investors may not fully understand the nuances of different national accounting policies and practices, and thus reach improper and potentially misleading conclusions from comparative analyses

3. Enabling international audit firms to standardize their staff training and provide better audit quality worldwide

4. Enhancing the consistency of global audit practices in addressing global accounting practices and their potential deficiencies

5. Mitigating the confusion associated with having to understand various reporting regimes

Several initiatives have been taken toward convergence of U.S. GAAP and IFRS, including (1) the Norwalk Agreement in October 2002 between the IASB and the FASB, in which both boards agreed to the development of high-quality and compatible accounting standards that could be used not only for domestic but also for cross-border financial reporting; (2) the SEC roadmap toward convergence and accounting standards; (3) the 2006 FASB/IASB Memorandum of Understanding, which sets achievement of goals of short-term convergence and medium-term convergence; (4) a study commissioned by the U.S. Treasury to analyze ways to expedite the convergence process; and (5) an SEC proposal to allow foreign firms to file their financial statements using IFRS without having to reconcile them to U.S. GAAP. There have been extensive and inconclusive debates over the past several years that the IFRS are making steady progress to becoming globally generally accepted standards for financial reporting. The FASB and regulators should work closely with their international counterparts, the IASB and the European Association for Listed Companies, to achieve convergence in financial reporting standards and practices.

Table 15.1 shows the extent of collaboration and joint projects between the FASB and the IASB. It appears that the time has passed for U.S. regulators, standard setters, the

Table 15.1   Trend In Convergence in Accounting Standards

Projects	Status	Description
Panel A: Convergence influenced by or toward the FASB		
Discounted activities	Completed	Further aligned international standards with U.S. GAAP regarding assets held for sale and the timing of classifications of operations as discontinued.
Depreciation on assets held for disposal or idle assets	Completed	Further aligned international standards with U.S. GAAP.
Panel B: Convergence influenced by or toward the IASB		
Inventories	Completed	The FASB ruled that abnormal manufacturing costs should be recognized as an expense, thus moving toward the IFRS standards.
Asset exchanges	Completed	Elimination of an exception in fair value measurement allows convergence with IFRS.
Voluntary changes in accounting policies	Completed	This project requires a "retrospective application" of voluntary changes in policy (not to be confused with a restatement).
Leasing	Future	The IASB is researching the effects of requiring all leases to be capitalized. The FASB is expected to join efforts with push from the SEC.
Intangible assets	Future	The IASB is researching the effects on requiring all internally developed intangible assets, such as patents and copyrights, on the financial statements. **It is not known whether the FASB will converge with this.**
Panel C: Joint projects of the FASB and the IASB		
Share-based payment	Completed	The FASB followed the lead of IFRS but with differences existing in treatment of income taxes; two are working together.
Business combinations and reporting noncontrolling interests	In progress	Developing standards to require the expensing of acquisition costs. Should provide better ability to reconcile accounting to U.S. GAAP.
Revenue recognition	In progress	Seeking to eliminate conflicts found in U.S. GAAP.
Financial performance reporting	In progress	Effort to unify income statement and define "financing" as mandatory usage and not allowing options.
Liabilities and equity	In progress	Modified approach has the FASB developing the foundation seeking to establish a method to account for financial items with both debt and equity characteristics and then a joint effort to become unified.
Insurance contracts	In progress	Modified approach with the IASB defining many insurance contracts as financial instruments. The FASB to join after initial report.
Income taxes	In progress	Both the FASB and IASB will adopt standards from each other.
Postretirement benefits	In progress	Joint effort to require balance sheets to identify the status of pension funding based on the fair value of the pension assets.

accounting profession, and public companies to advocate that companies worldwide use a version of U.S. GAAP. The current trends indicate a move toward the acceptance of IFRS throughout the world, including the United States. Unlike U.S. accounting standards, IFRS are regarded as principles-based standards as opposed to rules-based standards. It is expected that U.S. accounting standards will move toward the principles-based approach. The use of the principles-based approach in promulgating accounting standards necessitates effective application of principles-based monitoring and enforcement of accounting standards as well as the appropriate exercise of professional judgment. The use of principles-based accounting standards would assist both the FASB and the IASB in moving more quickly toward the convergence of accounting standards. The possible convergence in both financial reporting and auditing requires creation of a globally accepted set of enforcement procedures that while allowing national sovereign enforcement powers, coordinate global enforcement procedures through a multinational regulatory council similar to the Basel Committee for the global banking industry.

Three recent initiatives by the SEC may create a landscape for the move toward convergence in accounting standards. First, the SEC is exerting more control over the FASB by requiring a more formal role in FASB member nominations. The second is the SEC rule that allows foreign private issuers to file financial reports using IFRS as issued by the IASB without having to reconcile them to U.S GAAP. It is expected that FASB standard-setting activities will significantly diminish or be limited to nonpublic companies on full convergence in accounting standards, which would produce a single globally accepted set of accounting principles. Third, the SEC, in August 2007, issued a Concept Release to obtain information about the nature and extent of the public's interest in permitting U.S. issuers (public companies) to prepare their financial statements in conformity with IFRS, as published by the IASB, for purposes of complying with the commission's rules and regulations relevant to public companies.[27]

Pursuant to the SEC proposal to eliminate the current requirement that foreign private issuers filing their financial statements using IFRS also file a reconciliation of those financial statements to U.S. GAAP, the SEC staff made some observations based on the review of annual reports from more than one hundred foreign private issuers prepared in conformity with IFRS. The staff reviews consist of asking for additional information, revising their financial statement presentation, strengthening disclosure in future filings, and amending the reviewed filings.[28] The SEC's staff general observations concerning the application of IFRS are

1. The vast majority of companies asserted compliance with a jurisdictional version of IFRS.

2. The majority asserted compliance with IFRS as published by the IASB.

3. The independent auditor's opinion on the company's compliance with the jurisdictional version of IFRS was used by the company without opining on the company's compliance with IFRS as published by the IASB.

4. There are numerous variations in the language used by companies and their auditors in describing IFRS as applied in the financial statements. This requires more consistent and uniform language asserting compliance with IFRS as published by the IASB.

5. A number of different income statement formats were used by companies in the same jurisdiction and even in the same industries. Some inconsistencies include captions and subtotals, lack of proper explanation of the accounting policies used, and inadequate disclosures of determination and calculation of voluntary per share measures and their reconciliation to those measures in the income statement.

6. Some companies inappropriately characterized items as cash equivalents or misclassified cash flow items as investing rather than operating cash flows in the statement of cash flow.

7. There were inconsistent accounting treatments for particular transactions concerning mergers, recapitalizations, reorganizations, acquisitions, and minority interests.

8. Financial statements had inappropriate and inadequate notes.

9. Accounting for insurance contracts varied substantially.

10. There was inadequate disclosure and information on important financial reporting issues, including revenue recognition, intangible assets and goodwill, asset impairments, leases, contingent liabilities, financial instruments, and derivatives.

We should expect significant changes in financial reporting as both the FASB and IASB are moving toward convergence in their standards, and the SEC is promoting the idea of giving U.S. companies the choice between U.S. GAAP and IFRS compliance in their filings with the SEC. It is expected that U.S. companies interested in adopting IFRS are those that have overseen subsidiaries that already use IFRS. Smaller U.S. companies whose global competitors are using IFRS in their financial reporting may also be good candidates for IFRS adoption. Widespread adoption of IFRS by U.S. companies requires proper understanding of IFRS and readiness of those companies' management, board of directors, auditors, and investors to convert to a new set of standards. It is expected that countries worldwide will adopt IFRS in place of their domestic GAAP. The issue that remains to be resolved is the approach in adopting IFRS. Two general approaches are being suggested. The first approach is to require listed companies (both domestic and foreign) to use IFRS, and thus, financial statements, management assertions, and audit reports must be in conformity with IFRS. The second approach is to adopt all IFRS, with necessary changes made in tailoring to the business, legal, and regulatory environment of the country and using it as the country's GAAP for listed companies. Many countries have chosen, or are planning to choose, the second approach on the grounds that their legal and regulatory system requires conformity with the national GAAP. Their approach is a hybrid approach of dual reporting in financial reports of stating conformity with the national GAAP and also compliance with IFRS. Countries currently requiring the third approach for their listing companies are Australia and New Zealand. The SEC is expected to remove the reconciliation requirement for international firms traded on U.S. exchanges to file using IFRS by 2009. The move by the SEC can be regarded by many as the first step by the SEC to eventually allow listed companies to use IFRS in place of U.S. GAAP.

Future of Financial Reporting

On June 27, 2007, the SEC announced the establishment of an advisory committee to examine the U.S. financial reporting system.[29] The committee is designed to reduce unnecessary complexity to make financial information more useful and transparent for investors, reduce costs and unnecessary burdens for preparers, and better use technological advances to enhance all aspects of financial reporting. The current financial reporting process of focusing on historical financial information has become overwhelmingly complex and less relevant to investors and the capital markets. The SEC has directed the advisory committee to study all important aspects of financial reporting with a keen focus on the following areas before making recommendations to the commission:

1. The current financial accounting and reporting standard-setting process
2. The current regulatory compliance process by registrants and financial professionals with accounting and reporting standards
3. The current systems of disseminating financial information to investors
4. Factors that contribute to the unnecessary complexity of financial reporting and reduce the transparency of financial information to investors
5. Cost effectiveness and efficiency of current accounting and reporting standards
6. Relevance, applicability, and adoptability of IFRS
7. The use of advances in technology, including XBRL format, in the financial reporting process

The SEC Advisory Committee, in its interim report of February 2008, developed twelve proposals to improve the quality of financial reports based on the following five overriding themes:

1. Increasing emphasis on the investor perspective in the financial reporting system
2. Consolidating the process of setting and interpreting accounting standards
3. Promoting the design of more uniform and principles-based accounting standards
4. Creating a disiplined framework for the increased use of professional judgment
5. Taking steps to coordinate U.S. GAAP with IFRS[30]

Pension and OPEB Plans Accounting

The recent rash of pension defaults has raised serious concerns about the future of the PBGC. It is expected that defined benefit pension plans will continue to weaken because of insufficient returns on plan assets. Defined benefit pension plans are coming under more scrutiny by lawmakers, regulators, and standard setters because of weaker plans, high-profile bankruptcies, pension reform, and the FASB's new pension accounting standards. The first phase of the project completed by the issuance of SFAS No. 158 requires (1) eliminating the off balance sheet treatment of over- and underfunded benefit plans by requiring companies to include an asset or liability on their balance sheets to reflect the amount of over- or underfunded pension and OPEB, (2) moving significant pension and OPEB disclosures onto companies' balance sheets, (3) marginally improving transparency of defined pension benefit and OPEB plans by requiring recognition of funded or unfunded status of plans in the balance sheet, and (4) showing only the net differences in pension and OPEB plans' total assets and liabilities on a company's balance sheet.

In the second phase, the FASB is expected to overhaul accounting standards for pensions and OPEB. The FASB should expedite the second phase of the project by (1) addressing the perceived "glaring measurement problems," (2) providing guidelines for the measurement and recognition of future retirement benefit obligations to employees, and (3) addressing assumptions that companies are making in estimating future interest rates and salary inflation. Public companies are now required to recognize pension and OPEB liabilities in compliance with SFAS No. 158. State and local governmental entities would also be required to report on their OPEB according to the proposed GASB. Legislation, titled The Truth in Accounting Act, was introduced in April 2007 that would require the federal government to accurately disclose the nation's unfunded liabilities, including social security and Medicare, estimated to exceed $43 trillion in the next 75 years.[31]

The Use of Derivatives Speculation

Derivatives have been used to offset risk from fluctuations in interest rates and currency. A study shows that many high-profile companies are using derivatives for speculative purposes by actively taking positions in interest rate and currency derivatives on the basis of likely market movements.[32] These companies consider speculation as a profitable activity, and their CFO compensation-related incentives (not the CEO) are associated with the likelihood that the company engages in derivative speculations. Investors are not able to differentiate between derivatives used for risk management purposes and those used for speculation purposes. Companies with a governance structure that enables greater managerial power and fewer shareholder rights and those with stronger derivative internal controls are more likely to use derivatives for profit making rather than for speculative purposes. The current GAAP do not provide adequate guidance for companies to properly disclose their speculative activities, and thus, reported financial statements do not adequately reflect the company's speculative activities.

Enterprise Risk Management

ERM is gaining momentum as corporate governance and other rating agencies take into consideration a company's ERM framework. An effective ERM program enables companies to safeguard against potential downturns in the economy, volatile capital markets, investment losses, or souring business conditions. Traditionally, ERM has meant different things to different people. COSO has provided a uniform framework for companies of all sizes to tailor ERM components to their business processes. The effective implementation of an ERM framework requires companies to identify and assess the likelihood of their risks, determine the internal controls necessary to address the risks, and maximize control activities to minimize the effects of risks.

A study conducted by PricewaterhouseCoopers suggests that a successful ERM has the following six components supported by several subcomponents:

1. *Governance and organization*—An EMR framework should be an integral part of a centralized risk function led by a CRO. The CRO should have the full support of the company's board of directors and senior executives.

2. *Risk appetite and strategy*—Senior management, in consultation with the board, should establish objectives, business strategies, and appetite for risk in achieving these objectives.

3. *Policies and procedures*—The risk management framework, including its functional roles and responsibilities and related policies, should be clearly documented to ensure consistent application and compliance throughout the company.

4. *Risk management processes*—There should be well-established and effective functioning processes to regularly identify exposures, assess the related risks, establish the associated controls, and assess key controls and management issues and actions.

5. *Tools and technologies*—An effective ERM should be equipped with the necessary tools, technologies, and applications that support risk assessments, financial management and reporting, and planning and monitoring.

6. *Risk monitoring and reporting*—ERM framework should be monitored on an ongoing basis to capture changes in the company's risk profile and ways to address changes and incorporate them into the existing ERM framework. Information about the nature and effectiveness of the framework should be reported to senior management and the board periodically and as needed.[33]

ERM has recently received considerable attention and interest from public companies, the business community, and the accounting profession. Financial scandals of the early 2000s and recent world events, including the September 11 terrorist attacks, have generated more interest in the issue of overall ERM, including traditional risks (e.g., strategic, financial, operational, information security, reputational). Regulators, standard setters, COSO, and public companies should work closely to implement guidelines provided in the COSO framework on ERM. On May 9, 2007, the Institute of Management Accountants (IMA) issued a new Statement on Management Accounting (SMA) titled "Enterprise Risk Management (ERM): Tools and Techniques for Effective Implementation."[34] The SMA provides guidance to accountants to implement a cost-effective and risk-based approach to assess and manage risks to achieve their organization's objective and remain accountable to their shareholders.

XBRL-Generated Financial Reports

XBRL enables computer systems to assemble data electronically in instance documents, retrieve data directly from XBRL instance documents, and convert data to human-readable financial reports. The SEC, in 2004, established a voluntary XBRL filing program under its EDGAR system. The FDIC implemented an XBRL filing system for all its banks, and European financial institutions are using XBRL in more than twenty-five countries. In summary, XBRL is expected to reduce substantially manual effort in the preparation of financial statements, strengthen ICFR, improve financial statement comparability, and level the playing field for investors to gain access to real-time, online financial information. Despite the perceived benefits of XBRL, less than 100 of the 10,000 public companies have submitted an XBRL filing under the SEC's voluntary program as of June 2007. This low acceptance of XBRL can be explained by (1) a lack of knowledge or understanding of XBRL; (2) common misconceptions about costs, resources required, and technical proficiency; and (3) unrealized benefits.[35]

A move toward the global acceptance of XBRL for electronic business and financial reporting requires auditors to provide assurance on XBRL-generated financial statements, and thus, they will be engaged to conduct an integrated audit on XBRL-generated financial statements. This type of audit should be conducted in accordance with (1) PCAOB AS No. 5 on ICFR, (2) the PCAOB's Interim Attestation Standard (AT 101), and (3) the PCAOB's Staff Questions and Answers document on XBRL released in May 2005. The SEC has recently established the Interactive Disclosure office, which will work with all financial reporting participants worldwide.

The objective of an integrated audit on XBRL-generated financial statements is the same as other financial statement audits. The objective is to express an opinion on (1) the effectiveness of both the design and operation of internal controls over XBRL-generated financial reports, particularly the posting of XBRL instance documents on the Internet; and (2) the fair presentation of XBRL-generated financial statements in conformity with the selected XBRL taxonomy (e.g., U.S. GAAP, IFRS). The primary difference in the audit object of the conventional financial reports and XBRL financial reports is that the conventional statements and their internal control reports are presented at a particular point in time (e.g., the end of the fiscal year), whereas XBRL-generated statements and their related internal controls are on a real-time basis. This presents challenges to auditors in providing continuous assurance on XBRL-generated real-time financial statements and internal control reports. An important issue for regulators, standard setters, public companies, and the accounting profession is to decide on whether to require public reporting on (1) XBRL-generated financial statements and internal control reports at a point in time (periodic filing report dates, quarterly 10-Q or annual 10-K Form); or (2) XBRL-generated financial statements and internal control reports on a real-time basis. Regulators and standard setters should require public disclosures of both XBRL-generated financial statements and internal control reports at only periodic report filing dates. Companies, however, should use XBRL-generated financial statements and related internal controls on the real-time basis for internal purposes.

EMERGING AUDITING ISSUES

The viability of public accounting firms, their audit failures, and consequences of such failures on concentration and competition within the auditing profession and audit liability have been extensively reported. One obvious example of auditors' failure to fulfill their professional responsibility is the fraud at Refco, Inc., where both the legal counsel and auditors engaged in aiding and abetting fraud according to the report from an independent examiner appointed by a U.S. bankruptcy court.[36] The report indicates that the law firm Mayer, Brown, Rowe & Maw executed a series of fraudulent transactions, and the audit firms of Grant Thornton and Ernst & Young were negligent or engaged in aiding and abetting fraud. The requirement of public accounting firms to make their financial statements public enables the public to make an informed decision about their viability. Furthermore, a substantial reduction in the number of problematic audits of large companies and significant profits resulting from Section 404 audits in the post-SOX period should assist public accounting firms to secure their continued viability. The emerging auditing issues in the post-SOX period are (1) auditor independence, (2) auditor changes, (3) engagement letters, (4) audit failure, (5) integrated audit approach, (6) concentration of and competition in public accounting firms, (7) electronic financial reporting and continuous auditing, (8) confirmations, (9) audit report, and (10) auditor liability.

Auditor Independence

SOX and SEC rules have addressed auditor independence in several ways. The PCAOB also approved its proposal addressing auditor independence in performing tax services. The AICPA, in October 2005, issued Ethics Interpretation 101-15, Financial Relationships. This interpretation provides the definition of "direct" and "indirect" financial interests by auditors in their client's business and types of financial interests that are considered direct or indirect. Nonetheless, auditor independence remains a continuous challenging issue that should be further refined by regulators and the accounting profession.

Auditor Changes

Emerging corporate governance reforms, including SOX, SEC-related rules, and listing standards, require lead audit partner rotation every five years. Nevertheless, it appears that audit committees are seriously considering circumstances that warrant audit firm rotations, even though the existing corporate governance reforms do not require audit firm rotation. The trend in audit firm rotation in the post-SOX period does not support the perception that changing auditors reduces audit quality. The general perception is that audit firm rotation can be very costly, complex, and ineffective without adding much to the objectivity and independence of financial statement audits. However, a recent report shows that in the post-SOX period (from 2003 to 2005) about 6,543 public companies changed their audit firm, which is roughly one-third of all public companies, and particularly, about 11 percent of public companies (1,322) changed their audit firm in 2006.[37] These suggest that in reality public companies frequently change their auditors, and any mandatory rotation every several years (e.g., ten years) may not be a bad idea.

Engagement Letters

There is no requirement that the engagement letter (a written contract between the company and its independent auditor) must be signed by a member of the audit committee, and management has the authority to sign the letter. Best practices suggest that the engagement letter be reviewed, approved, or signed by the chairperson of the company's audit committee or a designated member of the committee. This practice ensures (1) a common understanding among the audit committee, management, and the independent auditor that the auditor works with management for the audit committee; and (2) the audit committee regularly evaluates the performance of the independent auditor.

Audit Failure

A review of high-profile financial scandals suggests that they were the result of failures in business, financial reports, and audit functions. These scandals demonstrate that as a company approaches business failure, the incentive to "cook the books" increases. If opportunities exist, management may engage in financial statement fraud and, through gamesmanship schemes, pressure auditors not to report discovered fraud, which in turn increases the likelihood of both reporting and audit failures.

Integrated Audit Approach

An integrated audit covers the audit of both ICFR and audit of financial statements. Large public companies hired registered public accounting firms in 2004 to conduct an integrated audit, which substantially increased the cost of the audit. The compliance cost of Section 404 is expected to decrease in the second year and onward because both auditors and companies are gaining experience with integrated audit, and the significant portion of the first-year implementation cost resulted from startup costs. Public companies and their auditors were also challenged by inadequate staffing, insufficient training, and lack of proper experience in conducting an integrated audit. The PCAOB provides auditors with a set of recommendations to improve their audit strategies, policies, procedures, and training in applying an integrated audit in its new AS No. 5. The SEC is planning to require compliance with both Section 404(a) and AS No. 5 for smaller companies, known as nonaccelerated filers, for their fiscal year ending on or after December 15, 2008.

Concentration of and Competition in Public Accounting Firms

Section 701 of SOX directs the GAO to study the factors contributing to consolidation in public accounting firms in the 1980s and 1990s in the United States.[38] The GAO report concludes that although there is no evidence of adverse impact of consolidation of accounting firms, further concentration in auditing firms would not be good for healthy competition in the profession. Regulators and standard setters should encourage public companies to use public accounting firms other than the Big Four (e.g., the Second Big Six) for their audit and permissible nonaudit services that improve competition in the auditing industry and would result in higher audit quality and lower audit cost.

The CEOs of the six largest international audit networks suggest the following for reducing concentration and improving competition in the auditing profession.

- *Focus enforcement*—Enforcement authorities should focus on penalties for individual audit failures and related auditor negligence and wrongdoing rather than penalizing the entire firm, because the loss of another major auditing firm could be detrimental to the financial health of the capital markets.
- *Liability reform*—Meaningful liability reform should promote competition and reduce concentration in the audit industry.
- *Scope of service reform*—Meaningful reform in relaxing the current scope of service restrictions should go beyond those measures needed to preserve auditor independence and objectivity.[39]

These suggested measures fail to realize that lack of proper enforcement through ineffective self-review, performance of conflicting consulting services, and relaxed regulations on auditor liability were the main cause of audit failures and the current concentration in the auditing profession from the Big Eight a few decades ago to the Big Four now.

Continuous Auditing

The use of the Internet has had a significant impact on companies' operations and financial reporting. The financial reporting process is moving toward electronic financial reporting as more companies use the XBRL format. The use of the XBRL format allows investors to have online, real-time access to their company's financial reports. The e-filing system using XBRL reporting is now required for financial institutions. It is expected that public companies will expeditiously move toward using electronic filing and financial reporting using the XBRL format, which would result in reducing the cost of financial reporting, improving the accuracy and transparency of financial reports, and also necessitating the utilization of electronic, continuous auditing.

A 2006 PricewaterhouseCoopers survey reveals that (1) half of the surveyed U.S. companies are using continuing auditing techniques in 2006, which is up 35 percent from that of 2005; and (2) of those companies that do not yet have continuous auditing techniques in place, more than 31 percent have implemented plans to do so.[40] This significant increase in the use of continuous auditing techniques will eventually change the way both internal and external auditors have traditionally conducted the audit.

Confirmations

Confirmations provide audit evidence about several management assertions, including valuation, allocation, existence, completeness, rights, or even absence of certain conditions (e.g., side agreement). Confirmation of accounts receivable is required under the existing auditing standards. Auditors should maintain control over confirmations to ensure the integrity and reliability of the process and reduce the possibility of receiving false or colluded information. Where electronic media is used during the confirmation process, auditors should verify the source and content. To do so, auditors can use service providers.

Audit Report

The current audit report approach "on or off," "comply/do not comply," "black or white," "pass or fail" audit opinion is not value relevant to investors. A better approach could be the degree of a company's compliance with GAAP. Investors may demand that auditors express their opinion on the overall financial health and future prospects of the company. Auditors should express their judgment on both financial and nonfinancial information in a more customized audit report. Any improvements in audit procedures in detecting material misstatements, a better auditing standard establishing auditors' responsibilities in detecting fraud, or improvements in audit reports should narrow the perceived expectation gap discussed in Chapter 9.

Auditor Liability

In the pre-SOX period, public accounting firms operated under an ineffective self-regulatory oversight function, and unfortunately in the post-SOX period, these firms are permitted to operate without many of the governance measures and financial reporting requirements mandated of public companies, such as an independent board of directors or trustees and periodic filing of financial statements. Such requirements would increase the oversight and transparency of public accounting firms and allow the market to assess their liability exposures. The Big Four and other public accounting firms, while enjoying substantial increase in their revenue in the post-SOX period, seek a liability cap or protection from lawsuits that investors file against them for flawed audits. It is difficult to assess whether auditor liability is in proportion to their capital, profitability, or participation in any problem or audit fortune. Malpractice suits and outstanding claims against the Big Four accounting firms in the United States have increased in the post-SOX period to more than $1 billion.

In summary, business is booming at the large global public accounting firms; their revenues have grown at a double-digit pace in the post-SOX era. However, auditing firms are still facing several challenges. The first and the most pressing challenge remains how to attract the best, brightest, and talented staff and how to provide them with adequate training to be competent and ethical in meeting the huge demand for audit and nonaudit services. The second challenge is the nature and extent of their liability for audit failures. Finally, the issue of auditor viability is yet to be adequately addressed. The viability issue includes the nature and extent of auditor challenges, the likelihood of their failures, the ramifications of such failures, and the development of contingency plans in case of failures. Nonetheless, shareholders should vote annually on the ratification of the independent auditor, and the proxy statements to shareholders should disclose any auditor limited liability conditions and terms.

Audit Implications of Convergence to IFRS

Two recent initiatives by the SEC in connection with the move toward convergence to IFRS encouraged the PCAOB to address audit implications of possible adoption of IFRS by U.S. companies and audit of IFRS financial statements in U.S. SEC filings.[41] The FASB and IASB, in the past decade, have worked toward convergence in their accounting standards and more toward globally accepted accounting standards. Nonetheless, there are still differences in their respective accounting standards, and if public companies worldwide are allowed to adopt IFRS for their financial reporting purposes, these differences should be resolved. The SEC in its Concept Release noted several areas that IFRS are not adequate such as proper accounting standards for exploration activities by oil, gas, and mining companies; accounting for insurance contracts; accounting for common control mergers; acquisition of minority interests; reorganizations; recapitalizations; and the presentation of the income statement. The challenges facing registered public accounting firms in auditing U.S. companies and FPIs that will file IFRS financial statements with the SEC are (1) what quality control policies and procedures should be required by foreign-associated audit firms whose clients are SEC registrants; (2) what inspection procedures should be considered for foreign-associated audit firms whose clients are SEC registrants; (3) do the differences between U.S. GAAP and IFRS warrant special audit attention; (4) what changes in the accounting curriculum, including textbooks in financial reporting and auditing, should be made to properly train future graduates in IFRS; and (5) what practical training and continuing education should be required for practicing CPAs who audit IFRS financial statements.

SUMMARY

Corporate governance reforms have made significant improvements in public companies' governance, financial reporting, and audit activities. Nonetheless, several challenges have remained: director independence and liability, CEO duality, executive compensation, shareholder democracy including majority voting, advisory vote on executive pay and access to proxy materials, and CEO turnover and succession. Financial reporting and auditing challenges include the need for more forward-looking corporate reporting focusing on both financial and nonfinancial KPIs in the areas of economic, governance, ethical, social, and environmental activities; convergence in accounting and auditing standards; financial restatements; auditor independence and liability; electronic financial reporting in XBRL format; continuous auditing; and integrated audit of financial statements and internal controls.

The key points of this chapter are

- Investor confidence in the global financial markets is the key driver of economic growth, global competition, and financial stability worldwide.

- U.S. regulators and their counterparts in Europe and on other continents should work together to assess the feasibility of convergence to improve the efficiency, effectiveness, and integrity of the global capital markets and prevent a global crisis that would eventually affect the economy and financial markets of countries worldwide.

- Corporate governance reporting should assist companies to restore investor confidence and public trust in governance, economic, ethical, social, and environmental performance.

- The higher the shareholdings of independent directors, the more incentives for them to monitor management activities to protect their own interests as well as the interests of other shareholders.

- Companies should integrate SOX compliance process into their corporate governance structure, risk and compliance process, internal controls, financial reports, and audit activities.

- The risk-based approach for assessing and auditing ICFR has been suggested for public companies, particularly for smaller companies using the COSO internal control framework.

- Antifraud prevention and detection controls and assessments addressed by SOX, SEC rules, and PCAOB auditing standards are only to relevant financial statement fraud.

- Several initiatives are taken toward an ultimate convergence of both accounting and auditing standards.

KEY TERMS

Basel Committee for Banking
    Supervision
corporate social responsibility
    (CSR)
corporate sustainability
    reporting
enhanced business reporting
    (EBR)

Global Reporting Initiative
    (GRI)
Governance Metrics
    International (GMI)
International Corporate
    Governance Network
    (ICGN)

International Financial
    Reporting Standards
    (IFRS)
International Monetary Fund
key performance indicators
    (KPIs)

REVIEW QUESTIONS

1. What is the purpose of the financial markets regulatory global dialogue that has been established between the EC and the United States?

2. What is the benefit to institutional investors in supporting the e-proxy?

3. What are the areas of business practices of private companies in which SOX has led to improvements?

4. What is the EBRC?

5. Explain how the FASB and the IASB have made convergence of accounting standards possible to a certain extent.

6. Describe the future of financial reporting and the move toward mandatory ICFR.

7. Explain the objective of an integrated audit on XBRL-generated financial statements.

8. What are the emerging auditing issues in the post-SOX period?

DISCUSSION QUESTIONS

1. Identify and discuss the key emerging corporate governance issues.

2. Keeping in mind the number of scandals that have come up in recent years, do you think regulators worldwide coming together and working to enhance the integrity and efficiency of global markets will help? Explain your answer.

3. Global corporate governance can be classified into three general categories of "close," "open," and "hybrid." Discuss the characteristics of these three categories.

4. The framework of corporate governance reporting and assurance is suggested by the GRI. Describe the GRI guidelines for corporate governance reporting.

5. Explain why the trend toward emphasis on SEE issues will continue to increase.

6. Identify and describe factors that may influence the future of financial reporting and auditing.

7. Discuss the extent to which convergence between U.S. GAAP and IFRS is possible.

8. Discuss the possibility of convergence in auditing standards to a single set of high-quality auditing standards.

NOTES

1. International Federation of Accountants (IFAC). 2003, July. Rebuilding Public Confidence in Financial Reporting. IFAC, New York.

2. PricewaterhouseCoopers. 2005, January. Building the European Capital Market 2005 (Downloadable PDF). Available at: www.pwc.com/pl/eng/inssol/publ/2005/ipo_capital_04.html.

3. Wüstemann, J. 2004. Evaluation and Response to Risk in International Accounting and Audit Systems: Framework and German Experiences. *Journal of Corporation Law* 29(2): 449–466.

4. International Corporate Governance Network (ICGN). 2005, July 8. ICGN Statement on Global Corporate Governance Principles. Presented at the 2005 ICGN annual conference, London. Available at: www.icgn.org/organisation/documents/cgp/revised_principles_jul2005.pdf.

5. Global Reporting Institute (GRI). 2002. Sustainability Reporting Guidelines. GRI, Boston. Available at: www.celb.org/ImageCache/CELB/content/travel_2dleisure/gri_5f2002_2epdf/vl/gri_5f2002.pdf.

6. Commission of the European Communities. 2003, May 21. Communication from the Commission to the Council and the European Parliament: Modernising Company Law and Enhancing Corporate Governance in the European Union—A Plan to Move Forward. Available at: europa.eu.int/eurlex/lex/LexUriServ/site/en/com/2003/com2003_0284en01.pdf.

7. Association of British Insurers. n.d. Disclosure Guidelines on Socially-Responsible Investment. Available at: www.abi.org.uk/Display/File/85/SRI_Guidelines.doc.

8. Goldman Sachs. 2005, August 26. Portfolio Strategy: The Growing Interest in Environmental Issues is Important to Both Socially Responsible *and* Fundamental Investors. Global Strategy Research. Available at: www2.goldmansachs.com/ideas/environment-and-energy/port-strat-growing-interest-pdf.pdf.

9. Goldman Sachs. n.d. Goldman Sachs Environmental Policy Framework. Available at: www2.goldmansachs.com/citizenship/environment/policy-framework.pdf.

10. United Nations Foundation. 2005, May 10. 2005 Institutional Investor Summit on Climate Risk. Available at: www.unfoundation.org/features/2005_nst_investor_summit_climate_risk.asp.

11. Pender, K. 2006, September 10. Board Drama in East. *San Francisco Chronicle* p. F-1. Available at: www.sfgate.com/cgi-bin/article.cgi?file=Chronicle/archive/2006/09/10/BUGJ9L1IPA1.DTL.

12. U.S. Securities and Exchange Commission (SEC). 2007, July 27. Shareholder Proposals Relating to the Election of Directors. Available at: sec.gov/rules/proposed/2007/34-56161.pdf.

13. U.S. Securities and Exchange Commission (SEC). 2007, July 26. Shareholder Choice Regarding Proxy Materials. Available at: www.sec.gov/rules/final/2007/34-56135.pdf.

14. Automatic Data Processing, Inc., Brokerage Services Group. 2005, November 22. A letter sent by ADP to the Chairman of the SEC regarding the e-proxy proposal.

15. AccountingWeb.com. 2005, January 10. Enron Directors Agree to Pay Part of $168 Million Settlement. Available at: www.accountingweb.com.

16. State Board of Administration (SBA) of Florida. 2006. Corporate Governance: Annual Report 2006. SBA of Florida, Tallahassee. Available at: www.sbafla.com/pdf%5Cinvestment%5CCorpGovReport.pdf.

17. Financial Reporting Council (FRC). 2006, November. The UK Approach to Corporate Governance. Available at: www.frc.org.uk/documents/pagemanager/frc/FRC%20The%20UK%20Approach%20to%20Corporate%20Governance%20final.pdf.

18. Committee of Sponsoring Organization of the Treadway Commission (COSO). 2006, July 11. Internal Control over Financial Reporting—Guidance for Smaller Public Companies. AICPA, Jersey City, NJ.

19. Jain, P. K., and Z. Rezaee. 2006. The Sarbanes-Oxley Act of 2002 and Security Market Behavior: Early Evidence. *Contemporary Accounting Research* 23(3): 629–654.

20. Committee on Government Reform. 2006, June 19. A Balancing Act: Cost, Compliance, and Competitiveness after Sarbanes-Oxley. Hearing before the Subcommittee on Regulatory Affairs. Available at: frwebgate.access.gpo.gov/cgibin/getdoc.cgi?dbname=109_house_hearings&docid=f:33393.pdf.

21. Glass Lewis & Co. 2007, February 27. The Errors of Their Ways: Restatements Trend Alert, Yellow Card Trend Alert. Available at: www.pbs.org/nbr/pdf/GlassLewis-Errors.pdf.

22. Anderson, A., P. Herring, and A. Pawlicki. 2005. EBR: The Next Step: Enhanced Business Reporting Will Improve Information Quality, Integrity and Transparency. *Journal of Accountancy* 199: 71–74.

23. Association of Certified Fraud Examiners (ACFE). 2004. 2004 Report to the Nation on Occupational Fraud and Abuse. ACFE, Austin, TX. Available at: www.acfe.com/documents/2004RttN.pdf.

24. PricewaterhouseCoopers. 2005, November. Global Economic Crime Survey 2005. Available at: www.pwc.com/ro/eng/ins-sol/survey-rep/PwC_2005_global_crimesurvey.pdf.

25. Ernst & Young. 2007, April. From Compliance to Competitive Edge: New Thinking on Internal Control. Available at: www.ey.com/Globa/assets.nsf/International/AABS_InternalControls2007/$file/InternalControlsSurvey2007_online.pdf.

26. PricewaterhouseCoopers. 2005. Predicting the Un-Predictable: Protecting Utilities Against Fraud, Reputation & Misconduct Risk. Available at: www.pwc.com/extweb/challenges.nsf/docid/f6d685397da561d3802571550031332a/$file/utilities_predicting_unpredictable.pdf.

27. U.S. Securities and Exchange Commission (SEC). 2007, August 7. Concept Release on Allowing U.S. Issuers to Prepare Financial Statements in Accordance with International Financial Reporting Standards. Available at: sec.gov/rules/concept/2007/33-8831.pdf.

28. U.S. Securities and Exchange Commission (SEC), n.d. Staff Comments on Annual Reports Containing Financial Statements Prepared for the First Time on the Basis of International Financial Reporting Standards. Available at: www.sec.gov/divisions/corpfin/ifrs_reviews.htm; U.S. Securities and Exchange Commission. 2007, July 2. Staff Observations in the Review of IFRS Financial Statements. Available at: www.sec.gov/divisions/corpfin/ifrs_staffobservations.htm.

29. U.S. Securities and Exchange Commission (SEC). 2007, June 27. Advisory Committee on Improvements to Financial Reporting. Available at: www.sec.gov/rules/other/2007/33-8817.pdf.

30. SEC Advisory Committee. 2008, February 14. Progress Report of the SEC Advisory Committee on Improvements to Financial Reporting, Available at: www.sec.gov/rules/other/2008/33-8896.pdf.

31. Accounting Web.com. 2007, April 12. Bill Requires Reporting Unfunded Federal Liabilities. Available at: www.accountingweb.com.

32. Geczy, C., B. A. Minton, and C. M. Schrand. 2005, November. Taking a View: Corporate Speculation, Governance and Compensation. Available at: papers.ssrn.com/sol3/papers.cfm?abstract_id=633081.

33. Horgan, P. 2007. ERM: No Longer a Nice-To-Have. *Journal of Reinsurance* Spring. Available at: www.pwc.com/Extweb/pwcpublications.nsf/docid/4E436509AB683713852572EB007E1C6D/$File/erm.pdf.

34. Institute of Management Accountants (IMA). 2007, May 9. Statement on Management Accounting. Enterprise Risk Management: Tools and Techniques for Effective Implementation. IMA, Montvale, NJ. Available at: www.grc-usa.com/whitpap/IMAERM_Tools.pdf.

35. Stantial, J. 2007. ROI on XBRL. *Journal of Accountancy Online* June. Available at: www.cpa2biz.com/News/Journal+of+Accountancy/2007/June+2007/XBRL.htm.

36. Mollenkamp, C., I. McDonald, and D. Reilly. 2007. Refco Report Sheds Light On Collapse. *The Wall Street Journal* July 12. Available at: online.wsj.com/article/SB118417698983663542.html.

37. Glass Lewis & Co. 2007, March 21. Speak No Evil, Yellow Card Trend Alert. Available at: www.glasslewis.com.

38. U.S. General Accounting Office (GAO). 2003, September. Accounting Firm Consolidation: Selected Large Public Company Views on Audit Fees, Quality, Independence, and Choice. GAO-03-1158. Available at: www.gao.gov/new.items/d031158.pdf.

39. International Audit Networks. 2006, November. Global Capital Markets and the Global Economy: A Vision from the CEOs of the International Audit Networks. Available at: www.deloitte.com/dtt/cda/doc/content/dtt_CEOVision110806(2).pdf.

40. PricewaterhouseCoopers. 2006, June 27. PricewaterhouseCooper's 2006 State of the Internal Audit Profession Study: Continuous Auditing Gains Momentum. Available at: www.pwc.com/extweb/pwcpublications.nsf/docid/1981a92e13dee3cf8525718b006de80.

41. Public Company Accounting Oversight Board (PCAOB). 2007, October 18. Standing Advisory Group Meeting: Audit Implications of IFRS Financial Statements in U.S. SEC Filings. Available at: www.pcaobus.org/Standards/Standing_Advisory_Group/Meetings/2007/10-18/IFRS_Briefing_Paper.pdf.

Index